Praise for

THOMAS JEFFERSON
A Strange Case of Mistaken Identity

"A fresh view of Jefferson's life and character. So much has been written about him that I find this remarkable."
—Virginius Dabney
Pulitzer Prize–winning author of *The Jefferson Scandals*

"The personality of Thomas Jefferson baffled his friends and eluded scholars. Now Alf Mapp brings us closer to the authentic Jefferson in this delightfully written and thoroughly researched biography."
—Paul C. Nagel
former Director, Virginia Historical Society
and author of *Descent from Glory*

"A heavyweight addition to the Jefferson shelves. It is worthy of Pulitzer Prize consideration."
—Ruth Walker, *The Virginian–Pilot*

"A magnificent biography. . . . To read this lively, well–written and deeply researched biography of Jefferson is to gain a new understanding of the life and character of this great American." **—The Hon. Sir Peter Ramsbotham, G.C.M.G., G.C.V.O.**
former British Ambassador to the United States

"What strikes me first about this biography is Alf Mapp's gift for narrative. Through the tangle of paradoxes and the welter of events, he weaves an exciting and absorbing story. This is a splendid achievement." **—Henry Taylor**
Pulitzer Prize–winning author of *The Flying Change*

"Will win a high place among Jefferson biographies. . . . Alf Mapp has acquired a narrative skill reminiscent of Douglas Freeman. With this book he becomes a top–rank biographer." **—Parke Rouse, *Newport News Daily Press***

"Who could fail to be moved and excited by this fresh account of a great libertarian? . . . we need this reminder of our common heritage by a writer, who like his subject, Jefferson, combines 'great vision, glowing eloquence, tremendous industry and wide–embracing humanity.'" **—Michael Barrett, OBE**
former Cultural Attache, British Embassy, Washington, D.C.

"Mapp takes his readers on an ebullient excursion into Revolutionary America, pumping red blood into parchment personalities."
—William Ruehlmann, *Norfolk Ledger–Star*

Also by Alf J. Mapp Jr.

The Virginia Experiment: The Old Dominion's Role In the Making of America

Frock Coats and Epaulets: Psychological Portraits of Confederate Military and Political Leaders

America Creates Its Own Literature

Just One Man

The Golden Dragon: Alfred the Great and His Times

THOMAS JEFFERSON IN 1800   Painted by Rembrandt Peale within a few months of Jefferson's inauguration as President on March 4, 1801, the portrait shows the statesman at age fifty-seven. Courtesy of the White House Historical Association; Photograph by the National Geographic Society.

THOMAS JEFFERSON

A Strange Case of Mistaken Identity

ALF J. MAPP JR.

Madison Books

New York   Lanham   London

Copyright © 1987 by

Alf J. Mapp, Jr.

Madison Books

4720 Boston Way
Lanham, MD 20706

3 Henrietta Street
London WC2E 8LU England

Printed in the United States of America

British Cataloging in Publication Information Available

Trade paperback edition published November 1989

Library of Congress Cataloging-in-Publication Data

Mapp, Alf J. (Alf Johnson), 1925–
Thomas Jefferson : a strange case of mistaken identity.
Bibliography: p.
Includes index.
1. Jefferson, Thomas, 1743–1826. 2. Presidents—
United States—Biography. I. Title.
E332.2M36 1987 973.4'6'0924 [B] 86–33335

ISBN 0–8191–7454–8 (pbk.: alk. paper)

All Madison Books are produced on acid-free paper.
The paper used in this publication meets the minimum requirements of American
National Standard for Information Sciences—Permanence of Paper for Printed Library
Materials, ANSI Z39.48–1984. ∞

To
RAMONA HARTLEY MAPP

Table of Contents

List of Illustrations

Frontispiece: Thomas Jefferson in 1800

Following page 240

1. Governor's Palace (restored), Williamsburg

2. George Wythe

3. Wren Building, College of William and Mary

4. Banastre Tarleton

5. Peyton Randolph

6. Patrick· Henry

7. Model for State Capitol

8. Virginia State Capitol

9. Monticello

10. Jefferson's First Plans for Monticello

11. Jefferson as Minister to France

12. William Short

13. Abigail Adams

14. John Adams

15. Maria Cosway

16. James Madison

17. Martha Jefferson Randolph

Acknowledgment

ANY ACKNOWLEDGMENT of help in the preparation of this book should begin with an expression of appreciation to Jefferson himself. His meticulous record-keeping and voluminous correspondence through a long life, while lengthening the process of research by increasing the volume of available information, have provided greater access to the facts than is enjoyed by the biographers of most people. I am equally grateful for the variety of his interests, the appeal of his personality, and the liveliness of his writing style—qualities that have made entertaining, and sometimes exciting, the many hours necessarily spent in his company while preparing this volume.

My gratitude to numerous memoirists, historians, and biographers who have contributed insights into the mind and character of this most fascinating of American heroes is expressed in some detail in the bibliography of this work.

My special appreciation goes to those people who have helped me directly in research and in preparation of the manuscript. Important among these are staff members of the Hughes Library of Old Dominion University, especially Benjamin F. Clymer, formerly head reference librarian; the Norfolk (Va.) Public Library, especially Mrs. Lucile Portlock, formerly head librarian of the Sargeant Room, and Miss Peggy Haile, assistant head librarian; the Portsmouth (Va.) Public Library, especially William A. Brown, III, Assistant Director, and Susan H. Burton, manager of the main branch; the library of Tidewater Community College, Frederick Campus; the Congressional Library, Washington, D.C.; the Library of the Pentagon; the Alderman Library of the University of Virginia; the library of the University of South Carolina and the Caroliniana Library of that institution; the library of the Virginia Historical Society; the Virginia State Library; the Earl Gregg Swem Library of the College of William and Mary; and Ms. Rebecca C. Whyley of the William and Mary Office of University Relations and Information.

Many people have typed portions of the manuscript but three deserve special commendation, not only for their skill but also for their labors beyond the call of duty. They are Mrs. Robbie Lee Atherholt, Ms. Sue Wallace, and Ms. Thea Krause.

I have consulted with various experts whose help is acknowledged in the annotation. Special thanks should go to two honored historians who read the entire manuscript before publication, making valuable suggestions and bolstering the author's confidence in presenting to the world a biography departing from traditional interpretations. Paul C. Nagel, formerly vice president for academic affairs at the University of Missouri and director of the Virginia Historical Society, has written respected works in the mainstream of American history and, as the author of *Descent from Glory: Four Generations of the Adams Family*, has chronicled the activities of a clan that furnished Jefferson some of his warmest admirers and keenest rivals. Virginius Dabney, a Pulitzer Prize-winning editor, author, and historian, is the writer of valuable works on every period of Virginia history and an important book on Jefferson.

It is a pleasure to express appreciation to Elizabeth Carnes, managing editor of Madison Books, for her resourcefulness, cooperation, and constant encouragement.

Finally, my gratitude goes out to my wife, Ramona Hartley Mapp, for the skill, knowledge, and patience which she brought to the task of indexing this volume. She is a part of everything I do which is of any importance, and it is to her that *Thomas Jefferson: A Strange Case of Mistaken Identity* is dedicated.

Alf J. Mapp, Jr.
Willow Oaks
Portsmouth, Virginia

For here we are not afraid to follow truth wherever it may lead. . . .

— Thomas Jefferson

I

THE PARADOXICAL PATRIOT

"THOMAS JEFFERSON still survives," John Adams pronounced from his death bed on the fiftieth anniversary of the Declaration of Independence. He did not know that the Virginian had died five hours earlier but, as has been pointed out many times, he was right in the larger sense that Jefferson lives on as an influence, and even an inspiration, in American life. Among American heroes, only Washington and Lincoln are commemorated more often in the names of streets, and schools, and public buildings of every kind. Among Presidents of the United States, only Lincoln is more frequently quoted.

Yet Jefferson survives as many figures and they are not clones. As quoted by various politicians, newspaper editors, and scholars, the separate Jeffersons often seem to be debating with each other—and not just as one sometimes argues with himself as Jefferson did in his famous "Dialogue of Head and Heart." The differences among some of these Jeffersons are fundamental. One Jefferson would find it as difficult to remain calmly in the room with another as the actual Jefferson did to be closeted in cabinet sessions with Alexander Hamilton.

It is the major premise of this book that the story of Thomas Jefferson in American history is a strange case of mistaken identity resulting in part from willful misrepresentation but even more from the wishful thinking of both admirers and detractors. The process has been facilitated by the fact that the mind and soul of Jefferson present, as Shakespeare said of one of his characters but might as truly have said of himself, a "largesse universal as the sun." The possibilities for identification with him are infinite, and learned scholars as well as aspiring politicians have succumbed to the temptation. It is one that we have steadfastly and consciously resisted in an attempt to chip away at the encrustation of legend to reveal some portions of the true Jefferson. We shall fail miserably if we do not also humbly bear in mind that we shall never discover the complete Jefferson. None of his contemporaries did, and the figure known to them has in part been altered beyond recapture, weathered by the random winds of history.

Alexander Hamilton, in one of the less derogatory portions of a description of Thomas Jefferson, said that the Virginian was "paradoxical." Hamilton, of course, was no more objective about Jefferson than Jefferson was about him. And Jefferson, in a letter to George Washington, who was trying to make peace between his two quarreling cabinet members, had already described Hamilton as "a man whose history, from the moment at which history can stoop to notice him, is a tissue of machinations against the liberty of the country which has not only received [him] and given him bread, but heaped its honors on his head.''

Nevertheless, a man's enemies, though they fail to appreciate him, may furnish valuable insights into his mind and character. And Hamilton was an uncommonly perspicacious observer who spent many hours studying Jefferson in an effort to predict his moves. The fact that the New Yorker was frequently baffled in the attempt, far from discrediting his observation that Jefferson was paradoxical, lends credence to it. Indeed, recognition of the paradoxical quality of Jefferson's mind and personality would seem to be the starting point for any approach to understanding him.

Certainly Jefferson is not easily known. Henry Adams must have been aware of the paradoxes defying easy analysis when he wrote:

Almost every other American statesman might be described in a parenthesis. A few broad strokes of the brush would paint the portraits of all the early Presidents with this exception, . . . but Jefferson could be painted only touch by touch, with a fine pencil, and the perfection of the likeness depended upon the shifting and uncertain flicker of its semi-transparent shadows.

The most celebrated of the paradoxes associated with Jefferson is that the author of the Declaration of Independence with its statement "that all men are created equal, that they are endowed by their Creator with certain unalienable rights, that among these are Life, Liberty and the pursuit of Happiness," was himself one of the great slaveholders of Virginia. Only the opposition of Deep South slaveowners and New England slave traders kept him from including a specific condemnation of slavery in the Declaration, and he repeatedly denounced the institution as "infamous"; but when one of his own slaves ran away in 1769 he offered a reward for his capture, and when his prize cook sought to remain in freedom in Paris after his master's return from his diplomatic post Jefferson persuaded the man to come back to Monticello.

No less paradoxical in the fact that Jefferson is claimed as a patron saint by both liberals and conservatives in American politics. In the early years of the Republic he was the leader of strict constructionists of the Constitution. Yet perhaps the boldest departure from strict construction by any President was his own action in the purchase and assimilation of the Louisiana Territory, anticipating by a quarter of a century the Supreme Court's broad construction ruling under his philosophical antithesis, John Marshall.

Though Jefferson is justly famed as an innovator in politics and scholarship, he was also a dedicated traditionalist. He was an eager disciple of the Enlightenment but much of his light came from the lamps of Greece and Rome. More than anyone else, he was responsible for the classical revival in American architecture. When Pierre L'Enfant was proposing boldly original plans for the new federal city, Jefferson wrote to President Washington, "Whenever it is proposed to prepare for the Capitol, I should prefer the adoption of some one of the models of antiquity, which have had the approbation of thousands of years . . . .''

Religiously, no less than politically, he appears a figure of puzzling contrasts. When charges of atheism were hurting his political career, his friends could not prevail upon him to deny the allegation. Yet he turns out to have been a closet theologian who anticipated by more than a century some of the interpretations by Albert Schweitzer in *Quest of the Historical Jesus.* In 1800 the *New-England Palladium* declared, "Should the infidel Jefferson be elected to the Presidency, the *seal of death* is that moment set on our holy religion, our churches will be prostrated, and some infamous prostitute, under the title of the Goddess of Reason, will preside in the Sanctuaries now devoted to the worship of the Most High." In 1964 Donald S. Harrington wrote of this same man, "He was passionately devoted to the gospel of Jesus, which stirred him to the depths of his being and was the most powerful motive force in his life."

Jefferson's morals have been as much the subject of confused comment as his theology. His intimate correspondence reveals that he was offended by Parisian adultery and, despite his admiration for Benjamin Franklin, was uncomfortable in the elder statesman's household because it included a mistress. Yet Jefferson has been accused by some historians of having an affair with the wife of artist Richard Cosway, of attempting to seduce the wife of a friend and neighbor, and of fathering the children of a slave.

Whatever Jefferson's doubts about Parisian sexual mores, he is often accounted a Francophile. And because of his unfavorable references to the English in comparison with the French he is frequently described as an Anglophobe. True, in a bitter moment some years after the Revolution he wrote that the English had to be "kicked into good manners" and the acid of his references to "that nation" comes burning through the time-browned lines of his copper-plate correspondence. Yet he advised his friend Lafayette to try to obtain for France a constitution modeled upon the British system of government, and the three men whom Jefferson called the "greatest" in history, and whose pictures he kept for inspiration—Bacon, Newton, and Locke—were all Englishmen.

Of course, the Virginian sought peace with all nations, worked to ameliorate the cruelty of criminal law, abhorred violence, and became physically sick at the sight of blood. Yet he wrote at the time of Shays' Rebellion: "What signify a few lives lost in a century or two? The tree of liberty must be refreshed from time to time with the blood of patriots and tyrants. It is its natural manure."

Whether Jefferson's view of history was sanguinary or sanguine, it was always international. Among the Founding Fathers only Dr. Franklin was so much a citizen of the world as he or gave such spirited allegiance to a republic of the intellect transcending national boundaries. And, probably more than any of his famous contemporaries, the Virginian was free of that parochialism that saw the Atlantic littoral as "the real United States." His vision of the Republic stretched from coast to coast long before its borders did. And yet, when the author of the Declaration of Independence wrote from Philadelphia of his homesickness for "my country," it was to the Old Dominion that he referred. In 1792, when as secretary of state he was the third highest executive officer of the federal government, he referred to the Congress of the United States as a "foreign legislature" and wrote that anyone recognizing that body in "a case belonging to the state [of Virginia] itself" should "be adjudged guilty of high treason and suffer death accordingly, by the judgement of the state court." Later he wished his grandson to complete his education within Virginia instead of at one of the universities to the north because "all the science in the world would not to me as a parent compensate the loss of that open, manly character which Virginians possess and in which the most liberal and enlightened of the Eastern people are deplorably deficient.''

His celebrated enthusiasm for the American West, which made him the prophet and engineer of national expansion and prompted the Lewis and Clark expeditions, never led him but once to venture more than fifty miles west of his Virginia birthplace.

The third President is often cited as a devotee of republican simplicity who, after spending the previous night at a boarding house, walked to his first inauguration. Nevertheless, he not only designed and built for himself the most elegant home in America but found it necessary, even when he was hard pressed for funds, to make lavish alterations in Parisian quarters that he did not expect to occupy for more than a year.

An age of egalitarian enthusiasm has quoted with relish Jefferson's scornful references to the ''cyphers of the aristocracy'' and his warnings to Washington and John Adams about the growth of aristocracy in the United States. One sometimes gets the impression that Jefferson, surrounded by elitists, stood almost alone in his faith in the people. We often forget that Jefferson himself was an aristocrat whose maternal family, the Randolphs, were one of Virginia's three most powerful clans, descended from nobility and royalty. We overlook the fact that his best friends were chosen from the aristocracy and that he liked the young people of his family to marry within their own social class, evincing special delight when they were wedded to their own cousins.

And while Jefferson cherished hopes for ''the perfectibility of man,'' there were limits to his confidence in the human mind unrefined by intellectual cultivation. In August 1776 he wrote to Edmund Pendleton to protest the dangers implicit in direct election of senators: ''I have ever observed that a choice by the people themselves is not generally distinguished for its wisdom. This first secretion from them is usually crude and heterogeneous.'' Although he would prefer limited terms for senators, ''I could submit tho' not so willingly to an appointment for life, or to anything rather than a mere creation by and dependence on the people.'' Many knowledgeable students of American history, told that this quotation was from either Hamilton or Jefferson, would unhesitatingly attribute it to the future leader of the Federalists, the Founding Father who openly declared in the Federal Convention of 1787 that the chief voice in government should be accorded the ''rich and well born'' as the ''mass of the people. . . seldom judge or determine right.'' The distrust of popular judgement expressed in the letter to Pendleton would not be ascribed to the author of the Declaration of Independence, which only the month before had proclaimed that ''all men are created equal.''

There are paradoxes in Jefferson's attitudes toward individuals as well as to people *en masse.* He has been justly praised for the veneration which he continued to cherish for George Washington after his political break with the President and for the eagerness with which he resumed his warm friendship for John Adams after years of political strife. But his youthful admiration for Patrick Henry was not strong enough to survive the political differences of later years which caused him to confide to Madison the hope that the orator would die before the next session of the legislature.

A recital of such paradoxes removed from context suggests one who might be more notable for eccentricity than for solid accomplishment. Certainly Jefferson was not great *because* of the paradoxes, but it may be equally inaccurate to say that he was great *in spite* of them. To be strictly accurate, we must restore part of the context of Hamilton's appraisal. He said not just that Jefferson was ''paradoxical,'' but that he was ''certainly a man of sublimated and paradoxical imagination.'' There is the key—in the individual imagination and experiences that refined and developed or (in the eighteenth-century sense) *sublimated* it.

The imagination was a creative and artistic one. Some of the sense of paradox vanishes when we cease to think of Jefferson as a statesman who was only adventitiously an artist. The truth of the matter is that he was first of all an artist despite the fact that American society in his day did little to encourage the breed; in another time and place he might have earned substantial fame without ever entering politics.

The paradoxical element shrinks further when the investigator goes back to Jefferson's own writings—formal and informal—and tries to rid himself of preconceptions as he reads. Some of the best scholars have been guilty of ignoring or deleting quotations from Jefferson in a way that distorts his sentiments and convictions. And some less conscientious writers have chosen to serve up titillating tidbits to the exclusion of a balanced diet of facts although even the spiciest assortment of hors d'oeuvre is not long satisfying to a strong appetite for knowledge and understanding. But some very able and honest historians have, perhaps unconsciously, suppressed some of Jefferson's views either out of filial piety for this Founding Father or because they could not bear his endorsement of philosophies in conflict with their own.

Even after we have reduced the area of paradox by recognizing that Jefferson was primarily an artist and by considering his opinions as objectively as we can, there remains a large body of conflicting views and actions attributable to this complex American. Some of these paradoxes vanish when we remind ourselves of the simple fact of chronology. When one of the most notable qualities of genius is a remarkable capacity for growth, why should we be surprised that Jefferson's views at fifty years were not always in harmony with those he had held at thirty? How many reflective people maintain one set of views unchanged through a long life?

By observing Jefferson as his creative imagination is shaped and reshaped we can detect patterns amid the apparent chaos. Sometimes when he seems to be shifting from left to right and back again with no consistency, he is actually spiraling upward to another plane of understanding and the movements to left or right are purely incidental.

In ensuing chapters we shall follow Jefferson from childhood to his roles as national leader and international seer. By witnessing the development of his creative imagination from his very early years onward, we shall have a much better opportunity to understand him than if we began to take him seriously only when he was first elected to the Virginia House of Burgesses. Even with this precaution, we shall not come near to understanding all the things about him that puzzle us. What parent is not sometimes mystified by the offspring that he has seen grow from infancy to adulthood?

So, in attempting to improve our comprehension of Jefferson, we must concede at the outset that baffling paradoxes must remain. We can only look at him from different angles in a great many lights, for his is the iridescence of the butterfly or moth whose wings may be purple from one view, green from another, and bronze from a third. Yet who can say that each perception is not valid or that all are not valid simultaneously?

The problem is vastly complicated because there are so many angles from which to view Jefferson. As a private person he was a traditionalist and an innovator, a bookworm and an accomplished horseman, a passionate lover of nature and of the opposite sex. In public roles he was one of the world's great statesmen, one of his country's greatest writers and its most influential architect, an enterprising agriculturist, a linguist and an ethnologist of international note, a pioneer paleontologist, and an historian read respectfully in Europe as well as North America. One recalls President John F. Kennedy's amiable hyperbole in telling an assemblage of American winners of the Nobel Prize that they composed the greatest aggregation of varied talents to dine at the White House since Thomas Jefferson had last sat there to eat alone.

But if the multiplicity of Jefferson's accomplishments makes it more difficult to ferret out his identity it also multiplies the fascination of the task. The universe of Jefferson expanded throughout his life and in many directions but there is a thread of continuity between the sixteen-year-old "T. Jefferson" who wrote his guardian about his longing for "a more universal acquaintance" with men and with fields of learning and the eighty-two-year-old "Th. Jefferson" who wrote a Dutch scientist that he was reluctantly interrupting his study of the classics to acquire newly published knowledge.

Nor were the public and the private Jefferson compartmentalized in mature life. The public servant and the votary of love were not radically different aspects of a schizophrenic personality. The Jefferson who, seeking a model for the capitol of Virginia, by his own admission spent hours gazing "at the Maison Carrée like a lover at his mistress" was the same Jefferson who a few months earlier had been unable to dismiss from his mind the marble smoothness of Maria Cosway's shoulders. The paterfamilias of Monticello who often provided his children and grandchildren too much protective shade for healthy growth was not far removed from the sage of Monticello who was sometimes too anxiously paternal in committing the infant Republic to liberty's care.

It is not surprising that Jefferson, as one of the most interesting persons in history, should be one of those most written about. If he has been unfortunate during his lifetime and since in inspiring detractors and overzealous admirers who have equally distorted his image, he has also been fortunate in finding able and patient biographers who were content to paint his portrait "touch by touch" in the manner recommended by Henry Adams and have foreborne to limn him in darker or brighter hues than fidelity to fact would warrant. Their work, and even that of some less sober scholars, has shed revealing light on the primary sources which another student of Jefferson must study for himself.

Because of their contributions, one of less than herculean stature has the temerity to attempt a herculean task—producing a life of Jefferson that, without straining after novelty, provides fresh and provocative interpretations of some aspects of his character. Such a work demands the reconciling of distillations of Jeffersonian scholarship that superficially may seem totally incompatible. There is need for a biography of Jefferson that gives due consideration to the passion, overt and sublimated, that was so vital a part of his personality. But there is no need for another book that attempts a case history of his sex life. Such a work can never replace a profound multivolume work of massive scholarship devoted to all aspects of Jefferson's thought. Indeed, in the foreseeable future, no book or books will make obsolete the most monumental of the studies of his life and times, the six volumes and nearly one and a half million words of Dumas Malone's great biography. But the understanding of the great American gained from study of that work can be enhanced by judicious consideration of some of the more valid intuitions inspired by modern psychology and some of the evidences of the passionate loves and hates of one who self-consciously dedicated his life to reason.

A synthesis is needed—a synthesis of traditional historical scholarship with the new scholarship that seems fresh because it returns to the still older tradition that nothing human is alien.

As one gets closer to Jefferson his faults increase in magnitude, but so do his virtues. The experience is by turns humbling and exhilarating. Often, when we add a little to our knowledge of Jefferson, we encounter new paradoxes. The historian is reminded of a statement by one of Jefferson's favorite heroes, Sir Isaac Newton, that the more he increased the island of his knowledge the more he enlarged the shoreline of wonder.

Nevertheless, examining Jefferson's life is a far from profitless enterprise. Not just because it gives us the opportunity to see momentous events in America and Europe through the eyes of an intimately concerned participant with an extraordinary range of interests. And not even just because he united genius and a charismatic personality, both of which are fascinating subjects for study. Jefferson, more than any other American, exemplified Plato's ideal of the philosopher-king, the governor who is also a devotee of wisdom. Though the terminology, particularly in translation, is monarchial, the kind of leader envisioned by Plato would fit as readily into the Republic of his dreams as into the most regal of the Greek city-states. He wrote: "the human race will not see better days until either the stock of those who rightly and genuinely follow philosophy acquire political authority, or else the class who have political control be led by some dispensation of Providence to become real philosophers."

Jefferson is a phenomenon rare, perhaps even unique, in the American Presidency. We will be rewarded by a survey of the armory of ideas that he brought in 1801 to the office of chief magistrate of the American Republic. He came to his command post with no comprehensive plan of attack on the problems of the nation or the world, for he was as much pragmatist as idealist, often more a tactician than a strategist. But he did bring a set of objectives chosen with one eye on the future and he adhered to them with remarkable consistency through a long public life. It is interesting to learn how he was led to these objectives—sometimes by the probings of reason, sometimes by the promptings of desire. Some ideas born of emotion were later ratified by intellect and experience. These ideas, whatever their origin, constitute a philosophy, not in a formal or academic sense, but a recognizable philosophy nonetheless, one bearing the distinctive stamp of America's Philosopher-King. Appropriately enough, one is reminded of Plato's own statement that a Philospher-King is "something of a paradox."

II

THE WORLD BECKONS

"**W**OULD YOU go back to your cradle and live over again your seventy years?"[1] From Massachusetts John Adams addressed the question to Jefferson in the spring of 1816, several years after the Virginian had completed his seventh decade.

"I say Yea," Jefferson answered. "I think with you that it is a good world on the whole, that it has been framed on a principle of benevolence, and more pleasure than pain dealt out to us. . . . I steer my bark with Hope in the head, leaving Fear astern."[2]

Characteristically, Adams, having gotten an answer to one question, pressed another. Would his old friend be willing to live his life over and over throughout eternity? Jefferson's response would not be influenced by any contagion of optimism, for Adams confessed that a perpetual cycle of existence would "terrify" him "almost as much as annihilation."[3] Jefferson, however, found pleasure in such a prospect—provided that he might exclude the years after sixty and before twenty-five. He qualified the statement only slightly, saying that he "might" be willing to start at some point before twenty-five although he would not consider reliving forever the years after sixty.[4]

In 1825, when Adams reverted to the same subject, Jefferson, now eighty-two, said that he would be willing to relive all but the last seven years.[5] By that time his memories of childhood and youth evidently had mellowed. Still there was no nostalgic longing in the spirit of "When I Was One and Twenty" and no fond remembrance of earlier years. Admittedly, adolescence is frequently a troubled period made more so by adult insistence that the suffering teenagers are enjoying the happiest days of their lives. But even childhood in a privileged society in an idyllic setting was not rendered golden by the alembic of Jefferson's memory. At least once as a mature man he seems to have been close to equating childhood and youth with old age as periods of life when pain outweighed pleasure.

Why should his early years have been unhappy? The evidence on which to base an informed opinion is scarce. We know a good deal about the colonial Virginia environment and a fair amount about the particular localities in which he grew to manhood. But we know little about the specific conditions of his home life. There is reliable information about his father but his mother is a shadowy figure whose faint image yields to the persistent *pentimento* of her distinguished ancestors. There is only room then for modest inference regarding the causes of Jefferson's early unhappiness.

He was born in one of the most beautiful parts of America in the season of its greatest beauty. By the old style calendar then prevailing and according to the political boundaries then extant, he began life on April 2, 1743, in Goochland County, Virginia.[6] By the new calendar he was born on April 13 of that year and, by the modern map, in Albemarle County. His birthplace was a modest frame house little distinguished from many another within Virginia's borders though probably above the common standard of the frontier.[7]

In contrast to the simplicity of man-made structures was the magnificence of the natural setting. Transplanted Englishmen had found here an exotic country where the plow exposed blood-red earth from which burgeoned every spring new green life of startling vividness. If the fields of Albemarle are savagely beautiful in the Gauguin-like clash of elemental colors, the majestic mountain backdrop, softly blue, gray, and green, has the luminous lyricism of Corot. In 1670 the explorer John Lederer, standing on the crest of this region's Blue Ridge Mountains, had thought that he saw a misty ocean extending to the western horizon. Today, one standing on Jefferson's own beloved mountaintop on certain spring days may look out upon the ranges of lesser hills like ice-blue waves sweeping in from the mists of the west to break far below his feet in the white foam of dogwood.

Jefferson was to remain all his life sensitive to the beauties of his native landscape. While he acknowledged that the arts of Europe excelled those of America in his time, he always maintained, even after crossing the Alps, that the Old World could not match the grandeur of the New World's scenery. Among the most eloquent romantic contributions to early American literature are his tribute to the sublimity of Natural Bridge and his description of the dramatic confluence of the Shenandoah and the Potomac at Harper's Ferry. It is likely that Jefferson's remarkable esthetic sensitivity was heightened by the beauty of his childhood surroundings.

The odds were good that he would attain a respectable position in the community, perhaps even a conspicuous one in the colony. In an agricultural society of pioneers and planters that put its trust in bloodlines as well as Providence, young Tom was generally acknowledged to spring from promising stock.

His father, Peter Jefferson, was an extraordinarily vigorous man of thirty-five years at the time of the boy's birth.[8] Tradition has ascribed to him impressive physical feats such as the simultaneous lifting of two hogsheads of tobacco, one in each hand. This particular tradition, perpetuated by both Jefferson descendants and professional historians, may have originated from a letter in which the patriarch reported that he could raise two hogsheads of tobacco with his two hands, that is, grow two hogsheads of the product with the help of two field hands. The likelihood of the less spectacular version is increased by the fact that in Peter Jefferson's time two such hogsheads would have weighed about a ton.

But, whatever the truth of this particular story, he must have been a man of great physical strength. Stories of muscular prowess cluster about his name. According to one, he singlehandedly pulled down a shed after three of his workers had failed in a concerted attempt. Members of his family recalled his frequently saying, "It is the strong in body who are both the strong and *free* in mind."[9] Physical strength was often essential to freedom in the frontier society in which Peter Jefferson moved. One of his favorite maxims would doubtless have been subscribed to by most of his neighbors: "Never ask another to do for you what you can do for your self."[10] In obvious respects, Peter Jefferson was very like those neighbors—though stronger, taller, more resourceful, nearer to the ideal to which they aspired.

But he also had a life which few of them shared—a life of the mind. He had had little formal education but he had found delight in books. In the words of his illustrious son, he was "eager about information."[11] He learned surveying and, with Professor Joshua Fry of the College of William and Mary, became one of the two greatest cartographers in the American colonies.[12] He was sufficiently accomplished in address to win the hand of Jane Randolph and the enthusiastic friendship of the powerful and elegant Tidewater clan to which she belonged. Thomas Jefferson all his life reverenced the memory of his father. He seems to have implied what his cousin John Marshall once said explicitly of his own father, that he never had a child who was his equal. Like Jefferson, Marshall was the scion of a marriage betweeen a frontier leader of small formal learning and a lady of proud Randolph descent.

So much has been written about the exalted status of the Randolphs that many people have assumed that Thomas's paternal antecedents were very humble folk. Such was not the case. Peter Jefferson could not have declared, as Junot, "I am my own ancestor." Peter's father, Thomas Jefferson II,[13] had been a prosperous planter before suffering reverses late in life. His financial troubles, however, did not endanger his social position in Henrico County, where he served as sheriff, militia captain, and for almost two decades as one of the "gentlemen justices." Among those who dined at his table were Randolphs, and Eppeses, and William Byrd of Westover, who would come to be known as the "premier gentleman of America." Thomas II was intimately involved in two prestigious institutions of Virginia society, having built an Anglican church at his own expense and maintained a racing mare. His identification in the first instance was so complete that the house of worship in his parish became known as Jefferson's Church. And he took his second interest so seriously that he carried a disputed race to court. He strengthened his position in the colony by marrying Mary Field, daughter of Major Peter Field of New Kent County, stepdaughter of Captain Henry Randolph, and granddaughter of Henry Soane, a former speaker of the Virginia House of Burgesses.

Thomas II's father, the first Thomas Jefferson of Virginia,[14] had left a modest plantation and several slaves upon his death in 1697. He was a surveyor of the highways in Henrico County, and evidently earned respect as a man of integrity and some competence in practical affairs as he was occasionally an executor of wills.

Of this first Thomas's antecedents little is certainly known. But this fact is not proof of their obscurity. The ancestral link was often lost in the course of seventeenth-century emigration to America, surviving usually only because of the peculiar eminence of the persons concerned or their close relatives, or because of bequests to those left behind in the old country. Thomas I may not have been an immigrant; a "Mr. Jefferson" had been a member of the first representative assembly in the New World, which had convened at Jamestown in 1619. But the relationship here is purely conjectural. A strong tradition that the Jefferson family had once lived near the mountain of Snowden in Wales influenced Peter Jefferson to give the same name to his property on the Fluvanna River. It now seems probable that the first Thomas's father and grandfather had been plantation masters in the West Indies, to which they had emigrated from Suffolk, England.

Contrary to frequent assertion, the author of the Declaration of Independence was interested in his British ancestry. In 1771 he commissioned a London agent to "search the Herald's office for the arms of my family. I have what I have been told were the family arms, but on what authority I know not. It is possible there may be none. If so, I would with your assistance become a purchaser, having Sterne's word for it that a coat of arms may be purchased as cheap as any other coat."[15] The humorous allusion to *Tristram Shandy* is the kind of deprecatory reference to genealogy still considered obligatory by many American gentlemen as a preface to serious inquiry concerning their ancestors.

In the same vein, Thomas Jefferson comments on the Randolphs in his autobiography: "They trace their pedigree far back in England and Scotland, to which let everyone ascribe the faith and merit he chooses." Jane, wife of Peter Jefferson and mother of Thomas, was the granddaughter of William and Mary Isham Randolph of Turkey Island on the James River. They were the ancestors of so many notables that they have come to be called "the Adam and Eve of Virginia."[16] Of course, at the time of Tom's birth in 1743, no one could have foreseen that their descendants would one day include, besides the newborn Jefferson boy and Peyton Randolph, who was still thirty-one years from presidency of the Continental Congress, Edmund Randolph, George Randolph, John Randolph of Roanoke, "Light Horse Harry" Lee, John Marshall, Robert E. Lee, and many nationally prominent people of the twentieth century.

But the Randolphs already had in Virginia a prestige rivaled only by the Lees, the Carters, and the Byrds. In his *Travels in North America,* published in 1787, the Marquis de Chastellux complained: "One must be fatigued with hearing the name of Randolph in traveling in Virginia (for it is one of the most ancient families in the country, a Randolph being among the first settlers) and is likewise one of the most numerous and rich. It is divided into seven or eight branches, and I am not afraid of exaggerating when I say that they possess an income of upwards of a million livres."[17]

Jane Jefferson brought her son a notable heritage through her grandmother Mary Isham as well as through the Randolphs. This line went back through Sir Henry de Greene, Lord Chief Justice of England in the fourteenth century, to the Saier de Quincy, one of the leaders of the Magna Charta barons of 1215; King David I of Scotland; Hugh Magnus of France, leader of the First Crusade; and the two greatest rulers of medieval Europe, Alfred the Great and Charlemagne.[18] How much of this Isham family lore was familiar to Jane we do not know.

In fact, we know little of Jane herself. She must have been very dear to her husband, for, in giving the name Shadwell to his home where Tom was born, Peter Jefferson perpetuated the name of the London parish that was her birthplace.[19] Twenty-three years before Tom's birth she had been baptized in St. Paul's. Her father, Isham Randolph, had then represented the Colony of Virginia as its Colonial Agent in England. He led a diverse life, as diplomat, sea captain, politician, military officer, planter, and father of eleven children. When Jane was small, he returned to his native Virginia, increasing his acres and serving as burgess and colonel of militia, and eventually as Adjutant General, or chief military officer, of the colony. In England as well as Virginia, he enjoyed some reputation as an amateur naturalist.

Jane was nineteen in 1739 when she left Dungeness, her father's house, as the bride of Peter Jefferson. The woods of Goochland were ablaze with the glories of a Virginia October as the couple rode to the smaller, less elegant, plantation that would be their home. The groom was thirteen years her senior, a common circumstance in that day. As the eldest of the numerous Randolph progeny, she was perhaps mature for her years. The man at her side had long enjoyed the respect and confidence of her family. Her father and his nephew had shared Peter's substantial bond when he had become sheriff.

Though falling far short of the wealth of the Randolphs, Peter was prospering. Four years earlier he had acquired a thousand-acre tract that included the future site of Monticello. The next year, in a curious transaction, he gained a homesite and two hundred acres from William Randolph in exchange for a bowl of arrack punch prepared by Henry Wetherburn of Williamsburg's Raleigh Tavern. By the time of Tom's birth in April 1743 Peter probably owned at least 1,550 acres in the area.[20]

Tom was the third child. He had been preceded by Jane, now three, and Mary, not yet two. It is unlikely that Tom enjoyed for long, if ever, the undivided attentions of a doting mother. He was one of ten children born to Mrs. Jefferson within a period of fifteen years, the middle child of five born within six years.[21] Whatever the demands on Jane the mother, Jane the sister gave young Tom a full measure of affectionate attention. Singing psalms to him, she introduced him to the pleasures of music, which remained a lifelong delight. She was an eager listener when he excitedly told of his readings. Many years later, Thomas Jefferson's grandchildren, recalling his loving recollections of his sister, implied that she had done more than anyone else in his childhood to stimulate his ambition. Perhaps the gentle refinement of the Randolphs came to young Tom more through association with Jane, the first-born, than through his mother, who was pregnant roughly four and a half of the first ten years of his life.[22]

Thomas's own earliest recollection dated from the age of two. He remembered being "handed up and carried on a pillow by a mounted slave" as the family moved to Tuckahoe.[23] This plantation had been the home of Colonel William Randolph, Jane Jefferson's cousin and Peter's good friend. As death neared, Randolph had asked Peter to assume personal charge of his estate and his only son, the infant Thomas Mann Randolph. For the next seven years the Jeffersons lived in this James River home, a few miles above Richmond, where Tom became accustomed to a more elegant environment than Shadwell provided. Peter never claimed for this service that disrupted his life any compensation beyond his support while he lived on the estate.

Tom's next memory was of going out at Tuckahoe, a year or two after moving there, and repeating the Lord's Prayer. The boy's dinner was vey late and he fervently hoped for a swift response to "Give us this day our daily bread."[24]

Colonel Randolph had provided that his son be educated at home by tutors. Tom shared the instruction, apparently along with the two little Randolph girls and those of his own sisters that could benefit. Elizabeth Jefferson, born eighteen months after Tom, could not. Her intelligence was painfully subnormal.[25] Some suggested that she was born before her mother had fully recovered from Tom's birth.

During the Tuckahoe years Peter Jefferson helped to survey what later came to be known as the Fairfax Line. This boundary marked the western limits of the Northern Neck Proprietary of Lord Fairfax, the peninsula bounded on the east by the Chesapeake Bay and lying between the Rappahannock and Potomac Rivers. The line was run across seventy-six miles of mountainous wilderness between the headwaters of the two rivers. Peter Jefferson was one of two surveyors whose names appeared on the resulting map of the Northern Neck that was sent to England.[26]

Tom seems to have been too young to have absorbed much detailed information about his father's exploits on this surveying expedition, but he eagerly listened to reports of another three years later, when he was six. With Colonel Joshua Fry, Peter Jefferson led a party that surveyed the Virginia-North Carolina boundary, carrying it ninety miles inland from the westernmost point reached by Colonel William Byrd in his famous expedition. Tom passed on to his own children stories of his father's battling wild beasts and finding enough refreshment sleeping in a hollow tree to fight off fatigue when his companions fell from exhaustion.[27]

Though Peter Jefferson may not have loomed as large in the view of his peers as in the wide eyes of his young son, he nevertheless gained great prestige from the success of the expedition. The Council of Virginia voted him and Colonel Fry each the sum of three hundred pounds beyond expenses. When a new map of the colony was ordered a few months later by the Lords of Trade, Jefferson and Fry were selected to draw it. Their map still stands as one of the monuments of cartography in British America.[28]

Shortly afterward Peter Jefferson and his family returned to Shadwell. Not long before they had left their old home, the part of Goochland in which it was located had become a portion of the new county of Albemarle. The new political entity was quick to recognize Colonel Jefferson's proven abilities. He became county lieutenant, a position frequently held by noblemen in England and by Byrds, Carters, and Lees in Virginia. And he was elected to the House of Burgesses.[29]

Much of the time Tom was not with his family at Shadwell. When he was nine his father placed him as a boarding student in the Latin school of the Reverend William Douglas, minister of Goochland's St. James Parish. From him the boy learned French, Latin, and Greek—with a Scottish burr.[30] But there had been time for learning at Shadwell, too. One who collected information directly from Tom's grandchildren said that before he was fourteen the boy had learned from his father "to sit his horse, fire his gun, (and) boldly stem the Rivanna" when it was boiling red in floodtime.[31] It has been observed that young aristocrats of Virginia's Golden Age, like the sons of the ancient Persian nobility, were taught to ride well, shoot straight, and tell the truth. Apparently shooting straight did not come as easily to Tom as the other accomplishments. When he was ten years old his father sent him into the woods with a gun to bring back a wild turkey. After many failures the child found one in a pen, tied it to a tree with his garter in defiance of the flapping wings, shot it, and returned with his prize.[32]

When Tom was fourteen, his school days in Goochland were ended by his father's death. This event may have been even more than normally traumatic for the boy, because the passage of years and friendship with the great of the world never diminished his veneration for Peter Jefferson.

The adolescent had the slender form and delicate features of his mother's family, but he was physically his father's child too. He was doubtless pleased when people noted that he had the "calm, thoughtful, firm eye" and the facial outline of Peter Jefferson.[33]

A change of scene and new labors may have aided Tom's adjustment to his loss. He was sent to the school of the Reverend James Maury, fourteen miles from Shadwell, at the base of the highest mountain of the Southwest Range. There, in a log school house almost engulfed by the wilderness and the brooding mountains, he learned Homer's lines about the "wine-dark sea" and recited the rolling periods of Cicero. Tom had not warmed to his former teacher but he had not realized the man's professional shortcomings until he had had the advantage of studying under Mr. Maury. The child of intelligent Huguenot immigrants, Maury had been broadly educated at the College of William and Mary. Besides conveying his enthusiasm for classical tongues, he ardently maintained that the English language was "as enchanting as any that was ever spoken by any of the different families of the earth."[34]

Only five boys comprised the class that bounced Hector's boasts from the log walls. One of these was young James Maury, the schoolmaster's son, who often spent the weekends at Shadwell with Tom. Another was Dabney Carr, who had a swift horse. Tom, who had a slow pony, was regarded as foolishly optimistic when he agreed to race with Dabney if he himself might pick the date. Though several of the students were quite quick in their formal studies, they did not realize until much later why Tom had chosen February 30.[35]

Not all of his hours away from study were spent in boyish frolics. He formed the habit of taking long walks in that rugged country, and he spent many hours playing the violin.

After two years Tom left the log school and returned to Shadwell. He had become a very promising classical scholar and his proficiency on the violin was obvious when he played as he and his sister Jane sang together at the family fireside in winter or on the banks of the Rivanna in the "soft summer twilight."[36]

But he had not retired quietly into the bosom of his family. A letter that he wrote to one of his legal guardians, John Harvey, on January 14, 1760, not only tells of his hunger for wider experience but also suggests that he had become the center of a busy social life:

> I was at Colo. Peter Randolph's [a cousin's] about a Fortnight ago, and my Schooling falling into Discourse, he said he thought it would be to my advantage to go to the College, and was desirous I should go, as indeed I am myself for several Reasons. In the first place as long as I stay at the Mountains the Loss of one fourth of my Time is inevitable, by Company's coming here and detaining me from School. And likewise my Absence will in a great Measure put a Stop to so much Company, and by that Means lessen the Expences of the Estate in House-Keeping. And on the other Hand by going to the College I shall get a more universal Acquaintance, which may hereafter be serviceable to me; and I suppose I can pursue my Studies in the Greek and Latin as well there as here, and likewise learn something of the Mathematics. I shall be glad of your opinion.[37]

Which of Tom's tactfully worded arguments convinced John Harvey we do not know. But in 1760, at the age of seventeen, the boy entered the College of William and Mary in Williamsburg.

On his way to the colonial capital, he stopped over for the Christmas holidays at the home of Colonel Nathan Dandridge in Hanover County.[38] Here there was much drinking of toasts and fiddling and dancing. Tom was for his age an accomplished violinist and he had had instruction from a dancing master. "Virginians will dance or die," observed a Yankee tutor in their midst.[39] But there was one guest at Dandridge's whose very "passion," as Tom afterward said, "was fiddling, dancing and pleasantry." Some would not have deemed him the most instructive companion for Tom, but the boy found him fascinating. This neighbor of Dandridge's laughed and joked as lustily as if he had not already, by the age of twenty-three, exhausted his inheritance, having been a husband since the age of eighteen and a father several times over, and failed twice as a storekeeper and once as a farmer. His most visible acquisition was a reputation as a ne'er-do-well. One would not have suspected that his father had imparted to him some portion of his own classical education or that his mother was regarded by the polished William Byrd as one of the most fascinating conversationalists in Virginia, although the young man did express his confidence that men's "naiteral" parts could be improved by "larnin." There were times when his voice rang out so sonorously that the young people flocked from other rooms to hear his anecdotes. But Tom seems to have been present even when various diversions reduced the audience to one.

They were a strangely contrasting pair. Both were tall and thin, but the older man's slightly stooped figure was gauntly rugged while Tom's slenderness seemed more fragile. The loud-talking stranger had hair as uncompromisingly black as a crow's wing while the soft-spoken youngster's hair was chestnut, auburn, or sandy, depending upon the angle of light. A superficial observer might have said that both were gray-eyed, but Tom's calm, reflective eyes were actually hazel while those of his companion gleamed like polished steel. The senior's coarse-featured face seemed almost bloodless whereas Tom's delicate features were enlivened by a ruddy complexion. The same thin-skinned sensitivity that made the teenager the easy victim of both sun and wind also heightened every blush.

When the two parted at the end of the holidays, Tom to go to Williamsburg and a college education and his new friend to return to the farm and he knew not what, they promised to meet again, perhaps in the colonial capital. Tom's remarkable companion would not forget him. And Thomas Jefferson would always remember his first meeting with Patrick Henry.

III

'SEMINARY OF SEDITION'

WHAT SEVENTEEN-year-old Tom Jefferson first saw when he rode into Williamsburg we do not know. But we can be sure that he found it wonderful. The five-day ride on horseback from Albemarle County was an odyssey to the boy who had never before ventured more than twenty miles from home, and the capital was a metropolis to one who until then had never "seen a town of more than twenty houses."[1] Duke of Gloucester Street, wide enough for several carriages to travel abreast, stretched for a mile between story-and-a-half houses and shops. At its eastern end stood the rose brick capitol, with its portico of Doric and Ionic columns.[2] At the western end was the triangular, brick-walled yard of William and Mary College with its three rose brick buildings, the twelve-dormered roof of the largest bearing a high cupola. The original plans for this building apparently had been drawn by Sir Christopher Wren, but probably the name of England's greatest architect meant nothing to Tom at this stage of his life. About two-thirds of the way from the college to the capitol was Bruton Parish Church, not yet distinguished by the tall spire that would have excited his awe but chastely impressive with its long windows set in mellow red brick made to seem ruddier by the surrounding white tabletop tombs. Stretching northward from Duke of Gloucester Street past the church was the Palace Green. And visible at the end of the level green was the Governor's Palace itself, rising grandly above its handsome brick outer walls and magnificently grilled gates, its tall lantern cupola soaring in two tiers above the steep hip roof.[3] Though Tom many years later would become disenchanted with the Georgian style, he must have been confident at this time that the Palace was the handsomest residence in the American colonies. And many far more sophisticated people would have agreed. In that elegant residence lived Francis Fauquier, Virginia's popular royal governor and one of the most polished gentlemen of the Empire.

But, however interesting the Palace, and the capitol where Tom's father had served as a Burgess and where his Randolph cousins continued to sit in the Council, these buildings surely did not hold for him the fascination that drew him to the college. He may have thought in passing that, like his father, he might some day be a Burgess. But in his seventeenth year he seems to have been more intent upon becoming a scholar.

Apparently Tom was housed in what has come to be known as the Wren Building, the central and largest of the college structures. Those familiar with the Georgian charm of its many-windowed façade will be shocked by Jefferson's later lumping of it with the mental hospital in Williamsburg as "rude, misshapen piles, which, but that they have roofs, would be taken for brick-kilns."[4] But by that time he was even describing the Governor's Palace as "not handsome" and saying of all Virginia, already adorned then by houses still considered among America's most beautiful, "The genius of architecture seems to have shed its maledictions over this land."[5] When he saw the architecture of England he concluded it was worse than America's, though maintaining that Paris was even less handsome than London.[6] But at seventeen Tom was probably far less critical than in later years, and even in that subsequent time he admitted that the capitol, the college, and the hospital for lunatics were the most impressive public buildings in Virginia. Whatever he thought of the Wren Building itself, he must have admired from its balcony the mile-long sweep of Duke of Gloucester Street to the capitol, enlivened as it was by pedestrians, people on horseback, ox carts, covered wagons, phaetons, and sometimes jostling herds of cattle. Of course, even that extensive view could not match the majesty of mountain vistas back home.

But the intellectual horizons were excitingly wider. The seven-man faculty included several who had been distinguished for scholarship at Oxford and Cambridge. Nevertheless, far more important than these in Tom's eyes was William Small, a twenty-six-year-old alumnus of the much less prestigious Aberdeen. It is chiefly to his momentous meeting with Jefferson that Small owes an honored place in history. Jefferson's autobiographical tribute to Small was all that the most egotistical teacher could hope for from an illustrious former student:

> It was my great good fortune, and what probably fixed the destinies of my life, that Dr. William Small of Scotland was then professor of mathematics, a man profound in most of the useful branches of science, with a happy and an enlarged and liberal mind. He, most happily for me, became soon attached to me and made me his daily companion when not engaged in the school, and from his conversation I got my first views of the expansion of science and of the system of things in which we are placed. Fortunately the philosophical chair became vacant soon after my arrival at college and he was appointed to fill it *per interim,* and he was the first who ever gave in that college regular lectures in ethics, rhetoric, and belles lettres.[7]

History has tended to echo Jefferson's high praise of Small without inquiring further into his character. But enthusiasm for the professor was far from unanimous in Williamsburg during his residence there, and there are reasons for considering him a much more complicated figure than the simple compound of sweetness and light that his prize pupil made him out to be. A profile sketch[8] of Small shows a long, pointed, boldly out-thrust nose and a receding brow and chin, as though the eagerly probing proboscis were outrunning the rest of his face. There were those who believed that the inquisitive nose was thrust into too many places where it had no business. It found its skeptical way into the operations of the college, the customs of society, and even those processes of nature which a largely clerical faculty thought should be beyond the profane inquiry of man. This very skepticism made him attractive to his adolescent charges, as did his stand as the lone faculty member opposed to the professors' assertion that each teacher had the right to punish any refractory student in the way he deemed most appropriate.[9] All the facts about Small also tend to make him seem a thoroughgoing hero to most of today's readers—a free spirit of the Enlightenment in a repressive environment.

But there was another side of his character. He seems to have been free of the common vices of the time and place. He specifically was not given to drunkenness, a problem of the William and Mary faculty dating back at least to the time when Colonel William Byrd, as a member of the Board of Visitors, had to rise distressingly early after a night of heavy drinking to consider the fate of a professor charged with the same offense. But Small eventually earned the enmity of the Board, even of those members who originally had welcomed him as an antidote to the heavy clericalism of the faculty. Some seven years after Jefferson first met Small the teacher would be charged with "assum[ing] the Physician Title of Dr." and dashing about the colony to practice his newly acquired arts on "some of the principal Gentlemen," to the neglect of his pedagogical responsibilities. Small made himself obnoxious to the Visitors by frequent demands for salary increases and for home-leave, on one occasion for eighteen months, in order to purchase scientific equipment for the college. Failure to grant his requests provoked from him remonstrances charging the officials with "Ingratitude and Inattention to his past service." In the midst of his running battle with them he applied for the position of president. His career at William and Mary culminated in an absence without leave of more than two years and a series of letters in which he berated the Rector and Board. What slights, real or imagined, may have provoked Small into such disgruntlement we do not know, but obviously Jefferson's beloved teacher was no gentle, self-neglectful "Mr. Chips."

Nevertheless, on the credit side, it must be recorded that he did secure for the college the finest collection of scientific equipment in America. And his worth to college and colony may well have been greater than the Board realized. He had no publications to prove his scholarship, but he must have had a stimulating mind. The two great American polymaths of the eighteenth century, Jefferson and Benjamin Franklin, united in his praise, and one of the greatest English polymaths of the period, Erasmus Darwin, composed an elegy in his honor. Small was accused of being disrespectful of many things, but so far as we can discover, never genius. He evidently discovered genius in teen-aged Tom.

The intellectual excitement of the Enlightenment must have come to the boy through Small. All his previous teachers had been Anglican clergymen, a group not enthusiastic about the new learning with its questioning of established institutions. From the Enlightenment Thomas Jefferson took his three greatest heroes, Bacon, Newton, and Locke. They remained his heroes for life.

From Francis Bacon, Viscount St. Albans, he learned to trust his own powers of observation and not to receive any opinion unquestioningly because of reverence for the source. He became aware of the Idols of the Cave, learning that each of us dwells in a cave of his own, his individuality, which "refracts and discolors the light of nature," so that he would not put too great trust even in his own views. He learned to examine most critically those beliefs which were especially pleasing to him. Particularly inspiring to an idealistic youth was Bacon's assertion that, if reason and learning were applied to the tasks of government in an earnest desire to improve society, all that humankind had done would be "but an earnest of the things they shall do."

Sir Isaac Newton presented nature as a model of harmony from which man might deduce laws for his own guidance. Newton's *Principia* gave rise to the famous Deist concept of a mechanical universe, a great clock invented, constructed, and set in motion by the Deity. This view, which made no allowance for miracles, was anathema to orthodox clergymen, so it is unlikely that Tom had heard of it from previous schoolmasters except by way of warning. It is ironic that so many thinkers influenced by Newton's view of the universe should have been branded heretics, for the physicist himself was deeply religious and wrote more volumes of theology than of science. Nature was his Revelation; in effect, he echoed the psalmist: "The heavens declare the glory of God: and the firmament sheweth his handiwork."[10]

John Locke, Tom's third hero, related the empiricism of Bacon and Newton to man's life as a political animal. *An Essay Concerning Human Understanding* alerted the youth to the beginning of modern psychology and fed his hopes for the improvement of humankind. Locke's argument that each human mind was a blank tablet (*tabula rasa*) until written upon by experience fed hopes (never abandoned by Jefferson) of lifting virtually all people through education. Through Locke or his adherents, Jefferson would be converted to the theory, prominent in the *Second Treatise of Civil Government*, that legitimate authority to rule was derived from the consent of the governed. This theory, of course, would gain far greater circulation through the document prepared by Jefferson than through all the lengthy expositions and advocacies of Locke and his fellow philosophers. The Declaration of Independence would also echo Locke's belief that in the "state of nature" all human beings were free and equal. But the brevity and declamatory style of the declaration would not permit inclusion of Locke's explanation that equality was a matter of rights and not of abilities. Through hortatory exegesis Jefferson would be cited in support of an idea that his reason could not accept.

After mature consideration, one must take at face value Jefferson's conclusion that his association with Small "probably fixed the destinies of [his] life." Not only did Small introduce the Virginian to the three men who would remain his great heroes. So great was the influence of one of these—Locke—that a leading scholar of American intellectual history and political theory has written that *An Essay Concerning Human Understanding* and the *Second Treatise of Civil Government* "undergirded all [Jefferson's] thought."[11] Small enlisted Jefferson in the Enlightenment and in so doing enrolled a legion. Few American historians would quarrel with the assertion of Franklin's biographer, Ralph Ketcham, that "Jefferson stands with Franklin as the supreme embodiment of the Enlightenment in the United States."[12] Crane Brinton goes further in the entry on the Enlightenment which he prepared for *The Encyclopedia of Philosophy;* surveying the world in search of an individual embodiment of that great movement, he concludes: "we could do much worse than to pick Thomas Jefferson."[13]

Ironically, during the years when Small was exerting his strongest influence on the future and earning his major claim to fame through his influence on his brilliant pupil, he was impatient to escape the backwater of Williamsburg and return to the mainstream of English intellectual life. Nevertheless, the professor's existence in the colonial capital was not all loneliness and intellectual frustration. Along with George Wythe, he was a frequent dinner companion of Governor Fauquier at the Governor's Palace.

At some time during his student days Jefferson, despite his youth, was added to the group. He seems to have made his debut at the Palace as a fiddler, but the Governor and his friends were soon listening to the youth's conversation more than to his music. These sessions became at least as important to Jefferson's education as his experience in the classroom. And how he enjoyed them! In the first place, the table fare provided a welcome escape from the college food which, probably mediocre at best, was the subject of widespread scandal and an official reprimand from the Board of Visitors.[14] Then too, Jefferson, who early developed a taste for elegance, must have delighted in almost every prospect from the time he crossed the polished marble floors gleaming beneath a blazing chandelier in the walnut-paneled foyer. Even in later years when he was critical of the Palace's exterior, he admitted that the interior was handsome. But the sparkle he loved best came from the talk at dinner table, especially when there were just four diners.

The Governor, in his mid-fifties, was the most delightful of hosts. The prominent circles under his eyes somehow deepened his look of sophistication without compromising their liveliness under the brows raised in perpetual inquiry.[15] Technically, he was not Governor but Lieutenant Governor, the higher title being reserved as a sinecure for an English nobleman who remained at home. There was even a story that the office of lieutenant governor was his by chance, being secured for him through the intervention of a great lord who took pity upon him after wiping him out at the gaming table.

The story was doubtless apocryphal but it found believers because Fauquier was too enthusiastic a gambler. His inveterate gaming was the only vice popularly imputed to him. And many years later, as a mature statesman, Jefferson would describe him as the ablest governor Virginia ever had. He had succeeded as soldier and as merchant, was prized as a polished ornament of drawing room and salon, and had evidenced sufficient scholarship to be elected a Fellow of the Royal Society. He sometimes outraged the ecclesiastical establishment of the colony with his outspoken skepticism, but he was generally popular with the great planters and their wives. The river barons who dominated Virginia valued wit and learning and good manners.[16] They thought they saw in Fauquier a pleasing reflection of themselves.

If Fauquier was a model man of the world, Wythe, though still only in his thirties, could have sat for a portrait labeled "The Kindly Savant." His spare figure was dominated by his large head which in turn was almost overwhelmed by the jutting brow of his balding dome. The swelling brain appeared to have stolen extra nutriment from his body. Only after becoming accustomed to the massive skull would one notice the large, wide open, dark gray eyes, bold Roman nose, and intriguing combination of rock-firm jaw and gentle mouth.[17] Wythe was a "home-grown" lawyer: he had not trained in London's Inns of Court like some of Jefferson's Randolph cousins, but had read law in the office of a county practitioner after some education at William and Mary.[18] Nevertheless, he was generally recognized as one of the two best courtroom attorneys in Virginia and second to none in knowledge of the law. He was already highly respected in the General Court and the House of Burgesses. He would later become famous as a signer of the Declaration of Independence and the most celebrated teacher of law in American history. But his interests ranged far beyond public affairs and his profession. A large patrimony had given him early leisure in which to pursue knowledge for its own sake. His tongue dealt as trippingly with even obscure characters in the histories and literatures of various nations as if they had been familiar inhabitants of Williamsburg.

Consider that, in addition to Fauquier and Wythe, the group included Tom's beloved mentor, Small, and there is less cause for surprise that Jefferson, even after his association with Benjamin Franklin, John Adams, and George Mason—not to mention his familiarity with Parisian salons—should have written:

> At these dinners I have heard more good sense, more rational and philosophical conversation, than in all my life besides. They were truly Attic societies.[19]

Not all of Tom's learning sessions were in the ancient Greek tradition of the symposium, with witty exchanges over brimming glasses. In the next century some of his fellow students would have called him a grind. John Page, his closest schoolmate, recalled in later years that he himself had never "made any great proficiency in any study, for I was too sociable, and fond of the conversation of my friends, to study as Mr. Jefferson did, who could tear himself away from his dearest friends, to fly to his studies."[20] Page may have been minimizing his own scholarship; besides cultivating at William and Mary a sociability that helped him to become governor, he acquired under Small's tutelage a lifelong enthusiasm for all branches of mathematics. But he was astounded at Jefferson's capacity to study for fifteen consecutive hours and then bounce back by exercising his mountain-trained long legs in a two-mile run.

If Jefferson was a grind, he was not a Gradgrind. He was not simply collecting facts to satisfy either his teachers or his own acquisitive instinct. He was enlarging his view of the universe. His was not a dull labor, but a passionate pursuit of understanding.

He seems to have been troubled with a passion for other pursuits as well. In recognition of the temptations of the capital, he sometimes called it Devilsburg. The meticulously balanced Georgian architecture of the town presented a face of imperturbable propriety, but the community had its Hogarthian haunts enlivened by lusty wenches and flowing spirits. Besides there were amusements innocent in themselves that through excess became vices. Some hint of Jefferson's adolescent experiences was given when he was President of the United States in a letter he wrote to his grandson Thomas Jefferson Randolph, then a college student. The grandfather expressed "great anxieties" for his namesake, and added, "your dangers are great." He continued:

> When I recollect that at fourteen years of age, the whole care and direction of myself was thrown on myself entirely, without a relation or friend qualified to advise or guide me, and recollect the various sorts of bad company with which I associated from time to time, I am astonished I did not turn off with some of them, and become as worthless to society as they were.

What had saved him?

> I had the good fortune to become acquainted very early with some characters of very high standing, and to feel the incessant wish that I could ever become what they were. Under temptations and difficulties, I would ask myself—what would Dr. Small, Mr. Wythe, Peyton Randolph do in this situation? What course is it will assure me their approbation? I am certain that this mode of deciding on my conduct tended more to correctness than any reasoning power I possessed.

Knowing the even and dignified line they pursued, I could never doubt for a moment which of two courses would be in character for them, whereas, seeking the same object through a process of moral reasoning, and with the jaundiced eye of youth, I should have often erred.[21]

The next part of Jefferson's letter is couched in phrases which suggest that his memory of what he asked himself in youth may have been more than a little tinged with the attitude and rhetoric of advanced years:

From the circumstances of my position, I was often thrown into the society of horse racers, card players, fox hunters, scientific and professional men, and of dignified men; and many a time have I asked myself, in the enthusiastic moment of the death of a fox, the victory of a favorite horse, the issue of a question eloquently argued at the bar, or in the great council of the nation, well, which of these kinds of reputation should I prefer? That of a horse jockey? A fox hunter? An orator? Or the honest advocate of my country's rights? Be assured, my dear Jefferson, that these little returns into ourselves, this self-catechising habit, is not trifling nor useless, but leads to the prudent selection and steady pursuit of what is right.

Besides telling something of the temptations that Jefferson faced as a youth, the letter is enlightening in other ways. It is interesting to know that, looking back, he saw himself at fourteen as thrown entirely upon his own resources "without a relation or friend qualified to advise or guide" him. Is there here an implied derogation of his mother? Some have been quick to say so, but Jefferson's comment need not imply a lack of either intelligence or concern on her part. It seems probable that Jane Randolph Jefferson was keen-witted; a strong tradition persists that her skill as a letter writer was much admired.[22] Though her almost continuous childbearing had deprived Tom of attention during much of his childhood, one is not therefore justified in assuming that she was not interested in him. Jefferson may have felt that his mother, as a lady of the aristocracy, was ill-prepared to warn him of the pitfalls of male lust for drinking, gaming, and wenching.

With his father's old friends and his own Randolph cousins available for occasional counsel, young Tom may not have been as completely alone as he thought he was. But in the case of Jefferson, as with Charles Dickens and other sensitive children who have felt entirely abandoned, the belief in his abandonment may have had an overpowering reality of its own that blotted out any mitigating effects of external reality. Certainly President Jefferson's strong recollection of his sense of aloneness as a child and as a young man is a measure of the trauma which he suffered at his father's death. It also may go far to explain why Jefferson, though willing in his last years to relive most of his life, would have chosen to omit the first two decades.

To what extent can we trust Jefferson's memory of the questions he had posed himself regarding life goals? It seems reasonable to assume that he did indeed decide not to be a jockey or a gamester. Jefferson was a lover of horses in a colony where it was said that people would walk two miles to a stable in order to ride one mile on horseback to their destination and where "sporting parsons" were sometimes accused of too much fondness for the race track. But Jefferson seems always to have been as disinclined to race as in the old days in Maury's school when he resolved to confine such activity to February 30. As for gaming, a great amusement of the Virginia gentry, Jefferson seems never to have indulged. Monticello, in its builder's lifetime, was one of the very few mansions of the Old Dominion in which a pack of cards could not be found. Perhaps the example of the gifted Fauquier wasting too many hours at the card table made a strong impression on his youthful friend. Jefferson was abstemious indeed, rarely drinking anything stronger than a glass of wine and having no use for the colony's chief product, tobacco.[23]

It seems strange, though, that he should have listed oratory with more frivolous pursuits before presenting as an alternative the honest advocacy of his country's rights. What more effective advocate than a great orator? There is ample reason, as we shall later see, to suppose that the youthful Tom had aspired to be an orator and denigrated oratory only in later life when problems of delivery frustrated his ambitions.

Tom had a friend who counted on natural powers of eloquence to reverse his own downward fortunes. About three months after Jefferson, on his way to enroll at William and Mary, had said goodbye to a drifting Patrick Henry, the young man from Hanover had called on him at Williamsburg in a state of high optimism. Henry jauntily announced that he had spent the interim studying law privately and had come to town to obtain his license.[24] Tom, who believed in exhaustive preparation, was even more astonished by what ensued. There were four examiners: George Wythe, Attorney General John Randolph, Peyton Randolph, and Robert Carter Nicholas. Predictably, Mr. Wythe, a most diligent scholar, refused to certify the applicant as adequately prepared. But Peyton Randolph signed for him and Henry then approached the attorney general. John Randolph, taken aback by Henry's uncouth appearance, was sure that examining him would be a waste of time, but Henry persisted, pointing out that he already had one signature and, under the law, needed only a second to qualify. Randolph's supposition that the young man had little formal learning was soon confirmed but Henry defended his opinions so eloquently that the attorney general, indicating his shelves of law books, exclaimed: "Behold the force of natural reason. You have never seen these books, nor this principle of law; yet you are right and I am wrong. And from the lesson which you have given me I will never trust to appearances again." Jefferson, a little disgusted with his cousins' easygoing ways, later reported: "Peyton and John Randolph, men of great facility of temper, signed his license with as much reluctance as their dispositions would permit them to show."

Henry's easy success did not cause Jefferson to relax his study habits. Though he rose at dawn he continued to study well past midnight with another earnest student, John Tyler.[25] Another young man, Frank Willis, of Gloucester County, delighted in overturning the book-laden table of the hardworking pair when he returned from nights of revelry in the town.[26]

But Jefferson was not unsociable. Besides Tyler and John Page, his companions among the students included Dabney Carr, his pony-riding friend from the days at Maury's school. And he belonged to the F.H.C. Society which kept even the basis of its acronym a secret from all but its six members, and which he admitted—or boasted—had "no useful object."[27]

When Jefferson completed his studies at William and Mary in 1762, the nineteen-year-old remained in Williamsburg to study law with George Wythe. Samuel Johnson once observed that law was a study which sharpened the mind by narrowing it. Jefferson was in no danger from this process. With the encouragement of his multi-sided teacher he continued to read in many fields outside the chosen discipline.[28] Besides *Coke upon Littleton* and *Institutes of the Lawes of England,* he read widely in Greek, Latin, French, and English literature. He delighted particularly in Homer, where he found elemental simplicity allied with the scope and cadence of the tides. The stark dignity and grand themes of Greek tragedy stirred his imagination. In Horace, too, he discovered great pleasure; perhaps the satire first appealed to his youthful spirit, but the Roman poet's picture of supreme contentment as found on his country estate amid books and friends and philosophical discussion must have been permanently limned in his imagination. The jeweled Renaissance richness of Shakespeare, the elaborate crewel work of his language, fascinated a young man already bewitched by words, and he shuddered at the filial impiety of Goneril and Regan in *King Lear*.[29] He learned to love the organ tones of Milton, the gracefulness of Dryden, and the concise correctness of Pope. He did not automatically enjoy anything called a classic. Petrarch was not at all to his taste, and he admired rather than relished Dante. But he loved the rapier play of Moliére and the lusty roastbeef humor of Sterne, Fielding, and Smollett. *Don Quixote* amused him and provided him with allusions for a lifetime. He copied favorite ballads from song sheets. With more serious purpose, he copied selections from the eloquence of the two most illustrious orators of the ancient world, Demosthenes and Cicero. He had not yet developed a contempt for oratorical prowess.

Indeed, in the spring of 1762, Jefferson found himself spellbound by an orator. Outasseté, a great Cherokee chief popularly known in Virginia as Outacity, had arrived in Williamsburg en route to England to visit "the Great King, his Father," and incidentally receive Oliver Goldsmith and have his portrait painted by Sir Joshua Reynolds. In Williamsburg he was received by the Governor and Council and entertained at dinner by the college. The chief was no stranger to Tom as the Indian leader had several times been a guest of Peter Jefferson at Shadwell. Tom frequently attended Indian gatherings in Williamsburg, but preternaturally fresh in his memory a half century later was the one in which Outasseté said farewell to his Tennessee tribesmen on the eve of his ocean voyage. Jefferson recalled to his friend John Adams:

The moon was in full splendor, and to her he seemed to address himself in his prayers for his own safety on the voyage, and that of his people during his absence. His sounding voice, distinct articulation, animated action, and the solemn silence of his people at their several fires, filled one with awe and veneration, although I did not understand a word he uttered.[30]

Jefferson was finding very personal uses for whatever eloquence he could muster. And his classical learning served not only to enlarge his intellect but also to furnish him with Greek and Roman code names for young ladies who caught his fancy. For information on this side of his life we are indebted largely to the letters he wrote during long vacations at Shadwell to his confidant John Page. These missives also reveal that, however mature Jefferson might seem when discussing abstruse matters with Fauquier, Small, and Wythe, he was very much the adolescent when confiding affairs of the heart to one of his peers. On Christmas Day, 1762, from a plantation house "an easy day's ride from Shadwell," he wrote Page:

This very day, to others the day of greatest mirth and jollity, sees me over-whelmed with more and greater misfortunes than have befallen a descendant of Adam for these thousand years past I am sure; and perhaps, after excepting Job, since the creation of the world.... I am sure if there is such a thing as a devil in this world, he must have been here last night and have had some hand in con-triving what happened to me. Do you think the cursed rats (at his instigation I suppose) did not eat up my pocketbook which was in my pocket within a foot from my head? And not contented with plenty for the present they carried away my Jimmy worked silk garters and half a dozen new minuets I had just got, to serve as I suppose as provision for the winter. But of this I should not have accused the devil (because you know rats will be rats, and hunger without the addition of his instigation might have urged them to do this) if something worse and from a different quarter had not happened.... When I went to bed I laid my watch in the usual place, and going to take her up after I rose this morning I found her, in the same place it's true but! Quantum mutatis ab illo! all afloat in water let in at a leak in the roof of the house, and as silent and still as the rats that had eat my pocketbook... I should not have cared much for this but something worse attended it: the subtle particles of the water with which the case was filled had by their penetration so overcome the cohesion of the particles of the paper of which my dear picture and watch paper were composed that in attempting to take them out to dry them Good God! mens horret referre! my cursed fingers gave them such a rent as I fear I shall never get over.[31]

In ensuing sentences, Jefferson revealed the plight of an intellectually precocious, but still emotionally immature, teenager chagrined at the overnight loss of his pocket-book, his fancy garters, and the picture of his "best girl," but not so overcome that he could not express his grief in lengthy Latin and Greek quotations. His sorrow at his misfortune was undoubtedly genuine but so probably was his delight in depicting himself bearing his great grief. The whole letter smacks a bit of a child's exclamation, "You should have seen me watching the train wreck!"

He resumed:

However, whatever misfortunes may attend the picture or lover, my hearty prayers shall be that all the health and happiness which heaven can send may be the portion of the original, and that so much goodness may ever meet with what may be most agreeable in this world, as I am sure it must in the next. And now although the picture be defaced there is so lively an image of her imprinted in my mind that I shall think of her too often I fear for my peace of mind, and too often I am sure to get through Old Cooke (Jefferson misspelled phonetically the name of Coke, author of his legal text) this winter: for God knows I have not seen him since I packed him up in my trunk in Williamsburg.

Here he digressed to complain of his studies, lament about life, and provide a broad hint about the sort of young man that might be more successful than he in winning the love of a beautiful young girl:

Well, Page, I do wish the Devil had old Cooke (Coke), for I am sure I never was so tired of an old dull scoundrel in my life. What! are there so few inquietudes tacked to this momentary life of ours that we must need be loading ourselves with a thousand more?... But the old fellows say we must read to gain knowledge; and gain knowledge to make us happy and admired. Mere jargon! No: And as for admiration, I am sure the man who powders most, perfumes most, embroiders most, and talks most nonsense, is most admired. Though to be candid, there are some who have too much good sense to esteem such monkey-like animals as these, in whose formation, as the saying is, the tailors and barber go halves with God Almighty: and since these are the only persons whose esteem is worth a wish, I do not know but that upon the whole the advice of those old fellows may be worth following.

Next he instructs his friend:

Write me very circumstantially everything which happened at the wedding. Was SHE there? Because if she were I ought to have been at the devil for not being there too.

The capitalized SHE was Rebecca Burwell, the young woman whose image was destroyed when the watch case was soaked. She was the sister of a college mate, Lewis Burwell, Jr., of Gloucester County. Tradition, without supplying particulars, says that she was beautiful. Bishop William Meade, a highly respected clergyman and chronicler of Virginia families and institutions, reported that she was of noble character and much more serious-minded than most young ladies. In Jefferson's letter to John Page she appears sometimes as R.B. and often under such pseudonyms as "Belinda," "Adnileb," ("Belinda" in reverse), and "Campana in die."[32]

Jefferson's thralldom to Rebecca Burwell was not such as to prevent him in the same paragraph from asking to be "remember[ed] affectionately" to the Misses Potter who were to be told "the better half of me, my soul, is ever with them" and from sending a special message to another girl:

Tell Miss Alice Corbin that I verily believe the rats knew I was to win a pair of garters from her, or they never would have been so cruel as to carry mine away.

Mixed with Jefferson's ardor was a large share of shyness. He entrusted his friend John Page with a mission that he might have been expected to take care of for himself:

I would fain ask the favor of Miss Becca Burwell to give me another watch paper, of her own cutting, which I should esteem much more though it were a plain round one, than the nicest in the world cut by other hands: however I am afraid she would think this presumption after my suffering the other to get spoiled. If you think you can excuse me to her for this I should be glad if you would ask her.

On January 20, back at Shadwell, Jefferson was complaining in a letter to Page:

> All things here appear to me to trudge on in one and the same round. We rise in the morning that we may eat breakfast, dinner and supper and go to bed again that we may get up the next morning and do the same: so that you never saw two peas more alike than our yesterday and today.[33]

After polite inquiries about a "Nancy" of whom Page was enamoured, Jefferson asked:

> How does R.B. do? What do you think of my affair or what would you advise me to do? Had I better stay here and do nothing, or go down and do less? . . . Inclination tells me to go, receive my sentence, and be no longer in suspense; but reason says, "If you go and your attempt proves unsuccessful you will be ten times more wretched than ever."

To add to his misery, he was suffering from some form of conjunctivitis, or, as he said, the whites of his eyes had been replaced by reds. He had not even the comfort of reading. He proposed, perhaps not entirely in jest, that he acquire a boat (he would name it *Rebecca*) in which he and Page could visit England, Holland, France, Spain, Italy, and Egypt, returning to the British provinces to the north. "This, to be sure, would take us two or three years and if we should not both be cured of love in that time I think the devil would be in it." Meantime, he would find relief in a trip to Williamsburg at the earliest opportunity.

Twenty-three days later the letter was still unsent and Jefferson added a lengthy postscript explaining that his eyes were as red as ever and that, in any event, he would not soon visit Williamsburg as he had learned that there was smallpox in the town. News of the marriage of mutual friends caused him to revert to his old plaint:

> Why cannot you and I be married too, Page, when and to whom we would choose? Do you think it would cause any such mighty disorders among the planets? Or do you imagine it would be attended with such very bad consequences in this bit of a world, this clod of dirt, which I insist is the vilest of the whole system?

Apparently Willis, the man about town and toppler of study tables, had joined Jefferson and Page in a pledge that the first to be married would treat the others, and Tom now asked: "Is there no probability of you or Willis's paying the infant (small bottle) of arrack we betted?"

The letter closed in adolescent hyperbole:

> I verily believe, Page, that I shall die soon, and yet I can give no other reason for it but that I am tired with living. At this moment I am writing I am scarcely sensible that I exist.

Evidently his ennui was genuine. He added another postscript, this time a brief one, before sending the letter on March 11, fifty days after beginning it.

On July 15 Jefferson was still at Shadwell, more anxious than bored, but still the laggard lover, still in a welter of ratiocination, and still hoping that John Page would rescue him. He wrote:

The rival you mentioned I know not whether to think formidable or not as there has been so great an opening for him during my absence. I say "has been" because I expect there is one no longer since you have undertaken to act as my attorney. You advise me to "go immediately and lay siege in form."[34]

Nevertheless, he was disturbed by Page's advice: "Go immediately and lay siege . . . ." Possible imminence of the dreamed-of meeting inspired thoughts of flight. Somewhat reproachfully he replied to his friend:

You certainly did not think at the time you wrote this of that paragraph in my letter wherein I mentioned to you my resolution of going to Britain. And to begin an affair of that kind now, and carry it on so long a time in form is by no means a proper plan. No, no, Page, whatever assurances I may give her in private of my esteem for her, or whatever assurances I may ask in return from her, depend on it they must be kept in private. Necessity will oblige me to proceed in a method which is not generally thought fair, that of treating with a ward before obtaining the approbation of her guardian. I say necessity will oblige me to it, because I never can bear to remain in suspense so long a time. If I am to succeed, the sooner I know it the less uneasiness I shall have to go through: If I am to meet with disappointment, the sooner I know it, the more of life I shall have to wear it off: and if I do meet with one, I hope in God and verily believe it will be the last. I assure you that I almost envy you your present freedom; and if Belinda will not accept of my service it shall never be offered to another.

Jefferson then reveals a Prufrockian plethora of fears, among them that a proposal refused by Rebecca or regarded askance by her family might cause him to lose his present privilege of visiting her freely—one which he does not seem to have indulged in often. Again he asks Page to pave the way for him, and says:

I should be scared to death at making her so unreasonable a proposal as that of waiting until I return from Britain, unless she could be first prepared for it. I am afraid it will make my chance of succeeding considerably worse.

Without so much as a switch of paragraph, Jefferson suddenly shifts to an attitude and style that eighteenth-century gentlemen in their chauvinism would have described as more manly:

But the event at last must be this, that if she consents, I shall be happy; if she does not, I must endeavor to be as much so as possible. I have thought a good deal on your case, and as mine may perhaps be similar, I must endeavor to look on it in the same light in which I have often advised you to look on yours. Perfect happiness I believe was never intended by the Deity to be the lot of any one of his creatures in this world; but that he has very much put in our powers the nearness of our approaches to it is what I as steadfastly believe.

Those brave words have been quoted by various biographers who chose to omit both the agonizing preamble and a concluding paragraph in which Jefferson announced his intention of returning to Williamsburg by the first of October and of building a small house with one room for himself and one for Page, or of building a large dwelling if Belinda should consent to be his wife.

Jefferson was in Williamsburg by October 6, if not before. That evening the long windows of the Raleigh Tavern glowed golden with candlelight, and the sounds of music, dancing, and laughter trailed out into Duke of Gloucester Street like an irresistible invitation. Inside the elegantly paneled Apollo Room, the lanky young man dancing with the beautiful girl was Thomas Jefferson.

The next day he wrote to Page:

In the most melancholy fit that ever any poor soul was, I sit down to write to you. Last night, as merry as agreeable company and dancing with Belinda in the Apollo could make me, I never could have thought the succeeding sun would have seen me so wretched as I now am. I was prepared to say a great deal. I had dressed up in my own mind such thoughts as occurred to me, in as moving language as I know how, and expected to have performed in a tolerably creditable manner. But, good God! When I had an opportunity of venting them, a few broken sentences, uttered in great disorder, and interrupted with pauses of uncommon length, were the too visible marks of my strange confusion.[35]

Some writers have concluded that Jefferson's tongue was hampered by intemperate drinking. This explanation seems unlikely. It is very much in conflict with his abstemious habits. And there is a much simpler interpretation. Anyone who cannot understand verbal confusion in the presence of a most desirable member of the opposite sex has forgotten what it is to be very young, or was possessed in youth of extraordinary confidence in his own charm. Jefferson obviously had no such armor plate of self-esteem. But he did have remarkable powers of recuperation. Before the end of the month he was writing from Richmond to a friend, Will Fleming:

Last Saturday I left Ned Carter's where I had been happy in other good company, but particularly that of Miss Jenny Taliaferro: and though I can view the beauties of this world with the most philosophical indifference, I could not but be sensible of the justice of the character you had given me of her. She has in my opinion a great resemblance of Nancy Wilson, but prettier. I was vastly pleased with her playing on the spinet and singing, and could not help calling to mind those sublime verses of the Cumberland genius.

Oh! how I was charmed to see
Orpheus' music all in thee.[36]

But he had not completely forgotten his Belinda:

I do not like the ups and downs of a country life: today you are frolicking with a fine girl and tomorrow you are moping by yourself. Thank God! I shall shortly be where happiness will be less interrupted. . . . Dear Will, I have thought of the cleverest plan of life that can be imagined. . . . You marry S(uke)y P(otte)r, I marry R(ebecc)a B(urwel)l . . . and get a pole chair and a pair of keen horses, practice the law in the same courts, and drive about to all the dances in the country together. How do you like it?

The problems of the desultory courtship were carried into the new year. On January 19, 1764, Jefferson wrote Page from Williamsburg a troubled letter in which he referred to Rebecca by means of a Greek anagram for Belinda and called her "he" throughout in a further effort at disguise. He revealed that he had opened his mind to Rebecca "more freely and more fully" on some occasion after the Apollo Room fiasco, making clear to her what he now called "the necessity of my going to England, and the delays which would consequently be occasioned by that. . . . I asked her no question which would admit of a categorical answer, but assured (her) that such questions would one day be asked. In short, were I to have another interview with (her) I could say nothing now which I did not say then. . . a visit could not possibly be of the least weight, and it is, I am sure, what (she) does not in the least expect."[37]

Four days later Jefferson, in great anxiety, wrote Page that he feared his earlier letter regarding Rebecca had fallen into other hands—evidently those of her relatives. He wished that he had followed Page's example and written in Latin, referring to his love as *campana in die* rather than by the Greek acrostic for Belinda. "We must fall on some scheme of communicating our thoughts to each other which shall be totally unintelligible to everyone but ourselves." He closed with the request that Page tell Rebecca for him, "I think as I always did." But he forestalled any more suggestions that he see her in person by adding, "I have sent my horses up the country, so that it is out of my power to take even an airing on horseback at any time."[38]

At eleven o'clock on the night of March 20 Jefferson sat down at his desk in Williamsburg and wrote to Will Fleming:

As the messenger who delivered me your letter informs me that your boy is to leave town tomorrow morning I will endeavor to answer it as circumstantially as the hour of the night and a violent headache, with which I have been afflicted these two days, will permit. With regard to the scheme which I proposed to you some time since, I am sorry to tell you it is totally frustrated by Miss R.B.'s marriage with Jacquelin Ambler which the people here tell me they daily expect. I say the people here tell me so, for (can you believe it?) I have been so abominably indolent as not to have seen her since last October, wherefore I cannot affirm that I know it from herself, though am as well satisfied it is true as if she had told me.[39]

This seems to be the first recorded instance of those severe migraine attacks from which Jefferson would suffer during various personal crises. The rather detailed presentation of this particular personal crisis may seem supererogatory since Jefferson soon recovered and, despite his gloomy forebodings, was able to love again. The matter deserves some consideration because of the fact that many of us, even though we may not have forgotten what it is to be an adolescent, may need to be reminded that Jefferson was also one. But it assumes greater importance for another reason. Jefferson's life could furnish an instance in support of Marcel Proust's theory, reiterated through seven volumes of *Remembrance of Things Past,* that one's first romantic love sets the pattern for all that follow. And the pattern is discernible not only in Jefferson's relations with the opposite sex but, with elaborate modifications, in situations where he was enamored of an ambition rather than a person.

The dictum, "Love is of man's life a thing apart; 'tis woman's whole existence," never applied to Thomas Jefferson. Even when he was merely in love with the idea of love and little given to action, each new passion consumed his thoughts.

Love notwithstanding, in the years of Wythe's tutelage he undoubtedly gave many more hours to the logic of law than to passion. Apparently the period from eight o'clock in the morning to noon usually was devoted entirely to legal studies.[40] Gradually "old Coke" came to seem less a devil and even assumed the lineaments of a friend. The afternoons, except for physical exercise, were spent with subjects related to the law—ethics, history, politics, and the like. In the evenings he studied literature and oratory. Demosthenes and Cicero he sought for "elevated style."

As he pursued his studies patiently year after year, he had the frustration of seeing his friend Patrick Henry leap to success at the bar through natural powers of eloquence that seemed to owe little to cultivation. Sometime during Jefferson's residence in Williamsburg, Henry formed the habit of staying with him when in town for court sessions. Jefferson once recalled: "On one occasion of the breaking up in November, to meet again in the spring, as he was departing in the morning, he looked among my books, and observed, 'Mr. J., I will take two volumes of Hume's *Essays,* and try to read them this winter.' On his return he brought them, saying he had not been able to get half way into one of them." Henry's ear was more attuned to the melodious bugling of hounds than to the seraphic strains of higher philosophy. And though he apparently liked the serious-minded young Jefferson, an hour or two of quiet conversation with the younger man was not Henry's idea of a festive evening. Jefferson afterwards wrote of his friend: "His great delight was to put on his hunting shirt, collect a parcel of overseers and such like people, and spend weeks together hunting in the 'piny woods,' camping at night and cracking jokes round a lightwood fire."

Jefferson much preferred the company at the Governor's Palace or at George Wythe's pleasant, dignified, Georgian house by the Palace Green. He came to venerate Wythe even more for his kindly and upright character than for his learning. In Williamsburg, and as Wythe's pupil, he found the study of law an exceedingly pleasant occupation. The legal studies that he began in 1762 he continued into 1766.[41]

By 1765 Henry was a veteran of five years' practice in the courts. Moreover, in that year he was elected to the House of Burgesses. His electioneering was helped by his having become a celebrity two years before. In 1763 the Reverend James Maury, Jefferson's boyhood teacher, had brought suit for back pay in what became famous as the Parson's Cause. Ministers of the Established Church in Virginia had been paid in tobacco, a legitimate medium of exchange. But when an anticipated increase in tobacco prices had promised to make it cheaper to pay them in cash, thus permitting especially low taxes for their support, the Burgesses provided for cash payment. The ministers contended that, by accepting payment in tobacco when it was disadvantageous to them, they had earned the right to payment in the same medium when it worked to their advantage. In the trial in Hanover County Court, presided over by Henry's father, Justice John Henry, the young Henry had not only attacked the clergy as "rapacious harpies" but also had warned that a king who would disallow colonial legislation of the kind he was defending would be a tyrant who forfeited "all rights to his subjects' obedience." The charge brought cries of treason from some in the courtroom. The jury, obliged to admit that the Reverend Mr. Maury had the law on his side, had awarded him damages—to the extent of one penny. Henry's daring and eloquence had immediately made his name known throughout Virginia. Mr. Maury, deprived of pay he believed rightfully his and publicly vilified besides, had not been entirely mollified by Henry's apology after adjournment of the court. The minister said Henry had told him that his "sole view in engaging in the cause, and in saying what he had, was to render himself popular."[42]

While Jefferson was imbued with the libertarian ideas then circulating in Williamsburg—as in Boston, Philadelphia, and London—there is no assurance that he approved Henry's conduct in the Parson's Cause. The younger man had great respect for his old teacher, and Maury's son had been a cherished boyhood companion.

Nevertheless, Jefferson was soon enthusiastic about something that Henry did as a legislator.[43] The hill country lawyer could not have launched his career as a burgess at a more exciting time.

No one would have thought so, though, until May 26, when most members of the House were so sure that they had concluded their business for the session that many had already gone home. But on that day arrived a copy of the Stamp Act resolutions passed by Parliament. They galvanized the Chamber. Ever since George III's proclamation of 1763 forbidding trade with the Indians and prohibiting the issuance of grants for land west of the Alleghenies, the very territory for which the colonists had just fought in the French and Indian War, there had been a growing feeling among the colonials that their needs were little understood and much neglected. The American Revenue Act of 1764 had increased the anxiety and resentment of the colonists; it was the first law passed by Parliament expressly for the purpose of collecting money in the colonies for the Crown. The same year had brought reorganization of the customs service to provide much tighter enforcement of the trade laws. Another parliamentary act of that year, the Currency Act, was designed principally as a curb for Virginia and stirred great animosity in the Old Dominion. It forbade issues of legal tender paper money in all the colonies, nullified all acts of colonial assemblies not in accord with its terms, and provided for dismissal from office, with permanent ineligibility for any government position, in the case of any colonial governor assenting to a legislative act contrary to the new law. Such paper currency issues had been forbidden in New England for thirteen years. Among the remaining colonies, Virginia was the chief issuer of paper money.

Now, on top of these causes for alarm, came the Stamp Act. It was a threat first of all because it touched so many aspects of life in an organized society: the tax applied to newspapers, pamphlets, broadsides, almanacs, legal documents, insurance policies, ship's papers, licenses, and (greatly to the inconvenience of Virginians) dice and playing cards. Even more disturbing was the fact that, as the first direct tax ever levied by Parliament upon the American colonies, the Stamp Act might be the forerunner of many

more direct taxes. Particularly frightening was the provision that punishments for violations could be imposed by courts of vice-admiralty. As these tribunals functioned without
juries, the right to trial by jury might be endangered.

There was, therefore, great tension when, in response to news of the Stamp Act,
George Johnston rose in the Burgesses to move that the House go into Committee of
the Whole to consider "steps necessary to be taken in consequence." Patrick Henry's
fire-eating reputation increased the excitement when he seconded Johnston's motion.
The suspense tightened when, with the Burgesses sitting as Committee of the Whole,
Johnston deferred to Henry and the freshman legislator rose, drew forth a sheet of paper,
and announced that he would present a series of resolutions.

There was no more fascinated spectator of the proceedings than Thomas Jefferson, who, with his friend John Tyler, stood just outside the chamber door. Henry's
lack of serious scholarship and apparent preference for illiterate companions had caused
Jefferson to wonder about his friend's abilities. The House of Burgesses was not a county
court. Was Henry about to make a fool of himself?

As Henry stood, his plain dress contrasted unfavorably with the fine tailoring of
his colleagues, but there was drama in the contrast. His voice was rich and melodious
as he asserted that by two royal charters granted by King James I, the colonists "are
declared entitled to all the privileges, liberties, and immunities of denizens and natural-
born subjects, to all intents and purposes as if they had been abiding and born within
the Realm of England."

So far Henry was on safe ground. Two great scholars in the House of Burgesses,
Richard Bland and Richard Henry Lee, had said and written as much on occasion. Nor
was he saying anything new when he protested taxation without representation. Colonel
Thomas Johnson had led a movement in Virginia in support of this principle as early
as 1653. But some conservatives frowned when Henry spoke of the right to self-
government which had "never been forfeited or in any other way given up" by the
people of Virginia. They did not like such talk unless it was admitted that the Assembly's
powers were ultimately derived from the sovereign.

In a strong resonant voice Henry climaxed his reading with: "Resolved, therefore,
that the General Assembly of the Colony have the only and exclusive right and power
to lay taxes and impositions upon the inhabitants of this colony and that every attempt
to vest such power in any person or persons whatsoever, other than the General
Assembly aforesaid, has a manifest tendency to destroy British as well as American
freedom."

When Henry sat down, veteran legislators sprang up to oppose his resolutions. A
motion that they be considered seriatim was passed. The fourth resolution squeaked
by with a margin of two or three votes. The fight on the fifth, which proclaimed that
the General Assembly of this colony had the exclusive right to tax its inhabitants, was
the crucial one.

Again Henry took the floor. He seemed transformed. His face was flushed and he
breathed heavily, but there was something else, too. His plain garb no longer made
him look awkward among the richly colored coats and waistcoats of his colleagues;
instead it gave him the gaunt dignity of the monitory figure in a morality play. He
thundered that self-taxation was essential to freedom. As his voice rose to a roar, subsided to a whisper, and rose to a roar again, the question was lifted out of its parochial

context. His auditors felt that they stood on a high plain swept by the winds of history. Then, with mounting emphasis, Henry shouted:

> "Caesar had his Brutus, Charles the First his Cromwell, and George the Third—"
>
> "Treason," shouted speaker John Robinson, his full face flushed.
>
> "And George the Third," said Henry, "may he never have either."[44]

Had he originally planned to end his sentence that way? In any event he had escaped the charge of treason without beclouding the import of his warning. As they stood for the vote on the fifth resolution, the members were visibly excited. The vote was twenty for Henry's resolution, nineteen against. Henry had defeated the chief leaders of the Tidewater aristocracy.

Jefferson was startled by the transformation in his normally placid cousin, Peyton Randolph, when that distinguished attorney rushed past him in exit, his multiple chins bobbing furiously as he exclaimed, "By God, I would have given five hundred guineas for a single vote!"

Governor Fauquier, when he learned what had happened, was surprised that "young, hot, and giddy" members had prevailed. But, despite his loyalty to his cousin and to the governor who had been his mentor in many things, Jefferson in his heart was aligned with the "young, hot, and giddy." Afterwards he wrote of Henry, "He appeared to me to speak as Homer wrote."[45]

IV

REVERBERATIONS OF A SOFT VOICE

THOUGH HENRY may have had, as Jefferson said, the eloquence of a Homer, in the spring of 1765 he lacked the cunning of a Ulysses. However blind or half-sighted the Titans of the Assembly may have seemed to the young orator, they were still more than a match for him. Though he deplored their monocular lack of perspective, their single-eyed concentration was a strength as well as a weakness. Their united force was now exerted to turn back, as quietly and efficiently as possible, the threat of the hill country lawyer who had already stirred "the young, hot, and giddy" even within the bastion of privilege. Defense of the Tidewater obligarchy was to them a matter of conscience as well as self-preservation. *Noblesse oblige* required that they continue to provide responsible leadership for the colony—never more so than in a time of crisis in relations with the mother country.

On May 30, the day after Henry's impassioned oratory and the adoption of his resolutions against the Stamp Act by the House sitting as Committee of the Whole, the Burgesses reconvened to consider as a legislature what they had already acted upon in Committee. Henry and Jefferson may well have felt some anxiety: the previous day the crucial fifth resolution had carried by only one vote. But the lines of contest held firm and the House formally adopted the resolutions by a vote of twenty to nineteen.[1]

Elated over his apparently easy triumph in his first battle with veteran legislators, Henry packed his saddle bags and rode back home. Jefferson was not so sanguine. He later recalled, "The next morning, before the meeting of the House, Colonel Peter Randolph, then of the Council, came to the Hall of Burgesses, and sat at the clerk's table till the House-bell rang, thumbing over the volumes of journals, to find a precedent for expunging a vote of the House, which he said had taken place while he was a member or clerk of the House, I do not recollect which. I stood by him at the end of the table a considerable part of the time, looking on as he turned over the leaves, but I do not recollect whether he found the erasure."[2] Jefferson therefore was not surprised to see Peyton Randolph on that last morning of May, all turbulence gone from his brow, move that the resolutions be expunged. As they had been adopted seriatim, they must be voted on one by one. Motions to expunge the first four failed. But these votes had little significance. The first four resolutions had been only an historical and

philosophical prologue to the fifth, which declared that only the General Assembly of
Virginia had the power to tax inhabitants of the colony. On the crucial vote, on the
fifth, the decision was to expunge the resolution. Jefferson's relatives and family friends
had done their work well.

    Before a month had passed, though, it became apparent that Henry had gained a
sort of triumph. Although every word of his fifth resolution had been removed from
the Journal of the House of Burgesses, it was blazoned on the pages of New England
newspapers whose readers knew nothing about the expunging.[3] By September 25,
General Thomas Gage, commander of His Majesty's armed forces in North America,
reported to his government that Henry's resolves "gave the signal for a general outcry
over the continent."[4] Ezra Stiles wrote that they "came abroad and gave fire to the
continent."[5] In that same autumn, George Washington, a Burgess from Virginia's Fairfax County, wrote to a friend: "The Stamp Act imposed on the Colonies by the Parliament of Great Britain engrosses the conversation of the speculative part of the colonists,
who look upon this unconstitutional method of taxation as a direful attack upon their
liberties, and loudly exclaim against the violation. What may be the result of this and
some other (I think I may add) ill-judged measures, I will not undertake to
determine."[6]

    By his own testimony Jefferson's enthusiasm for the mounting opposition to the
Stamp Act must have been great, even though his delight in the influence of Henry's
resolutions was tempered by regret that radical victory was painful to relatives he loved,
to George Wythe, and to Governor Fauquier, who had brought him so much pleasure
and instruction. But by late October when the fight reached its climax in Virginia with
Colonel George Mercer, distributor of stamps for the colony, being forced to resign
by an assemblage that Fauquier said he "should call a mob, did I know that it was chiefly,
if not altogether, composed of gentlemen of property,"[7] personal tragedy had intervened to deflect Jefferson's attention from the march of events.

    On October 1, a little more than three months past her twenty-fifth birthday, Jane
Jefferson had died. Jefferson seems to have been closer to this beloved sister than to
any other member of the family after his father's death. His mother never figured largely
in his reminiscences. Lucy, Anna Scott, and Randolph were too young for him to have
shared with them many experiences of growing up; Elizabeth was too retarded for con-
geniality. Mary had left home early to marry John Bolling. Martha, now nineteen, had
recently married Jefferson's old friend, Dabney Carr. Jefferson loved her and enjoyed
her companionship, but his association with her lacked the special quality of his relationship with Jane. She had shared his learning and fed his ambition. His family said
that "He ever regarded her as fully his own equal in understanding."[8] He composed
for her a Latin epitaph beginning, "Ah, Joanna, puellarum optima" — "Ah, Jane, finest
of girls."[9] He would frequently speak of her to his grandchildren and in old age, sitting in church, would be moved by a multitude of emotions when the congregation
sang a psalm which he had first heard in her sweet voice.[10]

    By early spring of 1766 Jefferson had determined upon a change of scene. Now
twenty-three, he was no longer proposing to John Page the idle dream of a voyage to
Europe and Africa, but sought to interest Francis Willis in a trip through the northern
colonies. Willis had matured into a young man who found amusement in more subtle
ways than upsetting study tables and Jefferson now found him a most agreeable compan-

ion. Jefferson was therefore not only disappointed but, as he said, "vexed," to discover that his former college mate had set out on the same journey a few weeks before without telling him of his plans.[11] It may be assumed that Jefferson had sought Page's company for the same trip. As it was, disappointed at not having a traveling companion, he set out alone in May.

A letter which he wrote to Page on the twenty-fifth from Annapolis revealed that the young man from Albemarle had so far found his first journey outside Virginia arduous. His words also showed that he had regained his sense of humor.

> Surely never did small hero experience greater misadventures than I did on the first two or three days of my traveling. Twice did my horse run away with me and greatly endanger the breaking of my neck on the first day. On the second I drove two hours through as copious a rain as ever I have seen, without meeting with a single house to which I could repair for shelter. On the third in going through Pamunkey, being unacquainted with the ford, I passed through water so deep as to run over the cushion as I sat on it, and to add to the danger, at that instant one wheel mounted a rock which I am confident was as high as the axle, and rendered it necessary for me to exercise all my skill in the doctrine of gravity, in order to prevent the center of gravity from being left unsupported, the consequence of which would according to Bob Carter's opinion have been the corruition of myself, chair and all, into the water. Whether that would have been the case or not, let the learned determine: it was not convenient for me to try the experiment at that time, and I therefore threw my whole weight on the mounted wheel and escaped the danger. I confess that on this occasion I was seized with a violent hydrophobia.[12]

He found Annapolis a beautifully situated city about the size of Williamsburg with "generally better houses" but "more indifferent gardens." His interest centered on the Maryland House, then in session in what he took to be "an old courthouse which, judging from its form and appearance, was built in the year one." Other visitors wrote disparagingly of this State House, which in a few years would be replaced by the handsome capitol which is today one of the most architecturally interesting buildings in the United States. But the building that Jefferson saw seemed an appropriate meeting place for the legislators that he observed:

> I was surprised on approaching it to hear as great a noise and hubbub as you will usually observe at a publick meeting of the planters in Virginia. The first object which struck me after my entrance was the figure of a little old man dressed but indifferently, with a yellow queue wig on, and mounted in the judge's chair. This the gentleman who walked with me informed me was the speaker, a man of a very fair character, and who by-the-bye has very little the air of a speaker. At one end of the justices' bench stood a man whom in another place I should from his dress and phis have taken for Goodall the lawyer in Williamsburg, reading a bill then before the house with a schoolboy tone and an abrupt pause at every half dozen words. This I found to be the clerk of the assembly. The mob (for such was their appearance) sat covered on the justices' and lawyers' benches, and were

divided into little clubs amusing themselves in the common chit chat way. I was surprised to see them address the speaker without rising from their seats, and three, four, and five at a time without being checked. When a motion was made, the speaker instead of putting the question in the usual form only asked the gentlemen whether they chose that such or such a thing should be done, and was answered by a yes sir, or no sir: and tho' the voices appeared frequently to be divided, they would never go to the trouble of dividing the house, but the clerk entered the resolution, I supposed, as he thought proper. In short every thing seems to be carried without the house in general's knowing what was proposed.[13]

One might assume that the young Virginian was hypercritical of the neighboring colony's legislature, but contemporaries from other colonies, indeed from Maryland itself, were often shocked by the parliamentary behavior of the lower house at Annapolis.

Before leaving the city for Philadelphia, Jefferson happily noted the "rejoicings here on the repeal of the Stamp Act."[14]

One of his primary reasons for visiting Philadelphia was to be inoculated against smallpox. The American metropolis was also the center of the medical profession in the colonies. Jefferson bore a letter of introduction from Dr. George Gilmer in Virginia to Dr. John Morgan: "Give me leave to introduce the bearer, my particular friend, Mr. Thomas Jefferson. I need say nothing to recommend him to your esteem; your penetrating genius will discover him to be a gentleman eminently worthy of your acquaintance."[15]

Dr. Morgan may have inoculated Jefferson against smallpox, though tradition says that Dr. William Shippen, Jr., did the job. Even in Philadelphia few physicians would dare to perform the act. The variolation of that day was far more dangerous than modern vaccination. Fatalities were so numerous that doctors debated whether the disease or the supposed preventive was the greater menace. It was generally believed that inoculated persons spread smallpox to others. Inoculation was forbidden by law in New York and had excited mob action in Boston. On the eve of the Revolution, debate over the practice would further exacerbate differences between Norfolk's rebels and tories. At the climax rebels would smash the windows of a tory mayor's residence and march the inoculated women and children of his family to the Pest House, last home of those suffering contagious terminal illnesses. Despite the constant threat of smallpox to seaports, Norfolk physicians would not administer the vaccine until 1802, four years after Edward Jenner first tested his safer cowpox method.[16] Young Jefferson, so hesitant in affairs of the heart and even in launching upon a profession, had shown himself surprisingly bold in support of an idea.

Whether or not Dr. Morgan administered the controversial preventive to his Virginia visitor, there is circumstantial evidence that he inoculated him with a fever from which he never recovered—an enthusiasm for the fine arts. Not yet thirty and still some years from winning his place in medical history, the firm-jawed, widow's-peaked Dr. Morgan looked the very model of dependable solidity.[17] But he had recently come back from Europe a zealot. The celebrated artist and art dealer James Byres had introduced him to "a perfection which I could not have imagined" —the temples, monuments, and sculptures of the ancient Greeks and Romans and their neoclassical imitators. "The soul is struck at the review," he exclaimed, "and the ideas expand." He was still excited about the Apollo Belvedere and the Laocoön. In his home he had the beginnings of an art collection that included copies of Raphael's cartoons and of Palladio's architectural sketches. He delighted in showing these and in sharing his library of art and architecture. Art historians have noted that Jefferson's intense interest in the fine arts apparently dates from his trip to Philadelphia.[18] Literary expressions of the Enlightenment he had discovered in Williamsburg under the genial tutelage of Small, Wythe, and Fauquier. Now, through Dr. Morgan, he may for the first time have become aware of the artistic riches of Europe.

The Philadelphian, only eight years Jefferson's senior, must have seemed to him quite sophisticated. Philadelphia itself was dazzling to the Virginian, who until recently had seen only one city, little Williamsburg. Home to about twenty thousand people, its brick buildings (some four stories tall) stretching almost two miles along the Delaware River, the Pennsylvania city was one of the largest communities in the British Empire. But even Philadelphia probably seemed provincial to Morgan. Before spending time in Paris and Rome, he had studied in Edinburgh. The "Athens of the North" was then a principal center of the Enlightenment and, with its fierce philosophical debates as hot as the political arguments in the colonies, a far livelier place than Oxford or Cambridge. Moreover, Morgan had met one of the world's greatest geniuses, a wizened old man with the glowing face of a transcendently intelligent monkey—Voltaire himself. We may be virtually certain that at the time of Jefferson's meeting with Morgan neither of the young men suspected that there was at that moment in the room in Philadelphia one who would later rank with the French *philosophe* as one of the Enlightenment's half dozen chief ornaments.

After Philadelphia Jefferson did not find New York forbiddingly large, nor was the intellectual climate so stimulating as in the metropolis he had just left. No New Yorker seems to have impressed him so much as a young man from Massachusetts who stayed at the same house where Jefferson found lodging.[19] He could not know then that Elbridge Gerry, just two years his senior, would become a famous statesman and diplomat as well as a politician sufficiently shrewd to be memoralized in the term "gerrymander." Jefferson certainly did not suspect that the most famous product of his own pen would some day bear Gerry's signature, along with those of fifty-four other distinguished Americans. He did know that this Harvard graduate, though handicapped by a stammer, was uncommonly bright.

By July 23, 1766, Jefferson was back in Williamsburg after a voyage down the coast from New York.[20] He returned for some months to his legal studies. In 1767 he was presented to the General Court of Virginia by Wythe and entered upon the practice of law. He was then twenty-four years old and, besides two years of education in the liberal arts at William and Mary, had studied law for about five years under America's greatest teacher of the subject. He should have been as well prepared for the profession as study in the colonies could make him. Indeed, his period of preparation had been remarkably long in that day when men usually entered early upon their life's work. As late as 1780 John Marshall would be admitted to the bar after no more than a few months' attendance upon Wythe's lectures. Henry's preparatory studies, as we have seen, were brief and informal. Many an attorney of that time had simply "read law" in the office of an established practitioner until he believed himself ready to be examined. The extraordinary length of Jefferson's preparation may be attributed to his almost preternatural thoroughness, but it might just as well be imputed to a desire to postpone a decisive step in his personal life.

A longer than customary period of study—but not the five years that Jefferson spent—might be explained by the fact that he began his practice in the General Court rather than the county courts. "General Court lawyers were the elite of Virginia lawyers."[21]

The General Court was the highest appellate court in Virginia, the capstone of justice in the colony. It sat only in the capitol in Williamsburg and consisted of the Governor and royal Council. As David John Mays wrote, "It was spoken of with awe by the youths who were preparing themselves for the profession of law, and all of the stories and traditions concerning it were drunk up avidly by the students and apprentices."[22]

The county courts, strictly courts of inferior jurisdiction, were presided over by gentlemen justices for the most part more notable for local success in the practical affairs of life than for any knowledge of legal intricacies.

One should not assume that a typical lawyer, upon losing his case in a county court, would appeal it to the General Court and personally plead his client's cause before that tribunal. An act of Assembly for 1761 prohibited attorneys practicing in the General Court from practicing also in the county courts. The only lawyers exempted were barristers, and they were defined as graduates of London's Inns of Court who were qualified to try cases before superior courts in England. Barristers were few in Jefferson's Virginia.[23]

As Jefferson had qualified to practice before the General Court and was not a barrister, he was automatically prevented from practicing in the county courts. Despite this fact, the legend has persisted since the publication of Henry S. Randall's valuable and generally reliable life of Jefferson in 1858 that, in addition to his appearances before the General Court, he had an extensive and highly remunerative practice in the county courts. The assumption has caused various scholars to conclude that Jefferson prospered more in his law practice than he actually did, and that he gained much politically useful knowledge of Virginia and of the nature of public opinion from riding the circuit. One respected historian stated without proof that an increase of county court cases compensated Jefferson for the loss of some practice in the General Court when the young lawyer's political opinions repelled prominent persons.[24] A twentieth-century scholar has said that Jefferson "appeared constantly before the county courts."[25] Another has specified that within five years he "had cases in no less than 53 of the 57 counties."[26] The most honored Jefferson biographer of our own time, a scholar justly respected for painstaking accuracy, nevertheless has declared that his hero's "business in the county courts was extensive" and "constituted a political education in itself."[27]

Almost as much as the famous description of President Jefferson in carpet slippers receiving His Britannic Majesty's ambassador, this venerable misconception has contributed to the image of the master of Monticello as a folksy democrat. Some have pictured him as taking an almost Lincolnesque delight in the bucolic exchanges of rustic forums. Some who have rhapsodized sentimentally over Jefferson's attachment to the county courts would be shocked to learn what he thought of most of the lawyers practicing in them. In 1779, when consideration was given to ending the prohibition against the same attorneys appearing before both the high tribunal and the inferior courts, Jefferson protested: "I think the bar of the General Court a proper and an excellent nursery for future judges if it be so regulated as that science may be encouraged and may live there: But this can never be if an inundation of insects is permitted to come from the county courts and consume the harvest."[28]

As might be expected, Jefferson was meticulous in preparing his cases. And his rivals at the bar could appreciate his learned reasoning and classical allusions. They included his teacher George Wythe, the flow of whose cogent arguments was sometimes slowed by their heavy freight of Greek and Latin quotations; Peyton Randolph, whose education at William and Mary had been supplemented by study at London's Middle Temple; Richard Bland, erudite historian and scholar of constitutional law; and Edmund Pendleton, who lacked a university education but as a polished orator outshone most of his peers. By no means were the twelve councillors who sat as judges all formally trained to the law but most, in addition to some familiarity with the English common law, had at least a nodding acquaintence with Greek and Roman philosophical works on justice. They were river barons, powerful representatives of the oligarchy that dominated the social, economic, and political life of the colony. A knowledge of polite literature was to them a class obligation. To be a stranger to Horace and Ovid could be as embarrassing as ignorance concerning the finer points of good horseflesh.

As an earnest disciple of the Enlightenment Jefferson enjoyed the General Court. He would have found no delight in haranguing an ignorant jury. Some of his colleagues could marshal the forces of reason or play upon simple emotions with equal pleasure and felicity. But not Jefferson. His fastidious mind rejected all appeals save to reason.

Other pursuits appealed to a more genial side of the relentlessly logical young attorney. He was a planter as well as a lawyer, and sometimes turned gratefully from interpretation of the common law to living in happy compliance with the laws of nature. In 1764 he had attained his legal majority and had come into his inheritance. At that point he stopped charging the expenses of his education against his father's estate; indeed even earlier he had scrupulously returned a portion of his expense funds, because of the conviction that he had wasted money.

Under the terms of Peter Jefferson's will, Thomas had the choice of either the home plantation on the Rivanna or the Fluvanna lands about twenty-five miles away on the south fork of the James River. The estates were of about equal size but the Rivanna lands loomed much larger than any other in his affections. The home itself at Shadwell, with its four hundred acres, would be his mother's for her lifetime. Altogether, with 2,650 acres on the Rivanna and other holdings elsewhere, he was the heir to more than five thousand acres.[29] Responsibilities also devolved upon him as the titular head of the family and as heir to Albemarle County's principal civic leader.

Jefferson gained quick cash by selling seven hundred acres in Amherst County almost as soon as he inherited them. In 1765 he began farming the Shadwell tract, renting slaves from his mother. He continued to operate his father's water mill. In the same year, when an act of assembly provided for "clearing the great falls of James River, the river Chickahominy," and the Rivanna for unimpeded transportation of produce, Jefferson was one of the trustees appointed to receive subscriptions. Actually his role was greater than this limited formal recognition might indicate. He seems to have given the proposal its principal impetus in the Rivanna district. Shortly before Jefferson became President of the United States he cited his part in the project as his first public service and one of his most important contributions to the general welfare.[30] At the time he must have delighted in the realization that he was exercising the same kind of leadership that his father would have in similar circumstances and that he was involved in something actual rather than hypothetical.

In 1766 Jefferson began keeping his garden book, a record of information useful to him as a practical farmer—facts to aid him in projecting the yield of his fields or the consumption of fodder by his livestock.[31] Prosaic lists were punctuated by notations of the blooming of purple hyacinths, bluebells, and wild honeysuckle.

At the same time, in a small, neat hand he carefully kept financial records of his agricultural operations, and of other matters for his mother, brother, and three sisters who remained at Shadwell. The twins, Anna Scott and Randolph, were only eleven.

In the summer of 1767, he began keeping portable account books in which he recorded even the most trivial personal expenditures. Had he been less efficient, his meticulous record-keeping in so many fields would have seriously impeded his accomplishments. He could have been like the man who was so busy keeping a diary that he had no time to live. Was a sense of the transitory nature of life responsible for his passion for recording all its manifestations?

Certainly his biographer has no right to complain. Because of Jefferson's penchant for record-keeping we can place precisely on the calendar many nonpublic events which otherwise would have gone undated or even unnoticed. Thus we know that in 1767, the same year he was admitted to the bar, he had begun to plant fruit trees on a beautiful mountaintop which he could see from the yard at Shadwell.[32] Evidently he was dreaming of building a home there. He had already named the site Monticello (Italian for "little mountain"). Three years before he had been adding Italian to his list of acquired languages which already included Greek, Latin, Anglo-Saxon, and French. From his beloved mountaintop the world appeared at its best—a place of sunshine shafts and gentle mists. In time, his orchards would make the mountaintop a scene of mellow fruitfulness. But beneath the pastel surface was the primitive vitality of the frontier, as rawly red as the earth turned up by the spades that dug in at his command.

In May of 1768 Jefferson, in exchange for wheat and corn, contracted for the leveling of his mountaintop by Christmas. Soon he was planting more fruit trees, carefully spacing them on the southeast slope. His plans were already well advanced to make his permanent home in sight of his birthplace. His attitude had changed since age twenty when he had confessed to Will Fleming, "I do not like the ups and downs of a country life" and had admitted that he found relief from boredom only in "frolicking with a fine girl." Having lived in a town and visited cities, he preferred a rural environment.

"Frolicking," however, evidently still had its attractions, and with embarrassing results.

For more than four months in 1768, Dr. Thomas Walker,[33] physician to Jefferson's family since the days of his childhood, was absent from Albemarle while participating with other colonial representatives, Sir William Johnson, and Iroquois chieftains in the conference that led to the signing of the Treaty of Fort Stanwix on November 5, and while traveling to and from the meeting place. Accompanying him as secretary to the Virginia commissioners was his son, John Walker, also a neighbor of the Jeffersons. John had been a boyhood friend of Thomas Jefferson's and a classmate at William and Mary. Jefferson had been one of John's groomsmen four years earlier when he had married Elizabeth Moore. Jefferson considered her a "handsome lady." Now, before undertaking the long journey to Fort Stanwix, John Walker made his will, naming Jefferson first among his executors. He asked his old friend to look after his wife and infant daughter.

Jefferson appears to have undertaken this responsibility in good conscience, visiting the Walker home frequently, and failing to perceive that precise moment at which the attractions of Elizabeth's company became a stronger motivation for his visits than his obligation to her husband.[34] All his life Jefferson loved to pay compliments. Imperceptibly, the polite language of gallantry became a declaration of infatuation. At some moment of physical closeness, Jefferson found her irresistible. Perhaps with a kiss, perhaps a caress, or both, he made toward his friend's wife an advance that he later admitted to have been improper. The episode would return to haunt both his personal and public life for many years to come. In that season of his discontent we can be sure that Jefferson's thinskinned cheeks were suffused with blushes of hot shame whenever he thought of how he had betrayed a trust. And he must have been thoroughly disconcerted by the realization that, far from being a complete man of reason, he was a creature of passion and impulse.

When the Walkers, father and son, returned to Albmarle, Jefferson resumed his friendly relations with them. If Elizabeth, or Betsy, as she was often called, viewed Jefferson with resentment or fear, she did not confide that fact to her husband.

Jefferson and Dr. Walker soon found themselves engaged in the same enterprise. Virginia's new royal Governor, the Right Honorable Norborne Berkeley, Baron de Botetourt, just arrived from England, promptly dissolved the existing Assembly and issued writs for the election of its successor. Thus, before mid-December the voters of Albemarle participated in an election to fill the two seats in the House of Burgesses allotted to that constituency. Besides the two incumbents, Dr. Thomas Walker and Edward Carter, a great planter, there was a third candidate, Thomas Jefferson.[35] Now twenty-five, Jefferson, besides having been influential in improving the Rivanna, was an increasingly prominent lawyer. His family name was not as prestigious as Carter's but it was more beloved in Albemarle.

One can easily imagine how uncomfortable the dignified and fastidious Jefferson was on election day. He had to appeal to an audience very different from the General Court. It was customary for the candidates to treat the electors to a copious flow of liquor, sometimes as much as a quart and a half per voter.[36] Like George Washington, another aloof gentleman on the hustings, Jefferson probably disapproved of the practice but complied because he did not wish to suffer in comparison with his opponents. One may well imagine that, as election day wore on, proceedings acquired a Hogarthian character. There was no secret ballot. Each voter, sometimes with measured enunciation, sometimes in slurred syllables, pronounced the names of his choices. Each of the favored candidates shook his hand and publicly thanked him. While one part of Jefferson's mind kept tally, the other must have wondered if the Greeks had conducted their experiment in democracy in the same fashion. Presumably he submitted with uneasy grace and a nervous smile to being carried about on his supporters' shoulders when, at the end of the day, he and Dr. Walker were declared the victors.[37]

In May of 1769 Jefferson took his seat in the House of Burgesses. Did his mind turn back four years to the day in 1765 when, standing in the doorway, he had thrilled to Henry's oratory and the excitement that it aroused? If he had ever dreamed of approaching that feat, he had long since abandoned the idea. His voice was persuasive in the quiet of the General Court and in conversation, but when he raised it so as to be heard out of doors or by a large audience, it had a peculiar husky quality that grated upon the ear. A more comfortable thought, perhaps, was that he was sitting in the Assembly where his father had sat, although Thomas in his autobiography would omit legislative service from the list of Peter's accomplishments.

The pomp and pageantry when the Assembly convened on May 8 must have impressed Jefferson, if only as evidence that His Majesty's government was giving serious consideration to events in Virginia. First of all, there must be significance in the fact that the new Governor was just that, a real Governor, not a Lieutenant Governor acting in the name of a sinecure-holder, as had been the case for so many years. And the baron was popular at court. Indeed, a right royal figure he cut in a pleasantly portly sort of way as he rode down Duke of Gloucester Street to the capitol, his kindly face smiling from the windows of a glittering coach drawn by six cream-white Hanoverian horses whose silver-mounted harness sparkled in the sun. A gift from His Majesty's uncle, the carriage had originally been built for the King himself and the royal arms had once decorated the doors now boldly blazoned with Virginia's escutcheon.[38]

The Council Chamber, rather than the lower house, was the setting for the meeting of Governor and Burgesses. The legislators were not receiving His Majesty's representative; he was receiving them. The handsome dark paneling was a foil for the baron's red-coated and gold-braided splendor.[39]

Peyton Randolph, a match for the Governor in dignity and more than a match in girth, made a brief speech reminding His Excellency of the House's "ancient rights and privilege." Jefferson, as a new member, may not have been aware of a small but significant departure from time-honored ritual in all this business. The Speaker "laid claim" to the "prerogatives" of the House; in earlier times he would have "petitioned."

The Governor's reply gained force and appeal from his benevolent countenance and from his unusually winning personality. As one who had never been outside the colonies, Jefferson could not judge the correctness of some sophisticated Virginians' observation that the Governor's manner was like that of George III in reading the address from the throne. But he was aware of Botetourt's effectiveness. Those whom Fauquier had called "the cool old members" of the Assembly had already established a warm social relationship with the baron, and he in turn had a strong sense of rapport with many of his audience. He had already reported to London concerning the Virginians that he liked "their style exceedingly." When Lord Botetourt told his audience that it was "a peculiar felicity" and "a great addition to the many honors I have received from my Royal Master" to bear a special message from the King, it was easy to believe that he was truly glad and did indeed feel honored.

The message was that His Majesty intended that, "for the future, his Chief Governors of Virginia shall reside within their government." Lord Botetourt concluded: "I have nothing to ask but that you consider well and follow exactly, without passion or prejudice, the real interests of those you have the honor to represent; they are most certainly consistent with the prosperity of Great Britain, and so they will ever be found when pursued with temper and moderation."[40]

The Burgesses found nothing to quarrel with in his statement, but it was unlikely that they could agree with his lordship on the "real interests" of their constituents. The Governor's diplomacy had softened the bluntness of the royal instructions to order the new Assembly "to desist from their unwarrantable claims and pretensions, and yield due submission to the supreme authority of Parliament."[41]

In these circumstances peculiar significance attached to what might in times of less tension have been a mere formality—the drafting of a formal reply to the Governor's address. There must, in consequence, have been some surprise when Edmund Pendleton used his considerable influence to have a new member, Jefferson, draw up the resolution specifying the points to be made in the reply to the Chief Executive.[42]

While still a law student, Jefferson had been introduced to Pendleton by Wythe. Pendleton had taken a great liking to the young man and had been impressed by his knowledge and verbal skill. Now he was eager to push him forward. Jefferson could scarcely have made his way in the House under better auspices. Twenty-two years his senior and seventeen years a legislator, Pendleton[43] had grown in the confidence of his colleagues through intensive application, the most dependable integrity, unfailing tact, and consistent levelheadedness. If women had had the vote he might have enjoyed even greater political success. They were always praising his handsome face and pleasant voice. And in those days when women's legs were hidden by long skirts and men's were revealed in silk hose, the girls liked to ogle Pendleton's limbs. Jefferson then regarded Pendleton as a conservative, but most of the Burgesses considered him a moderate. A mark of his standing in the House was his selection to second the nomination of Peyton Randolph as Speaker.

Pendleton undoubtedly guided Jefferson's hand in writing what proved to be the first of many state papers prepared by him. While his assigned task helped to bring Jefferson to public notice, it afforded little opportunity for display of his verbal talents. It was a job of ceremonial writing precisely attuned to the tenor and contents of the governor's address. It was certainly not a revolutionary document, for it proposed "that a most humble and dutiful Address be presented to his Excellency the Governor, returning Thanks for his very affectionate Speech at the Opening of this Session; Expressing our firm Attachment to His Majesty's sacred Person and Government, and a lively Sense of his Royal Favour. . . . " His Excellency was to be assured that, "if in the Course of our Deliberations, any matters shall arise, which may in any way affect the Interests of Great Britain, these shall ever be discussed on this ruling Principle, that her Interests, and Ours, are inseparably the same." Only in the last words of the concluding paragraph did Jefferson present, among the phrases of the sycophantic formula of ceremonial address, a gentle hint that the Virginians might contend with the Crown for principles of liberty. They would offer their "Prayers that Providence and the Royal Pleasure may long continue his Lordship the happy ruler of a free and an happy People."[44]

After unanimous adoption of the resolution, a committee was appointed to draft the actual reply proposed, and Jefferson was named to it. Pendleton then persuaded the committee to have Jefferson prepare the document.[45]

It is not hard to imagine the mingled anxiety and eagerness which the freshman legislator brought to the task. The previous two years had been ones of conflict between London and Williamsburg. By 1767 Chancellor of the Exchequer "Champagne Charlie" Townshend had replaced the ailing William Pitt in all but name as Prime Minister. Abolishing Pitt's distinction between external and internal taxation, Townshend had proposed to please his home constituents by reducing the British land tax and compensating for this loss by taxation of the American colonists. The Townshend Acts had become effective November 20, 1767, imposing new import duties on glass, lead, paints, paper, and tea.

Colonial legislators found little comfort in a preamble declaring that the funds thus obtained could be used for defense of the colonies and for "defraying the charge of the administration of justice and the support of civil government" in America. The same Acts provided for establishment of new Vice-Admiralty Courts and an American Board of Commissioners of the Customs. Townshend was getting what he wanted from the colonists while keeping the new taxes well within the realm of external taxation, a distinction that the colonials had insisted upon. But now the legislators of Virginia and other colonies were alarmed that the new system would make the royal Governors financially independent of the colonial Assemblies. In the colonies, as in England itself, legislative control of the purse strings was one of the few effective deterrents to tyranny. Apprehension was heightened when Parliament, reacting to the New York Assembly's refusal to appropriate beer and cider money for British troops stationed in their colony, suspended the legislature's powers.

The Virginia Assembly of 1768 had addressed a petition to the King, a memorial to the Lords and a remonstrance to Commons. The petition to the sovereign was only a vague appeal to his "fatherly goodness and protection." But the messages addressed to Parliament reiterated the principles of "no taxation without representation" which Virginians under the leadership of Colonel Thomas Johnson had advanced in the Northampton Declaration as early as 1652. "No power on earth," declared the Virginia Burgesses of 1768, "has a right to impose taxes upon the people or to take the smallest portion of their property without their consent, given by their representatives in Parliament." Since the colonies could not be represented in that body, right of self-taxation necessarily resided in the colonial legislatures. The "Suspending Act" aimed at New York was specifically cited as "more alarming" than measures directed toward the colonies in general.[46] The remonstrance to Commons warned that "exercise of anticonstitutional powers" anywhere in the empire might set a dangerous precedent for England herself.[47]

Obviously, the committee to draft these papers—headed by Richard Bland, and including Robert Carter Nicholas and Edmund Pendleton—had done its job well. The writers' colleagues thought so too. The three documents were unanimously approved by the Burgesses and concurred in by the Council. Also unanimous was the action of the Burgesses in pledging cooperation with Massachusetts in the defense of liberty. Moreover, they had instructed Speaker Randolph "to write to the respective speakers of the assemblies and representatives on this continent to make known to them our proceedings on this subject and to intimate how necessary we think it is that the colonies should unite in a firm but decent opposition to every measure which may affect the rights and liberties of the British colonies in America."[48]

Strong words! But when the legislators of 1768 had submitted these documents to the Governor for transmission to London, that post was not filled by a royal appointee. Fauquier's death had left as acting Governor the President of the Council, John Blair, an aged Virginia planter, who sent the papers to the English government with his own endorsement.

Now the document that Jefferson must prepare was a direct reply to the royal Governor in their midst, the first full Governor, rather than Lieutenant Governor, to serve in the colony in many years. The burden was a troubling one for a novice legislator. It is not surprising that Jefferson should have decided to insure the support of his fellow Burgesses by sticking very closely to his earlier composition, the resolution specifying the points to be made in the official reply. After all, this document had already won unanimous approval.

But when Jefferson presented his work to the committee, Robert Carter Nicholas[49] began ominously shaking his head. Nicholas was the Treasurer of the colony as well as one of its Burgesses. There was nothing particularly imposing in the appearance of this balding, delicate-featured man of average physique. But when he so much as murmured others strained to hear. He had a deserved reputation for uncommon common sense. His first and middle names recalled his grandfather, Robert (King) Carter of Corotoman, founder of Virginia's most powerful clan. He spoke with quiet assurance from an unassailable position of personal achievement, social prestige, wealth, political power, and proven integrity. His friends thought him a gifted writer, and he did nothing to discourage their opinion.

Jefferson, therefore, knew that his composition was in trouble as soon as Mr. Treasurer began shaking his head. The paper, Nicholas objected, stuck too closely to the wording of the resolution; the work required elaboration. As Jefferson laconically reported at a much later date, Nicholas was asked "to draw an address more in large, which he did with amplification enough, and it was accepted."[50] Jefferson was doubtless fully aware of the irony that his close adherence to the original resolution, which he had followed to insure acceptance of his writing, had helped to make it unacceptable. But he saw no humor in the situation. More than forty-five years later he wrote of the incident: "Being a young man as well as a young member, it made on me an impression proportioned to the sensibilities of that time of life."

The House sat as Committee of the Whole on May 16 to consider two threats to freedom. One was new, the citation in Parliament of authority to make colonists charged with treason stand trial in England. The second was an old subject of contention, taxation without representation.

As first consideration was given to the older threat Jefferson must have thought of the contrast between the unanimity of the House at this moment and the impassioned debate over the same issue that he had witnessed only four years earlier standing in the doorway of this very chamber. Not only was there now no dissent from resolutions asserting that the power to tax Virginians had always been "legally and constitutionally vested in the House of Burgesses," but the legislators turned proselyte. They resolved: "It is lawful and expedient to procure the concurrence of His Majesty's other colonies, in dutiful addresses, praying royal interposition in favor of the violated rights of America."

The other threat was dealt with no less forcefully:

> The seizing any person or persons residing in this colony, suspected of any crime whatsoever committed therein, and sending such person or persons to places beyond the sea to be tried, is highly derogatory of the rights of British subjects; as thereby the inestimable privilege of being tried by a jury from the vicinage, as well as the liberty of summoning and producing witnesses on such trial, will be taken away from the party accused.[51]

By unanimous vote, the Burgesses approved in regular session what they had done in Committee of the Whole and ordered that a copy of their address to the King be sent to the presiding officer of every legislature in North America.

If the Assembly had moved a considerable distance within four years to meet Patrick Henry, the populist leader himself had gone to surprising lengths to reach accord with his legislative colleagues. His conversation as well as his clothes were more closely tailored to the prevailing concept of propriety. For the parlors of Williamsburg, Henry had a diction and a supply of jokes different from those with which he approached his humbler constituents. The man who had so recently in the excitement of debate been charged with treason to the King was now appointed to a committee of three to draft an address to His Majesty. The chairman of that commitee was John Blair,[52] son of the Council President who had served as acting Governor between Fauquier's death and Botetourt's arrival. With all his forensic skill, trained in London's Temple and in Virginia's General Court, he had fought at the side of Nicholas and Bland against Henry's Stamp Act Resolutions in 1765.

The third member was Richard Henry Lee,[53] scion of a clan as prestigious as the Randolphs and scarcely less powerful than the Carters. Tall and spare, he had the strong-boned, proud-nosed, lofty-browed profile of an ideal Roman senator. At thirty-seven he was in the prime of life for a man of his day and only his black-gloved left hand, with its missing fingers, hinted at any physical imperfection. In formal education in England and in private reading in the library of his Westmoreland County mansion, he had schooled himself in the classics. Like Jefferson, he was afire with the excitement of the Enlightenment.

Lee had reigned supreme as the great orator of the House before Henry's spectacular debut. Now in sheer natural force the Northern Neck aristocrat had been eclipsed. Perhaps already Virginians, as they would with increasing frequency, were calling Lee a modern Cicero and Henry a Demosthenes. Like the Roman, Lee was learned and polished. Like the Greek, Henry thundered with the surge of the sea. Lee had not been present when Henry attacked the Stamp Act, but later had joined zealously in the fight against it. Nevertheless this belated activity could not erase from some minds the fact that, on the eve of the Stamp Act's passage, he had applied for the position of distributor. Some unkind persons suggested that his radical zeal sprang from a desire to live down his having been on the "wrong" side of one of the great issues of the day. But, like many rich sons of rich fathers in his time, Lee could discourse for hours with undimmed enthusiasm on the intellectually fashionable principles that he had imbibed among English levelers and Scottish egalitarians—provided the company was sufficiently polished. From his baronial estates in the Northern Neck he could ride in his handsome slave-driven equipage to Williamsburg to warn his fellow Virginians of the debilitating effects of the plantation system on both land and people. No age is unique in producing privileged persons who can happily dichotomize condemnation of their society and enjoyment of its fruits. The eighteenth century had its landau liberals as the nineteenth would have its carriage Communists.

If the sharp-tongued Lee had to alter his style considerably to participate in writing the committee's address to the King, Henry must have wrought a revolution within himself. In language reminiscent of the sycophancy of Ming courtiers, the committee, following a catalogue of grievances against Parliament, wrote:

Truly alarmed at the fatal tendency of these pernicious counsels, and with hearts filled with anguish by such dangerous invasions of our dearest privileges, we presume to prostrate ourselves at the foot of your royal throne, beseeching your Majesty, as our King and Father, to avert from your faithful and loyal subjects of America, those miseries which must necessarily be the consequence of such measures. After expressing our firm confidence in your royal wisdom and goodness, permit us to assure your Majesty that the most fervent prayers of your people of this colony are daily addressed to the Almighty, that your Majesty's reign may be long and prosperous over Great Britain and all your dominions; and that, after death, your Majesty may taste the fullest fruition of eternal bliss, and that a descendant of your illustrious house may reign over the extended British Empire till time shall be no more.[54]

Actually, the document was bolder than it seemed. All—Burgesses and the members of His Majesty's government alike—were acutely aware that the real target of criticism in such colonial missives was not so much the Commons as the King's ministers. The House adopted the address unanimously and without amendment, and ordered that it be published in English newspapers as well as dispatched to the King. Certainly it was not wanting in that "elaboration" which had been missed in Jefferson's efforts.

The great work done, the Burgesses turned to consideration of local grievances. The morning had worn on to an end, and a petition of certain planters in Brunswick County had just been referred to the proper committee when the Sergeant at Arms announced: "Mr. Speaker, a message from the Governor."[55]

Standing in the aisle, the clerk of the General Assembly read the message aloud: "Mr. Speaker, the Governor commands the immediate attendance of your House in the Council Chamber."

Jefferson and his colleagues followed hard-breathing Peyton Randolph upstairs to the Council Chamber. Seated in his high-backed chair, the Governor wore that look of intense gravity peculiar to the habitually genial in their most serious moments. "Mr. Speaker, and Gentlemen of the House of Burgesses, I have heard of your resolves and augur ill of their effect. You have made it my duty to dissolve you; and you are dissolved accordingly."

The Governor spoke not a word more. The stunned Burgesses filed downstairs, collected paper and personal belongings from the chamber in which they no longer had a right to meet, and then walked out onto the streets of Williamsburg.

A little later they reconvened in the Apollo Room of the Raleigh Tavern, on Duke of Gloucester Street. As Jefferson glanced from the set and serious faces of his colleagues to the gilded motto, "Hilaritas Sapientiae et Bonae Vitae Proles" (Jollity, Offspring of Wisdom and Good Living), gleaming gold against the storm-cloud lead-blue paneling over the fireplace, he must have been acutely aware of the irony. Did he find it hard to believe that less than six years before he had danced in this same long chamber with Rebecca Burwell? Where now he met with others to frame a reply in words and action to His Majesty's Royal Governor, to His Majesty himself, and to His Majesty's royal government in Parliament assembled, he had once fretted that he could not find the proper words to speak to a young lady to whom he was not even truly committed. Then he had been convinced that the crisis at hand in the Apollo Room was the most crucial of his life.

Peyton Randolph, so recently unanimously reelected Speaker of the House, was unanimously elected moderator of this assembly. The same face that Jefferson had seen distorted by swollen-cheeked, chin-bobbing frustration on leaving the House of Burgesses after the favorable vote on Henry's Stamp Act Resolutions now presided with dignity and composure over a group assembled in defiance of royal authority.

After a number of members had vented their exasperation over the threats to colonial liberties, a thirty-seven-year-old burgess from Fairfax rose and immediately gained respectful attention. No one anticipated brilliant oratory. George Washington[56] had never displayed any gift for spoken eloquence. Indeed, he had never been known to speak in public for more than fifteen minutes, and then in a quietly matter-of-fact way, though he lived in an age when legislators sometimes pulled out every elocutionary stop in orations lasting several hours. His authority derived in part from a remarkable presence compounded of towering physical stature with athletic grace, marmoreal dignity, and a rugged nobility of countenance. Fourteen years of no special distinction had followed his youthful hour of glory in the French and Indian War but people still regarded him as a person far above the ordinary. Only a few years hence, when he still had not proved his ability in large-scale military operations, a British officer who glimpsed him would say that if the tall Virginian stood beside any sovereign in Europe, the crowned head would appear to be his lackey. Abigail Adams later would think his appearance not "unworthy of a god." The respectful attention accorded Washington had another basis: he spoke rarely and always to the point.

This time Washington was the first speaker to present a constructive plan. It was not principally his creation. Some think it had been entrusted to him by Richard Henry Lee. In any event, it had at least been edited by one of the most brilliant men in America, Washington's Fairfax neighbor George Mason.[57] Though Washington disliked speaking in public, he was an oratorical exhibitionist compared with Mason. When Henry spoke, some of his audience almost swooned with excitement; when Mason spoke, he himself almost fainted in panic. Only the pressure of duty and his passionate adherence to threatened principles prodded and lured Mason away from his beautiful Gunston Hall, where this very domestic widower cherished his loving daughters, savored his excellent library, and nursed his gout. But, like Lee and Jefferson, he thrilled to the opportunity for political experiment in the spirit of the French and Scottish Enlightenment. Though he did not practice law in the courts, there were few in the world so learned as he in the legal lore of many nations. Some of Virginia's most active leaders constantly sought his counsel.

So it was not strange that Washington should advance a plan that bore the marks of Mason's editorship if not his authorship. It called for organization of associations whose members would be pledged to import no British goods except a few specified necessities. Groups of this kind had already been formed in the Northern colonies. They would work a much greater hardship on Virginia's plantation society with its heavy dependence on British manufactures than on the colonial societies to the North. In recognition of this problem the plan presented by Washington would allow the importation of cloth and sewing thread.

The motion was put and passed: "A Committee was appointed to prepare the necessary and most proper Regulations for that Purpose, and they were ordered to make their Report to the General Meeting the next Day at 10 o'Clock."[58] In the document presented next day by the committee, Mason and Washington's list of prohibited articles was included almost unchanged. No taxed article would be imported, and even taxed articles already in Virginia should not be purchased after September 1, 1769, so long as the tax on them remained. Also placed on the nonimportation list were many untaxed items classified as luxuries.

The importation of slaves would be forbidden after November 1. Some of the Burgesses, though virtually all were slaveholders, saw this matter as one of moral as well as economic and political significance. As early as 1736, Colonel William Byrd, one of Virginia's greatest river barons, had appealed to Parliament "to put an end to this unchristian traffick of making merchandise of our Fellow Creatures."[59] More recently, efforts by the General Assembly to pass laws restraining importation of Negroes had been vetoed by the crown.

Probably none of the Burgesses was more sensitive than Jefferson to the anomaly of their position as slave-owners contending for liberty as a God-given right. Into the Commonplace Book that he had kept since student days, he had copied from time to time the opinions of various historians, jurists, and philosophers on slavery as well as on man's duty to his fellows.[60] With him in Williamsburg now was his coachman, Jupiter, who had been with him in student days in this same city. Jupiter was his own age. He was more than a coachman; he was as indispensable a factotum as Figaro. He tended to many purchases and other errands. Sometimes Jefferson borrowed small change from his slave, always scrupulously noting the sums in his Account Books. And then there were slaves with whom the relationship was quite different, men like his shoemaker, Sandy. Jefferson had described him as hard drinking, hard swearing, "artful and knavish" two months earlier when he had advertised for him in the *Virginia Gazette* as a runaway slave and promised a reward to his captor.

The Association would end automatically when London abolished the taxes. Otherwise, dissolution could be achieved only by a general meeting of subscribers after a month's notice. But even an end to the Association would not free the individual subscribers in the General Meeting from their pledge not to import "any Manner of Goods, Merchandise, or Manufactures, which are, or shall thereafter be taxed by Act of Parliament, for the Purpose of raising Revenue in America."

The plan was adopted by the General Meeting and signed by ninety-four of 116 former Burgesses. Some members of the dissolved Assembly had already gone home. Others were not prepared to commit themselves with such finality. The minutes described the signers as "a great Number of the principal Gentlemen of the Colony then present."[61] And so they were. The names appeared in two columns, the first headed in accordance with customary procedure by the presiding officer, Peyton Randolph, and the other headed perhaps through chance by Patrick Henry. As Douglas Southall Freeman observed, it was "as if the old party and the new in the House of Burgesses, the defenders of the throne and the author of the 'Stamp Act resolution,' wished it to be known that they stood together in this pledge of resistance to what they considered arbitrary taxation."[62] But not quite all of Virginia's leadership was united, and some families reflected the division. John Randolph did not add his name to the list headed by Peyton. Jefferson was apparently the fifty-first signer. He was his cousin Peyton's protégé but, with appropriate if accidental symbolism, his name was sixth in the column headed by Patrick Henry, leader of "the young, hot, and giddy."

The work done that day in Williamsburg proved far-reaching. Marylanders, meeting at Annapolis on June 22, organized an Association modeled after Virginia's. South Carolina followed suit a month later and North Carolina on November 7 simply endorsed the Virginia Association.[63]

On that same day, November 7, a new House of Burgesses convened. Looking around at his colleagues, Jefferson saw little evidence that the Assembly was a new one. In almost every instance the voters had returned the members of the dissolved House. Noting who was absent, he concluded that just about the only former Burgesses punished by the electorate were those who had declined to sign the Association.[64]

In his speech, the Governor was his most benevolent self. And he gave the legislators concrete reasons for pleasure. He announced that the King had approved westward extension of the boundary between the Cherokees and land-hungry Virginians. More important, Botetourt said: "His Majesty's present administration have at no time entertained a design to propose to Parliament to lay any further taxes upon America for the purpose of raising a revenue, and . . . it is their intention to propose in the next session of Parliament to take off the duties upon glass, paper and colors, upon consideration of such duties having been laid contrary to the true principles of Commerce."

And then the Governor added something in that roundly vowing, heartily sincere manner that was so hard to resist:

> I will be content to be declared infamous if I do not to the last hour of my life, at all times, in all places, and upon all occasions, exert every power with which I either am or ever shall be legally invested, in order to obtain and to maintain for the Continent of America that satisfaction which I have been authorized to promise this day, by the confidential servants of our gracious Sovereign who, to my certain knowledge, rates his honor so high that he had rather part with his crown than preserve it by deceit.[65]

In a reply written by Nicholas and Pendleton, the House joined the Council in expressing "the highest regard for the Governor and an appreciation of the cordial relations thus re-established." There was gratitude to "the best of kings," "especially as we cannot doubt but the same wisdom and goodness which have already induced His Majesty favorably to regard the humble entreaties of his faithful subjects in America will still farther incline the royal breast to an exertion of His Majesty's gracious and benign influence toward perfecting the happiness of all his people."[66]

Though Jefferson liked the Governor and believed in his sincerity, he thought the Burgesses' reply was much too humble. He did not share Pendleton's belief that the Association was no longer needed.[67] He was convinced that smooth diplomacy could not iron out all the troublesome difficulties between the mother country and her colonies.

But diplomacy was tried on both sides. In December a ball was given in the Governor's honor by Mr. Speaker and the Burgesses. The nearly one hundred ladies present were full of Virginia politeness, but his lordship could not look at them without being reminded of the problems of office. They had forsaken their prized English silks and satins for the sturdy homespun of colonial looms.[68]

With adjournment of the Assembly on December 21, Jefferson could look back on an eventful year. He had entered the House of Burgesses and had begun to make his way there—albeit not as quickly as if he had been able to combine oratorical ability with his status as protégé of both the Speaker and Pendleton. There would remain for a long time the chagrin of the Burgesses' rejection of his reply to the Governor. But there was some consolation in the fact that his first state paper, prosaic document that it was, had been accepted. The hoarse, guttural quality of his voice[69] when raised in Assembly guaranteed that he would indulge in no flights of oratory despite his marked flair for eloquence (what a difference the twentieth century's amplifying systems might have made in his career!). But his voice was pleasantly conversational in small groups, and was listened to with respect in committee. As a member of the prestigious Committee of Privileges and Elections, chaired by Pendleton, he discussed matters concerning disputed returns and the official qualifications of Burgesses with such fellow members as Nicholas, Bland, Benjamin Harrison, Lee, and Washington.[70]

As Jefferson left Williamsburg for Albemarle, his mind was on another house—the one he was building at Monticello. Much has been said to the effect that Jefferson, in building on an almost inaccessible mountaintop, evidenced a desire to retreat from the rough struggles of the bristling plain. Perhaps so. He certainly liked to avoid conflict when he could without sacrifice of principle. But that is not the whole significance of Jefferson's choice. He chose his building site in the face of repeated reminders by well-meaning neighbors and experienced builders that no one in America or England had chosen such a site for an elegant mansion.[71] He quietly reminded them that now someone had.

V

FIRE ON THE HILL,
SNOW ON THE MOUNTAIN

STANDING IN the quiet Charlottesville street, Jefferson found it hard to believe what the excited slave was trying to tell him. How could Shadwell be in ashes? Just a little earlier this afternoon he had dined there with his family before riding into town on business. As soon as he absorbed the fact that his boyhood home was destroyed, he thought of his library— the law books essential to his profession, the record books important to his well-ordered life, his father's books and irreplaceable personal records, the volumes of literature, history, and philosophy that were old friends. "Were none of my books saved?"

"No, master, all lost," the servant commiserated. And then his face brightened. "But we save your fiddle."[1]

The day would come when Jefferson could tell the story as a humorous anecdote. But that day was not February 1, 1770, when he learned that a cheap fiddle had been rescued from the flames while his books and papers were permitted to burn. Nor was that day so soon as February 21 when he wrote John Page:

My late loss may perhaps have reac[hed y]ou by this time, I mean the loss of my mother's house by fire, and in it, of every pa[per I] had in the world, and almost every book. On a reasonable estimate I calculate th[e cost o]f t[he b]ooks burned to have been 200. sterling. Would to god it had been the money [; then] had it never cost me a sigh! To make the loss more sensible it fell principally on m[y books] of common law, of which I have but one left, at that time lent out. Of papers too of every kind I am utterly destitute. All of these, whether public or private, of business or of amusement have perished in the flames.

He explained the urgency of his problem:

I had made some progress in preparing for the succeeding general court, and having, as was my custom, thrown my thoughts into the form of notes, I troubled my head no more with them. These are gone, and 'like the baseless fabric of a vision, Leave not a trace behind.' The records also and other papers, which furnished me with states of the several cases, having shared the same fate, I have no foundation whereon to set out anew. I have in vain attempted to recollect some of them, the defect sometimes of one, sometimes of more circumstances, rendering them so imperfect that I can make nothing of them. What am I to do then in April? The resolutions which the court have declared of admitting no continuances of causes seemed to be unalterable. Yet it might surely be urged that my case is too singular to admit of their being often troubled with the like excuse. Should it be asked what are the misfortunes of an individual to a court? The answer of a court, as well as of an individual, if left to me, should be in the words of Terence, "homo sum; humani nil a me alienum puto."—but a truce with this disagreeable subject.[2]

While evidencing considerable maturity in the intervening years, this letter to Page is reminiscent in style of the account of his troubles which the sixteen-year-old Jefferson sent the same friend on that bleak Christmas Day when he woke to find his watch damaged and both Rebecca's picture and his fancy garters destroyed through the combination of voracious rats and a leaky roof. In each case he joined Latin with English and drew from the classics to express his frustration. Incidentally, the quotation from Terence that Jefferson included in his letter about the burning of Shadwell was remarkably applicable to himself. So wide was the range of his interests and sympathies that he might well have said, "Nothing human is alien to me."

In other ways, the letter was reminiscent of Jefferson's earlier correspondence with Page, even to a plea: "Am I never more to have a letter from you? Why the devil don't you write?"

After some compliments to Mrs. Page, Jefferson wrote how much he would like to be with the couple. "If this conflagration, by which I am burned out of a home, had come before I had advanced so far in preparing another, I do not know but I might have cherished some treasonable thoughts of leaving these my native hills. Indeed I should be much happier were I nearer to Rosewell. . . ." Rosewell was the handsome mansion of the Pages in Gloucester County.

He added: "I reflect often with pleasure on the philosophical evenings I passed at Rosewell in my last visits there. I was always fond of philosophy even in its dryer forms, but from a ruby lip it comes with charms irresistible. Such a feast of sentiment must exhilarate and lengthen life at least as much as the feast of the sensualist shortens it. In a word I prize it so highly that if you will at any time collect the same Belle assemblée, on giving me three days previous notice, I shall certainly repair to my place as a member of it."

Of course, we should not take too seriously Jefferson's talk of living anywhere but in Albemarle County. He was simply indulging in one of the many little pleasantries which were so much a part of his correspondence and conversation. But it is significant that when he was still in the midst of problems resulting from a great loss he was fondly recalling the pleasures of friendship and the delights of feminine beauty and looking forward to further enjoyment of them. More significant still is the account of his young brother-in-law, Dabney Carr, with which he closes his letter:

This friend of ours, Page, in a very small house, with a table, half a dozen chairs, and one or two servants, is the happiest man in the universe. He possesses

truly the art of extracting comfort from things the most trivial. Every incident in
life he so takes as to render it a source of pleasure. With as much benevolence
as the heart of man will hold, but with an utter neglect of the costly apparatus
of life, he exhibits to the world a new phaenomenon in philosophy, the Samian
sage in the tub of the Cynic.[3]

Once again Jefferson was romanticizing. While he himself would have shared
Pythagoras's enthusiasm for music, science, and social reform and hence would have
enjoyed the life of the Samian sage, it is inconceivable that the Virginian, with his love
of comfort and elegance, would have been content to live as Diogenes the Cynic reputedly did. It is hard indeed to picture Jefferson taking shelter in a tub turned on its side
and answering, when Alexander asked what he might do for him, "Just stand out of
my sunlight." What is important, amid Jefferson's usual hyperbole in informal correspondence with close friends, is the evidence that his attention was focused on the
ideal of domestic happiness.

But, if Jefferson had not found a life's companion, he enjoyed the comfort of
devoted friends. Page snatched up his pen to write a heartfelt reply though his own
household had been cast into "hurry and confusion" by the death of his mother-in-law
only an hour before.[4]

Thomas Nelson, Sr., lawyer, burgess, and secretary for the Virginia Council of State,
wrote: "As I have a pretty good collection of books, it will give me pleasure to have
it in my power to furnish you with any you may want." He also sent by the bearer
of his letter a collection of door and shutter hinges, mortice locks, and pulleys to hasten
the building of a new shelter.[5]

A younger Thomas Nelson, nephew of Mr. Secretary, wrote immediately upon learning of Jefferson's loss to assure him "nothing can give me so much pleasure as to render
you every service that is in my power." By March 6 he was assuring Jefferson that he
would transmit his order to the London bookseller "by the first opportunity" but
prudently suggested that a copy be sent by another vessel as well, not an uncommon
precaution in those days of uncertain voyagings. Most welcome of all was the assurance
that the General Court would indulge him with a continuance of his causes. "My father
says you may be certain of that, as the Court has frequently done it where there have
been good reasons for it."[6] "Father" was William Nelson, President of the Council, and
hence a particularly influential member of the General Court.

From George Wythe came a present of nectarine and apricot grafts and his best
grapevines, together with a message: "You bear your misfortune so becomingly that,
as I am convinced you will surmount the difficulties it has plunged you into, so I foresee
you will hereafter reap advantages from it several ways."[7] The praise of those we admire is important to all of us. To Jefferson it was almost essential.

As has often been lamented, the destruction of Jefferson's books and papers was
not only a blow to him but also a loss to his biographers. What we would give for some
of the meticulously kept records that perished in the flames! And how useful it would
be to know the names of the destroyed volumes that he prized as friends!

Fortunately, we do have means of reconstructing with reasonable accuracy much
of the mental furniture of which no flames could deprive Jefferson so long as his brain
remained intact. We have the Commonplace Book[8] into which he copied from read-

ings that struck his fancy, often appending his own comments on the text. He began it in his student days and kept it into 1776, apparently adding four leaves in 1824, making a total of 158 covered on both sides with his miniscule script.

How this book escaped the flames we do not know. Perhaps Jefferson carried it into town with him on the day that Shadwell burned, thinking that he might while away the time in reading some volume and making notes if his business should require waiting. Many years later, in answer to a correspondent, he sent some notations from the Commonplace Book, explaining: "They were written at a time of life when I was bold in the pursuit of knowledge, never fearing to follow truth and reason to whatever results they led, and bearding every authority which stood in their way. This must be an apology, if you find the conclusion bolder than historical facts and principles will warrant."[9]

Another clue to Jefferson's reading and evolving philosophy is the list of books that he compiled in 1771 for Robert Skipwith, a friend who requested his help in selecting a library of volumes "improving as well as amusing." As informative as the list itself was the accompanying explanation of choices. Moreover, besides the information derived from the Commonplace Book and the letter to Skipwith, there is the evidence implicit in Jefferson's other letters and compositions.[10] There are specific allusions and close paraphrasings pointing to works that influenced him.

One of the most impressive things about the list Jefferson prepared for Skipwith is its variety. No one should be surprised to find histories of Virginia, Robertson's histories of Scotland and of Charles V, Hume's history of England, Clarendon's account of the Rebellion, Bossuet's history of France, as well as Plutarch's *Lives,* Livy, Sallust, Tacitus, and Caesar. Some persons, mindful of Jefferson's involvement in the Enlightenment, might be surprised to see the Bible listed under ancient history. They forget that the great father of the Scottish Enlightenment, Francis Hutcheson, was a Presbyterian minister. Not unexpected would be the law books or the works of political and natural philosophy ranging from the ancient Romans to modern times. One who knew Jefferson's plans for Monticello would expect his inclusion of many books on the fine arts and art criticism. Certainly it was not unusual that a planter's library should hold various agricultural works, including Jethro Tull's *Horse-hoeing Husbandry.* But some might wonder at the large amount of poetry, drama, and fiction included. Besides such revered giants as Homer, Virgil, and Shakespeare, there were Terence, Ossian, Dryden, Pope, Milton, Moliére, Congreve, Rousseau, Smollett, Samuel Richardson, Henry Fielding, Goldsmith, Spenser, Gay, Swift, and Lord Lyttleton. And probably a great many people would not expect Jefferson's vigorous defense of imaginative literature. Referring to this listing, he wrote Skipwith:

A view of the second column in this catalogue would, I suppose, extort a smile from the face of gravity. Peace to its wisdom! Let me not awaken it. A little attention, however, to the nature of the human mind evinces that the entertainments of fiction are useful as well as pleasant. That they are pleasant when well written, every person feels who reads. But wherein is its utility, asks the reverend sage, big with the notion that nothing can be useful but the learned lumber of Greek and Roman reading with which his head is stored? I answer, every thing is useful which contributes to fix us in the principles and practice of virtue. When any signal act of charity or of gratitude, for instance, is presented either to our sight or imagination, we are deeply impressed with its beauty and feel a strong desire in ourselves of doing charitable and grateful acts also. On the contrary when we see or read of any atrocious deed, we are disgusted with its deformity and conceive an abhorrence of vice. Now every emotion of this kind is an exercise of our virtuous dispositions; and dispositions of the mind, like limbs of the body, acquire strength by exercise. But exercise produces habit; and in the instance of which we speak, the exercise being of the moral feelings, produces a habit of thinking and acting virtuously. We never reflect whether the story we read be truth or fiction. If the painting be lively, and a tolerable picture of nature, we are thrown into a reverie, from which if we awaken it is the fault of the writer.

I appeal to every reader of feeling and sentiment whether the fictitious murther of Duncan by Macbeth in Shakespeare does not excite in him as great horror of villainy as the real one of Henry IV by Ravaillac as related by Davila? And whether the fidelity of Nelson, and generosity of Blandford in Marmontel do not dilate his breast, and elevate his sentiments as much as any similar incident which real history can furnish? Does he not in fact feel himself a better man while reading them, and privately covenant to copy the fair example? We neither know nor care whether Laurence Sterne really went to France, whether he was there accosted by the poor Franciscan, at first rebuked him unkindly, and then gave him a peace offering; or whether the whole be not a fiction. In either case we are equally sorrowful at the rebuke, and secretly resolve we will never do so: we are pleased with the subsequent atonement, and view with emulation a soul candidly acknowledging its fault, and making a just reparation.

Considering history as a moral exercise, her lessons would be too unfrequent if confined to real life. Of those recorded by historians few incidents have been attended with such circumstances as to excite in any high degree this sympathetic emotion of virtue. We are therefore wisely framed to be as warmly interested for a fictitious as for a real personage. The spacious field of imagination is thus laid open to our use, and lessons may be formed to illustrate and carry home to the mind every moral rule of life. Thus a lively and lasting sense of filial duty is more effectually impressed on the mind of a son or daughter by reading King Lear, than by all the dry volumes of ethics and divinity that ever were written. This is my idea of well-written Romance, of Tragedy, Comedy, and Epic Poetry.[11]

The arguments used by Jefferson in defense of imaginative literature are not original with him. They are familiar to readers of Aristotle's *Poetics,* Horace's *Art of Poetry,* Sir Philip Sidney's *Apology for Poetry,* and other works scarcely less famous. But Jefferson restated the arguments in an appealing style, and they came with particular force from such an ardent collector of facts.

Jefferson considered Dr. Samuel Johnson's dictionary necessary to a well-fleshed library, but he found much fault with that work. He quarreled with the lexicographer's prejudice, not so much the kind revealed in definitions of "Excise" as "a hateful tax . . . adjudged [by] . . . wretches hired by those to whom excise is paid," or of "Pension" as "pay given to a state hireling for treason to his country." Jefferson was more concerned with what he saw as a prejudice in favor of the classical languages, one so strong as to cause Johnson to neglect Anglo-Saxon etymology. This reaction may be surprising in view of Jefferson's habit of interlarding his correspondence with Greek and Latin quotations. But he had also become an enthusiastic Anglo-Saxon scholar. It was just that so few people shared this language with him that its use in writing to friends would have been a hindrance to communication. He once explained that he began the study of Old English while a law student "by being obliged to recur to that source for explanation of a multitude of law-terms."[12] He had found in Fortescue Aland's preface to *Fortescue on Monarchies* a list of books for the study of Anglo-Saxon and, with their aid, had taught himself the language. Eventually Jefferson would devise a system for the teaching of Anglo-Saxon and would say that this study would have become a major pursuit of his life if other demands had not intervened.[13]

Jefferson's writings, both public and informal, reveal his self-conscious awareness of his Anglo-Saxon heritage. In view of his admiration of the greatest of the Anglo-Saxons, Alfred the Great, it is interesting that Jefferson apparently was unaware of his direct descent from this remarkable man. In any event, it is not surprising that he should have felt a spiritual kinship with one who was author, statesman, historian, geographer, translator, codifier of laws, and architect.[14]

The Commonplace Book and other writings reveal that Jefferson's appreciation of the Anglo-Saxons is much colored by Tacitus's portrayal of these Germanic tribesmen as sturdily virtuous practitioners of democracy. Jefferson saw the Anglo-Saxons as originators of the institutions of representative government and trial by jury. He saw the Norman French as corrupters of a superior culture. Jefferson tended to exaggerate the accomplishments of the Anglo-Saxons but his estimate was not nearly so wide of the mark as that of generations of historians who, until recent years, viewed these first Englishmen as tribesmen rescued from barbarism by the French. The best of recent scholarship reveals the Anglo-Saxons as culturally superior to their conquerors in all but engineering and military science and shows them to be originators of political institutions with which the Normans formerly were credited.[15]

But Jefferson did not scorn French contributions to political thought. His Commonplace Book contained no less than twenty-seven excisions from Montesquieu to a total of twenty-eight pages, more than for any other writer. Later this admiration for the author of *De l'Esprit des Lois* would wane and eventually turn to antipathy, principally because the baron repeatedly cited the British government as the best of models. Nevertheless, like some of the framers of the United States Constitution, Jefferson must have been influenced by Montesquieu's theory of the separation of powers—legislative, executive, and judicial—as a safeguard to liberty. A reader of Jefferson's *Notes on Virginia* may well see internal evidence of Montesquieu's theories of the influence of climate and geography on culture.[16]

Another Frenchman, Voltaire, is often quoted in the Commonplace Book. But, as Gilbert Chinard concluded after careful study of Jefferson's correspondence, there is little evidence that Voltaire exerted a strong influence on the Virginian. Of course, Jefferson, even unwittingly, may have been influenced by a sentence he copied from Voltaire ("Il est évident que sous le nom de Dieu, c'est le diable qu'un tel peuple adore"). For, as the Virginian wrote to John Adams in 1823:

I can never join Calvin in addressing *his God*. He was indeed an atheist, which

I can never be; or rather his religion was demonism. If ever man worshiped a false God, he did. The Being described in his five points is not the God whom you and I acknowledge and adore, the Creator and benevolent Governor of the world, but a demon of malignant spirit.[17]

Jefferson copied into his Commonplace Book a great variety of religious opinions. One gets the impression that in his twenties he was searching and sorting among religious convictions. He carefully copied excerpts from the religious thoughts of Locke and Shaftesbury,[18] but it is impossible to determine the extent to which he agreed with either. He was extremely reticent in matters of faith even when—as we shall see later—his silence cost him politically. Maybe he agreed at least with Shaftesbury's statement, "Men of sense are really of but one religion." When asked, "What religion?" the earl replied, "Men of sense never tell." There is stronger evidence that Jefferson shared another idea with Shaftesbury, the belief in a "moral sense" implanted in every human being of normal capacity.

This idea of the "moral sense" became the philosophical keystone of Shaftesbury's disciple, Francis Hutcheson. He was a Presbyterian minister of the third generation but he was not representative of that Calvinism of which Jefferson was so critical. Indeed, the Presbytery of Glasgow once tried him for teaching "false and dangerous" doctrines. First among these was his assertion that the moral goodness of one's actions could be measured by the degree to which they promoted the happiness of others. Second was his argument that it is possible to have a knowledge of good and evil without having a knowledge of God. But this knowledge was God-given. In terms of inherent moral sense, which was the most significant sense, all men were equal. The moral sense would tell us that virtue must be evaluated in social terms: "That action is best which accomplishes the greatest happiness for the greatest numbers."

And there was one of Hutcheson's followers, Thomas Reid, who asserted: "Moral truths, therefore, may be divided into two classes, to wit: such as are self-evident to every man whose understanding and moral faculty are ripe, and such as are deduced by reasoning from those that are self-evident."

Also of the "moral sense" school was Henry Home, Lord Kames, from whom Jefferson copied long passages and who appeared, on the list Jefferson prepared for Skipwith, under three separate headings—Law, Religion, and Criticism on the Fine Arts. Apparently Kames's *Essays on the Principles of Morals and Natural Religion* was one of the few books that survived the burning of Shadwell.[19] A copy of it still in existence bears marginal notes in Jefferson's handwriting that may date from student days in Williamsburg. Kames wrote: "There is a principle of benevolence in man which prompts him to an equal pursuit of the happiness of all."

Another Scotsman, Adam Smith, though a practitioner of "the dismal science" of economics, did not measure the effectiveness of government in terms of pounds and pence. He wrote: "All constitutions of government. . . are valued only in proportion as they tend to promote the happiness of those who live under them."

Where in the intellectual firmament does John Locke shine alongside the starry sweep—the veritable Milky Way—of the Scottish Enlightenment? Locke exalted the triumvirate of "life, liberty, and property." But he declared the business of life to be "the pursuit of happiness." Scholars argue as to whether Jefferson was familiar with Locke's

Two Treatises on Government. There is no positive evidence that he was. Garry Wills, in his *Inventing America,* emphasizes that this work of the English empiricist was not widely circulated in America.[20] But it seems unlikely that Jefferson, with his consummate intellectual curiosity and great concern with government, should have failed to read twin treatises in political philosophy that comprise one of the two most important works produced by one of his three chief heroes.

Nevertheless, whether or not he knew this particular work of Locke's, the idea that the authority of government was dependent upon the consent of the governed was available to him also through the writings of Jean-Jacques Burlamaqui and would soon be available through the writings of a fellow American, James Wilson. Besides, it had been enunciated in Parliament as early as 1613 by Sir Edwin Sandys, father of representative government in Virginia and hence on the North American continent. [21] Many such ideas, as Jefferson later would say, were "in the air." In any event, Jefferson was familiar with Locke's *Essay Concerning Human Understanding* and was both prescient and naive in his assumption of the wonders that could be wrought by public education's tracings on the waiting blank tablets of the human mind.

With what memorable phrases Jefferson's head rang after all this reading! "Life and liberty." "The pursuit of happiness." "Self-evident truths." And they were not just glittering ornaments to brighten somber discourse. They were terms specifically defined[22] in the writings of the Scottish Enlightenment, to which Jefferson had been introduced by William Small and which he continued to study with great avidity.

To what conclusion did these speculations lead? The words of Kames, Reid, Adam Smith, Burlamaqui—even those of Hume, whose atheistic writings were rescued from the authorities by the pious Hutcheson in the interest of free expression—all lead back to the surprisingly seminal Francis Hutcheson. And he preached that thoughts must be translated into action to increase the sum of human happiness. Sometimes the action must be drastic. He wrote:

> . . .as the end of all civil power is acknowledged by all to be the safety and happiness of the whole body, any power not naturally conducive to this end is unjust; which the people, who rashly granted it under an error, may justly abolish again when they find it necessary to their safety to do so.

Perusal of Jefferson's Commonplace Book reveals that he was busily collecting instances of colonies' refusing to be subjected to their mother governments. He noted that the Samians had with impunity asserted their independence of Athens by concluding a defensive alliance with Sparta.[23] He cited, too, the examples of Syracuse and Corcyra, which had "renounced their obedience" to Corinth.[24] He was intrigued by a reference to Mycenae's "throwing off dependence on Argos," and posed himself a question for research: "Were they a colony of Argos?"[25] He was certainly interested in peoples who had found it necessary "to dissolve the political bands which [had] connected them with another."

But Jefferson's mind was not entirely occupied with philosophy and politics in the autumn of 1770. While his Commonplace Book evidences his study of federations ranging from that of ancient Greece to the Helvetic body and the Union of Utrecht, his account books show his growing interest in another kind of union. There were times when his concern with dissolving bands yielded to a fascination with wedding bands. Jupiter was always being sent to buy theater tickets in Williamsburg. Also Jupiter was directed to buy hair powder and buckles by the same young master who, eight years before, disgusted that Rebecca Burwell preferred another, had written Page, "I am sure that man who powders most, perfumes most, embroiders most, and talks most nonsense, is most admired." Then he had been caustic about the "monkey-like animals. . .in whose formation. . .the tailors and barbers go halves with God almighty."

Jefferson's new interest had been foreshadowed when, in his letter telling Page of the burning of Shadwell, he had written of his brother-in-law Dabney Carr's becoming through marriage "the happiest man in the universe." Later there was much more specific evidence of the focus of Jefferson's thoughts in the letter he wrote in 1771 to Robert Skipwith suggesting a choice of books for that gentleman's library. He had concluded with an invitation to Skipwith and his wife to visit him at "Rowanty," evidently a playful reference to Monticello as the Arcadian Olympus, "mountain of the world and pivot of heaven":

> Come then and bring our dear Tibby with you; the first in your affections, and second in mine. Offer prayers for me too at that shrine to which, tho' absent, I pay continual devotion. In every scheme of happiness she is placed in the foreground of the picture, as the principal figure. Take that away, and it is no picture for me.[26]

Tibby (Mrs. Robert Skipwith) was the sister of Martha Wayles Skelton, twenty-three-year-old widow of Bathurst Skelton. Martha and her three-year-old son, John, apparently lived with her father, John Wayles, at his plantation, The Forest, in Charles City County, not a great many miles from Williamsburg. There, and in the capital, Jefferson paid court to her. It is not surprising that he found her attractive. Traditions from several sources[27] agree that she was beautiful. She is said to have been "a little above medium height, slightly but exquisitely formed"—like the Houdon statue of Diana that Jefferson so much admired. Randall wrote: "Her complexion was brilliant—her large expressive eyes of the richest shade of hazel—her luxuriant hair of the finest tinge of auburn."[28] There is testimony to her grace in dancing, on horseback, and in walking. Her singing voice was sweet (this may have reminded Jefferson of Jane) and her skill on the spinet and the harpsichord was much admired. She was also intelligent and well read, a lively conversationalist. No wonder Jefferson had rivals for her hand.

One day, according to a story[29] handed down in the Jefferson family, two of Martha's suitors met on her doorstep and were shown into the same room to wait until she was ready to see them. They had too much in common to have much to say to each other. As they waited in uneasy silence they could hear from the adjacent room the blended notes of harpsichord and violin. They knew who was playing the harpsichord. They probably guessed who was playing the violin. When they heard Martha's and Jefferson's voices joined in song, the two suitors listened restlessly through several stanzas, then exchanged glances, took their hats, and left.

Asking Mr. Wayles for Martha's hand probably held no terrors for Jefferson. Suitor and father had seen much of each other and got along well. In his autobiography Jefferson wrote:

> Mr. Wayles was a lawyer of much practice, to which he was introduced more by his great industry, punctuality and public readiness, than by eminence in the science of his profession. He was a most agreeable companion, full of pleasantry and good humor, and welcomed in every society. He acquired a handsome fortune...[30]

John Wayles was then a widower. Martha's mother, aristocratic Martha Eppes, had died soon after the daughter's birth. A second wife had died, leaving three daughters (one of them Mrs. Skipwith), and a third wife had died without issue. Wayles was not one to go long without female companionship.

As early as February 20, 1771, from the cottage at Monticello in which Jefferson lived while work proceeded on the main house, he had written his London agent: "The things I have desired you to purchase for me I would beg you to hasten, particularly the clavichord, which I have directed to be purchased in Hamburg because they are better made there and much cheaper."[31] By June 1 another letter made clear why the purchase of a keyboard instrument was so urgent. Explaining that he had waited to write again until he could be sure that the Association would remove importation restrictions on all but dutied articles, he begged leave to change his original order:

> I wrote therein for a clavichord. I have since seen a fortepiano and am charmed with it. Send me this instrument then instead of the clavichord. Let the case be of fine mahogany, solid, not veneered. The compass from Double G to F in alt., a plenty of spare strings; and the workmanship of the whole very handsome, and worthy the acceptance of a lady for whom I intend it.[32]

The piano was to be a wedding gift for Martha. The keyboard and violin duets begun in The Forest would be continued at Monticello. Incidentally, the first of the two letters to the London agent had also instructed him to "search the Herald's office for the arms of my family" and to purchase a coat of arms (which could be done if the applicant enjoyed sufficient status) if none was already registered.[33] In the letter with the revised order, he wrote: "I desired the favor of you to procure me an architect. I must repeat the request earnestly and that you would send him in as soon as you can."[34] The domestic instinct was stirring in Jefferson as strongly as in his brother-in-law, Dabney Carr, but Jefferson would not be content with the humble cottage about which he had rhapsodized earlier. While his thousands of acres, though ample, did not match the tens of thousands of the Carters and Lees, he would build a manor house as elegant as any in Virginia and as beautifully furnished. And as he contemplated marriage and progeny, family pride stirred in him. He was so eager to assume his new family responsibilities that he made an entry in his Account Book for little John Skelton in anticipation of the time when he would be his guardian in Martha's behalf. But apparently in June 1771, about a week and a half after Jefferson placed the order for the piano, John died.[35] He was Martha's only child.

Mourning for the child may have delayed the wedding with its attendant festivities.

In any event, Thomas and Martha Jefferson began a new year together. They were married at The Forest on New Year's Day 1772. Two clergymen and at least one fiddler played their parts in the ceremony.[36]

As was frequently the custom in that day, the couple lingered at the bride's home after the ceremony—not for hours but for days. The newlywed Jeffersons stayed for two weeks. On the way to Monticello they stopped over at Tuckahoe, Jefferson's second boyhood home, where Randolph cousins still lived. The delay was lengthened by the breaking down of their phaeton. After they left Tuckahoe, Jefferson for the first time became so absorbed in his daily life that he failed to make notes in his Account Book. At first the light covering of snow on the ground and sparkling encrustation on the branches of trees made the world a crystalline delight of virginal beauty. But as they rode on they found snow of greater and greater depth until finally it became an impediment. Eventually they were forced to abandon the phaeton and proceed on horseback. Toward the end of the day they stopped at Blenheim, Colonel Carter's plantation. But no Carters were there, and only an overseer was in charge. After a short rest they set out about sunset for Monticello. Most people in the area thought that Monticello was eight miles from Blenheim, but Jefferson, of course, knew that it was really "8.01 miles."[37] Riding through snow from eighteen inches to two feet deep, the Jeffersons may have found even one-hundredth of one mile a significant distance.

Arriving at Monticello late at night after ploughing up the mountain through snowdrifts, they found all lights out and no fires burning. The servants had retired to their own houses. Both bride and groom were depressed by "the horrible dreariness of such a house at the end of such a journey."

Jefferson did not wish to wake the servants. Quietly he and Martha entered the only habitable portion of the dwelling under construction, the small cottage at the end of what would be the south terrace of the completed mansion. "Part of a bottle of wine, found on a shelf behind some books, had to serve . . . both for fire and supper."[38] Soon their voices were joined in song, punctuated by laughter over the spartan character of their homecoming. And so began their first night alone under their own roof.

Martha, Jefferson soon learned, had many prosaic virtues as well as the gifts that had at first excited his admiration. She was a good manager of the servants and she kept household accounts as accurately as he had.

On September 27 Martha gave birth to a little girl. The Jeffersons named this child Martha, too, and began calling her Patsy. Jefferson, by now, often called his wife Patty.

The mother, her anxiety sharpened by the loss of one child, and the father, beset with all the apprehensions of a first-time parent, grew daily more miserable as Patsy seemed to waste away before their eyes. As month succeeded month it seemed less and less likely that she would see her first birthday. Then, when she was six months old, she "was recovered almost instantly by a good breast of milk."[39] The words are Jefferson's. He does not tell us whose good breast came to the rescue. Probably, as so often in plantation days, a black wet-nurse supplied the necessary nutrition. Seeing nature succeed where physicians had failed, Jefferson was confirmed in his prejudice against the medical profession. He once said that, whenever he saw two doctors in conference, he looked for a buzzard.[40]

Meanwhile, work went on with the building of a more stately mansion for Jefferson's growing family. The architect from England never came and Jefferson, more and more a student of architectural drawings, began executing designs of his own with a skill in draftsmanship reminiscent of his father. The design was altered through successive visions and revisions as he became increasingly a master of his newly acquired science. At times he did almost as much tearing down as building. Though the design was always consistently neoclassical and included a columned portico, it would grow progressively more Palladian in inspiration, with curves replacing many straight lines and sharp angles.[41]

But, through all the changes of building and rebuilding, the mountaintop itself was home. Jefferson loved to look toward the West in winter when he could see a snowstorm, "rising over the distant Allegheny, come sweeping and roaring on, mountain after mountain, till it reaches us, and then when its blast is felt, to turn to our fireside, and while we hear it pelting against the windows to enjoy the cheering blaze."[42] In the summer he delighted in standing above the storm and looking down upon the play of lightning in the clouds below.[43] At times, in defiance of all logic, one could almost believe oneself superior to fate.

But it was necessary to come down from the mountain to participate in the affairs of men. And Jefferson the public man had not been swallowed up in domesticity. He had attended a special session of the House of Burgesses called in the summer of 1771 by President William Nelson, acting governor after the death of Botetourt, to provide relief for sufferers from the "Great Fresh," the greatest flood in Virginia's history. In May the James, Rappahannock, and Roanoke Rivers, fed by mountain torrents, had overflowed their banks, destroying wharves, tobacco warehouses, and homes. In Richmond buildings had been swept aside by a forty-foot wall of water. The total financial loss to Virginians was estimated at two million pounds. The Burgesses moved quickly to provide compensation for "Sharers in [the] Melancholy Catastrophe."[44]

So great was concern over this Virginia disaster that the Burgesses were not as excited as they might otherwise have been over the killing of three civilians by British soldiers defending themselves from the attack of a Boston mob. Though the captain of the British guard had been acquitted in a Boston court after defense by no less a patriot than John Adams, John's cousin Samuel Adams, with the aid of an imaginative engraving by Paul Revere, had so orchestrated newspaper accounts and pulpit denunciations of the event that it had come to be known with abhorrence up and down the Atlantic seaboard as the Boston Massacre.

The meeting of the Burgesses necessarily brought together most of the Associators. As had been foreseen by Jefferson and others, they voted to dissolve the Association and lift the restrictions on all importations except "tea, paper, glass and painters' colors of foreign manufacture upon which a duty is laid for the purpose of raising a revenue for America." A group including Washington and Mason had called for consideration of the fact that it might not be "consistent with good policy to attempt keeping up a plan here which is now being dropped by all our sister colonies."[45]

The new Governor arrived in September 1771. He was John Murray, Earl of Dunmore, Viscount Fincastle, baron of Blair, of Moulin and of Tillymont. Those who placed faith in external symbols might have seen his red hair combined with flashing brown eyes as evidence of temper. They would have drawn conclusions too from his weak chin and petulant mouth. They might have seen arrogance in the way he looked down his long, sharp nose. They would have been most unscientific and quite unjustified and, in this instance, they would also have been completely right. But at first the leaders of Virginia society found him charming. They admired his graciousness and his familiarity with good literature. They did not know that, besides carrying the royal Stuart genes, he also carried the royal Stuart faith in the divine right of kings.[46]

Jefferson was elected to the new Assembly for which Dunmore issued writs of election and which convened February 10, 1772. The legislative session that winter was not nearly so notable as the weather. Virginia had in January perhaps the greatest blizzard that had thus far been recorded within its borders. Washington, who did not reach Williamsburg until March 2, said that the snow everywhere on his Mount Vernon plantation had been "up to the breast of a tall horse."[47] Throughout Virginia the spirit of revolt seemed as frozen as the rivers.

January 1773 began on a very different note. Ingeniously executed counterfeit notes and coins were discovered to be circulating in the colony. Fear of accepting bad currency almost strangled commerce. Consulted by the Governor, the Council advised the calling of the General Assembly to devise appropriate legislation. Meanwhile, they proposed, His Excellency should offer substantial rewards for apprehension of the counterfeiters and of any person knowingly attempting to circulate false currency. Dunmore agreed.

Shortly afterward some fifteen or sixteen Virginians were accused of comprising a counterfeiting ring under the leadership of a North Carolinian. On February 23 five of them were brought to the capital under heavy guard for questioning. One was released. The others, after a hearing before the court of neighboring York County, were remanded to the Williamsburg gaol.[48]

When the Assembly convened on March 4, the Burgesses' relief that the counterfeit ring had been broken was offset by their concern that the Pittsylvania County Court had been bypassed to bring Pittsylvania residents to trial in distant York County. Was not this violation of the right of vicinage distressingly suggestive of Parliament's threat to bring American colonists to London for trial? They protested to the Governor:

> The duty we owe our constituents obliges us, my Lord, to be attentive to the safety of the innocent as we are desirous of punishing the guilty; and we apprehend that a doubtful construction and various execution of criminal law does greatly endanger the safety of innocent men. We do therefore most humbly pray your Excellency that the proceedings in this case may not in future be drawn into consequence or example.[49]

The Governor, after expressing incredulity at the Burgesses' anxiety, submitted the question of the legality of his actions to the General Court. That conservative body upheld him. Some of the younger Burgesses were doubly disturbed by the course of events in Virginia, because they had heard that a Rhode Island Court of Inquiry had been empowered to transport "persons accused of offenses committed in America to places beyond the seas to be tried." They met one evening in a private room of the Raleigh Tavern to coordinate their strategy in the Burgesses. Among them were Jefferson, Patrick Henry, Richard Henry Lee, and his brother Francis Lightfoot Lee. And there was another, the new Burgess from Louisa, Jefferson's brother-in-law, Dabney Carr.[50] He was also his dearest friend and the man Jefferson most admired among all his living acquaintances. "His firmness," said Jefferson, "was inflexible in whatever he thought was right; but when no moral principle stood in the way, never had man more of the milk of human kindness, of indulgence, of softness, of pleasantry of conversation and conduct." Jefferson foresaw for him a great career as a statesman. Here was a man of "spotless integrity, sound judgement, handsome imagination, enriched by education and reading; quick and clear in his conceptions, of correct and ready elocution, impressing every hearer with the sincerity of the heart from which it flowed."[51] Ready elocution—that was the great gift which Jefferson lacked. Carr was making a reputation for eloquence in the courts. There were those who thought he might some day be Henry's greatest forensic rival in Virginia.[52]

Jefferson now made Carr his political protégé. Though only six months older than his friend, Jefferson was a veteran legislator whereas Carr was a newcomer. When someone, probably Richard Henry Lee, proposed the creation of a Virginia Committee of Correspondence, Jefferson was suggested as a good member to introduce the resolution providing for it. Evidently, since the group included Virginia's Demosthenes and Cicero, it was thought that Jefferson could bring to the job some asset more important then oratorical ability. This advantage may have been the respect and friendship of contending factions.

Jefferson was enthusiastic about the idea of an instrument to maintain communication between Virginia and her sister colonies. Massachusetts already had local committees of correspondence. In establishing a committee to speak for an entire colony, the Old Dominion would be taking the logical next step, one that might well inspire emulation in Massachusetts herself. But Jefferson did not covet the privilege of introducing the resolution. Just as Pendleton had once thrust Jefferson forward to prepare state papers that the veteran legislator might otherwise have presented, so Jefferson now made an opportunity for Dabney Carr to impress the House with his oratorical gifts in a role being urged upon Jefferson himself.[53]

Thus it was that on March 12, when the House resolved itself into a Committee of the Whole on the State of the Colony, Dabney Carr secured the floor. He said that "His Majesty's faithful subjects" had been so "much disturbed by various rumors and reports tending to deprive them of their ancient legal and constitutional rights" as to make necessary a "communication of sentiments" between Great Britain and the American colonies and among the colonies themselves. To this end he proposed the naming of eleven Burgesses to a Committee of Correspondence "in order. . .to remove the uneasiness and to quiet the minds of the people." The Committee would have the duty "to obtain the most early and authentic intelligence of all such acts and resolutions of the British Parliament, or proceedings of administration, as may relate to or affect the British colonies in America, and to keep up and maintain a correspondence and communication with our sister colonies respecting these important considerations."[54] From time to time it would report on these matters to the House.

Carr cited particularly the threat implicit for all colonists if a recent Rhode Island Court of Inquiry had indeed been empowered to transport Americans overseas to be tried for offenses committed in Rhode Island. Jefferson proudly noted that Carr spoke "with great ability, reconciling all to [his motion], not only by the reasonings, but by the temper and moderation with which it was developed."[55] Ready acceptance in Committee of the Whole was followed by unanimous adoption in the House. Peyton Randolph was made chairman of the newly created Committee and Carr found himself serving on it alongside such giant stalwarts as Robert Carter Nicholas, Richard Bland, Richard Henry Lee, Benjamin Harrison, Edmund Pendleton, and Patrick Henry, as well as his old friend Jefferson.

The next day Lord Dunmore prorogued the Assembly. The Burgesses were not dismayed. As Jefferson and Carr rode away from the capital they agreed that the previous day's work in Williamsburg would almost inevitably lead to a meeting of representatives from all the American colonies. Before long New Englanders would be reading the resolution with delight and Samuel Adams would exult in Virginia's "truly patriotic resolves" gladdening "the hearts of all who are friends of liberty."[56]

Governor Dunmore's evaluation was different as he wrote his report to London: "Your lordship will observe there are some resolves which show a little ill humor in the House of Burgesses, but I thought them so insignificant that I took no matter of notice of them."[57]

In May Jefferson was again in Williamsburg on business. Before he returned home Dabney Carr, then in Charlottesville, died of bilious fever. Apparently, he was buried at Shadwell before Jefferson could reach Albemarle.[58] This death must have been his hardest blow since the loss of his sister Jane. He grieved for his widowed sister Martha and her children and he lamented the passing of his own dearest friend. The event was rendered the more poignant by the fact that Dabney Carr had seemed on the threshold of a brilliant—perhaps even a great—career.

Jefferson recalled their early schooldays at Mr. Maury's. It was for the race between his own slow pony and Dabney's swift horse that he had set the date of February 30. There had been Elysian days when the two boys, on vacation, had carried their books up a wooded slope of Monticello to lie under a particular great oak, alternately studying and talking or gazing up at drifting clouds. They conceived such a fondness for this majestic tree that they pledged each other "that the one who survived should see that the body of the other was buried at its foot." Jefferson now had Carr's body disinterred from the grave at Shadwell and reburied beneath the beloved tree.[59] Later he wrote an inscription concluding: "To his Virtue, Good Sense, Learning and Friendship this stone is dedicated by Thomas Jefferson, who, of all men living, loved him most."[60] Jefferson's grief did not prevent his computing from the time consumed by the gravedigging that one laborer performing at that rate would require four days to dig up an acre.[61] Perhaps, amid reminders of the transitory quality of life, he sought comfort in hard facts.

Jefferson's household more than tripled overnight. He took in his sister and her six young children—three boys and three girls.[62]

Death struck the family again on May 28. John Wayles, Patty's father, died at the age of fifty-eight. There was mourning for the father that Patty loved and the father-in-law of whom Jefferson was genuinely fond. A material difference in their lives resulted from Patty's inheritance of about eleven thousand acres, greatly increasing their estates, and fourteen slaves. Among these slaves were a mulatto woman, Betty Hemings, reputedly the daughter of a slave woman and an English sea captain, and Betty's children. These children, as quadroons, were even lighter than their half-breed mother. There is substantial evidence in support of the general belief at the time that John Wayles was their father.[63] Thus Mr. and Mrs. Jefferson apparently were served by her deceased father's concubine and were waited upon by at least one slave who was Mrs. Jefferson's half-sister, as close kin to her genetically as the beloved Tibby Skipwith. As time passed, some people noted that Jefferson seemed particularly solicitous for the welfare of the light-skinned children of Betty Hemings who came with John Wayles' estates. At least four historians[64] have noted a radical change in 1772–73 in Jefferson's attitude toward mulattoes. He became fearful that miscegenation was a menace to American civilization.

There was another aspect of the legacy from John Wayles. The dead man had been heavily in debt to English merchants. It quickly became necessary to sell more than half of the inherited lands to pay off the Jeffersons' share of the indebtedness. From the purchasers Jefferson received notes, rather than cash, in accordance with a practice then quite prevalent in Virginia. Only later did Jefferson learn that the English creditors would not accept these notes in settlement. At the time it seemed that the Jeffersons' prosperity had increased substantially.[65]

Monticello itself continued to grow but a stranger might have wondered why Jefferson found so much peace there. The dust and litter of construction were a nuisance inside, and the yard was piled with bricks and lumber. The plantings took on a more permanent look than the dwelling itself.

A chance meeting at Monticello brought an exotic note to the gardens, kitchen, and dining table. A Florentine, Philip Mazzei, dined with the Jeffersons on a November evening of 1773 in the company of Thomas Adams, the English agent through whom Jefferson had ordered the pianoforte and whom he had asked to obtain a Jefferson coat of arms. Mazzei had fled his homeland after getting into trouble with the authorities because of his importation of such forbidden books as the works of Giordano Bruno, Rousseau, and Voltaire. In England he had met Benjamin Franklin and Thomas Adams, both of whom suggested that he would find a congenial home in America. Under Adams' patronage and with his companionship, Mazzei had sailed for Virginia with grapevines and a force of Italian laborers with a view to planting vineyards and building a wine industry. Adams had led him into the Shenandoah Valley, hoping to interest him in some property there. It was on their return that they dined at Monticello. With his interest in representatives of other cultures and his particular delight in anyone who shared his enthusiasm for the philosophes, Jefferson was an animated and charming host.

He was no less entertaining the next morning when he and Mazzei went for a long walk before the others were stirring. Jefferson showed the Italian some land suitable for his purpose and apparently offered to lend it to him. The Virginian coveted the opportunity to gain a cosmopolitan neighbor. The Florentine was enchanted by Jefferson's intellect and warmth, and by the fact that, though self-taught in the language, the American could converse easily with him in Italian. Upon their return to the house they were greeted by Adams who, after one look at Jefferson, said: "I see by your expression that you've taken him away from me. I knew you would do that." Jefferson only smiled and suggested that they all go into breakfast.[66]

Mazzei did indeed become a neighbor, and in fact a member of the Monticello household while his own house was being built. Fortunately, the construction job did not take as long as the building of Jefferson's mansion. The presence of a dozen Italian workmen as well as Mazzei enlivened the neighborhood. Soon Jefferson's men were cultivating Italian vegetables and using Italian-style tools. The rather prosaic wine cellars of Monticello were enriched with Italian wines. Jefferson gained further proficiency in the mellifluous Italian language and began wearing an Italian hunting coat like the one favored by Mazzei. Soon other Albemarle planters were wearing the same kind of coat and cultivating Italian delicacies in their garden plots.[67]

The new year of 1774 dawned with Jefferson living the life of a pastoral patriarch with his own vine and fig tree, his well-tilled acres, and his bondmen and bondwomen. The thirty-year-old plantation master was now enjoying what he later described as a life of "unchecquered happiness." He was in what was for him the dearest spot on earth, and for some time duty had not called him away. Dunmore, unhappy with the actions of the 1773 legislature, had continued to prorogue the Assembly. The most unmilitary Jefferson was now, as his father had been, colonel of the Albemarle militia, but the duties were not strenuous. At least he did not look ridiculous on a horse. In fact, Jefferson, generally much less athletic than most of the young men with whom he had grown up, was one of the most accomplished horsemen in the county. Best of all Jefferson's blessings was his marital happiness. The household was smoothly run under trying conditions (the constant building and the sudden additions of relatives and long-staying guests) and Patty was a witty, sprightly, and physically beautiful companion. In later years a granddaughter who had lived with the Jeffersons reported that Patty "had a vivacity of temper which might sometimes border on tartness, but which, in her intercourse with her husband, was completely subdued by her affection for him."[68] Of course, there was the missed companionship of Dabney Carr, and the serenity might have been even more unruffled if some of the little bondmen and bondwomen had not been siblings of his wife. But Jefferson had developed a habit of magnifying good things and brushing unpleasant ones from consideration.

Harsh reality, nevertheless, intruded from time to time. In his Account Book for 1774 appears a terse entry for March 1: "My sister Elizabeth was found last Thursday being Feb. 24." On February 21 and 22, earthquakes had shaken the buildings at Monticello. These occurrences, uncommon in the area, had sent most of the occupants scurrying for the safety of open spaces. No significant damage to structures occurred on either occasion, but after the second day, Elizabeth could not be found. The whole problem was complicated by her mental retardation. Under what conditions she was found we do not know. If she was still alive she did not live much longer. On March 7, one day after the second greatest flood in the history of the Rivanna, a violent boiling over of blood-red waters in a reminder that nature was not always benign, Elizabeth was buried in the red clay of the little cemetery that held Dabney Carr's remains. On the same day Jefferson sold two old bookcases to the Reverend Charles Clay, deducting from the price to compensate the minister for conducting the funeral service.

But there were vital stirrings that had nothing to do with earthquakes and that carried the seeds of life rather than destruction. There was another child in Patty's womb. On April 3, about an hour before noon, she gave birth to a little girl. The child was named Jane Randolph for her grandmother. This circumstance is particularly interesting in view of some biographers' efforts to make Jefferson appear hostile to his mother and to his whole Randolph heritage.

At this time of happiness Jefferson could not foresee that events of the very next month would deprive him of the uninterrupted domestic life which he prized and precipitate him for most of the rest of his life into the sort of public controversy that he sought to avoid.

VI

YEAR OF DECISION

IN THE spring of 1774, Jefferson, Virginia, and the American colonies all moved into a season of crisis.

Governor Dunmore, after repeated postponements, called the Assembly back into session in May. Early in their deliberations they received word of the Boston Port Bill, passed by Parliament to close the harbor in punishment for the Tea Party of the previous December. Despite Samuel Adams' propagandizing in behalf of the "Mohawks" who had dumped ninety thousand pounds of tea, leaving great windrows rising above the waters, Washington and Pendleton, like Benjamin Franklin, regarded the provocative action as lawless and the inexcusable destruction of private property. But even conservative Burgesses believed that Parliament's retaliation was inexcusably severe. Pendleton, who had earned the nickname "Old Moderation," viewed the Port Bill as "a common attack upon American rights." As he later reported, "we were in a flame and intended some spirited resolves, but postponed them till we should have finished the public business, lest an expected dissolution should leave that undone."[1]

Nevertheless, some of the Burgesses were afraid that, before the end of the session, the fires of resentment might have subsided among their graver colleagues. On the night of May 23, these bold members met privately in the Council Chamber under Henry's leadership. This bastion of conservatism was an odd meeting place for rebel strategists but it had a reference library that the more familiar rooms of the Raleigh Tavern could not supply. Jefferson was one of the group, along with the Lee brothers, Richard Henry and Francis Lightfoot, and one who was not a Burgess, George Mason.

The philosopher of Gunston Hall was still resisting calls to public office that would take him far from Fairfax County but his counsel was eagerly sought by Virginia's leaders of colonial resistance. He had played a major role in the framing of the Association. Though he was not a practicing lawyer, he was as well versed in constitutional law, including British and Roman precedents, as any man on the continent. Not even Wythe exceeded him in legal lore, and no one in Virginia wielded a more trenchant pen. The Burgesses were glad that private business had brought the gout-ridden, much afflicted wise man to Williamsburg at this time of legislative crisis. Probably for the first time Jefferson had the chance to take the measure of this strange figure, in appearance altogether the stout burgher except for the large and luminous brown eyes that seemed to miss nothing. Only duty could lure him from the limited comforts permitted by his many ailments. He responded particularly willingly to a call from Henry. Perhaps partly because his estimate of a great orator was influenced by his own fear of public speaking, he was coming to regard the Hanover lawyer as "the first man upon this continent."[2]

Not one of those present had had the opportunity to take his own full measure in comparison with leaders from the other colonies. Only later would it be realized that this tiny group included the two most eloquent orators and the two most eloquent penmen, and perhaps the most gifted constitutional scholar, of their generation in North America. Even the least remarkable of the group, Francis Lightfoot Lee, would earn a respected place in national history. Jefferson must have experienced an intense intellectual excitement apart from the chiaroscuro drama of the candlelit conspiracy in behalf of freedom.

Jefferson apparently was the chief originator of the plan adopted by these brilliant conferees. He proposed that Virginians observe a day of fasting and prayer because of what was happening in Boston and might happen elsewhere in the colonies. It would arouse "our people from the lethargy into which they had fallen. . .and alarm their attention."[3] At the same time, the move could not be construed as violent. A precedent was necessary, as it always is, to rebels who are not prone to revolution. They turned to the volumes of a Puritan historian who had been secretary to Oliver Cromwell. "With the help, therefore, of Rushworth,[4] whom we rummaged over for the revolutionary precedents and forms of the Puritans of that day, preserved by him, we cooked up a resolution, somewhat modernizing their phrases, for appointing the 1st day of June, on which the port bill was to commence, for a day of fasting, humiliation and prayer, to implore Heaven to avert from us the evils of civil war, to inspire us with firmness in support of our rights, and to turn the hearts of the King and Parliament to moderation and justice."

No one could fault them for praying that civil war might be averted, yet mentioning the possibility was one way of underlining the threat.

Who would have the honor of proposing the resolution? Either Henry, who initiated the meeting, or Jefferson, as author of the plan, would seem to be an appropriate choice. But Henry in 1774 was still known as the foe of the clergy in the Parsons' Cause and not the defender of the established church that he became; and Jefferson at this same time was a quoter of philosophical skeptics and not the biblical scholar that he became. "To give greater emphasis to our proposition, we agreed to wait the next morning on Mr. Nicholas, whose grave and religious character was more in unison with the tone of our resolution, and to solicit him to move it. We accordingly went to him in the morning. He moved it the same day. . . ."[5]

The resolution that Robert Carter Nicholas read to a hushed house was superior in precision, in chaste brevity, and in the musical march and majesty of its lines to anything commonly heard in legislative papers. The day of fasting and prayer was to be set aside "devoutly to implore the divine interposition for averting the heavy calamity which threatens destruction to our civil rights and the evils of civil war; to give us one heart and one mind firmly to oppose, by all just and proper means, every injury to American rights; and that the minds of His Majesty and his Parliament may be inspired from above with wisdom, moderation and justice to remove from the loyal people of America all cause of danger from a continued pursuit of measures pregnant with their ruin."[6] The views of Henry, Richard Henry Lee, and George Mason had once alarmed Nicholas. Jefferson's first attempt at writing a significant state paper had excited his contempt. How strange that, in this scene of the great drama unfolding in the relations between England and her largest American colony, Nicholas should read lines prepared for him by these four men—Henry, Lee, Mason, and Jefferson. In cadence and phrasing the resolution seems especially to bear the stamp of Henry, Mason, and Jefferson. The largest share of the credit for its production has long been accorded to Jefferson.

He and his colleagues had hit upon the method for leading reluctant rebels to decisive action—convincing them that they were doing no more than their ancestors had done in similar, well-documented crises. Sometimes the precedents might furnish fresh insights into current problems. At other times they might simply afford a comforting sense of not being in completely strange territory. So Virginians walked down a revolutionary path marked, and sometimes illumined, by the lights of the past.

The House approved the resolution without a dissenting vote.

Two days later, a little after three o'clock in the afternoon, the routine business of the Burgesses was interrupted by an expected message. "The Governor commands the House to attend his Excellency in the Council Chamber."[7] Probably with a sense of déjà vu, the members once again climbed the stairs behind portly, puffing Peyton Randolph.

Dunmore's dark eyes flashed as he confronted them:

Mr. Speaker and Gentlemen of the House of Burgesses, I have in my hand a paper published by order of your House, conceived in such terms as reflect highly upon His Majesty and the Parliament of Great Britain, which makes it necessary for me to dissolve you; and you are dissolved accordingly.[8]

The next day, as in May of 1769, the Burgesses reassembled in the Apollo Room of the Raleigh Tavern. Richard Henry Lee was ready with resolutions. They contained the warning that continuation of unconstitutional taxation might "compel us against our will to avoid all commercial intercourse with Britain." Even more significant was the declaration that "an attack made on one of our sister colonies to compel submission to arbitrary taxes is an attack made on all British America, and threatens ruin to the rights of all unless the united wisdom of the whole be applied. And for this purpose it is recommended to the Committee of Correspondence that they communicate with their several corresponding committees on the expediency of appointing deputies from the several colonies of British America to meet in general congress at such place annually as shall be thought most convenient, there to deliberate on those general measures which the united interests of America may from time to time require."[9]

The key word was "annually." Two colonial congresses had already been held and a third was proposed by leaders in Rhode Island, Pennsylvania, and New York. But the two held and the one proposed were all ad hoc assemblies. In approving Lee's resolutions, the Virginians went an important step farther than the representatives of any other colony. They proposed the establishment of an intercolonial assembly to meet with even greater regularity than had lately been the custom with some of the separate legislatures.[10]

That very evening, only one day after Dunmore had dissolved the House and a few hours after members had met in the Raleigh Tavern to pass resolutions of united resistance, the erstwhile Burgesses were hosts to Lady Dunmore at an elegant ball.[11] The invitation to the lady had been issued before the quarrel with her husband, and Virginia's urbane revolutionists would not think of being so rude as to rescind it. Certainly Jefferson, with his habitual courtesy to all and marked gallantry to women, would not have proposed snatching back the invitation. In a pageant of subtle silks and bright brocades, with powdered heads bowing and silver-buckled shoes gently tapping polished floors in the stately measures of the dance, the adversaries played roles as rigidly prescribed by convention as the boxwood mazes of the Governor's Palace. But no one knew the path out of the maze—nor to what it led.

The next day Jefferson participated in a meeting of the Committee of Correspondence that drew up a circular letter proposing an annual congress as "extremely important" and soliciting views from the other colonies.

Twenty-five Burgesses remaining in Williamsburg or convenient to it in nearby counties met on the morning of May 30 in response to an emergency call from Peyton Randolph. Dispatches from Boston, Philadelphia, and Annapolis told a tale of mounting crisis. Bostonians advocated a general colonial suspension of trade with Great Britain and the West Indies for the duration of the Port Act. Philadelphians pledged a generalized loyalty in high-sounding abstractions. The Maryland Committee of Correspondence endorsed Boston's proposals and sought opinions on cancellation of debts owed to British merchants and the boycotting of any colony that refused to join with a majority of others in such a plan of stiff resistance.

Many of the assembled Virginians thought it dishonorable to cancel their debts but were prepared to give sympathetic consideration to the other suggestions. And they were moved by Samuel Adams' plea from beleaguered Boston: "A thought so dishonorable to our brethren cannot be entertained as that this town will now be left to struggle alone." Still they did not feel that they could presume to represent all of Virginia. By unanimous consent, an invitation was issued to former Burgesses to sound out their constituents and meet in Williamsburg. The letter concluded: "Things seem to be hurrying to an alarming crisis, and demand the speedy, united council of all those who have a regard for the common cause." Jefferson was one of the signers of this document.[12]

He does not appear, however, to have lingered in Williamsburg until June 1, the day of fasting and prayer, when Burgesses remaining in town marched in a body to special services at Bruton Parish Church. Instead, he joined John Walker in a call for a special prayer service in their own Albemarle County parish of St. Anne's. As reports came in from various parts of Virginia, Jefferson was delighted with the effects of the call to fasting and solemn services. He saw it as "a shock of electricity, arousing every man and placing him erect and solidly on his centre."[13]

In ensuing weeks Jefferson labored to compose lengthy but spirited resolutions which he hoped would be approved by the freeholders of Albemarle. Then, backed by their endorsement, he would present the resolutions in much more extensive form at the convention in Williamsburg in August. If the Virginia convention approved, the powerful backing of the most populous of the colonies should go a long way toward securing adoption by a general congress of all the colonies. The dream was a heady one.

Albemarle freeholders, meeting in Charlottesville on July 26, confirmed Jefferson and Walker as their representatives. The process was virtually identical with that by which most of the former Burgesses were commissioned to represent their constituencies at the Williamsburg Convention. The notable thing about the Albemarle meeting was that it also adopted Jefferson's resolutions, just as he had planned. At least twelve other counties had adopted resolutions, but Jefferson's were astonishingly bold. They denied the right of Parliament to exercise authority over "the inhabitants of the several states of British America."[14] The resolutions that he had prepared for the convention went even farther. Not only did they address George III directly in a manner that most Englishmen would deem impudent, but in language far more audacious than Henry's which had provoked cries of "Treason!" Jefferson had written, "Should the people take upon them to lay the throne of your majesty prostrate, or to discontinue their connection with the British empire, none will be so bold as to decide against the right or the efficacy of such avulsion."[15]

As Jefferson set out on the road to Williamsburg he carried in his baggage a manuscript that many officers of the British government would have considered more incriminating than a dagger dripping with human blood. London had reasserted that Americans could be brought to England to be tried for treason.[16] Beheading was no longer the customary punishment upon conviction. The usual method was hanging, though sometimes the prisoner was cut down while still alive so that his intestines could be ripped out and burned before his eyes. Of course, there was always the possibility that the judges might find mitigating circumstances so that the accused might be imprisoned rather than executed. And also it was possible that Jefferson's resolutions would attract little attention in London, but this seemed unlikely if they should be adopted by a great congress of the colonies. Besides, if they were not noticed in England, what would they accomplish? For a young man who disliked controversy Jefferson had followed an unusual course. He had a great deal to think about as he rode along the hot, dusty Virginia roads. Suddenly his meditations were interrupted, and then again and again. Perhaps it was the heat, perhaps it was an infection or something he had eaten, or maybe it was the effect of emotional turmoil on a sensitive colon. At any rate, he had a bad case of diarrhea. There was nothing for him to do but head back to Monticello.[17]

But, if his flesh was weak, his spirit was strong. He could not appear in Williamsburg as the advocate of his own resolutions, but he could see that they reached the capital to speak for themselves. He sent one copy to Patrick Henry and another to Peyton Randolph.

Jefferson never learned what had happened to the copy entrusted to Henry. Apparently it was never heard of again. The resolutions may have been too bold even for the author of the Stamp Act Resolves or, just as likely, that negligent genius may have mislaid them on a tavern table. Jefferson later suggested that Henry might have been "too lazy" to read them, adding, "He was the laziest man in reading I ever knew."[18]

Peyton Randolph, though he deplored some of his cousin's provocative phrases, was careful to see that they received a hearing. In his role as presiding officer he informed the convention that he had received resolutions from a member "prevented by sickness" from offering it in person, and he "laid it on the table for perusal." "It was read generally by the members," Jefferson later noted, "approved by many, though thought too bold for the present state of things."[19] Edmund Randolph reported, "I distinctly recollect the applause bestowed on the most of them, when they were read to a large company at the house of Peyton Randolph." But he added that not all the paragraphs won equal approbation.

Some of Jefferson's friends were not willing to let his work sink into obscurity. Without consulting him, they had it printed in Williamsburg in pamphlet form. For Jefferson's working title, "Draft of Instructions to the Virginia Delegates in the Continental Congress," they substituted, "A Summary View of the Rights of British America Set Forth in Some Resolutions Intended for the Inspection of the Present Delegates of the People of Virginia Now in Convention." The by-line "by a native and member of the House of Burgesses" could not protect an anonymity already lost.[20]

Jefferson's pleasure in the circulation of his ideas was lessened because his work had been rushed to press before he had had the chance to give it a final editing. When he was taken sick, he had sent the two copies on to Henry and Randolph without taking time to fill in some blanks or to check on the accuracy of dates quickly culled from memory as he was composing.[21]

It was inevitable that, once published, Jefferson's proposals should excite considerable attention. In several respects they went beyond previous publications in the colonies and they were vigorously—in some cases, memorably—phrased. It began conventionally: "Resolved that it be an instruction to the said deputies when assembled in General Congress with the deputies from the other states of British America to propose to the said Congress that an humble and dutiful address be presented to his majesty begging leave to lay before him as chief magistrate of the British empire the united complaints of his majesty's subjects in America; complaints which are excited by many unwarrantable encroachments and usurpations, attempted to be made by the legislature of one part of the empire, upon those rights which God and the laws have given equally to all."[22] So far there was the traditionally humble form of address to the throne, familiar Enlightenment doctrine of God-given rights, and on the surface persistence in the convenient fiction that the colonists were the victims of a Parliament of whose usurpations a kindly, paternal king was unaware. But in the very next phrases Jefferson's statement became an indictment of the monarch himself: "To represent to his majesty that these his states have often individually made humble application to his imperial throne, to obtain thro' its intervention some redress of their injured rights; to none of which was ever even an answer condescended."

They ventured "humbly to hope that this their joint address, penned in the language of truth, and divested of those expressions of servility which would persuade his majesty that we are asking favors and not rights, shall obtain from his majesty a more respectful acceptance. And this his majesty will think we have reason to expect when he reflects that he is no more than the chief officer of the people, appointed by the laws, and circumscribed with definite powers, to assist in working the great machine of government erected for their use, and consequently subject to their superintendence."

Jefferson then proceeded to give George III a history lesson. And here he drew upon his Anglo-Saxon studies. We see the fruit of some of the facts and observations that he had copied into his Commonplace Book in earlier years. Jefferson wished "to remind him that our ancestors, before their emigration to America, were the free inhabitants of the British dominions in Europe, and possessed a right, which nature has given to all men, of departing from the country in which chance, not choice, has placed them, of going in quest of new habitations, and of there establishing new societies, under such laws and regulations as to them shall seem most likely to promote public happiness." In so doing, they were true to the traditions of their race and the general experience of mankind. "Their Saxon ancestors had under this universal law, in like manner, left their native wilds and woods in the North of Europe, had possessed themselves of the island of Britain (then less charged with inhabitants), and had established there that system of laws which has so long been the glory and protection of that country. Nor was ever any claim of superiority or dependence asserted over them by that mother country from which they had migrated. And were such a claim made it is believed that his majesty's subjects in Great Britain have too firm a feeling of the rights derived to them from their ancestors to bow down the sovereignty of their state before such visionary pretensions."

In saying that assertion of sovereignty (or if you will, a declaration of independence) by a colony was in accordance with "universal law," Jefferson was drawing upon his Commonplace Book notes on the history of Athenian and other Greek colonies. But he emphasized the Anglo-Saxon experience, underlining the parallels between Germanic emigration to Great Britain and British emigration to America:

And it is thought that no circumstance has occurred to distinguish materially the British from the Saxon emigration. America was conquered, and her settlements made and firmly established at the expense of individuals and not of the British public. Their own blood was spilt in acquiring lands for their settlement, their own fortunes expended in making that settlement effectual. For themselves they fought, for themselves they conquered, and for themselves alone they have right to hold. No shilling was ever issued from the public treasures of his majesty or his ancestors for their assistance, till of very late times, after the colonies had become established on a firm and permanent footing. . . . then, indeed, having become valuable to Great Britain for her commercial purposes, his parliament was pleased to lend them assistance against an enemy who would fain have drawn to herself the benefits of their commerce to the great aggrandizement of herself and danger of Great Britain.

Jefferson was being realistic in pointing out that, in the French and Indian Wars, Britain had acted from self-interest rather than from any special solicitude for Americans. He further punctured the popular British argument that the colonies owed much to the mother country because of the protection she had accorded them in that struggle; he reminded the King that England had often given such assistance to Portugal and other states with whom she was commercially involved, "yet these states never supposed that, by calling in her aid, they thereby submitted themselves to her sovereignty."

The point was cleverly made. In part of the argument, though, Jefferson was a better advocate than historian. The colonies could scarcely have succeeded without England's sponsorship at their inception or survived without her protection from European predators at a later period.

The transition to the next bold claim was so smoothly accomplished as almost to rob it of its radical aspect:

...settlements having been thus effected in the wilds of America, the emigrants thought proper to adopt that system of laws under which they had hitherto lived in the mother country, and to continue their union with her by submitting themselves to the same common sovereign, who was thereby made the central link connecting the several parts of the empire thus newly multiplied.

In other words, America's general congress would be as independent of Parliament as Parliament would be of any American assemblage. Acknowledgement of the same king would be the only official link between Britain and America. More than one hundred fifty years before the Statute of Westminster, Jefferson had anticipated the Commonwealth of Nations. Of course, the idea did not spring full-blown from his brain. His cousin Richard Bland as early as 1764 had published a pamphlet asserting that England and the American colonies were "coordinate kingdoms under a common Crown."[23] But Bland had not pursued the argument as forcefully as his fellow Virginian did now. Nor had he coupled his statement with a reminder that an errant king could be forced to pay the supreme penalty. Discussing the fate of the American colonists under the reign of the Stuarts, Jefferson said:

...not long were they permitted, however far they thought themselves removed from the hand of oppression, to hold undisturbed the rights thus acquired at the hazard of their lives and loss of their fortunes. A family of princes was then on the British throne, whose treasonable crimes against their people brought on them afterwards the exertion of those sacred and sovereign rights of punishment, reserved in the hands of the people for cases of extreme necessity, and judged by the constitution unsafe to be delegated to any other judicative.

Jefferson attacked the royal practice of granting to favorites—as in the case of Maryland to Lord Baltimore, Pennsylvania to Penn, Carolina and the Jerseys to groups of nobles—large portions of territory "which had been acquired by the lives, the labors and the fortunes of individual adventurers."

He charged that "a free trade with all parts of the world, possessed by the American colonists as of natural right, and which no law of their own had taken away or abridged, was next the object of unjust encroachment." He detailed the deleterious effects of Parliament's restrictions on American trade and manufactures and pointed out that London's legislators could subject Americans to many hardships not imposed on the people of Great Britain. He asked "with what moderation they are like[ly] to exercise power where [they] themselves are to feel no part of its weight."

He concluded his recital of historic and long-standing injuries:

...thus have we hastened thro' the reigns which preceded his majesty's, during which the violations of our rights were less alarming because repeated at more distant intervals, than that rapid and bold succession of injuries which is likely to distinguish the present from all other periods of American story. Scarcely have our minds been able to emerge from the astonishment into which one stroke of parliamentary thunder has involved us before another, more heavy and more alarming, is fallen on us. Single acts of tyranny may be ascribed to the accidental opinion of a day; but a series of oppressions, begun at a distinguished period and pursued unalterably thro' every change of ministers, too plainly prove a deliberate, systematical plan of reducing us to slavery.

He then cited an act for levying certain duties passed in the fourth year of George III's reign, the Stamp Act passed in the fifth year, the "act declaring the right of Parliament over the colonies" passed in the sixth, and the act for granting duties on paper, tea, and other commodities passed in the seventh.

Then he singled out "one other act passed in the same 7th year of his reign" that, "having been a peculiar attempt, must ever require peculiar mention." Of the act suspending the legislature of New York, Jefferson wrote:

One free and independent legislature hereby takes upon itself to suspend the powers of another, free and independent as itself, thus exhibiting a phaenomenon, unknown in nature, the creator and creature of its own power. Not only the principles of common sense, but the common feelings of human nature must be surrendered up, before his majesty's subjects here can be persuaded to believe that they hold their political existence at the will of a British parliament. Shall these governments be dissolved, their property annihilated, and their people reduced to a state of nature, at the imperious breath of a body of men whom they never saw, in whom they never confided, and over whom they have no powers of punishment or removal, let their crimes against the American public be ever so great? Can any one reason be assigned why 160,000 electors in the island of Great Britain should give law to four millions in the states of America, every individual of whom is equal to every individual of them in virtue, in understanding, and in bodily strength? Were this to be admitted, instead of being a free people, as we have hitherto supposed, and mean to continue, ourselves, we should suddenly be found the slaves, not of one, but of 160,000 tyrants, distinguished too from all others by this singular circumstance that they are removed from the reach of fear, the only restraining motive which may hold the hand of a tyrant.

Next Jefferson attacked the measure by which Boston, "a large and populous town whose trade was [its] sole subsistence, was deprived of that trade and involved in utter ruin." In this instance, misled by unreliable reports from New England, Jefferson made an inaccurate statement. He argued that there was no necessity for meting out any punishment to the town inasmuch as individuals could be punished for destruction of the tea. "If in this they did wrong, they were known, and were amenable to the laws of the land, against which it could not be objected that they [the laws] had ever in any instance been obstructed or diverted from their regular course in favor of popular offenders. They should therefore not have been distrusted on this occasion." Actually, of course, those who threw the tea overboard were disguised as Mohawk Indians, and officeholders of Boston conspired with the rest of the populace to protect the identities of the raiders.

Jefferson also raised the frightening prospect that, under an act for the suppression of riots and tumults, an American could be "stripped of his privilege of trial by his peers of his vicinage, removed from the place where alone full evidence could be obtained," and "without money, without counsel, without friends, without exculpatory proof," be "tried before judges predetermined to condemn." As the author of words for which he could be charged with treason, Jefferson was particularly vehement on this point. "The cowards who would suffer a countryman to be torn from the bowels of their society in order to be thus offered a sacrifice to parliamentary tyranny would merit that everlasting infamy now fixed on the authors of the act!"

The king was attacked for the negative as well as the positive use of his power. He was guilty of the "wanton exercise" in America of the veto over legislative acts which his predecessors, "conscious of the impropriety of opposing their single opinion to the united wisdom of two houses of parliament," had "modestly declined." Jefferson creatively proposed a new "great office" for His Majesty, "to resume the exercise of his negative power to "prevent the passage of laws by any one legislature of the empire which might bear injuriously on the rights and interests of another."

Jefferson weakened this section, however, by overstatement of the American case in an attack on George III's "shameful abuse" of the veto to perpetuate the institution of slavery in America. There had been, he reminded, "repeated attempts" to "exclude all further importations from Africa. Yet our repeated attempts to effect this by prohibitions, and by imposing duties which might amount to a prohibition, have been hitherto defeated by his majesty's negative: thus preferring the immediate advantages of a few British corsairs to the lasting interests of the American states, and to the rights of human nature deeply wounded by this infamous practice."

Insofar as his native Virginia was concerned, Jefferson was so far on solid historical ground. Virginia had legally recognized slavery only after two New England states had done so and in the eighteenth century the General Assembly of Virginia had repeatedly voted to restrain the importation of slaves only to be blocked every time by a royal veto. And, of course, less than four years before publication of Jefferson's *Summary View*, George III had instructed Virginia's Governor, "upon pain of the highest displeasure, to assent to no law by which the importation of slaves should be in any respect prohibited or obstructed."[24]

But then, carried away by zeal, Jefferson went so far as to say, "The abolition of domestic slavery is the great object of desire in those colonies where it was unhappily introduced in their infant state." There were in Virginia and all the other colonies many people who wished to end slavery and doubtless in most colonies a majority who wished to end the slave trade. But emancipation was not the consuming dream of whole populations anywhere. Jefferson would be reminded forcibly of this within less than two years.

Jefferson charged the King with delaying "for years" the consideration of acts of colonial assemblies and pointed out that because of the necessity for royal review, even in emergencies, "however immediate may be the call for legislative interposition, the law cannot be executed till it has twice crossed the Atlantic, by which time the evil may have spent its whole force."

The Virginian bore down hard on "a late instruction to his majesty's governor of the colony of Virginia, by which he is forbidden to assent to any law for the division of a county unless the new county will consent to have no representative in assembly."

That colony has as yet affixed no boundary to the Westward. Their Western counties therefore are of indefinite extent. Some of them are actually seated many hundred miles from their Eastern limits. Is it possible then that his majesty can have bestowed a single thought on the situation of those people, who, in order to obtain justice for injuries however great or small, must, by the laws of that colony, attend their county court at such a distance, with all their witnesses, monthly, till their litigation be determined? Or does his majesty seriously wish, and publish it to the world, that his subjects should give up the glorious right of representation, with all the benefits derived from that, and submit themselves the absolute slaves of his sovereign will? Or is it rather meant to confine the legislative body to their present numbers, that they may be the cheaper bargain whenever they shall become worth a purchase?

Next Jefferson attacked the King's "dissolution of representative bodies for doing their duty." He reminded his sovereign that "one of the articles of impeachment against Tresilian and the other judges of Westminster Hall in the reign of Richard the second for which they suffered death as traitors to their country, was that they had advised the king that he might dissolve his parliament at any time." But he made too sweeping an assertion when he said: "Since the establishment, however, of the British constitution at the glorious Revolution on its free and ancient principles, neither his majesty nor his ancestors have exercised such a power of dissolution in the island of Great Britain." Jefferson himself wrote in the margin of his personal copy of the pamphlet, "On further inquiry I find two instances of dissolutions before the parl. would of itself have been at an end. . . ." He referred to parliaments dissolved by King William in 1700 and 1701. Jefferson argued:

The feelings of human nature revolt against the supposition of a state so situated as that it may not in any emergency provide against dangers which perhaps threaten immediate ruin. While those bodies are in existence to whom the people have delegated the powers of legislation, they alone possess and may exercise those powers. But when they are dissolved by the lopping off one or more of their branches, the power reverts to the people, who may use it to unlimited extent, either assembling together in person, sending deputies, or in any other way they may think proper. We forbear to trace consequences further; the dangers are conspicuous with which this practice is replete.

Not only did Jefferson complain against the doubling of the royal price for purchasing and holding colonial lands, he also denied that the King had any right to charge anything for grants. Here he dug back into Anglo-Saxon studies and into those records of feudal usage which he had copied into his Commonplace Book. Whether or not he knew of his descent from William the Conqueror, Jefferson did know that he had noble lines of Norman blood. But in any contest between Normans and Saxons, whether of personalities or usage, he identified with his Saxon forebears. In this instance, he wrote of what he called "an error in the nature of our landholdings, which crept in at a very early period of our settlement. . . . In the earlier ages of the Saxon settlement feudal holdings were certainly altogether unknown, and very few, if any, had been introduced at the time of the Norman conquest. Our Saxon ancestors held their lands, as they did their personal property, in absolute dominion, disencumbered with any superior, answering nearly to the nature of those possessions which the Feudalists term Alloidal.''

Jefferson also pointed out that William made feudal grants of the lands of Saxon lords who fell at Hastings, "but still much was left in the hands of his Saxon subjects, held of no superior, and not subject to feudal conditions. . . . Feudal holdings were therefore but exceptions out of the Saxon laws of possession, under which all lands were held in absolute right. These, therefore, still form the basis or groundwork of the Common law, to prevail wheresoever the exceptions have not taken place. America was not conquered by William the Norman, nor its lands surrendered to him or any of his successors. . . . Our ancestors, however, who migrated hither, were farmers, not lawyers. The fictitious principle that all lands belong originally to the king, they were early persuaded to believe real, and accordingly took grants of their own lands from the crown. And while the crown continued to grant for small sums and on reasonable rents, there was no inducement to arrest the error and lay it open to public view. But his majesty has lately taken on him to advance the terms of purchase and of holding to the double of what they were, by which means the acquisition of lands being rendered difficult, the population of our country is likely to be checked. It is time therefore for us to lay this matter before his majesty, and to declare that he has no right to grant lands of himself.''

Jefferson further charged

That, in order to enforce the arbitrary measures before complained of, his majesty has from time to time sent among us large bodies of armed forces, not made up of the people here, nor raised by the authority of our laws. Did his majesty possess such a right as this, it might swallow up all our other rights whenever he should think proper. But his majesty has no right to land a single armed man on our shores; and those whom he sends here are liable to our laws for the suppression and punishment of Riots, Routs, and unlawful assemblies, or are hostile bodies invading us in defiance of law. . . . To render these proceedings still more criminal against our laws, instead of subjecting the military to the civil power, his majesty has expressly made the civil subordinate to the military. But can his majesty thus put down all law under his feet? Can he erect a power superior to that which erected himself? He has done it indeed by force; but let him remember that force cannot give right.

The long concluding paragraph of Jefferson's *Summary View* is a strange amalgam of the germane, the jejune, and the judgmental. Some of its sentences smack of the poster art of the pamphleteer and some are among the noblest written by any American of the eighteenth century:

These are our grievances which we have thus laid before his majesty with that freedom of language and sentiment which becomes a free people, claiming their rights as derived from the laws of nature, and not as the gift of their chief magistrate. Let those flatter, who fear: it is not an American art. To give praise where it is not due, might be well from the venal, but would ill beseem those who are asserting the rights of human nature. They know, and will therefore say, that kings are the servants, not the proprietors of the people.

In rhythm and antithesis, as in verbal precision, the foregoing passage is a model of rhetoric. The sentence "Let those flatter, who fear: it is not an American art," is an expression of native pride comparable in resonance to some of Shakespeare's tributes to Elizabethan England.

But immediately the writer addresses his sovereign in a naively hortatory and pedagogic tone:

> Open your breast, Sire, to liberal and expanded thought. Let not the name of George the third be a blot in the page of history.... The great principles of right and wrong are legible to every reader: to pursue them requires not the aid of many counsellors. The whole art of government consists in the art of being honest. Only aim to do your duty, and mankind will give you credit where you fail. No longer persevere in sacrificing the rights of one part of the empire to the inordinate desires of another: but deal out to all equal and impartial right. Let no act be passed by any one legislature which may infringe on the rights and liberties of another. This is the important post in which fortune has placed you, holding the balance of a great, if a well poised empire. This, Sire, is the advice of your great American council, on the observance of which may perhaps depend your felicity and future fame, and the preservation of that harmony which alone can continue both to Great Britain and America the reciprocal advantages of their connection.

The opportunity that the writer extends to the King is brilliantly conceived, but the manner of presentation is strange indeed for a man of Jefferson's customary tact. Why did he assume that any self-respecting prince would let himself be lessoned so?

Perhaps Jefferson was only technically addressing the King. Perhaps he was impelled by "a decent respect to the opinions of mankind" and addressed his own and future generations. Embedded in that final paragraph, so ill-conceived psychologically if intended for royal eyes, was a magnificent sentence whose luster has been not worn, but burnished, by the sweep of generations: "The god who gave us life, gave us liberty at the same time: the hand of force may destroy, but cannot disjoin them."

When first presented to the convention and published as a pamphlet, Jefferson's proposals did not speak for most Virginians, or most Americans. In retrospect he said: "Tamer sentiments were preferred, and I believe, wisely preferred, the leap I proposed being too long as yet for the mass of our citizens. The distance between these and the instructions actually adopted is of some curiosity, however, as it shows the inequality of pace with which we moved, and the prudence required to keep front and rear together."[25] But Jefferson certainly spoke *to* a great many Americans, and Englishmen as well. Besides the Williamsburg printing of *A Summary View*, editions were published in New York, Philadelphia, and Boston, and even twice in London with a dedication to the King.[26] In one summer Jefferson's fame became continental and then leaped the Atlantic. There is no indication, however, that George III ever read a line of the pamphlet. He was a conscientious monarch who spared himself no responsibility, but he was too busy carrying out such self-assigned tasks as memorizing the name and station of every officer in the royal navy to read the disgruntled scribblings of some obscure provincial in Virginia.

From Peyton Randolph, who had gotten his information from an agent of the House of Burgesses in England, Jefferson heard that his pamphlet had caused his name to be "inserted in a long list of proscriptions, enrolled in a bill of attainder commenced in one of the Houses of Parliament, but suppressed in embryo by the hasty step of events, which warned them to be a little cautious."[27] Research since has revealed no such proscription, and some historians have concluded that Jefferson was misinformed.[28] But for the rest of his life he preened himself that as early as 1774 he had been blacklisted as a particularly dangerous man along with Patrick Henry, John Adams, Samuel Adams, John Hancock, and others scarcely less notorious.

In that same August when Jefferson began building his fame, he took a drastic step that rid him of one distraction that had been taking too much time from his public career, his writing and scholarship, and his domestic life at Monticello. After seven years of practice he freed himself from the profession for which he had spent five years in preparation. On August 11 he turned over his law practice to his cousin Edmund Randolph. At that time Jefferson had 132 clients with active cases. He had earned a reputation for legal scholarship and for high competence at the bar without ever practicing the magic that can hold a court enthralled. His most publicized case, Howell vs. Netherland, April 1770, was not one calculated to elevate him in the estimation of the Virginia gentry. Jefferson represented without fee one Samuel Howell, a slave suing for freedom from his master. Howell's grandmother had been the daughter of a white woman and a black man and had been bound to servitude until the age of thirty-one. Howell's mother had been born during her own mother's period of servitude. The opposing attorney, none other than George Wythe, did not even have to speak in behalf of his client. Indeed, the court apparently stopped following Jefferson through an intricate legal and genealogical maze when he said, "Under the law we are all born free," and a little later, after admitting that one act had enslaved the first mulatto and a second had enslaved her issue, asserted that the third generation could not be deprived of its freedom except by some future legislation "if any should be found wicked enough."[29]

But now, in 1774, courtroom contests were behind him. He would plead for freedom, individual and national, in larger forums. Nevertheless, the many hours spent in the study of law had not been wasted. They had opened to him the world of Anglo-Saxon culture and the history of feudalism. They had given him an understanding of constitutional principles. They had helped to discipline his talents and had taught him how to marshal evidence in support of a proposition. And they had gained him the knowledge of the law that would be of inestimable value to him as a lawmaker.

The next forum for Jefferson's talents was the convention—really an unauthorized session of the House of Burgesses—held in March 1775 in Richmond. Actually, the meeting was held outside Richmond and across shallow Shockoe Creek. Though Richmond had long since outgrown the status of frontier outpost which it had at the time of its founding by Colonel William Byrd, it still could boast no building large enough to house a convention. It was fortunate, therefore, that St. John's Episcopal Church, a large frame structure of severe dignity, stood on a hill just outside the city. Not so easily overcome was the lack of comfortable hostelries such as the delegates would have enjoyed in Williamsburg. But Williamsburg would not have been a comfortable place with Governor Dunmore and his armed guard there.

With former desk mates as pew mates and Peyton Randolph named to the chair

by acclamation, the strange surroundings must soon have seemed to Jefferson less ecclesiastical than political. Even the rules and orders of the old House of Burgesses were
adopted *in toto*.

In accordance with those rules the Virginians debated for two days the recommendations of the Continental Congress which had met in Philadelphia. Congress, like Jefferson in his *Summary View*, had protested the revenue measures imposed since 1763,
the extension of vice-admiralty jurisdiction, the dissolution of colonial legislatures, and
the maintenance of standing armies amid peaceful citizens. But the language of its Declaration and Resolves was far more temperate than Jefferson's. The Congress had also formed
a Continental Association modeled after the Virginia Association. It pledged cessation
of all imports from Britain by December 1 and a complete end to the slave trade by
the same date. All consumption of British products and some luxury products of any
foreign origin would cease March 1, 1775. All export trade to Great Britain, Ireland,
and the West Indies would end September 1, 1775. Each county, town, or city was
to elect a committee to enforce the provisions of the Association, punishing offenders
by publicity and boycott. Any colony falling from faithfulness to the Association would
itself be boycotted.

Virginia delegates, during the two days of debate, were aware of reports that most
of the King's troops would be removed from Boston and that suffering English merchants were preparing to appeal to Commons to redress American grievances prompting
the Association. They knew too that bets of three to two "that the American acts will
be totally repealed" had been laid in a London coffeehouse. Nevertheless, at the conclusion of argument, they unanimously approved the recommendations of the Congress.

On the third day the Virginia delegates considered a Jamaican petition to the King
for which the Assembly of that colony sought a Virginia endorsement. Although the
document was an appeal for American rights, it indicated that Jamaicans would not resort
to arms in defense of their liberties. With individual colonies, just as Jefferson had said
was true with individual delegates, prudence was "required to keep front and rear
together." The leaders of the convention, not wishing to alienate even half-hearted
volunteers in the cause of American rights and yet unwilling to endorse a statement
forswearing armed resistance, devised an innocuous resolution complimenting their
brethren in Jamaica without signifying complete agreement.

Virginia's Old Guard had no chance to relax into self-congratulation over its efficient handling of the Jamaican resolution. Patrick Henry was demanding the floor and
they sensed that there would be trouble. He proposed additional resolutions:

> Resolved, that a well regulated militia, composed of gentlemen and yeomen,
> is the natural strength, and only security, of a free government; that such a militia
> in this Colony would forever render it unnecessary for the Mother Country to
> keep among us, for the purpose of our defense, any standing army; That the
> establishment of such a militia at this time is peculiarly necessary.... Resolved,
> therefore, That this Colony be immediately put into a posture of defense.[30]

Richard Bland replied. Age had added to the scholar's stoop of his tall frame. His
skin was as yellowed as the old parchments which he had searched so long for ancient
precedents. Nearly complete blindness now deprived him of eye contact with his au-

dience and his delivery was as halting as his walk. But his brain was one of the most agile in the room and the delegates were attentive. With the precision of a schoolmaster demonstrating the solution of a problem in Euclid, he dealt with Henry's arguments. He did not see how any good could be accomplished by talking of armed resistance when there was evidence that the Association might already be leading Parliament toward a realistic reappraisal of the American crisis.

Robert Carter Nicholas rose and gained the full attention of the convention. Some visitor from a distant colony, unaware of his prestigious compound of sagacity, integrity, family, and wealth, might well have wondered why this balding, very average-looking man with the undistinguished voice, could so rivet the attention of his colleagues. He warned that wild talk could imperil the chances of a satisfactory settlement.

Next to speak was Benjamin Harrison, a cousin of Nicholas's and like him a grandson of Robert (King) Carter. Six feet four inches tall and of majestic girth, Harrison did not look at all like Nicholas. The fifth of his name to serve in the House of Burgesses, he seemed at times to regard public office as his birthright. Military threats, he argued, were more likely to hinder than to advance the progress of liberty.

Edmund Pendleton rose to endorse Harrison's argument. His well-modulated tones seemed the very voice of reason.

Then Henry again got the floor. At first his speech was halting and deferential. But his words gathered momentum as he began to recite the colonists' grievances against London. A peculiar vibrant note of almost hypnotic power crept into his voice as he hurled at his listeners rhetorical questions about the arrogance with which their petitions had been spurned by the King.

Suddenly an Old Testament prophet seemed to inhabit Henry's tall, lean figure as he thundered, "We must fight! I repeat it, sir, we must fight; an appeal to arms and to the God of Hosts is all that is left us!" As he lowered his voice, it throbbed with a new, controlled excitement. "They tell us, sir, that we are weak—unable to cope with so formidable an adversary. But when shall we be stronger? Will it be the next week or the next year? . . . Sir, we are not weak if we make the proper use of those forces which the God of nature hath placed in our power. Three millions of people armed in the holy cause of liberty, and in such a country as that which we possess, are invincible by any force which our enemy can send against us. . . . The battle, sir, is not to the strong alone; it is to the vigilant, the active, the brave."

Sweeping his audience along on the torrent of his eloquence, Henry cried out: "Gentlemen may cry, Peace, peace—but there is no peace. The war is actually begun. The next gale that sweeps from the North will bring to our ears the clash of resounding arms!"

Back bowed and wrists crossed, Henry assumed the posture of a manacled slave. "Is life so dear, or peace so sweet, as to be purchased at the price of chains and slavery? Forbid it, Almighty God!"

. . . he slowly bent his form yet nearer to the earth, and said, "I know not what course others may take," and he accompanied the words with his hands still crossed. . . . After remaining in this posture of humiliation long enough to impress the imagination . . . , he arose proudly, and exclaimed, "but as for me,"— and the words hissed through his clenched teeth, while his body was thrown back, and every muscle and tendon was strained against the fetters which bound him . . . then the loud, clear, triumphant notes, "give me liberty," electrified the assembly. It was not a prayer, but a stern demand, which would submit to no refusal or delay. . . . And, as each syllable of the word "liberty" echoed through the building, his fetters were shivered; his arms were hurled apart; and the links of his chains were scattered to the winds. . . . His countenance was radiant; he stood erect and defiant; while the sound of his voice and the sublimity of his attitude made him appear a magnificent incarnation of Freedom. . . . After a momentary pause, only long enough to permit the echo of the word "liberty" to cease, he let his left hand fall powerless to his side, and clenched his right hand firmly as if holding a dagger with the point aimed at his breast. He stood like a Roman senator defying Caesar, . . . and he closed the grand appeal with the solemn words, "or give me death!" which sounded with the awful cadence of a hero's dirge . . . he suited the action to the word by a blow upon the left breast with his right hand, which seemed to drive the dagger to the patriot's heart.[31]

As Henry sat down, silence followed. Some felt dizzy. A man listening through a window called out, "Let me be buried at this spot."[32]

A few delegates rose to oppose their rumblings to Henry's thunder. Then Richard Henry Lee, tall, patrician-profiled, stepped forth like a Roman senator. In rolling Ciceronian periods and drawing on classical history, he seemed to add the weight of Roman law to the message that Henry had brought down from the mountain.

At this point Jefferson amazed the convention by asking to be heard. His own awareness of his limitations as an orator constricted his throat when he attempted to speak in any chamber larger than a committee room. What pain of embarrassment it cost him now to speak for Henry's resolution! He was following the two greatest orators in America. His voice came forth huskily and the palms of the large hands that gestured so awkwardly must have been wet with cold sweat. But Jefferson had done his homework well. He was sure of his facts and firm in his convictions. "He argued closely, profoundly and warmly," giving philosophical dignity, enhanced by his unmistakable earnestness, to the position taken by Henry and Lee.[33]

The fact that Jefferson had abandoned his usual silence in full assembly added to the effectiveness of his arguments before an audience already deeply stirred by Henry and Lee. Nicholas's keenly realistic mind immediately detected the drift of the Convention. It also told him that if the Convention was to take the militant step of authorizing a Virginia militia, it would be foolish to stop with the two regiments recommended by Henry—a force large enough for provocation but too small for defense. He therefore proposed the raising of a force of ten thousand to twenty thousand men.

Finally, Henry's resolution was amended, substituting for specific numbers the words, "such a number of men as may be sufficient." It passed.

Jefferson was appointed to a committee of twelve to prepare a plan for the militia. The group included Patrick Henry, Nicholas, and Harrison, as well as three experienced soldiers, Washington, Adam Stephen, and Andrew Lewis. The committee's report was submitted the next day, and the day after that it was debated, amended, and adopted. It called for the organization in each county of "one or more volunteer companies of infantry and troops of horse . . . in constant training and readiness to act in any emergency." The Tidewater counties, where equestrianship was one of the essential manly arts, were asked to concentrate on cavalry. The northern and western counties, where frontiersmen were supposed to glide swiftly and silently on moccasined feet, were urged to emphasize infantry. The volunteer companies would operate under their own county committees of defense until an emergency made it advisable to place them under a central command. Noting that "a proper provision of arms and ammunition has not been made, to the evident danger of the community in case of invasion or insurrection," the committee recommended that each county levy a head tax to remedy the deficiency. A central purchasing agency was established for those that needed help.

After adoption of the defense report, the Convention appointed a committee for the "encouragement of arts and manufactures." Later it turned to one of the principal items of business for which it had been called into session—election of delegates to the Second Continental Congress. The Convention reelected its seven delegates to the first congress—Peyton Randolph, Washington, Henry, Richard Henry Lee, Bland, Harrison, and Pendleton.

Jefferson could not reasonably have hoped to displace one of these men who had already served to general satisfaction. But it was natural for him to hope for election when the Convention on its last day, mindful of the fact that Randolph might have to be called back from Philadelphia to preside over another meeting in Virginia, proceeded to elect an alternate delegate. Jefferson was chosen. The results might be interpreted to signify that he was now one of the eight most prominent leaders in his colony. And there was a good chance that he might soon participate with the leaders of other colonies in deliberations in Philadelphia where, thanks to *A Summary View*, his fame had preceded him. What an exciting prospect! Like Chaucer's Clerk of Oxenford, "gladly would he learn and gladly teach."

Jefferson attached great importance to the approaching Second Continental Congress. Refusal of the New York Assembly to elect delegates to that conclave had prompted him to introduce in the Convention a resolution to "procure authentic information from the Committee of Correspondence for the Province of New York, or otherwise, whether their House of Representatives by any vote or votes whatsoever have deserted their confederacy. . . .[34] Here Jefferson had paused in the work of drafting, then scratched out "their confederacy" and substituted "the Union."

He was pertinacious in his pursuit. Virginia's own Committee of Correspondence would be instructed to determine, in the language of his resolution, "whether the other Colonies are to consider such vote or votes as declaring truly the sense of the people of their province in general, and as forming a rule for their future conduct; and if they are not so to be considered. . .then they inform us by their names and other sufficient descriptions, of the individuals who may have concurred in such vote or votes." A defection from the compact, he said, "would be a perfidy too atrocious to be charged on a sister colony but on the most authentic information." Significantly, Jefferson had at first written "states" instead of "colonies" and then, thinking better of it, had used the traditional term of reference.

VII

SELF-EVIDENT TRUTHS
IN A VIRGINIA ACCENT

I N THE predawn blackness of April 20, 1775, fifteen shadowy figures crept
stealthily past the small gardens and along the deserted streets of Williamsburg,
guided by the whispered instructions and silent gestures of their leader. They
had neither time nor inclination to luxuriate in the fragrance of a spring night
in Tidewater Virginia. Theirs was a serious business. It led them to the black
bulk of the Powder Magazine, the pointed-roofed, octagonal, brick structure that housed
the capital's ammunition and arms. A little later, escorted by these same men, a heavily
loaded wagon creaked its way out of town toward the James River. There the wagon's
contents were transferred to a naval vessel, H.M.S. *Fowey*.

The shadowy figures who thus crept anonymously into history were fifteen British
Marines and their captain. Their mission, to remove ammunition from the Powder
Magazine and store it aboard a British ship of war, was ordered by Governor Dunmore.
It was his response to the Virginia Convention's action of placing the colony in a military
posture.[1]

Discovery of the Governor's raid produced an angry mob that upon the cry "To
the Palace!" began boiling down Duke of Gloucester Street to the Governor's residence.
Peyton Randolph, with Nicholas's help, called the enraged throng to order as if they
had been boisterous legislators, and the two men persuaded them to disperse in exchange for a promise that the Common Hall, the city fathers, would make a formal
protest.

In confrontation with Dunmore, Randolph reminded him that the ammunition
stored in the Powder Magazine had been placed there for the colony's security and would
be needed immediately in event of a slave uprising. The Governor replied that he too
had been concerned over a possible slave revolt and so had removed the powder to
a place where it would be secure from rebel blacks. If needed, it could be brought back
within half an hour. Meanwhile it would be unwise in a time of public excitement to
place a large supply of gunpowder within reach of men who had already taken up arms.

Virginians were indeed in arms. At least fourteen companies of light horse had
gathered in Fredericksburg to ride on the capital. Soon they were joined by soldiers
in fringed hunting shirts who carried tomahawks as well as rifles. Messages of modera-

tion from Randolph, Richard Henry Lee, Pendleton, and Washington sowed doubts in the Fredericksburg camp. Angry men hesitated for several days and then dispersed after unanimously pledging "to each other to be in readiness, at a moment's warning, to reassemble, and by force of arms, to defend the law, the liberty and rights of this or any sister colony from unjust and wicked invasion." Had they delayed one more day before dispersing no one could have talked them out of marching on Williamsburg. For on that day, April 29, Virginians were told that a British column had marched to Lexington, Massachusetts "where they found a company of our militia in arms, upon which they fired without provocation, and killed six men, and wounded four others."

Patrick Henry made inflammatory speeches to volunteers at New Castle and Doncastle and marched on Williamsburg at the head of a force welded from both groups.

Dunmore added to the strength and color of his palace guard by enlisting sailors, marines, slaves, and even a few Indians. But Henry's and Dunmore's forces never met. Before the orator and his troops could enter the city they were met by an emissary from the Governor who paid him for the disputed powder. Henry accepted the bill of exchange, saying that he would present it to Virginia's delegates to the Continental Congress so that they might purchase more gunpowder.

Of course, Henry himself was one of those delegates. When he and colleagues set out for Philadelphia a few days later they were accompanied to Virginia's northern border by two independent companies of militia. On May 4 the Governor had issued a proclamation outlawing "a certain Patrick Henry, of the county of Hanover, and a number of his deluded followers."

Not long before the gunpowder crisis, a Virginia merchant had written, "The planters, especially the common sort of them, are in high spirits, so that they think little about the political dispute."[2] In Albemarle county there was a planter of an uncommon sort who was scarcely forgetful of the political crisis, though he did at times seem to be almost wholly absorbed in domestic affairs and farming pursuits. On May 7 he was not preoccupied with speculation on the role to be played by Virginia's delegates in the Congress to convene three days hence. He was most immediately concerned with the birth of a colt in his stables.[3] Of course, there may have been some allusion to the current crisis in his naming the newborn "Caractacus," presumably for the Welshman who battled the Roman conquerors. In any event, the eponymous Welshman was of royal descent and Jefferson seemed intent upon proving that his own Caractacus was equine royalty. Inside the cover of his Farm Book he compiled a genealogy for the colt. He rejoiced that, as the grandson of Old Fearnought, foremost stallion of his time in the Old Dominion, the colt "indisputably belonged to the first equine family of Virginia."[4] Despite his allegiance to ideals of equality and some later disparaging references to the "cyphers of the aristocracy," Jefferson retained much of his faith in the bloodlines of quadrupeds and bipeds alike. In young manhood he had copied into his Commonplace Book a quotation from Euripedes that most members of the Virginia gentry would have thought conveyed a truth commonplace indeed: "To be of the noble born gives a peculiar distinction clearly marked among men, and the noble name increases in lustre in those who are worthy."

Before the day's end Jefferson's thoughts had turned back to the division between the mother country and her American colonies, and to the possible rupture of longstanding friendships that might be entailed. He addressed a letter to his old teacher, William Small, now a resident of Birmingham, England. Jefferson informed his beloved mentor that he was sending him six dozen bottles of madeira, half by one ship, half by another. "I hope you will find it fine as it came to me genuine from the island and has been kept in my own cellar eight years."

In the next paragraph the letter abruptly changed tone. Jefferson told of fighting in the Boston area:

This accident has cut off our last hopes of reconciliation, and a frenzy of revenge seems to have seized all ranks of people. It is a lamentable circumstance that the only mediatory power acknowledged by both parties, instead of leading to a reconciliation his divided people, should pursue the incendiary purpose of still blowing up the flames as we find him constantly doing in every speech and public declaration. . . . A little knowledge of human nature and attention to its ordinary workings might have foreseen that the spirits of the people here were in a state in which they were more likely to be provoked than frightened by haughty deportment. And, to fill up the measure of invitation, proscription of individuals has been substituted in the room of just trial. Can it be believed that a grateful people will suffer those to be consigned to execution whose sole crime has been the developing and asserting their rights?[5]

After more in the same vein, Jefferson, in his rough draft, broke off with: "But for God's sake, where am I got to? Forever absorbed in the distresses of my country, I cannot for three sentences keep clear of its political struggles." In his copy, however, he eliminated this exclamation, while retaining in the carefully prepared letter the impression of having discontinued the political discourse upon suddenly becoming aware of his preoccupation. In the revised version, he concluded:

But I am getting into politics altho' I sat down only to ask your acceptance of the wine, and express my constant wishes for your happiness. This, however, seems secured by your philosophy and peaceful vocation. I shall still hope that amidst public dissension private frendship may be preserved inviolate, and among the warmest you can ever possess is that of your obliged humble servt.,

Th. Jefferson

Jefferson did not know that when he penned this letter, Small, of whose good health he had been assured several months earlier, was now dead.

Soon Jefferson was writing a far less personal letter, one of much greater interest to his countrymen. Governor Dunmore on May 12 summoned the House of Burgesses for June 1 to receive Lord North's Conciliatory Proposition, a proposal from the British ministry that London refrain from imposing taxation for support of civil government and the common defense on any colony whose assembly agreed to make a grant for those purposes. Only regulatory taxes would be imposed by Parliament. Jefferson reported to Williamsburg, knowing that within a few days he would be leaving for Philadelphia. Peyton Randolph, who had been elected president of the Second Continental Congress as of its predecessor, had left that post to preside over the House in

Williamsburg. Jefferson, as Randolph's alternate, was needed in Philadelphia.

In the ten days that Jefferson worked as a Burgess, he was one of the busiest legislators. He was a member of the committee that drafted a no-nonsense reply to the Governor's comments on the "alarming situation." The legislative document, which admitted the parlous state of affairs but laid the blame squarely on London, was presented in person by Jefferson and his fellow committeemen. Little in the paper bore the impress of Jefferson's style, with the possible exception of one sentence: "Money, my lord, is not a plant of the native growth of this country." Almost entirely Jefferson's work, however, was the much more important reply to Lord North's proposal. Peyton Randolph, in Jefferson's words, "was anxious that the answer of our assembly, likely to be the first, should harmonize with what he knew to be the sentiments and wishes of the body he had recently left. He feared that Mr. Nicholas, whose mind was not yet up to the mark of the times, would undertake the answer, and therefore pressed me to prepare an answer. I did so, and with his aid carried it through the house with long and doubtful scruples from Mr. Nicholas and James Mercer, and a dash of cold water on it here and there, enfeebling it somewhat. . . ."[6]

Actually Jefferson drafted the resolution prescribing the contents of the address to Lord North and had to leave for Philadelphia before the drawing up of the reply itself, but his prescriptions were so particular and were so faithfully followed that to all practical purposes he wrote the reply. It was a far more temperate document than A Summary View but no less firm.

He began:

Wishing nothing so sincerely as the perpetual continuance of that brotherly love which we bear to our fellow subjects of Great Britain and still continuing to hope and believe that they do not approve the measures which have so long oppressed their brethren in America, we were pleased to receive his Lordship's notification that a benevolent tender had at length been made by the British House of Commons towards bringing to a good end our unhappy disputes with the Mother Country. . .next to the possession of liberty, we should consider such Reconciliation the greatest of all human blessings. With these dispositions we entered into consideration of that Resolution: we examined it minutely; we viewed it in every point of light in which we were able to place it; and with pain and disappointment we must ultimately declare it only changes the form of oppression without lightening its burthen.[7]

He asserted:

The British Parliament has no right to intermeddle with the support of civil government in the Colonies. For us, not for them, has government been instituted here; agreeable to our Ideas provision has been made for such Officers as we think necessary for the administration of public affairs; and we cannot conceive that any other legislature has a right to prescribe either the number or pecuniary appointments of our Offices.

He discussed in succession a number of reasons for declining Lord North's offer:

Because to render perpetual our exemption from an unjust taxation, we must saddle ourselves with a perpetual tax adequate to the expectations and subject to the disposal of Parliament alone...

Because on our undertaking to grant money as is proposed, the Commons only resolve to forbear levying precuniary taxes on us; still leaving unrepealed their several acts passed for the purposes of restraining the trade and altering the form of Government of the Eastern Colonies; extending the boundaries and changing the Government and Religion of Quebec; enlarging the jurisdiction of the Courts of Admiralty, and taking from us the right of trial by jury; and transporting us into other Countries to be tried for criminal offenses. Standing armies too are still to be kept among us...

Because at the very time of requiring from us grants of money they are making disposition to invade us with large armaments by sea and land...

Because the proposition now made to us involves the interest of all the other Colonies. We are now represented in General Congress by members approved by this House where our former Union it is hoped will be so strongly cemented that no partial application can produce the slightest departure from the common cause. We consider ourselves as bound in honor as well as interest to share one general fate with our sister colonies, and should hold ourselves base deserters of that Union to which we have acceded, were we to agree on any measures distinct and apart from them.

Jefferson had developed a style of his own. Any competent analyst would have suspected that the reply from Virginia to Lord North was written by the author of *A Summary View*. The later composition nowhere attained the heights of eloquence occasionally reached by the earlier one but it was equally forceful, more concise, and free from the occasional immature expressions of emotion that marred its predecessor.

Without waiting for final adoption of the document he had composed, Jefferson climbed into his phaeton on June 11 and, accompanied by at least two servants, set out on the journey to Philadelphia. He probably also had with him, as on most of his journeys, a volume by Laurence Sterne and a tiny violin on which he could practice in public inns and welcoming homes without disturbing other people.

When he arrived in Philadelphia on June 21, Congress had already been in session six weeks. He received an enthusiastic welcome from the rest of the Virginia delegation, partly because he was the bearer of their expense money. But he was welcomed by delegates from other colonies as well. "His pamphlet 'Summary View of the Rights of British America' had been widely circulated among the delegates and had exerted an influence equaled by no other colonial literary production with the exception of James Wilson's 'Considerations on the Nature and Extent of the Legislative Authority of the British Parliament.' "[8] One of those who most admired Jefferson was John Adams, a rotund, roundheaded man who looked like one cannonball placed atop another and fired words like shots. Adams said that the Virginian "brought a reputation for literature, science (i.e. organized knowledge), and a happy talent of composition."[9] To a New England friend he wrote: "Though a silent member in Congress, he was so prompt, frank, explicit and decisive upon committees and in conversation—not even Samuel Adams was more so—that he soon seized upon my heart."[10] Though John

Adams was only eight years older than Jefferson, he had an avuncular attitude toward the younger man.

A complicated personality lived behind Samuel Adams' bold-nosed, open-eyed countenance. Less intellectual than his cousin John, he was also more impatient of routine business. As a tax collector in Massachusetts, he had left the records of his office a hopeless mess, but he had a genius for revolutionary intrigue and propaganda.

He had also pushed and pulled along the path of revolution another Massachusetts man, John Hancock, who now presided over the Congress as successor to Peyton Randolph. Handsome, wealthy, with prestigious connections, Hancock was willing to consider separation from Britain but he did not pant after social revolution.

On June 14 Jefferson saw Hancock's countenance transformed by what John Adams called "mortification and resentment" when Adams placed Washington's name before the Congress for the post of commander of the Continental Army then assembled outside Boston. Adams' preliminary praise of the man he was going to name had sounded to Hancock like an exact description of himself. Washington was so disconcerted that he bolted from the room.[11]

Washington's formal nomination and election came the next day. He said that he had never aspired to be commanding general. Some thought this statement was strange in that Washington was the only member of the Congress who regularly attended every session in a military uniform. The truth was that Washington had not wanted to be overlooked when a deputy commander was chosen. Probably Patrick Henry shared with Jefferson what Washington, with tears in his eyes, solemnly told him after accepting the appointment: "Remember, Mr. Henry, what I now tell you: from the day I enter upon command of the American armies, I date my fall, and the ruin of my reputation."[12]

The choice of Washington, though greatly facilitated by the respect he had inspired in the Congress, was largely engineered by the Adams cousins. They had listened seriously to what John called "the Frankfort advice." En route to Philadelphia, he and other New England delegates had been met at Frankfort, outside Boston, by delegates from the Middle Colonies who urged that Virginians be pushed forward into positions of leadership. Virginia was known as a reservoir of talent but so were several of the other colonies. The chief concern was that Virginia was the most populous of the colonies and at least potentially the most influential. Liberal delegates from Pennsylvania were particularly aware that many prominent Virginians suspected Massachusetts radicals of a largely selfish desire to draw the other colonies into conflict as a means of defending Boston. All agreed that it was necessary to have Virginia's manpower and wealth securely enlisted in the patriot cause. Other Southern colonies would follow Virginia's lead.[13]

Virginians were certainly playing principal roles in the Congress when Jefferson arrived. Henry and Lee were generally recognized as the greatest orators. Jefferson was confident, though, that there was room for thinkers and writers who were not spellbinders. As he sat in the white-paneled chamber of the State House he had before him the example of sixty-nine-year-old Benjamin Franklin, a stout little toby jug of wit and wisdom. Franklin was an early child of the Enlightenment. Jefferson had much in common with this thinker, writer, and inventor who refrained from making speeches but carelessly dropped phrases that circulated widely among the delegates.

A few days after Jefferson's arrival, a "Declaration on the Necessity of Taking Up

Arms" was presented by a committee on which Franklin served along with William Livingston, John Jay, Thomas Johnson, and John Rutledge of South Carolina, who was believed to be its principal draftsman. The Congress found the work unacceptable and added to the committee two penmen of reputation, John Dickinson, author of the popular *Letters from a Farmer of Pennsylvania*, and Jefferson.

The Virginian was asked to prepare a draft, but when he presented his work to the committee, Dickinson disapproved specifically and generally. Livingston also was unenthusiastic, as he had been about the earlier draft by Rutledge. "Both," he said, "had the faults common to our Southern gentlemen. Much fault-finding and declamation, with little sense or dignity. They seem to think a reiteration of tyranny, despotism, bloody &c. all that is needed to unite us at home and to convince the bribed voters of the North of the justice of our cause."[14]

Actually, while the charge of bombast might have been leveled against some portions of *A Summary View*, it does not seem applicable to Jefferson's draft for the committee in Philadelphia. Anyway, it was mostly Dickinson's opposition, rather than Livingston's, that delayed the committee's work for about two weeks.[15]

This period was a frustrating one for Jefferson although he evidently enjoyed midday dinner and supper at City Tavern, where he appears to have shared a table with about seven other delegates, among them Lee and Harrison. In his lodgings at the home of Benjamin Randolph, the cabinetmaker, he labored to make his phrases acceptable without sacrificing his arguments.

Dickinson, unyielding, was asked to produce a draft of his own. This he did, drawing heavily on Jefferson's work. Had Dickinson improved on Jefferson? The answer is mostly a matter of taste as the content is largely the same. This writer feels that, on balance, Dickinson hurt more than he helped. Certainly the replacement of the Virginian's clear introduction with a fuzzy one twice as long weakened the composition. Indeed, a London critic delightedly quoted this passage as evidence of the low quality of thought among the American rebels.[16]

But Dickinson at his best was a gifted writer and he added some memorable phrases. Perhaps the best was: "These devoted colonies were judged to be in such a state as to present victories without bloodshed and all the easy emoluments of statutable plunder." Good, too, is: "Our cause is just. Our Union is perfect. Our preparations are nearly completed. Our internal resources are great; and our assurance of foreign assistance is certain."

But some of Jefferson's finest phrases, as a result of Dickinson's rewriting, appeared marred, maimed, or at least hobbled, in the text finally adopted by Congress. Thus only in blunted form emerged Jefferson's assertion "The new ministry, finding all the foes of Britain subdued, took up the unfortunate idea of subduing her friends also." Lost was Jefferson's appealing recital of what had been accomplished by the cooperative efforts of Britain and America:

Proceeding thus in the fulness of mutual harmony and confidence, both parts of the empire increased in population and in wealth with a rapidity unknown in the history of man. The political institutions of America, its various soils and climates, opened a certain resource to the unfortunate and to the enterprising of every country, and ensured to them the acquisition and free possession of property.

That was an early statement of what would come to be known as "the American dream."

But Jefferson's words, in many cases close paraphrases of passages in his *A Summary View*, added strength to many parts of the document. A close examination of Jefferson's and Dickinson's separate drafts, together with the document adopted by the Congress, shows that the final product did not, as is often asserted and as Jefferson himself came to believe, consist of Dickinson's work with a few of Jefferson's paragraphs tucked on the end. Rather, Dickinson's words are heavily interlarded throughout with Jefferson's and gain distinction and force from the combination. Only slightly weakened by minor alteration was a passage in which Jefferson scored a telling point against Parliament:

By one act they have suspended the powers of one American legislature, and by another have declared they may legislate for us themselves in all cases whatsoever. These two acts alone form a basis broad enough whereon to erect a despotism of unlimited extent. And what is to secure us against this dreaded evil? The persons assuming these powers are not chosen by us, are not subject to our control or influence, are exempted by their situation from the operation of these laws, and lighten their own burthens in proportion as they increase ours. These temptations might put to trial the severest characters of ancient virtue: With what new armor then shall a British Parliament encounter the rude assault?

Missing from the final fair copy, however, was a passage in which Jefferson addressed a pointed reminder to those of the King's subjects who might feel they had nothing at stake in the American struggle for liberty:

When hostilities shall cease on the part of the aggressors, hostilities shall cease on our part also. For the achievement of this happy event, we call for and confide in the good offices of our fellow subjects beyond the Atlantic. Of their friendly dispositions we do not yet cease to hope, aware, as they must be, that they have nothing more to expect from the same common enemy than the humble favor of being last devoured.

While Jefferson was disappointed that his own draft was not accepted with only a few changes, he could still take pride in the fact that he was coauthor with Dickinson, no mean penman, of this important paper. The Congress was enthusiastic about the joint effort.

If Jefferson had been mean enough, he might have taken secret delight in a subsequent exchange on the floor between Dickinson and Benjamin Harrison. A second petition to the king, prepared by Dickinson and adopted by the Congress with only one significant alteration, a reference to itself, brought the Pennsylvanian to his feet, saying: "There is but one word in the paper, Mr. President, of which I disapprove, and that is the word 'Congress.' " Harrison rose above his fellow delegates like a whale surfacing. "There is but one word in the paper, Mr. President, of which I approve," he spouted, "and that is the word 'Congress' "[17]

Jefferson's aspirations for authorship were soon satisfied. The Congress named him with Franklin, John Adams, and Richard Henry Lee to the committee to draft resolutions on Lord North's Conciliatory Proposal. What a concentration of eloquence and scholarship in one small committee! Because of Jefferson's effective reply to Lord North from the Virginia House of Burgesses, he was asked by the rest of the committee to draft this reply from the Congress. He worked earnestly at his task, searching hard for the precise word in several instances, as indicated by the numerous changes in portions of his first draft. He brought forth a document similar to the one he had written for the House but with a greater variation than might have been expected in expression of the same ideas. The new version had its own eloquence, as when Jefferson wrote:

We are of opinion that the proposition contained in this resolution is unreasonable and insidious: Unreasonable, because, if we declare we accede to it, we declare without reservation, we will purchase the favour of Parliament, not knowing at the same time at what price they will please to estimate their favor: It is insidious because individual colonies, having bid and bidden again, till they find the avidity of the seller too great for all their powers to satisfy, are then to return into opposition, divided from their sister colonies whom the minister will have previously detached by a grant of easier terms, or by an artful procrastination of a definitive answer.[18]

Eloquent too was the statement: "A proposition to give our money, accompanied with large fleets and armies, seems addressed to our fears rather than to our freedom."

The committee was highly pleased with his work. The only significant change made was the addition of a paragraph by Dr. Franklin which strengthened the paper by pointing out the danger implicit in Parliament's claiming of the right to alter "all our charters and established laws, which would leave us without the least security for our lives or liberty." The resolutions were adopted by the Congress on July 31, 1775.

Jefferson cherished no naive hopes that king or Parliament would be persuaded by his writings. The reply to Lord North was designed partly to stimulate criticism in Great Britain itself of London's actions and even more to solidify colonial support for military defense. As early as June 26, Jefferson had written from Philadelphia to Francis Eppes in Virginia: "You will before this have heard that the war is now heartily entered into, without a prospect of accommodation but through the effectual interposition of arms."[19]

On August 1 Jefferson left Philadelphia for Richmond, where another Virginia Convention sat. He was in time for the election of delegates to the next Continental Congress. Patrick Henry, who had been commander in chief of the Virginia militia, and Washington, commander of the Continental Army, were ineligible. In these circumstances, Jefferson, with eighty-five votes, was third in the balloting, behind Peyton Randolph with eighty-nine and Richard Henry Lee with eighty-eight. Just behind Jefferson was Benjamin Harrison with eighty-three. Then there was a big dip with Jefferson's good friend Thomas Nelson, Jr., garnering only sixty-six, his cousin Richard Bland sixty-one, and his mentor George Wythe fifty-eight. Bland begged off because of physical infirmity, and Jefferson joined Henry in the effort to elect George Mason in his place, but Mason declined, recommending Francis Lightfoot Lee, who was chosen.

Before leaving Richmond Jefferson transacted one item of business that must have dramatized for him the widening gulf between old friends and kin as people chose sides in the coming struggle. In 1771 John Randolph, attorney general of Virginia, and Jefferson had entered into a curious agreement witnessed by Wythe, Henry, and others and filed with the General Court.[20] The document provided that if Randolph should predecease Jefferson, the younger man should inherit his fine violin and the music that went with it. If Randolph should outlive Jefferson he would be the inheritor of a portion of Jefferson's library equal in value to the violin. In August of 1775 it became apparent that the two men might become dead to each other. For John Randolph, who had served the colony faithfully and whose brother Peyton had presided over the revolutionary councils of both Virginia and America, found indissoluble his own allegiance to the crown. In sorrow, he was moving to England. Jefferson therefore had delivered to Carter Braxton the sum of thirteen pounds to be transmitted to John Randolph in payment for the violin.

Jefferson's almost personifying concern for the precious instrument is shown in his letter of August 25 with the request that Randolph entrust the violin to the bearer.

I believe you had no case to her. If so, be so good as to direct Watt Lenox to get from Prentis's some bays or other coarse woolen to wrap her in, and then to pack her securely in a wooden box.[21]

He then turned to a larger problem:

I am sorry the situation of our country should render it not eligible to you to remain longer in it. I hope the returning wisdom of Great Britain will e'er long put an end to this unnatural contest. There may be people to whose tempers and dispositions Contention may be pleasing, and who may therefore wish a continuance of confusion. But to me it is of all states, but one, the most horrid. My first wish is a restoration of our just rights; my second a return of the happy period when, consistently with duty, I may withdraw myself totally from the public stage and pass the rest of my days in domestic ease and tranquility, banishing every desire of afterwards even hearing what passes in the world. Perhaps ardour for the latter may add considerably to the warmth of the former wish. Looking with fondness towards a reconciliation with Great Britain, I cannot help hoping you may be able to contribute towards expediting this good work. I think it must be evident to yourself that the ministry have been deceived by their officers on this side the water, who (for what purposes I cannot tell) have constantly represented the American opposition as that of a small faction, in which the body of the people took little part. This you can inform them of your own knowledge to be untrue.

Referring to those who still wished a "reunion with their parent country," he wrote:

I am sincerely one of those, and would rather be in dependence on Great Britain, properly limited, than on any nation upon earth, or than on no nation. But I am one of those too who rather than submit to the right of legislating for us assumed by the British Parliament, and which late experience has shewn they will so cruelly exercise, would lend my hand to sink the whole island in the ocean.

He had a proposal:

If undeceiving the minister as to matters of fact may change his dispositions, it will perhaps be in our power by assisting to do this, to render service to the whole empire, at the most critical time certainly that it has ever seen. Whether Britain shall continue the head of the greatest empire on earth, or shall return to her original station in the political scale of Europe depends perhaps on the resolutions of the succeeding winter. God send they may be wise and salutary for us all!

I shall be glad to hear from you as often as you may be disposed to think of things here. You may be at liberty I expect to communicate some things consistently with your honor and the duties you will owe to a protecting nation. Such a communication among individuals may be mutually beneficial to the contending parties. On this or any future occasion if I affirm to you any facts, your knowledge of me will enable you to decide on their credibility; if I hazard opinions on the dispositions of men, or other speculative points, you can only know they are my opinions. My best wishes for your felicity attend you wherever you go, and believe me to be assuredly Your friend & servt.,

Th: Jefferson

John Randolph replied:

Tho we may politically differ in Sentiments, yet I see no Reason why privately we may not cherish the same Esteem for each other which formerly I believe Subsisted between us. Should any Coolness happen between us, I'll take Care not to be the first mover of it. We both of us seem to be steering opposite Courses; the Success of either lies in the Womb of Time. But whether it falls to my share or not, be assured that I wish you all Health and Happiness.[22]

Amid the fast-moving and sometimes heart-rending events of revolution Jefferson was able to see happenings in the long perspective of history. In 1774 he had become one of the prepublication subscribers to Ebenezer Hazard's printed collection of American state papers which, the New Yorker proposed, would "begin with Grant from Henry 7th, to John Cabot, and his Sons for making Discoveries; and will include every important public paper (such as Royal Grants, Charters, Acts of Parliament, &c. &c.) relating to America, of which either the original, or authentic Copies can be procured, down to the present time."[23] Included would be the Stamp Act and the various resolves prompted by it and "other Acts of the British Parliament for raising a Revenue among us by internal Taxation. . . ." In the spring of 1775 Jefferson offered Hazard copies of old documents from his own collection and generously offered his own services in hunting for Virginia manuscripts. "I had before begun a perusal of our ancient records, which however I can only carry on when my attendance in assembly calls me to our capital from which my ordinary residence is remote."[24] To Jefferson's activities as collector and historiographer we owe the preservation of many priceless records of American history. He sought information for the use of "all those concerned in the administration of government" and of "any historical genius which may happen to arise."

Jefferson enlarged his perspective, too, when he returned to his mountaintop and gazed out upon the distant successive ranges of the Blue Ridge, those cool blue waves frozen in the same timeless immobility when the first pioneers looked upon them, and the first Indians. And perspective was to be found, too, in the comfort of his family and the sense of continuity that it gave him. But during that September that he spent at Monticello his sense of continuity received a rude shock. Jane Randolph, the younger of his two little daughters, died. As so often when he suffered deep personal loss, he left only a stark formal record.

By October 2 he was back in Philadelphia to participate in the Continental Congress. Again he was housed at Benjamin Randolph's, sharing his lodgings this time with Peyton Randolph and Thomas Nelson, Jr. One evening Jefferson accompanied Peyton Randolph to dinner at a private home outside the city. In dismay, Jefferson saw Randolph's broad, benevolent features suddenly contort. The corpulent frame became inert. Jefferson was with him five hours later when he died of apoplexy.[25] As a college student in Williamsburg, Jefferson had sometimes faced temptation by asking himself what Peyton Randolph would do under similar circumstances. Afterwards, while retaining respect and affection for his older cousin, Jefferson had sometimes been impatient of Mr. Speaker's measured approach to revolution. Since then the rush of events had pressed Randolph into a quickened pace and experience had restrained Jefferson from headlong rushing so that the two often marched arm in arm as comrades.

Jefferson wrote John Randolph to inform him of Peyton's death. He referred also to a recent proclamation of George III declaring the American colonies in a state of rebellion and warning "traitors." Jefferson said that the Americans lacked "neither inducement nor power to declare and assert a separation. It is will, alone, that is wanting, and that is growing apace under the fostering hand of our King. One bloody campaign will probably decide, everlastingly, our future course; and I am sorry to find a bloody campaign is decided on."[26]

But an American declaration of independence, if it came, would not come this session. That became increasingly apparent as the weeks wore on. There was little to do but indecisive committee work while wishing for triumphs of the Continental Army or the entrance of Canada on the side of her sisters to the south.

When Congress was told on December 2 that one of America's heroes, Ethan Allen, had been placed in irons aboard a British vessel to be carried to England to be tried for treason, Jefferson was appointed to draft a public protest. He proposed a message to Major General Howe:

Should you think proper in these days to revive antient barbarism, and again disgrace our nature with the practice of human sacrifice, the fortune of war has put into our power subjects for multiplied retaliation. To them, to you, and to the world we declare they shall not be wretched, unless their imprudence or your example shall oblige us to make them so; but we declare also that their lives shall teach our enemies to respect the rights of nations. We have ordered Brigadier General Prescot to be bound in irons, and confined in close jail, there to experience corresponding miseries with those which shall be inflicted on Mr. Allen. His life shall answer for that of Allen, and the lives of as many others for those of the brave men captivated with him. We deplore the event which shall oblige us to shed blood for blood, and shall resort to retaliation but as the means of stopping the progress of butchery. It is a duty we owe to those engaged in the cause of their country, to assure them that if any unlucky circumstance, baffling the efforts of their bravery, shall put them in the power of their enemies, we will use the pledges in our hands to warrant their lives from sacrifice.[27]

But Jefferson began to realize that this declaration would never be sent to General Howe. The Congress was increasingly inclined to let General Washington handle the problem in his own way.

Jefferson seemed to be wasting his time in long, dull committee sessions. He missed terribly both his wife and little Patsy. He had written regularly to them but received replies quite irregularly. Wife and daughter, in his absence, were staying with Mr. and Mrs. Francis Eppes. Surely they were safe. But one child had already died and his wife had a delicate constitution. Not hearing from them was maddening. In November he wrote Francis Eppes:

I have never received the scrip of a pen from any mortal in Virginia since I left it, nor been able by any enquiries I could make to hear of my family. I had hoped that when Mrs. Byrd came I should have heard something of them, but she could tell me nothing about them. The suspense under which I am is too terrible to be endured. If anything has happened, for God's sake let me know it.[28]

The torment was too much and duty no longer constrained him to remain in Philadelphia when so little was being accomplished. On December 29, as the year neared its end, he headed back to Monticello.

While Jefferson was still en route home Governor Dunmore celebrated New Year's Day by bombarding Norfolk, Virginia's largest city. As the predawn cannonade began from His Majesty's ships in the harbor, British sailors and marines applied torches to wharves and warehouses. Virginia and North Carolina riflemen, who had entered the city after victory at nearby Great Bridge, began setting fire to dwellings in the town which, though it housed many patriots, had become notorious as a nest of tories.

Back at peaceful Monticello a few days later Jefferson must have found it difficult to believe reports that only one-fifth of the seaport's buildings remained after a night made hellish by flames, shouts, screams, drunken threats, random shots, and exploding gunpowder, as wildly neighing horses pulled heavy cartloads of cherished possessions over rough cobblestones. Some of the poorer inhabitants had trundled away on wheelbarrows the few things they could save. Many evacuees were forced to flee on foot. Some were singing.

However unreal the events seemed, Jefferson could not have been unaware of their significance. On December 18, Washington had told the Continental Congress that "the fate of America a good deal depends on Dunmore's being obliged to evacuate Norfolk this winter or not."[29] Now Dunmore had evacuated Norfolk after declaring martial law and ordering "every person capable of bearing arms to resort to His Majesty's standard, or be looked upon as traitor to His Majesty's crown and government." Dunmore was making easier that separation which so many Virginians anticipated and dreaded

For the time, though, Jefferson welcomed the concerns of domestic life. His fears for Patty and Patsy had proved groundless. And at Monticello they would be far from the guns of the fleet with which Dunmore had taken refuge. Jefferson began to stock his park with the beautiful white-tailed Virginia deer, large-eyed, elegantly slim-legged, their coats warmly brindle in the pale sunlight of winter. And another beautiful creature was added to the menage—another foal descended from Fearnought.

Still there was no escaping the dangers of war. Terrible events in Tidewater were brought closer by a letter which John Page had written before the burning of Norfolk:

> We care not for our Towns, and the Destruction of our Houses would not cost us a Sigh. I have long since given up mine as lost. I have not moved many of my Things away—indeed nothing but my Papers, a few Books and some necessaries for Housekeeping. I can declare without boasting that I feel such Indignation against the Authors of our Grievances and the Scoundrel Pirates in our Rivers and such Concern for the Public at large that I have not and can not think of my own puny Person and insignificant Affairs.[30]

With the coming of spring Jefferson must again face the problems of politics and war. He would have liked to participate in the Virginia Convention, which probably would be forging a constitution, partly because this work was near to his heart and partly because then he need not be so far from his family. But duty commanded him to return to Philadelphia. Nelson, who was accompanied by his wife, urged Jefferson to bring Patty with him, saying that Mrs. Nelson could nurse her, but Mrs. Jefferson was not well enough to travel so far. Jefferson was beset with anxiety in March as he tended to plantation affairs in preparation for the northward journey.

On the last day of the month tragedy struck, but not where Jefferson had feared. His mother, who was still living at Shadwell, suffered a sudden stroke and was dead within an hour. As with the death of his daughter, Jefferson recorded only the stark facts of the loss.

More eloquent evidence of his distress is the migraine attack which he now suffered. Apparently he had had the problem before, but never of the same duration and severity. His reluctance to discuss any personal disability makes it difficult to determine just what visual and other difficulties accompanied the horrendous headaches which apparently, day after day, lasted with little or no interruption from sunrise to sunset.[31] Modern medical science tells us that this condition most often afflicts the intelligent, ambitious, and conscientious. Particularly vulnerable are perfectionists. Attacks are most likely to follow periods of unusual tension. In this instance Jefferson was disabled for five weeks.

After a week's journey made especially disagreeable by the knowledge that he might be overcome by another attack anywhere along the road, he arrived in Philadelphia May 15 with his servant Bob. Perhaps the faithful Jupiter had been left behind to look out for the family. Jefferson still worried about his wife.

To his lodgings at Benjamin Randolph's, he brought the money that he had collected for the purchase of gunpowder for Virginia and for the relief of Boston's poor. He also brought with him the results of an informal survey in his part of the colony indicating that nine-tenths of the people wanted independence. Awaiting him was a letter from an old friend of his student days at William and Mary, Dr. James McClurg, asking Jefferson's help in obtaining for him the post of physician to the Continental Troops in Virginia. He added: "The notion of independency seems to spread fast in this colony, and will be adopted, I dare say, by [the] next convention. The electors of James City, it is said, are preparing instructions for the treasurer to vote in its favor."[32] Also awaiting Jefferson was a letter from John Page that was more forceful in its appeal: "For God's sake declare the colonies independent at once, and save us from ruin."[33]

On the very day that Jefferson arrived in Philadelphia the Virginia Convention, by unanimous vote, instructed its delegation to the Continental Congress to "propose to that respectable body to declare the United Colonies free and independent States . . . and that they give the assent of this colony . . . to whatever measures may be thought proper and necessary by the Congress for forming foreign alliances and a confederation of the colonies. . . ."[34] None of the other colonies had acted so boldly. (On April 12 the North Carolina Convention had authorized its delegates in Philadelphia to vote for an independence resolution if one should be introduced, but only Virginia had instructed its delegates to propose such a resolution.) Jefferson was seated in the Congress on June 8 when Richard Henry Lee, conscious that he was history's instrument, stood tall, surveyed the assembly with a piercing gaze, and then, hunching his shoulders and thrusting his patrician head forward in the classic stance of a Roman senator, called in a melodiously modulated voice for a declaration "that these united colonies are, and of right ought to be, free and independent States."[35]

Debate on the resolution revealed that although New Englanders were warm in support, the Middle Colonies (Maryland, Delaware, Pennsylvania, New Jersey, and New York) were not ready for independence. And although North Carolina's delegates had already been instructed to support such a move and Virginia was often regarded as the bellwether of the other Southern colonies, delegates from at least one of them, South Carolina, indicated that they were not prepared for a final break. Many delegates, though themselves "friends to the measure," thought they should not "take any capital step till the voice of the people drove us into it."[36] Decision on the resolution was deferred till July 1.

Meanwhile Jefferson wished that he could be in Virginia where things were done more decisively. The resolutions for independence adopted by the Virginia Convention had also provided "that a committee be appointed to prepare a Declaration of Rights, and such a plan of government as will be most likely to maintain peace and order in this colony, and secure substantial and equal liberty to the people." Jefferson wrote to Nelson, now back in Virginia:

> It is a work of the most interesting nature and such as every individual would wish to have his voice in. In truth, it is the whole object of the present controversy; for should a bad government be instituted for us, in future it had been as well to have accepted the bad one offered us from beyond the water without the risk and expense of contest.[37]

Jefferson thought that there was a legitimate reason for delaying official action on a constitution. He believed that the Convention lacked the legal authority to adopt one. Only delegates elected for the express purpose of framing a constitution would be legally qualified for the task. Frustrated in his desire to present his arguments in person in Williamsburg, he entrusted them to Edmund Randolph. But neither Jefferson's logic nor Randolph's polished persuasiveness was sufficient to change the Convention's mind.[38]

Discouraged but not dismayed, Jefferson began drafting a constitution to be submitted to the Convention. George Wythe, who left Philadelphia for Williamsburg in June, carried Jefferson's composition with him. On arrival he discovered that a draft by George Mason had already been approved in committee and presented on the floor. Some amendments were proposed, but Wythe realized that the delegates—hot, tired, and wearied with argument—were not disposed to wrangle long over niceties, much less to begin consideration of a substitute document. He therefore presented Jefferson's draft to them solely in the hope that they might draw upon it for amendments. Jefferson later was not happy to learn that the delegates had used only one part of his paper, the preamble, which they simply had attached to Mason's production.

Actually the constitution drafted by Mason poured the heady brew of revolution into the old bottles of established oligarchy. But there was no great loss to democratic government because Jefferson's draft was not adopted. His work did not differ radically from Mason's nor, for that matter, from constitutions adopted shortly afterwards in other states. As Jefferson later explained: "In truth, the abuses of monarchy had so much filled all the space of political contemplation that we imagined everything republican which was not monarchy. We had not yet penetrated to the mother principle, that 'governments are republican only in proportion as they embody the will of the people and execute it.' Hence, our first constitutions had really no leading principles in them."[39] As some political scientists today define a republic as any government not headed by a monarch, some may wish to substitute "democratic" for "republican" in Jefferson's statement. In effect, the new Constitution of Virginia made possible a continuation of the plantocracy that had ruled for generations. Like the constitutions of the other states, it reflected a colonial-bred fear of executive authority, tending to make the governor a figurehead. Jefferson's draft differed on this point only in giving the chief executive a little more appointive power.

Jefferson's work differed from Mason's chiefly in the matter of suffrage. It retained a property qualification for voters, in accordance with the general belief in the eighteenth century that the interests of society would be served best by those who had an economic stake in it. But Jefferson's plan also called for the granting of property to those who did not have any. Thus his system was somewhat analogous to that of twentieth-century corporations which have given stock to their employees to increase the workers' stake in the success of the company. If adopted, Jefferson's constitution would have given the privilege of voting to virtually every white male in Virginia. The system would still have been far short of democracy except in the Athenian sense, all citizens of Athens having been given the vote but only a minority being permitted to become citizens. As in Athens, all women and slaves would have been denied the franchise. Still, Jefferson's idea would greatly have enlarged the oligarchy.

Significant reforms were proposed in Jefferson's draft—abolition of the importation of slaves, prohibition of an established church, and equal rights for males and females in the descent of property. But, even if Jefferson's work had been laid before the Convention in time, these proposals undoubtedly would have been edited and amended out by his contemporaries. Their chief interest is as evidence of his thinking and of the boldness with which he was willing to implement it. To Jefferson the differences between his constitution and Mason's seemed monumental. He soon conceived the idea of remaking Virginia's government, however long the process might prove.[40]

He was, however, enthusiastic about Mason's Declaration of Rights, which had been adopted before the Constitution. The product of Mason's years of study in history, philosophy, and law rather than simply of the ten days of effort that directly produced the document, it is justly honored as one of the world's great state papers. As Roscoe Pound has observed, "The Virginia Bill of Rights of 1776 is the first and, indeed, is the model of a long line of politico-legal documents that have become the staple of American constitutional law."[41] In line of descent from the Virginia document are the Bills of Rights of the United States, France, and various Latin American republics, as well as the statement on human rights in the charter of the United Nations.

Some phrases in Mason's work apparently made a strong impression on Jefferson. Whether for that reason, or because the two men eagerly read the same philosophers and many expressions common to both were refinements of the intellectual currency of the time, Jefferson later used phrases strikingly similar to Mason's. Of course, Jefferson was quick to disclaim credit for originality in employing them. But Mason's words were like hammer strokes striking responsive chords in Jefferson with such phrases as "all men are by nature equally free and independent and have certain inherent rights . . . all power is vested in and consequently derived from the people . . . . government is, or ought to be, instituted for the common benefit, protection, and security of the people." What vibrations were prompted by Mason's statement that the rights of man included "the enjoyment of life and liberty, with the means of acquiring and possessing property, and pursuing and obtaining happiness and safety"?[42] Of course, Jefferson applauded the Declaration of Rights for calling for free and regular elections, a free press, and trial by jury, and for inveighing against general warrants, excessive bail, cruel and unusual punishments, hereditary office, and taxation without representation.

But Jefferson himself now had an opportunity to state important principles in glowing phrases in a public document. In the absence of Richard Henry Lee, presenter of the resolution for independence, who was called back to Virginia because of his wife's illness, Jefferson was made chairman of the Committee to prepare a Declaration of Independence for congressional consideration.[43] Elbridge Gerry, whom Jefferson had met on his first trip to Philadelphia, was now a delegate from Massachusetts. He eagerly reported a growing sentiment, even among the hesitant colonies, for separation from Great Britain. Jefferson thought that soon they would be ready to "drop from the parent stem."[44]

The other committee members were John Adams, Benjamin Franklin, Roger Sherman, and Robert R. Livingston. The last two Jefferson did not know well. A delegate from Connecticut where he was treasurer of Yale College, the sober-suited Sherman, sunken-eyed and lantern-jawed, comes down to us in a contemporary portrait looking like a Boris Karloff portrayal of a Nathaniel Hawthorne Puritan. Originally a cobbler, he had qualified for the bar at the age of thirty-three. Now fifty-five, he had retired from business to devote his time to his numerous public activities at every civic and political level. Contrasting with Sherman was Robert Livingston whose bold-featured face and distinguished manner bespoke the easy confidence of one born to success. The wealthy son of a justice of the New York supreme court, he had been educated at King's College for a career of public service rapidly advanced by the combination of cultivated ability and powerful connections.

Jefferson was the youngest of this committee of notables, with the exception of Livingston, who was three years his junior. Nevertheless, they all soon deferred to their chairman's ability as a thinker and writer, insisting that he prepare the principal draft of the Declaration. Franklin may have deferred largely because of the frustrations he had experienced as a penman for public bodies.[45] Adams had his own reasons for insisting that Jefferson be the author. According to the New Englander, the Virginian at first demurred, urging Adams himself to prepare the draft. When Adams refused in his blunt way, Jefferson asked why and drew from that cannonball of a man a swift succession of sentences delivered like shots on target. "Reasons enough."

"What can be your reasons?"

"Reason first: You are a Virginian and a Virginian ought to appear at the head of this business. Reason second: I am obnoxious, suspected, and unpopular. You are very much otherwise Reason third: You can write ten times better than I can."[46]

Jefferson, according to Adams, protested no further. Adams' insistence that a Virginian should "appear at the head of this business" was in accordance with the "Frankfort advice" that Virginia be shoved forward in the revolutionary movement to increase her commitment.

Jefferson's experience with legislative bodies in Virginia and in Philadelphia had taught him that his colleagues' unanimous assurance that he was the man to prepare the paper was no guarantee that they would later approve his work.

Once again, at the end of tedious days of conference, he devoted his evenings to composition. He no longer had rooms at Benjamin Randolph's. Soon after his arrival in Philadelphia in May, Jefferson had written Thomas Nelson, "I am at present in our old lodgings tho' I think as the excessive heats of the city are coming on fast, to endeavor to get lodgings in the skirts of the town where I may have the benefit of a freely circulating air."[47] He had rented the second floor of a three-and-a-half-story brick house recently built on the southwest corner of Seventh and Market Streets. The builder and owner, Jacob Graff, Jr., a newlywed brick mason, occupied the lower floor. Five windows on the east side helped to provide some of the ventilation Jefferson sought.[48]

Though he had left his lodgings with Benjamin Randolph, he had carried with him a useful example of his former landlord's cabinetmaking skill—a folding writing desk of Jefferson's own design. Of it he wrote: "It claims no merit of particular beauty. It is plain, neat, convenient, and, taking no more room on the writing table than a moderate quarto volume, it yet displays itself sufficiently for any writing."[49] When Jefferson, returning hot and tired from the daily sessions at the State House, climbed the stairs to his two rooms, he must have been tempted to go directly to his bed in the back room instead of to his writing desk in the parlor. But to his little portable desk he went, again and again, to work on his draft of the Declaration of Independence.

Jefferson said afterwards that he had consulted no book or pamphlet, but he had not eschewed these references in any futile attempt to be original. He drew on many sources. They were, however, so much a part of his mental furniture that he could call them to mind as readily as he might summon the images of familiar household objects.

He later defined his purpose as "not to find out new principles, or new arguments, never before thought of, not merely to say things which had never been said before, but to place before mankind the common sense of the subject, in terms so plain and firm as to command their assent, and to justify ourselves in the independent stand we are compelled to take. Neither aiming at originality of principle or sentiment, nor yet copied from any particular and previous writing, it was intended to be an expression of the American mind, and to give to that expression the proper tone and spirit called for by the occasion."[50]

One part of the Declaration Jefferson had already written—the indictment of the King and the catalogue of his offenses of commission and omission. He had rehearsed these in *A Summary View* (blaming Parliament more than Sovereign) and then had carefully detailed them in his proposed constitution for Virginia, from which they had been removed by legislative surgery for transplantation to the body of Mason's work, which they served as a preamble. Though Jefferson may simply have been writing from memory when he prepared the roster of complaints in the Declaration of Independence, the similarities are so marked as to suggest that he had the pages of his earlier work spread beside his little portable desk.

But if he copied most from himself, he seems to have drawn next most heavily from James Wilson. In his pamphlet *Considerations on the Nature and Extent of the Legislative Authority of the British Parliament*, published in 1774 but probably written as early as 1770, Wilson had said:

All men are by nature equal and free: no one has a right to any authority over another without his consent: all lawful government is founded in the consent of those who are subject to it: Such consent was given with a view to ensure and to increase the happiness of the government, above what they would enjoy in an independent and unconnected state of nature. The consequence is that the happiness of the society is the first law of every government.[51]

In the Declaration of Independence, Jefferson wrote:

We hold these truths to be self-evident, that all men are created equal, that they are endowed by their creator with certain inalienable rights, that among these are life, liberty and the pursuit of happiness. That to secure these rights, governments are instituted among men, deriving their just powers from the consent of the governed. That whenever any form of government becomes destructive of these ends, it is the right of the people to alter or to abolish it, and to institute new government, laying its foundation on such principles, and organizing its powers in such form, as to them shall seem most likely to effect their safety and happiness.

Jefferson's and Wilson's words, though not cut from the same die, would seem to issue from the same mint. In truth, they were rather drawn from the same treasury of expressions and thoughts which furnished the intellectual currency of Europe and America. Jefferson's words were no more like Wilson's than Wilson's were like Locke's, Hutcheson's, Lord Kames's, or Burlamaqui's. And Jefferson's paragraphs have a rhythmic grace, a processional stateliness, which Wilson's lack. They carry with them the sense of inevitability, of cosmic harmony, that distinguishes so much of the style of the King James Version of the Bible and the noblest passages of Abraham Lincoln's oratory.

The connotation of inevitability comports well with Jefferson's use of "self-evident." He borrowed the term from the Scottish Enlightenment but altered its application.[52] Hutcheson and his followers used the expression to describe what they believed to be inherent moral perceptions. A normal human being, they held, regardless of educational advantages or their lack, was capable of choosing in the ethical realm between right and wrong. The ignorant, it was argued, might serve as effectively on juries as their more lettered compeers because essential moral truths were not hidden from anyone. They were self-evident.

Jefferson made a more extravagant claim when he asserted that the equality of men was self-evident. Surely he had heard the proposition disputed many times, as, for example, when the court ruled against him in his "born free" case. Partly Jefferson was indulging in an apodictic style of debate in which emphatic asseveration might be substituted for close reasoning. But, above all, his statement that all men are born equal was by no means so sweeping an assertion as it might seem. As Jefferson himself pointed out in various writings, he did not cherish the delusion that all men were equal in ability to learn, or inventiveness, or athletic aptitude. But they were equal in their rights to life, liberty, and the pursuit of happiness. They might by their own actions forfeit these blessings. But they could not otherwise justly be deprived of them.

A modern scholar[53] has quite ingeniously sought to prove that Jefferson meant primarily that all men were equal in the most important faculty of humankind—moral sense. Whatever abstruse or sophistic reasoning they may employ, however, serious and capable historians do not, like some politicians and even some educators who should know better, say with casual casuistry that the multitalented Jefferson implied equality of human potential. He had convincing evidence to the contrary if he looked no farther than himself and his own siblings.

When Jefferson had completed his draft he showed it first to Adams and then to Franklin, each of whom suggested a few small changes which he accepted. The document, as Jefferson had fervently hoped, emerged from the full committee little changed and was presented to Congress on June 28. Sitting as Committee of the Whole, Congress on July 1 debated the Lee Resolution for Independence, action on which had been postponed to that date in hopes of gaining unanimous support for the separation. After nine hours of continuous argument, the vote was postponed to the next day. Then it was not unanimous because the New York delegates, bound by instructions from home, abstained. Nevertheless, John Adams, who had labored many months for independence, was exuberant. It was then that he wrote the famous letter to Abigail in which he said:

> The second day of July, 1776, will be the most memorable epocha in the history of America. I am apt to believe that it will be celebrated by succeeding generations as the great anniversary festival. It ought to be commemorated as the day of deliverance, by solemn acts of devotion to God Almighty. It ought to be solemnized with pomp and parade, with shows, games, sports, guns, bells, bonfires, and illuminations, from one end of this continent to the other, from this time forward for evermore.[54]

Obviously the act of declaring independence, made more urgent by the necessity of forming alliances which would enable the American colonies to survive, was more important to Adams than the style and manner in which Americans and the world were informed of the fact. But to the Congress the document itself was a matter of great importance. Jefferson was made acutely aware of this fact as he sat mostly in anguished silence, on July 2, 3, and 4, while Congress debated the political and literary merits of his composition. Listening sympathetically at his side, Franklin told him that he had long ago made up his own mind never to prepare another paper for submission to a public body. The older man also told him a humorous anecdote about a hatter who had altered his elegantly inscribed signboard so many times in obedience to individual criticisms that eventually it bore only his name and a picture of a hat.[55] Jefferson listened with his usual polite tact, but he was in no mood to enjoy a joke.

He was disappointed when the delegates excised his favorite historical argument that the American colonies had never owed any more allegiance to Great Britain than the Anglo-Saxons of England owed to the Germanic homelands from whence they had come. He regretted the deletion of a passage in which he said that repeated offenses had driven the Americans to an act of separation undesired and painful:

> These facts have given the last stab to agonizing affection, and manly spirit bids us to renounce forever these unfeeling brethren. We must endeavor to forget our former love for them, and to hold them as we hold the rest of mankind, enemies in war, in peace friends. We might have been a free and a great people together, but a communication of grandeur and of freedom it seems is below their dignity. Be it so, since they will have it: the road to happiness and to glory is open to us too; we will climb it apart from them, and acquiesce in the necessity which pronounces our eternal separation.[56]

But Jefferson was most chagrined at the reception accorded his passage on slavery, which he denounced in much the same language he had used in *A Summary View*. Not only did gentlemen from South Carolina and Georgia protest this section but delegates from some New England states feared that it would anger influential constituents who had grown rich in the slave trade. Some of these delegates were quick to point out their own opposition to the institution but believed it reckless to antagonize powerful men whose support for the new government was almost essential. At this juncture, as throughout the three days of debate, Adams supported Jefferson on every word.[57] Nevertheless, one-fourth of the document submitted by the committee had been deleted before the Declaration was adopted on July 4.[58]

Jefferson was relieved but far from exuberant. All the rest of his life he believed that his work had been weakened historically and rhetorically by congressional editing. He sent copies of his own draft to Richard Henry Lee and other friends that they might compare the merits of the two versions. They agreed that Jefferson's creation had been damaged. Most scholars since have suggested that the amendments improved the original work both in terms of literary excellence and of concession to the political realities of the day. Very recently, however, it has been argued that the judgement of Jefferson and his contemporaries was correct and Congress had indeed desecrated his masterpiece.[59]

Examining Jefferson's draft and the final Declaration phrase by phrase, some of us are inclined to feel that some changes were beneficial, others deleterious. While a phrase or two of Jefferson's expression of sorrow at parting from "our brethren" may sound a bit maudlin, the passage as a whole is one of noble pathos that lends appealing warmth to a state document. With a little editing, it might well have been left in. While we must concede the delegates' superior knowledge of their own constituencies, we must still regret the practical necessity—if it was that—that compelled the Founding Fathers to appear before the bar of history simultaneously proclaiming freedom as a God-given right and denying it to their human chattels and human cargoes. Some congressional substitutions of cooler phrases for Jefferson's more perfervid ones probably were improvements. Probably no one would quarrel with Congress's correction of the Virginian's habitual use of the apostrophe in the possessive "its" or of his custom of not capitalizing the first letter of a sentence; but we can regret mildly that someone— either the Congress or a careless copyist—changed "inalienable" to "unalienable." The part of the document that strikes us today as least noble is the section that his contemporaries considered most important—the indictments of King George.

It is in other portions that the Declaration rises to its greatest heights, elevated far above the provincial and the temporal. These portions survived the committee sessions and the congressional debates. Who could possibly wish to excise them? Men and women who have never set foot in America have been stirred by the words:

> When, in the course of human events, it becomes necessary for one people to dissolve the political bands which have connected them with another, and to assume among the powers of the earth the separate and equal station to which the laws of nature and of nature's God entitle them, a decent respect to the opinions of mankind requires that they should declare the causes which impel them to the separation.

And even a generation calloused to dishonor in high places finds inspiration in the vow:

> and for the support of this declaration we mutually pledge to each other our lives, our fortunes, and our sacred honor.

Many have pointed out the similarities between Jefferson's prose in the declaration and that of Locke, Hutcheson, Wilson, Mason, and others. Some have even gone so far as to charge plagiarism. They forget that Jefferson, when he finally signed the Declaration of Independence, did so not as its author but as one of fifty-five delegates to the Congress in Philadelphia. His avowed purpose, as we have seen, was to produce "an expression of the American mind." Julian Boyd has said that, "even if Jefferson had 'copied from any particular and previous writing' . . . the most that would be proved by this is that he had failed to be original in an enterprise where originality would have been fatal."[60] And Boyd adds:

> The greatness of his achievement, aside from the fact that he created one of the outstanding literary documents of the world and of all time, was that he iden-

tified its sublime purpose with the roots of liberal traditions that spread back to England, to Scotland, to Geneva, to Holland, to Germany, to Rome, and to Athens. In the fundamental statement of national purpose for a people who were to embrace many races and many creeds, nothing could have been more appropriate than that the act renouncing the ties of consanguinity should at the same time have drawn its philosophical justification from traditions common to all.[61]

Plagiarism? A comparison of the Declaration of Independence with various possible sources, some of them copied in his own Commonplace Book, reveals many striking parallels and some duplicate phrases. But they are so perfectly compressed and integrated, both in logical structure and in unifying rhythm, in Jefferson's Declaration that they comprise an original work of art no less than T. S. Eliot's compounds of sources ranging from a duchess' diary to phrases from Frazer's *Golden Bough*. But had Wilson expressed at least two years ahead the essence of Jefferson's Declaration? Jefferson, in his glowing Declaration, no more plagiarized the Pennsylvanian's quite adequate prose than Shakespeare, in *The Tempest*, plagiarized William Strachey's straightforward account of the wreck of the *Sea Venture*.[62] In each instance the ideas and even many of the words are the same. But in each case a prosaic work has been lifted to new heights where the light of the imagination can play around it. It has drawn divine fire, and its effulgence can never be mistaken for the soft glow of a domestic candle.

VIII

'WITH A SINGLE EYE . . .'

O LD MODERATION was disappointed in his protégé. Edmund Pendleton, who had sometimes been troubled by Jefferson's youthful radicalism, was not disturbed that the young friend he had first launched in the writing of state papers had now become author of the Declaration of Independence. In fact, Pendleton lamented that some of Jefferson's too conciliatory "brethren" had weakened the original draft. Pendleton himself had become first a reluctant revolutionist and then a spirited one. Indeed, he had served as chairman of the Committee of Safety that governed Virginia in the interim between Dunmore's departure and the establishment of a new constitutional government.

His concern now was not that Jefferson might continue his activities but rather that he might withdraw from them. Delegates who had served in Philadelphia with Jefferson said that, all the while, he had agonized over his wife's health and lamented his absence from Virginia. Hearing that the younger man found few attractions in any public responsibilities far removed from home, Pendleton had hoped to induce him to accept a high judicial post in Virginia or to play some prominent part in the new state government. Finding no eagerness in Jefferson's response, Pendleton on August 10, 1776, wrote to him:

> I am extremely concerned to hear your disagreeable situation is rendered more so by the indisposition of Mrs. Jefferson. May heaven restore her health and grant you a joyful meeting. I am not able to answer your reasons for not engaging in the Judiciary, not having adopted that kind "that another shall be compelled to serve in an office that I must be excused from." However, I can but lament that it is not agreeable and convenient to you, for I do not assent to your being unqualified, tho' I readily do to your usefulness in the State Representative body, where having the pleasure of Mrs. Jefferson's company, I hope you'll get cured of your wish to retire so early in life from the memory of man, and exercise your talents for the nurture of our new State Constitution, which will require all the attention of its friends to prune exuberances and cherish the plant.[1]

Pendleton, as an orphan adopted into the Virginia aristocracy by the powerful Robinson clan, had the convert's dedication to the ideals of his class. Prominent among those was noblesse oblige. The Virginia plantocracy of the eighteenth century was one of the most responsible oligarchies in the history of western civilization. Like all rulling elites, it was at times arrogant but it strongly held that the privileges of leadership and of superior advantages must be paid for in community service. The extent of one's services should be proportionate to one's advantages. Jefferson's advantages of birth and training were great indeed. His services should be commensurate, but all his various learning seemed only to provide him with the conversational baubles of the dilettante, the private toys of the solitary scholar. Or so it seemed to Pendleton when he believed that his protege might retire from public service at the age of thirty-three after a seven-year career climaxed by the writing of the Declaration of Independence.

Jefferson's term in Congress would expire in August. He had written to Pendleton, as president of the Virginia Convention, as well as to Dr. George Gilmer, serving in that convention as acting delegate from Albemarle in Jefferson's absence, informing both that he did not wish to be reelected to the Congress. As luck would have it, when the balloting for the Virginia delegation took place, Pendleton had not received the letter addressed to him and Dr. Gilmer was absent. But Jefferson, determined to retire from the Congress, had prepared for such eventualities. Edmund Randolph personally addressed the Convention to present Jefferson's appeal to be relieved. Despite this plea, however, Jefferson was reelected, even though the Convention had reduced the delegation from seven to five.[2]

When he learned that he had been fourth in balloting in which Harrison and Braxton had lost out altogether, he was not flattered to be reelected over his own objections. Doubtless his sensitivity was exacerbated by the searching and mauling to which his Declaration was being subjected by the Congress. On July 1 he had written William Fleming:

It is a painful situation to be 300 miles from one's country, and thereby open to secret assassination without a possibility of self defense. I am willing to hope nothing of this kind has been done in my case, and yet I cannot be easy. If any doubt has arisen as to me, my country will have my political creed in the form of a "Declaration &c." which I was lately directed to draw. This will give decisive proof that my own sentiment concurred with the vote they instructed us to give.[3]

Thoroughly homesick and with the earwig of anxiety always gnawing in his brain, Jefferson was determined not to accept reelection or any other employment that would take him out of Virginia. Supposedly, if he accepted another term, there would be various opportunities to return to Monticello and the wife not well enough to come to him. But there were supposed to have been similar opportunities in the term now drawing to an end and he had found that, when urgent committee responsibilities did not compel his attendance, the absence of fellow delegates from Virginia made his presence necessary to obtain a quorum. In an official letter to Pendleton as chairman of the Virginia Convention, Jefferson thanked that body for the "continued confidence" of which he was actually so skeptical, then wrote:

I am sorry the situation of my domestic affairs renders it indispensably necessary that I should solicit the substitution of some other person here in my room. The delicacy of the house will not require me to enter minutely into the private causes which render this necessary. I shall with cheerfulness continue in duty here till the expiration of our year by which time I hope it will be convenient for my successor to attend.[4]

A biographer longs in vain for substantial clues to the exact state of Patty's health and of Jefferson's domestic affairs which delicacy forbade him to "enter minutely into." In any event, worried as Jefferson was, he continued conscientiously and doggedly to render yeoman service in such matters as helping to draw up rules of procedure for the Congress, joining his Virginia colleagues in attempting to settle their state's boundary dispute with Pennsylvania, proposing with John Adams a revision of the articles of war, and answering numerous queries and requests from his constituents.

By September 3 the arrival in Philadelphia of Richard Henry Lee, assuring the Virginia delegation of a quorum, freed Jefferson to return home. Anticipating his departure, on August 29 he had paid his rent in full to Mrs. Trapp, duly recording the transaction on one of the blank pages provided for the purpose in his copy of *The Philadelphia Newest Almanack, For the Year of Our Lord 1776.*[5] From the same source we know that he was returning home bearing gifts ranging from female clothing to a doll, as well as purchases in line with his own researches. On July 4 he had bought a thermometer and seven pairs of women's gloves, and had given one shilling and six pence to charity. Paper, pamphlets, and books accounted for much of his expenditure in Philadelphia, but he had also bought spurs and a straw hat, and in June, when he had found little amusement in the tedious debates of the Congress, he had paid a shilling to see a monkey. With great relief he now squared all accounts in the city and rode homeward through a countryside just touched with the first flames of autumnal red and gold.

Six days later he held Patsy in his arms and hugged his children to him. When he waked next day to see morning gilding his beloved mountains he was surely even more strongly confirmed in his determination to eschew responsibilities that would imprison him in distant cities. He had never, however, intended abruptly to abandon public life altogether as Pendleton had feared. The older man had urged upon him the nurture and pruning of Virginia's new constitution and a hand in reformation of the "too sanguinary" criminal code. For these tasks Jefferson had enthusiasm and he proposed to play an active role in his state's legislature. But there must be no distant duties.

About a month later Jefferson and his family were comfortably settled in George Wythe's home on the Palace Green in Williamsburg. Wythe had given them the use of the house while he served in the Congress in Philadelphia and Jefferson served in the Virginia Assembly. The Georgian brick mansion, four-square as its master, held for Jefferson many fond memories from his student days. So did the Palace itself, which he could see from the front windows. He could follow public duty and at the same time be with his family amid familiar surroundings in his beloved Virginia.

Hoofbeats that broke the quiet on October 8 shattered this comforting certainty. With the staccato insistence of the hoofbeats, the great world was knocking on Jefferson's door. The messenger had been dispatched by the Congress in Philadelphia. It was surely with foreboding that Jefferson broke the seal on the letter from John Hancock, President. The first sentence justified his fears: "The Congress having appointed you to fill a most important and honorable department, it is with particular pleasure I congratulate you on the occasion." The letter continued:

By the enclosed Resolves you will perceive, that Doctor Franklin, Mr. Deane, and yourself, are chosen Commissioners at the Court of France, to negotiate such Business as the Congress shall entrust you with. For this Purpose, Letters of Credence, and Instructions will be delivered to Doctor Franklin, and Duplicates forwarded to you and Mr. Deane. You will therefore, be pleased to acquaint me, by the Return of the Express, who brings you this, at what Time and Place it will be most convenient for you to embark, in Order that a Vessel may be sent to take you on Board. A suitable Vessel, will, in the mean Time, be provided here for the Accommodation of Doctor Franklin, it being judged most prudent, that you should sail in different ships.[6]

Hancock appealed to Jefferson's patriotism and sense of duty in a way that made refusal difficult:

As it is fully in your Power, so I am persuaded it is the favorite wish of your heart, to promote the interest and happiness of your country; and that you will, in particular, render her the great services which she so fondly expects from you on this occasion.[7]

Jefferson agonized for three days before replying:

It would argue great insensibility in me could I receive with indifference so confidential an appointment from your body. My thanks are a poor return for the partiality they have been pleased to entertain for me. No cares for my own person, nor yet for my private affairs would have induced one moment's hesitation to accept the charge. But circumstances very peculiar in the situation of my family, such as neither permit me to leave nor to carry it, compel me to ask leave to decline a service so honorable and at the same time so important to the American cause. The necessity under which I labor, and the conflict I have undergone for three days, during which I could not determine to dismiss your messenger, will I hope plead my pardon with Congress; and I am sure there are too many of that body, to whom they may with better hopes confide this charge, to leave them under a moment's difficulty in making a new choice.[8]

Jefferson's service in the House of Delegates began on October 11, the day he wrote to decline his diplomatic appointment. He was soon immersed in legislative affairs. Under the State Constitution, written in the long shadow of executive tyranny, power centered in the legislature. Patrick Henry, whose voice had reverberated through the legislative halls and reached through windows and doors to collect audiences outside, was now "cabined, cribbed, confined" within the Governor's Palace, from which the echoes of his pronouncements seldom traveled so far as the Capitol. Unlike Jefferson, the new Governor had in mind no plans for reform of laws or institutions. In the act of declaring their independence, the American people had overtaken Henry's radicalism. He dreamed of no revolution beyond the winning of freedom from England. But even if he had, he could have done little to implement his ideas. He could no more escape the constitutional maze that hedged his steps than he could leap over the geometrical walls of boxwood in the Palace's formal gardens.

That Jefferson as a highly respected legislator could exert far more influence in shaping the new government than Henry could as Governor became apparent on November 5 when the delegate from Albemarle, by joint action of House and Senate, was named chairman of a Committee to Revise the Laws of the Commonwealth.[9] When Pendleton had written to Jefferson on July 22 to urge him to accept a high judicial post, he had added: "You are also wanting much in the revision of our laws and forming a new body, a necessary work for which few of us have adequate abilities and attention."[10]

Jefferson was already busy with reform. On his first day in the House, he had asked leave to bring in a bill for the establishment of courts of justice. This proposal, designed to restore local operations of justice disrupted by war, was not welcomed by most of his colleagues. Courts could enforce the payment of debts. Tobacco, the popular medium of exchange as well as the principal cash crop in Virginia, was almost worthless at this point and debt-ridden planters feared summonses. Three days later he had introduced a bill against entails, an action on which he prided himself for the rest of his life.

Entailment was a process by which the succession of an estate could be determined for generations, with no inheritor having the privilege of bequeathing it as he desired or even selling or otherwise disposing of it. The practice, centuries old, was intended to preserve large estates intact so that in each generation some bearer of the family name would have the lands and wealth to support the honor of the house. Thus there were baronial domains along the rivers and bayshores that barred the small farmer from hope of easy access to the waterways. There were some estates so large as to invite mismanagement by all but the ablest and most energetic at a time when industrious small landholders—some even relatives of the local river baron—lacked the acreage for practicable rotation of planted and fallow fields. Besides, an end to entails would free some land-poor inheritors of large estates from the fearful burden of non-productive fields extending to the horizon. Only by action of the General Assembly could the possessor of an entailed estate divide it among his heirs contrary to the provisions of his inheritance, or sell part of his plantation to secure funds to repair his barns, refurbish his house, or build a profitable grist mill. Jefferson saw his proposal as putting the ax to the overgrown tree of plantocracy whose great shade denied a place in the sun to so many smaller growths.[11]

The bill to abolish entails was quickly passed. Few members of the aristocracy fought to preserve the old system. Its most active defender was Pendleton, who may have wished momentarily that he had not so strongly urged Jefferson to take a prominent role in reforming the laws of the state. In any event, the abolition of entail probably did not initiate the drastic social and economic changes in Virginia that Jefferson liked to think of its inaugurating. Many estates in Virginia, like Peter Jefferson's in which Thomas shared, were not entailed. Entail was probably becoming the exception rather than the rule.

Building the momentum of reform, however, was more important to Jefferson than any specific measure. No time must be lost. A little later he would write:

... It can never be too often repeated, that the time for fixing every essential right on a legal basis is while our rulers are honest, and ourselves united. From the conclusion of this war we shall be going down hill. It will not then be necessary to resort every moment to the people for support. They will be forgotten, therefore, and their rights disregarded. They will forget themselves, but in the sole faculty of making money, and will never think of uniting to effect a due respect for their rights. The shackles, therefore, which shall not be knocked off at the conclusion of this war, will remain on us long, will be made heavier and heavier, till our rights shall revive or expire in convulsion.[12]

With high hope early in the new year Jefferson rode to Fredericksburg for the first meeting of the Committee to Revise the Laws of the Commonwealth. On January 13, 1777, he sat down with the other members—Pendleton, Wythe, Mason, and Thomas Ludwell Lee—for what he himself described as "the first and only meeting of the whole committee."[13]

The first question discussed was whether they should "attempt to reduce the whole body of the law into a code, the text of which should become the law of the land." Pendleton, the habitual defender of tradition, surprised Jefferson by calling for a completely new code of laws. Thomas Ludwell Lee, who shared his brother Richard Henry's liberalism, seconded the suggestion. Jefferson, Wythe, and Mason opposed the proposal. Jefferson argued that if a completely new code were produced "every word and phrase in that text would become a new subject of criticism and litigation until its sense should have been settled by numerous decisions; . . . in the meantime, the rights of property would be in the air."[14] He agreed with Wythe and Mason that such an undertaking would be too bold. Sometimes Jefferson may have been more comfortable as a radical when there were stout conservatives to slow the forward rush. He and his two like-minded colleagues argued that the common law, "the law preceding the existence of the statutes," should not be meddled with "further than to accommodate it to our new principles and circumstances." Their view prevailed.

The entire committee agreed "to take up the whole body of statutes and Virginia laws, to leave out everything obsolete or improper, insert what was wanting, and reduce the whole within as moderate a compass as it would bear . . . ." There would be another reduction—"to the plain language of common sense, divested of the verbiage, the barbarous tautologies and redundancies, which render the British statutes unintelligible." Exempted from this process of paraphrase would be "the ancient statutes, particularly those commented on by Lord Coke, the language of which is simple, and the meaning of every word so well settled by decisions as to make it safest not to change words where the sense was to be retained." Jefferson had acquired great respect for "old Coke" since student days when he had consigned the eminent jurist to the devil as "an old, dull scoundrel."

At thirty-three years of age Jefferson was the principal agent of legal reform in Virginia.[15] Apart from his leadership of the Committee, he was incessantly busy drafting bills dealing not only, as we have seen, with courts of justice and entails, but also with such controversial subjects as the established church, the importation of slaves, naturalization, and representation, as well as a myriad of smaller matters. Not all of his proposals found easy passage. He drafted his Statute of Virginia for Religious Freedom in 1777, but found that the time was not yet ripe for its introduction. Virginia had never been conspicuous for religious intolerance in that intolerant age, but its people were not yet prepared to accept the idea that there was no religious view whose expression should in any way "diminish, enlarge, or affect" the "civil capacities" of the speaker or writer. This was true even though Jefferson, in an adroit preamble, turned the tables on those who would charge him with impiety; he condemned the "impious presumption" of any who "assumed dominion over the faith of others." Jefferson also had to defer his efforts for gradual emancipation of the slaves, but he was one of the leaders of opinion who helped to make Virginia in 1778 the first American state to prohibit the importation of slaves; indeed, in the words of J.H. Ballagh, "the first community in the civilized modern world to prohibit the pernicious traffic."[16]

Jefferson was less successful in the same year when he and Mason introduced legislation to give small settlers (including squatters) an advantage over speculative companies in the western lands. From a variety of motives, selfish and patriotic, ranging from speculative interests and fear of depressing the value of eastern lands to Washington's fear that prospective soldiers would be lured from the Army, most of the great planters rallied behind Harrison and Pendleton to defeat the proposal.

Not only did Jefferson introduce a number of reform bills: he also was the prompter and author of such bills introduced by other legislators. Apparently he even secured certain committee appointments so that he could attach amendments embodying his pet projects to bills acted on by those committees.[17] Julian P. Boyd, after the most thorough study of the subject yet made, concludes: ". . .it is safe to say that Jefferson was, as author or chief advocate, responsible for the introduction and adoption of more bills than any other single member of the General Assembly in the years 1776 to 1779. In the variety of subjects touched upon, in the quantity of bills drafted, and in the unity of purpose behind all of this legislative activity, his accomplishment in this period was astonishing. He was in himself a veritable legislative drafting bureau."[18]

The sheer mass of his legislative work would be imposing even if he had not also been busy with the work of the Committee to Revise the Laws of the Commonwealth. Viewed in conjunction with this concurrent activity it is astounding. Jefferson had converted his committee to the view "that our whole code must be reviewed, adapted to our republican form of government, and, now that we had no negatives of Councils, Governors, and Kings to restrain us from doing right, it should be corrected, in all its parts, with a single eye to reason, and the good of those for whose government it was framed."[19]

The task was staggering, even for so gifted a quintet. But the committee soon was reduced to three. Mason, though his knowledge of constitutional law far exceeded that of most attorneys, "excused himself as, being no lawyer, he felt himself unqualified for the work, and he resigned soon after. Mr. Lee excused himself on the same ground, and died, indeed, in a short time."[20] Jefferson, Wythe, and Pendleton therefore apportioned the work among themselves. It was ironic that as they set to work in earnest, Jefferson, who had been the pupil of one and the protégé of the other, was actually as well as technically chief of the triumvirate.

Many meetings of the three would be held in Williamsburg to bring their collective judgments to bear on difficult points. But they would spend much time alone on their separate parts of the labor. Jefferson would work with the English statutes from earliest times into the reign of Henry VIII, plus most of the work originally assigned Mason and Lee, including matters of slavery and criminal law. Pendleton would deal with both English statutes of later date and Virginia Acts of Assembly. The versatile Wythe would work with a number of matters outside the provinces of his colleagues.[21]

Some questions were settled before the conferees left Fredericksburg. The death penalty would be reserved for "Treason and Murder (and no other Crime)." Manslaughter would be punished by forfeiture and labor. Suicide was not to incur forfeiture but to be "considered as a disease."[22] The bodies of those executed for petty treason or parricide would be "delivered over to surgeons to be anatomized." This last proposal may have had its inspiration in Jefferson's spirit of scientific inquiry.

A spirit of humanity informed such proposals as the repeal of "the Act which makes concealment by the mother of the death of her bastard child amount to evidence of her having murdered it." In the same category was the provision that protection or comfort of the accused by a parent, child, or wife not be "deemed misprision or treason." Apparently, since the word "wife" rather than "spouse" was used, the committee did not consider the possibility that a woman might commit treason and be protected by her husband.

Another enlightened proposal on which the committee agreed and which Jefferson enthusiastically championed was that male and female descendants should share equally in the division of intestate estates.

At variance with the humane and progressive spirit of most of the changes was the proposal that bestiality, sodomy, and rape be punished by castration. Apparently before assigning so severe a punishment for bestiality, the committee considered Jefferson's argument that public ridicule would almost always curb any urge toward intercourse with four-footed mates but evidently this deterrent was finally regarded as insufficient. Perhaps one or two conferees gave in on this point to gain another. Castration for rape seemed to be more in accord with the ancient principle of *lex talionis*, under which an injury to the body of a victim would be repaid by a legally imposed injury to a comparable portion of the aggressor's anatomy. Or it might be analogous to an ancient provision that in cases of assault the offending member, whether hand, foot, or otherwise, be sacrificed. In any event, as far back as the time of Alfred's Law in ninth-century England, castration as a punishment for rape was reserved for those cases in which a slave assaulted a slave, and then only because a slave would be unable to make financial compensation to the injured party. Still, Jefferson and his associates would probably have argued that castration was not only a perfect safeguard against recidivism but also a more humane punishment than execution.

Jefferson's committee did not bring forth any integrated code of law instantly identifiable and in this respect comparable to the codes of Hammurabi, Justinian, Alfred, and Napoleon. Such a feat would have been impossible even if the committee had consisted of Moses, Solon, and Blackstone. In the first place, the Virginians were operating within a legislative framework and could not, in the fashion of old-time monarchs, create a body of law by fiat. Secondly, they were acting for a people more sophisticated in self-government than the Babylonians, the subjects of the Byzantine Empire, the Anglo-Saxons, or even the future subjects of Napoleon.

The great accomplishment of Jefferson and his committee was to initiate and then to guide, at first together and later severally and with the aid of newcomers to government, a series of legal reforms great and small all tending to the enlargement of individual freedom and opportunity. Whether or not Jefferson was a great democrat, he was certainly a great civil libertarian. His spirit and his scholarship inform hundreds of Virginia statutes, some of which were enacted into law long after his own service as a legislator. Many of these individual measures are now of interest only to the legal antiquarian. They are as obscured by the mists of history as the foothills of the Blue Ridge by October's blue veils. But rising majestically into view are certain peaks that soar into the universal empyrean. Among these are Jefferson's Statute for Religious Freedom which in his lifetime was translated into foreign languages and came to be recognized as one of the great documents of human liberty. Another was his plan "for the more general diffusion of knowledge," which was not enacted in his lifetime and was never enacted in precisely the terms he advocated, but which proved the most seminal proposal in the history of American public education.

Considered radical and democratic in Jefferson's time, his plan seems conservative and elitist to many people in our own. The daughters as well as the sons of all citizens would have the opportunity to learn reading, writing, and arithmetic for three years without charge in the lowest level of public schools. These institutions he called "hundred" schools, reaching back to 1619 for the term used to designate legislative districts in Virginia and in turn derived from the Anglo-Saxon. (Indeed, the whole concept of free education for boys and girls of even the humble classes dated back to Alfred, but the ninth-century king's schools for "all the free-born youth now in England who have the ability"[23] had disappeared at the time of the Norman Conquest if not before.)

Jefferson's scheme, beyond primary grades, would not affect the education of the financially well-off. As before, they would be able to go as far academically as their families' resources and their own abilities could carry them. But for some of the less fortunate his plan could make a world of difference. At the second level would be the grammar schools, one for each ten of the hundred schools. Private pupils whose parents could afford the board and tuition might attend on a paying basis. But there would also be a limited number of State scholarships. From the children of the poor attending the ten primary schools in a grammar school district, an appointed educational administrator would select to be educated at public expense one boy "of the best and most promising genius and disposition." A twentieth-century American marvels that the opportunity to go beyond the third grade should have been granted to only one boy, and never a girl, from each group of ten primary schools. But many of Jefferson's contemporaries criticized his "optimistic" assumption that the children of the poor, except in the rarest instances, could pursue education profitably beyond the three "R's."

After one year in grammar school the least promising third of the scholarship holders, or "foundationers," would be dropped. At the end of the second year, free education would end for all except one foundationer adjudged "best in genius and disposition." He would be educated at public expense for four more years. From those completing the extra four years there would be chosen at two-year intervals and from each county a single student "of the best learning and most hopeful genius and disposition, who shall be authorized...to proceed to William and Mary College; there to be educated, boarded, and clothed, three years." The whole scheme might more readily be seen as a liberal reform if Jefferson had not observed, "By this means twenty of the best geniuses will be raked from the rubbish annually, and be instructed at the public expense, so far as the grammar schools go."[24]

The choice of the word "rubbish" to describe the intellectually inept seems strange for Jefferson, who ordinarily was particularly sensitive to human feelings, had had a retarded sister, and often insisted that he could learn something from anybody. But there is the mitigating circumstance that the term was not a reflection of class prejudice. Jefferson freely admitted that there were "cyphers of the aristocracy" and argued that nature had sown genius among the poor and humble as well as the rich and well-born.

He explained:

> The ultimate result of the whole scheme of education would be the teaching all children of the state reading, writing, and common arithmetic: turning out ten annually of superior genius, well taught in Greek, Latin, geography, and the higher branches of arithmetic: turning out ten others annually, of still superior parts, who, to those branches of learning, shall have added such of the sciences as their genius shall have led them to: the furnishing to the wealthier part of the people convenient schools, at which their children may be educated, at their own expense.—The general objects of this law are to provide an education adapted to the years, to the capacity, and the condition of every one, and directed to their freedom and happiness.[25]

In calling for instruction in Greek and Latin as early as the fourth year of school, Jefferson was not departing from the system prevailing in his day. Indeed, the Kingswood School near Bristol, England, in 1768 included in the first year not only the study of Latin and Greek grammar but also the reading of Caesar, Virgil, and the Greek Testament.[26]

But he did depart from custom in the curriculum for the first three years: "Instead. . . of putting the Bible and Testament into the hands of the children at an age when their judgements are not sufficiently matured for religious enquiries, their memories may here be stored with the most useful facts from Grecian, Roman, European and American history. The first elements of morality too may be instilled into their minds; such as, when further developed as their judgements advance in strength, may teach them how to work out their own greatest happiness, by showing them that it does not depend on the condition of life in which chance has placed them, but is always the result of a good conscience, good health, occupation, and freedom in all just pursuits."[27]

Jefferson noted:

> The learning of Greek and Latin, I am told, is going into disuse in Europe. I know not what their manners and occupations may call for: but it would be very ill-judged in us to follow their example in this instance. There is a certain period of life, say from eight to fifteen or sixteen years of age, when the mind, like the body, is not yet firm enough for laborious and close operations. If applied to such, it falls an early victim to premature exertion; exhibiting indeed at first, in these young and tender subjects, the flattering appearance of their being men while they are yet children, but ending in reducing them to be children when they should be men. The memory is then most susceptible and tenacious of impressions; and the learning of languages being chiefly a work of memory, it seems precisely fitted to the powers of this period, which is long enough too for acquiring the most useful languages ancient and modern.[28]

Modern research confirms the theory that a foreign language is best learned in the early years.

Jefferson added:

I do not pretend that language is science. It is only an instrument for the attainment of science. But that time is not lost which is employed in providing tools for future operation: more especially as in this case the books put into the hands of the youth for this purpose may be such as will at the same time impress their minds with useful facts and good principles.[29]

He expressed special concern for the talents of intelligent poor children whose abilities would "perish without use if not sought for and cultivated."[30]

Finally, he argued:

But of all the views of this law none is more important, none more legitimate, than that of rendering the people the safe, as they are the ultimate, guardians of their own liberty. For this purpose the reading in the first stage, where they will receive their whole education, is proposed, as has been said, to be chiefly historical. History by apprising them of the past will enable them to judge of the future; it will avail them of the experience of other times and other nations; it will qualify them as judges of the actions and designs of men; it will enable them to know ambition under every disguise it may assume; and knowing it, to defeat its views. In every government on earth is some trace of human weakness, some germ of corruption and degeneracy, which cunning will discover, and wickedness insensibly open, cultivate, and improve. Every government degenerates when trusted to the rulers of the people alone. The people themselves therefore are its only safe depositories. And to render even them safe their minds must be improved to a certain degree. This indeed is not all that is necessary, though it be essentially necessary.

If the College of William and Mary was to be the capstone of education in Virginia, it too must be reformed. Jefferson proposed changes deemed radical in both America and Europe. He moved to eliminate the two chairs of divinity and to add chairs of law, medicine, history, and—some thought this the height of absurdity—*modern* languages.

Jefferson's plan for the diffusion of knowledge included also the establishment of a state library in Richmond with a collection of maps as well as books for public use. Moreover, the public library would be combined with an art gallery of paintings and statues.[31] To Jefferson's scheme for the diffusion of knowledge—from the primary schools, through the college and including the library and gallery—the reply of his fellow legislators was, "The state cannot afford it." The movement toward advanced public education proceeded slowly everywhere. Not until 1936 was Jefferson's idea for a state museum of art realized anywhere in the United States, and then appropriately enough it came in his own native Virginia.[32]

Jefferson's habit of pressing for things that his countrymen were not ready for and persistently reminding them of responsibilities they were not prepared to acknowledge might have been expected to make him extremely unpopular. There were those whom he irritated. Landon Carter, an intellectual great planter of the Northern Neck, wrote to George Washington: "Was any man in your camp to say who is the greatest drunkard and most pernicious to society, he who only drinks at night and is perhaps ashamed of it in the morning, or he who gets drunk...at mid-day..., I dare say the midnight drunkard would be the most to be respected."[33] He concluded that Jefferson must be a midday drunkard. Otherwise, there was no accounting for the proposals he made in broad daylight in public assemblies.

But Carter was very much an exception in his enmity to the tall, red-haired delegate from Albemarle. Though the Assembly had divided into two bitterly contesting factions, the conservative side headed by Benjamin Harrison and the liberal led by Richard Henry Lee, both groups continued to seek Jefferson's friendship and advice. He worked in harmony on committees with representatives of both. He had a remarkable gift for pressing his views in the face of opposition without losing either respect or friendship. Lee, writing to him from Philadelphia, confided his determination not to be driven from office by conservative enemies in Virginia, thanked Jefferson for "the only satisfactory account" of the proceedings of the Assembly, and signed himself "your affectionate friend."[34] Edmund Pendleton, one of the staunchest conservatives, in the same letter in which he disagreed with Jefferson on certain legal reforms, referred to his intertwined feelings of regard for his friend and his country, and said: "You hurt those feelings when you sometimes speak of retiring. You are too young to ask that happy quietus from the public, and should at least postpone it 'til you have taught the rising generation the forms as well as the substantial principles of legislation."[35] When a bill introduced by Jefferson rotated Lee out of his post in Philadelphia, the ousted congressman fumed at Harrison for his part in the affair but remained on the best of terms with the gentleman from Albemarle.[36]

Jefferson did not try to be all things to all people. By his writings and by his conversation he made his controversial views well known. But the animated expression of his convictions was consistently tempered by his courtesy and by respect for his opponents. There was no need for him to dissemble to find common ground with both camps. He was conservative in his love of tradition and liberal in his enthusiasm for experiment. Above all he was believed to be incorruptible, by the temptations of fame and power as well as those of wealth.

Public affairs did not completely consume Jefferson's time and thoughts in 1777, 1778, and 1779. On May 28, 1777, after a long period of anxiety about Patty's health, a son was born to the Jeffersons. Added to the other joys of fatherhood was the prospect of passing on the family name to a future master of Monticello. But the child died on June 14. Though Jefferson labored long and hard over revision of the laws, he took a leave of absence from the House of Delegates, because of responsibilities and anxieties that held him at home. Despite his absences, he was reelected to the House in April 1778 and attended from May 12 to June 1. This time he was nominated for speaker of the House but lost, 51 to 23, to Benjamin Harrison.

Any possible eclipse of political fortunes seemed overshadowed in his consciousness by the eclipse of the sun which he observed from his mountaintop on June 24 with the aid of a recently purchased theodolite. Once again, too, he was absorbed in the building of his home, contracting for three stone columns for a portico and ordering one hundred thousand red bricks, more than had already gone into the structure.

Jefferson was evolving an architectural style of his own, a version of the Palladian that dotted Europe from Italy to England but distinguished from the original by bold patterns of beige stone contrasting with red brick that presented a far livelier appearance than the uniformly colored stone monuments of the continent.

He was adding to his family as well as his house. A third daughter, Mary (who soon came to be called Polly) was born August 1, 1778.

In November Jefferson returned to the House of Delegates, but only reluctantly. On several occasions during the fall session he was ordered taken into custody by the sergeant-at-arms to compel his attendance. At least twice he had to pay fines to secure his release.[37] How can we explain such seeming laxity on the part of one normally so conscientious as Jefferson and so hardworking? Was he ill at times but willing to be thought negligent rather than admit a constitutional frailty? Were there domestic problems that he considered none of the public's business? Maybe Jefferson, in his independent way, was confident that he was doing his duty and considered appearance secondary. More than any of his colleagues, he was a legislator who did his homework, but it was quite literally *home*work. Toiling away under his own roof, he was preparing judicial reforms whose significance would dwarf the accomplishments of his colleagues.

The extent of his labors was suspected by a few colleagues in the House, but some of his former associates in Philadelphia were beginning to regard him as self-indulgent. John Adams, with whom he had begun a spirited correspondence, wrote: "Your country is not yet quite secure enough to assure your retreat to the delights of domestic life."[38] Richard Henry Lee did not soften the asperity of his message: "It will not perhaps be disagreeable to you in your retirement sometimes to hear the events of war, and how in other respects we proceed in the arduous business we are engaged in."[39]

Some of the news must have been disturbing to Jefferson in his retirement. It is not surprising that Washington, who had his troubles with Congress and whose ill-supplied troops left bloody footprints in the snows of Valley Forge the horrible winter of 1777-78, should have asked impatiently, "Where is. . .Jefferson?" But Jefferson was privy to certain important war measures that were hidden from all his friends in Philadelphia and nearly all in Virginia. Governor Patrick Henry had authorized George Rogers Clark to raise seven companies of fifty men each and attack the British fort of Kaskaskia in the Illinois country. So great was the necessity for secrecy that the plan was confided to only three legislators—Wythe, Mason, and Jefferson—who agreed that if the expedition proved successful they would press in the Assembly for a reward of three hundred acres of land to each participant.[40]

This was the start of the heroic campaign in which Clark, by a rare combination of military sagacity, diplomatic skill, and dogged endurance, won the Northwest Territory for the United States. Whether Jefferson, who was not one of Henry's cronies, was one of only three confidants chosen by the Governor in this matter or whether Clark enlisted Jefferson's aid in convincing the Governor, the young statesman's admission to the secret council was a tribute not only to his trustworthiness but also to his influence in the legislature. Jefferson's colleagues might occasionally compel his participation in their deliberations, but nobody was trying to oust him.

Retrospectively, John Adams said that the contest for men's minds had been a more important part of the Revolution than the struggle on the battlefields. Jefferson concentrated on the herculean task of legal reform with an intensity that seemed to render him oblivious to the enemy fleets that patrolled Virginia's vulnerable, river-corridored, ill-defended coasts. In his assiduous mining of precedents while the war raged around him, he reminds us of Henry Timrod's striking image:

> As men who labor in that mine
> Of Cornwall, hollowed out beneath the bed
> Of ocean, when a storm rolls overhead,
> Hear the dull booming of the world of brine
> Above them, and a mighty muffled roar
> Of winds and waters, yet toil calmly on,
> And split the rock, and pile the massive ore,
> Or carve a niche, or shape the archèd roof....[41]

The war came to Jefferson in January 1779. Enemy troops entered Albemarle County, albeit as conquered rather than conquerors. Some four thousand British and Hessian soldiers taken prisoner in Burgoyne's surrender at Saratoga, October 1777, had been quartered in Massachusetts. But the rigorous winters and the scarcity of food in the area caused the Congress to order their removal to Virginia. Colonel John Harvie, a member of the Congress, offered as a campsite his land on Ivy Creek, about four miles west of Charlottesville. Thus, after a march of 628 miles over frozen roads, the prisoners arrived in Albemarle County shortly after New Year's Day.[42] Jefferson, as county lieutenant, and doubtless with a great deal of personal curiosity, visited the campsite. A good hater when dealing with the enemy on paper, he was immediately moved to compassion when he saw actual human beings shivering in the cold rain outside unfinished barracks. He was revolted at the sight of the decayed food thrust before them. At once he began to become acquainted with individuals and to enlist aid in improving their living conditions. He thought Major General William Phillips, the chief British officer, insufferably arrogant, and matched that gentleman's formal politeness with his own. But he soon made friends with the highest ranking Hessian, Major General Baron Frederick Adolphus Riedesel.

About a month after the prisoners arrived, the baron was joined by his wife and three children and they all moved into the home of Mazzei, who had sailed to Europe as an agent for Virginia. The baroness proved to be a statuesque Teutonic beauty whom Jefferson found attractive although he generally seems to have preferred slender elegance. Virginia ladies, accustomed to riding sidesaddle with slippered feet dangling, were amazed at the apparition of this Valkyrie riding booted and spurred over the hills of Albemarle.[43]

Soon the Riedesels were frequent visitors at Monticello, along with two other Hessians, Captain Baron von Geismar and Jean Louis de Unger. The baroness sang Italian airs, accompanied on the violin by Captain Geismar. Jefferson, playing the violoncello, sometimes joined Geismar in a string duet. And Jefferson and Unger enjoyed philosophical discussions. To Jefferson these informal parties at Monticello must have been reminiscent of the feasts of music and philosophy he had enjoyed at the Governor's Palace in Fauquier's administration. In August 1777 Jefferson had written Franklin, then in Paris: "I wish my domestic situation had rendered it possible for me to have joined you in the very honorable charge confided to you. Residence in a polite court, society with literati of the first order, a just cause, and approving God will add length to a life for which all men pray and none more than your most obedient and humble servant."[44] Jefferson had not been able to go to Europe. But the tides of war, against all probability, had deposited a bit of Europe on a hillside in his native Albemarle, and he was happily taking advantage of the situation.

When in March there was talk of removing the prisoners from the Charlottesville area, they were unhappy at the prospect and Jefferson protested to Governor Henry. The British and Hessians, he said, were spending $30,000 a week to "great and local advantage." As for the welfare of the prisoners themselves, "Of 4,000 people it would be expected according to ordinary calculations that one should die every day. Yet in the space of nearly 3 months there have been but 4 deaths among them." These people were no threat to the American cause and were contentedly tending their gardens. "Does not every sentiment of humanity revolt against the proposition of stripping them of all this and removing them into new situations . . .?"[45] Jefferson also appeared in their behalf before the Council of State. The prisoners were permitted to remain.

In April Jefferson was reelected to the House of Delegates. He was on hand when the session commenced May 3. This session would be a vital one. In June, he would report with Wythe and Pendleton the proposed Revisal of the Laws of Virginia to which he had sacrificed so much candle wax. This legislative bundle would include "the Bills for Proportioning Crimes and Punishments, for the More General Diffusion of Knowledge, for Amending the Constitution of the College of William and Mary, and for Establishing Religious Freedom." The way must be prepared.

There was another reason, too, for Jefferson to be on hand early. He was to be placed in nomination for the office of Governor. Having served three terms, Henry was ineligible to succeed himself. Jefferson had not sought the office and he still had qualms about it. Any enthusiasm he might have mustered was dampened by the fact that nomination would place him in rivalry with his old friend John Page whose name had also been advanced, along with that of General Thomas Nelson, a distinguished soldier. But if there were those determined to nominate Jefferson, he was not disposed to acquiesce easily in defeat. (When he had been reelected to the Congress in defiance of his expressed wishes, he had brooded over the narrowness of his margin of victory.) John Page would be formidable competition; besides being President of the Council and Lieutenant Governor, he was one of the most popular men in Virginia. And General Nelson's military record would be a powerful asset in seeking to become a wartime Governor.

When the two houses of the General Assembly balloted in joint session on June 1, the vote was Jefferson, 55; Page, 38; Nelson, 32.[46] Though Jefferson led he was eight votes short of a majority. Before the second ballot, Nelson's name was withdrawn, and it became apparent that many of his supporters were shifting to Page. Tension gripped the Assembly as the second ballot began. The final vote was Jefferson, 67; Page, 61.[47]

Jefferson could not have failed to notice Page's absence from the crowd of well-wishers surrounding him. He must therefore have been pleased the next day when he received a note from his old friend:

I would have waited on you to congratulate you on your Appointment yesterday had I not been under an Engagement to return Home with Mazzei. I attended at your Lodgings today as soon as our Board adjourned, but you were not at Home. I am unhappily obliged to be at Gloster Court tomorrow, and therefore think it proper, notwithstanding our Intimacy and Friendship, to inform you of this; lest till I can have the Pleasure of conversing freely with you, you might be induced to suspect that I am influenced by some low dirty feelings and avoid seeing you to conceal that Embarrassment which might be the Result of them. I can assure you However that I have such Confidence in your good Opinion of my Heart that were it not for the World who may put a wrong Construction on my Conduct I should scarcely trouble you with this Apology.[48]

Jefferson replied:

It had given me much pain that the zeal of our respective friends should ever have placed you and me in the situation of competitors. I was comforted however with the reflection that it was their competition, not ours, and that the difference of the numbers which decided between us, was too insignificant to give you a pain or me a pleasure (had) our dispositions towards each other been such as to have admitted those sensations. I know you too well to need an apology for any thing you do, and hope you will for ever be assured of this; and as to the con- structions of the world, they would only have added one to (the many sig)ns for which they are to go to the devil. As this is the first, so I hope it will be the last instance of ceremony between us.[49]

Old friendships secure and new duties awaiting him, Jefferson, who at times had seemed unaware of the war raging around him, became the wartime leader of the most populous American state.

IX

HORSEBACK GOVERNOR

S VIRGINIA'S new Governor, Jefferson found himself in familiar physical surroundings. Undoubtedly, in his student days when he was so frequently a guest of Governor Fauquier, he did not foresee that the Palace would one day be his home. It was then the official residence of the royal governor and no native Virginian had been appointed to that office except Thomas Lee, who had died in 1750 before he could enter upon his duties.[1] But however strange it might seem to be the occupant of this particular mansion, there was nothing strange to him in its design and appointments. Its interior had been altered significantly since Fauquier had lived there, but Jefferson himself was apparently the author of the changes. Architectural sketches by him show that he redesigned the foyer, adding a corner fireplace and a corner closet to transform the room into a demi-octagon like the salon of Monticello. Precisely when Jefferson executed this and other changes in design is not known. It might have been in the administration of the colony's last royal Governor, Lord Dunmore, for whom he sketched an addition to the College of William and Mary, or during the terms of the first Governor of the Commonwealth, Patrick Henry, who found the official residence less liveable than imposing.[2] Jefferson, largely through the beauty of Monticello, had acquired an architectural reputation that brought requests from private as well as official sources.

But however much Jefferson was at home in the physical structure of the Governor's Palace, he definitely was not comfortable in the office itself. Barely more than two weeks after his election, he thanked Richard Henry Lee for his congratulations but added: "In a virtuous government, and more especially in times like these, public offices are what they should be, burthens to those appointed to them which it would be wrong to decline, though foreseen to bring with them intense labor and great private loss."[3]

He showed that he was not just dealing in conventional generalities when in the same letter he said:

It is a cruel thought that when we feel ourselves standing on the firmest ground in every respect, the cursed arts of our secret enemies, combining with other causes, should effect, by depreciating our money, what the open arms of a powerful enemy could not. What is to be done? Taxation is become of no account, for it is foreseen that notwithstanding its increased amount there will still be a greater deficiency than ever. I own I see no assured hope but in peace or a plentiful loan of hard money.

To whom did Jefferson refer as "secret enemies"? The speculators about whom Lee complained? Or the legislators who kept printing more and more paper money as a solution to the problem of inflation? Jefferson deplored the practice, but he was powerless to do anything about it. He was also powerless to collect the new taxes—a poll tax, taxes on slaves, carriages, liquors, imports, and retail stocks—which the Assembly sought to impose on a people who had gone to war over taxation.

Before the end of the month Jefferson was confiding even to Major General William Phillips, highest-ranking British officer interned in Albemarle: "The hour of private retirement, to which I am drawn by my nature with a propensity almost irresistible, will be the most welcome of my life."[4] As the leader of a rebel commonwealth, Jefferson faced some of the same problems that would vex governors of Southern states in the Civil War. A people who had seceded from a government that they believed tyrannical were so jealous of their individualism and so suspicious of all authority that they could not be led to cooperate adequately with a government lacking the appeal of ancient ties and enduring custom. The problem was compounded by a state constitution that made the legislature the center of power. Even much of the daily administration became government by committee because the Assembly had created for the Governor a Council of State, a body theoretically advisory but actually supervisory. Administration was further hobbled by a Board of War and a Board of Trade owing their appointments to the Assembly and subordinate to the Council of State as well as to the Governor. Creation of these two boards had been recommended by Jefferson's Committee for the Revisal of the Laws of Virginia. As an architect altering the political structure he had not provided so well for his comfort as a future Governor as when he had planned the remodeling of the palace.

The Congress had levied assessments for its operations and for maintenance of the Continental Army that would have strained Virginia's finances even without the problem of supplying shoes, clothing, tents, arms, and munitions to its own militia. Learning that the financial crisis was equally severe in other states brought no cheer to Jefferson. At a time when so much depended upon voluntary exertions, citizens were inclined to rest on their oars. Hadn't Burgoyne surrendered? And wasn't France now at the side of America with her wealth, her armies, and her fleets?

Some Americans, Virginians included, were beginning to feel that the Congress was almost as much their enemy as England. Rumor had it that Spain was prepared to join with France in support of the United States if the new republic would cede its claim to Florida and control of the Mississippi. But the leaders of Congress reportedly had not accepted the offer, so antagonizing the French minister that he was preparing to return to Paris. The report contained just enough plausibility, with a little genuine truth, to persuade even the sophisticated. Governor Jefferson himself, finding "a pretty general opinion prevailing that peace and the independence of the thirteen states are now within our power," talked of ignoring Congress and restoring lines of communication through the old Committees of Correspondence so that the states might negotiate directly with the French minister.[5] He realized that Spanish control of the Mississippi might eventually necessitate a war between the American states and Spain but, he argued, "It would surely be better to carry on a ten years war some time hence than to continue the present an unnecessary moment."[6]

Despite his irritation Jefferson was prudent enough to await word from some of Virginia's delegates to Congress before taking drastic action, believing that they "would think no obligations of secrecy under which they may have been laid sufficient to restrain them from informing their constituents of any proceedings which may involve the fate of their freedom and independence."[7]

The Governor showed similar restraint in appraising the conduct of the British who, just before he assumed office, had raided the Hampton Roads area. An expedition dispatched from New York under Admiral Sir George Collier had sent ashore a landing force that captured Fort Nelson on the Elizabeth River and occupied Portsmouth with its vital shipyard. A British raiding party dispatched from Portsmouth had captured Suffolk, Virginia's chief depot of military supplies. With most of the local patriots serving elsewhere, southeastern Virginia had been practically helpless as the invaders sacked, looted, and plundered.

The immediate crisis was now past. Jefferson had called out the militia and temporarily held back two thousand Virginia recruits headed for the Continental Army. But Collier had withdrawn from Virginia and the recruits had been sent to South Carolina where the national need was greater. Now, as Jefferson explained in the same letter to William Fleming in which he discussed the rumor about Congress blocking the peace, he had to determine amid all the emotions of war exactly what had happened in Hampton Roads: "Some resolutions of Congress came to hand yesterday desiring an authentic state[ment] to be sent them of the cruelties said to have been committed by the enemy during their late invasion. . . . Though so near the scene where these barbarities are said to have been committed I am not able yet to decide within myself whether there were such or not. The testimony on both sides is such as if heard separately could not admit a moment's suspension of our faith."[8]

In another matter of alleged British barbarities Jefferson was not nearly so objective. George Rogers Clark's expedition in the Northwest Territory had exceeded all reasonable expectations. After an incredible two-hundred mile march, part of it through shoulder-high flood waters, Clark had employed a daring ruse and clever diplomacy to obtain the surrender of Lieutenant Colonel Hamilton and the British garrison at Vincennes. Virginians now had won control of the Illinois country and shortly organized it as a new county. News of the victory gladdened the beginning of Jefferson's administration. The captured colonel, preceded by his reputation as "Henry Hamilton, the Hairbuyer," eventually arrived in Williamsburg with two aides. All three officers were in chains. Ordinarily, by the prevailing rules of civilized warfare, these officers would have been paroled within Williamsburg and, pending eventual exchange, would have been tendered the same courtesies enjoyed by the Saratoga prisoners interned in Albemarle. But Hamilton reportedly had incited the Indians to brutal attacks on white settlers and had offered bounties for American scalps. At this distance from events it is virtually impossible to determine the justice of the charges. At least one scholar[9] has concluded that the British officer was a much maligned, "brave and high-minded soldier" while others have tended to echo the original charges. In any event, Clark believed the worst reports of him, and so did Jefferson and the Council of State.

General William Phillips, who in his internment in Albemarle had benefited from

Jefferson's courtesy and kindness, sought the release from irons of his fellow officer. The communication to the Governor and Council was enclosed in a letter from one of Jefferson's Albemarle neighbors, Theodorick Bland. Jefferson explained that the Council was pained to hesitate "on my request from General Phillips whose polite conduct has disposed them to every indulgence consistent with the duties of their appointment. The indiscriminate murder of men, women and children with the usual circumstances of barbarity practiced by the Indian savages was the particular task of. . . Hamilton's employment, and if anything could have aggravated the acceptance of such an office and have made him personally answerable in a high degree it was that eager spirit with which he is said to have executed it and which if the representations before the Council are to be credited seems to have shown that his own feelings and disposition were in union with his employment."[10]

Bland and Jefferson continued to correspond on the subject, Bland's next letter being an eccentric one including another request: "Having been informed that since your Excellency's appointment to the government of this Commonwealth your residence will be chiefly if not entirely at the seat of government, you will pardon me if (tempted by the perpetual view of your delightful seat from my lowly and I may say dirty cottage) I should venture to ask a preference should you be disposed to permit any other than your family to occupy it."[11]

Meanwhile, the Council of State officially declared itself "called on by that justice which we owe to those who are fighting the battles of their country, to deal out at length miseries to their enemies, measure for measure, and to distress the feelings of mankind by exhibiting to them spectacles of severe retaliation where we had long and vainly endeavored to introduce an emulation in kindness. . . ."[12] Accordingly, Hamilton and his two aides were ordered "put into irons, confined in the dungeon of the public jail, debarred the use of pen, ink, and paper, and excluded all converse except with their keeper." Jefferson did not merely acquiesce. In his next letter to Bland, he said, "I enclose you the reasons which have induced the Council to [act] with such rigor with. . . Hamilton and the others there. It is impossible for any generous man to disapprove his sentence."[13]

Jefferson and the Council were far from alone in their attitude. The Governor's report to the Congress brought from Richard Henry Lee the comment: "The reasons assigned for Hamilton's treatment are strongly and pointedly set forth. His fate is well merited."[14] Jefferson's report to Washington, saying, "It will add much to our satisfaction to know it meets with your approbation," brought the general's assurance that he "most fully authorize[d] the Treatment decreed."[15]

Then Phillips appealed on a point of law. Wasn't the treatment accorded Hamilton outlawed by the officer's formal capitulation? Hamilton, Lieutenant Governor of Detroit as well as an officer of His Majesty's forces, had surrendered in reliance on the generosity of his enemies. Jefferson transmitted these arguments to Washington and the Congress, seizing on the word "generosity" to make his own argument: "Generosity, on a large and comprehensive scale, seems to dictate the making a signal example of this gentleman."[16] The British must be taught better conduct. Under these circumstances harsh treatment of Hamilton and his aides became "an act of benevolence."

Finally Washington, foreseeing a succession of reprisals and counter reprisals, advised the Governor that while Hamilton might properly be confined to a room, he probably should not be kept in irons. Jefferson was in Albemarle when the message from Washington arrived, and the Council of State lost no time in removing the shackles. Upon Jefferson's return he agreed with the Council that the three prisoners should be paroled within limits. But the Britishers balked at a parole restriction forbidding them to say anything against the United States. Jefferson then ordered them back to jail until they changed their minds. Under the circumstances, he maintained, their confinement was voluntary. Washington in the autumn suggested that compromise might be discreet. Jefferson, in a letter of October 8, replied, "In every event I shall resign myself to the hard necessity under which I shall act."[17]

Not until a year later was the Hamilton affair settled when Jefferson, after a stubborn insistence that the British officer was too dangerous to be at large, yielded to Washington's pleas that he be exchanged as part of a plan that would benefit Virginians imprisoned on Long Island. But first Hamilton had to sign a parole including the statement at which he had balked.

One can say with Dumas Malone, "There was no trace of sentimental weakness here; in this matter he [Jefferson] was hard as iron."[18] One can even argue that, in calling for reprisals for British treatment of American prisoners, Jefferson was commendably consistent with his earlier position as a member of the Congress. But it is hard to deny the validity of Nathan Schachner's argument that the vein of iron would "have been more appropriate in connection with other matters relating to the governorship."[19]

Certainly Jefferson, as Governor of a hard-pressed Commonwealth already invaded by the enemy, spent an unconscionable amount of time and energy in matters relating to one captured lieutenant colonel. Washington was as strong-willed as Jefferson, but in his prime he did not let personal emotion distort his perspective in great matters. The position taken by Jefferson in the Hamilton affair was not materially different from that assumed initially by Washington himself and virtually all the leaders of the Virginia Assembly and the Continental Congress. It was his adamant refusal to depart from that position—even though compelling reasons for a reassessment mounted on every side—that set Jefferson apart from his colleagues. The differences between will and wilfulness can be scarcely distinguishable, less a matter of inherent quality than of the nature of the adversary and the milieu. As in the examples of Jefferson Davis and Woodrow Wilson, hardheadedness can be a source of both strength and weakness in a leader. The difference between heroic determination and plain pigheadedness is often in the eye of the beholder.

Though the Council of State as a whole continued to advise Jefferson and, as in striking the shackles from Colonel Hamilton, even to act for him in his absence, three members soon came to exercise more influence on his decisions than the rest of their colleagues put together. One of these, as might be expected, was John Page, who had been his personal friend longer than anyone else in public life. Another was John Walker, his Albemarle neighbor. The third was James Madison,[20] a young man with whom Jefferson had barely been acquainted not long before.

Though evidently the least prepossessing of the three, Madison soon became Jefferson's chief advisor. Then twenty-seven years old, not more than an inch or two above five feet in height, weighing about a hundred pounds, Madison had a pleasant face distinguished by a high, balding forehead which he tried to cover in part by pulling a peak of hair down in the middle. Obviously he had qualifications that overcame his lack of presence. He had served on the Orange County Committee of Safety, of which his father had been chairman, and had been elected in 1776 to the Virginia Constitutional Convention. His father's prominence might have helped him that far up the ladder, but in the convention his own talents quickly made him one of the most prominent young members. His reputation had been augmented by a term in the House of Delegates. He had failed of reelection, but for a reason with which Jefferson could sympathize. He had refused to follow the custom of treating the electorate to rum and punch. In November 1777, however, his former colleagues had attested their confidence by electing him to the Council of State.

The Governor soon learned why this quiet little man was so highly esteemed. When any question of state arose he seemed to be familiar with the principal legal precedents and could place each in its specific historical context. His impromptu explanations were better organized and more precisely worded than the most carefully prepared exegeses of most of his able contemporaries. He delivered his opinions in totally humorless fashion, with solemn dignity but not a trace of pomposity. Such was the clarity of his dispassionate expression that he seemed the very embodiment of reason.

But Madison had still more surprises for Jefferson. When the Governor saw him socially, as he did with increasing frequency, he discovered one of the wittiest conversationalists he had ever known. A flexible little smile playing around the corners of the gentle mouth was the signal for a dexterous riposte, not delivered in malice but for the sheer fun of fencing. When Jefferson and Madison were together, the eloquent flow of anecdote, punctuated by apt allusions to history and to modern and classical literature, provided a rich feast for anyone intellectually equipped to appreciate it.

The better acquainted he became with Madison, the more Jefferson discovered in common with him. He was a graduate of the College of New Jersey, now Princeton University, where he had been introduced to the Scottish Enlightenment as Jefferson had at William and Mary. Plagued by illness and fascinated by philosophy and theology, the twenty-year-old Madison had remained at college a half-year beyond graduation to read in those subjects under the guidance of the president, Dr. John Witherspoon, who was both his Small and his Wythe. Like Jefferson's professor of natural philosophy, Witherspoon was an authentic Scottish product of the Enlightenment. And like Jefferson's old law professor, the Princeton educator was also a statesman (he signed the Declaration of Independence) who was participating with his former student in building a new nation. Like Jefferson, Madison had performed precociously on the public stage despite temptations to withdraw to a life of quiet scholarship.

For five years after leaving Princeton Madison lived in near seclusion on his father's plantation, studying philosophy, theology, and law while he fought an uncertain battle with respiratory illness and nerves. In a time of discouragement he had confided to a friend that he did not know why he was preparing for a profession when he probably would not live to practice it. Now strengthened by horseback riding and apparently more happily oriented philosophically, Madison walked with a bouncy step and in private displayed a humor equally bouncy, in public a marmoreal calm.

The Governor was fortunate in having the advice of Madison as well as other able members of the plantocracy. Incidentally, in 1779 Jacquelin Ambler, who had married the Belinda who had once driven Jefferson to distraction, joined the Council as one of his constitutional advisers. What changes the years had brought! But Jefferson was still being driven to distraction—this time by problems that seemed insoluble despite all the resourcefulness he and his advisers could muster. Feeding Virginia's soldiers seemed to call for another miracle of the loaves and fishes. Unable to increase production of foodstuffs when so much manpower was going into armies, the Governor and Council tried at least to stop the flow of food from the State. Jefferson issued a proclamation placing an embargo on beef, pork, corn, wheat, grain, and flour. But profiteers continued to ship provisions, largely unhindered by policing worthy of the name. Some of Virginia's soldiers were clad in lacy rags. And some had to hope that empty guns would look formidable enough to frighten the enemy.[21]

Some states were ignoring calls from the Continental Congress rather than denude their own defenses. All of them at times put their own threatened people ahead of the national interest. Virginia gave more freely to the nation than most, but in the summer of 1779, when the Commonwealth expected a British invasion, it commandeered for the emergency certain Continental arms arriving within its borders. A heated complaint from Congress provoked from the Governor no apology but a verbal offensive. The arms in question, he said, were Virginia's due. Seven battalions had been raised in Virginia's extremity and these men could not be sent into battle unarmed. "In this situation of things a vessel, loaded with arms, seemed to be guided by the hand of Providence into one of our harbors. They were, it's true, the property of our friends, but of friends indebted to us for those very articles. They were for the common defense, too, and we were a part of the Body to be defended."[22]

At this juncture the year was dying on a darkening landscape. Washington himself had warned that large-scale invasion of Virginia was imminent. Every wind of winter brought the howl of alarums. Now was a time for the Governor to be as bold in ordering preparations as in speaking up to the Congress about the diversion of arms to Virginia's need. But in this crisis Jefferson was concerned with the constitutional niceties that limited the executive. Addressing Benjamin Harrison, Speaker of the Assembly, in his own capacity as Governor and spokesman for the Council, Jefferson wrote: "It is our duty to provide against every event and the Executive are accordingly engaged in concerting proper measures of defense."[23] They desired to summon the militia to defend both banks of the James River, but there were great difficulties. Money was short. And, too, the men would take it ill to be called out in such cold weather, especially if after all there should be no invasion. These considerations, Jefferson wrote, "induce us to refer to the decision of the General Assembly."[24]

Jefferson might as well have said "defer" rather than "refer." Constantly he deferred to the Assembly, making no effort by personal decisiveness to redress the constitutionally enshrined imbalance between the legislative and executive branches.

Washington soon reported that his warning had been premature, but all realized that eventually there would be a sizeable invasion. In May 1780 the Assembly granted to the Governor and Council emergency powers to be exercised for limited periods. These included authority to call out up to twenty thousand men, directing them anywhere in the State or even sending them beyond its borders. The Governor and Council were also authorized to commandeer horses, wagons, boats, tent linens, cattle, and agricultural produce for military purposes, paying fair market value. Suspected troublemakers, in the event of invasion or insurrection, could be removed or imprisoned without due process of law. But if executive action had to be taken by the Governor and Council acting together, a quick executive response to an emergency still seemed unlikely. For more than a month, Jefferson had been unable to obtain a quorum of the Council and in the period from April 7 to May 13 no business was conducted by the executive offices.[25]

On September 8, following two British victories in South Carolina, Cornwallis invaded North Carolina. Conquest of that state would open the road to victory in Virginia, for the Old Dominion could not count on significant aid from the Continental army. A few months before, Washington had reported to Congress "... the country exhausted; the people dispirited; the consequence and reputation of these states in Europe sunk; our enemies deriving new credit, new confidence, new resources."[26] And when he had penned these words of discouragement he had not known that by nightfall two Connecticut regiments would be in armed mutiny. On September 13, amid all these troubles, Jefferson wrote to Richard Henry Lee:

> The application requisite to the duties of the office I hold is so excessive, and the execution of them after all so imperfect, that I have determined to retire from it at the close of the present campaign. I wish a successor to be thought of in time who to sound Whigism can join perseverance in business and an extensive knowledge of the various subjects he must superintend. Such a one may keep us above water even in our present moneyless situation."[27]

Richmond had replaced Williamsburg as the capital of Virginia and the executive mansion was a plain frame house that was a far cry from the elegance of either the Governor's Palace or Monticello. Jefferson had once sponsored legislation to move the government from Williamsburg to some more central location, apparently hoping thereby to diminish the political influence of the great Tidewater river barons. But it was the movement of the war up through the Carolinas toward Virginia that finally gave effective impetus for the change. Now Richmond itself might not be safe from the enemy. Continental Generals Greene, Gates, and Steuben made desperate pleas to Jefferson from their threatened positions in the Carolinas. In answer to one such appeal, Jefferson had offered to Greene militia drawn from four counties, and already encamped on Virginia's southern border. The qualification that he appended in a letter to Steuben did little to encourage in the generals a belief that Virginia's very civilian Governor understood their problems. He would send the men "provided they can be induced to go willingly. The length of their march heretofore and having been some time in service seems to give them a right to be consulted."[28]

Yet an insurrection the following summer in what is now Southwest Virginia led Jefferson to order Colonel William Campbell to "take in hand these Parricides" and to instruct Judge Charles Lynch that "the most vigorous, decisive measures should be continued for seizing everyone on whom probable proof of guilt shall appear."[29] Small offenders should be released if they turned State's evidence, but the leaders and officers should be tried for high treason. Ordinarily, as executive, he shrank from encroachment upon the prerogatives of the legislature, but when his dander was up he could even instruct the judiciary.

When Gates left his post in the field to come to Richmond and appeal to the Governor face to face for more help, Jefferson refused to promise what he did not believe he could deliver and instead told the already agitated officer to "look forward to much difficulty and a perplexed department."[30] The prophecy was fulfilled. Gates was so perplexed when most of the Virginia militia sent to his aid arrived without guns that he informed the Governor: ". . . your Excellency will be necessarily led into an enquiry [into the disappearance of supplies] as it carries exceedingly the appearance of neglect or fraud."[31]

Virginia was not alone in the ineptness of its government. North Carolina, although the war was actually being fought within its borders, seemed to be giving no more aid to the continental cause than Virginia. And Washington was finding Northern citizens unbelievably lax.

Jefferson's problems were larger than those of most Governors. Virginia had given its greatest soldiers, from Washington down, to fight in other states. War raged to both the north and south and generals in the two theaters made rival demands on the Commonwealth's slender and rapidly diminishing resources. The Congress could not agree as to where Virginia's help was most desperately needed. Virginians thought it was most necessary in Virginia itself. Many of her finest troops had helped to defend New England, New Jersey, New York, and Pennsylvania. Some of her best soldiers had been captured far from home when Charleston surrendered. Now Virginia itself seemed about to become the principal battleground of the war.

Jefferson appeared to carry the principles of democracy to ridiculous extremes in dealing with the militia, but he knew better than Steuben the temper of the ordinary Virginia soldiers. They were not like the European peasants that the baron had found obedient from habit. Almost the only discipline they had known in manhood was self-imposed and they were fighting for independence. In the next century their rebel descendants in the Army of Northern Virginia would be electing their own regimental officers and otherwise behaving in most unmilitary fashion on almost every occasion except actual battle, when they proved themselves one of the great armies of history.

An experienced warrior in the Governor's chair, exhibiting in frequent appearances before both soldiers and civilians a rough and ready knowledge culled from camps and bought from battlefields, might have succeeded if the Constitution had given him sufficient power or if he had felt no philosophical compunctions about seizing it. But Jefferson was not such a man and he was not privileged to work in such a context. So what did he do? He tried to make sense of all the demands upon him, but when he could not he turned to things of which he could make sense. And the character of his interests was testimony to his faith that Virginia and the United States would survive the challenge of arms. He was intent on winning the battle for the human mind. On July 26, 1780, when it seemed that Virginia was about to be overrun by the British its Governor had written to James Madison in happy excitement about Wythe's full-fledged school of law at William and Mary: "Our new institution at the College has had a success which has gained it universal applause. Wythe's school is numerous. They hold weekly courts and assemblies in the capitol. The professors join in it, and the young men dispute with elegance, method and learning. This single school, by throwing from time to time new hands, well principled and well informed, into the legislature, will be of infinite value."[32]

And Jefferson saw that the winning of the West would be important to America and that he could make a contribution to this enterprise. He not only approved George

Rogers Clark's plans to build a fort at the confluence of the Mississippi and Ohio Rivers but sent detailed instructions for the project. He at once grasped the significance of a point not only vital to frontier defense but important to protection of the great volumes of commerce that would one day move over these heartland watercourses to the port of New Orleans. He also urged Clark to foster friendship with any Indian tribes not yet committed to war against the United States. At the same time he did not wish Clark to be tempted into inciting Indian attacks against the British: "Notwithstanding their base example we wish not to expose them to the inhumanities of a savage enemy. Let this reproach remain on them, but for ourselves we would not have our national character tarnished with such a practice."[33] And toward the inhabitants of the French villages he urged "a mild conduct" and their introduction to American laws that they might be impressed strongly "with the advantages of a free government." Jefferson was looking confidently above and beyond the smoke of battle to more distant fields of national conquest.

And what did the Governor do when insoluble problems ambushed him from every tangled thicket of red tape and morass of financial depression, and hostile armies continued an almost steady progress toward his capital? What did he do in those dark days when his hopes for the new law school and his plans for winning the West could fill only a portion of the troubled hours? Why, he devoted himself to answering some questions about the resources and institutions of Virginia which the French government had directed to him through Francois, Marquis de Barbé-Marbois, Secretary of Legation in America. Identical questionnaires went to selected citizens of the other states, but apparently Marbois received no more than superficial replies from all but Jefferson. Virginia's Governor plunged into profound research at the end of 1780, and on March 4, 1781, with his State invaded and its government preparing to retreat into the hills on horseback, he took time to apologize to Marbois that he had made only a start on the project but assured him that soon he would be able to begin work in earnest. When Jefferson finished his *Notes on the State of Virginia,* he had produced a full-scale book designed to tell Europeans and Virginians themselves what Virginia, and indeed the United States, was like. He had produced a scientific work enlisting the interest of some of the world's greatest savants, a philosophical and even prophetic treatise on the American dream, and an eloquent classic of American literature.

Meanwhile the fate of the State of Virginia, on which Jefferson was so busily taking notes, was very much in doubt. After the routing of the Continental Army at Camden, South Carolina, on August 16, 1780, Gates galloped toward Virginia with British hoofbeats almost echoing his own. To his appeals for help, Jefferson replied that he would send more men "as fast as they come out of the hospital."[34]

In September Jefferson was warned that as Cornwallis raced northward Sir Henry Clinton was preparing to sail southward, the two great British forces joining in a pincer operation with Virginia as its apparent object.

A few days before the first of these warnings was penned to the Governor, he had written a letter to the Chevalier de la Luzerne, commander of America's French allies in the field, which revealed at once a grasp of strategic possibilities and high statesmanship in the national interest. Though Jefferson suggested that dispatch of the French fleet to Chesapeake Bay might be a significant factor in national defense now that the British armies were preparing to concentrate in Virginia, he emphasized that the anticipated effect on the common fortunes of all the states should be the sole determinant:

> The interest of this state is intimately blended so perfectly the same with that of the others of the confederacy that the most effectual aid it can at any time receive is where the general cause most needs it. Of this you yourself, Congress, and General Washington are so perfect judges that it is not for me to point it out. . . . If their action in the north will have more powerful influence toward establishing our Independence, they ought not to be wished for in the south, be the temporary misfortunes there what they will.[35]

Jefferson was not kept long in suspense. On October 20 a British fleet of sixty sail entered Chesapeake Bay with five thousand troops commanded by Major General Alexander Leslie. Three days later they landed a considerable force at Newport News and seized and ravaged nearby Hampton. Almost simultaneously infantry and cavalry were landed on the opposite shores of Hampton Roads at Portsmouth. By the third of November between 2,500 and three thousand troops were concentrated near the vital shipping town.[36] A British outpost was established in Suffolk, troops were sent into Princess Anne County, and the building of fortifications was soon underway. Only Cornwallis' orders to Leslie to join forces with him on his northward march caused the invading troops to reembark on November 15. Jefferson was relieved that Virginia had been saved but embarrassed that its salvation had been effected by the enemy's change of plans rather than its own defensive capability. He knew that only scattered foot soldiers, underarmed and with little of the cartridge paper essential to ammunition, had stood between Richmond and the British cavalry.

Jefferson now proposed to the Council of State the creation of a standing army. They were not ready for so radical a measure. Had they not already assigned three thousand men to serve in the Continental Army for three years or the duration, using as bait the promise of a healthy slave to every fighter for freedom?

Discouraged, Jefferson talked of resigning, but Page and others argued against it, suggesting that he would be deserting his post in crisis. Jefferson stayed on. He was now in his second term, scheduled to end in June 1781.

Unable to beef up the defense forces, he had addressed another grave problem, the lack of military intelligence from the South. He had set up a relay system of horsemen between the invaded area of the Carolinas and the Virginia capital. With the same careful calculation that he brought to everything from the building of Monticello to his experiments in agricultural science, Jefferson had concluded that news should travel from the Southern battlefields to him at the rate of 120 miles every twenty-four hours. At the Southern terminus of this line of communication the Governor would need a reliable officer, one who was, as he said, "sensible" and "judicious."

For this post he chose a twenty-two-year-old colonel who, after worthy service with the Continental Army, had returned to Virginia with a letter of recommendation from General Washington and an earnest desire to serve in the defense of his native state. The tall, open-faced young Virginian had already won Jefferson's notice to the extent that the Governor had found time to guide him in legal studies. Thus James Monroe became the protégé of Thomas Jefferson, who was already the younger man's hero.[37] The Governor perhaps found such admiration particularly appealing in a time when he seemed unheroic in his own eyes. He certainly seemed unheroic to many of his fellow Virginians. Some thought that he should take personal command of the militia and lead it into the field. Fortunately, Jefferson was not overmastered by any impulse to military glory.

A happy family event briefly provided relief from the pressing gloom of public emergencies. On the night of November 30, Martha gave birth to a girl who was christened Lucy Elizabeth. Joyful tidings went out to kith and kin.

But all the news that traveled north by Jefferson's relay system was bad. In the last eight months of the Governor's administration, bad became worse. On the last day of that miserable year, 1780, he learned that another fleet, presumably British, had entered Chesapeake Bay. The message, which Jefferson received from a horseman at eight o'clock on that quiet Sunday morning, was to give him a New Year's Eve of fateful indecision. It was really a note which a Hampton merchant had addressed to General Nelson, who in turn forwarded it to the Governor. Twenty-seven sail had been sighted, but the merchant could not be sure that they were British.[38]

Two days had elapsed between the sighting and Jefferson's receipt of the report. If the ships were the enemy's, precious time had been lost. Of course, there was the possibility that the vessels were the long-awaited warships of France come to sweep the bay of invaders. But if they were indeed British, they still might not be engaged in any large-scale operation. By coincidence William Tatham, of General Nelson's staff, was in Richmond when the message arrived and, upon hearing of it, called on the governor. As he drew rein at the official residence, Jefferson was walking out with all the casual aplomb of any townsman intent on nothing more than a Sunday morning stroll. Yes, the Governor confirmed, he had been informed of the presence of warships in the bay. But probably nothing more than a foraging party would be sent ashore. Until he had more facts he would not alarm the country by calling out the militia.[39]

As it was Sunday and the Council was scheduled to meet in regular session the following day, Jefferson did not call a special meeting. He did ask the general to investigate the report and wrote to coastal militia officers, alerting them to a possible emergency and soliciting further information. He also stationed horsemen to relay intelligence swiftly. When he reported these measures to the Council on Monday, they approved his actions and adjourned. Jefferson was determined not to play the role of Chicken Little, and the Council seemed to sympathize completely.

The next morning Jefferson received from Colonel Nathaniel Burwell the shocking news that a considerable British naval force had entered the James River. If the British were merely searching for food, they seemed prepared to devour Virginia. In the Council's name, the Governor directed half of the militia of three nearby counties and a sizeable portion of the militia of three others to concentrate for the defense of Petersburg. The arms and military stores in that city were surely the enemy's target. Meanwhile, the materiel should be moved to Richmond. Gunpowder still at the powder mills should be moved to Westham, seven miles from the capital. British troops held in Virginia under the conventions of war should be dispatched north to Maryland. Legislators rode away in all directions to assume militia duties in their separate counties. So quiescent Richmond became like an ant hill when the sole of a boot looms over it.

By now Jefferson was virtually certain that the enemy aimed at Petersburg. Richmond might be the next target. But his optimism was not easily shaken. When the night of January 3 brought news that the British had anchored off Jamestown, the Governor seized upon the possibility that the old capital, now a farm community, was their chosen destination.[40] Jamestown was rich in history but in little else.

At five o'clock a rapping on the door and the hasty lighting of candles in the predawn darkness waked the Governor from his dream of peace. The British ships were on the move again, headed up river toward Richmond. He hastily convened the remaining members of the Council and ordered all the militia of nearby counties to assemble at Westham. Evening brought news that the British had landed downstream at Westover, the elegant mansion of the Byrds and an appropriate way station on the river road to Richmond. Jefferson ordered that the convention prisoners be hurried north to Maryland without any further delay for assembling baggage. Benedict Arnold, the hated traitor and (more important) a formidable general, was leading nine hundred troops toward Richmond, bent upon capturing Virginia's political leaders as well as the capital. Jefferson was in the saddle, supervising the loading of stores in Richmond and riding directly to the arms foundry to take charge of the removal of supplies to Westham. At one o'clock on the following morning, having revealed an energy and decision that must have surprised some of his colleagues, he arrived at Tuckahoe, the Randolph plantation where he had spent part of his childhood. Here he could clasp Martha to his chest before dropping into the sleep of exhaustion. He had sent her and the children to go on ahead to this place of refuge which should be more secure than any building in Richmond.[41]

By one o'clock on the afternoon of January 5 Arnold, after an unopposed twenty-five-mile dash from Westover, entered Richmond. He was disappointed to discover that the Governor and Council and all legislators had left the city. There were no defending soldiers. Arnold's men broke into the Governor's house. They spared the furniture but made merry with the contents of his wine cellar. Destroying the powder magazine in Richmond, Arnold sent an infantry regiment and thirty horse posthaste after the last wagons carrying materiel to Westham, then burned the foundry and ancillary facilities for arms manufacture.

Jefferson, drawing on unsuspected reserves of energy, was even more busy on the fifth than Arnold. Early in the morning he took his family across the James to Fine Creek, his father's first farm, a less conspicuous and therefore presumably a safer refuge than Tuckahoe. From there he had galloped to Westham where he had succeeded in removing valuable stores before the arrival of Arnold's troops. He then pressed on to Steuben's headquarters but, finding the general gone, rode back toward Westham to speed the evacuation of supplies. When his exhausted horse stumbled to a halt, the Governor borrowed another and streaked on. He labored on into the night, infusing workers with some of his own energy. Through his efforts, fifteen tons of munitions were saved. Sometime before dawn he caught a little sleep in a friendly house.

He was up early on the sixth and in the saddle again, tirelessly urging forward cumbersome wagons that seemed to proceed at a bovine pace. In the evening, having done all that he could to make up for the precious days initially lost by his and the Council's optimism, he rejoined Martha and the children at Fine Creek.

The next day Arnold, learning that militia were going into action and that Generals Steuben and Nelson were marching rapidly toward him from Petersburg, put the torch to various public buildings and private homes in Richmond, seized slaves (among them ten of Jefferson's) and retreated to Westover and the protection of the guns of His Majesty's ships. Greatly augmented by militia that Jefferson had alarmed, prodded, and inspired into action as he galloped about the countryside, Steuben and Nelson pursued Arnold to Westover. There they were hopelessly disadvantaged under the guns of the royal navy, so they merely concentrated on seeing that no British raiding parties left the plantation. Frustrated by wasteful inactivity, Arnold and his men at last returned to their ships and sailed down river to a then obscure little community named Yorktown.

That same day, January 8, Jefferson rode out to survey the damage wrought in the nightmare week since he had strolled forth on a quiet Richmond sabbath, pausing to assure a member of Nelson's staff that there was no apparent reason for alarm. Now a cold rain, heavy at times, added to the dismal aspect of the ravaged land. He knew that Richmond had been devastated. When he drew rein at Westham and later at Manchester, across the James from the capital, the scene was essentially the same—gray ashes under gray skies. The incessant rain drummed at his consciousness with the insistence of a host of regrets that could not be dismissed.

The next morning Jefferson entered Richmond. Gaping windows stared aghast from blackened ruins. Buildings left standing amid the devastation emphasized the caprice of the destroyers. Two hundred militiamen hastily assembled to defend the city had fled before a British force estimated by Jefferson as fifteen hundred infantry and fifty to 120 horse. Even if the estimate was high the city's amateur defenders had been outnumbered at least five to one by the onrushing professionals.

Jefferson convened the Council in what seemed a city of the dead. Three members answered his summons. Each day he and they met and adjourned in a seemingly endless ritual. Finally, on January 19, the return of a fourth member made a quorum. Jefferson made an official report of what all knew informally—that, after their devastating raids, the unscarred British had dropped down river from Westover, sailing in majestic disdain past the feeble batteries on the shore. The Council approved the Governor's proposal that paroles enjoined upon "peaceable citizens" by the British be voided by general proclamation and that the embargo on provisions for the invader be continued. Jefferson was vulnerable to finger pointing but no member of the Council could lift a finger unstained by its part in the disaster.

Jefferson now became as obsessed with the punishment of Arnold as he had once been with the chastisement of Henry Hamilton. On the last day of that bleak January he wrote to General J.P.G. Muhlenberg, who almost exactly three years before had preached his farewell sermon at Woodstock, shed his clerical robes in the pulpit to reveal his officer's uniform, and marched out of the church into history. There could be no doubting this man's patriotic zeal.

You will readily suppose that it is above all things desirable to drag Arnold from those under whose wing he is now sheltered. On his march to and from this place I am certain it might have been done with facility by men of enterprise and firmness. I think it may still be done though perhaps not quite so easily. Having peculiar confidence in the men from the Western side of the mountains, I meant as soon as they should come down to get the enterprise proposed to a chosen number of them, such whose courage and whose fidelity would be above all doubt. Your perfect knowledge of those men personally, and my confidence in your discretion, induce me to ask you to pick from among them proper characters, in such number as you think best, to reveal to them our desire, and engage them to undertake to seize and bring off this greatest of all traitors. . . . I will undertake if they are successful in bringing him off alive, that they shall receive five thousand guineas reward among them, and to men formed for such an enterprise it must be a great incitement to know that their names will be recorded with glory in history. . . .[42]

One portion of Jefferson's original draft he himself crossed out as perhaps a little excessive:

I shall be sorry to suppose that any circumstances may put it out of their power to bring him off alive after they shall have taken him and of course oblige them to put him to death. Should this happen, however, and America be deprived of the satisfaction of seeing him exhibited as a public spectacle of infamy, and of vengeance, I must give my approbation to their putting him to death. I do this considering him as a deserter from the American army, who has incurred the pain of death by his desertion, which we have a right to inflict on him and against which he cannot be protected by any act of our enemies. I distinguish him from an honorable enemy, who, in his station, would never be considered by me as a justifiable object of such an enterprise. In event of his death, however, I must reduce the reward proposed to 2000 guineas, in proportion as our satisfaction would be reduced.[43]

This time, however, the Governor did not persist in his obsession regarding Arnold nearly so long as he had in his desire to see "the hairbuyer" chastised. He soon reverted to broader goals and statesmanlike foresight. The "peculiar confidence in the men from the Western side of the mountains" that he had professed to Muhlenberg extended far beyond such matters as the capture of Arnold. More than any other statesman in America, he grasped the possibilities of the western lands. Despite needs close to home he made provisions for another expedition in the Northwest by George Rogers Clark. And in generous terms he relayed to Congress Virginia's reiteration of what was, whether viewed as an act of magnanimity or of enlightened self-interest, one of the most remarkable offers made by any sovereign state in modern history.

When Richard Henry Lee had introduced in the Congress on June 7, 1776, a resolution for independence he had coupled with it a proposal that "a plan of confederation be prepared and transmitted to the respective colonies for their consideration and approbation." Articles of Confederation and Perpetual Union had been formally adopted by the Congress on November 15, 1777, and two days later dispatched to each State for action. But ratification had lagged; some of the States feared the magnification of Virginia's influence in some not too distant day when her population, already the largest in the Union, would be increased by settlement of the western lands she claimed. Mindful of the necessity for a more effective government than the loose alliance centered in Philadelphia, Virginia offered to cede to the new Union all the vast territory north of the Ohio River—land won by the enterprise, sweat, and blood of Virginians. With a prophetic insight remarkable for a humiliated chief magistrate seated in a violated house amid the ruins of his capital as he awaited a still larger invasion, Jefferson wrote to the

President of the Congress: "This single event (ratification), could it take place shortly, would overweigh every success which the Enemy have hitherto obtained and render desperate the hopes to which those successes have given birth."[44]

In February, Jefferson received an explosive letter from General Gates who was as upset by his loss to Cornwallis as the Governor was over his own humiliation by Arnold. But, whereas Jefferson's wrath was directed against the American turncoat, Gates' vehemence was vented on his fellow American rebels, and particularly on their elected officials:

> If Lord Cornwallis conquers the southern and eastern parts of North Carolina and extends his posts of communication to Portsmouth, (Virginia), you must expect the weight of the war will penetrate into your bowels, and cause such inflammation there as may (if timely remedies are not applied) consume the life blood of the state. Have you cried aloud to Congress, and to *The Commander in Chief of The Army,* for succor? Have they listened to your cry? If they have not, are you doing the best thing for yourselves? Military wisdom has ever heretofore been imputed to Virginia. Is there a rottenness in the State of Denmark? Find it out, and cut it off.[45]

Despite Gates' vexation, he was not entirely unsympathetic. He added: "This is the letter of one chess player to another, not the letter of General Gates to Governor Jefferson. I am now at my unhappy private house; you are acting in the busy scene of public life, and in the most exalted station, in which I sincerely wish you all honor and success. Happiness I know you cannot have."

Jefferson replied: "I have been knocking at the door of Congress for aids of all kinds, but especially of arms, ever since the middle of summer. The Speaker, Harrison, is gone to be heard on that subject. Justice indeed requires that we should be aided powerfully. Yet if they would repay us the arms we have lent them we should give the enemy trouble though abandoned to ourselves."[46]

He also told Gates: "Arnold lies still at Portsmouth with 1500 men."[47] Arnold may actually have had two thousand or more. Since January 20 he had dug in at Portsmouth to await the arrival of Cornwallis from the South. HMS *Charon* was stationed off Craney Island where it could at any time block navigation to the Elizabeth River, which flowed between Norfolk and Portsmouth. Other British warships blockaded the waterfront from downtown Portsmouth to the adjacent village of Gosport with its important shipyard.[48]

Jefferson received almost daily reminders from various military officers and civil officials that the success or failure of the Revolution might well depend on what happened in Virginia within the next few months. And everyone seemed to think that the chief responsibility for what happened in Virginia devolved upon the Governor. The Assembly was not due to convene again until March. The Council no longer sought the initiative but seemed quite willing for Jefferson at last to assume responsibility for everything so long as he did not interfere too drastically with the normal lives of private citizens.

Steuben's choleric temper was not improved by Arnold's escape. He had proposed even before the traitor's raid that Hoods, a strategic spot on the James River below Richmond, be fortified to protect the capital. Arnold's successful move on the city and his continued presence in Virginia, soon to be vastly augmented, gave additional urgency to the recommendation. The general asked the Governor for forty slaves and ten mechanics to build the fortifications. Jefferson indicated his willingness to supply the work force by February 7. But the Council apparently was unwilling to authorize the Governor to impress men for this service. Thus no workers were available when the deadline arrived, and an angry Steuben demanded an explanation: "Three weeks are now elapsed since the enemy went down the river. In this time the work could have been half finished. If government think the work unnecessary [or if] they have it not in their [power] I have only to beg they would for my own justification give me their opinion in writing. . . . My wish is to prevent a repetition of the disgrace but as I can do nothing without the assistance of the government, I must beg your Excellency to give me answer to this that I may have it in my power to justify my own conduct."[49] Steuben's frustration apparently was increased by the fact that he had reported to Washington on February 1 that the work would be "begun in a few days."

In view of the fact that Jefferson often has been charged with obtuseness, lethargy, or insensitivity in regard to Steuben's plan for erecting fortifications below Richmond, it is simple justice to quote portions of his reply other than the usually cited: "The Executive have not by the laws of this State any power to call a freeman to labor, even for the public, without his consent, nor a slave without that of his master."[50]

Jefferson began his letter with great politeness: "I have been honored with your letter of yesterday's date. Your representation of the importance of erecting a small work at Hoods was considered by the Executive as an evidence of your friendly attention to the defense of the State and was by them as you desired laid before the assembly."[51]

He explained:

The Assembly, pressed in time, did not, as far as I am informed, take it under consideration. The invasion which took place just before their rising prevented any thing further being done till the departure of the enemy from this place, and the return of the Executive to it. The proposition of undertaking the work which you then again renewed was approved of by them, and they determined to procure if possible the several articles necessary for carrying it into immediate execution according to the plan and estimate prepared. I think however you misapprehended us when you understood it was agreed that the 40 Negroes and 10 artificers required should be furnished by the five nearest counties and be at the spot on the 7th inst. It does not occur to me or to any Gentlemen of the Council that the 7th or any other day was fixed on for their assembling: and that we could not have agreed that the 40 Negroes and 10 artificers should be furnished by the five nearest counties may be deduced from the conversation which you will recollect to have passed between us the evening before you last went to Cabin-Point. You informed me you meant to call for 20 militia from each of the [five] circumjacent counties to come to Hoods with their hoes and axes to erect the work but to notify to them at the same time that you would receive 10 Negroes in their room: and you asked me whether you must apply to government for authority to do this. I answered that such an application would produce no effect, as it had been the subject of conversation at the Council Board that day, and the Board was of opinion we had no right to call out the militia to do fatigue duty. You then replied you would do it of your own authority and throw yourself on the Assembly for a justification. I repeat this conversation thus particularly to satisfy you that we could not have agreed that the five neighboring counties should produce these laborers and of course that we stand discharged of having failed to fulfill such an agreement.

Jefferson added:

Sensible that a necessary work is not to be abandoned because their means are not so energetic as they could wish them and on the contrary that it is their duty to take those means as they find them and to make the most of them for the public good, they propose to pursue this work, and if they cannot accomplish it in a shorter, they will in a longer time.

Jefferson did not remind Steuben that fortification of Hoods had been a project of the Governor's at least as far back as the preceding November, when he had written Speaker Harrison: "Hoods on James River has been considered as very capable of opposing the passage of vessels. In pursuance of this plan all supernumerary guns have been withdrawn from Portsmouth, Hampton, and York, and some progress has been made in constructing a battery at Hoods."[52] The same letter relates that Jefferson, on his own initiative, had asked Colonel J.C. Senf, an engineer, to observe the site and make suggestions.

Jefferson's letter to Harrison on the matter had been read in the House of Delegates on the day it was written. The matters discussed were referred to a committee that reported December 2. Senf's report was tabled.[53] Then, as the Governor related, Arnold's invasion upset all timetables.

Jefferson informed Steuben that he personally had authorized Colonel Senf to "search among our artillery officers for one whom he would choose" to erect the fortification "under his direction and that this officer should immediately proceed to hire slaves in the neighborhood of Hoods, where I thought it more likely the people would be willing to hire as the work respected their safety more immediately. He did so, and sent a Captain Allen on this business. . . . Colonel Senf informed me that he had himself engaged 8 or 10. Four carpenters were assigned to Colonel Senf at this place, the several articles of tools . . . were procured for him here, a boat to carry them down, and I took for granted that they went."[54]

There is no blinking the fact that Jefferson, like the members of the Council, had at first underestimated the threat from Arnold and had lost precious time. But before the blow fell he had sensed the importance of fortifying Hoods and after the disaster he had taken the initiative in proceeding with its fortifications. It is almost inexplicable that even admiring biographers of Jefferson in our own time have seized upon a single quotation lifted from the context of his letter to Steuben and used it as evidence of the Governor's failure to grasp the realities of Virginia's defense as late as February 1781.

Jefferson had learned a lesson during Arnold's invasion. The Governor who directed so many practical details from horseback while retaining the broad perspective of national needs bore little resemblance to the figure he had been—a war leader more distinguished by sangfroid than acuity. Jefferson was no Alexander to cut the Gordian knot of legal red tape. But increasingly, while complying technically, he circumvented the regulations of a government constituted as a debating society.[55]

Steuben appeared February 15 at a meeting of the Council that Jefferson called to hear the general's plea for cooperation with the French fleet expected to arrive soon off the Virginia capes. The Council authorized the Governor to take certain measures for the fortification of Hoods, which he had already initiated on his own responsibility. Then the stout, balding baron with the pugilist's nose[56] explained the opportunities presented by the anticipated arrival of the French ships. As usual his personal appeal face to face had a magnetism to offset the repellent quality of his letters. Steuben climaxed his presentation with a request that all armed vessels already in the James River be impressed into service to help the French. The Council seemed unshaken by the request, Jefferson breathed a sigh of relief, and the German parted from the Virginians with warm good will on both sides.

Imagine, then, Jefferson's embarrassment the next day when he found it necessary to write to the general:

> I make no doubt from what passed in council in your presence you were led to believe as I was that I should be advised to impress immediately all armed vessels in James River to cooperate with the French force. The board however decide against an impress, so that I am only to endeavor to engage the willing. I mention this to you that nothing more may be expected than is likely to be obtained from this measure.[57]

In any event, the incident should have left the general with a better understanding of the Governor's problems.

Legislatures are notoriously erratic, and the Council of Virginia was no exception. The Council not only opposed requests by Jefferson when it feared that individual independence would be circumscribed but also balked at proposed expenditures as not being absolutely essential. Yet it graciously granted his request for funds to purchase for public use a set of the 28-volume French *Encyclopédie*. It was then the world's greatest single compendium of facts, was imbued with a revolutionary philosophy that many thought shocking, and had ten volumes devoted to mouth-watering plates illustrating everything from the latest inventions to monuments of architecture. Jefferson had wanted to buy it for himself, but had found the price prohibitive. It may safely be assumed that he got more use out of the *Encyclopédie* than any other member of the public. But the Governor, whose growing reputation as a scholar had just recently brought him election to the governing council of the American Philosophical Society, headed by Benjamin Franklin, was already engaged in projects to share his learning with his countrymen.

Before the end of February, heartening news arrived from General Washington that not only would a strong French fleet confront Arnold's ships but that an army under command of the celebrated Marquis de Lafayette, now at twenty-four in his fifth year as a major general, would do battle with Cornwallis, whose forces were moving rapidly toward Virginia behind Greene's retreating army. Virginia would willingly have foregone the honor of being the decisive battlefield of the Revolution. But, if the battle was to be fought within her borders, it was reassuring to have such help. Meanwhile, deficient in both men and arms, Virginia had the task of holding out until help arrived.

A bitter blow to the state's morale and fighting strength came when the French fleet was intercepted by the British navy just off the Virginia capes and driven back to Newport, Rhode Island. Virginians therefore were frustrated in their attempts to retake Portsmouth. That base with its ship facilities was almost ideally suited to the needs of the British invader. The redcoats moved up the James in mid-April, occupied Williamsburg, and proceeded up the Appomattox River to Petersburg. Muhlenburg and the militia fought hard but their strength was insufficient to keep the British from entering the city on April 25 and burning warehouses there as well as in Warwick and at Chesterfield Courthouse. Major General William Phillips, who had arrived in Portsmouth on March 26 with 2,600 men, had superseded Arnold as part of a British upgrading of the entire Virginia operation. Cornwallis, about to invade the Old Dominion with his great southern army, was so confident that conquest of Virginia would mean control of all the American states that he had proposed abandonment of New York so that all British forces might be concentrated in the area of the Chesapeake Bay.[58]

Washington had sent Lafayette to Virginia with three regiments of light infantry from New England and New Jersey but, without the support of a naval arm and of the 1,200 French soldiers it was expected to deliver, the marquis faced an impossible task. Lafayette entered Richmond from the north just as the British occupied the village of Manchester on the south bank of the James opposite the city. The British hesitated to cross under fire. Lafayette knew that he was too weak to do more than stand his ground. The death of General Phillips on May 13 and the resumption of command by Arnold may have lengthened British hesitation. Lafayette hoped desperately that "Mad Anthony" Wayne, who was marching from Pennsylvania with reinforcements, would arrive before Cornwallis entered Virginia. But before Wayne could join forces with the Frenchman, Cornwallis entered the State, linking with Arnold at Petersburg on May 20. Thus Lafayette, with about 3,000 ill-equipped soldiers, was opposed by 7,200 well-equipped Britishers. He lamented to Washington, "I am not strong enough even to get beaten."[59] Cornwallis reportedly exulted, "The boy cannot escape me."[60]

Jefferson had tried to prepare Lafayette for the same sort of difficulties that had vexed Steuben. He had written him, "Mild laws, a people not used to prompt obedience, a want of provisions of war and means of procuring them, render our orders often ineffectual, oblige us to temporize and when we cannot accomplish an object in one way to attempt it in another." He had said in a later letter, "I know that you will be satisfied to make the most of an unprepared people, who have the war now for the first time seriously fixed in their country and have therefore all those habits to acquire which their Northern brethren had in the year 1776."[61]

Lafayette seemed to understand. Indeed, he and Jefferson became good friends. The younger man had great charm and an animation that made him seem handsome despite his unusual slant-back forehead. Each man respected the other's intellectual interests and unfailing courtesy.

Neither their combined nor separate ruminations on Virginia's plight, however, brought any comfort. Lafayette could only refuse to accept every provocation to battle other than mere skirmishing.

For two months, harassed by increasing demands for food, clothing, arms, and ammunition that were not available, Jefferson had given orders that were seldom obeyed. When his nineteen-week-old daughter, Lucy Elizabeth, died on the morning of April 15 there had been no time for mourning.

Jefferson had left Richmond on May 15, joining his family at Tuckahoe, and then retreated slowly westward to Albemarle with the tattered remnants of his government. From April 26 to May 10 he had repeatedly convened the Council and never had a quorum. On that date those legislators still remaining in Richmond had agreed to meet two weeks later in Charlottesville. From May 24 to May 30 Jefferson regularly called the Council to order with a single member present, and later the two adjourned. On May 30 another Council member, William Fleming, his friend since school days and at one time second only to Page as his confidant in problems of romance, joined his colleague and Jefferson. But then the original attendant, George Webb, decided that he was needed more elsewhere and left the next day. On May 31, June 1, and June 2, Jefferson followed with Fleming the ritual of convening and adjourning. Jefferson had officially resigned on June 1. By this time the members of the State government had dispersed on horseback among the Virginia hills. After June 2, concluding that his term had expired, Jefferson ceased to report to the improvised Council chamber.[62]

Word of Jefferson's resignation must have been very late in reaching some of the fleeing legislators. It is not surprising that Cornwallis still thought of him as Governor. From his headquarters in Hanover County, His Lordship dispatched Lieutenant Colonel Banastre Tarleton to capture Jefferson and the Assemblymen. On June 3 Tarleton set out for Charlottesville with 180 dragoons and seventy mounted infantry.

Tarleton's name was well known throughout the American states. Now in his mid-twenties, he had entered His Majesty's armed forces at the beginning of the Revolution, quickly distinguishing himself in Cornwallis' campaigns in the North before earning in the South a reputation for "dash, daring" and ruthlessness.[63] Included in his green-coated force (we too easily assume that all British wore red coats) were American tories who thirsted for their "erring" brothers' blood. In a theatrically heroic portrait[64] by Sir Joshua Reynolds, Tarleton appears as a Georgian dandy, his calves encased in shiny boots, his stocky thighs in skin-tight trousers, his short green jacket hugging the contours of his muscular torso, the face beneath the plumed helmet an embodiment of macho arrogance tinged with a subtle effeminacy finding concrete expression in the spit curls that sufficed for sideburns.

Late on the night of June 3 Tarleton and his men jingled and jangled into Louisa Court House some forty miles from Charlottesville, and up to the local hostelry, Cuckoo Tavern.[65] There men and horses took refreshment and rested awhile. A large-framed young man of boyishly open countenance was drinking in the tap room when the clatter of hooves, clinking of harness fastenings, and clanking of swords abruptly roused him from his ease to take a quick glimpse outside. Immediately guessing the identity of the riders and their mission, he stole out silently, mounted his horse and rode off. He was Jack Jouett, a militia captain, and he was determined to reach Charlottesville before Tarleton so that he could warn the Governor and other leaders.

The area was Jouett's native briar patch and he knew backroads and woodland paths unknown to Tarleton. His scarlet militia coat torn by clutching branches, he rode furiously through overarched forest roads that the bright moonlight penetrated only in patches. When Tarleton's troop took to the road again they were traveling by a longer route than Jouett and also took time to destroy several supply wagons. About 4 a.m. they stopped at Castle Hill, Thomas Walker's estate, surprising there not only the doctor but also several legislators staying with him. Meanwhile, Jouett rode into Charlottesville, alarming the town, and riding up the mountain to Monticello. At daybreak he reined in his panting horse at the steps of the mansion and was soon pouring out the fearful news to Jefferson. The Governor took it quite calmly, graciously thanking the young militia captain and insisting that he take a glass or two of madeira. Apparently unruffled, Jefferson sat down to a leisurely breakfast with his family and his guests, the speakers of both houses of the Assembly and several other legislators. Afterwards the guests took their leave and Jefferson sent his family on a journey of fourteen miles to the Coles plantation, Enniscorthy, where they would remain till the emergency was past. At Monticello he began packing his most important papers. He had always regretted the loss of papers in the fire at Shadwell. This time there was not only the danger of loss but also the possibility that information useful to the enemy would fall into their hands.

He was still methodically occupied with the task about two hours later when another militiaman arrived with word that the British were expected momentarily. This time Jefferson strapped on a light sword and rode part way down the mountain. Then he tied his horse among some trees and trained his telescope on the streets of Charlottesville. No sign of Tarleton's men there. He started to ride back up to the mansion but focused once more on the thoroughfares of the town. This time they were aswarm with green-coated dragoons and red-coated infantry. Jefferson spurred his horse onto a woodland trail and galloped away.

Because of Jouett's quick action, knowledge of the country, and superb horsemanship, leaders important not only to Virginia but to the American Republic escaped the enemy's grasp. Some legislators were captured, but these were regarded as of little importance and were soon released. One of them was a frontiersman elected to the Virginia House of Delegates from the large, sparsely settled western county of Kentucky—none other than Daniel Boone.[66] But Benjamin Harrison, Thomas Jefferson, and Patrick Henry escaped. According to persistent tradition,[67] one body of legislators warned by Jouett were berated by the mistress of a farm house where they took refuge. As she warmed to her denunciation, she shrilled: "They tell me one of you ran away so fast that he didn't even get both boots on. What would Patrick Henry think?" At that moment, it is said, Patrick Henry, unrecognized by her among her unwelcome guests, shoved his bootless leg farther beneath the concealing table.

One of the ironies of history is that Paul Revere's ride, metamorphosed into the galloping rhythms of Henry Wadsworth Longfellow, has all but drowned out in the clatter of hooves on New England cobblestones the story of Jack Jouett's remarkable exploit. Yet Jouett, in an almost incredible forty-mile dash over wilderness trails, saved the author of the Declaration of Independence, another signer of that great document, and the oratorical firebrand of the Revolution, besides enough legislators to reassemble farther west in Staunton as the duly constituted government. But Revere, justly honored as a great silversmith, pioneer industrialist, and loyal patriot, was captured before he ever reached Concord, and his ride was completed by a Dr. Samuel Prescott who had encountered the Bostonian by accident while returning from a courting engagement. Nevertheless, today Prescott is almost forgotten and the name of Jack Jouett is little known while some years ago a Massachusetts community apparently thought it profitable to erect a highway marker proclaiming, "This is the route that Paul Revere would have taken on his famous ride in April 1775 if he had not gone by way of Lexington and Concord."

Patrick Henry not only remained free, thanks to Jouett's warning, but became the dominant figure in the legislature that met west of the Blue Ridge in Staunton. General Thomas Nelson was that body's choice to succeed Jefferson as Governor. The Assembly appropriately enough voted to present Captain Jouett an "elegant sword and pair of pistols."[68] Among the Assembly's resolves was another echo of Tarleton's raid: "Resolved, That at the next session of the Assembly an inquiry be made into the conduct of the Executive of this State for the last twelve months."[69]

The author of the motion was George Nicholas, an obscure young legislator from Henry's county, Hanover. Henry lent his oratorical gifts in support of the measure, which may well have been instigated by him. The resolution was voted for by Jefferson's friends as well as his enemies. Despite the fact that Jefferson had been almost too dilatory in departing from Monticello, rife rumor had him fleeing in cowardly haste. Typical of the comments bruited was one in a letter written by Miss Betsy Ambler, daughter of Rebecca Burwell, the "fair Belinda" of Jefferson's youth. Though Miss Ambler thought it only proper that her father, the Councillor, should flee and remain in hiding because "the public office which he holds makes it absolutely necessary for him to run no risk of falling into the hands of the enemy," she found nothing "more laughable than the accounts we have of our illustrious Governor, who, they say, took neither rest nor food for man or horse till he reached Carter's Mountain."[70] Jefferson's friends voted for the resolution in hopes that an investigation would clear him of any imputation of cowardice.[71]

Jefferson did not know for sure why the resolution had carried. In view of his sensitivity about failure to be reelected to Congress even after declaring he did not wish to be returned, it is easy to imagine his anguish on this occasion. At least, even though it might not yet be wise to return to his beloved Monticello, he could spend this trying time in the privacy of Poplar Forest, a plantation he owned ninety miles from Charlottesville.[72] And there was comfort in the news that Monticello had been left largely unravaged by the invader. But there were other woes. Even his favorite horse, Caractacus, had unseated him at almost the same time that the leaders of the Commonwealth seemed to be rejecting him. The resulting fall broke his arm, confining his movements for six weeks, giving him more time to brood, providing a throbbing obbligato of pain as the leitmotif of his troubled thoughts.

A letter from the Congress informing him that, in company with John Adams, Benjamin Franklin, John Jay, and John Laurens, he had been appointed a minister plenipotentiary to negotiate peace with England through the offices of Catherine the Great, Empress of All the Russias, was no consolation. He craved the respect and affection of his fellow Virginians. He gave no thought to accepting the diplomatic appointment but instead persuaded Isaac David, member of the House of Delegates from Albemarle, to resign so that he might take his place and thus plead his case in person before the legislators.[73]

Before going to Staunton he wrote to young Mr. Nicholas for a detailed statement of formal charges, saying, "It could not be intended first to stab a reputation by a general suggestion under a bare expectation that facts might be afterwards hunted up to bolster it."[74]

Nicholas replied, "You consider me in a wrong point of view when you speak of me as an accuser."[75] He explained:

> As a freeman and the representative of free men I considered it as both my right and duty to call upon the executive to account for our numberless miscarriages and losses so far as they were concerned in or might have prevented them. In doing this I had no private pique to gratify, and if (as I hope it may) it shall appear that they have done everything in their power to prevent our misfortunes I will most readily retract any opinion that I may have formed to their prejudice.

Not until December 12, 1781, did the new Assembly consider the resolution of inquiry into Jefferson's conduct as Governor. By then Cornwallis had abandoned his base at Portsmouth to proceed to Yorktown, assuring his superiors that the move should hasten the end of the war. On October 19, with the aid of a French fleet under De Grasse, the prophecy had been fulfilled spectacularly, but not precisely in the way his lordship had envisioned.

Washington warned that Cornwallis's surrender did not necessarily mean the end of the war, that England could send other armies to America, but less cautious Americans concluded that independence had been won. People were no longer so eager for scapegoats. Jefferson's many labors for the American cause were remembered. The House unanimously passed a generous resolution:

> Resolved, That the sincere thanks of the General Assembly be given to our former Governor, Thomas Jefferson, Esq. for his impartial, upright, and attentive administration of the powers of the Executive, whilst in office; popular rumors gaining some degree of credence, by more pointed accusations, rendered it necessary to make an inquiry into his conduct, and delayed that retribution of public gratitude, so eminently merited; but that conduct having become the object of open scrutiny, tenfold value is added to an approbation, founded on a cool and deliberate discussion. The Assembly wish therefore, in the strongest manner, to declare the high opinion which they entertain of Mr. Jefferson's ability, rectitude and integrity, as Chief Magistrate of this Commonwealth; and mean by thus publicly avowing their opinion, to obviate all future, and to remove all former, unmerited censure.[76]

We may be sure that Jefferson was not disposed to quibble over a single word of the resolution, even the misuse (or miscopying) of "retribution," which normally would have offended his meticulous verbal sense.

In retrospect, he did not consider young Nicholas worthy of his wrath. He said of him in a letter penned on Christmas Eve: "The trifling body who moved this matter was below contempt; he was more an object of pity. His natural ill-temper was the tool worked with by another hand. He was like the minnows that go in and out of the fundament of the whale. But the whale himself was discoverable enough by the turbulence of the water under which he moved."[77]

After this time Jefferson continued to acknowledge Patrick Henry's peerless abilities as an orator but apparently spoke of his character only in terms of revulsion.

How bad had been Jefferson's administration as Governor? The apparent ineffectualness of the Commonwealth's efforts within its own borders stands in sad contrast to the accomplishments of individual Virginians in field and forum—Washington as Commander in Chief of the victorious Continental Army, Patrick Henry as the voice of Revolution, George Mason as the author of the Declaration of Rights, George Rogers Clark as Winner of the West, Richard Henry Lee as introducer of the resolution for independence, Jefferson himself as the author of the Declaration of Independence, not to mention the achievements of such adopted Virginians as Daniel Morgan and John Paul Jones. The record of individual contributions was not equaled by any other State. But within Virginia were dissension, profiteering, malingering, and military naiveté.

The story, however, was not very different in any of the thirteen States. Even Jefferson would have been amazed if he could have known that in the twentieth century a prominent historian, after a comparative study of Revolutionary records from New England to Georgia, would conclude that Virginia was in the vanguard of States contributing to the Continental Army and "excelled all her sister States in devoting 'land, property and manufacturing' to naval purposes."[78]

These facts Jefferson, still on the defensive despite the House's handsome acknowledgement, could not know. But of one thing he did feel sure. To Edmund Randolph's importunity that he return to public life Jefferson had replied: "I have taken my final leave of everything of that nature. I have retired to my farm, my family and books, from which I think nothing will evermore separate me."[79]

X

'DIVINE DISCONTENT'

JEFFERSON WAS not, like Alfred the Great, fitted by nature and training to fight back from holdings reduced to less than thirty acres in a swamp until he had freed his kingdom of hordes of invaders. The Virginian had not been reared in the hard school of war that had made his Anglo-Saxon ancestor a general at sixteen. Besides, this particular achievement of Alfred's appears to have been unique in Western, if not in world, history. But Jefferson shared with the ninth-century monarch at least one characteristic extremely rare among war leaders. While waging war he also cultivated assiduously the arts of civilization. As we have seen, between enemy invasions of the Commonwealth and with the whole American Revolution hanging in a doubtful balance, he was actively concerned with expanding the curriculum at the College of William and Mary, providing public library facilities, preserving and annotating historical documents, and doing personal research into a dozen fields of knowledge for production of his classic *Notes on the State of Virginia*.

Perhaps, along with the mature perspective that kept Jefferson mindful of the needs of the future as well as the exigencies of the moment, he was motivated in these intellectual concerns by a desire to escape more frustrating realities. But there was something else involved—that "divine discontent" which will not permit some minds to rest so long as there are better ways to be found and new realms to explore. In less exalted terms, Jefferson himself said he had a "canine appetite" for knowledge.

Jefferson's intellectual enthusiasms and his passionate devotion to civil and religious liberty infuse his correspondence from adolescence into old age just as they do his public papers. But evidence of these interests is nowhere so concentrated, nor so buttressed with erudition, as in his *Notes on the State of Virginia*.

The title is misleading. Even insofar as Jefferson confined his writing to a description of the history, geography, government, flora and fauna of Virginia, he was dealing not alone with the territory embraced by the present borders of the Commonwealth but with all lands explored, settled, and claimed by Virginians at the time of the Revolution—approximately a third of the North American continent. Additionally, Jefferson went far beyond this scheme. Possessed of a versatile and speculative mind quick to perceive relationships among virtually all branches of knowledge, he theorized—often brilliantly—in matters of botany, zoology, geology, anthropology, and political and moral philosophy. It is not surprising that the breadth of the work amazed many

Europeans who saw America in the time-honored way of those who wonder, "Can any good thing come out of Nazareth?"

Moreover, though the largely statistical portions of the book have no more style than an almanac, many of its constituent essays have an Addisonian polish and clarity, while some of the pleas for liberty have the sinewy terseness of Jonathan Swift and a few passages of natural description anticipate by several decades the most effective prose of the English Romanticists. Some excerpts from the book were printed in anthologies as early as the nineteenth century; but even most students of American writing were unaware of the literary merits of the work as a whole until Gilbert Chinard in 1929 hailed it as "one of the first masterpieces of American literature."[1] Since then many critics have agreed.

That Jefferson should have produced a work of such breadth and quality within a period of less than eleven months, seven of which he spent as Governor of a war-torn State and four as an embarrassed retiree preparing a detailed defense against his detractors, a period that brought the severe illness of his wife and death of his daughter, the evacuation of his capital and flight from his home before an invader seeking his capture, not to mention the fall from a horse that broke his arm and confined him for six weeks—that he should have accomplished so much against such odds—is little short of astonishing. Yet such is the case.

Jefferson began work on the book following the British invasion of Tidewater Virginia in October 1780. After a second invasion in January 1781 forced the evacuation of the capital, he merely explained to Marbois, whose inquiries had prompted the work: "Hitherto it has been in my power to collect a few materials only, which my present occupations disable me from completing. I mean, however, shortly to be in a condition which will leave me quite at leisure to take them up...."[2] When he returned to Monticello from Poplar Forest in August 1781 the manuscript was complete except for a few articles for which he needed information from members of the Assembly convening in October. From Richmond on December 20 he dispatched the full manuscript to Marbois, who must have been surprised at what his queries had produced.[3]

The reader is still surprised. The specificity of Jefferson's accounts would be expected by anyone familiar with the detailed records he kept of farm operations and of the building of Monticello. But the occasional lift from the prosaic to a highly charged lyricism is something that few people expect from one of the principal apostles of the Enlightenment. At one point Jefferson is dryly informing us that the Potomac River is "$7\frac{1}{2}$ miles wide at the mouth; $4\frac{1}{2}$ at Nomini Bay; 3 at Acquia," and so on, followed by a dutiful report on the sounding of its depth at various stations.[4] But just a few pages later he describes the river with an eloquence that surpasses those natural descriptions by James Fenimore Cooper that elicited Balzac's admiration, and attains a sublimity that invokes comparison with Chateaubriand, bursting full volume upon the reader with the suddenness of the mighty stream itself as it issues from the mountains:

> The passage of the Potomac through the Blue Ridge is perhaps one of the most stupendous scenes in nature. You stand on a very high point of land. On your right comes up the Shenandoah, having ranged along the foot of the mountain an hundred miles to seek a vent. On your left approaches the Potomac, in

quest of a passage also. In the moment of their junction they rush together against the mountain, rend it asunder, and pass off to sea. The first glance of this scene hurries our senses into the opinion, that this earth has been created in time, that the mountains were formed first, that the rivers began to flow afterwards, that in this place particularly they have been dammed up by the Blue Ridge of mountains, and have formed an ocean which filled the whole valley; that continuing to rise they have at length broken over at this spot, and have torn the mountain down from its summit to its base. The pile of rock on each hand, but particularly on the Shenandoah, the evident marks of their disrupture and avulsion from their beds by the most powerful agents of nature, corroborate the impression. But the distant finishing which nature has given to the picture is of a very different character. It is a true contrast to the foreground. It is as placid and delightful, as that is wild and tremendous. For the mountain being cloven asunder, she presents to your eye, through the cleft, a small catch of smooth blue horizon, at an infinite distance in the plain country, inviting you, as it were, from the riot and tumult roaring around, to pass through the breach and participate of the calm below. Here the eye ultimately composes itself; and that way too the road happens actually to lead.[5]

Similarly he describes the Natural Bridge of Virginia, which he had acquired by purchase of a 157-acre tract in Rockbridge County in 1775, in terms prosaic enough for one writing about a phenomenon sometimes listed among the "Seven Natural Wonders of the World": "The fissure, just at the bridge, is by some admeasurements, 270 feet deep, by others only 205. It is about 45 feet wide at the bottom, and 90 feet at the top; this of course determines the length of the bridge, and its height from the water." But the patient recorder of statistics becomes in the same paragraph the enthusiastic celebrator of "the most sublime of Nature's works." He relates the thrill of personal experience: "Though the sides of this bridge are provided in some parts with a parapet of fixed rocks, yet few men have resolution to walk to them and look over into the abyss. You involuntarily fall on your hands and feet, creep to the parapet and peep over it. Looking down from this height about a minute gave me a violent headache."[6] In a later amendment to the original manuscript Jefferson wrote: "It is impossible for the emotions arising from the sublime to be felt beyond what they are here. So beautiful an arch, so elevated, so light, springing, as it were, up to heaven! The rapture of the spectator is really indescribable."[7]

From nature's architecture Jefferson turned to that of man. Like so many outstanding architects, he was highly critical of any school but his own. It was in *Notes on the State of Virginia* that he characterized the Wren Building of the College of William and Mary and the Hospital in Williamsburg as "rude, mis-shapen piles, which, but that they have roofs, would be taken for brick-kilns." The capitol he found "tolerably just in its proportions and ornaments, save only that the intercolonnations are too large." Even the Governor's Palace, as we have seen earlier, he described as "not handsome without" though "spacious and commodious within" and "capable of being made an elegant seat."[8] He was so in love with the architectural styles of classical Greece and Rome and with Andrea Palladio's Renaissance adaptations of them that he regarded even the neo-Palladian masterpieces of Sir Christopher Wren as disgusting perversions. He complained that in courthouses and churches (and here one is reminded that he had worshiped in Williamsburg's Bruton Parish Church) "no attempts are made at elegance." Then he added:

> Indeed it would not be easy to execute such an attempt, as a workman could scarcely be found here capable of drawing an order. The genius of architecture seems to have shed its maledictions over this land. Buildings are often erected, by individuals, of considerable expense. To give these symmetry and taste would not increase their cost. It would only change the arrangement of the materials, the form and combination of the members. This would often cost less than the burthen of barbarous ornaments with which these buildings are sometimes charged. But the first principles of the art are unknown, and there exists scarcely a model among us sufficiently chaste to give an idea of them.[9]

His optimism reasserted itself, however: "Architecture being one of the fine arts, and as such within the department of a professor at the college, according to the new arrangement, perhaps a spark may fall on some young subjects of natural taste, kindle up their genius, and produce a reformation in this elegant and useful art."[10] This was one of several instances in which Jefferson cited the enlarged curriculum at William and Mary as a harbinger of progress without claiming credit for the changes which he had initiated.

Even this optimism was modified by decided reservations about the future of domestic architecture: "But all we shall do in this way will produce no permanent improvement to our country while the unhappy prejudice prevails that houses of brick or stone are less wholesome than those of wood."[11]

Certainly Jefferson himself had used brick and stone very imaginatively in his own home, contrasting red brick of Albemarle clay with buff stone trim in a way that added great liveliness to the dignity of symmetrical Palladian façades. The colors also blended well with the landscape and, as we have seen, Jefferson even leveled off the top of his peak in such a way that the low dome of Monticello seemed to become the summit of the mountain. In adapting a European mode for American use he was fully aware of the desirability of conforming to the esthetic demands of the environment.

Though the still incomplete structure of Monticello, the remodeling of the foyer of the Governor's Palace, and a few designs for friends were so far his chief architectural achievements, Jefferson was on his way to becoming America's greatest architect of the day and the father of the whole neoclassical movement in the United States. Some today would give this self-educated amateur who never charged for his services a still higher rank among architects. Nigel Nicolson featured Monticello as one of thirty-six European and American residences in *Great Houses of the Western World,* citing Jefferson's originality in using octagon designs "imparting 'movement' to the whole building" and achieving effects of light and shade "softening and humanizing the classicism of the porches."[12] Dictionaries and encyclopedias of world architecture differ in their evaluations of his talents but few ignore him. In 1976 a poll of the American Institute of Architects placed him above Louis Sullivan, Frank Lloyd Wright, and all other American architects as the creator in the University of Virginia of the nation's greatest architectural achievement.[13]

Furthermore, like Britain's famous Adam brothers, Jefferson was a pioneer in design-ing interior furnishings to harmonize with his architectural plans. In Monticello he de-signed complementary valances, draperies, wooden furniture, drinking cups, and silver candlesticks. Of course, he was also his own landscape gardener. The Marquis de Chastellux may have exaggerated in saying, "Mr. Jefferson is the first American who has consulted the fine arts to know how he should shelter himself from the weather."[14] But certainly none before him or in his time consulted them to more ad-vantage or with so great inspiration to his countrymen.

Jefferson was as interested in weather as in shelter. He made pioneer studies of rainfall, temperature, and climate, recording detailed personal observations at Monticello, in Williamsburg, and at Philadelphia, and exchanging information with residents of other States and of Europe.[15] These studies led him to reflections on clothing and other in-sulation against the cold. He analyzed the reasons for the differing properties of linen, cotton, fur, and feathers as conductors and retainers of heat.[16]

Even more interesting to Jefferson than the shelter or clothing of the New World were the people themselves, the transplanted Europeans and Africans, and the aborigines. As historian, linguist, and anthropologist, he examined the life of each ethnic group.

He anticipated Arnold Toynbee's interest in the "sea changes" experienced by cultures transplanted from the Old World to the New. Few people in the world in his time enjoyed so sweeping a perspective of the unity and variety of Anglo-Saxon culture. Englishmen lacked the requisite knowledge of American institutions and Americans the knowledge of English origins in Germanic Europe to see, as Jefferson so clearly did, the two great westward migrations of Anglo-Saxon culture as related events spanning twelve centuries.

He is justly honored (though not often enough) as "the earliest American student of Anglo-Saxon language and institutions."[17] In his *Notes on the State of Virginia* he wrote, in connection with curriculum reforms at William and Mary: "To the professor-ships usually established in the universities of Europe, it would seem proper to add one for the ancient language and literature of the North, on account of their connec-tion with our own language, laws, customs, and history."[18] Jefferson's reference was to "the old Germanic languages, especially Old English or Anglo-Saxon." He was the instigator of the addition of such studies to the curricula of both William and Mary and the University of Virginia. His *An Essay Toward Facilitating Instruction in the Anglo-Saxon and Modern Dialects of the English Language,*[19] published posthumously, has proved stimulating to scholars in both the nineteenth and twentieth centuries. Some of his theories about the teaching of Old English find confirmation in the methods de-vised in the second half of the twentieth century by the eminent philologists Albert H. Marckwardt and James L. Rosier.[20] In his own life, Jefferson's Anglo-Saxon studies enriched his appreciation of his native tongue, added depth to his scholarship in the law, and were so much a part of him that, as we have seen, he drew heavily upon them as penman of the Revolution, infusing the drama of his own time with a high sense of history lifting it above the exigential.

Yet Jefferson's pride in his own ethnic heritage did not blind him to the splendor of other cultures. His enthusiasm for French civilization was such that some of his coun-trymen would call him a Francophile, and the art, architecture, and mellifluous language of Italy excited his ardent admiration.

He was rare among Americans of his generation in appreciating the cultures of the Indian nations inhabiting North America. Enjoying wider circulation in the United States than Rousseau's concept of the "noble savage" was the popular belief that "the only good Indian is a dead Indian." Of course, an example of tolerance had been set by Jefferson's father in entertaining chiefs in his home, and one moonlit night at Williamsburg when Jefferson heard the farewell address of Outassété to his people, he had acquired a lifelong respect for the Indians' genius for oratory. He included in the *Notes* the speech of Logan, a Mingo chief whose family were murdered by whites.[21] The dignified lament, concluding with "Who is there to mourn for Logan?—Not one," became a favorite of American anthologists and elocutionists. Once, when Jefferson was accused of having fabricated the speech in order to ascribe the gift of high eloquence to an Indian and thus refute Buffon's thesis that man and all other creatures degenerated in the New World, the Virginian replied: "But wherefore the forgery? Whether Logan's or mine, it would still have been American. . . . He would have a just right to be proud who could with truth claim that composition. But it is none of mine; and I yield it to whom it is due."[22]

Jefferson was quite concerned with Buffon's assertions, which the Virginian neatly summarized:

> 1. That the animals common both to the old and new world, are smaller in the latter. 2. That those peculiar to the new, are on a smaller scale. 3. That those which have been domesticated in both, have degenerated in America: and 4. That on the whole it exhibits fewer species. And the reason he thinks is, that the heats of America are less; that more waters are spread over its surface by nature, and fewer of these drained off by the hand of man. In other words, that *heat* is friendly, and *moisture* adverse to the production and development of large quadrupeds.[23]

Jefferson replied in *Notes:*

> I will not meet this hypothesis on its first doubtful ground, whether the climate of America be comparatively more humid? Because we are not furnished with observations sufficient to decide this question. And though, till it be decided, we are as free to deny, as others are to affirm the fact, yet for a moment let it be supposed. The hypothesis, after this supposition, proceeds to another; that *moisture* is unfriendly to animal growth. The truth of this is inscrutable to us by reasonings a priori. Nature has hidden from us her modus agendi. Our only appeal on such questions is to experience; and I think that experience is against the supposition. It is by the assistance of *heat* and *moisture* that vegetables are elaborated from the elements of earth, air, water, and fire. We accordingly see the more humid climates produce the greater quantity of vegetables. Vegetables are mediately or immediately the food of every animal: and in proportion to the quantity of food, we see animals not only multiplied in their numbers, but improved in their bulk, as far as the laws of their nature will admit.[24]

He also challenged the count's claim that "nature is less active, less energetic on one side of the globe than she is on the other." "As if," said Jefferson, "both sides were not warmed by the same genial sun; as if a soil of the same chemical composition, was less capable of elaboration into animal nutriment; as if the fruits and grains from that soil and sun, yielded a less rich chyle, gave less extension to the solids and fluids of the body, or produced sooner in the cartilages, membranes, and fibres, that rigidity which restrains all further extension, and terminates animal growth. The truth is, that a Pigmy and a Patagonian, a Mouse and a Mammoth, derive their dimensions from the same nutritive juices. The difference of increment depends on circumstances unsearchable to beings with our capacities. Every race of animals seems to have received from their Maker certain laws of extension at the time of their formation. Their elaborative organs were formed to produce this, while proper obstacles were opposed to its further progress. Below these limits they cannot fall, nor rise above them. What intermediate station they shall take may depend on soil, on climate, on food, on a careful choice of breeders. But all the manna of heaven would never raise the Mouse to the bulk of the Mammoth."[25]

Jefferson proceeded to a specific refutation, animal by animal, of charges that American animals were smaller than their Old World counterparts and, besides compiling categorical statistics, eagerly collected skeletons and skins to send to Europe as specimens. But of primary concern to him was the imputation that human beings attained neither the physical nor mental growth in America that was customary in Europe. His method of refutation was not the whimsical way of Benjamin Franklin who seated French and American guests on opposite sides of his dinner table and, when the question of relative stature arose, asked all to stand, whereupon the Americans towered over their opposite numbers. The wily host had anticipated the question and loaded his guest list with tall Americans and short Frenchmen. Jefferson compiled facts on Americans of European descent, but devoted special attention to the aborigines. He submitted evidence that they were tall, long-limbed, well-informed, and intelligent. He even was at pains to assert that their "generative organs" were just as large as those of Europeans. To the charge that they lacked the sexual ardor of Europeans, Jefferson retorted that their exertions in hunting and warring drained some of the passion and energy that might otherwise have gone into concupiscence, and that the chivalric customs of most tribes restrained them from the rape of female prisoners that was an accepted concomitant of war in the Old World.[26]

His studies of the Indians ran much deeper than the compiling of census data. He was a serious student of their languages, tribal organization, and anthropology.

He was a pioneer in the investigations that he initiated in comparative linguistics, not only among the aborigines of North and South America but also with the peoples of Europe and Asia. He cannily observed of the Indian nations, "A knowledge of their several languages would be the most certain evidence of their derivation which could be produced."[27] He even suggested that some ancestors of the American Indians might have entered the country in much earlier times by a land bridge from Asia.

Discussing linguistic evidence of both unity and differentiation among the North American Indians, Jefferson wrote lines that have less value as scientific explication than as a revelation of his own philosophy:

Very possibly there may have been anciently three different stocks, each of which multiplying in a long course of time, had separated into so many little societies. This practice results from the circumstance of their having never submitted themselves to any laws, any coercive power, any shadow of government. Their only controls are their manners, and that moral sense of right and wrong, which, like the sense of tasting and feeling, in every man makes a part of his nature. An offense against these is punished by contempt, by exclusion from society, or, where the case is serious, as that of murder, by the individuals whom it concerns. Imperfect as this species of coercion may seem, crimes are very rare among them: insomuch that were it made a question, whether no law, as among the savage Americans, or too much law, as among the civilized Europeans, submits man to the greatest evil, one who has seen both conditions of existence would pronouce it to be the last: and that the sheep are happier of themselves, than under care of the wolves. It will be said, that great societies cannot exist without government. The savages therefore break them into small ones.[28]

Jefferson had turned archeologist in pursuit of information on the Indians. In the *Notes* he told of exploring a burial mound "situated on the low grounds of the Rivanna about two miles above its principal fork, and opposite to some hills, on which had been an Indian town. It was of a spheroidical form, of about 40 feet diameter at the base, and had been of about twelve feet altitude, though now reduced by the plough to seven and a half, having been under cultivation about a dozen years. Before this it was covered with trees of twelve inches diameter, and round the base was excavation of five feet depth and width, from whence the earth had been taken of which the hillock was formed."[29]

The sense of adventure shines through the dispassionate prose in which he tells of his discovery:

I first dug superficially in several parts of it, and came to collections of human bones, at different depths, from six inches to three feet below the surface. These were lying in the utmost confusion, some vertical, some oblique, some horizontal, and directed to every point of the compass, entangled, and held together in clusters by the earth. Bones of the most distant parts were found together, as, for instance, the small bones of the foot in the hollow of a skull; many skulls would sometimes be in contact, lying on the face, on the side, on the back, top or bottom, so as, on the whole, to give the idea of bones emptied promiscuously from a bag or basket, and covered over with earth, without any attention to their order. . . . There were some teeth which were judged to be smaller than those of an adult; a skull, which, on a slight view, appeared to be that of an infant, but it fell to pieces on being taken out, so as to prevent satisfactory examination; a rib, and a fragment of the under-jaw of a person about half grown; another rib of an infant; and part of the jaw of a child, which had not yet cut its teeth. This last furnishing the most decisive proof of the burial of children here, I was particular in my attention to it. It was part of the right-half of the under-jaw. The processes, by which it was articulated to the temporal bones, were entire; and the bone itself firm to where it had been broken off, which, as nearly as I could judge, was about the place of the eyetooth. Its upper edge, wherein would have been the sockets of the teeth, was perfectly smooth. Measuring it with that of an adult, by placing their hinder processes together, its broken end extended to the penultimate grinder of the adult. This bone was white, all the others of a sand color. The bones of infants being soft, they probably decay sooner, which might be the cause so few were found here.[30]

Jefferson "made a perpendicular cut through the body of the barrow" and found four "plainly distinguishable" strata. There may have been a thousand skeletons. He examined the visible evidence in terms of prevalent theories regarding these mounds:

The bones nearest the surface were least decayed. No holes were discovered in any of them, as if made with bullets, arrows, or other weapons. . . . Every one will readily seize the circumstances above related, which militate against the opinion, that it covered the bones only of persons fallen in battle; and against the tradition also, which would make it the common sepulchre of a town, in which the bodies were placed upright, and touching each other. Appearances certainly indicate that it has derived both origin and growth from the accustomary collection of bones, and deposition of them together; that the first collection had been deposited on the common surface of the earth, a few stones put over it, and then a covering of earth, that the second had been laid on this, had covered more or less of it in proportion to the number of bones, and was then also covered with earth; and so on. The following are the particular circumstances which give it this aspect. 1. The number of bones. 2. Their confused position. 3. Their being in different strata. 4. The strata in one part having no correspondence with those in another. 5. The different states of decay in these strata, which seem to indicate a difference in the time of inhumation. 6. The existence of infant bones among them.[31]

Not only was Jefferson one of North America's first archeologists, as distinguished from mere curious diggers, but he "anticipated by a century the aims and methods of modern archaeological science."[32]

Jefferson's studies—linguistic, ethnological, and anthropological—all led him to believe that the Indian was probably the equal of the Caucasian in native intelligence. Apparent differences in intelligence between the two ethnic groups he attributed to differences in education, not merely that the education of the Indian was in many respects inferior to that of the European or his American descendant, but that each group was trained to use its intelligence in different ways.

This conclusion of Jefferson's was the same as that reached by a scientific and versatile Virginia planter and political leader of an earlier generation, William Byrd II of Westover. Byrd also had said that he believed the Negro to be naturally as intelligent as the Caucasian, suspecting that apparent racial differences in intellect were the result of culture.[33] Jefferson was not prepared to go that far.

His attitude toward blacks was liberal enough to excite anger in his own day though conservative enough to cause dismay in ours. But what could be more ironic than to lift Jefferson out of his own time to judge him in the context of ours and then pronounce him intolerant?

Reporting in the *Notes* that Virginia's population of 567,614 was divided on the ratio of nearly 11 to 10 between free inhabitants and slaves, Jefferson wrote, "Under the mild treatment our slaves experience, and their wholesome, though coarse, food, this blot in our country increases as fast, or faster, than the whites."[34] He related the record of royal vetoes of Virginia's legislative efforts to end the slave trade and then boasted: "In the very first session held under the republican government, the Assembly passed a law for the perpetual prohibition of the importation of slaves. This will in some measure stop the increase of this great political and moral evil, while the minds of our citizens may be ripening for a complete emancipation of human nature."[35]

He was less optimistic in a later portion of the book, but still not completely pessimistic:

The whole commerce between master and slave is a perpetual exercise of the most boisteroius passions, the most unremitting despotism on the one part, and degrading submission on the other. Our children see this, and learn to imitate it; for man is an imitative animal. This quality is the germ of all education in him. From his cradle to his grave he is learning to do what he sees others do. If a parent could find no motive either in his philanthropy or his self-love, for restraining intemperance of passion towards his slave, it should always be a sufficient one that his child is present. But generally it is not sufficient. The parent storms, the child looks on, catches the lineaments of wrath, puts on the same airs in the circles of smaller slaves, gives a loose to his worst of passions, and thus nursed, educated, and daily exercised in tyranny, cannot but be stamped by it with odious peculiarities.

The man must be a prodigy who can retain his manners and morals undepraved by such circumstances. And with what execration should the statesman be loaded, who permitting one half the citizens thus to trample on the rights of the other, transforms those into despots, and these into enemies, destroys the morals of the one part, and the amor patriae of the other. For if a slave can have a country in this world, it must be any other in preference to that in which he is born to live and labor for another: in which he must lock up the faculties of his nature, contribute as far as depends on his individual endeavors to the evanishment of the human race, or entail his own miserable condition on the endless generations proceeding from him.

With the morals of the people, their industry also is destroyed. For in a warm climate, no man will labor for himself who can make another labor for him. This is so true, that of the proprietors of slaves a very small proportion indeed are ever seen to labor. And can the liberties of a nation be thought secure when we have removed their only firm basis, a conviction in the minds of the people that these liberties are of the gift of God? That they are not to be violated but with his wrath? Indeed I tremble for my country when I reflect that God is just: that his justice cannot sleep for ever: that considering numbers, nature and natural means only, a revolution of the wheel of fortune, an exchange of situation, is among possible events: that it may become probable by supernatural interference! The Almighty has no attribute which can take side with us in such a contest.

But it is impossible to be temperate and to pursue this subject through the various considerations of policy, of morals, of history natural and civil. We must be contented to hope they will force their way into every one's mind. I think a change already perceptible, since the origin of the present revolution. The spirit of the master is abating, that of the slave rising from the dust, his condition mollifying, the way I hope preparing, under the auspices of heaven, for a total emancipation, and that this is disposed, in the order of events, to be with the consent of the masters, rather than by their extirpation.[36]

In discussing the revision of the laws of Virginia, in which he had played the leading role, Jefferson cited a plan to emancipate all slaves born after passage of a proposed act. He explained: "The bill reported by the revisors does not itself contain this proposition; but an amendment containing it was prepared, to be offered to the legislature whenever the bill should be taken up, and further directing, that they should continue with their parents to a certain age, then be brought up, at the public expense, to tillage, arts or sciences, according to their geniuses, till the females should be eighteen, and the males twenty-one years of age, when they should be colonized to such place as the circumstances of the time should render most proper, sending them out with arms, implements of household and of the handicraft arts, seeds, pairs of the useful domestic animals, &c. to declare them a free and independent people, and extend to them our alliance and protection, till they shall have acquired strength; and to send vessels at the same time to other parts of the world for an equal number of white inhabitants; to induce whom to migrate hither, proper encouragements were to be proposed."[37]

He said:

It will probably be asked, Why not retain and incorporate the blacks into the state, and thus save the expense of supplying, by importation of white settlers, the vacancies they will leave? Deep rooted prejudices entertained by the whites; the thousand recollections, by the blacks, of the injuries they have sustained; new provocations; the real distinctions which nature had made; and many other circumstances, will divide us into parties, and produce convulsions which will probably never end but in the extermination of the one or the other race.

To these objections, which are political, may be added others, which are physical and moral. The first difference which strikes us is that of color. Whether the black of the negro resides in the reticular membrane between the skin and the scarf-skin, or in the scarf-skin itself; whether it proceeds from the color of the blood, the color of the bile, or from that of some other secretion, the difference is fixed in nature, and is as real as if its seat and cause were better known to us. And is this difference of no importance? Is it not the foundation of a greater or less share of beauty in the two races? Are not the fine mixtures of red and white, the expressions of every passion by greater or less suffusions of color in the one, preferable to that eternal monotony, which reigns in the countenances, that immovable veil of black which covers all the emotions of the other race? Add to these, flowing hair, a more elegant symmetry of form, their own judgment in favor of the whites, declared by their preference of them, as uniformly as is the preference of the Orangutan for the black women over those of his own species. The circumstance of superior beauty, is thought worthy attention in the propagation of our horses, dogs, and other domestic animals; why not in that of man?

Besides those of color, figure, and hair, there are other physical distinctions proving a difference of race. They have less hair on the face and body. They secrete less by the kidneys, and more by the glands of the skin, which gives them a very strong and disagreeable odor. This greater degree of transpiration renders them more tolerant of heat, and less so of cold, than the whites. Perhaps too a difference of structure in the pulmonary apparatus, which a late ingenious experimentalist has discovered to be the principal regulator of animal heat, may have disabled them from extricating, in the act of inspiration, so much of that fluid from the outer air, or obliged them in expiration, to part with more of it. They seem to require less sleep. A black, after hard labor through the day, will be induced by the slightest amusements to sit up till midnight, or later, though knowing he must be out with the first dawn of the morning. They are at least as brave, and more adventuresome. . . . They are more ardent after their female: but love seems with them to be more an eager desire, than a tender delicate mixture of sentiment and sensation. Their griefs are transient. Those numberless afflictions, which render it doubtful whether heaven has given life to us in mercy or in wrath, are less felt, and sooner forgotten with them. In general, their existence appears to participate more of sensation than reflection.[38]

Jefferson summarized:

Comparing them by their faculties of memory, reason, and imagination, it appears to me, that in memory they are equal to the whites; in reason much inferior, as I think one could scarcely be found capable of tracing and comprehending the investigations of Euclid; and that in imagination they are dull, tasteless, and anomalous. It would be unfair to follow them to Africa for this investigation. We will consider them here, on the same stage with the whites, and where the facts are not apocryphal on which a judgment is to be formed. It will be right to make great allowances for the difference of condition, of education, of conversation, of the sphere in which they move. Many millions of them have been brought to, and born in America. Most of them indeed have been confined to tillage, to their own homes, and their own society: yet many have been so situated, that they might have availed themselves of the conversation of their masters; many have been brought up to the handicraft arts, and from that circumstance have always been associated with the whites. Some have been liberally educated, and all have lived in countries where the arts and sciences are cultivated to a considerable degree, and have had before their eyes samples of the best works from abroad. The Indians, with no advantages of this kind, will often carve figures on their pipes not destitute of design and merit. They will crayon out an animal, a plant, or a country, so as to prove the existence of a germ in their minds which only wants cultivation. They astonish you with strokes of the most sublime oratory; such as prove their reason and sentiment strong, their imagination glowing and elevated.

But never yet could I find that a black had uttered a thought above the level of plain narration; never see even an elementary trait of painting or sculpture.[39]

He did concede: "In music they are more generally gifted than the whites with accurate ears for tune and time, and they have been found capable of imagining a small catch." But then he added: "Whether they will be equal to the composition of a more extensive run of melody, or of complicated harmony, is yet to be proved."[40] The whole statement smacks very much of that tired cliché of racial discussions, "They have a wonderful sense of rhythm." Jefferson had not had the opportunity to hear the compositions of W. C. Handy, Scott Joplin, or Duke Ellington.

Turning to another art, Jefferson observed: "Misery is often the parent of the most affecting touches in poetry. Among the blacks is misery enough, God knows, but no poetry. Love is the peculiar oestrum of the poet. Their love is ardent, but it kindles the senses only, not the imagination."[41] Jefferson's fellow Virginian, George Washington, might here have entered a caveat. He had been so impressed with the young black Phyllis Wheatley's poetic effusions in the manner of Alexander Pope that he had invited her to read them to his staff. Jefferson had not overlooked the Massachusetts marvel. He wrote: "Religion has indeed produced a Phyllis Wheatly; but it could not produce a poet. The compositions published under her name are below the dignity of criticism. The heroes of the Dunciad are to her as Hercules to the author of that poem."[42]

Discussing with familiarity the recently published letters of a black born on a slave ship, Jefferson wrote: "Ignatius Sancho has approached nearer to merit in composition; yet his letters do more honor to the heart than the head. . . . Upon the whole, though we admit him to the first place among those of his own color who have presented themselves to the public judgment, yet when we compare him with the writers of the race among whom he lived, and particularly with the epistolary class, in which he has taken his own stand, we are compelled to enroll him at the bottom of the column."[43] Of course, there was then no Richard Wright, Ralph Ellison, James Baldwin, or Ernest Gaines.

Turning to the suggestion that the conditions of slavery rather than any inherent deficiency might be responsible for the apparent inequality of blacks and whites, Jefferson cited evidence that Roman slaves even in the reign of Augustus had enjoyed fewer advantages than the blacks held in bondage in Virginia in his own day. "Yet notwithstanding these and other discouraging circumstances among the Romans, their slaves were often their rarest artists. They excelled too in science, insomuch as to be usually employed as tutors to their master's children. Epictetus, Terence, and Phaedrus were slaves. But they were of the race of whites. It is not their condition, then, but nature, which has produced the distinction."[44]

In pronouncing the black intellectually inferior to the white, Jefferson was voicing an opinion with which in that age nearly every white, and probably nearly every black, would have agreed. But then he proceeded to take issue with the commonly voiced opinion that blacks were by nature thievish and in general morally inferior to whites:

Whether further observation will or will not verify the conjecture, that nature has been less bountiful to them in the endowments of the head, I believe that in those of the heart she will be found to have done them justice. That disposition to theft with which they have been branded, must be ascribed to their situation, and not to any depravity of the moral sense. The man, in whose favor no laws of property exist, probably feels himself less bound to respect those made in favor of others. When arguing for ourselves, we lay it down as a fundamental, that laws, to be just, must give a reciprocation of right: that, without this, they are mere arbitrary rules of conduct, founded in force, and not in conscience: and it is a problem which I give to the master to solve, whether the religious precepts against the violation of property were not framed for him as well as his slave? And whether the slave may not as justifiably take a little from one, who has taken all from him, as he may slay one who would slay him? That a change in the relations in which a man is placed should change his ideas of moral right and wrong, is neither new, nor peculiar to the color of the blacks.[45]

He concludes: "Notwithstanding these considerations which must weaken their respect for the laws of property, we find among them numerous instances of the most rigid integrity, and as many as among their better instructed masters, of benevolence, gratitude, and unshaken fidelity."[46]

Convinced that the Negro equaled the Caucasian in moral stature, which Jefferson considered the most important measure of human worth, he nevertheless believed that an intellectual disparity would make unwise the mingling of the races in freedom and social equality. "Among the Romans," he said, "emancipation required but one effort. The slave, when made free, might mix with, without staining the blood of his master. But with us a second is necessary, unknown to history. When freed, he is to be removed beyond the reach of mixture." To prevent such mixture, they must be colonized apart.[47]

Jefferson was temporarily blinding himself to the miscegenation that had already taken place in many instances; he evidently did not see before him the dark faces of his wife's half sisters who served at Monticello. If he did think of this matter at all, he must have drawn a measure of security from the law under which a little black admixture could make a white officially a Negro but a similar infusion from a Caucasian could not officially make a black white. In a later generation, Booker T. Washington would observe that Negro blood must be the strongest blood in the world as even a little of it would make anyone a Negro. Yet had not Jefferson himself passionately challenged this idea in Howell v. Netherland in 1770 when he had fought for the freedom of his mulatto client?

Jefferson was not at ease with his conclusions about blacks. In fact, he rendered them quite tentative before quitting the subject:

The opinion, that they are inferior in the faculties of reason and imagination, must be hazarded with diffidence. To justify a general conclusion, requires many observations, even where the subject may be submitted to the anatomical knife, to optical glasses, to analysis by fire, or by solvents. How much more then where it is a faculty, not a substance, we are examining; where it eludes the research of all the senses; where the conditions of its existence are various and variously combined; where the effects of those which are present or absent bid defiance to calculation; let me add too, as a circumstance of great tenderness, where our conclusion would degrade a whole race of men from the rank in the scale of beings which their Creator may perhaps have given them. To our reproach it must be said, that though for a century and a half we have had under our eyes the races of black and of red men, they have never yet been viewed by us as subjects of natural history. I advance it therefore as a suspicion only, that the blacks, whether originally a distinct race, or made distinct by time and circumstances, are inferior to the whites in the endowments both of body and mind.[48]

In thus admitting that blacks as an ethnic group might possibly equal whites in native capacity, Jefferson was departing not only from the convictions of his class in Virginia but from virtually all those Americans from Massachusetts to Georgia who, whether as slave traders or slaveholders, had been closely associated with the nation's black population. Today, some people have difficulty in realizing that Jefferson's few tentative demurrers to his own suppositions about Negro capacities were once regarded as bold challenges to fiercely defended dogma.

Though Jefferson had grave doubts about racial equality, he seemed to accept the equality of the sexes as a matter beyond argument among the enlightened. In evaluating the level of society among the Virginia Indians, he said: "The women are submitted to unjust drudgery. This I believe is the case with every barbarous people. With such, force is law. The stronger sex therefore imposes on the weaker. It is civilization alone which replaces women in the enjoyment of their natural equality."[49]

Of course, there were some women who could have told him that even the civilized society of the United States did not allow their sex "the enjoyment of their natural equality." Both Abigail, the wife of John Adams, and Hannah, the sister of Richard Henry Lee, demanded that women be allowed to vote. Actually, the eighteenth century was not as repressive of feminist rights as the nineteenth would be. Women in the United States operated hostelries and other businesses. In both America and England they helped to edit publications for readers of both sexes. Jefferson was careful to train the minds of his own daughters and personally was attracted to women of intelligence and education. Apparently the fact that Martha was well read was one of her attractions. After all, Jefferson had grown up in the belief, which he never abandoned, that his beloved sister Jane was his own intellectual equal. This recognition does not seem to accord well with Jefferson's suggestions at times that women were better off not involved in politics, but one must remember that he also indicated sometimes his belief that scholars could lead happier and more useful lives apart from affairs of government. He thought it a pity that such a brilliant scientist as his friend David Rittenhouse should accept state office in Pennsylvania and lamented that he himself had been snatched from useful studies by political demands.

Yet Jefferson's political activities were part and parcel of his life as a scholar. For him the contest for votes was largely a necessary adjunct to the struggle for ideas. During the Revolution, according to a contemporary reporter, the epitaph of John Bradshaw, president of the commission that sentenced Charles I, was "often seen pasted up in the houses of North America."[50] The inscription, a thrilling tribute to martyrdom in the interest of liberty, was said to be "engraved upon a cannon at the summit of a steep hill near Martha Brae in Jamaica." The fact that Bradshaw had not been buried in Jamaica did not inhibit one whit the circulation of the story. Thomas Jefferson suspected that the epitaph was a fabrication by Benjamin Franklin, who was at least as much propagandist as philosopher and not above a little mythologizing in behalf of democracy. Later evidence has lent weight to his suspicions.

But Jefferson was so impressed with the last words of the "epitaph," whatever their origin, that he tried to have them adopted as Virginia's motto and, failing that, adopted them as the personal motto surrounding the monogram on his seal: "Rebellion to tyrants is obedience to God." Later Jefferson was to express a similar idea in even more memorable words of his own: "I have sworn upon the altar of God eternal hostility to every form of tyranny over the mind of man."[51] Freedom of the mind was, to him, at least as vital as freedom of speech and press. The mind must be freed from the tyranny of censoring governments, but it must be freed also from the domination of ignorance and superstition.

Nowhere is his devotion to freedom more apparent than in his labors for religious liberty. In the *Notes* Jefferson related that the General Assembly of Virginia in October 1776 had "repealed *all acts of parliament* which had rendered criminal the maintaining any opinions in matters of religion, the forbearing to repair to church, and the exercising any mode of worship; and suspended the laws giving salaries to the clergy, which suspension was made perpetual in October 1779." He did not tell of his own part in these reforms.[52]

But he did tell of his high hopes that Virginia would repeal its own act of Assembly of 1705 providing that "if a person brought up in the Christian religion denies the being of a God, or the Trinity, or asserts there are more Gods than one, or denies the Christian religion to be true, or the scriptures to be of divine authority, he is punishable on the first offense by incapacity to hold any office or employment ecclesiastical, civil, or military." For the second offense there were additional punishments, most of them seldom if ever invoked in those days, but one of them a constant threat to the parent who publicly voiced unorthodox religious opinions—ineligibility for guardianship. Jefferson commented: "A father's right to the custody of his own children being founded in law on his right of guardianship, this being taken away, they may of course be severed from him, and put, by the authority of a court, into more orthodox hands. This is a summary view of that religious slavery, under which a people have been willing to remain, who have lavished their lives and fortunes for the establishment of their civil freedom."[53]

The law was not as harsh as those restricting political freedom in some states, especially the theocracies of New England. Not only was it easier on Christian offenders, but Jews were exempt from persecution under the Virginia enactment as it applied specifically to those "brought up in the Christian religion." But it was not as broad as the laws of Pennsylvania and New York, which contained no provision for the legal establishment of religion. The fact that the Virginia law was sparingly applied was no guarantee that such moderation would always prevail. Turning impassioned advocate in the midst of his philosophical disquisition, Jefferson urged:

> Let us too give this experiment fair play, and get rid, while we may, of those tyrannical laws. It is true, we are as yet secured against them by the spirit of the times. I doubt whether the people of this country would suffer an execution for

heresy, or a three years imprisonment for not comprehending the mysteries of the Trinity. But is the spirit of the people an infallible, a permanent reliance? Is it government? Is this the kind of protection we receive in return for the rights we give up? Besides, the spirit of the times may alter, will alter. Our rulers will become corrupt, our people careless. A single zealot may commence persecutor, and better men be his victims. It can never be too often repeated, that the time for fixing every essential right on a legal basis is while our rulers are honest, and ourselves united. ... The shackles, therefore, which shall not be knocked off at the conclusion of this war, will remain on us long, will be made heavier and heavier, till our rights shall revive or expire in a convulsion.[54]

Many of Jefferson's contemporaries were shocked when he wrote: "The legitimate powers of government extend to such acts only as are injurious to others. But it does me no injury for my neighbor to say there are twenty gods, or no god. It neither picks my pocket nor breaks my leg."[55]

To the assertion that a nonbeliever should at least be restrained from propagating error, he replied:

Constraint may make him worse by making him a hypocrite, but it will never make him a truer man. It may fix him obstinately in his errors, but will not cure them. Reason and free enquiry are the only effectual agents against error. Give a loose to them, they will support the true religion, by bringing every false one to their tribunal, to the test of their investigation. They are the natural enemies of error, and of error only. Had not the Roman government permitted free enquiry, Christianity could never have been introduced. Had not free enquiry been indulged, at the era of the reformation, the corruptions of Christianity could not have been purged away. If it be restrained now, the present corruptions will be protected, and new ones encouraged.

Was the government to prescribe to us our medicine and diet, our bodies would be in such keeping as our souls are now. Thus in France the emetic was once forbidden as a medicine, and the potato as an article of food. Government is just as infallible too when it fixes systems in physics. Galileo was sent to the inquisition for affirming that the earth was a sphere: the government had declared it to be as flat as a trencher, and Galileo was obliged to abjure his error. This error however at length prevailed, the earth became a globe, and Descartes declared it was whirled round its axis by a vortex. The government in which he lived was wise enough to see that this was no question of civil jurisdiction, or we should all have been involved by authority in vortices. In fact, the vortices have been exploded, and the Newtonian principle of gravitation is now more firmly established, on the basis of reason, than it would be were the government to step in, and to make it an article of necessary faith.

Reason and experiment have been indulged, and error has fled before them. It is error alone which needs the support of government. Truth can stand by itself. Subject opinion to coercion: whom will you make your inquisitors? Fallible men; men governed by bad passions, by private as well as public reasons. And why subject it to coercion? To produce uniformity. But is uniformity of opinion desirable? No more than of face and stature. . . . Difference of opinion is advantageous in religion. The several sects perform the office of a censor morum over each other. Is uniformity attainable? Millions of innocent men, women, and children, since the introduction of Christianity, have been burnt, tortured, fined, imprisoned; yet we have not advanced one inch towards uniformity. What has been the effect of coercion? To make one half the world fools, and the other half hypocrites.[56]

The Statute of Virginia for Religious Freedom, which Jefferson had drafted in 1777, had not yet been enacted. And, of course, he had no plans to remain in the legislature where he could steer its passage. But he had won converts. Foremost among these was James Madison, who was prepared to use all the parliamentary arts of conciliation and battle necessary to secure enactment. That might not come for several years, but come it would. Jefferson was confident that the progress of enlightenment would win acceptance for this work whose composition he bracketed with his authorship of the Declaration of Independence.

He was justly proud of this document which had the Declaration's soaring appeal to universal principles without its abrupt descent into name calling. The statute was written by one who, as the preamble declared, was "well aware that Almighty God had created the mind free; that all attempts to influence it by temporal punishments or burthens, or by civil incapacitations, tend only to beget habits of hypocrisy and meanness, and are a departure from the plan of the Holy Author of our religion, who, being Lord both of body and mind, yet chose not to propagate it by coercions on either, as was in his Almighty power to do." It asserted: "The impious presumption of legislators and rulers, civil as well as ecclesiastical, who, being themselves but fallible and uninspired men have assumed dominion over the faith of others, setting up their own opinions and modes of thinking as the only true and infallible, and as such endeavoring to impose them on others, hath established and maintained false religions over the greatest part of the world, and through all time."[57] It also stated, "To compel a man to furnish contributions of money for the propagation of opinions which he disbelieves is sinful and tyrannical." And: "Even the forcing him to support this or that teacher of his own religious persuasion" would be a deprivation of liberty.

One of the most memorable statements was: "Our civil rights have no dependence on our religious opinions, more than on our opinions in physics and geometry; . . . therefore the proscribing any citizen as unworthy the public confidence by laying upon him an incapacity of being called to offices of trust and emolument, unless he profess or renounce this or that religious opinion, is depriving him injuriously of those privileges and advantages to which in common with his fellow citizens he has a natural right; that it tends also to corrupt the principles of that very religion it is meant to encourage, by bribing, with a monopoly of worldly honors and emoluments, those who will externally profess and conform to it."[58]

Fears that some unauthorized religious teachings might incite to harmful acts were answered by declarations that "it is time enough for the rightful purposes of civil government for its officers to interfere when principles break out into overt acts against peace and good order; and finally, that truth is great and will prevail if left to herself, that she is the proper and sufficient antagonist to error, and has nothing to fear from the conflict, unless by human interposition disarmed of her natural weapons, free argument and debate, errors ceasing to be dangerous when it is permitted freely to contradict them."[59]

The statute concluded:

> *Be it therefore enacted by the General Assembly*, That no man shall be compelled to frequent or support any religious worship, place or ministry whatsoever, nor shall be enforced, restrained, molested, or burthened in his body or goods, nor shall otherwise suffer on account of his religious opinions or belief; but that all men shall be free to profess, and by argument to maintain, their opinions in matters of religion, and that the same shall in no wise diminish, enlarge, or affect their civil capacities.

So intense were Jefferson's feelings about religious liberty that he attached to the statute a statement that is a surprising departure from parliamentary practice: "And though we well know that this Assembly, elected by the people for the ordinary purposes of legislation only, have no power to restrain the acts of succeeding Assemblies, constituted with powers equal to our own, and that therefore to declare this act irrevocable would be of no effect in law, yet we are free to declare, and do declare, that if any act shall be hereafter passed to repeal the present, or to narrow rights hereby asserted . . ., such act will be an infringement of natural right."[60]

The Act for Establishing Religious Freedom would eventually be printed in a pamphlet in Paris and in various editions of the *Notes on the State of Virginia* and would become celebrated throughout the world. It would win Jefferson many admirers and some inveterate foes. He called his fight for religious freedom the "severest" of his life. It would cause him to the end of his life, and after, to be charged with atheism. Holding consistently to his declaration that religion was a private matter, Jefferson refused, despite the urging of family and friends, to defend himself by public revelation of his views. To some members of his family and to a few fellow intellectuals he would confide his beliefs. At one time in youth and early manhood Jefferson appears to have been flirting with, if not temporarily mated to, agnosticism. Further study and reflection eventually brought him to an unorthodox but personally important religious faith. He seems to have entered that stage by the time he wrote the statute and certainly by the time he defended the principle of religious freedom so eloquently in *Notes on the State of Virginia*.

That work, written originally as a reply to a set of specific questions from a French diplomat, was so interesting and provocative that it began circulating as originally written and in translation, without the writer's authorization. Apparently, like an earlier Virginian, William Byrd II, Jefferson was reluctant to present to the world "an unlicked literary cub." Even when he autographed a few presentation copies for friends he urged each recipient to "put them into the hands of no person on whose care and fidelity he cannot rely to guard them against publication."[61] At length he had to cooperate with an authorized edition to prevent unauthorized publication. Then he added the map of Virginia which his father had produced with Joshua Fry. The loyal son insisted that this chart was worth more than all the rest of the book.

Critics appreciated the map but they did not accept Jefferson's comparative evaluation of chart and text. *Notes on the State of Virginia* is still recognized as one of the Enlightenment's most important productions, American or European. It is valuable intrinsically and as a revelation of the mind of one who was an eloquent writer; a wise philosopher; a far-seeing statesman; an American pioneer in archaeology, paleontology, and comparative linguistics; a scientific agriculturist; a skilled inventor; America's first significant scholar of Anglo-Saxon culture; a distinguished historian and archivist; a serious musician who amid multifold duties found time for years to practice on the violin almost daily; and an architect of international importance.

How did such a phenomenon appear fifty miles from the wilderness frontier of a new country? Despite the easy assumptions of those who have researched only superficially the milieu of Jefferson's Virginia, he was not an anomaly in a society of leather-lunged Squire Westerns. We should not take too seriously Jefferson's occasional strictures on the lack of intellectual activity among his acquaintances. Genius, even when associated with benevolence, is sometimes impatiently ungenerous in appraising its associates. Albert Einstein privately deplored the fate that had placed him in "a village of intellectual pygmies"—when he was a member of the Princeton Institute for Advanced Study. Though Jefferson's fellow Virginians of the plantocracy might spend many hours chasing the fox, they also spent many hours pursuing knowledge. And the Eureka of the successful seeker of truth was not drowned by the halloos of happy hunters. Even Jefferson's old friend John Page, regarded in his time as more devoted to the social than to the liberal arts, had a lifelong passion for higher mathematics and delighted in Latin puns. And Jefferson's Virginia friends included Richard Henry Lee, with his extensive knowledge of history and the classics, besides the immensely learned Richard Bland, George Wythe, George Mason, and James Madison. One of Jefferson's severest political critics, Landon Carter, was a classical scholar and scientific researcher.

The planter tradition in Virginia fostered broad education, both theoretical and practical, as part of a gentleman's equipment. A man should be a good judge of horseflesh and at the same time no stranger to Aristotle's or Shakespeare's remarks on the subject. This tradition had not suddenly flowered in Jefferson's generation, though it was then that it attained its most impressive efflorescence. In the generation before,[62] Robert (King) Carter, richest of the river barons, had found time amid multifarious agricultural, business, political, and military affairs to carry on a correspondence studded with classical allusions and including a letter to England pointing out errors in the Latin text from which his son was studying. Ralph Wormeley, described as "the greatest man in the government, next the Governor" in the last decade of the seventeenth century, was a serious student of political and moral philosophy, versed not only in such standards as Bacon, Locke, and Cicero, but also Seneca, Pythagoras, and Henri duc de Rohan. One of the chief men on the Council with Carter and Wormeley was Colonel Richard Lee, who read voraciously in five languages and sparked his conversation with apt quotations from Epictetus, Erasmus, Valleius Paterculus, and Flavius Arrianus. A fellow councillor and one-time acting Governor, William Byrd II, had one of the two largest libraries in the American colonies, was perhaps the most graceful writer in America in his time, and, as we have seen, was so keen a student of science as to be admitted to the Royal Society at the age of twenty-two.

Jefferson was not rare, or even unusual, among Virginia political leaders in possessing diverse intellectual interests. He was more impressive than others in the full panoply of his concerns and in the international stature of his achievements in several fields. Basically, the intellectual differences between Jefferson and other talented members of his society were matters of degree. Intellectually, he was the most conspicuous product of that society. He shared also the sense of noblesse oblige that tempered the arrogance and acquisitiveness of the planter oligarchy. But here, too, there was a difference—perhaps also a difference of degree, but if so, carried so far as to be a difference in kind. Many of Jefferson's colleagues felt, besides a kindly concern for their neighbors, a gentlemanly sense of responsibility to the state and concern for individual rights such as that expressed with such convincing moderation by Marcus Aurelius. They had not, with a zealot's passion, "sworn upon the altar of God eternal hostility to every form of tyranny over the mind of man."

XI

RETREAT FROM THE WORLD

BOUT THE time that François Marbois was registering astonishment over the richly various mind revealed in Jefferson's *Notes on the State of Virginia* another Frenchman, also named François, was experiencing the amazement of discovery in the presence of the author himself. François Jean, Marquis de Chastellux, traveling in North America and recording his adventures and observations for publication in a book that would become famous, stopped over in the spring of 1782 at Monticello. The marquis was a critical man—in architectural matters almost as critical as his host. Monticello he damned with faint praise: "This house... is rather elegant, and in the Italian taste, though not without fault."[1] But the architect and master of Monticello he found most impressive. The marquis was prepared to be impressed with the fact that Mr. Jefferson practiced several civilized arts. After all, the fellow was an American, and one viewed an American practitioner of the arts much as Dr. Samuel Johnson looked upon a woman preaching: "It is like a dog walking on its hind legs. It is not done well, but it is wonderful that it is done at all." But Chastellux who, as a nobleman, a general, a member of the French Academy, and an enthusiastic traveler, had enjoyed the opportunity of talking with some of the most distinguished men in the world, soon was captivated by Jefferson's personality and awed by his intellect.

At first the Virginian seemed coolly and correctly courteous but then the warmth came through and the conversation coruscated. "Let me describe to you," wrote the marquis, "a man not yet forty, tall, and with a mild and pleasing countenance, but whose mind and understanding are ample substitutes for every exterior grace. An American, who without ever having quitted his own country, is at once a musician, skilled in drawing, a geometrician, an astronomer, a natural philosopher, legislator and statesman."[2] There was about Jefferson a rarefied atmosphere, "and it seemed as if from his youth he had placed his mind, as he had done his house, on an elevated situation, from which he might contemplate the universe."[3]

Chastellux thought Jefferson's situation an enviable one. The Virginian had leisure for the employment of his versatile genius as well as scientific equipment and a large and select library to aid him. His windows looked out upon noble prospects and the Virginia countryside was one great blossoming garden. When he stepped outside, graceful deer came up to eat Indian corn from his extended hand. Mrs. Jefferson was "mild and amiable" despite being almost nine months pregnant. The Jefferson children already in the world, ten-year-old Patsy and four-year-old Polly, were "charming." There were six other children in the household, the offspring of his sister Martha, widow of his old companion Dabney Carr. Jefferson was a loving father to all and their teacher in everything from simple sums for the younger to Virgil for the oldest.[4]

One evening after the children and Mrs. Jefferson had retired, Chastellux and his host had a memorably delightful time. Casual allusions revealed a mutual enthusiasm for the poems of Ossian. In 1773 Jefferson, influenced no doubt by his passion for the literatures of northern Europe, had pronounced the supposedly ancient bard the greatest poet of all time.[5] Like most intellectuals of the day, the Virginian had been completely deceived by James McPherson's hoax in offering his own writings as translations from the works of a writer in less polished but also less corrupt times. Once Jefferson's enthusiasm had been almost as great as that of Napoleon, who carried a volume of Ossian on each campaign. Chastellux and Jefferson were seated with a bowl of punch when they fell into conversation about the poems. Chastellux happily recalled: "It was a spark of electricity which passed rapidly from one to the other. . . . We recollected the passages in those sublime poems which particularly struck us. . . . In our enthusiasm the book was sent for, and placed near the bowl, where, by their mutual aid, the night far advanced imperceptibly upon us."[6]

Jefferson's life was not as carefree as it seemed to Chastellux. At least two things were worrying him—persistent prodding to return to public life, and his wife's troubled health that gave him an additional reason for staying at home.

He refused to be a candidate for election to the House of Delegates in the session beginning May 6. When the voters of Albemarle elected him anyway, he addressed to the Speaker of the House a letter in which he declined to serve.[7] Edmund Randolph, attending the session at which Jefferson's note was read, promptly reported to James Madison: "Mr. Jefferson has. . .tendered a resignation. This they refuse to accept, grounding the refusal upon his own principles, delivered on a similar occasion."[8]

Madison did not join in begging Jefferson to reconsider. He wrote Randolph: "Great as my partiality is to Mr. Jefferson, the mode in which he seems determined to revenge the wrong he received from his country does not appear to me to be dictated either by philosophy or patriotism. It argues, indeed, a keen sensibility and strong consciousness of rectitude. But this sensibility ought to be as great towards the relentings as the misdoings of the legislature, not to mention the injustice of visiting the faults of this body on their innocent constituents."[9]

Jefferson's letter to the Speaker was received by his old William and Mary classmate John Tyler, newly elected to that office. He wrote Jefferson, "the Constitution in the opinion of the members will not warrant the acceptance of your resignation," and added, more threatening than pleading:

I am sorry most sincerely for my country that she is deprived of your services, and I am sorry for myself in particular, that I could not have the pleasure of yielding to you the office which I hold, and which you could fill with so much more propriety. However, I suppose your reasons are weighty, yet I would suggest that good and able men had better govern than be governed, since 'tis possible, indeed highly probable, that if the able and good withdraw themselves from society, the venal and ignorant will succeed. I am sure you can readily discover how miserable a situation the country would be reduced to, and how wretched the reflection to a person of sense and merit. In times of peace men of moderate abilities perhaps might conduct the affairs of the State, but at this time when the Republic wants to be organized and requires but your influence to promote this desirable end, I cannot but think the House may insist upon you to give attendance without incurring the censure of being seized.[10]

Perhaps the letter that most troubled Jefferson was one from his young protégé James Monroe, who had been elected to the House of Delegates and had written, all eagerness and hero worship, on the very day that Jefferson had penned his resignation, "how very anxiously I wish your arrival and how very sincerely I join the better part of this community in my desire that a few days more will give us your aid in the House and society to your friends."[11] When Monroe wrote again five days later he had learned of Jefferson's intentions and was far less deferential:

It is publicly said here that the people of your county informed you they had frequently elected you in times of less difficulty and danger than the present to please you, but that now they had called you forth into public office to serve themselves. This is a language which has been often used in my presence and you will readily conceive that as it furnishes those who agree on the fundamental maxims of a republican government with ample field for declamation, the conclusion has always been, you should not decline the service of your country. The present is generally conceived to be an important era which of course makes your attendance particularly necessary, and as I have taken the liberty to give you the public opinion and desire upon this occasion, and as I am warmly interested in whatever concerns the public interest or has relation to you it will be unnecessary to add it is earnestly the desire of, Dear Sir, your sincere friend and servant.[12]

The approval of his family and friends was even more important to Jefferson than to most people, and few things delighted him more than the worshipful admiration of the young. He could not bear with equanimity having his image tarnished in the eyes of a young admirer. Jefferson replied to Monroe:

It gives me pleasure that your county has been wise enough to enlist your talents into their service. I am much obliged by the kind wishes you express of seeing me also in Richmond, and am always mortified when any thing is expected from me which I cannot fulfill, and more especially if it relate to the public service. Before I ventured to declare to my countrymen my determination to retire from public employment I examined well my heart to know whether it were thoroughly cured of every principle of political ambition, whether no lurking particle remained which might leave me uneasy when reduced within the limits of mere private life. I became satisfied that every fibre of that passion was thoroughly eradicated.

I examined also in other views my right to withdraw. I considered that I had been thirteen years engaged in public service, that during that time I had so totally abandoned all attention to my private affairs as to permit them to run into great disorder and ruin, that I had now a family advanced to years which require my attention and instruction, that to this was added the hopeful offspring of a deceased friend whose memory must be for ever dear to me who have no other reliance for being rendered useful to themselves and their country, that by a constant sacrifice of time, labor, loss, parental and friendly duties, I had been so far from gaining the affection of my countrymen, which was the only reward I ever asked or could have felt, that I had even lost the small estimation I before possessed: that however I might have comforted myself under the disapprobation of the well-meaning but uninformed people yet that of their representatives was a shock on which I had not calculated: that this indeed had been followed by an exculpatory declaration, but in the meantime I had been suspected and suspended in the eyes of the world without the least hint then or afterwards made public which might restrain them from supposing I stood arraigned for treasons of the heart and not mere weaknesses of the head. And I felt that these injuries, for such they have been since acknowledged, had inflicted a wound on my spirit which will only be cured by the all-healing grave.[13]

Having explained his feelings, Jefferson proceeded to refute any supposition that the House had the legal right to reject his resignation and compel his attendance. He argued, "Offices of every kind, and given by every power, have been daily and hourly declined and resigned from the declaration of independence to this moment." Jefferson wrote "declaration of independence" in lower case but he must have been aware that the reference would be a reminder of his services as author of that great document. He argued also that the claims of public service could never be construed to demand that the individual surrender to the state "his whole existence."[14]

If we are made in some degree for others, yet in a greater are we made for ourselves. It were contrary to feeling and indeed ridiculous to suppose a man had less right in himself than one of his neighbors or all of them put together. This would be slavery and not that liberty which the bill of rights has made inviolable and for the preservation of which our government has been changed. Nothing could so completely divest us of that liberty as the establishment of the opinion that the state has a *perpetual* right to the services of all its members. This to men of certain ways of thinking would be to annihilate the blessing of existence; to contradict the giver of life who gave it for happiness and not for wretchedness, and certainly to such it were better that they had never been born. However with these I may think public service and private misery inseparably linked together, I have not the vanity to count myself among those whom the state would think worth oppressing with perpetual service. I have received a sufficient memento to the contrary. I am persuaded that having hitherto dedicated to them the whole of the active and useful part of my life I shall be permitted to pass the rest in mental quiet.[15]

A distinguished biographer has written that "there was no occasion for him to go into legalities, as he proceeded to do," and has said "this extraordinary communication cannot be understood except on the background of extreme anxiety. His natural sensitivity had been abnormally heightened."[16] But actually there was very good reason for him to set forth legal arguments against being forced to attend the deliberations of the House despite his resignation. As we have seen, the Speaker of the House, in very lightly veiled words, had threatened him with this very circumstance.

There is no doubt, however, that Jefferson was extremely anxious when he wrote the letter. In the last paragraph he revealed: "Mrs. Jefferson has added another daughter to our family. She has been ever since, and still continues, dangerously ill." The little girl, born at one o'clock on the morning of May 8, had been named Lucy Elizabeth, as had the daughter who had died the year before.

Apparently Jefferson's letter to Monroe was the last that he wrote for seventy-nine days.[17] He had been nursing his beloved Patty since early May, watching the large eyes grow larger in the wasting face. The painful vigil continued through the summer.

One day Patty, propped up, penned a few lines:

"Time wastes too fast: every letter I trace tells me with what rapidity life follows my pen. The days and hours of it are flying over our heads like clouds of windy day, never to return more—everything presses on. . . ."

She paused in midsentence, perhaps because of fatigue, perhaps because her memory flagged. She knew that her husband could complete the lines. They were from *Tristram Shandy*, a book that he had read so often that he knew many passages by heart. Jefferson finished the sentence in heavier ink:

". . . and every time I kiss thy hand to bid adieu, every absence which follows it, are preludes to that eternal separation which we are shortly to make."[18]

On September 6 Jefferson recorded in his account book: "My dear wife died this day at 11:45 a.m."

Behind the terse record was a story of overwhelming grief. Jefferson's eldest daughter, Patsy, then three weeks shy of her tenth birthday, became for a month "his constant companion."[19] Many years later she wrote her account:

> As a nurse, no female ever had more tenderness or anxiety. He nursed my poor mother in turn with Aunt Carr and her own sister—sitting up with her and administering her medicines and drink to the last. For four months that she lingered, he was never out of calling; when not at her bedside, he was writing in a small room which opened immediately at the head of her bed. A moment before the closing scene, he was led from the room almost in a state of insensibility by his sister Mrs. Carr, who, with great difficulty, got him into his library, where he fainted, and remained so long insensible that they feared he never would revive.
>
> The scene that followed I did not witness; but the violence of his emotion, when almost by stealth I entered his room at night, to this day I dare not trust myself to describe. He kept his room three weeks, and I was never a moment from his side. He walked almost incessantly night and day, only lying down occasionally, when nature was completely exhausted, on a pallet that had been brought in during his long fainting fit. My aunts remained constantly with him for some weeks, I do not remember how many. When at last he left his room, he rode out, and from that time he was incessantly on horseback, rambling about the mountain, in the least frequented roads, and just as often through the woods. In those melancholy rambles, I was his constant companion, a solitary witness to many a violent burst

of grief, the remembrance of which has consecrated particular scenes of that lost home beyond the power of time to obliterate.[20]

Burial had been in the little forest-enclosed family cemetery on the mountain slope at Monticello that already held the remains of their dead children and Dabney Carr. By custom the ceremony would have been attended by family, friends, all the house servants, and any field workers who wished to come. Just a little before Mrs. Jefferson's death, the house servants had filed past her bed in farewell. Jefferson placed above the grave "a plain horizontal slab of white marble" inscribed:

> To the memory of
> Martha Jefferson,
> Daughter of John Wayles;
> Born October 19th, 1748, O.S.
> Intermarried with
> Thomas Jefferson
> January 1st, 1772;
> Torn from him by death
> September 6th, 1782:
> This monument of his love is inscribed.[21]

Beneath the inscription were two lines in Greek, taken from the apostrophe of Achilles to Patroclus over Hector's corpse, in the twenty-second book of the *Iliad:* The lines may be translated:

If in the next world men forget their dead,
Yet will I even there remember my dead companion.

Some have seen the use of a Greek inscription as "an ostentation of learning on a most inappropriate occasion," and others have defended it as a device that "revealed his devotion to the initiated while veiling it from the vulgar gaze."[22] The explanation does not seem consistent with Jefferson's personality as revealed in informal correspondence. There is nothing to suggest that he regarded those who did not know Greek as *ipso facto* more insensitive than those who did. A great many people in his day could read Greek; Jefferson's own familiarity with the classics, Latin and Greek, was such that he thought a translation unnecessary.

All are correct, however, in supposing that Jefferson regarded his loving relationship with his wife as a very personal matter. Some close friends never heard him mention her name after her death. Some time before his own death he disposed of her letters. After his demise, Randall tells us, "in the most secret drawer of a private cabinet which he constantly resorted to, were found locks of hair, and various other little souvenirs of his wife, and of each of his loving and lost children—down to those of the latter who died youngest—'with words,' says a member of his family in describing the fact to us, 'of fond endearment, written in his own hand upon the envelopes of the little mementos.' They were all arranged in perfect order, and the envelopes indicated their frequent handling."[23]

The needs of those dear to him finally drew Jefferson back into the lifestream. Colonel Archibald Cary was having inoculations for smallpox given at Ampthill, his handsome Georgian mansion about five miles below Richmond. He invited Jefferson to bring his own children and the young Carrs to take advantage of the protection. Jefferson could not deny them. He carried them to Ampthill and stayed on, becoming the chief nurse as the house became a hospital.[24]

He was still there on November 25 when he received a letter from Robert Livingston in Philadelphia informing him that the Congress had again appointed him one of the Ministers Plenipotentiary for negotiating peace with Great Britain.[25] The action, on motion by James Madison, was unanimous. Madison had suggested that "the death of Mrs. Jefferson had probably changed the sentiments of Mr. Jefferson with regard to public life, and that all the reasons which led to his original appointment still existed."[26]

This time there was no hemming and hawing, backing and filling, before Jefferson replied. The very next day he wrote: "I will employ in this arduous charge, with diligence and integrity, the best of my poor talents, which I am conscious are far short of what it requires. . . . Your letter finds me at a distance from home, attending on my family under inoculation. This will add to the delay which the arrangement of my particular affairs would necessarily occasion. I shall lose no moment, however, in preparing for my departure, and shall hope to pay my respects to Congress . . . at some time between the twentieth and the last of December."[27]

He wrote the same day to Chastellux, who had written him a letter of condolence:

It found me a little emerging from that stupor of mind which had rendered me as dead to the world as she was whose loss occasioned it. Your letter recalled to my memory that there were persons still living of much value to me. If you should have thought me remiss in not testifying to you sooner how deeply I had been impressed with your worth in the little time I had the happiness of being with you, you will, I am sure, ascribe it to its true cause, the state of dreadful suspense in which I had been kept all the summer and the catastrophe which closed it.[28]

"Before that event," Jefferson continued, "my scheme of life had been determined. I had folded myself in the arms of retirement, and rested all prospects of future happiness on domestic and literary objects. A single event wiped away all my plans and left me a blank which I had not the spirits to fill up. In this state of mind an appointment from Congress found me, requiring me to cross the Atlantic, and, that temptation might be added to duty, I was informed at the same time from his Excellency the Chevalier de la Luzerne that a vessel of force would be sailing about the middle of December in which you would be passing to France. I accepted the appointment and my only object now is so to hasten over those obstacles which would retard my departure as to be ready to join you in your voyage, fondly measuring your affections by my own and presuming your consent."

Great as was Jefferson's grief, he could no longer deny life. As deeply ingrained in his nature as the occasional need to retreat was the alternate need for shared activity. Now, after the greatest loss he had known, one that for a while had made family and friends fear his permanent withdrawal from the world, the life force asserted itself with corresponding power through every intellectual and social channel. Duty summoned. Rewarding friendships beckoned. A whole continent, long familiar through his studies and the pictures of its natural and architectural wonders, glowing with the cultural riches of milleniums, yet virgin to his own experience, awaited him with the promise of adventure. Much as he loved America, and especially his own Virginia, it would be good to put an ocean between him and the scenes of his recent tribulations, public and private. He would soon stand on the windswept deck of a fine ship, his nostrils filled with the salt scent of an element older than the continents of Old World and New with their mundane demands. Surely the figurehead of such a vessel would look a good deal like Hope.

XII

RETURN TO THE FRAY

THE TRANSITION from Virginia to Paris was not nearly so swift as Jefferson had expected. The fault was not his. Committing his business affairs to Francis Eppes, his brother-in-law, and Nicholas Lewis, a trusted friend, he set out on the road to Philadelphia on December 19, 1782, with ten-year-old Patsy. Arriving eight days later, he found that upper Chesapeake Bay was frozen and the *Romulus*, upon which he was to sail for France, had not been able to enter the port of Baltimore, much less proceed farther north.[1]

Meanwhile Jefferson, no longer a recluse, was busy with renewed friendships and various purchases and small matters of business that signified renewed commitment to life. He and Patsy were staying at the same boarding house as James Madison, now a member of the Congress, and the two Virginians resumed those long, far-ranging, spirited conversations which earlier had been a delight to both of them. Jefferson also visited the headquarters of the Philosophical Society, of which he was now a councillor, and made a contribution to its expense fund. He bought books, for him always an appropriate way of celebrating good fortune or assuaging depression. He had his sword and gunlock mended. He had his watch repaired. He bought maps of the continent that for some months would be his home.[2]

Hoping to expedite his journey by boarding ship in Baltimore, Jefferson left Philadelphia with Patsy on January 26. Two days were lost because of misinformation about a ferry, and as a result they did not reach Baltimore until five days of traveling through cold and rough weather spent, he wrote Madison, "in the most execrable situation in point of accommodation and society which can be conceived."[3]

While he waited for the ice to break up so that he could go aboard the *Romulus*, he made among the purely practical purchases two others that indicated his continuing recovery from the isolation of grief; he bought a chess set and tickets to a play.

The weather turned colder and the *Romulus* was obliged to fall down the bay to a position about twelve miles south of Baltimore. On February 6 the impatient Jefferson attempted to reach the vessel in a small boat. Following in the wake of another small craft they had proceeded "with tolerable ease" about halfway to their ship when the influx of the tide "closed on us on every side and became impenetrable to our little vessel, so that we could get neither backwards nor forwards."[4] Jefferson, who hated to be held immobile when he had no amusement, was most unhappy until a sloop forced its way through the ice and carried them to the *Romulus*.

After remaining aboard all night he returned to shore. The commander of the French ship had informed him that "the enemy, having no other employment at New York, have made our little fleet their sole object for some time" and had twenty-five ships lying in wait, "a most amazing force for such an object."[5] In a letter[6] to Madison, the Minister Plenipotentiary explained his plight and requested instructions from the Congress. He could embark from Boston ("Would to God I had done this at first; I might now have been half-way across the ocean"); "stay here with patience till our enemies think proper to clear our coast. . . . It may not be till the end of the war"; return to Virginia and await favorable circumstances for sailing from York or Hampton; request the protection of the British flag and sail from Baltimore; or simply await a truce. To request a flag from the enemy, if consistent with the dignity of the United States, seemed to him the best proceeding. But he added, "I shall acquiesce in anything."

Madison replied that he agreed with Jefferson's choice of expedients but was not yet able to transmit official instructions from the Congress. He did, however, send in code some information regarding John Adams, who would be the Virginian's fellow minister in negotiations with England: "Congress yesterday received from Mr. Adams several letters dated September not remarkable for anything unless it be a display of his vanity, his prejudice against the French Court and his venom against Dr. Franklin."[7]

Baltimore may have been fully capable of furnishing intellectual companionship while Jefferson awaited word from the Congress, but if so he did not find it.[8] Of course Williamsburg and Philadelphia, and even Richmond when the legislature was in session, had raised his expectations of urban intellectual environment. That was still a time when an influx of legislators could be counted upon to raise the cultural level of a community.

Jefferson's estimate of the Virginia General Assembly at that time, however, was not high. Some of its best leaders had been drained off to the Congress in Philadelphia and others were serving in the army. In a letter to Edmund Randolph on February 15 Jefferson expressed pleasure that his cousin was considering being a candidate for election to the legislature: "Indeed I hear it with as much pleasure as I have seen with depression of spirit the very low state to which that body has been reduced. I am satisfied there is in it much good intention, but little knowledge of the science to which they are called. I only fear you will find the unremitting drudgery, to which any one man must be exposed who undertakes to stem the torrent, will be too much for any degree of perseverance. I sincerely wish you may undertake and persevere in it."[9]

He also expressed the wish that Randolph would soon be joined in the Assembly by Madison and William Short, a bright young man becoming another Jefferson protégé. He strongly wished an infusion of new minds into the Assembly, particularly because he believed the legislators in the previous session had been "led into a declaration of a doctrine of the most mischievous tendency."[10]

Seeking to justify measures excluding a return to the state by Tory refugees and providing for reversion of their property to the Commonwealth, the lawmakers had cited "the dissolution of the social contract on a revolution of government, and much other little stuff by which I collect their meaning to have been that on changing the form of government all our laws were dissolved, and ourselves reduced to a state of nature." He had been disturbed to see such a stand assumed by the legislators of Vermont; he was even more disturbed to see it approached by those of Virginia. "For my part, if the term *social contract* is to be forced from theoretical into practical use, I shall apply it to all the laws obligatory on the state, and which may be considered as contracts to which all the individuals are parties." He would make the lawmakers sick of their own medicine.

He confided to Randolph another worry:

> I find also the pride of independence taking deep and dangerous hold on the hearts of individual states. I know no danger so dreadful and so probable as that of internal contests. And I know no remedy so likely to prevent it as the strengthening the band which connects us. We have substituted a Congress of deputies from every state to perform this task: but we have done nothing which would enable them to enforce their decisions. What will be the case? They will not be enforced. The states will go to war with each other in defiance of Congress; one will call in France to her assistance; another Great Britain, and so we shall have all the wars of Europe brought to our own doors. Can any man be so puffed up with his little portion of sovereignty as to prefer this calamitous accompaniment to the parting with little of his sovereign right and placing it in a council from all the states...?[11]

Suggesting what might be accomplished by Randolph in league with such men as Madison and Short, he added:

> My 'humble and earnest prayer to Almighty god' will be that you may bring into fashion principles suited to the form of government we have adopted, and not of that we have rejected, that you will first lay your shoulders to the strengthening the band of our confederacy and averting those cruel evils to which its present weakness will expose us, and that you will see the necessity of doing this instantly before we forget the advantages of union, or acquire a degree of ill-temper against each other which will daily increase the obstacles to that good work.[12]

Obviously Jefferson was not so revolutionary as many of his brethren, especially when the shift was from theory to practice. He foresaw chaos if the "state of nature theory" were carried too far and he perceived the need for a truly federal government. As in his work on revision of the laws of the Commonwealth, he refused to walk as a statesman into some areas into which he strode with unslackened pace as an intellectual.

While Jefferson admonished other people to busy themselves in public service, he himself remained frustrated in his attempts to pursue his own appointed task. Reports from Britain suggested that peace might come before he could reach the negotiating table. Congress hesitated. Then came a resolution informing him that "it is the pleasure of Congress, considering the advices lately received in America, and the probable situation of affairs in Europe, that he...not proceed on his intended voyage until he shall receive their further instructions."[13]

While he continued to wait in Baltimore, he averted boredom by writing letters. Patsy, too, had taken to correspondence. Her father suspected from what he knew of her "hierogliphical writing" that the recipients would need "an interpreter from Egypt."[14]

One letter that Jefferson wrote after his return to Philadelphia in March dealt with a matter that had troubled his conscience, or at least his sense of propriety. While on a visit to Baltimore, Abner Nash, Governor of North Carolina, had offered Jefferson partnership in a land speculation scheme. The governor and some associates were purchasing the escheated lands of North Carolina Tories at a conveniently low price for resale at a high one. Jefferson obviously had found the offer tempting. On March 11 he wrote Nash: "I consider it as one of those fair opportunities of bettering my situation which in private prudence I ought to adopt, and which were I to consider myself merely as a private man I should adopt without condition or hesitation."[15] But there was still a possibility that he would participate in the peace negotiations and also a chance that the escheated lands of those who had been loyal to the Crown would be one subject of discussion in those negotiations. Under the circumstances, he thought that he should not enter into any business enterprise that might "lay (his) judgement under bias." In thus renouncing the opportunity—especially when his finances had been strained by the building and furnishing of Monticello—Jefferson evidenced, for one of his generation, an extraordinary scrupulosity regarding conflict of interest.

The letter to which he himself most eagerly awaited a reply was undoubtedly the one he addressed to the Congress on March 13 seeking to learn whether recent dispatches "may have enabled (them) to decide on the expediency of continuing or of countermanding my mission to Europe."[16] Jefferson seemed determined not to regain a reputation for being uncooperative. He wrote Robert R. Livingston, President of the Congress, "I take the liberty of expressing to you the satisfaction it will give me to receive their ultimate will as soon as other business will permit them to advert to this subject."[17]

Livingston officially informed Jefferson on April 4 that by resolution of April 1 Congress had declared that it considered "the object of his appointment so far advanced as to render it unnecessary for him to pursue his voyage, and that Congress are well satisfied with the readiness he has shown in undertaking a service which, from the present situation . . ., they apprehend can be dispensed with."[18] Eight days later Jefferson and Patsy headed back to Monticello in the phaeton.

They stopped over in Richmond for two weeks and Jefferson lobbied among the legislators in behalf of a new constitution for Virginia and a stronger federation of the thirteen states. He was comfortable with the members to a degree that might not have seemed possible to him a year earlier. And there was a balm for the ego in handsome action by a Virginia institution. The College of William and Mary had awarded him the honorary degree of doctor of civil law, citing him as "most skilled both in private and public law; of exceptional love for his country; illustrious not only in other matters but especially in championing American liberty; and so imbued with letters, whether popular or recondite and abstruse, that all the fine arts seem to foregather in one man; these arts are adorned by the greatness of his mind, which proposes nothing with regard to ostentation, everything with regard to conscience, and for a deed well done he seeks his reward not from popular acclaim but from the deed itself."[19] The engrossed parchment with ribbon and seal was rendered more precious because one of the five signatures was that of his old teacher George Wythe.

Back at Monticello, Jefferson continued his work of "championing American liberty." Encouraged by legislative interest in calling a new constitutional convention in Virginia, he began drafting a proposed constitution for the Commonwealth. He had always been disappointed that he had not been in Williamsburg in 1776 when the document prepared by Mason had been adopted and that his own model draft had arrived too late for any use except the tacking of the preamble onto Mason's work. When Jefferson was frustrated in the execution of a project to which he was strongly committed, he remained alert—for years if need be—to any opportunity to complete his original design. In the more than six years which had intervened since Jefferson's first draft, study and experience had combined to suggest to him many changes. Particularly his administrations as Governor had taught him the futility of having a chief executive who was the creature of the legislature. Accordingly, in the draft that he completed in the summer of 1783, he proposed:

> The powers of government shall be divided into three distinct departments, each of them to be confided to a separate body of magistracy; to wit, those which are legislative to one, those which are judiciary to another, and those which are executive to another. No person, or collection of persons, being of one of these departments, shall exercise any power properly belonging to either of the others, except in the instances hereinafter expressly permitted.[20]

The legislature would be bicameral, the members of each house being chosen, in effect, by vote of all free male citizens.

The Governor would be selected by joint ballot of both houses of the Assembly, would serve a term of five years, and would be ineligible for a second term.[21]

A veto power was provided, not to be exercised by the Governor alone, but by a Council of Revision including the chief executive together with two Councillors of State and a judge from each of the three superior courts—Chancery, Common Law, and Admiralty.[22]

Jefferson included provisions for freedom of religion and offered a proposal for freedom of the press that was revolutionary in its sweep: "Printing presses shall be subject to no other restraint than liableness to legal prosecution for false facts printed and published."[23]

The legislature would be forbidden "to ordain death for any crime but treason or murder, or military offenses." They also would be prevented from passing *ex post facto* laws or bills of attainder, and from permitting "the introduction of any more slaves to reside in this state, or the continuance of slavery beyond the generation which shall be living on the thirty-first day of December, one thousand eight hundred: all persons born after that day being hereby declared free."[24]

Terse and unqualified was a provision: "The military shall be subordinate to the civil power."[25]

The movement toward a new constitutional covention in Virginia became stalled. But the ideas embodied in Jefferson's draft percolated into the consciousness of many influential Virginians and other Americans and finally, through publication in Paris, into the intellect of Europe. Many of Jefferson's proposals were embodied in later constitutions of the Commonwealth, the United States, the Confederate States of America, and various republics in Europe, South America, Asia, and Africa. Others, not yet adopted, are still proposed by reformers. The author of the document never doubted the significance of his work.

The same summer that saw Jefferson at work on his new constitution for Virginia also saw him elected to an office that would take him away from his state. On June 6, 1783, Virginia legislators named him to the Commonwealth's congressional delegation for the session beginning November 1.

Meanwhile, at Monticello he lovingly catalogued the library that he would soon be leaving. He now had 2,640 volumes, which he classified according to a modified version of a system proposed by Francis Bacon. The categories, based upon the intellectual faculties, were: I, Memory (history and biography); II, Reason (philosophy, "moral and mathematical"); and III, Imagination (the fine arts). His library—even if one did not include the volumes of music by such composers as Bach, Haydn, Vivaldi, and Purcell—was one of the largest and most various in America.[26]

On October 15, Jefferson took a farewell look at the russet and gold of his leather bindings and finally at the russet and gold of his beloved mountains. With three matching horses, two hitched to the phaeton and the third as a relief, he set out with Patsy and a servant for Philadelphia.

Arriving two weeks later he found that Congress, made apprehensive by the mutiny of unpaid soldiers, had fled to Princeton. Deeming the danger small, he left Patsy at the same boardinghouse where they had previously stayed and where she had made friends, secured a dancing master for her, and rode on to Princeton. There he was frustrated by the discovery that the Congress, still fearful of "sunshine patriots," was moving on to Annapolis.

But now he had to return to Philadelphia before proceeding to the Maryland capital. Mrs. Trist, at whose boardinghouse he had left Patsy, was herself preparing to leave Philadelphia. New living arrangements would have to be made for the child. He found quarters for her with Mrs. Thomas Hopkinson, the elderly mother of Francis Hopkinson, a signer of the Declaration of Independence and the author of a series of satires, most celebrated among them *The Battle of the Kegs*. He was also a prominent composer for the harpsichord. Soon Patsy was dancing with his children and those of David Rittenhouse while Hopkinson served as a harpsichordist.[27]

Jefferson was pleased that he could leave Patsy in such cultured company. Besides his accomplishments as author and musician, Hopkinson had learned other arts and sciences while obtaining baccalaureate and master's degrees from the College of Philadelphia and, perhaps more important, at the dinner table of his father, Thomas, first president of the American Philosophical Society. Rittenhouse, of course, was a prominent member of that society, as well as a fellow of the Royal Society of London and an internationally famous astronomer. Although Patsy was placed in such an intellectually stimulating environment, Jefferson was leaving nothing to chance and her tutors. In a letter from Annapolis after joining his congressional colleagues, he sent her a schedule to be followed from shortly after rising to bedtime: "From 8 to 10, practice music. From 10 to 1, dance one day and draw another. From 1 to 2, draw on the day you dance, and write a letter next day. From 3 to 4, read French. From 4 to 5, exercise yourself in music. From 5 till bedtime, read English, write, etc."[28]

The regimen would not have been considered unusually severe for boys at a good preparatory school of the period,[29] but it was unusual for an eleven-year-old girl. Jefferson, however, was educating his daughter as he would a precocious son. He not only introduced her to some of his favorite fiction, such as *Don Quixote* and *Gil Blas*, but to factual works that even so enlightened a Frenchman as Marbois regarded as strange fare for a young lady. To the diplomat's expressions of surprise Jefferson replied: "I am obliged in it to extend my views beyond herself and consider her as possibly at the head of a little family of her own. The chance that in marriage she will draw a blockhead I calculate at about fourteen to one, and of course [conclude] that the education of her family will probably rest on her own ideas and direction without assistance. With the best poets and prose writers I shall therefore combine a certain extent of reading in the graver sciences."[30] Even before Patsy was old enough to receive suitors, her father was looking askance at her unmaterialized husband.

Jefferson's letters to Patsy were full of anxious admonitions to be always busy, to improve her spelling, to write to him every week, and to listen so attentively to her conscience that she would "never do or say a bad thing. . . . Our maker has given us all this faithful internal Monitor, and if you will always obey it, you will always be prepared for the end of the world, or for a much more certain event, which is death. This must happen to all: it puts an end to the world as to us, and the way to be ready for it is never to do a wrong act."[31] He even was exacting about details that one might expect an absent father to overlook:

. . . above all things, and at all times let your clothes be clean, whole, and properly put on. Do not fancy you must wear them till the dirt is visible to the eye. You will be the last who will be sensible of this. Some ladies think they may under the privileges of the dishabille be loose and negligent of their dress in the morning. But be you from the moment you rise till you go to bed as cleanly and properly dressed as at the hours of dinner or tea. A lady who has been seen as a sloven or slut in the morning will never efface the impression she made with all the dress and pageantry she can afterwards involve herself in. Nothing is so disgusting to our sex as a want of cleanliness and delicacy in yours. I hope therefore the moment you rise from bed, your first work will be to dress yourself in such a style as that you may be seen by any gentleman without his being able to discover a pin amiss. . . .[32]

Even in separation, Jefferson was still the pater familias, not only directing a stream of letters to Patsy, but also making frequent inquires about the two younger girls, Polly and Lucy Elizabeth, who remained in Virginia in the care of his sister-in-law, Mrs. Eppes. Nor did he neglect to write to his younger nephew Peter Carr, now a student at Walker Maury's school. He sent him a copy of Homer and wrote: "I am anxious to hear from you, to know how your time is employed, and what books you read. You are old enough to know how very important to your future life will be the manner in which you employ your present time. I hope therefore you will never waste a moment of it."[33] The many admonitions were softened by a promise: "You may be assured that nothing shall be wanting on my part which may contribute to your improvement and future happiness."

The same letter contains a hint of a quality in Jefferson that, together with his fascinating conversation and sensitivity to others' feelings, may have had a great deal to do with the charm which he exercised over so many women of all ages:

. . . it is proper for you now to begin to learn those attentions and that complaisance which the world requires should be shown to every lady. The earlier you begin the practice of this, the sooner it will become habitual, and with the more ease to yourself will you enter on the public stage of life, and conduct yourself through it. You will find that on rendering yourself agreeable to that sex will depend a great part of the happiness of your life: and the way to do it is to practice to every one all those civilities which a favorite one might require.

The letter closes with the advice: "If you can find means to attract the notice and acquaintance of my friend Mr. Madison, lately returned to your neighborhood from Congress, he will be a most valuable patron to you. His judgment is so sound and his heart so good that I would wish you to respect every advice he would be so kind as to give you, equally as if it came from me."

By this time, Madison appears to have become Jefferson's best friend since the death of Dabney Carr. Jefferson greatly regretted Madison's departure from Annapolis. He corresponded with him on personal matters and affairs of state. He particularly hoped that Madison would sound out George Mason to determine whether the squire of Gunston Hall shared their belief in the need for a strengthened federal constitution. "Is he determined to sleep on or will he rouse and be active?"[34] Now that Jefferson had returned to public responsibility, he wanted every other able man to do likewise.

Most were not nearly active enough to suit him. Though Congress was supposed to have reconvened at Annapolis on November 26, representatives from only six states were present as late as December 11. Seven constituted a quorum. Nine would be necessary for ratification of the peace treaty. When that number would be present, he wrote Madison, seemed "as insusceptible of calculation as when the next earthquake will happen."[35] The matter was urgent. A clause in the peace treaty signed September 3, 1783, rendered it ineffective unless ratifications by the signatories were exchanged within six months of that date.

England might be glad for the treaty to fall through. The United States had obtained extraordinarily favorable terms about which the British might be having second thoughts. They had not only agreed to recognize American independence but also to accept an expansion of the new nation's borders, surrendering frontier forts and granting other concessions, including a guarantee that Americans might continue to fish off Newfoundland and Nova Scotia. In return the ministers of the United States had agreed only that all debts owed by Americans to British creditors would be validated as would the far less numerous debts owed by Englishmen to Americans, and that Congress would "earnestly recommend" to the several states restoration of the property and rights of Americans who had remained loyal to the Crown. France was displeased that the United States had negotiated without consulting her, and, for all Jefferson knew, she might be happy to frustrate ratification. He was more involved in the matter than most of the little band of congressmen who waited anxiously for their colleagues. He was chairman of the committee on the treaty.

He was also chairman of the committee of arrangements for the public ceremonies on December 23 when Washington came to Annapolis to resign his commission as commander in chief of the Continental army. Jefferson was ill and possibly missed the ball given by the Maryland Assembly in the general's honor. Washington not only drank thirteen toasts proposed by his hosts and a fourteenth one that was his own idea, all without the slightest loss of dignity, but danced every set of the ball so that, as a contemporary said, "all the ladies might. . .get a touch of him."[36]

Jefferson was present in the State House at noon the next day when Washington formally submitted his resignation.[37] The nineteen or twenty congressmen present sat with their hats on as the general, wearing his blue and buff uniform and escorted by Charles Thomson, strode through their midst to the front of the chamber. Then the doors were opened to ladies who filled the gallery and distinguished gentlemen who crowded the chamber below, many standing with their backs pressed close to the walls. When presented, Washington bowed and the congressmen doffed their hats in salute. In appearance he was the ideal of Anglo-Saxon kingliness; in manner he had the simple republican dignity of an ancient Roman magistrate. But, after all, even *his* composure at this moment was less than marmoreal. The manuscript from which he read his farewell trembled visibly and he soon had to grasp it in both hands.

Almost at the end his voice broke, but he recovered and concluded in a firm voice: "Having now finished the work assigned me, I retire from the great theater of action; and bidding an affectionate farewell to this august body under whose orders I have so long acted, I here offer my commission, and take my leave of all the employments of public life."

After the Congress had formally adjourned and the spectators had left, Washington, who had stepped into an anteroom, returned to the chamber to shake hands with each delegate. Many had been brushing away tears almost from the beginning of the general's farewell. Jefferson described the moment as "affecting."[38] He himself was an emotional man. There is no reason to suppose he was dry-eyed on this occasion.

The same letter in which he reported the event to Governor Benjamin Harrison expressed his "extreme anxiety at our present critical situation." The arrival of a Rhode Island delegate had raised the number of states represented to seven, but "the departure of a member two days hence leaves us with only six states and of course stops all business. We have no certain prospect of nine within any given time; chance may bring them in, and chance may keep them back. In the meantime only a little over two months remain for their assembling, ratifying, and getting the ratification across the Atlantic to Paris."[39]

As so often when Jefferson was troubled and anxious, his health suffered. On New Year's Day he wrote Madison, "I have had very ill health since I have been here and am getting rather lower than otherwise."[40]

While Jefferson worried about the absence of some congressmen he found it difficult to tolerate the presence of others. "Our body," he later wrote in his autobiography, "was little numerous, but very contentious. Day after day was wasted on the most unimportant questions. A member, one of those afflicted with the morbid rage of debate, of an ardent mind, prompt imagination, and copious flow of words, who heard with impatience any logic which was not his own, sitting near me on some occasion of a trifling but wordy debate, asked me how I could sit in silence, hearing so much false reasoning, which a word should refute? I observed to him, that to refute indeed was easy, but to silence impossible; that in measures brought forward by myself, I took the laboring oar, as was incumbent on me; but that in general, I was willing to listen; that if every sound argument or objection was used by some one or other of the numerous debaters, it was enough; if not, I thought it sufficient to suggest the omission, without going into a repetition of what had been already said by others: that this was a waste and abuse of the time and patience of the House, which could not be justified. And I believe, that if the members of deliberate bodies were to observe this course generally, they would do in a day, what takes them a week." He concluded, "It is really more questionable than may at first be thought whether Bonaparte's dumb legislature, which said nothing, and did much, may not be preferable to one which talks much and does nothing."[41]

Yet he seemed to think congressional loquacity almost inevitable: "If the present Congress errs in too much talking, how can it be otherwise in a body to which the people send one hundred and fifty lawyers, whose trade it is to question everything, yield nothing, and talk by the hour? That one hundred and fifty lawyers should do business together ought not to be expected."[42]

Some delegates now argued that, regardless of the rules, ratification by seven states should suffice. A few said that, even if the number did not meet the legal requirements, the British need never be apprised of the fact. Three went so far as to give "notice that when the question should be put they would call the yeas and nays, and show by whose fault the ratification of this important instrument should fail, if it should fail."[43] Jefferson insisted that such a move would be both risky and dishonorable. He opposed their resolution with one of his own and informed them that he would "place that also on the journals with the yeas and nays as a justification of those who opposed the proposition."[44]

Jefferson's proposal was that, if one more state's delegates should arrive, the Congress should then travel to Philadelphia to convene at the bedside of the South Carolina delegate who was too ill to come to Annapolis. Thus the votes of nine states would be available. If an eighth state's delegates did not arrive, however, he had another plan. He moved that a resolution approved by seven states be sent the American plenipotentiaries in Europe together with instructions to seek an extension of time for ratification and with authorization to present the seven-state resolution only if ratification by nine states had not arrived by the deadline. The resolution made no effort to deceive the British about the questionable binding force of such a document. It frankly stated: "The States now present in Congress do declare their approbation and, so far as they have power, their ratification of the said treaty." Such provisional ratification was to be superseded by definitive ratification when the votes of nine states could be mustered.[45]

This method was never resorted to. On January 14, twelve days after Jefferson's motion, the delegates from New Jersey and New Hampshire arrived and the treaty was promptly ratified. Though the American documents reached Europe just past the deadline, the British did not quibble. After a final exchange in May, peace was official.

The chief significance of Jefferson's proposal is that the apparent need for such a motion underlined his warning in *Notes on the State of Virginia*: "It can never be too often repeated that the time for fixing every essential right on a legal basis is while our rulers are honest and ourselves united. From the conclusion of this war we shall be going down hill."[46]

Jefferson's proposal also showed something else. He was as firmly rooted as ever in his integrity, but he was no longer so rigidly doctrinaire in seeking solutions as when he had been Governor. There were hints that, when the nation's welfare was at stake, he might even evidence a flexibility commensurate with his imagination.

On the day the treaty was ratified Jefferson wrote Patsy: "I have received two or three letters from you since I wrote last. Indeed my health has been so bad that I have been able scarcely to read, write or do anything else." He was delighted with the letter she had written him in French but disappointed that her drawing master had discontinued his lessons. The instructor was unwilling to accept payment for the little that he had been able to teach her, but Jefferson told his daughter, "I would wish him to receive it, because if there is to be a doubt between him and me which of us acts rightly, I would choose to remove it clearly off my own shoulders."[47]

A few days later he must have felt much more like writing. On January 20 he sent Madison a letter of some 2,400 words telling of books he was trying to buy for his correspondent, making observations on paleontology and meteorology, reporting on the steps by which ratification of the peace treaty was obtained, speculating on the results of Virginia's cession to the United States of lands north of the Ohio River, and advocating development of internal waterways. He said that he hoped Madison was using the library at Monticello ("I beg you to make free use of it") and concluded: "Monroe is buying land almost adjoining me. Short will do the same. What would I not give you could fall into the circle? With such a society I could once more venture home and lay myself up for the residue of life, quitting all its contentions which grow daily more and more insupportable. Think of it. To render it practicable only requires you to think it so. Life is of no value but as it brings us gratifications. Among the most valuable of these is rational society. It informs the mind, sweetens the temper, cheers our spirits, and promotes health. There is a little farm of 140 acres adjoining me . . . . Once more think of it."[48]

Before the end of February Jefferson and Monroe were even closer neighbors than they would be in Albemarle. They rented joint quarters and hired a French servant. Jefferson, who once had demonstrated a remarkable ability to maintain friendships in both factions of the Virginia Assembly, now found little to like about any of the Virginia delegation to Congress except Monroe and Samuel Hardy, both of whom he found honest and good tempered. John Mercer he saw as voluble and vain. Arthur Lee, apparently fractious by nature, had quarreled with him about ratification of the treaty. In general the quality of the Congress had sunk far below the previous high level.[49]

Though Jefferson found little zest for his congressional duties, he worked hard at them, drafting more than thirty papers. Most important of these was the Ordinance of 1784, which he drew up as chairman of a committee to prepare a plan for temporary government of the western lands. This, the first territorial ordinance of the United States,[50] was formally proposed by Jefferson on March 1. It embodied a concept that he had enunciated even before the Declaration of Independence—that the States should not subject the western lands to the same colonial status which they themselves had fought to escape. New states organized in the western territory would be equal partners of those on the Atlantic Seaboard. The United States should renounce imperialism in its continental expansion. If this procedure had not been followed, what became the continental expanse of the United States would undoubtedly have been balkanized.

Jefferson proposed the formation of fourteen new states. The names of two, Illinoia and Michigania, survive today with slight modifications. Others, strange hybrids of Indian and classical origin, among them Assenisipia and Polypotamia, were strangled by twisted tongues.

More important than the names suggested were the provisions for evolution to statehood with self-government every step of the way. Even more vital was the provision that slavery should not exist after 1800 in the new states. Such a measure could have had an incalculable influence on American history, but it was defeated by a single vote. Also beaten down was Jefferson's attempt to forbid hereditary titles in the new states. His report, as adopted on April 23, was mangled by amendments. It was never implemented. In his frustration Jefferson could not know that his thoughtfully composed report would become the basis for the historic Northwest Ordinance of 1787.

A variety of other legislative matters claimed Jefferson's attention. Robert Morris, the famous Philadelphia financier, had called upon Congress to adopt a standard monetary unit. Jefferson had suggested the same need in 1776. Individual states had their own currencies, and in addition the coins of Spain, Portugal, France, Holland, and of course England, circulated widely. Making change in the United States was not a simple task for any schoolboy. But the unit proposed by Morris—1/1440 of a dollar—was not likely to simplify the process.

Jefferson, therefore, offered a counterproposal, with characteristic thoroughness working out a decimal system of coins whose parts and multiples could be computed easily, yet whose values would so closely approximate those of familiar coins that the transistion would be almost painless.[51] He also gave great attention to the sizes of the coins, knowing that popular acceptance would go in tandem with convenience. A dollar comparable to the Spanish coin of that name was his basic unit. Then there would be a silver dime, a copper penny, and a ten-dollar gold piece. Morris offered a compromise between his scheme and Jefferson's, but it greatly impaired the convenience and utility of Jefferson's plan, and the Virginian did not accept it. He laid the question before the public in a pamphlet setting forth his original design, together with Morris's arguments against it, and his own replies to Morris. The informed public saw the superiority of Jefferson's system, and it was eventually adopted by the Congress. In his enthusiastic agrarianism, he was surely pleasurably aware of the irony that a Philadelphia financier had been bested at his own game by a Virginia farmer.

The Congress was ready to deal with another question which Jefferson had raised in earlier years—the fact that, as Congress was the executive as well as the legislature, its periodic adjournment left no functioning governmental authority for the United States. As chairman of a committee to deal with the problem Jefferson proposed appointment of a Committee of States which would be empowered to conduct during recesses any business which a seven-state quorum could transact when Congress was in session.[52] His plan was adopted. It was far from a model of efficiency but it went as far as the Congress, still fearful of executive tyranny, was prepared to go.

Jefferson's advice was also sought by one more distinguished than any of his Congressional colleagues. George Washington, president pro tempore of the Society of the Cincinnati, an organization of veteran officers from the Revolution, had learned that formation of the group had aroused anxiety in many quarters. Its name was a reminder that most of the patriot officers, like Cincinnatus of Roman history and legend, had turned aside from the plow to grasp the sword in their country's defense and then had returned to the farm. But mere nomenclature could not reassure many Americans concerned that membership was restricted to those who had been officers in the Continental Army and to their male descendants. Jefferson's fears of an officer caste system and of the hereditary principle involved may have been heightened by the fact that he himself had been a civilian in the war.

Nevertheless, the letter in which he replied on April 16 to an inquiry from Washington was dispassionate and well reasoned. Unlike some congressmen, he saw no selfish scheme in formation of the organization. "When the army was about to be disbanded, and the officers to take final leave, perhaps never again to meet, it was natural for men who had accompanied each other through so many scenes of hardship, of difficulty and danger . . . to seize with fondness any propositions which promised to bring them together again at certain and regular periods. . . . I doubt, however, whether in its execution it would be found to answer the wishes of those who framed it, and to foster those friendships it was intended to preserve. The members would be brought together at their annual assemblies no longer to encounter a common enemy, but to encounter one another in debate and sentiment. Something I suppose is to be done at those meetings, and however unimportant, it will suffice to produce difference of opinion, contradiction and irritation. The way to make friends quarrel is to pit them in disputation under the public eye. An experience of near twenty years has taught me that few friendships stand this test; and that public assemblies where everyone is free to speak and to act, are the most powerful looseners of the bands of private friendship. I think therefore that this institution would fail of its principal object, the perpetuation of the personal friendships contracted through the war."[53]

He feared that the hereditary basis for membership would threaten the state constitutions, which were based on "denial of a preeminence by birth." He objected, too, that "a distinction is kept up between the civil and military which it is for the happiness of both to obliterate." He also was disturbed by the creation of such a strong pressure group, reflecting "that being an organized body, under habits of subordination, the first obstructions to enterprise will be already surmounted; that the moderation and virtue of a single character has probably prevented this revolution from being closed as most others have been by a subversion of that liberty it was intended to establish; that he is not immortal, and his successor or some one of his successors at the head of this institution may adopt a more mistaken road to glory."[54]

No less interesting than Jefferson's opinion about the new veterans' organization is the revelation, in the letter's concluding paragraph, of his attitude toward his own political career:

I consider the whole matter as between ourselves alone, having determined to take no active part in this or anything else which may lead to altercation, or disturb that quiet and tranquillity of mind to which I consign the remaining portion of my life. I have been thrown back by events on a stage where I had never more thought to appear. It is but for a time however, and as a day laborer, free to withdraw or be withdrawn at will.[55]

Washington must have been gratified that Jefferson would not join in public criticism of the Society of the Cincinnati, but he was not content to let the matter rest. When the general passed through Annapolis in May on his way to Philadelphia to preside over a national convention of the organization, he sat up past midnight discussing the matter with Jefferson. The younger man did not know whether he had influenced the old soldier until later when he learned that Washington, using phrases reminiscent of Jefferson's own, had opposed the hereditary provision for membership and had told the convention that he would resign unless it was removed.[56]

Jefferson's intimation that his own public career might be nearing an end probably was prompted by bad health and an inability to shake for long the melancholy that had descended upon him with Patty's death. G. K. van Hogendorp, a youthful Dutchman with all the eagerness, shrewdness, and innocent insolence of a young Boswell, had met the Virginian in Annapolis while touring America in search of facts and celebrities. Even the praise of Jefferson he had heard in Boston had not prepared him for the brilliance and variety of an intellect that he had to admit would have been rare in Europe. And he was almost as deeply impressed with the American's personal qualities. Shortly after their meeting, he wrote: "Even your cool and reserved behavior prepossessed me in favor of you. I valued so much the more every little mark of esteem that I could perceive in your conversation."[57] In later notes published at the Hague, he revealed an understanding of Jefferson's mood at the time:

> Mr. Jefferson, during my attendance at the session of Congress, was more busily engaged than anyone. Retired from fashionable society, he concerned himself only with affairs of public interest, his sole diversion being that offered by belles lettres. The poor state of his health, he told me occasionally, was the cause of this retirement; but it seemed rather that his mind, accustomed to the unalloyed pleasure of the society of a lovable wife, was impervious since her loss to the feeble attractions of common society, and that his soul, fed on noble thoughts, was revolted by idle chatter. . . . He has the shyness that accompanies true worth, which is at first disturbing and which puts off those who seek to know him. Those who persist in knowing him soon discern the man of letters, the lover of natural history, law, statecraft, philosophy, and the friend of mankind.[58]

Hogendorp wrote Jefferson a letter so compounded of hero worship, bold intrusion, and youthful egotism that the Virginian must have been tempted to say, "Down, boy, down!" Instead he replied:

> Your observation on the situation of my mind is not without foundation: yet I had hoped it was unperceived, as the agreeable conversations into which you led me often induced a temporary inattention to those events which have produced that gloom you remarked. I have been happy and cheerful. I have had many causes of gratitude to heaven, but I have also experienced its rigors. I have known what it is to lose every species of connection which is dear to the human heart: friends, brethren, parents, children—retired, as I thought myself, to dedicate the residue of life to contemplation and domestic happiness, I have been again thrown by events on the world without an object on which I can place value. For those which are distant I am excluded by reason and reflection. The sun of life having with me already passed his meridian, with you he is ascending, and I sincerely participate of your rising prospects. Your thirst after knowledge, your capacity to acquire it, your dispositions to apply it to the good of mankind, with the ardent spirits of youth necessary to support a man against the impediments opposed to him, give your country much to hope from the continuance of your life.[59]

Despite his busy involvement in public affairs and his ill health Jefferson had written many pages in answer to the young man's questions on tobacco culture, the history of American finance, and the port of Norfolk.

Suddenly once again Jefferson felt the scattered resources of his spirit being pulled into focus like iron filings in a magnetic field, and again the magnet was Paris. On May 7 Congress adopted instructions drafted by Thomas Jefferson to be sent to American Commissioners who would negotiate treaties of amity and commerce with the principal nations of Europe. Now some Southern congressmen were demanding that two Southerners be appointed to join Adams, Franklin, and Jay, who were already in Europe. The states below the Potomac, it was argued, had special commercial needs not understood by diplomats from the North.

While a compromise was being worked out news arrived that John Jay was returning home. Congress promptly chose him as Secretary of Foreign Affairs, a post for which Jefferson had once been nominated, and elected Jefferson to the vacated post of Commissioner. A letter which Jefferson received on this occasion from John Tyler, who had once written threateningly to him about his absence from the House of Delegates, seems to have been representative of the high favor which the erstwhile unpopular Governor now enjoyed with his fellow Virginians: "God send you safe to the destined port, continue you there in health and happiness, as long as you choose to stay, and waft you back to your native country, where you will always be acceptable to the good and virtuous."[60]

Not nearly so welcome was a letter from Madison telling him that Mazzei was on his way to Annapolis to solicit Jefferson's aid in securing appointment to a European consulate. Mazzei hunting over the hills of Albemarle in an Italian shooting jacket (soon copied by Jefferson and his neighbors) and Mazzei hunting for political preferment were two different creatures. The first may have been an agreeable companion and a fair shot, but the second was a contentious aspirant ready to fire his blunderbuss at all who stood between him and the object of his aim.

Madison, ever the faithful friend, had convinced the Italian that he should call upon Patrick Henry and the Governor before leaving the state, hoping thus to delay his arrival in Annapolis until after the adjournment of Congress.[61] Madison wrote that Mazzei, when last in Europe, had conceived a great enmity toward Franklin and had alleged "that the exquisite cunning of the old fox has so enveloped his iniquity that its reality cannot be proved by those who are thoroughly satisfied of it. It is evident from several circumstances stated by himself that his enmity has been embittered if not wholly occasioned by incidents of a personal nature. Mr. Adams is the only public man whom he thinks favorably of or seems to have associated with—a circumstance which their mutual characters may perhaps account for."[62] Nevertheless, Madison believed, "however dreadful an actual visit from him might be to you in a personal view it would not produce the public mischiefs you apprehend from it."[63]

There was no question of Jefferson's apprehension. He had written Madison that he found "alarming" the news of Mazzei's approach. "I tremble at the idea. I know he will be worse to me than a return of my double quotidian headache."[64] Here is a hint that the illness that had recently plagued Jefferson had involved his migraine attacks.

Perhaps partly because of Mazzei's approach, Jefferson made haste to depart. He did not take time to visit the daughters and the nephews and nieces in Virginia before sailing. He did send them warm messages of love. And he asked Madison to accept as "a tender legacy" fourteen-year-old Peter Carr. Among other things, he wished him to see that the boy obtained a good mastery of Latin, Greek, French, Italian, and—his own special linguistic enthusiasm—Anglo-Saxon.[65]

He also charged his friend with another responsibility—to work in the Virginia Assembly to have the slave tax applied to Continental requisitions so that Virginia would be paying her share of United States government expenses. "Virginia must do something more than she has done to maintain any degree of respect in the Union and to make it bearable to any man of feeling to represent her in Congress. . . . There is no man who has not some vice or folly the atoning of which would. . . pay his taxes."[66] Harsh words for the state he loved so dearly, and that had so generously parted with her western lands in the common interest when Pennsylvania, New Jersey, and Rhode Island refused to surrender their smaller and less valid claims. But in every major undertaking Jefferson demanded of everyone or everything with which he identified, be it child of his loins or mother state, precisely what he demanded of himself—unalloyed perfection.

For his personal secretary Jefferson chose his protégé William Short, who at twenty-five was already a member of the Executive Council for Virginia. "If I am enabled to offer you no other advantage than a bed and board free," the new Commissioner wrote, "I am also enabled to assure you I shall give you very little trouble."[67] Short's reply was prompt and of the sort that Jefferson loved: "My determination is what it has long been, to accompany you in any capacity whatsoever."[68]

Jefferson hoped to sail from Boston about June 20. The intervening time would be none too ample for a first-hand investigation of the industry and commerce of the Northern states so that he could speak knowledgeably of these activities as well as about Southern trade and agriculture in European negotiations.[69]

First, though, he returned to Philadelphia for Patsy. She could learn much in Paris and besides he wanted her with him. He tried to arrange for a private printing of his *Notes on Virginia*, not yet published, but the Philadelphia printer of his choice could not promise delivery before Jefferson sailed. Therefore he would have it printed in Europe. He was eager to have it read by personal friends in America and by European scholars, but dreaded, as we have seen, the heated controversy that could be provoked by general publication.

Closely related to one of the immediate objects of the book, refutation of Buffon's theory that all living things degenerated in the New World, was Jefferson's purchase in Philadelphia of a panther's tawny hide—a large one.[70] Presenting it to Buffon as a gift would be a graceful way of compelling his attention to the fact that America had animals that compared favorably in size with their European counterparts. In line with the same purpose, he had a standing order with George Rogers Clark for mammal skeletons of impressive size regardless of the cost of packaging and transportation. Sometimes the elegant foyer of Monticello, cluttered with crates, bones, and elks' antlers, resembled the packing room of a natural history museum.

His correspondence with Clark contains another evidence of the tenacity with which he held to favorite ideas and enterprises, awaiting the opportunity to promote them.

On December 4, 1783, in a letter thanking the general for some shells and seeds from the western territories, Jefferson had pointed out the desirability of "exploring the country from the Mississippi to California." He said, "How would you like to lead such a party? Though I am afraid our prospect is not worth asking the question."[71] Nearly a score of years later, when the general had retired but Jefferson was in a position of power, the statesman's repetition of the question sent Meriwether Lewis and George Rogers Clark's brother William westward on one of history's most famous and fruitful expeditions of exploration.

Jefferson and Patsy at the end of May rode by coach from Philadelphia to New York. While there he bought a Spanish dictionary as an aid to reading his old favorite *Don Quixote* in the original. Thence he proceeded to Connecticut, where he visited about a dozen communities within a week.[72] Probably the highlight was the day he spent with Ezra Stiles, scholarly and energetic president of Yale College, to whom Jefferson bore a letter of introduction from his old congressional colleague Roger Sherman. Stiles soon found that Sherman had not exaggerated in saying, "He is a gentleman of much philosophical as well as political knowledge—and I doubt not you will be very agreeably entertained with his conversation."[73] The Virginian could satisfy with specific information his host's eager inquiries about the administration, curriculum, and faculty salaries at William and Mary. Though Stiles, through his broad interests, had contributed to the secularization of Yale, he may, as a former professor of divinity, have deplored the dropping of that subject at the Virginia college.

Stiles pumped his visitor for all sorts of information on the different elements—ethnic, social, and economic—of the Old Dominion's population. He recorded in his diary Jefferson's prediction that, because of the diffusion of land ownership, "the plebeian interest will prevail over the old aristocratical interest in that state." Stiles showed Jefferson the college library and the institution's scientific apparatus. The Virginian enthusiastically described in minute detail a British invention for the production of electricity. He also described the great bones dug up on the Ohio and boasted that his own collection included a thigh bone three feet long and a tooth weighing sixteen pounds. Stiles was accustomed to meeting distinguished people but he devoted about six hundred words in his diary to his conversations with Jefferson, concluding, "The Governor is a most ingenious naturalist and philosopher, a truly scientific and learned man, and every way excellent."[74]

Next Jefferson went to Rhode Island. When he left Providence for Dedham and Boston, he "was attended a few miles from town by a number of the principal inhabitants."[75] After several days in Boston he toured Massachusetts and New Hampshire with letters of introduction from Elbridge Gerry, whom he had met at a boarding-house on his first trip to New York and who had later served in Congress with him and signed the Declaration of Independence. Everywhere hospitality was lavished upon him. Everywhere people were delighted with him. More than sixteen years later Samuel Adams said that his wife was still talking about "the pleasure and entertainment" that Jefferson had brought to Boston before embarking for Europe.[76]

Jefferson learned that another Mrs. Adams, Abigail, was sailing within thirty-six hours to join her husband, John. He wished to change plans in order to accompany her but could not speed last minute preparations.[77] He did take time before sailing to write to Gerry thanking him for his kindness and leaving for him in appreciation an elegant traveling desk with silver fittings.[78] On July 5, 1784, fifteen days past the anticipated date, he boarded the *Ceres* and sailed for Europe.

XIII

PARIS AND LIFE

ABOARD THE *Ceres* there were only six passengers, including the two Jeffersons; their black servant, James Hemings; and Colonel Tracy, owner of the vessel. Patsy later recalled, "The voyage was as pleasant as fine weather, a fine ship, good company, and an excellent table could make it."[1] For three days they were becalmed off the banks of Newfoundland, but even this setback was turned to advantage. They feasted on some of the finest fresh fish in the world, throwing part of the catch overboard "for want of salt to preserve it." When the sails filled again, Jefferson was busy keeping a daily log, recording temperature and wind direction. He noted the wide wheeling gannets, big as geese; shark fins cutting the water; whales swimming past in primeval majesty.[2] Despite the delay they landed in Plymouth, England, only nineteen days after leaving Boston.

For the first time Jefferson was in a truly foreign country, though at times, in spite of his internationalism, he had regarded any place outside Virginia as foreign. He was not sentimental about being in the land of his ancestors. In fact, he had hoped to transfer to a vessel for the French coast instead of landing in England. But it was necessary to find a physician for Patsy who had been running a fever for several days.[3]

They remained about a week in Plymouth, until Patsy recovered. On the third day she was improved enough for Jefferson to ride off to Farnham, Titchfield, and Gosport while she apparently remained at Bradley's Crown Inn in Portsmouth.[4]

On July 31 they crossed the stormy channel to Havre (a most unpleasant trip for one of Jefferson's sensitive equilibrium) and began the journey by easy stages through the wheatlands and villages of France to Paris. With the eye of a farmer as well as that of an artist Jefferson noted the signs of intense cultivation, the long-settled air of the villages with their stone houses, the permanent aspect of the occasional chateau, even the time-tamed appearance of the forests. Nature had a far more disciplined look than in America. They spent two days in the ancient town of Rouen, whose towers looked down upon a meandering Seine in no hurry to leave that peaceful plain to keep a rendezvous with the sea. On August 5 and 6 they rode up the Seine valley. The second day they entered the town of Saint-Germaine-en-Laye with its huge chateau and spreading terrace and glimpsed the domes and spires of Paris.[5] Jefferson was no lover of great cities; he viewed them as festering sores on the body politic. But he was a lover of culture and diversity, and Paris was the market town for the arts of the world. We can be sure that his excitement was irrepressible.

A little later they were crossing the Pont de Neuilly (Jefferson pronounced it the handsomest bridge in the world), a graceful structure like a series of long, low gazelle leaps across the Seine. Soon their carriage wheels were rattling on the broad pavements of the Champs-Elysées, which appealed to Jefferson's enthusiasm for great vistas. That day they found lodgings in the Hotel d'Orleans, adjacent to the Palais Royal, home of Louis Philippe Joseph d'Orleans, Duc de Chartres and future Duc d'Orleans. The duke had extended his grounds by dispossessing some of his neighbors and, with the aid of the famous Victor Louis, had created great public gardens in a spacious pilastered enclosure beautified by trees, sculpture, and elaborately dressed ladies of fashion drawn to a spot that was becoming "the capitol of Paris." The clink of trowels and rap of hammers still broke in upon the beauty and quiet of the scene, but Jefferson could visualize how grand it would be when completed. Soon he was thinking how desirable it would be to develop a square in the same fashion in Richmond.[6]

Despite the fascination of the scene, Jefferson moved in a few days to another Hotel d'Orleans, this one in the Rue des Petits Augustins, thus becoming one of the earliest, if not the first, of distinguished American writers to reside on the Left Bank. James Hemings was no longer the only servant with him. He had already engaged a *valet de chambre* named Marc. And the new valet would not be laying out the plain apparel of a Virginia gentleman. Jefferson was quick to buy lace ruffles and a new dress sword and belt.[7]

More in keeping with his usual purchasing habits were his visits to the bookstores that crowded the Left Bank—five of them in one street alone. Never before had he reveled in such literary largesse. By his own testimony, "While residing in Paris I devoted every afternoon I was disengaged, for a summer or two, in examining all the principal bookstores, turning over every book with my own hands, and putting by everything related to America, and indeed whatever was rare and valuable to every science."[8] As the term "science" then denoted any scholarly discipline, the range of his selections was far greater than the term would suggest to most modern readers. Apparently he spent the equivalent of about five days' rent before concluding his first visit to a Paris bookstore.

But even the teeming shelves of the Left Bank, so richly redolent of ink and leather, could not satisfy his appetite for long. "For such works as could not be found in Paris" he placed standing orders with booksellers of London, Amsterdam, Frankfort, and Madrid.[9] His progress in Spanish was such that the treasures of that language were now open to him. He once told John Quincy Adams, son of John Adams, that he had learned Spanish in the nineteen days of his Atlantic crossing. Though young Adams recorded the claim in his diary, he added, "But Mr. Jefferson tells large stories."[10] Be that as it may, it would be hard to exaggerate Jefferson's lust for learning. The tall American who could reach the high shelves without a ladder was becoming one of the best-known figures among the bookstalls of Paris, and his name was well known to the leading booksellers of half a dozen nations. And he was celebrated as much for knowing his own mind as for his enthusiasm. "When I name a particular edition of a book," he wrote a London bookseller, "send me that edition and no other. . . . I disclaim all pompous editions and all typographical luxury; but I like a fine white paper, neat type, and neat binding, gilt and lettered in the modern style."[11] It was not that his esthetic appreciation failed to embrace the physical appearance of books as well as their contents, but, he told a fellow Virginian, as one who "labored grievously under the malady of

Bibliomania," he necessarily "submitted to the rule of buying only at reasonable prices, as a regimen necessary to that disease."[12]

Soon Jefferson was a producer as well as a consumer of books. He engaged Philippe-Deny Pierres, a Parisian printer whose rates were much lower than those of his Philadelphia counterparts, to run off two hundred copies of *Notes on Virginia* for private distribution. Later he consented somewhat reluctantly to the production by a less reliable Paris printer of a French translation of the work by the Abbé Morellet. Eventually the Statute of Virginia for Religious Freedom was printed not only in English, but also in French and Italian, winning high praise from intellectuals and stimulating great interest in the author.

The doors of Paris salons opened to him like welcoming arms. He gloried in the conversational feasts which offered the added pleasure of the exotic, though he insisted that the intellectual quality of the talk was no better than he had known in Williamsburg at Governor Fauquier's table with Small and Wythe.[13]

One of the most interesting of those to whom Jefferson's writings provided an introduction was Buffon, the famous naturalist whose theory that all life degenerated in the New World had prompted a spirited refutation in the *Notes*. Incensed as he was by the Frenchman's disparagement of America, Jefferson nevertheless acknowledged him to be "the best informed of any naturalist who has ever written." Buffon was the father of natural history as a unified science and perhaps had a more comprehensive view of the physical sciences than any other person of his time. Jefferson sent the *Notes* to the great scientist through the good offices of Chastellux, with whom the Virginian had happily renewed his friendship, and followed it with the gift of the large panther skin purchased in Philadelphia.

Regretting that his health prevented him from calling on the giver, Buffon invited Jefferson and Chastellux to dine with him in the Intendant's House, where he lived as superintendent of the royal gardens. As an enthusiastic gardener fascinated by the surroundings, the American was not displeased with his host's unusual habit of remaining in his study until dinner time and receiving "no visitors under any pretense" while giving his guests free run of house and grounds. When Chastellux and Jefferson chanced upon their host in the gardens they pretended not to see him. Jefferson seems to have been a little apprehensive of the evening ahead but such thoughts were dispelled when he was welcomed to dinner by the man whose rugged features were illumined by so much kindly intelligence: "He proved himself then, as he always did, a man of extraordinary powers in conversation. He did not declaim; he was singularly agreeable."[14]

The eminent Frenchman found Jefferson interesting and entertained him on other occasions. They seem always to have discussed science; Jefferson customarily talked with each person about that person's specialty. With Buffon, as with others, he appears to have held his own. Once they argued about chemistry—a science still in its infancy more than two centuries after its emergence from alchemy but only a decade after the discovery of oxygen. Buffon said that it was just another species of "cookery." Jefferson insisted that it was "big with future discoveries for the utility and safety of the human race."[15]

From time to time the Virginian contributed the skeleton of some large American mammal to the Cabinet du Roi, the national museum of natural history that Buffon directed, and he never lost an opportunity to point out in his diplomatic way various flaws in Buffon's theory of New World degeneracy. Eventually, the Frenchman promised to make amends in a future edition of his *Histoire Naturelle*.[16]

Much as Jefferson enjoyed his conversations with the savants of Paris, his visits to bookstores, his trips to such theaters as he had never known before, his attendance of classical concerts, and his introduction to opera, which he savored although the noises emitted by some of the heroines resembled "the agonizing struggles for breath in a dying person,"[17] he was too much imbued with the work ethic to neglect responsibilities. On the advice of the Marquise de Lafayette, whose husband was in America, he enrolled Patsy in the school of the Abbaye de Panthemont. The student body included both Protestants and Catholics drawn from various countries by the institution's high reputation. He shopped with his eleven-year-old daughter for dresses and bonnets and lingerie,[18] acquiring a knowledge of things to which most American men were strangers.

He was equally thorough in discharging public responsibilities. He crossed the Seine to Passy to confer with his fellow commissioner Dr. Franklin who was then living in one of the wings of the Hôtel de Valentinois, a large and handsome villa amid extensive grounds. Now seventy-eight years old, big-domed, with long, wispy hair—like some latter-day Merlin who had lured electricity from the skies—Franklin had aged but would be unmistakable anywhere, an ethnic group of one. He greeted with happy cordiality the only American who equaled him in versatility, but did not show him around the garden terraces that ran down to the river. The Pennsylvanian suffered so from the gout and from "the stone" in his bladder that, although he "praised the fine view and looked at the beauties of the garden below," he "never stirred a step to descend and walk about in them."[19] Together they stared across the river at the park and buildings of the Royal Military School and discussed the military and economic security of the United States. There would be other visits to the sage of Passy. Before this one was concluded, they sent an invitation to John Adams, the third commissioner, then at the Hague, to join them in Paris.

On September 15, 1784, Jefferson, looking taller and thinner than ever in the company of his two rotund companions, Franklin and Adams, entered the white and gold rococo magnificence of the French Foreign Ministry at Versailles to present to Charles Gravier, Comte de Vergennes, "the Commission of the United States in Congress assembled authorizing them to negotiate and conclude a supplementary treaty between the United States and His Most Christian Majesty." The foreign minister, a very polite man whose gentle smile seemed contradicted by the vertical frown marks above the bridge of his nose, was far more observant of Jefferson than of the Virginian's companions. He had dealt with them before, finding Adams impatient and doctrinaire, preferring Franklin as a man of the world who had taken the trouble to understand France.[20]

Jefferson's household eventually included William Short, his personal secretary; Colonel David Humphreys, the tall, dark, somewhat pompous Connecticut man who was Secretary of Legation; and four servants. One of the most versatile men of his age, Jefferson nevertheless never mastered the art of looking after himself. Though he placed strong philosophical emphasis on republican simplicity, he always required a great deal of personal service. And he was a far cry from his father who, while on a surveying expedition, had slept in a hollow tree. As we have seen, Thomas Jefferson's idea of frugal living was buying crates of books in untooled leather bindings with simple gilding.

He stretched his income almost to the breaking point by acquiring a fine wine cellar, apprenticing James Hemings to an excellent French chef, buying a handsome carriage with green morocco lining that put the old phaeton to shame, and (just before maximum expansion of his household) leasing on October 16 a town house on the cul-de-sac Tait-bout. With it came a courtyard and two gardens, but no furniture. Leaving more utilitarian purchases to Marc, replaced as *valet de chambre* and promoted to *maître d'hôtel*, Jefferson went on a shopping spree for furniture, carpets, linens, silver, and china that consumed more than his annual salary as commissioner. Nothing daunted, he spent further to remodel the practically new interior.[21] One member of his staff was a *frotteur*, or rubber of floors. When the handsome tile or parquet had been waxed, he would attach brushes to his shoes and glide over the increasingly shiny surfaces with the graceful aplomb of an ice skater.[22]

Such was life at Hôtel Têtebout, as Jefferson, with characteristic disregard for the native spelling, called his new home.

Not until a little later did he learn that just before he moved into the new house tragedy again had struck his family. A letter dated October 13 from his sister-in-law Elizabeth Wayles Eppes informed him: "A most unfortunate whooping cough has deprived you and us of two sweet Lucys within a week. . . . Your dear angel was con-fined a week to her bed; her sufferings were great, though nothing like a fit. She retained her senses perfectly, called me a few moments before she died, and asked distinctly for water."[23] A following letter by Francis Eppes reported of his daughter and Jeffer-son's, "They suffered as much pain, indeed more, than ever I saw two of their ages experience."[24] Fortunately, Polly, though she also had caught the disease, had recovered.

The news was a heavy blow for a very loving and family minded man. Much later he wrote to Elizabeth Thompson, a native Virginian living in England: "My history, since I had the pleasure of seeing you last, would have been as happy a one as I could have asked, could the objects of my affection have been immortal. But all the favors of fortune have been embittered by domestic losses. Of six children I have lost four, and finally their mother."[25]

He had suffered migraine attacks for the first six weeks after his arrival in Paris. Caught up in the intellectual and esthetic delights of the city, he had begun to regain his health though the dampness of the climate still brought respiratory congestion. Now he was once again precipitated into mourning.

But he did not withdraw from the world. He paid frequent visits to Patsy's school to see that she was not lonely and was delighted to find her happily wearing her crimson uniform and answering to the affectionate nickname of Jeffy. John and Abigail Adams were living in the village of Auteiul outside Paris, and Jefferson often visited them there and invited them to dinner in turn. While the Virginian respected Franklin's far-ranging mind and liked him personally, he found the Adamses' quiet family life far more con-genial than the Pennsylvanian's more unorthodox lifestyle. John Adams in turn admired Jefferson's "abilities and steadiness" and Abigail, an outspoken woman of pronounced opinions, grew steadily fonder of the courtly and considerate Virginian. Young Abby received that warm deference which Jefferson gave to women of every age, and John Quincy, at seventeen manifesting the brilliance which was to distinguish him always, hung so much upon Jefferson both at Auteiul and in Paris that the senior Adams later told his friend, "He appeared to me to be almost as much your boy as mine."[26]

For a time the three commissioners met every day at Passy. Franklin's already considerable respect for Jefferson increased with each new revelation of the younger man's well-organized genius. The old diplomat was pleased by the rumors that, upon his retirement as minister to France, Jefferson would succeed him.[27] The Virginian was uncomfortable when Franklin jested freely with his women and he abhorred his cynical view of females (the venerable incorrigible had advised a young friend to settle upon an old mistress who would appreciate his favors since "all cats are gray in the dark" and had taken comfort in the fact that a woman's bottom often remained smooth after the rest of her had become rough or wrinkled). But Jefferson did not bristle with moral indignation in the American minister's presence as did Adams, and he had a far better working relationship with him.[28]

But soon the meetings at Passy and the attendance of levees in Paris began to seem to Jefferson a quaint masquerade with little point or substance. The court of Louis XVI was concerned with the domestic affairs of France and the problems and opportunities presented by the plenipotentiaries of great and ancient states. The three commissioners from the infant confederation on the edge of the North American wilderness were, Jefferson concluded, "the lowest and most obscure of the whole diplomatic tribe."[29]

Instead of despairing and doing nothing, he began to compose a model treaty of commerce and amity that could be presented with modifications to each of the score of nations they might approach. To this task he brought the same talents for clarity and organization, and the same high zeal for humanitarian reform, that had distinguished his labors in the recodification of Virginia laws.

Three such treaties were already in existence, one negotiated with the United Netherlands by Adams and the other two (with France and Sweden) by Franklin. More agreements were urgently needed. In freeing themselves from colonial exploitation as part of the British Empire, the Americans had also cut themselves off from a closed system of commerce that had advantages as well as disadvantages. New arrangements must be made if there were to be dependable markets for American goods. Not only were the markets of the Old World controlled by European states that had little confidence in the ability of the United States to meet its responsibilities or perhaps even to survive, but the much nearer markets of the West Indies and other areas of the New World were controlled by the same colonial powers. To make an effective breakthrough the United States needed not only to make new treaties but to conclude supplementary ones with France, Sweden, and the Netherlands.

In a letter to his colleagues Jefferson addressed the problem in language reminiscent of that which he had used in introducing his proposals for reform of Virginia's laws: "Will it not be better to take up the subject as it were anew, to arrange the articles under classes, and while we are reforming the principles to reform also the language of treaties, which history alone and not grammar will justify? The articles may be rendered shorter and more conspicuous by simplifying their style and structure."[30] Jefferson altered the phrasing of this first draft, perhaps because of the implied criticism of treaty texts already prepared by Franklin and Adams. In any event, as Julian Boyd has observed, "if he gave up the words in his rough draft, he did not give up the intent."[31]

His model treaty was a big improvement in both "style and structure" over those prepared by his colleagues, though both, especially Franklin, were gifted writers. Jefferson's improvements were the reflection of an ordered mind. His talent for classification asserted itself as he marshaled topics under appropriate heads and subheads. And the rigorous economy that he could exercise with words so much more effectively than with money reduced by one-third the length of some paragraphs in, for instance, the treaty with Sweden.[32] Working within the restraints of diplomatic usage, he found no room for vaulting phrases or intellectual leaps into the empyrean of ideality. But the task demanded imagination nonetheless—the ability of the mind to free itself from time-honored forms and approach afresh the task of composing a treaty. There was innovation, too, in the humanitarian note struck in Articles 23 and 24. The first provided:

> If war should arise between the two contracting parties the merchants of either country then residing in the other shall be allowed to remain nine months to collect their debts and settle their affairs, and may depart freely, carrying off all their effects without molestation or hindrance: and all women and children, scholars of every faculty, cultivators of the earth, artisans, manufacturers and fishermen, unarmed, and inhabiting unfortified towns, villages, or places; whose occupations are for the common subsistence and benefit of mankind, shall be allowed to continue their respective employments, and shall not be molested in their persons nor shall their houses or goods be burnt or otherwise destroyed, nor their fields wasted by the armed force of the enemy into whose power, by the events of war, they may happen to fall: but if any thing is necessary to be taken from them for the use of such armed force, the same shall be paid for at a reasonable price.[33]

Article 24 embodied a convention for the humane treatment of prisoners of war. They were to be kept "in wholesome situations" and were not to be "put into irons, nor bound, nor otherwise restrained in the use of their limbs."[34] They were to have opportunities for fresh air and exercise and their rations and medications were to be of the same quality as those issued to the captor's own troops. Each party would have a commissary of prisoners permitted to check on the welfare of its nationals imprisoned by the other. "And it is declared that neither the pretense that war dissolves all treaties, nor any other whatever, shall be considered as annulling or suspending this. . . article, but on the contrary that the state of war is precisely that for which they are provided, and during which they are to be as sacredly observed as the most acknowledged articles in the law of nature or nations."[35]

The American commissioners presented the proposed treaty on November 10, 1784, to the Prussian minister in Paris, together with a written defense of the innovative humanitarian measures. This document, probably also prepared by Jefferson,[36] argued: "This article, being in favor of humanity, by softening and diminishing the calamities of war, we think it will be honorable to the first powers who agree to it, and more particularly so to His Majesty the King of Prussia, if he whose subjects are known to be so well defended by his power and abilities as to make the stipulation of any favor for them during war unnecessary, should be the foremost in setting the example of agreeing to such an article."[37] Along with this appeal to Frederick's pride in his reputation as an enlightened monarch and his military prowess was a tactful reminder of a good reason for retaining American friendship: "The part too which engages not to commission privateers nor make prizes of merchant ships will, we think, show the disinterestedness of the United States, since their situation is suited to prey with ease on the rich commerce of Europe with the West Indies, which must pass before their doors, while their own, consisting of lumber and provisions, is of so little value . . . that the loss in that kind of war is vastly inferior to the profit, which was demonstrated in their late contest with Britain, whose mighty fleets were insufficient to protect their trade from the depredations of a people as able and expert seamen as themselves."[38]

Frederick the Great's bright, bulging eyes scanned with approval the report on the treaty's humanitarian provisions. When the king's endorsement was conveyed to the American commissioners on January 24, 1785, John Adams was almost ecstatic. He told the Prussian minister, "I am weary of the slow motions of other courts and states as much as I admire the dispatch, intelligence, and decision of that of Berlin."[39] He praised "the Platonic philosophy" of the articles, a reference which must have surprised Jefferson, who seems to have had an antipathy to Plato. Adams thought they embodied at least as good a "lesson to mankind" as the writings of the Attic philosopher and, when backed by the king of Prussia, would have a more beneficent influence than the teachings of either Plato or Sir Thomas More.

Later Jefferson proposed to the sympathetic Adams an enlightened measure that he realized was "beyond our powers, and beyond the powers of Congress too." Indeed he was so acutely aware of its prematurity that he told Adams he would not reveal it to "any other mortal living."[40] Jefferson's suggestion was for treaties of reciprocity extending full rights of citizenship to the citizens of one nation when in the territory of the other, a measure that would be regarded as radical when proposed by Sir Winston Churchill in the twentieth century.

But, while Jefferson dreamed of reforms extending far into the future, he was very much concerned with what was possible in his own time. He confided to Monroe in a letter in June of 1785 that, in working for treaties between the United States and other nations, he had a purpose transcending the facilitation of trade, important as that was: "You see that my primary object in the formation of treaties is to take the commerce of the states out of the hands of the states, and to place it under the superintendence of Congress, so far as the imperfect provisions of our constitution will admit, and until the states shall by new compact make them more perfect."[41] He explained: "Congress, by the Confederation, have no original and inherent power over the commerce of the states. But by the 9th article they are authorized to enter into treaties of commerce. The moment these treaties are concluded the jurisdiction of Congress over the commerce of the states springs into existence, and that of the particular states is superseded so far as the articles of the treaty may have taken up the subject." Jefferson believed that a strengthening of federal power was essential to preserve the United States. Once again the former strict constructionist governor was evidencing his willingness to abandon strict construction when the nation's security was at stake.

Though alive to the intellectual currents of Europe and a keen student of its politics, Jefferson found his thoughts turning increasingly to his native land. He examined each public question in the light of its probable influence on American affairs, each scientific innovation in terms of its utility to his own country. And he was particularly concerned with developments in Virginia. He wrote freely concerning the politics of his state to Monroe and Madison, employing a code of his own devising.[42] The secrecy was undoubtedly a good idea in view of the frequency with which dispatches were opened by curious and sometimes hostile persons, but the impression is inescapable that Jefferson the diplomat enjoyed this method of communication as much as Jefferson the college boy had when conveying the secrets of his courtship to John Page. In one coded letter to Madison he expressed the hope that, unsatisfactory as the Virginia Constitution was, proposals to frame a new one at that time would not be acted upon. "While Mr. Henry lives," he said, "another bad constitution would be formed and forever on us. What we have to do I think is devoutly to pray for his death."[43] In the meantime, they must "prepare the minds of the young men."

Other actions of Virginia's legislators also drew his thoughts to the Old Dominion. The General Assembly had voted to erect a statue of George Washington and thought that only a European sculptor would be worthy of what they regarded as the greatest American subject. As late as the 1920s President Coolidge, when asked to commission American art works, would ask, "Can't we get all the art we need from France?" But there was more justification for this attitude at a time when America's leading sculptors were carvers of wooden figureheads for sailing ships. The legislators, through Governor Harrison, asked Jefferson's help in finding an artist in marble and he replied: "There could be no question raised as to the sculptor who should be employed, the reputation of Monsieur Houdon, of this city, being unrivaled in Europe. He is resorted to for the statues of most of the sovereigns in Europe."[44]

Jefferson had sent for Houdon to discuss plans for the statue and had been quite pleased with the stocky, balding artist who on superficial observation might have passed for an innkeeper. Franklin, whose aid also had been requested by the Virginians, and Jefferson were convinced after conversations with the sculptor that "no statue of General Washington which might be a true evidence of his figure to posterity could be made from his picture."[45] Jefferson joyfully reported, "Monsieur Houdon, whose reputation is such as to make it his principal object, was so anxious to be the person who should hand down the figure of the general to future ages, that without hesitating a moment he offered to abandon his business here, to leave the statues of kings unfinished, and to go to America to take the true figure by actual inspection and mensuration."[46] Already, in the infant United States, kings were accorded that peculiar prestige which they seem to enjoy among the citizens of republics. "We believe, from his character," Jefferson wrote of Houdon, "that he will not propose any very considerable sum for making this journey, probably two or three hundred guineas, as he must necessarily be absent three or four months and his expenses will make at least a hundred guineas of the money. When the whole merit of the piece was to depend on this previous expenditure, we could not doubt your approbation of the measure, and that you would think with us that things which are just and handsome should never be done by halves."[47]

To Washington, who heartily disliked posing for portraits, but whose ear was ever sensitive to the call of duty, Jefferson had written, "I trust that, having given to your country so much of your time heretofore, you will add the short space which this operation will require to enable them to transmit to posterity the form of a person whose actions will be delivered to them by History."[48]

Arrangements for the statue, eventually erected in the Virginia State Capitol where it is today prized as the most valuable portrait sculpture in the United States, consumed many hours of Jefferson's time in conference and correspondence. Soon he was finding delight in visits to Houdon's studio, where the heads of state were ranged in solemn conclave with an occasional philosopher among them, and Diana tripped lightly by in naked innocence of the marble visages turned toward her.

Houdon himself, only two years older than Jefferson, was much to his liking. Both pursued excellence with an avidity that left far behind the fast fading landmarks of pecuniary consideration. Houdon's straightforward portraiture, free of the superfluous decoration indulged in by the sculptor's immediate predecessors, must have appealed to Jefferson through its classic Roman quality. There were the same individuality and revelation of personality that distinguished the best of the Roman work. And there was a heightened animation that surpassed the Romans, because Houdon had learned or devised techniques that they had not known. In place of symmetrical hollows for the pupils of the eyes he had little openings as irregular as dental cavities, so that from a distance they appeared to twinkle with the light of life. And on the heads of men he let some of his tool marks remain in a way that imparted added vigor: see the intelligence, half mischievous, half benign, that glows from the wrinkled face of Voltaire in the busts and especially in the full-length seated figure. In contrast, polished smoothness characterized the marble busts of Diana and the full-length statue which caught her swift motion as effectively as the images of Voltaire arrested his fleeting expressions. The complete nudity of the figure apparently was considered too bold even for the Paris Salon,[49] but the exquisite refinement of face and body with slenderly elegant legs and small piquant breasts like finialed Palladian domes captivated Jefferson. He purchased a small plaster model and carried it back to America, but apparently never displayed it at Monticello; instead he gave it to a friend with the advice that "its nudity may be an objection to some."[50]

Jefferson did not like all statues undraped, or even classically draped. There was a proposal that Houdon's statue of Washington show him in toga, or perhaps even bare-chested. Jefferson was relieved when Washington himself rejected the idea, consenting to be depicted instead in his uniform as commander of the Continental army. From Paris the commissioner wrote his fellow Virginian, "I think a modern in antique dress as just an object of ridicule as a Hercules or Marius with a periwig and *chapeau bras*" (tricorn hat).[51]

Jefferson also criticized contemporary drapery as he found it in France. He thought that the elaborate costumes of many of the fashionable ladies of Paris were symbolic of the essential frivolity of society in the capital. Though he loved French art and scholarship, he deplored an artificiality and sensuality that he contrasted with American naturalness. If only Old World sophistication could be united with New World artlessness! Jefferson was one of the first Americans to articulate the inner conflict later expressed so vividly by Henry James, Edith Wharton and others. He set forth his views in an entertaining letter to Charles Bellini, professor of modern languages at the College of William and Mary:

Behold me at length on the vaunted scene of Europe! It is not necessary for your information that I should enter into details concerning it. But you are perhaps curious to know how this new scene has struck a savage of the mountains of America. Not advantageously I assure you. I find the general fate of humanity here most deplorable. The truth of Voltaire's observation offers itself perpetually, that every man here must be either the hammer or the anvil. It is a true picture of that country to which they say we shall pass hereafter, and where we are to see god and his angels in splendor, and crowds of the damned trampled under their feet.[52]

In a romantic threnody for Europe's lost innocence and a celebration of America's Paradise regained, Jefferson ignored the existence of bucolic cunning to match metropolitan guile:

> While the great mass of the people are thus suffering under physical and moral oppression, I have endeavored to examine more nearly the condition of the great, to appreciate the true value of the circumstances in their situation which dazzle the bulk of the spectators, and especially to compare it with that degree of happiness which is enjoyed in America by every class of people. Intrigues of love occupy the younger, and those of ambition the more elderly part of the great. Conjugal love having no existence among them, domestic happiness, of which that is the basis, is utterly unknown. In lieu of this are substituted pursuits which nourish and invigorate all our bad passions, and which offer only moments of ecstasy amidst days and months of restlessness and torment. Much, very much inferior this to the tranquil permanent felicity with which domestic society in America blesses most of its inhabitants, leaving them to follow steadily those pursuits which health and reason approve, and rendering truly delicious the intervals of these pursuits. In science, the mass of people is two centuries behind ours, their literati half a dozen years before us. Books, really good, acquire just reputation in that time, and so become known to us and communicate to us all their advances in knowledge. Is not this delay compensated by our being placed out of the reach of that swarm of nonsense which issues daily from a thousand presses and perishes almost in issuing?[53]

Then he entered some items on the credit side for Europe:

> With respect to what are termed polite manners, without sacrificing too much the sincerity of language, I would wish (my) countrymen to adopt just so much of European politeness as to be ready [to] make all those little sacrifices of self which really render European manners amiable, and relieve society from the disagreeable scenes to which rudeness often exposes it. Here it seems that a man might pass a life without encountering a single rudeness. In the pleasures of the table they are far before us, because with good taste they unite temperance. They do not terminate the most sociable meals by transforming themselves into brutes. I have never yet seen a man drunk in France, even among the lowest of the people.

Enthusiasm seized his pen:

> Were I to proceed to tell you how much I enjoy their architecture, sculpture, painting, music, I should want words. It is in these arts they shine. The last of them particularly is an enjoyment, the deprivation of which with us cannot be

calculated. I am almost ready to say it is the only thing which from my heart I envy them, and which in spite of all the authority of the decalogue I do covet.

Finally, one part of Jefferson's mind viewed dispassionately his own passion, concluding: "But I am running on in an estimate of things infinitely better known to you than to me, and which will only serve to convince you that I have brought with me all the prejudices of country, habit and age."

About a fortnight later Jefferson compared America and Europe in replying to an American who had requested from him the name of the continent's "best seminary for the education of youth." Jefferson replied that, if one must send an American youth abroad for his education, the choice probably would lie between Geneva and Rome. He apparently did not even consider any place in France. And he cautioned: "It is true that the habit of speaking the modern languages cannot be so well acquired in America, but every other article can be as well acquired at William and Mary College as at any place in Europe. When college education is done with and a young man is to prepare himself for public life, he must cast his eyes (for America) either on Law or Physic. For the former where can he apply so advantageously as to Mr. Wythe? For the latter he must come to Europe; the medical class of students therefore is the only one which need come to Europe."[54]

He pursued the subject further:

Let us view the disadvantages of sending a youth to Europe. To enumerate them all would require a volume. I will select a few. If he goes to England he learns drinking, horse-racing and boxing. These are the peculiarities of English education. The following circumstances are common to education in that and the other countries of Europe. He acquires a fondness for European luxury and dissipation and a contempt for the simplicity of his own country; he is fascinated with the privileges of the European aristocrats, and sees with abhorrence the lovely equality which the poor enjoy with the rich in his own country: he contracts a partiality for aristocracy or monarchy; he forms foreign friendships which will never be useful to him, and loses the season of life for forming in his own country those friendships which of all others are the most faithful and permanent: he is led by the strongest of all the human passions into a spirit for female intrigue destructive of his own and others' happiness, or a passion for whores destructive of his health, and in both cases learns to consider fidelity to the marriage bed as an ungentlemanly practice and inconsistent with happiness: he recollects the voluptuary dress and arts of the European women and pities and despises the chaste affections and simplicity of those of his own country; he retains through life a fond recollection and a hankering after those places which were the scenes of his first pleasures and of his first connections; he returns to his own country, a foreigner, unacquainted with the practices of domestic economy necessary to preserve him from ruin; speaking and writing his native tongue as a foreigner, and therefore unqualified to obtain those distinctions which eloquence of the pen and tongue ensures in a free country.

Sounding very much like a late nineteenth-century Midwesterner, this eighteenth-century American in Paris concluded:

It appears to me then that an American coming to Europe for education loses in his knowledge, in his morals, in his health, in his habits, and in his happiness. I had entertained only doubts on this head before I came to Europe: what I see and hear since I came here proves more than I had even suspected. Cast your eye over America: who are the men of most learning, of most eloquence, most beloved by their country and most trusted and promoted by them? They are those who have been educated among them, and whose manners, morals and habits are perfectly homogeneous with those of the country.

Jefferson's saving sense of perspective, which had so often spared him from becoming a crank or an ideologue, asserted itself in the end: "Did you expect by so short a question to draw such a sermon on yourself? I dare say you did not. But the consequences of foreign education are alarming to me as an American. I sin therefore through zeal whenever I enter on the subject. You are sufficiently American to pardon me for it."

The reference to sex as "the strongest of all the human passions" suggests that perhaps the American widower was sometimes casting a warmer than Platonic eye on those voluptuous beauties he deplored. At least we know that he spoke from bitter personal knowledge when he warned of the effects of Parisian luxury on simple domestic economy. When a fellow countryman sought to borrow money from him for a passage back home, promising to repay immediately upon arrival in Philadelphia, Jefferson replied:

> Your letter of this day distresses me not a little as it finds me utterly unable to give you the assistance needed. My outfit here, for the articles of furniture, clothes and carriage only has cost me fifteen hundred guineas. No allowance of this kind being made I have been obliged to run in debt for it. The uneasiness which this has given me for some time past has preyed on my spirits night and day. And indeed my situation is not a little delicate. The laws not giving remedy against me, the first creditor whom I can neither pay nor prevail to wait, carries his complaint to the king immediately, and exposes me of necessity to censure and recall. These circumstances have not only reduced me to a rigid economy, but render it impossible for me either to advance money or further hazard my credit. I am fully sensible that this information may be distressing to you, and this increases the pain with which I communicate it. I am unhappily in a condition to feel much for your difficulties without a power to lessen them.[55]

Jefferson's indebtedness had not arisen from riotous living but from the application of the philosophy which he had expressed to Governor Harrison in making arrangements for Houdon's statue of Washington. He firmly believed that "things which are just and handsome should not be done by halves."

Though the Congress of the United States did not indicate its approbation of Jefferson by substantially increasing his pay, it did signify its confidence in another way. On May 2, 1785, he received a letter from John Jay notifying him that on March 10 he had been elected to succeed Franklin as United States Minister to France.[56]

In the summer Franklin returned to America and Adams left for London to serve as United States minister there. By then Jefferson had presented his credentials to Vergennes, with whom he had already had many dealings and would have many more. By now he may have arrived at the conclusion he would communicate to Madison about a year and a half later that the French Foreign Secretary, though he had played the principal role in committing France to support of the United States in the Revolution, was no friend of democracy: "He is a great minister in European affairs, but has very imperfect ideas of ours (and) no confidence in them. His devotion to the principles of pure despotism renders him unaffectionate to our governments but his fear of England makes him value us as a makeweight. He is cool, reserved in political conversation, free and familiar on other subjects, and a very attentive, agreeable person to do business with. It is impossible to have a clearer, better organized head; but age has chilled his heart."[57]

Three days after presenting his credentials to Vergennes the new American minister delivered his letter of credence in a private audience with Louis XVI where, as Jefferson reported to Jay, he had gone "through the other ceremonies usual on such occasions."[58] The king was not stupid and was basically decent, but it must have been disagreeable to Jefferson to bow and scrape to this fat and lethargic young man, eleven years his junior, whom court etiquette prevented from returning the compliment.

Other aspects of his mission proved quite agreeable. He became a polished diplomat, at home amid the mirrored glitter of Versailles as well as among the salons and the savants. Indeed, his brilliant conversation and his *Notes on Virginia* were earning him a reputation as a polymath. The learned Mr. Jefferson as successor to the learned Dr. Franklin was a good advertisement for American culture. The Virginian did not impress his idiosyncrasies of dress on the popular mind as had his predecessor. There was no fad for Jefferson hats as there had been for Franklin caps. Jefferson would never have been recognized in the streets by as many people as identified Franklin, who had grown almost to be a caricature of himself. But he became very popular among the aristocrats and upper middle class, who valued intellect and manners. His kindness appealed to all classes.[59] His path to social success was smoothed in part by Chastellux and in large measure by the Lafayettes. When the Virginian was new in France, Lafayette had written from America: "My house, dear sir, my family, and anything that is mine are entirely at your disposal and I beg you will come and see Mde. de Lafayette as you would act by your brother's wife. Her knowledge of the country may be of some use to Miss Jefferson whom she will be happy to attend in everything that may be agreeable to her. Indeed, my dear sir, I would be very angry with you if either you or she did not consider my house as a second home."[60]

That home was a great meeting place for Americans, including some aboriginal ones. Two young braves, an Oneida and an Onondaga, were members of the household.[61] The Marquis ostentatiously sprinkled his speech with Americanisms and even kept a retainer in full Indian regalia. Though the general was a bit of a poseur, there was worth beneath his mask of worth, much as the true lineaments of benevolence lay beneath Lord George Hell's mask of benevolence in Beerbohm's story. Early in his ministry Jefferson wrote Madison, "I take him to be of unmeasured ambition but that the means he uses are virtuous."[62] Two years later he wrote of the Frenchman's "canine appetite for popularity and fame," but noted, "He has a great deal of sound genius, is well remarked by the king."[63] He also wrote: "The Marquis de Lafayette is a most valuable auxiliary to me. His zeal is unbounded and his weight with those in power great."[64]

Well might Jefferson be grateful. Perhaps his two most significant achievements as minister were projecting an American image of intelligence and urbanity that strengthened confidence in the revolution-born republic and securing trade concessions from the French government. Lafayette, like Chastellux, accelerated the image-building by giving Jefferson exposure to the most influential people in France. In the matter of trade agreements he facilitated arrangements that might have been impossible without his help.

Overseas trade was vital if the United States was to survive as a national entity. With England in no mood to promote the fortunes of her former colonies, France seemed the chief hope. Yet the French government had severely limited importation of rice, whale oil, salt fish and meats, and tobacco, and was largely shutting the United States out of the West India trade. The proximity of the West Indies had made commerce with the islands a principal American objective. The rice planters of South Carolina, the fishermen of New England, and the tobacco growers of Virginia were badly hurt by the restrictions on specific commodities.

Drawing on his study of the American economy, including information gained on his New England tour, and meshing this knowledge with what he had learned about French industry, Jefferson in a personal interview in August 1785 urged upon Vergennes the importance of quickly placing "the commerce between France and America on the best footing possible." Having had no response, Jefferson wrote the Foreign Minister a detailed letter on the same subject, using as an excuse the Virginian's supposed distrust of his own ability to express himself clearly "in a language I speak so imperfectly."[65]

Much of the letter was in the style of French diplomacy, as in the sentence, "We fervently invoke Heaven to make the king's life and happiness the objects of its peculiar care, and that he may long be relieved in the burthen of government by your wise counsels." But the body of the letter was a closely reasoned argument buttressed by statistics and revealing a considerable knowledge of French fiscal policies and the national economy. Having demonstrated benefits to accrue to France as well as to the United States as a result of increased trade between the two nations, Jefferson said: "It is with sincerity I add that warm feelings are indulged in my breast by the further hope that it would bind the two nations still closer in friendship, by binding them in interest. In truth no two countries are better calculated for the exchanges of commerce. France wants rice, tobacco, potash, furs, ship-timber. We want wine, brandies, oils, and manufactures. There is an affection too between the two people which disposes them to favor one another. If they do not come together then to make the exchange in their own ports, it shows there is some substantial obstruction in the way." The American Minister had a diplomatic way of telling the government of His Most Christian Majesty that it was doing something wrong.

The letter was a skillful reply to Vergennes' complaint that American commerce "covered the Thames" but did not find its way to the ports of France. But shafts of logic and rays of friendship both failed to penetrate the wall of royal self-interest. The king had granted a monopoly of the tobacco trade to the Farmers-general who paid him handsomely for the privilege. Robert Morris of Pennsylvania had in turn obtained from them a monopoly of the American tobacco trade with France. Southern tobacco growers were doubly the victims of monopoly. Similarly, New England sellers of whale oil had to pay the French government duties three times those paid by the Hanseatic ports.

Jefferson appealed to Lafayette for help and the Frenchman took the matter directly to the Comptroller General. As a result duties on whale oil for American shippers would be reduced to the level of those for the Hanseatic cities for one year, provided that the cargo was carried in either American or French vessels. The concession was a limited one, but the machinery of reciprocity had been oiled.

Jefferson was quick to supply another idea in a letter to Vergennes: "Both nations perhaps may come into the opinion that their friendship and their interest may be better cemented by approaching the conditions of the citizens reciprocally to that of *natives*, as a better ground of intercourse than that of *the most favored nation*. I shall rest with hopes of being authorized in due time to inform your Excellency that nothing will be wanting on our part to evince a disposition to concur in revising whatever regulations may on either side bear hard on the commerce of the other nation."[66]

When Vergennes saw Jefferson at the Court of Versailles some days later, the Frenchman complained once again that Americans were trading more with their former enemy, England, than with their ally, France. Jefferson laid aside subtlety: "Merchants will not and cannot trade but where there is to be some gain. . . . The commerce between two countries cannot be kept up but by an *exchange* of commodities."[67] He then cited in quick succession French impediments to the importation of American rice, furs, and tobacco. Even with whale oil, where a better arrangement existed, provisions were for only one year. Jefferson was not encouraged by Vergennes' parting reply that there could be no promises.

But he did not give up. Once again he appealed to Lafayette, who had already initiated organization of a committee of prominent Frenchmen to promote Franco-American trade.

Lafayette reported to Jefferson in March 1786 that he had addressed the French Committee on American Tobacco and that they had requested a written copy of his remarks on the desirability of ending the monopoly: "I am considered as one that has got a very strange idea—and don't think I can get anything now but the hatred of the financeering people. But as [an associate] was telling me in his botanic style, I am sowing seeds which will bear fruit in time."[68]

The Monticello orchardist was not impressed. Too many seedlings of hope had been nipped by the frosty politeness of the French Court. But on May 30, 1786, with the bloom of spring, came a message from Vergennes that the Morris monopoly on tobacco could be broken to the extent of 15,000 hogsheads per annum.[69] The amount was not impressive, but at last a breach had been made.

By that time Jefferson had completed a sudden and unexpected trip to England. About the end of February Colonel William Stephens Smith, secretary and aid to John Adams, had arrived on Jefferson's doorstep with a letter from his employer entreating Jefferson to come to London "without loss of time. The Portuguese Minister has received his instructions from his Court [regarding the proposed treaty], and we may here together conduct and finish the negotiation with him, I suppose in three weeks. But there is another motive more important. There is here a Tripolitan ambassador with whom I have had three conferences. . . . Your visit here will be imputed to curiosity, to take a look at England and pay your respects at Court and to the Corps Diplomatic."[70]

John Adams had acquired some of his Cousin Samuel's love of intrigue, but there was no question this time of his genuine concern and even agitation. "There is nothing to be done in Europe of half the importance of this," he wrote, "and I dare not communicate to Congress what has passed without your concurrence. What has been already done and expended will be absolutely thrown away and we shall be involved in a universal and horrible war with these Barbary States, which will continue for many years, unless more is done immediately. I am so impressed and distressed with this affair that I will go to New York or to Algiers or first to one and then to the other, if you think it necessary, rather than it should not be brought to a conclusion. Somebody must go to New York, one of us, or Humphries or Smith in order to persuade Congress of the necessity of doing more. Then somebody must go to Holland to obtain the means, and then somebody perhaps to Algiers to make use of them. The Tripolitan might be persuaded to go with him."[71]

Colonel Smith filled in the details of recent developments in a matter that had long troubled Jefferson. The four Barbary States—Morocco, Algeria, Tunisia, and Libya— that rimmed the northern coast of Africa west of Egypt had been centers of highly organized piracy at least since the sixteenth century. Cruisers owned by rich subjects and manned by a respected class of reises, or professional captains, preyed on Mediterranean commerce, sharing a tenth of the value of their prizes with the reigning deys. The prizes included crews and passengers. The affluent could buy their freedom; the poor were condemned to slavery. Even Englishmen who proudly sang "Rule, Britannia! Britannia, rule the waves" paid tribute occasionally to the deys to insure that Britons never would be slaves. Great and ancient states accepted submission to this blackmail as a way of life.

Jefferson could not. When several American vessels and their crews were seized by the Barbary pirates during his first year as an American Commissioner, he had written General Nathanael Greene that he was "absolutely suspended between indignation and impotence."[72] When the United States was meekly reduced to ransoming its citizens and Congress even took pride in the fact that the price was lower than might have been expected, Jefferson demanded that the Republic place itself in a position to punish the pirates. In a letter to Jay in August 1785 he argued: "Weakness provokes injury and insult, while a condition to punish it often prevents it. This reasoning leads to the necessity of some naval force, that being the only weapon with which we can reach an enemy. I think it to our interest to punish the first insult, because an insult unpunished is the parent of many others."[73]

Even lacking a truly strong navy, the United States should be able to resist Barbary demands, he insisted. He wrote Monroe: "We ought to begin a naval power, if we mean to carry on our own commerce. Can we begin it on a more honorable occasion, or with a weaker foe? I am of opinion Paul Jones with half a dozen frigates would totally destroy their commerce, not by attempting bombardments. . .but by constant cruising and cutting them to pieces by piecemeal."[74]

Congress had decided instead to negotiate "an amicable treaty," purchasing peace as cheaply as possible. Eighty thousand dollars, it was reported to Jefferson, had been appropriated to pay the ransoms of Americans already captured and to buy protection from such depredations in the near future. One Thomas Barclay was being sent as special agent to deal with Morocco while one John Lamb was dispatched to negotiate with Algiers.

Jefferson quickly drafted a proposed treaty with the Barbary States and sent a copy to John Adams in London. The treaty required each Barbary ruler "to release all citizens of the United States now in captivity within his dominions, and to restore all property which has been taken by any of his subjects from citizens of the United States." It also made "all persons belonging to any vessel of war public or private . . . responsible in their persons and property" for any injury done the people, vessels, or effects of the other party. And it provided, "No vessel of his majesty shall make captures or cruise within sight of the coasts of the United States."[75]

In the accompanying note Jefferson told Adams, "My anxiety is extreme indeed as to these treaties. What are we to do? We know that Congress have decided ultimately to treat. We know how far they will go."[76] But, he reminded Adams, their word of Congress' decision was still unofficial. And Mr. Lamb, after five months, still had not arrived. If he did not arrive on either of the packets currently expected, why not exercise their own powers as ministers plenipotentiary and appoint someone who would bargain hard with the pirate kings? John Paul Jones would be a good emissary. "If we look forward to the very probable event of war with those pirates, an important object would be obtained by Captain Jones's becoming acquainted with their ports, forts, tactics, &c."[77] Once again the strict constructionist, when the welfare of the nation was at stake, was prepared to take bold action not explicitly authorized. He had learned lessons as a frustrated Governor.

Jefferson had begun to solicit the cooperation of other small nations in curbing the piratical operations of the Barbary States when, to his disappointment, Lamb arrived in Paris. Lamb and Barclay, following Congress's instructions, were to negotiate if Jefferson and Adams approved their appointment. Negotiations with Morocco proceeded smoothly. The American ship immediately in question and its cargo and crew were returned to the United States through Spain, and assurances were given that United States commerce would not be preyed upon in the near future. But no progress was made with Algiers. Two American ships remained in Algerian hands and twenty-two American citizens remained Algerian slaves.

A Jefferson granddaughter said in later years that her grandfather never gave up an idea or a friend. The generalization is a little sweeping, but one of the Virginian's most notable characteristics was the pertinacity with which he held to favorite ideas in the face of years of discouragement. Therefore, when he left Paris for London in March of 1786 in response to Adams' urgent plea, he cherished hopes that at last there could be some settlement with the Barbary States consistent with national honor. As it turned out, his hopes were frustrated again. Tunisia's swarthy ambassador sought a treaty for one year at a cost of 12,500 guineas or a "perpetual peace" for 30,000 guineas. Ten percent of either sum would go into his own pocket.[78]

Adams and Jefferson reported to Jay:

We took the liberty to make some inquiries concerning the grounds of their pretensions to make war upon nations who had done them no injury, and observed that we considered all mankind as our friends who had done us no wrong, nor had given us any provocation.

The Ambassador answered us that it was founded on the laws of their Prophet, that it was written in their Koran, that all nations who should not have acknowledged their authority were sinners, that it was their right and duty to make war upon them wherever they could be found, and to make slaves of all they could take as prisoners, and that every Musselman who should be slain in battle was sure to go to Paradise.[79]

Between puffs on a two-foot long pipe[80] he had given them a fearsome account of his countrymen's predatory operations, telling the two Americans "that it was a law that the first who boarded an enemy's vessel should have one slave more than his share with the rest, which operated as an incentive to the most desperate valor and enterprise, that it was the practice of their corsairs to bear down upon a ship, for each sailor to take a dagger in each hand and another in his mouth, and leap on board, which so terrified their enemies that very few ever stood against them, that he verily believed the devil assisted his countrymen, for they were almost always successful."

Jefferson and Adams had asked time to consider and sought fresh instructions from their government. The Tripolitan ambassador had told them that "Tunis would treat upon the same terms, but he could not answer for Algiers or Morocco." Whatever the United States government might do at this juncture, Jefferson had not given up. If he ever had an opportunity to bring the Barbary pirates to their knees, he would seize it at once.

Negotiations with the Portuguese ambassador, delayed because of that diplomat's illness, necessitating an extension of Jefferson's stay in England, bore only false fruit. A treaty was negotiated but it proved unacceptable to the Court in Lisbon.

Still Jefferson was repaid for the pains of six days' travel in bad weather, including the dreaded crossing of the Channel. The reunion with the Adamses was a happy one. Despite Madison's warnings about Adams' testiness, the New Englander and Jefferson had gotten along even better in Europe than in Philadelphia.[81] Adams seems to have been more charming in the company of Abigail, partly because he was happier when with her and partly because her humor complemented his seriousness. Jefferson enjoyed Abigail's wit and pungent phrasing. He had relished his exchange of letters with John after the Adamses left Paris for London, but Jefferson was especially pleased when Mrs. Adams initiated a correspondence with him. The two were always shopping for each other in their respective capitals. On at least one occasion he bought shoes for her. At the same time he sent a bisque figure of Mars for her dinner table, saying, "They offered me a fine Venus, but I thought it out of taste to have two at table at the same time."[82] Jefferson may have been laying it on a bit thick. A portrait[83] painted by Mather Brown the year before shows her with bright blue-grey eyes and a look of intelligence and animation but the long nose is large nostriled and the mouth is more remarkable for firmness than beauty. There can be little doubt, however, that her personality was fascinating.

Certainly Jefferson's regard for her was at least matched by hers for him. She called him "one of the choice ones of the earth."[84] From London she had written him: "Nobody ever leaves Paris but with a degree of tristeness. I own I was loth to leave my garden because I did not expect to find its place supplied. I was still more loth, on account of the increasing pleasure and intimacy which a longer acquaintance with a respected Friend promised, to leave behind me the only person with whom my Companion could associate with perfect freedom and unreserve, and whose place he had no reason to expect supplied in the land to which he is destined."[85] Jefferson had written to John Adams: "The departure of your family has left me in the dumps. My afternoons hang heavily on me."[86]

So there was an exciting reunion in Grosvenor Square. It was almost as if Jefferson were being reunited with his own family.

A very different reception awaited him at Court where Adams had arranged for his friend to be received. Adams was fond of recounting his own first reception at St. James when he had talked of restoring "the old good nature and the old good humor between people, who, though separated by an ocean and under different governments, have the same language, and a similar religion and kindred blood." Adams was convinced that there had been a tremor of emotion in the King's voice when he said, "I must say that I not only receive with pleasure the assurance of the friendly dispositions of the United States, but that I am very glad the choice has fallen upon you to be their minister."[87] This account, despite Jefferson's suspicions of the British government, may have led him to expect a friendly welcome when he was accompanying Adams. But surely the Virginian must have recalled the very personal terms in which he had excoriated George III in the Declaration of Independence.

In any event, His Majesty evidently had not forgotten. In the high-ceilinged chamber of St. James' while many eyes watched, Adams and Jefferson were announced and bowed to the corpulent monarch whose heavy white eyebrows bristled startlingly from his red face. Abruptly they found themselves facing the royal back.[88] In the months and years that followed, Jefferson's comments on George III and on Englishmen generally were more acrimonious than before. A year later he wrote Colonel Smith: "Of all nations on earth, they require to be treated with the most hauteur. They require to be kicked into common good manners."[89]

But Jefferson's prejudice did not bar admiring friendships with individual Englishmen. One of these was Dr. Richard Price, a clergyman who was also a favorite of Abigail Adams'. About a year before he had sent Jefferson by Franklin a copy of his booklet *Observations on the Importance of the American Revolution*. In response to Jefferson's letter of thanks, the liberal divine had written: "The eyes of the friends of liberty and humanity are now fixed on (America). The United States have an open field before them, and advantages for establishing a plan favorable to the improvement of the world which no people ever had in an equal degree."[90] He also favored reciprocal trade agreements with the United States, though he thought that influential opinion in Britain was strongly against them. It is not surprising that Jefferson found congenial company on the two occasions that he dined with him during the London visit.

Although one of his principal objects in England was the conclusion of commercial treaties, Jefferson shared Price's pessimism about the venture. From London, Jefferson reported to Jay:

> With this country nothing is done; and that nothing is intended to be done on their part admits not the smallest doubt. The nation is against any change of measures; the ministers are against it, some from principle, others from subserviency; and the king more than all men is against it. If we take a retrospect to the beginning of the present reign we observe that amidst all the changes of ministry no change of measures with respect to America ever took place: excepting only at the moment of the peace, and the minister of that moment was immediately

removed. Judging of the future by the past, I do not expect a change of disposition during the present reign, which bids fair to be a long one as the king is healthy and temperate. That he is persevering we know. If he ever changes his plan it will be in consequence of events which neither himself nor his ministers at present place among those which are probable. Even the opposition dares not open their lips in favor of a connection with us, so unpopular would be the topic. It is not that they think our commerce unimportant to them. I find that the merchants here set sufficient value on it. But they are sure of keeping it on their own terms. No better proof can be shown of the security in which the ministers think themselves on this head, than that they have not thought it worthwhile to give us a conference on the subject, though on my arrival we exhibited to them our commission, observed to them that it would expire on the 12th of the next month, and that I had come over on purpose to see if any arrangements could be made before that time. Of the two months which then remained, 6 weeks have elapsed without one scrip of a pen, or one word from a minister except a vague proposition at an accidental meeting.[91]

Whatever the impediments to an exchange of goods between England and the United States, Jefferson was determined to promote the commerce of ideas. He hoped to leave with some choice spirits in England an understanding and appreciation of American institutions. He became friendly with Sir John Sinclair and learned from him some of the latest developments in scientific agriculture. Though he disliked the factory system and prophesied that factory workers might one day challenge the government, Jefferson shopped the manufactories for ideas. He was fascinated with the possibilities of steam and predicted that in the United States it would be used to propel boats. Benjamin Vaughan, an English friend of Benjamin Rush's, became his informant on various mathematical and scientific instruments.[92]

And Jefferson began buying such instruments as if they had been books. He purchased a solar microscope to explore the microcosm, a globe telescope to search the macrocosm. He also bought a protractor, a thermometer, and a camp theodolite. He ordered a model of a portable copying press. He bought several of the new upright oil lamps, sending one to Charles Thomson and another to Richard Henry Lee.[93] This model was even better than a similar one of French manufacture that he had sent earlier to James Madison, expressing his delight over all that the new invention could mean to a fellow insomniac.

He shopped for many relatives and friends, taking much time and pains to please. From one couple with whom he visited in England he took orders for shopping in Paris. These were John Paradise, a Greek-born scholar unfortunate in business, and Lucy Ludwell, his Virginia-born wife. Paradise was an obliging man who promised to instruct the American Minister by mail in the pronunciation of modern Greek, which Jefferson hoped would afford clues to pronunciation of the classic tongue. Lucy Paradise was a highly eccentric and unstable person whose demands upon Jefferson, together with the exigencies from which he had to rescue her well-meaning husband, eventually reached such a total as to comprise the chief material of a hefty volume by a twentieth-century biographer.[94] All services, from purchasing a harpsichord to obtaining financial credit, were performed with no hint of martyrdom. Jefferson's generally agreeable nature may have been rendered even more so by the facts that Mrs. Paradise was considered beautiful and that she called him "the first character in...North America."

There were pleasant associations with many people, but undoubtedly Jefferson's happiest hours in England were those he spent with members of the Adams family. "Oh, to be in England, Now that April's there," Browning would rhapsodize in "Home-thoughts from Abroad." In John Adams' company Jefferson explored the delights of an English April, loving every live–green and blossoming moment of it. He took even greater delight in the gardens than Adams did. The Virginian always had in hand as a guide Thomas Whately's *Observations on Modern Gardening* and he made detailed notes of his own.[95] Jefferson was a romantic relishing spontaneous acquaintance with beauty but he was also a man of the Enlightenment who believed in reinforcing "the first fine careless rapture."

As almost always, unless he was viewing classical or neoclassical buildings, he was highly critical of the architecture of the manor houses and palaces set amid the land-scaped grounds, but the beauty of the gardens themselves exceeded his expectations. In a memorandum, he noted of Whately: "I always walked over the gardens with his book in my hand, examined with attention the particular spots he described, found them so justly characterized by him as to be easily recognized, and saw with wonder that his fine imagination had never been able to seduce him from the truth."[96] Jefferson had admired French landscaping but he liked the English kind even better. The geometrical beauties of Gallic gardens were a pleasing extension of architecture, but there was something even more appealing in the British compromise with what Words-worth would call a "sportive wood run wild." Soon after leaving England he wrote John Page: "The gardening in that country is the article in which it surpasses all the earth. I mean their pleasure gardening. This, indeed, went far beyond my ideas."[97]

Consistent with his preference for the natural, he noted of Chiswick, property of the Duke of Devonshire, "The garden shows still too much of art." Esher-Place, a blend of tree clumps and hollows, he pronounced "a most lovely mixture of concave and convex."[98] After a detailed description of the 2,500 acres of Blenheim he concluded, "Art appears too much."[99] At Kew he was so impressed with the Archimedes screw for raising water that he drew a diagram of it.[100]

The gardens at Twickenham were small—only five acres—by comparison with the royal and baronial parks, but he found them especially interesting, both intrinsically and because three and a half acres comprised the original garden of Alexander Pope. Here the frail gnome had held court among the beauty and nobility of fashionable England in a triumph of wit and industry over deformity and pain. Jefferson particularly noted: "Obelisk at bottom of Pope's garden, as monument to his mother. Inscription, 'Ah! Editha, matrum optima....' "[101] Strangely, Jefferson biographers appear to have overlooked the parallel between this monument and the one that Jefferson had planned in 1771 to commemorate his sister Jane. In his Account Book he had outlined plans for a small Gothic temple "at the spring on the north side of the park" with an altar bearing, as we have seen earlier, the inscription "Ah! Joanna, puellarum optima..."

This little temple was only part of elaborate plans for a burial ground steeped in Gothic romance that seemed to anticipate Coleridge. Amid prosaic entries in the Account Book he wrote: "Choose out for a burying place some unfrequented vale in the park, where is 'no sound to break the stillness but a brook, that bubbling winds among the weeds; no mark of any human shape that had been there, unless the skeleton of some poor wretch, who sought that place out to despair and die in.' Let it be among ancient and venerable oaks; intersperse some gloomy evergreens." One half of the grounds would be reserved for the burial of his own family, the remainder for servants and "strangers." The exit was to "look on a small and distant part of the blue mountains." The sides of the altar in the center of the temple were to be of turf, the top of plain stone. He added, "very little light, perhaps none at all, save only the feeble ray of an half extinguished lamp." Near a cascade would be another temple with a roof "Chinese, Grecian, or in the taste of the Lantern of Demosthenes at Athens." Under it would be an Aeolian harp, "covered from the weather" and so concealed that visitors would not see the source of the plaintive chords that reached their ears.

At the age of twenty-eight Jefferson had been luxuriating in esthetic melancholy. But then life had reasserted its claims. "This would be better," he wrote. "The ground above the spring being very steep, dig into the hill and form a cave or grotto. Build up the sides and arch with stiff clay. Cover this with moss. Spangle it with translucent pebbles from Hanovertown, and beautiful shells from the shore at Burwell's ferry. Pave the floor with pebbles. Let the spring enter at a corner of the grotto, pretty high up the side, and trickle down, or fall by a spout into a basin, from which it may pass off through the grotto. Reclining on a couch of moss would be a sculptured figure, the Nymph of the grot. The grounds in general would be planted in grass interspersed with jessamine, honeysuckle, and sweetbriar." He wrote a note to himself: "Keep in it deer, rabbits, peacocks, guinea poultry, pigeons, etc. Let it be an asylum for hares, squirrels, pheasants, partridges, and every other wild animal (except those of prey). Court them to it by laying food for them in proper places. Procure a buck elk to be, as it were, monarch of the wood; but keep him shy, that his appearance may not lose its effect by too much familiarity. A buffalo might be confined also."[102] Still romantic, but in a happier vein, reminiscent of the unity of life rather than the universality of death.

In view of these earlier plans for Monticello it is not surprising that, during his tour of English gardens in 1786, Jefferson took particular delight in the cascade at Blenheim, [103] and admired the two temples at Stowe while regretting the removal of the grotto since Whately's visit.[104] Jefferson was still thinking of the landscaping of Monticello. "My inquiries," he said in his memorandum of the tour, "were directed chiefly to such practical things as might enable me to estimate the expense of making and maintaining a garden in that style."[105] His ideas were now chaster than in 1771. Maturing taste and economic necessity alike would prune the luxuriance of his original plans. But he still would make his home one of the most beautifully landscaped places in America, artfully fitting to the contours of his Virginia mountain the drapery of English-style plantings.

Jefferson's tour with Adams included historical places as well as gardens. At Stratford-on-Avon they visited the grave of William Shakespeare and his dwelling, where they were shown a chair said to have belonged to the poet. "We cut off a chip according to custom,"[106] Adams wrote, leaving uncertain whether one chip was taken by each of the tourists or they shared a souvenir between them. Their enthusiasm caused them to extend their travels. From Buckingham, Adams wrote his wife: "We have seen magnificence, elegance and taste enough to excite an inclination to see more."[107]

Back in London, Jefferson shared the Adamses' pleasure in the company of three popular American-born portraitists, John Trumbull, John Singleton Copley, and Mather

Brown. Doubtless their comments, as well as his own increased viewing of masterpieces since arrival in Europe, contributed to the growing sophistication of his notes on specific works of art.[108] Before leaving London he had his own likeness painted by Brown, probably at the request of the Adamses, who had sat for him earlier and were enthusiastic about the results. The Jefferson portrait[109] adorned the Adamses' living quarters and Jefferson eventually received a copy.

Probably the first portrait for which he posed, it is the most elegant we have of him but perhaps the least forceful. It looks very much like Brown's other paintings of male subjects, virtually all of whom appear preeminently as men of fashion. The powdered hair is so precisely rolled over the ears as to resemble a fancy wig, an article for which Jefferson appears to have had no use. The black coat contrasting with the white ruffles at wrists and neck recalls Mrs. Adams' account of Jefferson's sartorial plight a few days after receiving a newly tailored suit of clothes in Paris. "There is now court mourning," she wrote, "and every foreign minister with his family must go into mourning for a prince of eight years old, whose father is an ally of the King of France. This mourning is ordered by the court and is for eleven days only. Poor Mr. Jefferson had to hie away for a tailor to get a whole new black silk suit made up in two days; and at the end of eleven days should another death happen, he will be obliged to have a new suit of mourning (of another material) because that is the season when silk must be left off." She explained that in Paris, "to be out of fashion is more criminal than to be seen in a state of nature, to which the Parisians are not averse."[110] The portrait seems to show one of those dandies of whom the youthful Jefferson had remarked that in their making the tailor and the barber had gone halves with the Almighty.

Abigail was glad that they at least would have Jefferson's portrait to assuage their sadness after his leave-taking on April 26. Without the slightest hint of impropriety on either side and with no scintilla of threat to her adoring relationship with John, she had grown to love the tall Virginian. Her husband, for his part, was being separated from his most cherished companion in Europe. Colonel Smith, the young secretary of legation, already in love with daughter Abigail and soon to become her husband, joined the rest of the family in enthusiasm for Jefferson and sorrow at his parting.[111] Jefferson was glad to leave London for a friendlier capital, but he would sorely miss the vicarious taste of family life that he had been afforded.

Even Paris, however, had lost some of its charm. Some months before his trip to London, Jefferson had rented a much more spacious dwelling, the formally handsome Hôtel de Langeac[112] with its elegant, sunburst-ceilinged oval salon.[113] He had adorned his walls with beautiful paintings. But despite these pleasing aspects, life was becoming a chore as well as an extravagance. He complained that it "called for an almost womanly attention to the details of the household."[114]

The trouble was, of course, that he was homesick, even among the fine and culinary arts of Paris. He cultivated Indian corn in his little garden just off the Champs-Elysées "for the use of my own table, to eat green in our manner."[115] He sent back to Albemarle County for a seed ear of the "small ripe corn we call hominy corn" as well as for seeds of the sweet potato, watermelon, and cantaloupe. He also requested from Virginia "a dozen or two bacon hams."[116] In answer to a Virginia friend's letter he wrote: "I thank you again and again for the details it contains, these being precisely of the nature I would wish. Of political correspondents I can find enough. But I can persuade nobody to believe that the small facts which they see passing daily under their eyes are precious to me at this distance: much more interesting to the heart than events of higher rank. Fancy to yourself a being who is withdrawn from his connections of blood, of marriage, of friendship, of acquaintance in all their gradations, who for years should hear nothing of what has passed among them, who returns again to see them and finds the one-half dead. This strikes him like a pestilence sweeping off the half of mankind. Events which had they come to him one by one and in detail he would have weathered as other people do, when presented to his mind all at once are overwhelming. Continue then to give me facts, little facts, such as you think everyone imagines beneath notice, and your letters will be the most precious to me. They will place me in imagination in my own country, and they will place me where I am happiest."[117]

There would be comfort in reuniting his little family. Ever since the death of Lucy Elizabeth and Polly's serious illness he had longed to bring to Paris the one daughter remaining in Virginia.[118] But the same heightened anxiety for her welfare that made him desperate to have her with him also fed his imagination of the perils of her voyage. He feared the North Atlantic in winter and in the turbulent equinoxes; therefore the crossing must be made between April and July. The vessel must be neither untried nor deteriorated; it must have made at least one prior crossing but be not more than five years old. There was also the danger of illness on the voyage when the services of a good physician would not be available; after all, Patsy had been sick on the way to France. Certainly the servant accompanying her should be someone who had already had smallpox.[119] All of these requirements were impediments to quick transit.

But there were more besides. Eppington had become the child's home. Left there at the age of six by a father she would not see for three years, she had come to regard the Eppeses as her family. Aunt Eppes seemed more her parent than the dimly featured father who fired letters of admonition at her from the other side of the world. The little Eppes cousins were dearer to her than the sister who now seemed scarcely real. Jefferson was shocked to be told in a letter from his little girl that she was sorry he had asked her to join him. If there was to be a reunion he and Patsy must return to her; she could not go to them.[120]

Being very fond of the child and fearful of the traumatic effects of her father's insistence, both Mr. and Mrs. Eppes hoped that he would relent. But Jefferson persisted, and with a surprising lack of tact and understanding in one normally so richly endowed with those qualities. "I know, my dear Polly," he wrote, "how sorry you will be and ought to be, to leave [your uncle and aunt] and your cousins but your sister and [I] cannot live without you, and after awhile we will carry you back again to see your friends in Virginia. In the meantime you shall be taught here to play on the harpsichord, to draw, to dance, to read and talk French, and such other things as will make you more worthy of the love of your friends. But above all things, by our care and love of you, we will teach you to love us more than you will do if you stay so far from us. . . . When you come here you shall have as many dolls and playthings as you want for yourself or to send to your cousins. . . . I hope you are a very good girl, . . . that you never suffer yourself to be angry with anybody, that you give your playthings to those who want them . . . . Remember too as a constant charge not to go out without your bonnet because it will make you very ugly and then we should not love you so much. If you will always practice these lessons we shall continue to love you as we do now, and it is impossible to love you more."[121] Little of Jefferson the diplomat or Jefferson the captivator of female hearts comes through in this letter. It is not surprising that it brought no sudden softening of Polly's adamant opposition. Jefferson complained much of the loneliness of his situation.

Of course, there were compensations in being in Paris. He was convinced it was the intellectual capital of the world. Nowhere else had he heard so much beautiful music, and music was one of his chief passions. Even though most treaty-making efforts proved fruitless, there were other opportunities to serve his country and state, and some of these enterprises appealed to his scholarly and esthetic proclivities.

Upon his return from London, Jefferson helped to revise the entries on the United States and some of the separate states in the great *Encyclopédie Méthodique*. These sections had been entrusted to Jean Nicolas Démeunier, who sent Jefferson lists of questions to which the American minister prepared detailed answers. Eventually he examined Démeunier's manuscript and suggested so many revisions that the final product seems to have been a collaboration. William Short, after paying tribute to Démeunier's talents in a letter to William Nelson, wrote: "What he had said under the head of the Etats Unis was as erroneous and as false as might be expected from a man who had made the Abbé Raynal his model, and his own lively imagination his guide. Fortunately he has candor, and after putting this article under Mr. Jefferson's inspection, he readily struck out and altered the most flagrant errors. It remains at present as different from what he had written it, as to matters of fact, as virtue from vice, and as to reflections it is changed from censure to eulogy."[122] Short was staggered by the thought that, except for Jefferson's presence in Paris, what promised to be the world's most prestigious compendium of universal knowledge would have disseminated gross misinformation about the United States. "Is it not melancholy reflection, my dear Nelson, that writings of this sort, that books that we are taught to worship from our infancy, should be merely the works of hazard and uncertainty?"

Not quite so happy, from Jefferson's point of view, was his collaboration with François Soulés in preparing a revised edition of the French historian's *Histoire des troubles de l'Amérique Anglaise*.[123] Though the work was primarily a military history of the American Revolution, it also passed judgment on the political and cultural development of the United States. Soulés did not accept Jefferson's suggestions as uncritically as Démeunier had. The historian did accept the American's account of the legislative background of the Declaration of Independence and of other matters of which the minister had direct knowledge. Jefferson's pleasure in Soulés' assertion that "the members of the first Continental Congress would have done honor to Athens and Rome" undoubtedly was offset by his conclusion that "since then persons of mediocrity had come to the head of American affairs, proving that philosophy had not yet made great progress there and that the American electorate were already as corrupt as in the old world."[124] Jefferson must have squirmed a little at the Frenchman's assertion that American ministers plenipotentiary "had exhibited a pomp and style scarcely compatible with the role of philosophers" and that Americans in pursuit of elegance had "contracted enormous debts."[125] Jefferson was not given to pomp but he did love style.

One of the Virginian's most pleasurable services to his native state was in the designing of the capitol. Actually, the leaders of the Commonwealth had not asked Jefferson to be the architect. They had thought that he would be the intermediary in their dealings with a distinguished French artist, as when he had obtained Houdon's services in sculpting a statue of Washington. But Jefferson himself was an architect, albeit a self-taught one, and he had very strong ideas about what sort of structure should crown one of Richmond's seven hills[126] as a symbol of Virginia's government. As he hoped that the government itself would be in the classic mold of Greece and Rome, he believed that the capitol should reflect these influences. He therefore obtained the services of Charles-Louis Clérisseau, an architect who was an enthusiastic student of classical buildings. Jefferson's suggestions were so numerous and sound, and so eagerly pressed, that he became a collaborator instead of an agent. He soon dominated the cooperative effort to such an extent that he became the chief architect, with Clérisseau's draftsmen executing Jefferson's designs.

For his model the Virginian used his favorite classical building, the Maison Carrée in Nimes, a Roman structure of Greek inspiration which he told the members of the government in Richmond was "allowed without contradiction to be the most perfect and precious remain of antiquity in existence."[127] While retaining the principal proportions of the Roman structure he substituted an Ionic portico for the Corinthian and replaced with neoclassical fenestration the engaged pilasters on the sides. In addition to letting in air and light barred by the first-century design, Jefferson's plan gained in graceful simplicity over ornateness. Many consider it superior to the original in beauty and dignity.

Certainly Jefferson was satisfied. In a letter accompanying the plans sent to the General Assembly he rejoiced that he had based them on a "model already devised and approved by the general suffrage of the world."[128] He wrote of his designs to Dr. John Currie: "They are simple and sublime. More cannot be said. They are not the brat of a whimsical conception never before brought to light, but copied from the most precious, the most perfect, model of ancient architecture remaining on earth."[129]

Strangely enough, in all the months Jefferson had been in France he had not yet found time to visit the building at Nimes that he so admired, but knew it only through sketches and paintings. When he did visit the building a little later he wrote that he gazed at it "whole hours. . .like a lover at his mistress."[130]

The country where he now served was full of art and architecture which he saw through a lover's eyes. But the first excitement of the French adventure had worn off and he was no longer happy. France was not Virginia, the Maison Carrée was not a woman, and he was nobody's lover. He did not know that this last circumstance was about to change.

XIV

HEAD, HEART, AND GLANDS

JEFFERSON MUST often have wondered how different his life might have been if he had not accepted an invitation to visit the Paris grain market. How could he possibly have suspected that so ostensibly prosaic an occasion would launch him upon the greatest romantic adventure of his life, one that would leave him permanently marked both mentally and physically?

The invitation came from John Trumbull, whom he had met in London, and who now, in August and early September of 1786, was staying in Paris with Jefferson. The painter was studying the Virginian's face and figure, for he would be the most important actor in the artist's monumental painting of the signing of the Declaration of Independence.[1] The Halle aux Bleds was no ordinary grain market; it was a monument to the architectural skill of J.-G. Legrand and Jacques Molinos. Arthur Young described it as "a vast rotunda, the roof entirely of wood, upon a new principle of carpentry . . . so well planned and so admirably executed that I know of no public building that exceeds it in either France or England."[2] The principle of carpentry was not really new; it was borrowed from the Renaissance architect Philibert Delorme.[3] New or not, it would have interested Jefferson. His passion for architecture was great, and his interest in technical innovations was matched by his reverence for traditional forms. His aid had been enlisted in the planning of a public market for Richmond; the Halle aux Bleds might be a good source of ideas.[4]

Still he hesitated to accept Trumbull's invitation. The enthusiastic young New Englander was always dilating on the "merits and talents" of Mr. and Mrs. Cosway, a couple of artists he had met in Paris.[5] Richard Cosway was generally considered England's finest miniaturist. His best model was his beautiful wife, Maria, herself a talented artist. Trumbull was eager for Jefferson to meet them before their stay in Paris ended. The American minister was always too busy for a meeting. He kept telling himself that he "had no occasion for new acquaintance."[6] Now Trumbull told him that the Cosways would accompany them to the market. Jefferson started not to go, then decided he would not pass up the opportunity to see this "wonderful piece of architecture" in the company of his Connecticut friend who, besides being an artist, had some claim to being an architect.

The day was bright. Inside the Halle aux Bleds sunshine flooded through windowed spaces between supporting ribs that radiated from the lantern of the dome. Transported with enthusiasm, Jefferson praised the sight as "the most superb thing on earth" and exclaimed that it was "worth all he had yet seen in Paris." But privately one part of his mind admitted that his ecstasy owed more to the way the sunlight touched the gold of Maria Cosway's hair than to any other feature of the celebrated interior lighting. And surely her large, luminous eyes were bluer than the sky glimpsed through the overhead windows. The slender figure before him, exquisite as fine porcelain but all too obviously human flesh, made the dome, remarkable as it was, seem a mere "parcel of sticks and chips."[7]

There was something irresistible in her strange combination of languor and animation. Which was more beautiful, the smoothly curving cheek or the slender hand it rested upon? In this twenty-seven-year-old were mingled, devastatingly, childhood innocence and womanly grace as in some of Greuze's milkmaids. But she was really quite sophisticated. From those perfect lips—cupid's bow above, a little sensual fullness below—flowed words in a soft voice tinged with an Anglo-Italian accent gained from early years in Florence with her English parents. She knew many eminent artists, including Jacques Louis David, Jefferson's favorite French painter. Her numerous famous admirers included England's Prince of Wales, a wit and a celebrated collector of beautiful objects in many forms. Her own intelligence drew on the arts and languages of several nations.[8]

As Jefferson came nearer and nearer to exhausting his catalogue of the building's unusual features, he was casting about desperately for some way of prolonging his time with the enchantress. Everyone in the party, it soon developed, had another engagement, including Jefferson himself. He had accepted a dinner invitation from the estimable but sadly wrinkled Duchesse de la Rochefoucauld d'Anville. Surely he could not dine with her when he might be eating with Maria Cosway. Jefferson was animated with the special intensity that came to him with discovery of a compelling idea or a fascinating woman, and it must have given him the magnetism he usually radiated on such occasions. Soon he had persuaded Trumbull and both Cosways to cancel their engagements so that the little party might have dinner together. He himself, ordinarily so scrupulous about the truth, sent word to the venerable duchess that, just as he was leaving for his appointment with her, "dispatches came to hand which required immediate attention." In Jefferson's own words, "Lying messengers were . . . dispatched into every quarter of the city with apologies."[9]

Probably they ate at the Palais Royal, which had progressed in elegance since Jefferson's first arrival in Paris when the carpenters and masons had still been busy completing its construction. Even then Jefferson had considered it one of the principal ornaments of the city. It was a huge mall with pleasing gardens and shops offering every kind of merchandise. Just a little later, Sebastien Mercier would say: "There is no spot in the world comparable to it. Visit London, Amsterdam, Madrid, Vienna; you will see nothing like it: a prisoner could live here free from care for years with no thought of escape."[10] Not the least among its attractions were the many beautiful women of fashion who frequented the area. Jefferson had no trouble telling who was loveliest among them at the moment.

She appeared even more strikingly beautiful because of the foil at her side. Richard Cosway was noticeably shorter than she, even though she was not tall, and contemporaries described his face as simian. He habitually wore coats of startlingly bold colors.

The couple must have suggested a beautiful lady with her pet monkey. Jefferson was not the first to think that the magnificent Maria was wasted on such a spouse.[11]

Reluctant to separate himself from such a charming companion, Jefferson apparently proposed that they all drive to Saint-Cloud. In any event they visited the park there with its arbored arches and tree-lined avenue and stared at the Chateau de Bellevue, built for Madame de Pompadour but now the residence of Louis XVI's aunts.[12]

With night falling, the members of the party still did not return to their separate lodgings but visited Ruggieri's in the Montmartre area. There Italian pyrotechnicians presented elaborate shows combining pantomime with their specialty. On the program that night were "The Forges of Vulcan beneath Mount Etna" and "The Combat of Mars." As fountains of fire exploded against a dark velvet sky Jefferson's attention must have been torn between the coruscating spectacles and the beautiful features they illuminated. There was charm in Maria's every expression or gesture of surprise or delight.[13]

Their day did not end as the last fireworks dissolved in the night. They visited the celebrated harpist Julie Krumpholtz, and apparently heard her perform.[14] Maria herself was a harpist, pianist, singer, and composer. Jefferson's admiration mounted.

At last the day was over by anyone's reckoning. Everyone went home. "If the day had been as long as a Lapland summer day," he afterwards reflected, they "would still have contrived means, among [them], to have filled it."[15]

In any event, he contrived to be with Maria some part of almost each succeeding day while the Cosways remained in Paris. Sometimes Richard Cosway was busy with portrait painting.[16] On September 9 Trumbull left Paris for Germany.[17] Increasingly Jefferson and Maria were alone in their sightseeing. As they explored Paris and the countryside they also explored each other's lives and interests. He was fascinated by what he learned of her. She probably told him, as she did others, that she had been the sixth child born to her parents, the Hadfields, and that four of her predecessors had met mysterious deaths at night. "One day a maid servant went into the nursery, took me in her arms, and said, 'Pretty little creature, I have sent four to Heaven; I hope to send you also.' "[18] An alert governess reported the incident and the girl was committed to an insane asylum. Maria probably was fully aware of the effect on her admirers when they reflected that her life might have ended so early. There is no reason to suppose that Jefferson was an exception.

The Virginian wondered what so many had wondered: Why, with her youth, her beauty, and her talents, had she married Richard Cosway? Granted, he was a gifted portraitist, but with his eccentricities of feature and dress and effeminate manner he seemed an unlikely match.

Mr. Cosway was forty-four years of age, about a year older than Jefferson. At the time of the Virginian's meeting with the couple, they had been married about three years. Jefferson learned what the fashionable world of London already knew—that, after her father's death, Maria had married the absurd little man out of economic necessity. Her mother had talked her out of entering a nunnery in Italy and into going to England with her. Mrs. Hadfield, for her part, had acted upon the urging of her friend, the popular artist Angelica Kauffmann. Miss Kauffmann knew that Maria, before the age of twenty, had been elected to the Academy of Fine Arts in Florence. The older artist introduced the younger one to London society and to fellow painters. One of these was Richard Cosway, who married her, settling upon her 2,800 pounds and promising to support her penniless mother.[19]

He ensconced his bride in a London mansion rich with thick Persian carpets, ebony, mother-of-pearl, jasper, and lapis lazuli. Jefferson must have heard the rumor that the Prince of Wales had a secret tunnel between this residence and his own. There is no reason to suppose the report was true, but the fact that it was widely circulated evidences the extent to which Maria had captured the imagination of English society. Her presence drew more commissions for her husband's brush.[20]

Jefferson must soon have learned that there was no love between husband and wife. James Northcote said that Maria "always despised" her husband. Some thought that Richard Cosway had little interest in women except as models, whether for his elegant portrait miniatures or for the erotic scenes with which he secretly and lucratively adorned snuffboxes. Some even thought that he found young men more agreeable than young women.[21]

Jefferson's realization that Maria's marriage was unhappy and the strong suspicion, if not confirmation, that her husband was habitually unfaithful to her would have gone a long way toward easing his conscience as his infatuation grew. He had already been far gone in love when he returned home after the day that began with the visit to the Halle aux Bleds. When he had "looked back to the morning it had seemed to have been a month agone."[22]

In the days that followed, he took Maria on one little expedition after another to some favorite spot in Paris or its environs. Sometimes it was to the Bois de Boulogne, where he loved to ride or walk along the wooded paths which in their geometrical precision differed so from the woodland trails of Albemarle. Sometimes they returned to Saint-Cloud. The nagging voice of reason warned him that he should be more cautious because she would soon be gone and he always "rack[ed his] whole system" when parted from those he loved. "The separation would in this instance be the more severe" as he would probably never see her again.[23]

But the liquid syllables of her Anglo-Italian speech could drown the voice of reason. And he lost all perspective when gazing into those blue eyes. The frank enjoyment of his company expressed in her voice, her gaze, her smiles was an elixir to this man who at the age of forty-three had been prepared prematurely to forsake the amusements of the world and even to avoid making new friends. Whether or not Jefferson knew that James Boswell had complained that Maria Cosway treated adoring men "like dogs" and that Peter Pindar had saluted her beauty in verse, he did know that she was the subject of frequent and flattering notice in the gossip columns of London, that she was much admired by the Prince of Wales, that she was, in short, the toast of the British capital.[24] And yet, among all the delights of Paris, she seemed to find more pleasure in him than in anyone or anything else. A few months before he had approached life in the spirit of one serving time. Now he was gloriously alive. Even to be tortured occasionally by frustration and by thoughts of the almost inevitable end to the new excitement seemed better than experiencing the long dull ache of loneliness.[25]

By the fifth of September he was quite deaf to any admonitions of reason. On that day he took Maria through the Bois, stopping at the Bagatelle, an earth-hugging but elegant casino, the "house of the wager" built by the king's brother on a bet with the queen that it could not be completed within sixty days.[26] Jefferson was gambling more on one pair of blue eyes than he ever would on the eyes of any pair of dice. In fact, though he took chances in politics and romance, Jefferson was not a gambler in the conventional sense.

Next on the same journey they visited the Château de Madrid, which dated from the reign of Francis I, a curious time when Frenchmen had built some of the most elegantly refined dwellings in the world and made urinals of their great fireplaces and graceful staircases.[27] There was no hint of grossness now. A half-circle of venerable trees outlined a royal esplanade before a façade whose decoration of varnished tiles glittered in the bright sun. The chateau yielded a magnificent panorama ranging from where the Pont de Neuilly made its gazelle leaps across the Seine on one side to where Mont Valérien rose in gentle majesty on the other.[28]

Even more wonderful than any day they had yet shared was September 7, when they went to St. Germain. "How beautiful was every object!" Jefferson later recalled. Over the Pont de Neuilly they rode and over wooded heights along the Seine until, near Bougival, they stopped to look at the Machine de Marly, a seventeenth-century engineering monument that raised the river's waters until they flowed into the cascades and fountains of Versailles and the Château de Marly. When Jefferson had viewed the works in 1784, the hydraulic mechanism had excited his admiration. Now both he and Maria delighted in the rainbows in the great sheets of water thrown up by the apparatus.[29]

They rode three miles uphill from Marly to the town of St. Germain, site of the huge royal chateau, birthplace of Louis XIV, that Jefferson had seen on his first ride from the Channel to Paris. From the terrace they could see the Aqueduct of Marly and, beyond, the spires of the capital.

Back to Marly they rode to walk among the gardens of the Sun King's rural retreat. The general plan of the Palace, with six small pavilions leading up to it on either side, made an indelible impression on Jefferson's architectural imagination.[30] They wandered among the trees and shrubbery. Though Jefferson probably admired the many handsome statues he also doubtless found their forms inferior to the one at his side. The setting was idyllic. Madame Vigee-Le Brun, who had captured so much beauty in her canvases, pronounced the place "a more beautiful spot than any I had seen in my life."[31]

Afterwards they dined at a provincial inn where Petit, Jefferson's *maitre d'hotel* had had supper laid out for them. Before returning to Paris they wandered through the informal, English-style gardens of the residence at Louveciennes built for Madame du Barry.[32]

Of all their journeys, the most memorable for both was the one on September 16 to the Desert de Retz, an *anglo-chinois* garden about four miles from St. Germain. As a talented amateur gardener Jefferson may have been intrigued by the fact that this celebrated beauty spot represented the triumph of a wealthy amateur, Monsieur de Monville, over the best competitive efforts of the professionals. There was charm in the plantings and in the grotto, but there was fascination supreme in the giant ruined column[33] that had been constructed to satisfy a love of antique grandeur in decay. Sixty-five feet in diameter, the fluted, irregularly decapitated structure towered to a height of four stories. A staircase spiraled upward through a central stairwell affording access on each floor to semicircular and elliptical chambers decorated in the classically chastened rococo of Louis XVI. Windows in the fluting admitted sunlight. Jefferson exclaimed, "How grand the idea excited by the remains of such a column!"[34]

In a later letter to Maria he reminded her of the beauty of the spiral staircase they had climbed, and summarized the day: "Every moment was filled with something agreeable. The wheels of time moved on with a rapidity of which those of our carriage gave but a faint idea, and yet in the evening, when one took a retrospect of the day, what a mass of happiness had we traveled over!"[35] After saying how he loved to retrace "all those scenes" of perfect delight, he asked a question that would be at least irrelevant, perhaps even contradictory, if we did not interpret it symbolically according to the code of romance: "The day we went to St. Germains was a little too warm, I think, was not it?"[36]

On the second day after so much soaring happiness, Jefferson was perhaps quite literally brought to earth. He was walking at the time with a companion. Circumstantial evidence indicates that it was Maria.[37] The occasion of accident was a strange one for a man who, though once a great walker and always a good horseman, was not athletic. He failed in the attempt to jump over a fence, and either dislocated or broke his wrist. His physical suffering was great; his mental anguish was greater. It was quite possible that, carried away by a feeling of youthful exuberance in the company of his young love, he rashly attempted a feat that suddenly dramatized the age gap. A month later, writing with his left hand to William Stephens Smith who had asked the cause of the injury, Jefferson said: "How the right hand became disabled would be a long story for the left to tell. It was by one of those follies from which good cannot come, but ill may."[38]

Immediately after the accident, Jefferson was attended by two surgeons. But their ministrations brought no relief.

As Jefferson nursed his pain there was no word from Maria. We can be sure that he tortured himself with reflections that she might now see him as a ridiculous figure rather than a romantic one. We can imagine the eagerness two days later with which he tore open a letter, awkwardly pressing his left hand into service, when he recognized Maria's handwriting. The note[39] began in her inexact but expressive English and ended in fluent Italian: "I hope you don't always judge by appearances or it would be much to my disadvantage this day, without my deserving it. It has been the day of contradiction. I meant to have had the pleasure of seeing you *twice*, and I have appeared a monster for not having sent to know how you was, the *whole day*. I have been more uneasy than I can express."

She explained: "This morning my husband killed my project I had proposed to him, by burying himself among pictures and forgetting the hours. Though we were near your house, coming to see you, we were obliged to turn back, the time being much past that we were to be at St. Cloud to dine with the duchess of Kingston. Nothing was to hinder us from coming in the evening. But alas! My good intention proved only a disturbance to your neighbors, and just late enough to break the rest of all your servants and perhaps yourself. I came home with the disappointment of not having been able to make my apologies in *propria persona*. I hope you feel my distress instead of accusing me. . . . We will come to see you tomorrow morning if nothing happen to prevent it!"

She concluded in a vein sure to please Jefferson: "Oh, I wish you was well enough to come to us tomorrow to dinner and stay the evening. I won't tell you what I shall

GOVERNOR'S PALACE (RESTORED), WILLIAMSBURG   As a college student, Jefferson was in demand at Governor Fauquier's parties, first as a fiddler and then as a conversationalist. In 1779 he moved in as second Governor of the Commonwealth of Virginia. Courtesy of the Colonial Williamsburg Foundation.

GEORGE WYTHE Statesman as well as scholar, Jefferson's beloved teacher proudly signed the Declaration of Independence written by his former student. Courtesy of the Virginia State Library.

WREN BUILDING, COLLEGE OF WILLIAM AND MARY Here, in America's second oldest college, sixteen-year-old Thomas Jefferson was introduced to the philosophy of the Enlightenment. Courtesy of Joseph and Margaret Muscarelle Museum of Art, College of William and Mary in Virginia.

BANASTRE TARLETON   Colonel, later General, Tarleton led his British cavalry up the mountain to
Monticello to capture Governor Jefferson. Warned by Captain Jack Jouett, the Governor finished a leisurely
breakfast and trained his telescope on the approaching soldiers before fleeing to safety. Courtesy of The
Metropolitan Museum of Art.

PEYTON RANDOLPH   When in doubt as a youngster, Jefferson used to ask himself what this cousin would do in a similar situation. Randolph became Speaker of the Virginia House of Burgesses and President of the First Continental Congress. Courtesy of the Independence National Historical Park Collection.

PATRICK HENRY   An enthralled young Jefferson thought that Henry spoke "as Homer wrote," but an older Jefferson was tempted to pray for the orator's death before the next session of the legislature. Courtesy of the Colonial Williamsburg Foundation.

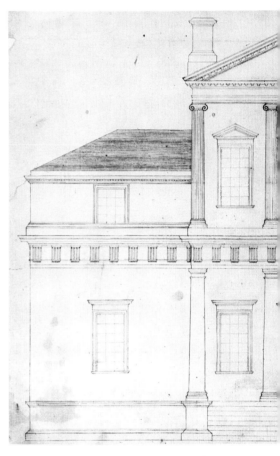

MODEL FOR STATE CAPITOL   This plaster model, made in France under Jefferson's direction, is housed today in the State Capitol in Richmond, Virginia. It was inspired by a Roman ruin in Nimes, France which Jefferson said he gazed at for "whole hours . . . like a lover at his mistress." Courtesy of the Virginia State Library.

MONTICELLO "All my wishes end where I hope my days will end, at Monticello." Courtesy of the Virginia State Library.

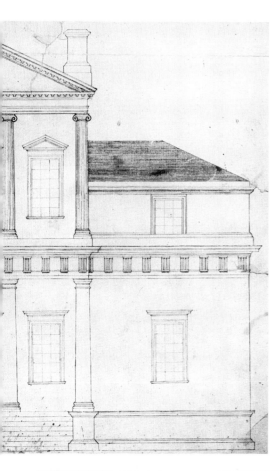

JEFFERSON'S FIRST PLANS FOR MONTICELLO Before he conceived the idea of adding a Palladian dome that made American architectural history, Jefferson designed a more traditionally classical Palladian house. Courtesy of the University of Virginia Library.

VIRGINIA STATE CAPITOL The central structure, completed in 1792, was designed by Jefferson. The wings, planned to harmonize with the original building, were added in 1904-05. Courtesy of the Virginia State Library.

JEFFERSON AS MINISTER TO FRANCE   Thus the American diplomat appeared in 1789 to his friend Jean-Antoine Houdon, eighteenth century Europe's greatest sculptor. Courtesy of the Museum of Fine Arts, Boston.

WILLIAM SHORT   Personal secretary to Jefferson, Short was also his protégé and at times almost a surrogate son. Courtesy of Joseph and Margaret Muscarelle Museum of Art, College of William and Mary in Virginia. "Gift of Mary Churchill Short, Fanny Short Butler and William Short."

ABIGAIL ADAMS   Mrs. Adams was a strong admirer of the tall Virginian who compared her to Venus and bought her silk stockings — until a misunderstanding ended the friendship. Courtesy of the Massachusetts Historical Society.

JOHN ADAMS   Jefferson's revolutionary comrade, Adams became his political enemy and then again his friend before being linked with him in one of American history's strangest coincidences. Courtesy of The Bettmann Archive.

MARIA COSWAY London gossip said that the Prince of Wales had built a tunnel between his house and Mrs. Cosway's, but it was in Paris that she had a romantic adventure with Jefferson which brought her sleepless nights and left him, in his own words, "more dead than alive." Courtesy of the New York Public Library.

JAMES MADISON Jefferson cherished him as a friend and relied on him as a political lieutenant. He also enjoyed the luxury of privately proposing extreme solutions to public problems, depending on Madison to urge restraint. Courtesy of the Colonial Williamsburg Foundation.

MARTHA JEFFERSON RANDOLPH This gifted daughter of Thomas Jefferson loved her husband, Thomas Mann Randolph, but wrote to her father: "I have made it my study to please him in everything and do consider all other objects as secondary to that except my love for you." Courtesy of The Bettmann Archive.

have; temptations now are too cruel for your situation. I only mention my wish if the executing them should be possible. . . . I would serve you and help you at dinner, and divert your pain after dinner by good music." She well knew that the most delicious foods would not tempt him so much as the prospect of being assisted at table by her. If she played or sang after dinner, Jefferson would have an excuse for riveting his gaze upon her even in the presence of her husband.

Whether he was able to come to dinner, we do not know. But he was soon seeing Maria again. On or before October 4 he persuaded her to accompany him on a ride, insisting that the jolting of the carriage would do him no harm. He received an even greater jolt when she told him that her husband had decided to leave Paris very soon.

That night Jefferson was kept awake by the pain in his wrist—and his heart. In the morning he wrote Maria a note whose broken words and shaky letters proclaimed the difficulties of the unpracticed left hand: "I have passed the night in so much pain that I have not closed my eyes. It is with infinite regret, therefore, that I must relinquish your charming company for that of the surgeon whom I have sent for to examine into the cause of this change. I am in hopes it is only the having rattled a little too freely over the pavement yesterday. If you do not go today I shall still have the pleasure of seeing you again. If you do, God bless you wherever you go. Present me in the most friendly terms to Mr. Cosway, and let me hear of your safe arrival in England. Addio Addio."

At the bottom of the page, in a handwriting particularly emphatic despite its inconsistent slant, he added: "Let me know if you do not go today."[40]

Jefferson was not made more comfortable by Maria's reply: "I am very, very sorry indeed. . . for having been the cause of your pains in the [night]. Why would you go? And why was I not more friendly to you and less to myself by preventing your giving me the pleasure of your company? You repeatedly said it would do you no harm. I felt interested and did not insist. We shall go, I believe, this morning. Nothing seems ready, but Mr. Cosway seems more disposed than I have seen him all this time. I shall write to you from England. . . . I beg you will think us sensible to your kindness, and that it will be with infinite pleasure I shall remember the charming days we have passed together, and shall long for next spring. . . . You will make me very happy if you would send a line to the *post restante* at Antwerp, that I may know how you are."[41]

So there would be no more meetings this year—if ever. She was leaving Paris now without even telling him goodbye in person.

Such an ending was intolerable. The worrisome wrist would have to take its chances. Jefferson summoned a cabriolet and rattled off to the Cosways'. He accompanied them out of Paris along the broad Porte St. Denis with its noble trees and triumphal arches marking the victories of Louis XIV. At the Pavillon de Saint-Denis, a toll house with a neoclassical portico, they all halted for a last meal together.[42] The farewell was not satisfactory. Not only was Mr. Cosway present, but so was Monsieur d'Hancarville, an author of books on classical antiquities and one of Maria's ardent admirers. But it was Jefferson who, though he did not have the use of his right arm, helped Maria into her carriage.

A few days later, in a letter to her, he described his feelings at that moment: "Having performed the last sad office of handing you into your carriage at the Pavillon de St. Denis, and seen the wheels get actually into motion, I turned on my heel and walked, more dead than alive, to the opposite door, where my own was awaiting me. Mr. Dan-querville (d'Hancarville) was missing. He was sought for, found, and dragged downstairs. We were crammed into the carriage, like recruits for the Bastille, and not having soul enough to give orders to the coachman. He presumed Paris our destination and drove off. After a considerable interval silence was broke with a 'Je suis vraiment afflige du depart de ces bons gens.' This was the signal for a mutual confession of distress."[43]

He added discreetly: "We began immediately to talk of Mr. and Mrs. Cosway, of their goodness, their talents, their amiability, and though we spoke of nothing else, we seemed hardly to have entered into matter when the coachman announced the Rue St. Denis, and that we were opposite Mr. Danquerville's (sic). He insisted on descend-ing there and traversing a short passage to his lodgings. I was carried home."

He pictured himself seated by his fireside, "solitary and sad," and said, "The follow-ing dialogue took place between my Head and my Heart." What follows is one of the most anthologized specimens of the literary dialogue genre so popular in the seven-teenth and eighteenth centuries. It is also, as Julian Boyd has observed, "one of the notable love letters in the English language."[44] Jefferson wrote the nearly nine thou-sand word missive with his left hand. By now it seemed almost certain that the wrist was actually broken. Twenty visits by the surgeons would do little to hasten the slow process of natural healing. He eventually became resigned to the prospect that he would never again enjoy the full use of the injured member. That he drove himself to write so much so effectively under such painful conditions is eloquent testimony to the strength of his interest in Maria Cosway. It is also one more evidence of Jefferson's tendency after an initial period of shock (he wrote several days after the parting) to fight disappointment and grief with purposeful activity.

The dialogue begins:

Head. Well, friend, you seem to be in a pretty trim.

Heart. I am indeed the most wretched of all earthly beings. Overwhelmed with grief, every fiber of my frame distended beyond its natural powers to bear, I would willingly meet whatever catastrophe should leave me no more to feel or to fear.

Head. These are the eternal consequences of your warmth and precipitation. This is one of the scrapes into which you are ever leading us. You confess your follies indeed: but still you hug and cherish them, and no reformation can be hoped, where there is no repentance.

Heart. Oh my friend! This is no moment to upbraid my foibles. I am rent into fragments by the force of my grief! If you have any balm, pour it into my wounds: if none, do not harrow them by new torments. Spare me in this awful moment! At any other I will attend with patience to your admonitions.[45]

The lament from the Heart of the forty-three-year-old Jefferson just parted from Maria Cosway—that he was "the most wretched of all earthly beings" and "overwhelmed with grief"—is remarkably like the lovelorn complaint of the nineteen-year-old Tom Jefferson—that he was "overwhelmed with more and greater misfortunes than have befallen a descendant of Adam for three thousand years . . . and perhaps, after excepting Job, since the creation of the world." The persistent leitmotif of the Heart throbs through nearly a quarter of a century.

The major difference between the epistolary threnodies of 1762 and 1786 is in the Head's counterpoint. In the earlier writing, the Head strove for detachment but with little success. The more mature Head is far more insightful. To the Heart's protest ("Spare me in this awful moment! At any other I will attend with patience to your admonitions"), the Head replies: "On the contrary I never found that the moment of triumph with you was the moment of attention to my admonitions. While suffering under your follies you may perhaps be made sensible of them, but, the paroxysm over, you fancy it can never return." Again the Head reproves: "Thou art the most incorrigible of all the beings that ever sinned! I reminded you of the follies of the first day, intending to deduce from thence some useful lessons for you, but instead of listening to these, you kindle at the recollection, you retrace the whole series with a fondness which shows you want nothing but the opportunity to act it over again."

Like the teenaged Jefferson, the mature man, even in the midst of his agitation, was attentive to literary style. Not surprisingly, his expression had improved greatly with the years. In the later writing there are a few foreign phrases but there is no ostentatious display of linguistic erudition. The older man wears the mantle of learning with an easy grace.

Jefferson is careful to appeal to Maria's ambition and esthetic sense in the course of the dialogue. The Head reminds the Heart that, even if Maria should return to Paris the next year, her stay would be brief and in any event the Atlantic eventually will part them. "What is to follow? Perhaps you flatter yourself they may come to America?" The Heart rises to sublimity in reply:

> God only knows what is to happen. I see nothing impossible in that supposition, and I see things wonderfully contrived sometimes to make us happy. Where could they find such objects as in America for the exercise of their enchanting art? Especially the lady, who paints landscape so inimitably. She wants only subjects worthy of immortality to render her pencil immortal. The Falling Spring, the Cascade of Niagara, the passage of the Potomac through the Blue Mountains, the Natural Bridge. It is worth a voyage across the Atlantic to see these objects; much more to paint, and make them, and thereby ourselves, known to all ages. And our own dear Monticello, where has nature spread so rich a mantle under the eye? mountains, forests, rocks, rivers. With what majesty do we there ride above the storms! How sublime to look down into the workhouse of nature, to see her clouds, hail, snow, rain, thunder, all fabricated at our feet! And the glorious sun, when rising as if out of a distant water, just gilding the tops of the mountains, and giving life to all nature!

Next he considers the possibility that some circumstance might someday cause Maria to seek refuge in his beloved hills. But discretion, requiring him to include Mr. Cosway in his remarks, gives an unintentionally humorous aspect to his protestations of love:

> I hope in God no circumstance may ever make either seek an asylum from grief! With what sincere sympathy I would open every cell of my composition to receive the effusion of their woes! I would pour my tears into their wounds:

and if a drop of balm could be found at the top of the Cordilleras, or at the remotest sources of the Missouri, I would go thither myself to seek and to bring it. Deeply practiced in the school of affliction, the human heart knows no joy which I have not lost, no sorrow of which I have not drunk! Fortune can present no grief of unknown form to me! Who then can so softly bind up the wound of another as he who has the same wound himself? But Heaven forbid they should ever know a sorrow!

A few paragraphs later, the Head lectures the Heart:

I wished to make you sensible how imprudent it is to place your affections, without reserve, on objects you must so soon lose, and whose loss when it comes must cost you such severe pangs. Remember the last night. You knew your friends were to leave Paris today. This was enough to throw you into agonies. All night you tossed us from one side of the bed to the other. No sleep, no rest. The poor crippled wrist too, never left one moment in the same position, now up, now down, now here, now there; was it to be wondered at if all its pains returned? The surgeon then was to be called, and to be rated as an ignoramus because he could not divine the cause of this extraordinary change.

In fine, my friend, you must mend your manners. This is not a world to live at random in as you do. To avoid these eternal distresses, to which you are for ever exposing us, you must learn to look forward before you take a step which may interest our peace. Everything in this world is matter of calculation. Advance then with caution, the balance in your hand. Put into one scale the pleasures which any object may offer; but put fairly into the other the pains which are to follow, and see which preponderates. The making an acquaintance is not a matter of in-difference. When a new one is proposed to you, view it all round. Consider what advantages it presents, and to what inconveniences it may expose you. Do not bite at the bait of pleasure till you know there is no hook beneath it. The art of life is the art of avoiding pain.

He continues in stoic vein:

The most effectual means of being secure against pain is to retire within ourselves, and to suffice for our own happiness. Those which depend on ourselves are the only pleasures a wise man will count on for nothing is ours which another may deprive us of. Hence the inestimable value of intellectual pleasures. Ever in our power, always leading us to something new, never cloying, we ride, serene and sublime, above the concerns of this mortal world, contemplating truth and nature, matter and motion, the laws which bind up their existence, and that eter-nal being who made and bound them up by these laws. Let this be our employ. Leave the bustle and tumult of society to those who have not talents to occupy themselves without them. Friendship is but another name for an alliance with the follies and the misfortunes of others. Our own share of miseries is sufficient: why enter then as volunteers in those of another? Is there so little gall poured into our own cup that we must needs help to drink that of our neighbor? A friend dies or leaves us: we feel as if a limb was cut off. He is sick: we must watch over him, and participate of his pains. His fortune is shipwrecked: ours must be laid under contribution. He loses a child, a parent or a partner: we must mourn the loss as if it was our own.

The Heart replies:

And what more sublime delight than to mingle tears with one whom the hand of heaven hath smitten! To watch over the bed of sickness, and to beguile its tedious and its painful moments! To share our bread with one to whom misfortune has left none! This world abounds indeed with misery: to lighten its burthen we must divide it with one another. But let us now try the virtues of your mathematical balance, and as you have put into one scale the burthens of friendship, let me put its comforts into the other. When languishing then under disease, how grateful is the solace of our friends! How are we penetrated with their assiduities and attentions! How much are we supported by their encouragements and kind offices! When Heaven has taken from us some object of our love, how sweet is it to have a bosom whereon to recline our heads, and into which we may pour the torrent of our tears! Grief, with such a comfort, is almost a luxury! In a life where we are perpetually exposed to want and accident, yours is a wonderful proposition, to insulate ourselves, to retire from all aid, and to wrap ourselves in the mantle of self-sufficiency! For assuredly nobody will care for him who cares for nobody. But friendship is precious not only in the shade but in the sunshine of life: and thanks to a benevolent arrangement of things, the greater part of life is sunshine.

Again the Heart speaks: "Let the gloomy monk, sequestered from the world, seek unsocial pleasures in the bottom of his cell! Let the sublimated philosopher grasp visionary happiness while pursuing phantoms dressed in the garb of truth! Their supreme wisdom is supreme folly: and they mistake for happiness the mere absence of pain. Had they ever felt the solid pleasure of one generous spasm of the heart, they would exchange for it all the frigid speculations of their lives, which you have been vaunting in such elevated terms."

Concluding sections of the dialogue furnish interesting clues to Jefferson's philosophy of life—at least in the autumn of 1786. The Heart takes over and has the final word. To the Head it says: "Respect for you has induced me into this discussion, and to hear principles uttered which I detest and abjure. Respect for myself now obliges me to recall you into the proper limits of your office. When nature assigned us the same habitation, she gave us over it a divided empire. To you she allotted the field of science, to me that of morals. When the circle is to be squared, or the orbit of a comet to be traced; when the arch of greatest strength, or the solid of least resistance is to be investigated, take you the problem: it is yours: nature has given me no cognizance of it. In like manner in denying to you the feelings of sympathy, of benevolence, of gratitude, of justice, of love, of friendship, she has excluded you from their control. To these she has adapted the mechanism of the heart. Morals were too essential to the happiness of man to be risked on the incertain combinations of the head. She laid their foundation therefore in sentiment, not in science. That she gave to all, as necessary to all: this to a few only, as sufficing with a few."

Some notable historians have asserted that the Head is triumphant in the dialogue. The usually astute Julian Boyd not only sees the Head as victorious in this exchange but asserts that with Jefferson the Reason was "a sovereign to whom the heart yielded a ready and full allegiance, proud of its monarch and happy in his rule."[46]

Surely the stereotype of Jefferson as a thoroughgoing Enlightenment figure must be responsible for this interpretation. If the "Dialogue" were the work of someone otherwise unknown to history, no one would conclude that its author intended to give the Head sovereignty over the Heart.

A pertinent passage is interesting both as a refutation of the theory that Jefferson wished to make the Heart a servant of the Head and as a revelation of his attitude toward his fellows. Addressing the Head, the Heart says:

> A few facts . . . will suffice to prove to you that nature has not organized you for our moral direction. When the poor wearied solider, whom we overtook at Chickahominy with his pack on his back, begged us to let him get up behind our chariot, you began to calculate that the road was full of soldiers, and that if all should be taken up our horses would fail in their journey. We drove on therefore. But soon becoming sensible you had made me do wrong, that though we cannot relieve all the distressed we should relieve as many as we can, I turned about to take up the soldier; but he had entered a bye path, and was no more to be found: and from that moment to this I could never find him out to ask his forgiveness. Again, when the poor woman came to ask a charity in Philadelphia, you whispered that she looked like a drunkard, and that half a dollar was enough to give her for the ale-house. Those who want the dispositions to give, easily find reasons why they ought not to give. When I sought her out afterwards, and did what I should have done at first, you know that she employed the money immediately towards placing her child at school.

Anyone who asserts that Jefferson in this composition advocated the dominion of Head over Heart will have a hard time twisting to his purpose the next example offered by this passionate leader of the American Revolution: "If our country, when pressed with wrongs at the point of the bayonet, had been governed by its heads instead of its hearts, where should we have been now? Hanging on a gallows as high as Haman's. You began to calculate and to compare wealth and numbers: we threw up a few pulsations of our warmest blood: we supplied enthusiasm against wealth and numbers: we put our existence to the hazard, when the hazard seemed against us, and we saved our country: justifying at the same time the ways of Providence, whose precept is to do always what is right, and leave the issue to Him. In short, my friend, as far as my recollection serves me, I do not know that I ever did a good thing on your suggestion, or a dirty one without it. I do for ever then disclaim your interference in my province." Not only does Jefferson leave the last word to the Heart, but he says in a concluding note to Maria, "I thought this a favorable proposition whereon to rest the issue of the dialogue. So I put an end to it by calling for my nightcap."

Before reaching that point he had acquiesced in the "law of our existence" that we have "no pleasure without alloy." He had said: "True, this condition is pressing cruelly on me at this moment. I feel more fit for death than life. But when I look back on the pleasures of which it is the consequence, I am conscious they were worth the price I am paying." He comforted himself with "expectations of [the Cosways'] promised return. Hope is sweeter than despair, and they were too good to mean to deceive me. In the summer, said the gentleman; but in the spring said the lady: and I should love her forever, were it only for that!"

Before Maria received Jefferson's letter she had sent him a note appended to four pages from John Trumbull. On first opening the message and seeing her signature, Jefferson assumed that the entire letter was from her. Stung by disappointment, he reproached her for sending a letter "of four lines only instead of four pages. I thank you for the four lines, however, because they prove you think of me. Little indeed, but better a little than none."[47] "Diable!" he exclaimed, in a style recalling the repeated imprecation "The Devil!" in his teenaged letters when he deemed a correspondent neglectful.

In reply to Jefferson's long "Dialogue" she wrote affectionately but without passion: "[Your letters] will never be long enough. When in the long winter evenings there is left some idle moment, sacrifice it to me, to sending me news of yourself. I can hardly wait to receive a letter from your right hand. . . . My husband sends you a thousand compliments. . . . I shall never forget your attentions to us. Sometimes we shall mention our contemplated tour next year, either to Paris or to Italy. Many things can prevent its execution, but even greater impossibilities have been carried out. Accept my best wishes for your health and happiness and believe me your much obliged and affectionate friend."[48]

But, about two and a half weeks later, when no new letter had arrived from Jefferson, she wrote in a very different vein. She had reverted to Italian, as she had said she did in moments of stress. The Virginian would have had no difficulty in translating: "What does this silence mean? I have awaited the post with so much anxiety and lo each time it arrives without bringing me any letters from Paris. I am really worried. I fear lest it be illness or that your arm is worse, I think of a thousand things at once except that my friends should so soon have forgotten me; if you are contemplating making me another big gift of a long letter, I shall beg you to send them to me shorter but more frequent. I no longer have the patience to wait and I am venturing to take up the pen without being sure whether I am to complain, whether I am to reprove, or whether I am to implore patience, to express my mortification and anxieties of this disappointment. Perhaps a letter is en route; in the meantime I shall complain because it delays so long in arriving."[49]

The letter becomes increasingly emotional: "When we separate, after the pain of separation is past, one lives in continual anxiety. One does not receive letters. One imagines a thousand misfortunes. If some mishap occurs one cannot run with succour or comfort, nor receive news of it. . . . Night thoughts, before the fire, and when the imagination is well warmed up, one could go cool off in a river. . . . When I began this I intended to say only three words but unconsciously I have arrived this far without even knowing what I have said, but when women begin talking it is difficult to hold them back, even if they are aware of their saying foolish things. . . . I receive in this moment two letters from Paris, but not from you."

Jefferson's own loneliness was particularly distressing. Pain kept him awake nights and prodded his imagination to torment him. Every time he wrote to a friend or to someone with whom he had business the awkwardness of his effort was a reminder of his "folly." His injury wore sorely on his nerves. It even prevented his fulfilling some of his functions as American minister. The Commonwealth of Virginia, acting through Jefferson, had commissioned Houdon to execute two busts of Lafayette, one to be placed in Richmond and the other to be presented to the City of Paris. Some diplomatic maneuvering by Jefferson had been necessary to win the King's permission for the French city to accept. But when the day came for the formal ceremony of presentation Jefferson was not well enough to take part. He was represented by William Short who was impressed most by the excitement of the honoree's wife. "I am persuaded," he wrote, "she did not receive more pleasure on the night of her marriage."[50] European journalists seemed to be impressed with almost every aspect of the event.[51]

Though Jefferson's activities temporarily were limited, his earlier diplomatic efforts were bearing fruit. Comptroller General Charles-Alexandre de Calonne, on October 22, wrote Jefferson a letter formally summarizing the various concessions to American commerce which his government was prepared to make.[52]

Before the end of the year Jefferson again was seizing the initiative in matters of wide scope and complexity. On December 1 he proposed to the Ambassadors of Russia and Portugal a concert of powers against the Barbary States. He called for a naval force jointly sponsored by the United States and some European powers to scour the Mediterranean of pirates. The enterprise would be directed by diplomatic representatives of the cooperating powers.[53] Whatever his government might do, Jefferson personally was committed to a policy of defense rather than tribute.

His personal life, too, was returning to something approaching normal—though it had never really been normal since Patty's death. For a short while there had been the excitement of discovering Maria and of enjoying her company—hours encapsulated in the awareness of impending frustration, and made the sweeter for it like grapes nestled in their sour skins. Physical pain and mental anguish, so long his bedfellows at the time of parting and since, had gradually faded like ghosts but, like ghosts, sometimes reappeared. By year's end there doubtless were times when he waked to a new morning with his old freshness of spirit before memory settled the sense of loss upon him like an oppressive yoke. But there was still hope. "In the spring, said the lady."

Maria did not come in the spring, but still she might come in the summer. And in the spring came another whom Jefferson loved. He had persisted in his efforts to bring Polly to France. Finally in May of 1787 the Eppses placed her on a vessel for Europe. At least, Jefferson, whatever his blunders in dealing with his daughter, was not the author of the strategy that got her aboard. She visited the ship with her young cousins and played on its decks with them for a day or more. Falling asleep after vigorous exercise, she waked to find the craft underway and all of her relatives missing. The only truly familiar person accompanying her was the slave Sally, young sister of James Hemings who served in Jefferson's Paris household as he had at Monticello.[54]

Sally apparently was not mature enough to provide much comfort for the little girl. Fortunately, the captain, Andrew Ramsay, was a fatherly man. After safe arrival in London, he replied to Jefferson's letter of appreciation for his care of Polly: "Indeed any person whose care she was put under must have been void of feeling if they neglected her. Her sweet dispostion and good nature demanded every attention; and her vexation and the affliction she underwent on leaving her aunt made it necessary to be attentive at first for I was afraid of her getting sick, but she soon got over it and got so fond of me that she seldom parts with me without tears, and indeed I am almost the same way with her."[55]

In a letter informing the Eppses of Polly's arrival in good health, Jefferson told of Ramsay's kindness: "Mrs. Adams writes me she [Polly] was so much attached to him that her separation from him was a terrible operation. She has now to go through the same with Mrs. Adams. I hope that in ten days she will join those from whom she is no more to be separated."[56]

Jefferson himself did not go to London to meet his daughter and escort her to Paris. He pleaded as an excuse the pressure of accumulated diplomatic business following a study tour of France. This may have been the primary reason, though one suspects that also he may have been reluctant to go where he would be expected to visit Mrs. Cosway at a time when the Head had temporarily asserted a perilous ascendancy over the Heart and where he would be under the watchful eyes of Abigail Adams and her friends. In any event, Mrs. Adams sent him a scolding letter for sending his French *maitre d'hotel*, Petit, to do what he should have done himself:

> If I had thought you would so soon have sent for your dear little girl, I should have been tempted to have kept her arrival here, from you a secret. I am really loth to part with her, and she last evening upon Petit's arrival, was thrown into all her former distresses, and bursting into tears, told me it would be as hard to leave me as it was her Aunt Epps. She has been so often deceived that she will not quit me a moment lest she should be carried away. Nor can I scarcely prevail upon her to see Petit. Though she says she does not remember you, yet she has been taught to consider you with affection and fondness, and depended upon your coming for her. She told me this morning, that as she had left all her friends in Virginia to come over the ocean to see you, she did think you would have taken the pains to have come here for her, and not have sent a man she cannot understand. I express her own words. I expostulated with her upon the long journey you had been, and the difficulty you had to come and upon the care, kindness and attention of Petit, whom I so well knew. But she cannot yet hear me.[57]

Mrs. Adams continued in a vein that Jefferson must have found both reassuring and troubling:

> She is a child of the quickest sensibility, and the maturest understanding, that I have ever met with for her years. She had been 5 weeks at sea, and with men only, so that on the first day of her arrival, she was as rough as a little sailor, and then she being decoyed from the ship, which made her very angry, and no one having any authority over her, I was apprehensive I should meet with some trouble. But where there are such materials to work upon as I have found in her, there is no danger. She listened to my admonitions, and attended to my advice and in two days was restored to the amiable lovely child which her aunt had formed

her. In short she is the favorite of every creature in the house, and I cannot but feel Sir, how many pleasures you must lose by committing her to a convent. Yet situated as you are, you cannot keep her with you.

She sounded another ominous note: "The girl she has with her wants more care than the child, and is wholly incapable of looking properly after her without some superior to direct her."

Mrs. Adams had asked Petit to stay a few days longer, so that Polly could become accustomed to him and so that there would be an opportunity for Jefferson to communicate a change of plans. "I have not the heart to force her into a carriage against her will and send her from me almost in a frenzy, as I know will be the case unless I can reconcile her to the thoughts of going and I have given her my word that Petit shall stay until I can hear again from you. Books are her delight, and I have furnished her out a little library, and she reads to me by the hour with great distinctness, and comments on what she reads with much propriety."

Jefferson had already written Mrs. Adams: "By this time she will have learned again to love the hand that feeds and comforts her, and have formed an attachment to you. She will think I am made only to tear her from all her affections. I wish I could have come myself. The pleasure of a visit to yourself and Mr. Adams would have been great additional inducement."[58]

Jefferson's next letter to Mrs. Adams was still tactful but unbudging: "If she were to stay till she should be willing to come, she would stay till you cease to be kind to her, and that, Madam, is a term for which I cannot wait."[59]

When Petit had reserved places in the stage and paid for them, Mrs. Adams accepted the inevitable. But she did not miss the opportunity to let Jefferson know of his daughter's unhappiness: "She says, 'If I must go, I will, but I cannot help crying so pray don't ask me to.' I should have taken great pleasure in presenting her to you here, as you would then have seen her with her most engaging countenance. . . . I never saw so intelligent a countenance in a child before. . . . I can easily conceive the earnest desire you must have to embrace so lovely a child after so long a separation from her."[60]

On July 15 Jefferson, as he informed Mrs. Adams, "had the happiness of receiving" his daughter. But the joy was mitigated by the inescapable realization that Polly had rather be somewhere else. "Among the first things she informed me of," he told Abigail, "was her promise to you that after she should have been here a little while she would go back to pay you a visit of four or five days. She had taken nothing into her calculation but the feelings of her own heart which beat warmly with gratitude to you. She had fared very well on the road, having got into favor with gentlemen and ladies so as to be sometimes on the knee of one, sometimes of another." Snatching at fragile straws, he added, "She had totally forgotten her sister, but thought, on seeing me, that she recollected something of me."[61]

When a separate note for Polly dropped out of one sent to Jefferson by Mrs. Adams in September, the little girl "flushed, she whitened, she flushed again, and in short was in such a flutter of joy that she could scarcely open it."[62] Jefferson assured Mrs. Adams, "At this moment she is in the convent, where she is perfectly happy."

Whether or not Polly was "perfectly happy," her father certainly was not. To Wilson Miles Cary, back in Virginia, he wrote about a month after Polly's arrival in Paris: "Time, absence, and comparison render my own country much dearer, and give a luster to all it contains which I did not before know that it merited. Fortunatus's wishing cap was always the object of my desire, but never so much as lately. With it I should soon be seated at your fireside to enjoy the society of yourself and family."[63] On the same day he wrote his Albemarle neighbor George Gilmer: "I shall be very happy to eat at Penpark some of the good mutton and beef. . . with yourself and Mrs. Gilmer and my good old neighbors. I am as happy nowhere else and in no other society, and all my wishes end, where I hope my days will end, at Monticello. Too many scenes of happiness mingle themselves with all the recollections of my native woods and fields to suffer them to be supplanted in my affection by any other. I consider myself here as a traveler only, and not a resident. My commission expires the next spring, and if not renewed, I shall of course return then. If renewed, I shall remain here some time longer. How much I cannot say; yet my wishes shorten the period. . . . My daughters are importunate to return also."[64]

Something other than homesickness contributed to Jefferson's unhappiness: "The accident of a dislocated wrist, badly set, has I fear deprived me forever of almost every use of my right hand. Nor is the extent of the evil as yet known, the hand withering, the fingers remaining swelled and crooked, and losing rather than gaining in point of suppleness. It is now eleven months since the accident. I am able, however, to write, though for a long time I was not so."[65]

In the letter to Gilmer and in correspondence with many other people Jefferson excused delay, as he had his failure to go to London in person for his daughter, by citing his recent absence from Paris on a tour and the resultant pressure of accumulated work. His travels, from February 28 to June 10, had taken him through southern France and northern Italy. The trip had been undertaken partly on the advice of his physicians, but a more compelling reason had been his desire to learn things that would enable American agriculturists—as he said, "the mass of our countrymen"—"to adapt their productions to the market." He always wished to discover markets for them and "endeavor to obtain favorable terms of reception." He was eager to find seeds and plants to be transferred to American soil.[66] His love of arts and antiquities would be satisfied by such a journey, but he seems to have had a puritanical need to pay for these pleasures by studying things that his countrymen would consider useful. Maybe the conscience of this very time-conscious man smote him for the days lost to duty when he had escorted Maria Cosway and nursed his injured wrist.

He made the trip in his own carriage, depending on post horses along the way. At the outset he was "pelted. . .with rain, hail, and snow."[67] Only now and then were there "a few gleamings of sunshine to cheer." He carried no servant with him, preferring to pick up on the journey one to whom he would be a stranger. In the course of the tour he explained his purpose and *modus operandi* in a letter to Lafayette: "I am constantly roving about to see what I have never seen before and shall never see again. In the great cities I go to see what travelers think alone worthy of being seen; but I make a job of it, and generally gulp it all down in a day. On the other hand, I am never satiated with rambling through the fields and farms, examining the culture and cultivators, with a degree of curiosity which makes some take me to be a fool, and others to be much wiser than I am. . . . I have often wished for you. I think you have not made this journey. . . . And to do it most effectually you must be absolutely incognito, you must ferret the people out of their hovels as I have done, look into their kettles, eat their bread, loll on their beds under pretense of resting yourself, but in fact to find if they are soft. You will feel a sublime pleasure in the course of this investigation, and a sublimer one hereafter when you shall be able to apply your knowledge to the softening of their beds, or the throwing a morsel of meat into the kettle of vegetables."[68]

Jefferson's concern for the downtrodden is in character, but it is difficult to picture this fastidious man, who even wiped off his horse with a handkerchief before mounting, lolling in strange beds in hovels.

His traveling incognito may have been motivated by something in addition to a quest for undisguised facts. His psyche had suffered and he had a need for escape from the society in which the suffering had occurred.

To Madame de Tott, a prominent French painter and one of a half dozen Parisian women with whom Jefferson carried on mild flirtations, he wrote[69]: "You know . . . that you have been in Paris and its neighborhood constantly since I had the pleasure of seeing you there; yet I declare you have been with me above half my journey, I could repeat to you long conversations, word for word, and on a variety of subjects. When I find you fatigued with conversation and sighing for your palette and pencil, I permit you to return to Paris awhile and amuse myself with philosophizing on the objects which occur. The plan of my journey, as well as of my life, being to take things by the smooth handle, few occur which have not something tolerable to offer me." He then gives an example which illustrates his desire for escape as much as his faculty for accommodation:

[The Auberge, in Marseilles] in which I am obliged to take refuge at night presents in the first moment nothing but noise, dirt, and disorder. But the Auberge is not to be too much abased. True; it has not the charming gardens of Chaville without, nor its decorations, nor its charming society within. I do not seek, therefore, for the good things which it has not, but those which it has. A traveler, says I, retired at night to his chamber in an inn, all his effects contained in a single trunk, all his cares circumscribed by the walls of his apartment, unknown to all, unheeded and undisturbed, writes, reads, thinks, sleeps, just in the moments when nature and the movements of his body and mind require. Charmed with the tranquility of his little cell, he finds how few are our real wants, how cheap a thing is happiness, how expensive a one pride.

Carried away with enthusiasm, Jefferson begins to sound more like Henry David Thoreau, less like the luxury-loving master of Monticello. One in his circumstances, he asserts, "views with pity the wretched rich, whom the laws of the world have submitted to the cumbrous trappings of rank: he sees him laboring through the journey of life like an ass oppressed under ingots of gold, little of which goes to feed, to clothe, or to cover himself; the rest gobbled up by harpies of various description with which he has surrouded himself. These, and not himself, are its real masters. He wonders that a thinking mind can be so subdued by opinion, and that he does not run away from his own crowded house and take refuge in the chamber of an inn."

Jefferson explains that his mind enjoys "no middle ground" between "the society of real friends and the tranquility of solitude." And even in his solitary journey there is need for compromise with harsh reality. "Thus reconciled to my Auberge by night, I was still persecuted by day with the cruel whip of the postilion. How to find a smooth handle to this tremendous instrument? At length, however, I found it in the callous nerves of the horse, to which these terrible stripes may afford but a gentle and perhaps a pleasing irritation, like a pinch of snuff to an old snuff taker." Jefferson was too ardent an advocate of change to be a Dr. Pangloss, but there is something Panglossian in his determined quest of serenity at this particular stage of his life.

Before many more lines he is giving up the discussion of any philosophy whatsoever:

> I should go on, Madam, detailing to you my dreams and speculations, but that my present situation is most unfriendly to speculation. 4,350 market women (I have counted them) brawling, squabbling, jabbering patois, 300 asses braying and bewailing to each other, and to the world, their cruel oppressions, 4 files of mule carts passing in constant succession, with as many bells to every mule as can be hung about him, all this in the street under my window, and the weather too hot to shut it. Judge whether in such a situation it is easy to hang one's ideas together.

The first month of Jefferson's journey took him through Burgundy, where he noted the white cattle and red wine; Beaujolais, "the richest country I ever beheld . . . , thick sown with farm houses [and] chateaus" and the home of a nude statue of Diana by Michael Angelo Slodtz that captivated the Virginian; Nimes, where he found himself under the spell of Roman civilization; and Aix-en-Provence, where for four days he tried without effect the warm waters prescribed by his physicians.[70]

If the waters of Aix-en-Provence did not refresh him, the architectural beauties of Nimes did. To the Comtesse de Tessé, he wrote: "Here I am, Madam, gazing whole hours at the Maison Carrée, like a lover at his mistress. The stocking weavers and silk spinners around it consider me as an hypochondriac Englishman about to write with a pistol the last chapter of his history. This is the second time I have been in love since I left Paris. The first was with a Diana . . . in the Beaujolais, a delicious morsel of sculpture . . . . This, you will say, was in rule, to fall in love with a fine woman; but with a house! It is out of all precedent! No, madam, it is not without a precedent in my own history. While at Paris I was violently smitten with the Hotel de Salm, and used to go to the Tuileries almost daily to look at it . . . . From Lyons to Nimes I have been nourished with the remains of Roman grandeur."

After indulging in humorous banter and delivering serious observations on government, he revealed the depth of his immersion in that antique world which had lapped teasingly at his youthful imagination long ago in Williamsburg.

"From a correspondent at Nimes you will not expect news. Were I to attempt to give you news, I should tell you stories a thousand years old. I should detail to you the intrigues of the courts of the Caesars . . . . I am immersed in antiquities from morning to night. For me the city of Rome is actually existing in all the splendor of its empire. I am filled with alarms for the event of the eruptions daily making on us by the Goths, Ostrogoths, Visigoths and Vandals, lest they should reconquer us to our original barbarism. If I am sometimes induced to look forward to the eighteenth century, it is only when recalled to it by the recollection of your goodness and friendship. . . ."

A very pretty little compliment of the rococo sort then fashionable. But Jefferson could be recalled to his own century by political intrigue as well as by romantic imagining. At Nimes, by prearrangement, he met a revolutionary minded Brazilian. Jefferson told Secretary of State Jay: "I [wrote] to the gentleman. . .that I would go off my road as far as Nimes, under the pretext of seeing the antiquities of that place, if he would meet me there."[71] If Jefferson's visit to the Roman ruins was only a pretext, he was unexpectedly carried away by his own ruse. Perhaps once again, his esthetic propensities warring with his utilitarian convictions, he was deceiving himself. He transmitted to Jay a good deal of information on conditions in Brazil derived from conversation with the stranger and added: "I took care to impress on him through the whole of our conversation that I had neither instructions nor authority to say a word to anybody on this subject, and that I could only give him my own ideas as a single individual: which were that we were not in a condition at present to meddle nationally in any war; that we wished particularly to cultivate the friendship of Portugal, with whom we have an advantageous commerce. That yet a successful revolution in Brazil could not be uninteresting to us. That prospects of lucre might possibly draw numbers of individuals to their aid, and purer motives our officers, among whom are many excellent. That our citizens, being free to leave their own country individually without the consent of their governments, are equally free to go to any other." Jefferson told of similar conversations in Paris with one who professed to be a revolutionary: "He had much the air of candor, but that can be borrowed, so that I was not able to decide about him in my own mind." Jefferson's diplomacy had acquired a French subtlety.

But he was still at heart a Virginia planter. As he traveled through southern France he noted carefully whether the soil was reddish, brown, or mulatto, and whether it was "rich," "bad to middling," or "rocky and poor." The large hills of Champagne reminded him of Elk Hill and Beaverdam Hills in Virginia. Near Marseilles, after leaving Aix, he saw on the road "one of those little whirlwinds which we have in Virginia." Everywhere he made specific notes on climate and crops.[72]

Departing from his original itinerary, he made a foray into northern Italy, spending about a month in travel around Turin, Milan, and Genoa. The last was "the spot at which I turned my back on Rome and Naples. It was a moment of conflict between duty which urged me to return, and inclination urging me forward."[73] This time agriculture, whale oil, and the demands of diplomacy won out over the lure of antiquities.

The return to Marseilles from Genoa was by sea, never an ideal mode for Jefferson, and he became extremely ill during his two days on the waves before a change of wind forced them to land at Noli. Even then the trip was scarcely less rocky for he had to ride a mule up the cliffs to a wretched lodging. His next stop was a still worse tavern, but by this time, with the return of health, he had so far recovered his spirits as to admire the changing beauty of the sea, alternately black, blue, and green, that had so lately been his enemy. He was still, however, in a mood for withdrawal. "If any person wished to retire from [his] acquaintance, to live absolutely unknown, and yet in the midst of physical enjoyments, it should be in some of the little villages of this coast, where air, water, and earth concur to offer what each has most precious."[74] He traveled on by mule day and night until he reached the Canal of Languedoc, which joined the Mediterranean to the Atlantic. He made detailed, illustrated notes of the mechanics of the canal.

He also was alive to its esthetic delights:

"I dismounted my carriage from its wheels, placed it on the deck of a light bark, and was thus towed on the canal instead of the post road. That I might be perfectly master of all the delays necessary, I hired a bark to myself by the day and have made twenty to thirty-five miles a day, according to circumstances, always sleeping ashore. Of all the methods of travel I have ever tried, this is the pleasantest. I walk the greater part of the way along the banks of the canal, level, and lined with a double row of trees which furnish shade. When fatigued, I take seat in my carriage where, as much at ease as if it were my study, I read, write and observe. My carriage being of glass all round admits a full view of all the varying scenes through which I am shifted, olives, figs, mulberries, vines, corn and pasture, villages and farms. I have had some days of superb weather, enjoying two parts of the Indian's wish, cloudless skies and limpid waters: I have had another luxury which he could not wish since we have driven him from the country of mockingbirds, a double row of nightingales along the banks of the canal in full song. This delicious bird gave me another rich treat at Vaucluse. Arriving there a little fatigued, I sat down to repose myself at the fountain which, in a retired hollow of the mountain, gushes out in a stream sufficient to turn three hundred mills. The ruins of Petrarch's (chateau) perched on a rock two hundred feet perpendicular over the fountain, and every tree and bush filled with nightingales in full chorus. I find Mazzei's observation just, that their song is more varied, their tone fuller and stronger than on the banks of the Seine. It explains to me another circumstance, why there never was a poet north of the Alps and why there never will be one. A poet is as much a creature of climate as an orange or a palm tree. What a bird the nightingale would be in the climates of America! We must colonize him thither."[75]

When he entered Brittany, Jefferson's sensitivity to beauty was blunted by his awareness of human sufferings. "The villages announce a general poverty, as does every other appearance. Women smite on the anvil and work with the hoe, and cows are yoked to labor." He was always depressed at the sight of people ground down by heavy tasks, but especially so if they were women. He noted with particular poignancy the occasional earring or decorative scarf with which one of these weary ones proclaimed her humanity even under the weight of animal burdens.[76] He considered hard labor for women a sign of a backward society.

In Touraine his scientific curiosity vied with his appreciation of the nightingales' song. Here he investigated Voltaire's theory of the spontaneous generation of shells without animal bodies. He concluded that a determination of the question "must wait till further and fuller observations."[77] Jefferson's travel notes, if no other evidence were available, would reveal his curiosity to be as far ranging as that of Voltaire himself, though without the cockiness that caused the French philosophe to volunteer to write everything under A and B in the great *Encyclopédie*.

Two days after leaving Tours Jefferson was back in Paris. He found a letter from Maria Cosway who desperately wondered whether he was "gone to the other world."[78] He replied that he "took a peep only into Elysium. I entered it at one door, and came out at another, having seen, as I passed, only Turin, Milan, and Genoa. I calculated the hours it would have taken to carry me on to Rome. But they were exactly so many more than I had to spare. Was not this provoking? . . . But I am born to lose everything I love. Why were you not with me? So many enchanting scenes which only wanted your pencil to consecrate them to fame. Whenever you go to Italy . . . have your palette and pencil ready, for you will be sure to stop in the passage at the Chateau de Saorgio. Imagine to yourself, madam, a castle and village hanging to a cloud in front. On one hand a mountain cloven through to let pass a gurgling stream; on the other a river, over which is thrown a magnificent bridge; the whole formed into a basin, its sides shagged with rocks, olive trees, vines, herds, &c. I insist on your painting it.''

With more urgency, he asked: ''When are you coming here? If not at all, what did you ever come for? Only to make people miserable at losing you. Consider that you are but four days from Paris. . . . Come then, my dear madam, and we will breakfast every day á l'Angloise, hie away to the Desert, dine under the bowers of Marly, and forget that we are ever to part again.''[79]

Whether or not Maria should return to Paris this year, another young lady Jefferson loved was on her way. As we have seen, his little daughter Polly arrived in Paris in the middle of July. And, as we have also seen, her fresh arrival from Virginia apparently stirred new nostalgia for home. Jefferson seems to have become impatient of the bustle and stir of Paris that once had fascinated him. In September he formed the habit of retreating to the hermitage of the lay brothers on Mont Calvaire (Valérien), sometimes for a week or more, when the press of work was great. There he would labor hard at his paper work, taking time out for strolls in the gardens (where no talking was allowed) and for dinner (where there was lively conversation with other guests). There was also, as at home, a view from a mountaintop.[80] He sampled the wine from the brothers' vineyards and sent Abigail Adams a dozen pairs of silk stockings from their manufactory.

But, however agreeable Jefferson found the hermitage on a short-term basis, he was far from forsaking all the attractions of this world. Using again one of his favorite images, that of Fortunatus's wishing cap, he had told Maria, ''If I had it, I question if I should use it but once. I should wish myself with you and not wish myself away again.''[81] Therefore he was depressed when Maria wrote him: ''I do not know that we shall come to Paris this year. I fear not. My husband begins to doubt it, just at the time when one should begin to prepare to leave. You cannot believe how much this uncertainty displeases me, when I have everything to fear against my desire. Why promise? Why lead me to hope?''[82]

When at summer's end it became evident that Richard Cosway definitely would not return to Paris in 1787, Maria took a bold step. She came without him. Arriving on August 28, she took up residence with the Princess Lubomirski, cousin to the King of Poland and mistress of one of the great Paris salons. Apparently Maria and Jefferson returned to the parks and gardens which they had formerly found delightful. Jefferson, or somebody, or something, was occupying a great deal of her time and thought.[83] From London, Trumbull wrote the Virginian: ''Pray tell her that *three* posts have passed in which no one of her friends has received a single line from her, that Lady Lyttleton, Mr. C[osway], her sister, and all the world are not only angry at her for not writing, but suffer all the distress of anxiety lest illness or accident of any kind should have occasioned her silence. I am commissioned to scold her heartily. Will you permit me to transfer the commission and to beg that you will execute it with all due severity and elegance. From you I am sure of its effect.''[84]

Jefferson replied playfully: ''I showed to Mrs. Cosway the part of your letter respecting her, and begged her to consider the scold as hanging over head till I could get a machine for scolding invented, because it is a business not fit for any human heart, and especially to be directed on such subjects as her."[85]

Some have assumed that, on meeting again in Paris, Jefferson and Maria Cosway found the fires of love reduced to dying embers. The return to the haunts of the previous year could be viewed as an unhappy attempt at warmed-over romance. Others have suggested that the two consummated their affair and then began to cool off. There is also the possibility that either Jefferson or Maria, or perhaps both, suddenly became uneasy about the entanglements and embarrassments into which their relationship might be leading them. Perhaps Jefferson did not relentlessly press against all obstacles to the extent that he did in pursuing some other goals. Whatever the state of affairs, he found it frustrating on November 13 when he wrote Trumbull: "Mrs. Cosway is well but her friends are not so. They are in continual agitation between the hopes of her stay and the fear of her recall. A fatality has attended my wishes, and her and my endeavors to see one another more since she has been here. From the mere effect of chance, she has happened to be from home several times when I have called on her, and I, when she has called on me. I hope for better luck hereafter."[86]

Evidently his luck did not improve. There are tantalizing hints of discord in a note, apparently of December 1, from Mrs. Cosway: "If my inclination had been your law I should have had the pleasure of seeing you more than I have. I have felt the *loss* with displeasure, but on my return to England when I calculate the time I have been in Paris, I shall not believe it possible."[87]

She invited Jefferson to breakfast on Saturday, December 8, but when he arrived he found she had already left for England. There was only a note written the night before: "I cannot breakfast with you tomorrow; to bid you adieu once is sufficiently painful, for I leave you with very melancholy ideas. You have given, my dear sir, all your commissions [for the performance of little favors in London] to Mr. Trumbull, and I have the reflection that I cannot be useful to you who have rendered me so many civilities."[88]

Two days after her departure she wrote from London: "You promised to come to breakfast with me the morning of my departure and to accompany me part of the way. Did you go? I left Paris with much regret. Indeed, I could not bear to take leave any more. I was confused and distracted; you must have thought me so when you saw me in the evening. Why is it my fortune to find amiable people where I go, and why am I to be obliged to part with them! 'Tis very cruel. I hope our correspondence will be more frequent and punctual than our meetings were while I was in Paris. I suspected the reason, and would not reproach you since I know your objection to company. You are happy you can follow so much your inclinations. I wish I could do the same. I do all I can, but with little success. Perhaps I don't know how to go about it."[89]

There is here the clear suggestion that Jefferson was unwilling to share with others the hours he spent in Maria's company. As a married woman much observed and talked about, she seems to have envied Jefferson's masculine freedom.

Maria's failure to keep her breakfast engagement, Jefferson told her in a letter of January 31, 1788, "spared me indeed the pain of parting, but it deprives me of the comfort of recollecting that pain."[90] He let Maria know, though, that he had found a comforter in Angelica Church, wife of John Church, M.P., and sister-in-law of Alexander Hamilton. A London beauty almost as celebrated as Mrs. Cosway herself, she was a close friend of Maria's. Indeed, Maria had written Jefferson, "She calls me her sister. I call her my dearest sister. If I did not love her so much I should fear her rivalship, but no, I give you free permission to love her with all your heart, and shall feel happy if I think you keep me in a little corner of it when you admit her even to reign Queen."[91] She pressed him for his real opinion of Mrs. Church, who had arrived in Paris soon after Maria's departure. Jefferson replied: "I never saw her before but I find in her all the good the world has given her credit for. I do not wonder at your fondness for each other. I have seen too little of her, as I did of you. But in your case it was not my fault, unless it be a fault to love my friends so dearly as to wish to enjoy their company in the only way it yields enjoyment, that is, en petite comité. You make everybody love you. You are sought and surrounded therefore by all. Your mere domestic cortege was so numerous that one could not approach you quite at . . . ease. Nor could you so unpremeditatedly mount into the phaeton and hie away to the Bois de Boulogne, St. Cloud, Marly, St. Germain. . . ."[92]

Meanwhile, Jefferson continued to find some comfort in Angelica Church's "goodness"—enhanced as it was by bright eyes, delicate features, and a graceful figure. When she returned to London he bracketed her with Maria in a message to John Trumbull, who had written of Mrs. Cosway, "She is angry yet she teases me every day for a copy of your little portrait—that she may scold *it* no doubt."[93] Jefferson could almost envy Trumbull for being in London since its overcast was relieved by two bright beauties. The American minister wrote his friend: "Say everything soft and affectionate for me to Mrs. Cosway and Mrs. Church. They are countervail to you for the want of a sun."[94]

When Maria wrote Jefferson on March 6 she was almost incoherent at times. Despite her English ancestry, English was only her second language and in moments of passion its flow was checked and twisted in ways that did not afflict her voluble Italian. "I have waited some time to see if I could recover my usual peace with you," she wrote, "but I find it is impossible yet, therefore must address myself to you still angry. Your long silence is impardonable. . . . My war against you is of such a nature that I cannot even find terms to express it. . . . I begin to run on and my intention was only to say *nothing,* send a blank paper as a lady in a passion is not fit for anything." The next words, though quite legible, are too confused to be interpreted with any certainty. Then she says, "What shall you do when you [are] much farther away? I can't bear the idea—will you give Mr. Trumbull leave to make a copy of a certain portrait he painted at Paris? It is a person who hates you that requests this favor. . . . Though I am angry, I can hardly end my letter. Remember I do you justice by not thinking of you now."[95] The note was unsigned but the handwriting was unmistakably Maria's—as though Jefferson needed that clue.

Before Jefferson could receive this message, he had left Paris because of a crisis larger than a lovers' spat. The inability of the United States government to collect sufficient money from the individual states had led it to the verge of bankruptcy. A French firm had seized United States military stores in France for nonpayment of debt. Another blow to American finances was a new ban on the importation of whale oil.

These matters would have been of great concern to anyone in the United States government, but they would normally have been a matter of immediate responsibility for John Adams, who had been charged with management of financial transactions for

American diplomatic establishments in Europe. But now Adams, newly elected Vice President of the United States, was preparing to return to America, and had told the bankers to deal with Jefferson in the immediate future. Jefferson afterwards stated his plight: "I had no powers, no instructions, no means, and no familiarity with the subject."[96]

Adams thought it necessary to take formal leave of the government at the Hague before leaving Europe. News of his departure from London came to Jefferson on the very day the Massachusetts diplomat was scheduled to arrive in Holland. "A consultation with him and some provision for the future was indispensable while we could yet avail ourselves of his powers. For when they would be gone, we should be without resource.... " Jefferson at once dispatched a letter to Adams in care of the American agent at the Hague:

> Our affairs at Amsterdam press on my mind like a mountain.... I am so anxious to confer with you on this...and get some effectual arrangement made in time that I determine to meet you at the Hague. I will set out the moment some repairs are made to my carriage. It is promised me at about three o'clock tomorrow; but probably they will make it night, and that I may not set out till Tuesday morning. In that case I will be at the Hague Friday night. In the meantime you will perhaps have made all your bows there. I am sensible how irksome this must be to you in the moment of your departure. But it is a great interest of the U.S. which is at stake and I am sure you will sacrifice to that your feelings and your interest. I hope to shake you by the hand within twenty-four hours after you receive this.[97]

Jefferson wrote Short of his anxiety on the trip:

> After two days of prosperous journey I had a good gleam of hope of reaching this place [the Hague] in the night of the third day. In fact however I got on the third day only to within eight hours land journeying and the passage of the Moerdyke. Yet this remnant employed me three days and nothing less than the omnipotence of God could have shortened this time of torture. I saw the Saturday passing over, and, in imagination, the packet sailing and Mr. Adams on board. And it was not till Sunday my anxieties were ended by finding him here. We are setting out this morning for Amsterdam, where if we fail in the principal object, I shall at least have the solace of easing my own shoulders of the burthen.[98]

The Virginian was inexperienced in financial negotiations and he was not about to assume the primary responsibility in discussions of such importance. He was determined that Adams, who had learned to speak the language of bankers, should present the American position in initial conferences.

Nevertheless he differed with Adams on a fundamental of American policy. The Amsterdam moneylenders, who had been purchasing what Adams called "immense quantities of American paper," now insisted that it be "acknowledged and paid in Europe." Before he knew that he would be joined in Holland by Jefferson, Adams had written that he felt obliged to put his colleague on guard "against the immeasurable avarice of Amsterdam as well as the ungovernable rage of speculation.''[99] He could not resist adding, ''I feel no vanity in saying that this project never would have been suggested if it had not been known that I was recalled.'' He was convinced that any threat implicit in the bankers' demand for payment in Europe was a bluff. ''It appears to me totally impossible that you or I should ever agree to it, or approve it, and so far as I can comprehend it is equally impossible for the Board of Treasury or Congress to consent to it. . . . The Continental Certificates and their interest are to be paid in America at the Treasury of the United States. If a precedent is set of paying them in Europe, I pretend not to sufficient foresight to predict the consequences. They appear, however, to me to be horrid. If the interest of one million dollars is paid this year in Europe, you will find the interest of ten millions demanded next year.''

He concluded: ''My dear friend, farewell. I pity you in your situation, dunned and teased as you will be. All your philosophy will be wanting to support you. But be not discouraged. I have been constantly vexed with such terrible complaints and frightened with such long faces these ten years. Depend upon it, the Amsterdammers love money too well to execute their threats. They expect to gain too much by American credit to destroy it.''

Jefferson was determined not to be left in so pitiable a situation and he strongly disagreed with Adams about resisting payment in Europe. The Virginian was not sure that the Dutch bankers were bluffing. America's dependence on them was greater than their dependence on America. Was it not better, he asked, to satisfy these financiers regarding the place of payment and obtain a desperately needed new loan that would preserve the credit of the United States for two more years? On the expiration of that period the financial position of the United States should be greatly improved because of the power of the new federal government to collect taxes not collectible under the old Confederation.[100] Then the nation could afford to be more independent.

Jefferson pressed Adams to negotiate a loan in line with this policy. The New Englander refused. Jefferson, as Adams explained to Abigail, ''would take no denial.'' The ambassador to London seems never before to have suspected that his colleague in Paris was more than a match for him in stubbornness. Adams was neither the first nor the last person to be deceived by Jefferson's preference for ''taking the smooth handle.'' Finally, Adams gave in and initiated negotiations for the needed loan. He was still vexed when he left Amsterdam on March 21, finding comfort only in the reflection that he had been mistreated. Jefferson remained for nine more days to complete negotiations, leaving in a glow of satisfaction with the effectiveness of his diplomacy in a field where he was a novice.[101] It is amazing that Jefferson had been able to exercise so much influence over the redoubtable Adams in a situation in which the younger man was so dependent on the elder's special knowledge.

The arguments with Adams and negotiations with the bankers had not consumed all of Jefferson's mental energies while in Amsterdam. He had made copious and precise notes, accompanied by pencil sketches, on a great diversity of things.[102] He was fascinated by a way of placing wooden joists and brick arches to obtain greater strength in building, a method of fixing a flagstaff or mast, the design of windows that opened for air without admitting rain, the construction of a kind of dropleaf table he had not previously seen. He was intrigued by a lantern that occupied the place of the middle pane of glass over a street door and thus gave ''light equally into the antechamber and the street." He gave special attention to "a machine for drawing light empty boats over a dam" and to sawmills powered by the wind. He admired two ingenious canal bridges. He sketched a Dutch wheelbarrow which he observed to be "very convenient for loading and unloading."

When he visited Hope's House, the principal banking firm in Amsterdam, his eye was on the forms of architecture as well as those of finance. He sketched the facade with its two-story, Tuscan-columned portico.

One of the structures that most interested him housed birds rather than people. He described in detail with exact measurements the impressive aviary of an Amsterdam merchant.

He also made notes on the character, reputation, and abilities of the principal merchant brokers of the city as well as on aspects of Dutch economy. Altogether, his industry and acuity were such that the notebook might be taken for the production of a committee whose members had roamed Amsterdam in pursuit of their separate predilections.

His notes after leaving Amsterdam to return to Paris through Germany reveal an equally insatiable and informed curiosity. He comments on architecture, topography, soil, crops, trees, people, livestock, wines. Precise statistics are given throughout, but now and then the prosaic facts are gilded with a poetic imagination.

Before setting out on the return journey Jefferson had included in a letter to John Trumbull a message for Mrs. Cosway and Mrs. Church which, because it treated them as a matched pair, must not have been very pleasing to either: "Give my love to Mrs. Church and Mrs. Cosway. Tell them they will travel with me up the Rhine, one on each hand, and for this I shall be indebted not to any goodness of theirs, but to my own imagination, which helps me cheerily over the dull roads of this world."[103] His travel notes make no mention of phantom companions but do describe the Rhine as "sublime." But, much as he admired natural beauty and noble ruins, he could not shut his eyes to the signs of poverty among the peasants. The unhappiness of others always disturbed him.

At Dusseldorf he reveled in an art gallery which he found "sublime," sketched a gate at the elector's chateau as it actually was and as he thought it should be redesigned, described and compiled statistics on the celebrated Westphalian hogs, noting with at least as much amusement as irritation: "Well informed people here tell me there is no other part of the world where the bacon is smoked. They do not know that we do it."[104] "We," of course, were Virginians.

He confessed his fascination with ancient ruins and vainly sought the "remains of the encampment of Varus, in which he and his legions fell by the arms of Arminius," but he was equally interested in the very modernly equipped palace of the Elector of Treves which had a central heating system. He was fascinated to find "large rooms very well warmed by warm air conveyed from an oven below, through tubes which open into the rooms." He also sketched an oil and vinegar cruet whose shape pleased him.

He entered Frankfort amid rain, hail, and snow, but found a warm welcome from Baron von Geismar, who as a young captive Hessian captain in the Revolution had played violin duets with him at Monticello. Jefferson now knew that his injured wrist would never permit him to play the instrument satisfactorily again. At nearby Hanau he had another reunion with Hessians whom he had befriended during their captivity.

He wrote Short that he had found in this country "a set of men absolutely incorruptible." These were the German postilions "whom nothing on earth," including money, could induce to proceed at more than a walk. He bemoaned his "retarded" progress, but delighted in his surroundings. "The neighborhood of this place has been to us a second mother country. It is from the Palatinate on this part of the Rhine that those swarms of Germans have gone who, next to the descendants of the English, form the greatest body of our people. I have been continually amused by seeing here the origin of whatever is not English among us. I have fancied myself often in the upper parts of Maryland and Pennsylvania."

At Heidelberg he praised the Schloss as "the most noble ruin I have ever seen." He was also impressed with the famous "tun of Heidelberg," which he measured personally, concluding that it would hold 283,200 bottles of wine.

At Strasbourg he was ecstatic over "the steeple of the cathedral which I believe is the highest in the world, and the handsomest." His activity here may be inferred from the advice he later gave friends: "Go to the very top of it; but let it be the last operation of the day, as you will need a long rest after it."[105]

Recrossing the Rhine at Strasbourg, he was again in France. Here he noticed that the plowman's labor, as he plodded behind a team of oxen, was made unnecessarily hard by the clumsy shape of the moldboard. Jefferson's inventive mind turned at once to the design of an ideal plow. He analyzed the function of the moldboard "to receive the sod after the share has cut under it, to raise it gradually and reverse it." He sketched his design with exact measurements and directions for its manufacture.[106] Later at Monticello he would test the product and improve it until he brought forth his internationally honored "plow of least resistance."

On the night of April 23, 1788, a day after sketching his invention, he rode down the broad, tree-lined, eminently civilized avenues of Paris to his home. A vast pile of letters awaited him. Among them was Maria Cosway's almost incoherent declaration of anger which had arrived after his hasty departure for Amsterdam. The next day he replied in a letter whose tone indicates that, whatever his distraught state in an earlier stage of their relationship, his emotions were now under much better control than hers:

> I arrived here, my dear friend, the last night, and in a bushel of letters presented me by way of reception, I saw that one was of your handwriting. It is the only one I have yet opened, and I answer it before I open another. I do not think I was in arrears in our epistolary account when I left Paris. In affection I am sure you were greatly my debtor. I often determined during my journey to write to you: but sometimes the fatigue of exercise, and sometimes a fatigued attention hindered me. At Dusseldorf I wished for you much. I surely never saw so precious a collection of paintings. Above all things those of Van der Werff affected me the most. His picture of Sarah delivering Agar to Abraham is delicious. I would have agreed to have been Abraham though the consequence would have been that I should have been dead five or six thousand years.[107]

Agar (the biblical Hagar) was pictured as a seminude blonde with that newly nubile look which Jefferson had admired in some statues of Diana.

Jefferson said that Carlo Dolce, as well as Van der Werff, had become "a violent favorite. I am so little of a connoisseur that I preferred the works of these two (artists) to the old faded red things of Rubens. I am but a son of nature, loving what I see and feel, without being able to give a reason, nor caring much whether there be one." Here Jefferson sounds very much like the twentieth-century man of affairs who boasts that he doesn't know art but does know what he likes. He may have abandoned one of the first rules of artistic criticism, to judge by presentation rather than subject. Jefferson never seems to have been enamored of heavily upholstered beauty or what T.S. Eliot called "pneumatic delights."

When Mrs. Cosway read, "At Heidelberg I wished for you too; in fact, I led you by the hand through the whole garden,"[108] she doubtless recalled that he had expressed a wish to sail up the Rhine holding hands with both her and Mrs. Church. There was little comfort in the lines, "At Strasbourg I sat down to write to you, but for my soul I could think of nothing at Strasbourg. . . ."

He relayed the news that the Princess Lubomirski, with whom she had stayed on her most recent visit to Paris, had moved into another house. "When you come again, therefore, you will be somewhat nearer to me, but not near enough, and still surrounded by a numerous cortege, so that I shall see you only by scraps as I did when you were here last. The time before we were half days, and whole days together, and I found this too little." Thus Jefferson served notice that he could not spend an inordinate amount of time in lovesick correspondence with a woman who seldom could spare him her undivided attention when he was present in person.

Some believe that Jefferson had cooled to Maria because he had found a new love, and they do not mean the elegant Angela. Fawn M. Brodie in *Thomas Jefferson: An Intimate History* suggests that when Jefferson wrote Mrs. Cosway about his delight in Van der Werff's representation of Abraham's concubine he was really longing for his own—the slave girl Sally Hemings.[109] Mrs. Brodie goes so far as to suggest that when Jefferson alluded to mulatto soil eight times in the twenty-five pages of notes on his 1788 tour he was thinking not so much of the hills and valleys of France and Germany as of Sally's smooth mulatto contours.[110] She even implies that, when Jefferson's thoughts near the end of his journey turned toward improvement of the plow, he was thinking of his slave girl waiting to be plowed upon his return to Paris.[111] Garry Wills, noting that "mulatto" was the term for a precise soil shade (yellowish brown), cites the fact that Jefferson used the term "red" seven times in the journal of his 1788 tour and thirty-eight times in the notes on an earlier trip in France. He then asks facetiously, "Does this mean he was entertaining incestuous anticipations of the arrival of his red-haired daughter?"[112]

The case for Sally's having been Jefferson's mistress is based largely on the writings of James Callender, a notorious dealer in character assassination who was employed by the Virginian's political enemies during his first term as president of the United States, and a demonstrably inaccurate memoir published in the *Pike County* (Ohio) *Republican* in 1873. Long dismissed by serious historians, Callender's charges were dusted off by Mrs. Brodie and polished to a high gloss with the aid of the latest techniques in psychohistory.[113] She and others have offered as further proof that certain slaves growing up at Monticello are said to have borne a physical resemblance to Jefferson and that at least one also shared his putative father's predilection for fiddling. Of course, there is no reason for surprise that some blacks born at Monticello should show a family resemblance to its master when one considers that his nephews Peter and Samuel Carr confessed that they had fathered some of Sally's numerous progeny. In fact, Jefferson's granddaughter Ellen Randolph called her cousin Samuel "the most notorious good-natured Turk that ever was master of a black seraglio kept at other men's expense."[114]

Some with imaginations less restrained than Mrs. Brodie's have suggested that Jefferson had Sally accompany his daughter to Europe so that he might consummate his passion for the slave girl. Since Sally was fourteen or fifteen when she arrived in France in 1787 and Jefferson had not seen her for more than three years, one is asked to believe that even amid the caresses of the cultivated belles of Paris he had pined for an ignorant serving girl whose eleven- or twelve-year-old charms were indelibly burnt into his brain. We cannot even suppose that this juvenile paramour was extraordinarily precocious. As we have seen, Abigail Adams, shocked that Polly should have been entrusted to so inept a servant, wrote: "The girl she has with her wants more care than the child, and is wholly incapable of looking properly after her without some superior to direct her."

Callender's relationship with Jefferson, his attempts to blackmail the statesman, and the subsequent publication of charges that the celebrated apostle of liberty had compelled a helpless slave to submit to his mad passion will be discussed later where chronologically appropriate. Suffice it to say for the moment that anyone who imagines Jefferson at this time turning away from the beautiful and accomplished Maria Cosway because of his absorption in Sally is not only making a claim that would be laughed out of court for lack of sufficient evidence but one totally inconsistent with Jefferson's character, taste, and temperament as exhibited in other circumstances.

Undoubtedly the females that Jefferson was most eager to embrace upon his return to Paris were his two daughters. During his travels he had written them letters filled with love and admonitions—both in extravagant proportions.

But there was waiting for him an old love for which he felt more than infatuation. He had dedicated himself to her defense and now he found her endangered. Ever since he had "sworn upon the altar of God eternal vigilance against every form of tyranny over the mind of man" he had felt that his responsibility to defend Liberty exceeded the confines of national boundaries.

One of Liberty's greatest devotees in France was Jefferson's friend Lafayette. He was active in pushing for governmental reforms that would ease the burdens of the poor, reduce the powers of the King, and increase the influence of the bourgeoisie. Through his friendship with the marquis and other distinguished Frenchmen of liberal sentiments, Jefferson was in touch with the growth of revolutionary ideas in France.

He witnessed on May 5, 1789 the opening session of the Estates General, a spectacle that dramatized class conflicts. Gouverneur Morris, who had obtained a ticket of admission from Jefferson, thought "there was displayed everything of noble and of royal in this titled country."[115] He noted: "A great number of fine women and a very great number of fine dresses ranged round the hall." In the high fashion of the time these dresses would have had huge skirts of various hues, the sheen of silk and satin interlaced with threads of gold and silver. The ladies' elaborate coiffures would have added at least a foot to their height.

Upon his throne on a dais sat Louis XVI, rotundly regal in his robes. To his left and a little below him sat Marie Antoinette, an elegant woman who carried her heavily coiffured head proudly on her slender, vulnerable neck. The backdrop was of "gold-fringed violet velvet embroidered with fleur-de-lis of gold."[116] Surrounding them were the princes of the blood and the princesses with their retinues. Behind the throne was "a cluster of guards of the largest size, dressed in ancient costume taken from the times of chivalry." Below the stage and to the left sat the marshals of France, their slight movements marked by the glancing lights from their medals. Opposite them, resplendent in their own decorations, were the ministers of state. "In front of the ministers . . . sat the representatives of the clergy, . . . priests of all colors, scarlet, crimson, black, white, and gray, to the number of three hundred. In front of the maréchals of France, on benches facing the clergy, sat an equal number of representatives of the nobility dressed in a robe of black, waistcoats of cloth of gold, and over their shoulders so as to hang forward to their waist, a kind of lappet about a quarter of a yard wide at the top and wider at bottom, made of cloth of gold. On benches which reached quite across the hall and facing the stage, sat the representatives of the people, clothed in black."

In the space between the glittering nobles and richly robed clergy and directly in front of the people's representatives (black-clad as for a burial service), stood the heralds at arms clasping those outmoded weapons, their staves, wearing on their vestigial surcoats the emblems of a vanished chivalry. Jefferson gave no detailed description of the scene. He simply wrote that, "had it been enlightened with lamps and chandeliers, it would have been almost as brilliant as the opera."

Jefferson realized that the people might be preparing to bury the monarchy but he still thought that a funeral might be premature. He noted: "The King's speech was what it should have been, and very well delivered. . . . The Noblesse, on coming together, show that they are not as much reformed in their principles as we had hoped they would be." Although some reformers hoped for cooperation by the lower clergy, there were fears that their superiors might impede unification of the Assembly. The clergy and the nobility might withdraw. "But I shall not consider even that event as rendering things desperate. If the King will do business with the Tier Etat [the Third Estate, the People], which constitute the nation, it may be well done without priests or nobles."[117]

Jefferson had applied for extended leave from his Paris post and eagerly awaited word that it had been granted, but the excitement of events unfolding in France partially compensated him for the delay. With his diplomatic contacts with the government and his personal friendship with such of its prominent critics as Lafayette and La Rochefoucauld he was in an unusual position to know what was going on among both the monarchial establishment and the Patriot Party. The notes that he sent back to the United States at this time not only were of value then to his government but have remained important to historians of the French Revolution. The celebrated French historian Hippolyte Adolphe Taine paid a high tribute to the American ambassador's powers of observation and analysis when he wrote in 1865 that an Englishman, an Irishman, and an American—Arthur Young, Edmund Burke, and Thomas Jefferson—had evidenced more understanding of what was happening in France than any of the twelve hundred members of its National Assembly.[118]

Two weeks after the convening of the Estates General, the three orders were sitting in separate chambers and could not reach agreement on whether voting should be by orders or by individual members. The higher clergy and a majority of the nobility wanted it to be by orders whereas the Third Estate were unanimous for individual balloting. Jefferson wrote: "All the world is conjecturing how they are to get over the difficulty. Abundance are affrighted, and think all is lost, and the nation, in despair at this unsuccessful effort, will consign itself to tenfold despotism. This is rank cowardice."[119]

He attended the sessions regularly. On June 2, accompanied by Short, he was comparing notes with Lafayette and Rabaut de St. Etienne, a liberal leader. "The idea was started," Jefferson said, "of the King's coming forward in a *séance royale*" and presenting "a charter containing all the good in which the parties agree." Representatives of each of the three orders, it was hoped, would sign the document. This idea apparently originated with Jefferson. In any event he drafted such a document. Among other things it provided for annual meetings of the Estates General and assigned that body control over taxes and appropriations. There were guarantees of civil rights and freedom of the press. Jefferson advocated that, upon general endorsement of the charter, the Assembly adjourn until the anniversary of its convening.[120]

Events bypassed the effort. The Third Estate announced that if the nobility and clergy would not join in the work of legislation, they would go on without them. On June 17 they assumed the name National Assembly. After hearing the day's debates, Jefferson wrote Jay: "The fate of the nation depends on the conduct of the King and his ministers. Were they to side openly with the Commons, the revolution would be completed without a convulsion by the establishment of a constitution totally free and in which the distinction of Noble and Commoner would be suppressed."[121]

But Jefferson did not let his ardent hopes lead him into false assumptions. He did not believe that the King and his ministers would show that much boldness and foresight. "The King is honest and wishes the good of his people, but the expediency of an hereditary aristocracy is too difficult a question for him. On the contrary, his prejudices, his habits, and his connections decide him in his heart to support it." He believed that the Queen and the Princes were ready to join with the nobility. If the King were to make such a move the result would be the financial ruin of the monarchy and perhaps its toppling in civil war. But he did not believe that Louis would take such a step. He believed that the lower clergy and a few of the nobles would join the Commoners to draft a constitution. But there would be too many powerful nobles and ecclesiastics working against such a government. Jefferson thought a possible solution would be the creation of a bicameral legislature with one chamber corresponding to Britain's House of Lords.

A limited constitutional monarchy with a bicameral Parliament was also the desire of Jacques Necker, minister of finance and chief minister of the government. Jefferson got on well with him and believed him an honest and sensible man but thought his abilities were exaggerated. A vain person, the Swiss-born banker and politician jealously guarded the popularity that he had won in his adopted country. The long-chinned, solemn-faced statesman was not nearly so interesting to Jefferson as Madame Necker, who kept a lively salon, and their twenty-three-year-old daughter, Madame de Staël, already well on her way to becoming one of Europe's most brilliant and fascinating women. Necker's chief lieutenant was the foreign minister, the Comte de Montmorin, with whom Jefferson had negotiated consular conventions favorable to the United States. Jefferson particularly esteemed him as a reliable man of good will.

More than in the ministry, however, the American put his confidence in the National Assembly, whose members he found "cool, temperate, and sagacious." He recorded with satisfaction the Assembly's boldness when, locked out of their meeting hall, they convened in a nearby indoor tennis court and took an oath not to disperse until they had produced a constitution. When some nobles and many clergymen joined the Assembly, Jefferson wrote Jay: "This great crisis being now over, I shall not have matter interesting enough to trouble you with as often as I have done lately."[122] All Paris, it seemed, miscalculated, and even the shrewdly observant American minister was no exception.

He continued to be an almost totally admiring spectator of the Assembly's deliberations until one day when a speech by its foremost orator, the Comte de Mirabeau, shocked him into consternation. Though Mirabeau was a count and the son of a marquis, there was more of grossness than of aristocracy in the thick features of his pock-marked face. Originally he had sought election as a representative of the nobility and had won a seat among the commons only after being rejected by his own class. Before winning fame as an economist, he had been sentenced to death for seduction and abduction of another man's wife and had served abroad as a secret agent. Now, having escaped many dangers in many roles, he was the darling of the people and, impelled by the eloquence that caused him to be hailed as "the Shakespeare of oratory," was moving rapidly toward leadership of the Assembly. Though nominally a supporter of Necker's, he was really working to unseat him. That became evident in the particular speech that disturbed Jefferson.

Before launching upon his oration, Mirabeau stood monolithic before the Assembly, no narrowness of neck weakening the massive line of large head upon huge body. Even the pockmarks of his face added to the granite quality of visage as he appraised his audience through eyes heavy-lidded as a Buddha's. Soon all that was cold stone vanished. He was a creature of fire, breathing flaming words that singed first one adversary and then another. This time not even Necker was exempt. A shortage of bread had led to riots. What was the chief minister doing while the people went hungry? Monsieur Necker, Mirabeau asserted, had received from Ambassador Jefferson an offer to furnish corn and flour from his country. Necker, the orator said, had refused.[123]

This statement was untrue. Jefferson was indignant at being made the instrument of injury to a decent man. He was also much concerned that the American government should be precipitated into an internal French quarrel. To Lafayette, who requested clarification, Jefferson wrote: "I know not how Monsieur de Mirabeau has been led into this error. I never in my life made any proposition to Mr. Necker on the subject: I never said I had made such a proposition. . . . I must beg leave to avail myself of your friendship and of your position, to have a communication of these facts made to the honorable assembly of the nation of which you are a member. . . ."[124] Jefferson also sent copies of the letter to Necker and Montmorin.[125]

Mirabeau freely told the Assembly all that the American minister's letter said and laid it on the table for inspection. Lafayette reported to Jefferson: "Somebody undertook to translate it, and the House called for the reading of the translation. I confess

I thought it indelicate, if not for Mirabeau's feelings at least for my own, that a man who had already said everything that was in the letter against himself be once more submitted to the reading of it, when nothing was left but what he had read himself. I therefore said that as M. de Mirabeau had literally translated your expressions I took a second reading to be useless. Necker and Montmorin are very angry with me for it."[126] The next day Lafayette wrote to Jefferson: "M. de Mirabeau's affair brought me under difficulties and almost a quarrel with the ministry."[127] He also said, perhaps only partly in jest, that he might yet have to ask Jefferson to claim him as an American citizen.

Lafayette was attempting to frame a Declaration of Rights. It was based largely on George Mason's Virginia Declaration of Rights, which Jefferson had circulated in France. The marquis sought his American friend's help with his composition. Jefferson suggested that Lafayette remove from the list of man's inalienable rights "property" and "the care of his honor."[128] More aware of popular attitudes than the nobleman, Jefferson saw that both references would have for many Frenchmen an irritating connotation of aristocracy.

The concluding article of Lafayette's draft, asserting the right of successive generations "to examine and, if necessary, to modify the form of government"[129] seemed to echo Jefferson's Declaration of Independence. At this distance, in view of the close association of Enlightenment figures from France and the United States, it is difficult to say who influenced whom. It must have been difficult even in their own generation. Distinguished historians have cited Jefferson's letter[130] of September 6, 1789, to James Madison as an example of radically original thought, yet there is strong evidence that its central idea was simply borrowed from an Englishman and amplified by Jefferson. The American minister wrote:

The question whether one generation of men has a right to bind another, seems never to have been started either on this or our side of the water. Yet it is a question of such consequences as not only to merit decision, but place also, among the fundamental principles of every government. The course of reflection in which we are immersed here on the elementary principles of society has presented this question to my mind; and that no such obligation can be so transmitted I think very capable of proof.—I set out on this ground, which I suppose to be self evident, *'that the earth belongs in usufruct to the living'*: that the dead have neither powers nor rights over it. . . .

What is true of every member of the society individually, is true of them all collectively, since the rights of the whole can be no more than the sum of the rights of the individuals. . . .

On similar ground it may be proved that no society can make a perpetual constitution, or even a perpetual law. The earth belongs always to the living generation. They may manage it then, and what proceeds from it, as they please, during their usufruct. . . .

This principle that the earth belongs to the living, and not to the dead, is of very extensive application and consequences, in every country, and most especially in France.

But Jefferson was not thinking ultimately of France. He told Madison:

> Turn this subject in your mind, my dear sir, and particularly as to the power of contracting debts; and develop it with that perspicuity and cogent logic so peculiarly yours. Your station in the councils of our country gives you an opportunity of producing it to public consideration, of forcing it into discussion. At first blush it may be rallied, as a theoretical speculation: but examination will prove it to be solid and salutary. It would furnish matter for a fine preamble to our first law for appropriating the public revenue; and it will exclude at the threshold of our new government the contagious and ruinous errors of this quarter of the globe, which have armed despots with means, not sanctioned by nature, for binding in chains their fellow men.

Biographers have undoubtedly been right in calling the idea radical, but they seem to have erred in calling it original. Jefferson wrote from his sickbed, apparently following one of his severe migraines. The physician in attendance was Dr. Richard Gemm, a tall Englishman erect in body and rigid in doctrine. Gemm's republican philosophy and association with French reformers had made him suspect in official circles in Paris.[131] The doctor had left with Jefferson a briefly stated proposition which quite obviously was the basis for the diplomat's letter to Madison. Gemm had written:

> That one generation of men in civil society have no right to make acts to bind another, is a truth that cannot be contested. The earth and all things whatever can only be conceived to belong to the living. The dead and those who are unborn can have no rights of property.[132]

There is no reason whatever to suppose that Jefferson was trying to advance the idea as his own peculiar invention. Indeed, Gemm's proposition apparently was enclosed with the letter to Madison.

It has been suggested that Lafayette, rather than Madison, was the principal person for whom Jefferson's elaboration of the proposition was intended.[133] Certainly there was no reason for Jefferson to include for Madison's benefit the specific suggestions for application in France which comprised a large part of the message. Confined to his bed, Jefferson was unable to take part in deliberations in which his advice was sought. Forced to rely on the written word, he had to be especially discreet because of his diplomatic position. He might have communicated with Lafayette through a letter addressed to Madison.

Whatever the reasons behind Jefferson's letter at the time, the idea that the earth belonged to the living was part of the intellectual baggage that he brought back from France. Back in the United States he did not press for specific radical reforms because of this idea, but he did not discard it. As a tenet of political philosophy it differed greatly from Edmund Burke's conserve assumption that society is a compact among the dead, the living, and the unborn.

The Declaration of Rights adopted by the National Assembly about six weeks later adheres closely to American models, especially the work of Mason and Jefferson. To Madison, Jefferson wrote: "It is impossible to desire better dispositions towards us than prevail in this assembly. Our proceedings have been viewed as a model for them on every occasion; and though in the heat of debate men are generally disposed to contradict every authority urged by their opponents, ours has been treated like that of the Bible, open to explanation but not to question."[134] If the American experience was the Frenchmen's Bible, Jefferson sat among them as prophet, apostle, and exegete.

Diplomatic considerations whispered a need for restraint, but enthusiasm urged him to accept the triple role. Lafayette, seeking to keep together the two factions of the Patriot Party, the constitutional royalists and the republicans, asked Jefferson to invite leaders of both groups to his home in an effort to prevent civil war: "I beg for liberty's sake you will break every engagement to give us a dinner tomorrow, Wednesday. We shall be some members of the National Assembly—eight of us whom I want to coalize as being the only means to prevent a total dissolution. . . . Those gentlemen wish to consult you and me. . . . I depend on you to receive us."[135] Jefferson gave the dinner. His guests included Jean-Joseph Mounier, chief of the constitutional monarchists. Mounier respected the American as one "known for his lights and virtues, who had at the same time the experiences and the theory of institutions proper for the maintenance of liberty."[136]

Supper was early. As Jefferson later remembered, it was about four o'clock when, "the cloth being removed, and wine set on the table, after the American manner, the Marquis introduced the objects of the conference, by summarily reminding them of the state of things in the Assembly, the course which the principles of the Constitution were taking, and the inevitable result, unless checked by more concord among the Patriots themselves."[137] The discussions "continued till ten o'clock in the evening, during which time I was a silent witness to a coolness and candor of argument unusual in the conflicts of political opinion, to a logical reasoning and chaste eloquence disfigured by no gaudy tinsel of rhetoric or declamation, and truly worthy of being placed in parallel with the finest dialogues of antiquity, as handed to us by Xenophon, by Plato, and Cicero."[138] When Jefferson was enthusiastic he was not given to understatement. Doubtless, portions of the discussion were brilliant. It is difficult to believe that he did not deceive himself when he recalled that he sat silent through six hours of scintillating conversation on matters that greatly interested him. Whatever Jefferson's role, Lafayette, Mounier, and he himself all seem to have been convinced that it was important.

However elated Jefferson may have been that evening, he was in a chastened mood the next morning: "Duties of exculpation were now incumbent on me. I waited on Count Montmorin the next morning, and explained to him, with truth and candor, how it had happened that my house had been made the scene of conferences of such a character."[139] Jefferson, as we have seen, respected the Foreign Minister's ability and character and cherished his good opinion for personal as well as official reasons. It was not easy to reveal these possible indiscretions to such a man. But the confession brought no frowns to Montmorin's honest face. "I already knew everything which had passed," he said. "I earnestly wish you would habitually assist at such conferences. I am sure you should be useful in moderating the warmer spirits and promoting a wholesome and practical reformation only."[140]

The French diplomat's startling candor drove the American into diplomatic jargon. Or perhaps Jefferson, having already planned his little speech, simply went ahead with it. "I know too well the duties I owe to the King, to the nation, and to my own country," he said, "to take any part in councils concerning their internal government. I shall persevere, with care, in the character of a neutral and passive spectator, with wishes only, and very sincere ones, that those measures might prevail which would be for the greatest good of the nation."[141]

He was still hopeful that the revolution would be peaceful but he was well aware that violence was boiling beneath the crust of custom. There had already been eruptions. On July 14 Jefferson had been visiting with his good friend Mme. de Corny when her husband returned with the news that he had been ordered to take possession of the arms at the Hôtel des Invalides but the people had seized them. He then had gone with five others to the Bastille to demand the arms there. Before the mild-mannered de Corny could fully grasp what was happening, "the people rushed against the place, and almost in an instant were in possession of a fortification, defended by one hundred men, of infinite strength, which in other times had stood several regular sieges, and had never been taken.... They took all the arms, discharged the prisoners and such of the garrison as were not killed in the first moment of fury. [They] carried the Governor and the Lieutenant Governor to the Gréve (the place of public execution), cut off their heads, and sent them through the city in triumph to the Palais Royal."[142] At the same time, in another quarter of Paris, an official had been seized while in the performance of his duties and summarily beheaded.

Jefferson had had bars and bells placed on his windows. He had written to Montmorin: "My hotel having been lately robbed, for the third time, I take the liberty of uniting my wish with that of the inhabitants of this quarter that it might coincide with the arrangements of the Police to extend to us the protection of a guard.... Other houses in the neighborhood have been robbed as well as mine."[143]

With the announcement of the King's dismissal of Necker and his ministry and the substitution of men "noted for the Turkish despotism of their characters,"[144] popular anxiety increased. As a precaution, the government sent about a hundred German cavalry to the Place Louis XV and backed them with about two hundred Swiss. "This drew people to the spot, who thus accidentally found themselves in front of the troops, merely at first as spectators; but, as their members increased, their indignation rose. They retired a few steps and posted themselves on and behind large piles of stones, large and small, collected in that place"[145] for the building of a bridge. By coincidence, Jefferson in his carriage passed at that moment through the lane formed by the stern-visaged troops on one side and the angry-faced people on the other. Hardly had his carriage emerged from between the hostile files when the people showered the troops with stones. Jefferson did not linger as the cavalry charged while the Swiss remained immobile. A little later he learned that the horsemen had retreated toward Versailles. That night angry mobs of men and women, armed with guns and bludgeons, and almost any tools that could be used as weapons, roamed the geometrically ordered streets of the City of Light.

Jefferson had warned Jay that civil war might be precipitated in France by any of several factors—the shortage of bread, the financial failure of the government, the anticipated flight of Louis XVI from his capital. But he believed that violence on a national scale might yet be averted. He abhorred the spirit and judgment of those who held that the King was "wilfully criminal" and should be executed. Jefferson later said that he had his own idea of what to do: "I should have shut up the Queen in a convent, putting harm out of her power, and placed the King in his station, investing him with limited powers, which, I verily believed, he would have honestly exercised, according to the measure of his understanding."[146]

Though a romantic and sensitive to feminine beauty, Jefferson did not see the Queen in a luminous cloud of sentiment as did Burke, who wrote: "Surely never lighted on this orb, which she hardly seemed to touch, a more delightful vision. . . . I thought ten thousand swords must have leaped from their scabbards to avenge even a look that threatened her with insult."[147] Jefferson wrote: "The King was now become a passive machine in the hands of the National Assembly, and had he been left to himself, he would have willingly acquiesced in whatever they should devise as best for the nation. A wise constitution would have been formed, hereditary in his line, himself placed at its head, with powers so large as to enable him to do all the good of his station, and so limited as to restrain him from its abuse. This he would have faithfully administered, and more than this, I do not believe, he ever wished. But he had a Queen of absolute sway over his weak mind and timid virtue, and of a character the reverse of his in all points. This angel, as gaudily painted in the rhapsodies of Burke, with some smartness of fancy, but no sound sense, was proud, disdainful of restraint, indignant at all obstacles to her will, eager in the pursuit of pleasure, and firm enough to hold to her desires, or perish in their wreck. . . . I have ever believed that, had there been no Queen, there would have been no revolution."[148]

But, if there must be a great national bloodletting in France, Jefferson would not see it. His request for leave had been granted at long last. He blamed no one for the delay, realizing that the transformation from a confederation to a federal union had temporarily paralyzed certain operations or, as he himself more picturesquely said, "the metamorphosis through which our government was then passing from its chrysalid to its organic form suspended its action in a great degree."[149]

The ever-helpful Trumbull had secured for Jefferson, his daughters, and his servants a passage directly to Virginia. The *Clermont*, a merchant vessel of 230 tons, was bound for Norfolk under Captain Nathaniel Colley, a resident of that city. For the fee of 120 guineas, the three Jeffersons, James and Sally Heming, and Petit had the ship entirely to themselves except for officers and crew.[150]

Patsy and Polly would not be returning to France; it was not the safest place now for young ladies. Besides, according to family tradition, Jefferson was fearful of keeping either girl in a convent school since one of them had recently expressed the desire to become a nun.[151] But Jefferson himself might return. After, he had not resigned, only obtained a leave of absence. Still he must have thought return improbable. Short, who would be in charge of the diplomatic offices during his superior's absence, bet Jefferson a beaver hat that he would be back.[152] Under the circumstances of uncertainty the returning minister left a large part of his furnishings in Paris. Nevertheless, there was much baggage to take with him and there were many things to ship, ranging from wines for Jay and Washington and books for Franklin and Madison to eight Houdon busts of John Paul Jones intended for scattered destinations.

There was an Houdon bust of Jefferson himself, one of the great Frenchman's masterpieces. To this work of art, more than to anything else, we are indebted for a clear idea of how Jefferson looked at the time of his departure from France. There are also, of course, the small oil portraits by Trumbull (he had to paint one for Angela Church in addition to the one for Maria Cosway). If their hues may be relied upon, Paris nightlife had not drained the apple-cheeked look that Jefferson had brought from the Virginia countryside. But the Houdon bust, the third-dimensional creation of one of the most renowned portraitists in history, tells us much more. The face is one of the strongest that Houdon ever sculpted. In the jutting chin and muscular jaws, even in the penetrating gaze of the large, deep-set eyes, there is an air of resolution. And there is a great sense of vitality; in the bristling brows; the eager, forward set of the head; the somewhat disciplined compression of a generous and apparently mobile mouth. H. H. Arnason, the distinguished art historian, says of the sculptured likeness, "It is at once a face of decision, of sensitivity, and the face of an aristocrat."[153]

Arnason is right, but there is something more in the face—something not apparent in earlier portraits but obvious in later ones, though never again quite so well expressed. The face of the 46-year-old Jefferson leaving France in 1789 was that of a man who had traded precocity for wisdom. Somehow, in a new social and intellectual milieu, he had discovered himself and had come to terms with what he had found. There is no science of physiognomy that can accurately read all these things in a face, but a discerning artist who is a good friend of the subject may read them in innumerable expressions and gestures and tones of voice and translate them into a work of art. The letters written by Jefferson before and after arriving in France, taken in the aggregate, tell in a thousand nuances the same tale of maturation.

When Jefferson embarked at Havre on October 7, 1789, after a delay of ten days occasioned by equinoctial gales and saw the coast of France recede from sight, probably forever, his thoughts must have been similar to those he expressed in his autobiography:

"A more benevolent people I have never known, nor greater warmth and devotedness in their select friendships. Their kindness and accommodation to strangers is unparalleled, and the hospitality of Paris is beyond anything I had conceived to be practicable in a large city. Their eminence, too, in science, the communicative dispositions of their scientific men, the politeness of the general manners, the ease and vivacity of their conversation, give a charm to their society, to be found nowhere else. In a comparison of this with other countries, we have the proof of primacy which was given to Themistocles after the battle of Salamis. Every general voted to himself the first reward of valor, and the second to Themistocles. So, ask the travelled inhabitant of any nation, in what country on earth would you rather live?—Certainly, in my own, where are all my friends, my relations, and the earliest and sweetest affections and recollections of my life. Which would be your second choice? France."[154]

Jefferson had found a second home. More important, he had found himself.

XV

STRUGGLE OF TITANS

AFTER STORMS that delayed sailing from Cowes, the *Clermont* had crossed the Atlantic to Norfolk within twenty-six days, less than half the anticipated time. The sun shone so brightly on smooth seas that even Jefferson, after five or six days of seasickness, rejoiced in a sense of well-being. He delighted in being aboard a vessel "remarkably swift, strong, stiff as a church" and captained by "a bold but judicious seaman." Some days later he pronounced the voyage "prosperous and pleasing beyond what was possible to be hoped."[1] Fate was saving its jolts for the very end.

They found the American coast guarded by a wall of fog. They could not even tell whether a pilot was waiting for them. "After beating about for three days," Captain Colley "determined to run in at a venture without having seen the capes."[2] At ten o'clock at night, afraid he was running aground, he cast anchor. "The wind rose, the vessel drifted down, dragging her anchors one or more miles." But the *Clermont* had passed the capes and was now in Chesapeake Bay. Jefferson and the others aboard could not then know that ships captained by less venturesome sailors had been blown off the coast and would be forced to remain at sea three or four weeks longer. The *Clermont* still had to beat up against a head wind that ripped away its topsails. Hardly had passengers and crew recovered from this shock when an onrushing brig suddenly loomed before them. The *Clermont*'s helmsman barely averted a collision.[3]

Attaining the shelter of Lynnhaven Inlet and then debarking in Norfolk in the forenoon of November 25, Jefferson must have rejoiced that his tribulations were over. But his relief was premature. Two hours after his party left the ship it was afire. All of their baggage, including Jefferson's public accounts which he would entrust to no hand but his own, was still aboard. The ship was soon reduced to a hull and the crew had begun scuttling it as the only means of controlling the flames when suddenly the yellow tongues began withdrawing. The hull was saved. Jefferson's hopes rose with the revelation that the walls of the state rooms "alone of all the internal partitions [had] escaped burning." Could the baggage have been saved? The thick walls of the trunks had "saved their contents from the excessive heat." But the escape was a wonder. "The powder in a musket in [the same] room was silently consumed."[4]

After experiencing storm and smoke and fog, Jefferson was greeted by several strangers come out of the mist to hail him by an unaccustomed title. One wonders if the mind of this devotee of Shakespeare turned back to the first scene of *Macbeth*. In their turn, his callers must have been moved to exclaim like the three witches: "Good sir, why do you start and seem to fear things that do sound so fair?" For the strangers were Norfolk's Mayor Robert Taylor and some aldermen and they welcomed Jefferson as Secretary of State. The returning diplomat did not even know what a Secretary of State was but he had determined to revert to private life as soon as possible and the title had an ominous ring.

When he learned the significance of the designation, it proved an even greater shock than the burning of the vessel on which he had come. In the new administration headed by George Washington as first President under the new Constitution, the most prestigious subordinate position would be Secretary of State. The office would unite the duties of chief administrative assistant in domestic matters with all the administrative and diplomatic responsibilities of John Jay's former job as Secretary of Foreign Affairs.[5]

The formal address delivered by the mayor praised Jefferson highly, returned "our unfeigned thanks for the many eminent services you have rendered the State during your residence abroad," and expressed the hope that he might be "as happy in the important station" he was "now called to by a grateful country" as he had "been successful in (his) negotiations."[6]

Jefferson had returned to a Norfolk very different from the town of flourishing docks and numerous neat brick buildings that at the start of the Revolution had comprised the largest city in Virginia. The former town had been burned as "a nest of tories." As the former owners of lots where warehouses and stores had stood often lacked the means to rebuild, the properties had been leased for seven years to entrepreneurs who were unwilling to erect expensive structures on such a short-term basis. Wooden shacks, therefore, replaced the more substantial buildings.[7]

Jefferson, in his reply to the mayor, seized upon the essential fact—that, however inelegant the town's appearance, it *was* rebuilding. "I am happy," he said, "that circumstances have led my arrival to a place which I had seen before indeed in greater splendor, but which I now see rising like a Phoenix out of its ashes to that importance to which the laws of nature destine it. Peculiarly favored by nature in situation and climate, fostered by our special government, and protected by that general one to which we have so wisely confided our greater concerns, we have ever ground to hope the future welfare of your city. That your particular happiness, gentlemen, may be mingled in the general stream of its prosperity is my sincere prayer. As for my mite of service, it has not been worthy the notice you so kindly take of it."[8]

In Jefferson's personal situation, there was evidence of Norfolk's growth and overcrowding. He and his party were able to stay at Lindsay's Hotel only thanks to some gentlemen who vacated their rooms as a courtesy to the distinguished visitor.[9]

A few days later Jefferson and his entourage were ferried across Hampton Roads to the city of Hampton. They drove through Williamsburg, a place filled with memories of the days when he had marveled at the erudition of Wythe and Short, the sophistication of Governor Fauquier and his own Randolph cousins. Five years in Europe had taught him that the Virginians he had known would not have been dwarfed by the stage of Europe. But he could have reflected that now he had surpassed all of them in erudition and perhaps in sophistication too. Whether such thoughts occurred to him we shall never know; it was not the sort of thing that he would put into writing.

By easy stages, spending evenings at the hearthsides of friends, Jefferson and his companions proceeded to Richmond. December of 1789 was an interesting time to be in the capital. Both houses of the General Assembly were in session and there was therefore the opportunity of renewing acquaintances with people from all over Virginia. A committee from each chamber waited upon him with an address of welcome and commendation. The memory of the bitterest day in his public life, when the legislature had launched an investigation of his administration as Governor, must have provoked conflicting emotions, sweetening the present moment by contrast with the past but also tempering present delight with reflections on the fickleness of public favor.

There were reasons, however, for him to be pleased with his state's legislators. The Virginia House of Delegates had ratified amendments to comply with the provisos laid down by the State Convention ratifying the Constitution, and the Senate seemed certain to follow suit.

Most of the credit for this success was due to Madison. Jefferson's diminutive friend had grown greatly in public stature during the American minister's years abroad. In informal discussions, in committee meetings, and in plenary sessions in Philadelphia in 1787 he had pleaded so knowledgeably and logically for the Virginia Plan of federal government that posterity would remember him as "the Father of the Constitution." Virginia's Edmund Randolph and George Mason had refrained from signing the document adopted. Striving for ratification in convention back in Virginia, Madison had persuaded Randolph to support ratification after all, but had failed to win over Mason who now disgustedly called Randolph "Young Benedict [Arnold]." Furthermore Madison had faced the wrathful oratory of Patrick Henry who had thundered his opposition in the midst of a severe storm that shook the meeting hall, so that the very elements had seemed to reverberate to his Jovian roar. Madison, standing so low that some of the delegates could not see him above the heads of their colleagues and referring to notes concealed in the hat that he held before him, had employed soft spoken reasonableness so effectively that the Federationists had defeated the Antis led by Henry. Madison had promised that if the Constitution went into effect he would work as hard for the addition of a bill of rights as he had for ratification. He was the author of the amendments for the protection of individual rights that had already passed in Virginia's lower house and were headed for passage in the upper.

Jefferson reported these matters in a letter to Short, but added: "Anti-federalism is not yet dead in this country. The gentlemen who opposed retain a good deal of malevolence towards the new government. Henry is its avowed foe. He stands higher in public estimation than he ever did, yet he was so often in the minority in the present Assembly that he has quitted it, never more to return unless an opportunity offers to overturn the new Constitution."[10]

Concerning at least one thing connected with the government of the Commonwealth, Jefferson was confident. He observed with great satisfaction the construction of the State Capitol on one of Richmond's seven hills. He wrote Short that it would "be worthy of being exhibited alongside the most celebrated remains of antiquity."[11] Jefferson's enthusiasm, whenever existent, was always evident. But in this instance it was even greater than most people suspected. They thought that he rejoiced in securing for his native Commonwealth a copy of one of the most impressive Roman monuments, little suspecting that his was the secret pride of creation. Not until 1915 was there a sufficient collation and analysis of evidence to justify a prominent architectural historian,

Fiske Kimball, in writing: "Indeed we now see clearly that Jefferson's insistence on the exactness with which he had followed the Maison Carée was largely to prevent further tampering with his design, and that the design really departed from its model in almost every way—in dimensions, in proportion, in ordonnance, and in detail."[12] The resulting "Palladianized Roman" structure would be hailed as "the first monument of the classical revival in America."[13]

For Jefferson there was the thrill of pioneering, albeit, as he usually preferred, within a traditional framework. He had not yet produced the work that would be cited in 1976 by a jury of forty-six distinguished practitioners, historians, and critics in the field as "the proudest achievement of American architecture over the past 200 years."[14] But he must have been excited by the knowledge that for the first time he had produced something "not merely Palladian." He was moving into a tasteful eclecticism that many would eventually call "Jeffersonian."

After leaving Richmond, Jefferson stopped at Eppington to visit his in-laws. Polly must have had an emotional reunion with her Aunt Eppes. Here Jefferson learned news of the family and close friends that must have whetted his appetite for Monticello.

Breaking in on pleasant anticipations was a letter, delivered at Eppington, from George Washington. Before he broke the seal, Jefferson knew of course that it was a formal request that he accept the post of Secretary of State. The domestic duties of the office, he learned, would include administration of all business in that category except war and finance. Jefferson was confident in foreign policy, but he thought the domestic burden would be formidable. He told Washington so in a letter that he wrote on December 15 from the Skipwith home, another stop on the way to Monticello. But he did not flatly refuse to serve: "It is not for an individual to choose his post. . . you are to marshal us as may be best for the public good."[15]

His little party arrived home on December 23. A letter to his overseer had announced his approach and the word had spread from farm to farm among his plantations that the master was due. The servants and field hands requested, and were granted, a holiday. Long before he arrived, they had assembled at Monticello. As time passed, they impatiently walked down the mountain for an earlier meeting. When Jefferson's carriage-and-four appeared, a shout went up from men, women, and children. Laughing and crying, they thronged the carriage. Some unhitched the horses and vied with each other for places along the shafts. Black faces glistened with effort even in the December air and the vehicle rolled onward and upward to the accompaniment of delighted whoops.[16] The moment must have been an emotional one for the man whose earliest recollection was of loving black arms lifting him up for a journey.

Then came Monticello's familiar roof, well known to his mind's eye long before it materialized for others to see. Next the compact elegance of the entire house, capping the mountain with the red bricks made from its own red earth. The carriage stopped at the foot of the lawn in front of the house.

As Patsy and Polly descended, attention shifted from their father to them. They had changed more dramatically than he in the years of absence. The crowd parted like the Red Sea to let them pass. There were gasps of admiration for Polly, an animated eleven-year-old, and Patsy, a young woman of seventeen, tall like her father and more stately than graceful.

But Jefferson himself was not permitted to walk to the door. Once again, as in his infancy, he was lifted up by strong black arms, this time a multitude of them, and carried to the house. Laughing and weeping slaves kissed his hands and feet.[17]

The return to Monticello and its innumerable associations must have intensified the sentiments which Jefferson had communicated to Madison before leaving France: "You know the circumstances which led me from retirement, step by step, and from one nomination to another, up to the present. My object is to return to the same retirement. Whenever, therefore, I quit the present, it will not be to engage in any other office, and most especially any one which would require a constant residence from home."[18]

This feeling was reinforced when he looked through the multipaned windows, so beautifully proportioned to his own design, to his beloved mountains, each smooth as a whale's back rising grandly from the morning mists. It was strengthened too by the delight in the faces of his servants. And it was further augmented when some of his Albemarle County neighbors addressed him in a memorial congratulating him on twenty years of consistently valuable public service and themselves on having launched him on that career by electing him to the House of Burgesses. Among the signers were many longtime residents of the county and at least one newcomer, James Monroe.[19] This promising protégé would be a welcome addition to the Albemarle circle of friends.

To the memorial from his neighbors Jefferson replied:

We have been fellow-laborers and fellow-sufferers, and heaven has rewarded us with a happy issue from our struggles. It rests now with ourselves to enjoy in peace and concord the blessings of self-government so long denied to mankind: to show by example the sufficiency of human reason for the care of human affairs and that the will of the majority, the natural law of every society, is the only sure guardian of the rights of man. Perhaps even this may sometimes err but its errors are honest, solitary and shortlived. Let us then, my dear friends, for ever bow down to the general reason of society. We are safe with that, even in its deviations, for it soon returns again to the right way. These are lessons we have learned together. We have prospered in their practice, and the liberality with which you are pleased to approve my attachment to the general rights of mankind assures me we are still together in these its kindred sentiments.[20]

Implicit in the next paragraph was an admission that he probably would not remain indefinitely in retirement from public life:

Wherever I may be stationed by the will of my country it will be my delight to see, in the general tide of happiness, that yours too flows on in just place and measure. That it may flow through all time, gathering strength as it goes, and spreading the happy influence of reason and liberty over the face of the earth, is my fervent prayer to heaven.

Madison visited at Monticello soon after Jefferson's return and added his persuasive voice to Washington's urgency. Jefferson feared that the new post would involve more domestic than foreign affairs. Madison, who by now was closely associated with Washington, assured Jefferson that the case would be otherwise. He also wrote

Washington about Jefferson's doubts.[21]

Again Washington wrote his chosen appointee: "I consider the successful administration of the general government as an object of almost infinite consequence to the present and future happiness of the citizens of the United States. I consider the office of Secretary for the Department of State as *very* important on many accounts, and I know of no person who, in my judgement, could better execute the duties of it than yourself."[22]

The last statement was undoubtedly true. Foreign affairs would be the most important work of the office. In this field the only Americans with significant experience except Jefferson were Franklin, whose health was bad; Adams, who was newly elected Vice President; and John Jay, who was to be named Chief Justice.

From New York, Madison wrote Jefferson of the "universal anxiety" with which his decision was awaited.[23] The master of Monticello sent Washington his acceptance.

While Jefferson was wrestling with the offer of the secretaryship and voicing concern over the domestic responsibilities associated with it, domestic matters of much narrower scope were also occupying his mind. Patsy was betrothed to her cousin Thomas Mann Randolph, Jr. Just when the tall, dark, twenty-one-year-old[24] man began his courtship is not known. He had been a student at Edinburgh when Patsy and her father were living in Paris. Family tradition says that he visited her at that time. Research by William H. Gaines, Jr. suggests otherwise.[25] In any event, Randolph was back in Virginia when the Jeffersons returned, and he became a frequent visitor.

Even if personal contacts had been few, he would have been far from a stranger in family-conscious Virginia. His father had been the ward of Peter Jefferson, and also one of Thomas Jefferson's playmates at Tuckahoe. Despite his occasional complaints about the aristocracy, the squire of Monticello favored wise inbreeding in his family as well as among his horses. Besides, young Randolph had varied intellectual interests and was an intelligent conversationalist.[26] Jefferson knew little or nothing of the suitor's temperament, but may have assumed that the son had his father's genial disposition. Accordingly, Jefferson wrote to the sire: "The marriage of your son with my daughter cannot be more pleasing to you than to me. Besides the worth which I discover in him, I am happy that the bond of friendship between us, as old as ourselves, should be drawn closer and closer to the day of our death."[27] To friends in Europe he sent word that the groom was a young man who in family, fortune, and personal worth was all that he could desire for his daughter.

There is every reason to believe that Jefferson was completely sincere in all these expressions of satisfaction. At the same time, we may be sure that on February 23 when the tall, reddish-haired girl who looked so much like him took the vows of marriage, the moment was a stressful one for so possessive a father.

Colonel Randolph deeded to his son 950 acres in Henrico County and forty slaves. Jefferson deeded to Patsy and her heirs a thousand acres in Bedford County, six families of slaves, and some livestock.[28]

Jefferson's generous gifts to his daughter were not evidence of prosperity. The pay of United States ministers in foreign capitals was too small to meet the expenses even of the frugal Adamses; it was far too small for the luxury-loving Virginian. His lands were his principal source of income and his eye quickly told him that they were poorer than when he had left them for public duties an ocean away. He sought a loan from Amsterdam bankers with whom he had conducted official business and through Richmond agents made arrangements with his English creditors to pay off over a period of seven years the debts inherited with, or related to, his father-in-law's estate.[29] In Paris he had lain awake nights worrying about debts. He knew now that a few bad seasons could necessitate the selling of Monticello, could even push him to the edge of bankruptcy.

Patsy, her husband, and her sister remained at Monticello on March 1 when Jefferson set out in the phaeton on the journey to New York City and his new duties. He stopped in Richmond for a week, completing arrangements with his English creditors and bolstering republican faith with his firsthand observations of European monarchies. From there he went to Alexandria, where he received an official welcome similar to the one in Norfolk and made a gracious reply. The warm reception was followed that night by a cold snow eighteen inches deep. Leaving his phaeton to be sent by water, a mode of travel he never favored for himself, he chose to "bump it myself in the stage to my journey's end."[30]

During a stopover in Philadelphia he called on Franklin, now bedridden and near death. The wasting of the flesh had transformed the familiar plump-cheeked face, at once grandfatherly and cherubic, into a visage lank and spectral, an impression strengthened by the long, straggling wisps of white hair. But head and heart were still very much alive. Jefferson recorded: "My recent return from a country in which he had left so many friends, and the perilous convulsions to which they had been exposed, revived all his anxieties to know what port they had taken, what had been their course, and what their fate. He went over all in succession with a rapidity and animation almost too much for his strength."[31]

After the older man's curiosity was satisfied there was a pause, and his friend then told him that he was glad to hear Franklin was writing his autobiography. The elder statesman replied, "I will give you a sample of what I shall leave." He then "directed his little grandson (William Bache), who was standing by the bedside, to hand him a paper from the table, to which he pointed." Franklin passed the sheaf of papers to Jefferson, telling him to take it and read it at his leisure. The Virginian glanced at the pages and promised to be careful to return them. "No, keep it," Franklin instructed. Not certain of the sick man's meaning, Jefferson again glanced at the manuscript, folded it for his pocket, and said, "I will certainly return it." Once again, Franklin insisted, "No, keep it."

Jefferson would remember the circumstances vividly many years later. Associated with them would be a mystery never completely resolved.[32] But, quite apart from these facts, the moment was a solemn one. Franklin was a great man and had been a good friend. Jefferson surely realized that he probably would never see him again.

Upon reaching New York City on Sunday, March 21, Jefferson called upon another great man—George Washington. It was about one o'clock when the President, just returned from church, received his fellow Virginian in the executive residence on Broadway.[33] Washington's monumental dignity was not dependent on uniforms. In mufti he looked "like an uncrowned king." The half a decade since Jefferson had seen him had done more than deepen the horizontal lines in the old commander's brow; it had added to his greatness. After leading his country to a military victory that had made independence possible, he had presided over the convention that framed its constitution, and then had been called by unanimous electoral vote to the position of chief magistrate. As always, Jefferson felt an admiration bordering on veneration.

But this respect did not make the younger man at all reticent two days later about giving advice to the President. At that time the two discussed various problems of foreign policy administration and touched upon the possibility of negotiations with Spain to insure American navigational rights in the Mississippi. Then, and in the next few days, Jefferson reverted to a question that had vexed him since his earliest experiences as an envoy in Europe and advocated federal action to free Americans enslaved by the Barbary pirates. He had already pointed out the locations that he preferred for consulates. He now pushed the unusual proposal that, of United States diplomats abroad, only the representative to Versailles be given ministerial rank. Elsewhere American ministers would definitely be at the foot of the table, and he thought it better to have a chargé d'affaires respected in that modest category than a minister snubbed in a more elevated one. The President was inclined to disagree on this point; he had not abandoned hope that an American minister would be well received in England.

The President also had a practical political reason for avoiding any suggestion that he did not wish the American representative at the Court of St. James's to have ministerial rank. Congress, which preferred the dignity of that designation, had before it a bill for "providing the means of intercourse between the United States and foreign nations." Involved in debate was whether determination of the rank of diplomatic representatives was the prerogative of the executive or the legislature. Jefferson advised Washington, as had Madison and Jay, that the Senate had only the power to accept or reject a Presidential nominee, not to prescribe the appointee's rank. But practical considerations hedged the President's exercise of this power. Congress must appropriate the money for maintenance of each diplomatic establishment and therefore must be placated. If the nation's legislators wanted the chief American diplomat in London to be designated "minister," then perhaps wisdom would dictate that they should be gratified.[34]

The President consulted his Secretary of State on matters other than foreign affairs. In these early days of the Administration, there were no formal cabinet sessions. Washington requested the opinions of each Secretary not only on that department head's specialty but also on other governmental matters, but these opinions were usually solicited individually.

Besides Jefferson, the department heads were Henry Knox, Secretary of War; Alexander Hamilton, Secretary of the Treasury; Edmund Randolph, Attorney General; and Samuel Osgood, Postmaster General. A fat-jowled major general of proven patriotism, Knox was knowledgeable chiefly in Washington's principal area of expertise—military affairs. His advice, therefore, seldom provided a point of view new to the President. Samuel Osgood was quite adequate for his post but his range of experience was narrow. The President's chief reliance within the executive department, therefore, was in Jefferson, Hamilton and Randolph.

Washington was well acquainted with Randolph. The handsome Roman features, together with the almost black eyes and exotically dark complexion that marked his descent from Powhatan and Pocahontas, combined with his mellow voice and urbane grace to make him a glamorous and fascinating figure. This personal attractiveness could make the thirty-six-year-old statesman a persuasive advocate for the Administration, but Washington was interested primarily in more solid qualities. He had known this appointee since the young man's boyhood. His brilliant record as a law student, his valuable work at the Constitutional Convention and in the fight for ratification, his leadership as Governor of Virginia, and his subsequent prominence at the bar were proof of his abilities. Washington had come to know him well through frequent personal association under conditions of stress when Randolph had served as his military aide. He had accepted the position of Attorney General in the fledgling government not in answer to the promptings of ambition (few would consider the job a step up for a former Governor of Virginia) but at considerable sacrifice of income and personal comfort.[35]

Even greater than Washington's reliance on Randolph, however, would be his dependence on Jefferson and Hamilton. Next to the President himself, they were the giants of the Administration. Devoted to the ideal of democratic government without factionalism, Washington did not suspect that these two magnetic Secretaries would become the focuses of political polarization. Of course, he could never foresee that popular opinion for generations would make them the simplistic symbols of opposing philosophies so that through history they would ride a seesaw of public esteem. Merrill Peterson makes a convincing case for his assertion that "Alexander Hamilton's place at any period on the imaginary scale that charts American reputations is always a good index to Jefferson's"[36] Because many Northerners were wont to blame secession on Jeffersonian democracy, the Virginian's reputation "merely survived" the Civil War whereas that of Hamilton, the strong advocate of centralized government, "was remade by it."[37] James A. Garfield said in Congress in 1865, "The fame of Jefferson is waning and the fame of Hamilton is waxing, in the estimation of the American people."[38] A little later, Massachusetts Senator Henry Cabot Lodge said of Jefferson and Hamilton, "We balance one man with his opposite and the health of the state depends on the see-saw."[39] The precipitate plunge of Hamilton's reputation in the Great Depression of the 1930's, an era ill-attuned to the bold exponent of capitalist domination, was matched by the sudden rise of Jefferson's prestige and the rapid advancement of plans for a national memorial to him comparable to those to Washington and Lincoln.

In Hamilton, Jefferson found a worthy antagonist. The New Yorker was contemptuous of the common man, and certainly he himself was far from ordinary. Almost everything about him was, for better or worse, superior, exotic, or at least different. Of course, there were those who thought his aristocratic sympathies incongruous. John Adams once described him as the "bastard son of a Scotch peddler." But Hamilton described himself as the son of a West India merchant "of respectable connection in Scotland." There was truth in both versions. His mother had been jailed for being "twice guilty of adultery" before going to live with James Hamilton XV, whom she did not marry. James, an unsuccessful merchant who had sprung from a branch of the ducal family of Hamilton, was the grandson of Sir Robert Pollock, "created Baronet of Nova Scotia by Queen Anne in 1702."[40]

Now thirty-four years old, Alexander Hamilton looked much more like the heir of Scottish lairds than the product of a disgraced union in a colonial outpost of the British West Indies. He was so slender and boyish in figure that people often mistakenly assumed him to be short, but his large head with its "reddish fair hair" pulled back into a queue would have graced a medallion and his carriage was military—like that of an officer walking past the cheerers of his victory. The ruddiness of his cheeks was emphasized by his fair complexion, which in turn was a foil for the "dark, almost violet, deep-set eyes." He might have seemed a little too much of a pretty boy, a fop in a Fragonard painting, except for the firmness of his jaw.[41]

It was appropriate that his mahogany desk in the Treasury Department should be decorated with the carved heads of young women,[42] like so many trophies boldly displayed. He was reputed to have made many conquests, among them his wife's sister, a noted beauty, that same Angelica Church who had fascinated Thomas Jefferson in Paris. She once wrote to Hamilton's wife, "I love him very much and, if you are as generous as the old Romans, you would lend him to me for a little while."[43] Rightly or wrongly, some thought she had borrowed him.

But Hamilton was no bon vivant. From early years he had been driven by an unresting ambition that had earned him a local reputation as a journalist and writer of amorous verse when he was still in his teens. His abilities had inspired fellow islanders to raise a fund to send him to America to obtain an education and make his fortune. At King's College, later Columbia University, he distinguished himself as a scholar.

The real acceleration of his career, however, began with the Revolution. At thirteen, hungering for glory, he had written, "I wish there was a war."[44] At twenty-two he was a lieutenant colonel on Washington's staff, but fretted rather than rejoiced at his reputation as chief penman at headquarters. Repeatedly he sought a separate command, once writing Washington, "I explained to you candidly my feelings in respect to military reputation and how much it was my object to act a conspicuous part in some enterprise that might perhaps raise my character as a soldier above mediocrity."[45] His request was granted in time for him to command with distinction at Yorktown.

Being the son-in-law of Major General Philip Schuyler, one of New York's richest aristocrats, helped him to launch a political career (by election to Congress in 1781) and a successful law practice. His own abilities, though, were his principal assets. As a delegate to the Annapolis Convention in 1786 he had written the report that prompted the Constitutional Convention of 1787. With Madison he had worked for ratification, writing at white-hot speed the campaign documents that comprised more than half of what became recognized as a classic of political philosophy, *The Federalist*. Against what appeared to be insuperable odds, he had won the fight for ratification by the New York convention.

Now Washington had named him Secretary of the Treasury. The President was convinced of both his genius and his courage. And not just the animal courage that displays itself in the excitement of physical conflict. The story was that Hamilton had stood firm but could not stop his knees from knocking when he first faced enemy fire. "What's the matter, Mr. Hamilton, are you afraid?" a more experienced soldier had taunted. "Yes, I'm afraid," Hamilton replied, "and if you were half as scared as I am you would run."

Washington's estimate was not extravagant. A few years later a very shrewd appraiser of men, the French statesman Talleyrand, would write, "I consider Napoleon, Fox, and Hamilton the three greatest men of our epoch, and if I were forced to decide among the three, I would give without hesitation the first place to Hamilton."[46]

Perhaps the prince was influenced in part by Hamilton's authoritarian philosophy. Jefferson had a hint of the Treasury Secretary's turn of mind in the early days of the Administration when they were still cooperating in friendly fashion. Hamilton asked the identity of three men whose portraits he saw in the Virginian's office. "The three greatest men the world has ever produced," Jefferson answered, "Bacon, Newton, and Locke." With equal finality Hamilton countered, "The greatest man in history was Julius

Caesar.''[47]

While Washington had intimate knowledge of Hamilton's virtues, he was also aware that his Treasury head could be difficult. When Hamilton was the general's aide, Washington complained on one occasion that the young man had needlessly kept him waiting. Hamilton resigned immediately and even haughtily rebuffed an overture from the commander-in-chief until General Schuyler and others persuaded him to be more reasonable.[48]

In Washington's eyes such temperamental qualities were more than offset by Hamilton's grasp of finance and government, his remarkable efficiency, and his appealing eloquence.

When Hamilton and Jefferson met in New York in 1790, apparently for the first time, Hamilton appears to have respected the Virginian's reputation. Jefferson probably knew Hamilton principally as a brilliant collaborator with Madison.

But Hamilton and Madison were no longer collaborators. The Secretary of the Treasury, when he had submitted to the Congress on January 14 his first Report on the Public Credit, had provoked a fight with members led by Madison. No one could deny the importance of the problem with which it dealt—the debt inherited from the Confederation—nor deny the pressing need for action. Indeed, there was no quarrel with Hamilton's approach to one-half of the problem, the foreign debt. He proposed that the foreign and domestic debts be funded at par, permitting creditors to exchange depreciated securities for newly issued interest-bearing bonds. The foreign debt, owed chiefly to the French and the Dutch, had been a great embarrassment to both Jefferson and Adams during their service in Europe. Thinking Americans realized that the new government would have little credibility if it did not deal efficiently with this problem. Opposition in the Congress was stirred by Hamilton's second proposition, that the Federal government assume, to the extent of $21,500,000, debts incurred by the several states during the Revolution.

While Hamilton's plans for dealing with the foreign debt met with general approbation, his proposal for funding the domestic debt stirred the bitter opposition of debtors and farmers who would be forced to sell their securities at great loss and to the tremendous profit of urban speculators.

Even more vigorous was the opposition of Southerners of virtually every class to Hamilton's proposal that the Federal government assume the states' war debts. Most of the Southern states were well launched upon plans for paying off their indebtedness. They were not willing to have the Federal government tax them to pay off the enormous debts of the New England states, which so far had done little to meet their financial obligations.

Madison and other far-seeing statesmen looked beyond the exigencies of the moment to what they regarded as a still more important reason for opposing assumption. They foresaw that such a policy would strengthen the central government and weaken the role of the states.

That development would be no accidental consequence of Hamilton's fiscal policies. Establishing public credit and gaining fiscal respectability for the United States were two of his major purposes. There was a third, the magnification of the federal government's power through the uniting of capitalist interests throughout the nation.

The Virginia delegation, led by Madison, spearheaded the opposition. On this issue

he broke with the Administration of his fellow Virginian; and Washington's prestige
and Hamilton's energetic advocacy were not quite enough to save the Treasury plan.
The vote in the House was 29 for, 31 against.

But the indefatigable Hamilton did not accept the decision as final. Jefferson foresaw
that the Treasury Secretary would press for the plan in another form. Nor was he so
strongly opposed to it as Madison and some other of his fellow Virginians. In a letter
to his son-in-law, Thomas Mann Randolph, he confided, "It appears to me one of those
questions which present great inconveniencies whichever way it is decided: so that
it offers only a choice of evils."[49] It was important, he thought, to settle the issue one
way or the other even though there was no satisfactory solution. It was one of two
vexing questions that were holding up the business of the Congress. The other was
the permanent location of a national capital. He conceived that the two matters might
be dealt with together and settled by compromise.

This opportunity was enhanced by the geographical alignment of contending forces.
The assumption scheme, as we have seen, was favored principally by the Northern states
and opposed by the Southern. The Northern states also wanted the national capital permanently located in Philadelphia, New York, or some other Northern city while
Southerners, especially Virginians, wanted it on the Potomac. The contest for the capital
was further complicated by the fact that Philadelphia and New York were working against
each other for designation as temporary capital, pending readying of a permanent one.
Pennsylvania delegates were approaching Southerners to offer votes for a permanent
capital on the Potomac in exchange for votes for a temporary capital for fifteen years
in Philadelphia. Perhaps, thought Jefferson, there could be another trade between North
and South, one involving Southern acceptance of a modified form of the assumption
proposal and of Philadelphia as temporary capital in exchange for location of the permanent capital on the Potomac. Failure to achieve such a compromise, Jefferson wrote
his son-in-law, would result in "an unqualified assumption and the permanent seat on
the Delaware."[50]

Jefferson therefore was in a receptive mood one day in June when, on the way
to the President's house, he was stopped in the street by Hamilton,[51] who was alive
with the excitement that animated him when he was pressing a new scheme. He not
only walked with the Virginian to his destination but detained him further. For half
an hour the tall, slightly shambling, long-limbed figure and the shorter, militarily erect
one strode back and forth in front of Washington's residence in earnest conversation.
Hamilton's excitement seemed not that of eagerness, but of desperation. He reviewed
the already familiar problems of economic disaster and legislative inaction, but added
a more chilling warning. He feared that some of the states, disgusted with the course
of events, were on the verge of seceding. Looking up into Jefferson's face, he argued,
"The members of the Administration ought to act in concert." Jefferson, he urged, by
getting his friends to support assumption, could save the Union. The Virginian's mind
must have flashed back to those heady days in Paris when his house had been the meeting
place for leaders of the two factions of Revolutionaries. He invited Hamilton to dine
with him and some friends the next day and discuss the problem as "reasonable men."

Jefferson said later that he himself talked little at the dinner.[52] This report probably
would have been received with incredulity by Pennsylvania's Senator William Maclay,
who had expressed vehement opposition when Jefferson approached him with a sug-

gestion that votes be traded on the capital and assumption measures. Maclay had reported that the Virginian, on another occasion, "spoke almost without ceasing." The senator gives us a description of Jefferson at that time, but the impression received by the guests may have been more favorable; Maclay was a backwoodsman who opposed Jefferson politically and lamented that the squire of Monticello "had been long enough abroad to catch the tone of European folly." He wrote: "Jefferson is a slender man. . . . his clothes seem too small for him, he sits in a lounging manner on one hip commonly, and with one of his shoulders elevated much above the other; his face has a sunny aspect; his whole figure has a loose, shackling air . . . . even his discourse partook of his personal demeanor. It was loose and rambling, and yet he scattered information wherever he went, and some even brilliant sentiments sparkled from him."[53]

However much or little Jefferson talked, he provided at the dinner party an ambience of amity suitable for trading.[54] And at his invitation the group included not only Virginia Congressmen Alexander White and Richard Bland Lee but also the foremost opponent of Hamilton's schemes, James Madison. Hamilton won from Madison and others an agreement that some of the Southerners, in the national interest, would switch their votes and support assumption. But, as the shrewd little Madison insisted, such a reversal would be so unpopular with their constituents that "some concomitant measure should be adopted to sweeten it a little to them." To nobody's great surprise, Hamilton offered to get his supporters to vote that the permanent capital of the United States be located on the Potomac River in Virginia. Both White and Lee agreed to vote for assumption. Jefferson said that White consented "with a revulsion of stomach almost convulsive."[55]

In July Congress made Philadelphia the temporary capital while determining that the permanent capital should be located in a ten square mile area on the Potomac. In the same month the House voted for assumption. On August 4 the funding provision became the law of the land. Obviously Jefferson's dinner party had done a great deal more than give Alexander White a bad case of indigestion.

Jefferson later described the settlement cynically: "The assumption was passed and 20 millions of stock divided among the favored states, and thrown in as a pabulum to the stock-jobbing herd. This added to the number of votaries to the Treasury, and made its chief the master of every vote in the legislature which might give to the government the direction suited to his political views."[56] At the time, though, Jefferson seems to have been pleased with both the compromise and his part in it. Virginia had gained the capital. And she had lost nothing on assumption; the details of the transaction were so delicately balanced that she would receive exactly the same sum that she paid out.

Jefferson's satisfaction was not shared by members of the Virginia General Assembly who, under the leadership of Patrick Henry, adopted on December 16 resolutions of opposition to assumption. The plan, they argued, would establish and tend to preserve a moneyed interest. It would make agriculture subordinate to commerce. Moreover, it would undermine the very federal system which it was supposed to strengthen. One of the milder observations in the resolutions drew the most vigorous response from Hamilton. The legislators had declared that they found no clause in the Constitution authorizing Congress to assume the debts of states. Hamilton wrote an associate: "This is the first symptom of a spirit which must either be killed, or will kill the Constitution."[57]

Though Jefferson had cooperated with the Treasury Secretary in passage of assumption, he was much closer in political philosophy to the protesting Virginians. Increasingly,
he saw a strict construction of the Constitution as one of the chief safeguards of the
federal system and of liberty itself. The matter seemed particularly vital because of
changes in the American climate of opinion during his absence in Europe. He later wrote:

> When I arrived at New York in 1790 to take a part in the Administration, being
> fresh from the French Revolution while in its first and pure stage, and consequently
> somewhat whetted up in my own republican principles, I found a state of things
> in the general society of the place which I could not have supposed possible. Be-
> ing a stranger there, I was feasted from table to table at large set dinners, the par-
> ties generally from twenty to thirty. The revolution I had left, and that we had
> just gone through in the recent change of our own government, being the common
> topics of conversation, I was astonished to find the general prevalence of mon-
> archical sentiments, insomuch that in maintaining those of republicanism, I had
> always the whole company on my hands, never scarcely finding among them a
> single co-advocate in that argument, unless some old member of Congress
> happened to be present.[58]

Jefferson took hope, however, from the character of Washington, writing to
Lafayette:

> I think, with others, that nations are to be governed according to their own
> interests; but I am convinced that it is their interest, in the long run, to be grateful,
> faithful to their engagements even in the worst of circumstances, and honorable
> and generous always. If I had not known that the head of our government was
> in these sentiments, and that his national and private ethics were the same, I would
> never have been where I am.[59]

Increasingly, though, Jefferson became convinced that Hamilton was a secret monarchist and, far from being neutral toward other nations, was an active partisan of England
in any matters of Anglo-French competition. Historians long thought that the Virginian
was a little obsessed in attributing monarchical views to the Treasury Secretary, but
recent revelations from Hamilton's correspondence have confirmed Jefferson's
suspicions.[60]

Amid troubling philosophical discords, the Secretary of State found some satisfaction in precise scientific considerations. The House of Representatives had asked him
for proposals for uniform weights and measures to apply everywhere within the United
States. Jefferson was eager to inaugurate a decimal system of weights and measures comparable to his decimal system of currency. Not even a month-long series of his sunrise-
to-sunset headaches kept him from the task. As he later reported, "What had been
ruminated in the day under a paroxysm of this most excruciating pain, was committed
to paper by candlelight, and then the calculations were made."[61]

Once again Jefferson turned his imagination to a task and brought forth something
quite different from what more conventional minds had anticipated. Realizing that
matter, subject to expansion and contraction, could not provide an invariable standard,

he fastened upon motion as a more reliable one. The motion of the earth on its axis, determining sidereal days that could be divided into seconds, would furnish a more stable basis. A pendulum could be set so that its oscillations would precisely mark the seconds, and each such movement would itself be a measure of length. He accepted the suggestion of a scientific-minded Philadelphian that a "uniform cylindrical rod of iron" be substituted for the more traditional pendulum, specifying that it be "of such length as, in latitude 45°, in the level of the ocean, and in a cellar, or other place, the temperature of which does not vary through the year, shall perform its vibrations in small and equal arcs in one second of mean time."[62] Jefferson was striving for truly universal standards, ones that would be adopted in virtually all the capitals of the world.

Although he was twenty-five years away from mathematical studies and many miles from a mathematical library, laboring under excruciating pain and resultant fatigue, he prepared an elaborate report marred only by an error in cubing the foot measure, causing a discrepancy of ten thousandths of a foot in one place and one millionth in another. These he corrected in an addendum.[63]

Jefferson's report won high praise from prominent Americans, among them Robert R. Livingston and President Ezra Stiles of Yale. The scholarly Yankee, who had been captivated when the Virginian visited him in Hartford before sailing for France, had corresponded ever since. Now he began teaching the new system and was moved to hope that the Secretary of State would succeed Washington as Chief Magistrate.[64] But politicians were not so enthusiastic as scholars. Before Jefferson's proposals ever emerged from the committee of one house, France had adopted its own metric system which was attracting an international following. Though Jefferson was disappointed, he did not regret his valiant labors. His plan was studied by Talleyrand and Condorcet and other prominent Europeans. The author's reputation for scholarship was enhanced throughout the Western world.

Another outlet for his scientific proclivities was afforded when "An Act to Promote the Progress of the Useful Arts" was approved in April 1790, creating the United States patent system, to be supervised by a Board of Arts consisting of the Secretaries of State and War and the Attorney General. Because of his knowledge and reputation, Jefferson was from the first the dominant figure in the triumvirate, adjudicating rival claims and rejecting inventions too imitative or useless to merit patenting. The principles laid down by Jefferson established precedents influential to this day in the operations of the Patent Office. Jefferson's philosophy admitted the value of exclusive patents and copyrights for limited periods as an incentive to invention and scholarship, but in the long run placed the public interest above individual property rights in ideas. He was eloquent in the presentation of his position.

> . . . If nature has made any one thing less susceptible than all others of exclusive property, it is the action of the thinking power called an idea, which an individual may exclusively possess as long as he keeps it to himself; but the moment it is divulged, it forces itself into the possession of everyone, and the receiver cannot dispossess himself of it. Its peculiar character, too, is that no one possesses the less, because every other possesses the whole of it. He who receives an idea from me, receives instruction himself without lessening mine; as he who lights his taper at mine, receives light without darkening me. That ideas should freely spread from

one to another over the globe, for the moral and mutual instruction of man, and improvement of his condition, seems to have been peculiarly and benevolently designed by nature.[65]

He concluded:

Inventions then cannot, in nature, be a subject of property. Society may give an exclusive right to the profits arising from them, as an encouragement to men to pursue ideas which may produce utility, but this may or may not be done according to the will and convenience of the society, without claim or complaint from anybody.

In the last days of 1790 Congress moved from New York to Philadelphia, and the Pennsylvania metropolis, in conformity with the compromise worked out at Jefferson's dinner table, became the temporary capital of the United States. If he couldn't be in Virginia the Philadelphia environment was as agreeable to Jefferson as any other in America. Here was the home of the American Philosophical Society and of such "ingenious speculators" as Charles Thomson and David Rittenhouse.

Actually Jefferson had been in Philadelphia since November 20 after spending two months at Monticello. He had need of the peaceful respite, for his residence in Philadelphia was at first Mrs. House's Boardinghouse, the home of most of the Virginia delegation in Congress and a much better center for conviviality and disputation than for concentrated study of governmental problems.[66] He had leased a four-story house[67] on High Street, unofficially known as Market Street, but the dwelling was still under construction. Desperate for privacy, on December 11 he took possession of two completed rooms, preferring the sound of carpenters driving nails to the more intrusive sound of politicians hammering home arguments. He increased his quarters room by room as the workmen progressed.

Confusion was magnified December 22 when he received twenty-seven drayloads of crates containing his furnishings shipped from France. Aside from carefully separating wine and books from other goods according to a true Gallic priority, his French packer had employed no discernible system. In one crate were such uncongenial tenants as Jefferson's files, a leather bag of tools, his bedroom commode, and a supply of macaroni and raisins.

Jefferson was not always neat; he habitually littered the floor with books and papers when he was researching and writing. But he had an orderly sense of categorization, so that he was disturbed at being unable to discover any logical order in the crating in addition to being vastly inconvenienced by having to unpack many cases to assemble the components of a single piece of furniture. For six weeks he tore open crates and delved into their mysterious interiors, doubtless impeding the goings and comings of carpenters and plasterers as much as they hindered his progress, turning his attention from statuettes and bolsters and stoves and nectarines to attend to the needs of departmental clerks. All this with the debris of unpacking mounting higher around the long legs of the hapless Secretary of State—ramparts of paper extensive enough to hide an army, hay and straw enough for its cavalry. And with every swing of the constantly opening doors, another blustery battalion of the fierce Philadelphia winter invaded the unfinished house.

During this same period of physical confusion, Jefferson was turning out knowledgeable state papers reducing complex subjects to clear and simple language, producing them with a rapidity reminiscent of his astonishing career as a legislative drafts- man in the House of Burgesses. Often throughout his mature life his mind seemed to operate with a logical precision independent of physical suffering or distraction.

Soon he had surrounded himself with the elegance that was at least as necessary to him as comfort. The crimson and blue damask curtains would have overwhelmed almost any furnishings except the damask-covered gilded chairs and ormolu-decorated tables and cabinets that transformed a Philadelphia apartment into a Paris salon. The Houdon heads that gazed serenely from their pedestals must have been more at home than some of the congressional callers.

In stark contrast to the interior of Jefferson's house was an office that seemed more suitable for Bob Cratchit than for the Secretary of State. A plain three-story brick building on the northwest corner of Market and Ninth, diagonally across from his home, housed the Department of State.[68] Venetian blinds and green curtains were the most notable concessions to comfort and beauty. Fireplaces and stoves provided warmth in the bleak surroundings of bare floors and plain tables where clerks sat in Windsor chairs, each with quill in hand. Many more quills were available near the ink wells and shakers of blotting sand. Stacks of paper and parchment skins awaited their future efforts as did (quite literally) a great quantity of red tape. A "Secretary's Room," or private office, was about as plain as the main room. Under these circumstances Jefferson might have preferred to do his paperwork at home even if this practice had not been his lifetime habit when feasible. In fact he even kept at home the official communications from American diplomats, following the custom of some Virginia county clerks who carried the records home at night for safekeeping. Not surprisingly, he chose to receive foreign diplomats at home rather than in the spartan offices of his department.

Most of his diplomatic problems centered on relations with Great Britain and France and were exacerbated by the rivalry between them. His public snubbing by King George III, no less than his experiences in the Revolution, had engendered hostility toward the British. But within his first eight months as an active member of the cabinet Jeffer- son had made a statement revelatory at once of his prejudice and his determination not to let it interfere with his official duties:

> Still as a political man they shall never find any passion in me either for or against them. Whenever their avarice of commerce will let them meet us fairly half way, I should meet them with satisfaction, because it would be for our benefit; but I mistake their character if they do this under present circumstances.[69]

The two chief matters demanding attention in Anglo-American relations were those of commercial intercourse and United States territorial integrity. Although a commer- cial treaty existed with France, one had not been agreed upon with Great Britain. The question of territorial integrity had not been solved by the Treaty of Paris in 1783. Although that document defined the new Republic's territory as extending northward to British North America, it did not define the southern limits of British territory. A great deal more imperial pink brightened the maps of North America used in London's

Whitehall than covered those that adorned the walls of Jefferson's drab offices in Philadelphia. And what were American rights of navigation in the Mississippi, which provided the western boundary? Besides, the British had never given up some of their outposts in the Northwest and seemed to be inciting the Indians there to hostile activity.

Jefferson proposed to deal with the two great issues simultaneously. Why not use the stick of commercial discrimination to punish Great Britain for her territorial infringements, at the same time extending the carrot of reciprocity as a reward for cooperation? Madison and many other congressmen already favored discrimination.

Jefferson had hardened some of his views into writing during the previous July when the Nootka Sound affair had threatened a full-bloom crisis. Spanish seizure of British ships near Vancouver Island had raised the specter of war between Great Britain and Spain. Both countries' territories bordered the United States. Thoughtful Americans had realized the dangers to the infant Republic, still as unsteady on its legs as a newborn colt, when two such strong neighbors began jostling each other. The situation had been further complicated by the apparently imminent involvement of an American ally, France, who was also allied with Spain. Jefferson had realized that, if England should seize the Floridas and Louisiana from the Spanish, the United States would be surrounded on land and sea by Britain's bristling guns. In letters to American diplomats in England, Spain, and France he gave an unsentimental appraisal of American dangers and opportunities, subordinating to his country's interest all sentimental regard for a favorite ally or resentment toward a former enemy. Freedom to navigate the Mississippi, he insisted, was essential to American survival. The right of survival was beyond question. So, therefore, was the American right to free navigation of the great river. That right should be secured by diplomacy if possible, by force if necessary. He was prepared to guarantee all Spanish territory west of the Mississippi in exchange for cession to the United States of all Spanish America east of that boundary. He explored the possibilities of French help, in case of war between England and Spain, to obtain the island of New Orleans, gateway to the Mississippi. But he was even willing, if necessary, to stand by while Britain seized the lands of one erstwhile ally, Spain, and fought a still dearer one, France, if the American jugular could thus be protected. To Gouverneur Morris, the United States representative in London, he wrote, "We wish to be neutral *if they will execute the treaty fairly and attempt no conquests adjoining us.*"[70]

The vision of a republic embodying humankind's aspiration for freedom fired Jefferson's idealism. To the service of that idealism he dedicated the almost inexhaustible ingenuity of a pragmatic mind. As eager as he was for his country to cultivate the arts of peace, he was ready for the United States to go to war if that was the only way to prevent Louisiana and the Floridas from falling under British sway. But so long as he could find intelligent reasons for hope of peace, he would advocate neutrality. He would try, however, to make England buy American neutrality. The purchase price would be abandonment of British outposts in the Northwest and agreement on a commercial treaty acceptable to the United States. The price could include the naming of a British minister to the United States instead of an informal representative.

Besides writing these views to American diplomats in London, Paris, and Madrid, Jefferson included them in a written reply to President Washington's solicitation of advice from him, the other cabinet members, Vice President Adams, and John Jay.

The Nootka crisis had gradually faded. George Beckwith, the British representative, who had arrived in the United States at the height of the excitement, remained for twenty-one months. Jefferson did not receive him. Such recognition would have been inappropriate for a man with no official credentials. But Hamilton, with Washington's consent, conferred with Beckwith often. How often is suggested by the frequency with which "Number Seven," Beckwith's code name for Hamilton, appeared in the Englishman's dispatches to his government.

Madison continued to advocate in Congress a policy of discrimination to obtain concessions from the British, and Hamilton through his followers in the House worked to block its adoption. Jefferson and Madison were increasingly close associates. Indeed, Jefferson suggested that his friend leave the noise and confusion of the boarding house and move in with him. Jefferson said that at his house there was enough of everything, too much of solitude.[71] Madison had declined, but they frequently went horseback riding together.

An incident involving one of Jefferson's horses had strengthened the bond between the two. He had bought the animal from his younger friend but it had suddenly died before the actual transfer of money. Jefferson had insisted on paying anyway despite Madison's protestations. In fact, he had overpaid and had to accept a refund from Madison.[72] In such incidents people learn a great deal about each other. As the days passed, the two Virginians talked in perfect confidence while riding or over supper, planning for the nation's good as they saw it and scheming to thwart Hamilton's interference. Occasionally they were joined by the new senator from Virginia, a like-minded man who had been a Jefferson protégé, James Monroe. For a time congressional support of the policy of discrimination was almost steadily strengthened by Jefferson's and Madison's efforts, but eventually, in February 1791, Hamilton and his friends prevailed.

In the same month another division of opinion emphasized the philosophical differences between the secretaries of State and Treasury. In the previous December Hamilton had submitted to the House of Representatives his *Report on the National Bank*, which called for establishment of a Bank of the United States modeled after the Bank of England. He believed that a banking system centered in a privileged institution acting as a banker to the government and including widely dispersed private banking firms would both strengthen the national government and bond it more strongly to the business community. The bank would be an amalgamation of public and private interest. The government would subscribe to 20 percent of the stock but the institution would be controlled by private stockholders. The bill passed and Washington, troubled by Madison's arguments against it, had to decide whether to sign it into law. He sought from each cabinet member an opinion in writing on the constitutionality of the measure. Jefferson on February 15 submitted his opinion that the proposal was unconstitutional.

His legal arguments were cool and precise, but his opposition was emotional as well as intellectual. He had confided his fears a few days before in a letter to George Mason: "What is said in our country of the fiscal arrangements now going on?"[73] Once again, as in earlier years, Jefferson meant Virginia when he said "our country." "Whether these measures be right or wrong abstractly, more attention should be paid to the general opinion." The Virginia plantation master's suspicion of urban capitalists came through as he used strong language: "The only corrective of what is corrupt in our present form of government will be the augmentation of the numbers in the lower house, so as to get a more agricultural representation, which may put that interest above that of the stock-jobbers." With an almost religious zeal, Jefferson sought to drive the money–changers from the temple of democracy.

Attorney General Randolph had already expressed his firm conviction that the National Bank bill was unconstitutional when Jefferson wrote his reply to Washington. Thus the Secretary of State, along with Madison and Randolph, became part of a trio of Virginians making an orchestrated attack on the bank.

In his reply to the President, Jefferson methodically listed the three things that the bill was designed to do. It would form a corporation with functions crossing state lines and challenging state authority. In effect, it would grant a monopoly. It would authorize directors of this new corporate monopoly to make regulations superseding in some instances the laws of the states. He then examined these provisions in the light of an amendment to the Constitution of the United States which had not yet been formally adopted but was assured of passage. He anticipated that it would be the Twelfth Amendment, and so designated it, but it became the Tenth Amendment: "The powers not delegated to the United States by the Constitution, nor prohibited by it to the States, are reserved to the States respectively, or to the people." "To take a single step beyond the boundaries thus especially drawn around the powers of Congress," Jefferson argued, "is to take possession of a boundless field of power, no longer susceptible of any definition."[74]

Did the National Bank bill move beyond the limits set by the Tenth Amendment? He anticipated the argument that its provisions were somehow justified by Congress's constitutional power to lay taxes and borrow money. He replied that "this bill neither borrows money nor ensures the borrowing of it. The proprietors of the bank will be just as free as any other money holders to lend or not to lend their money to the public." What of the contention that authority to establish the bank was implicit in the constitutional provision (Article I, Section 8) that "The Congress shall have power to lay and collect taxes, duties, imports, and excises, to pay the debts and provide for the common defense and general welfare of the United States?" Jefferson insisted that the clause simply authorized Congress to impose taxes to provide for the "general welfare"; it did not authorize Congress to do anything it conceived to be a contribution to the "general welfare." So broad an interpretation "would reduce the whole instrument to a single phrase." That single phrase, so interpreted, could cover anything Congress might dream of doing. If the framers of the Constitution had intended so broad an interpretation, they need not have gone to the trouble of spelling out separately the various powers reserved to the national legislature. The authors of the Constitution had "intended to lace [the Congress] up straitly within the enumerated powers and those without which, as means, those powers could not be carried into effect." He clinched this argument with a reminder to Washington, who had presided over the Constitutional Convention of 1787, that that body had rejected a proposal authorizing Congress to incorporate canal companies, turning it down specifically on the grounds that by extension such a grant of power could be used to justify incorporation of banks.

Jefferson knew that another constitutional clause, if broadly interpreted, could be used to justify almost any legislation that ingeniously led Congressmen wished to pass. Hamiltonians were already arguing that the authority to establish a national bank was implicit in the provision empowering Congress "to make all laws which shall be necessary and proper for carrying into execution the foregoing (enumerated) powers.'' Jefferson pointed out that all of the enumerated powers could "be carried into execution without a bank." Establishment of a bank, therefore, was certainly not "necessary" to execution of any of the enumerated powers. Therefore authorization for a national bank was certainly not implicit in the cited clause. Even if such a bank should prove *convenient*, and he did not believe it would, *convenience* would not be *necessity*. Convenience could "swallow up all the delegated powers." The Constitution restricted Congress to "those means without which the grant of power would be nugatory."

Having urged his view energetically, Jefferson concluded with an observation that relieved it of any dye of fanaticism. Although he disapproved of the bank bill, even apart from his conviction that it was unconstitutional, he thought that, unless Washington was similarly convinced of its unconstitutionality, the President should sign it because "a just respect for the wisdom of the legislature would naturally decide the balance in favor of their opinion."

Jarred into uncertainty by Jefferson's negative opinion following upon Randolph's, Washington went so far as to ask Madison to prepare a veto message to be ready if needed. The President sent Hamilton the letters written by Randolph and Jefferson so that the Secretary of the Treasury could consider their arguments in composing his own opinion.

Hamilton took a week to reply. Even so, he dedicated one sleepless night to composing his statement. He knew that he must muster all his persuasive skills to convince the President. In so doing he produced, doubtless quite consciously, a philosophical document of lasting interest. Many scholars think that, more than any of his contributions to *The Federalist,* it was his masterpiece. In addressing Jefferson's arguments Hamilton gave the doctrine of "implied powers" its most eloquent expression and prefigured John Marshall's historic interpretations of the Constitution. The New Yorker wrote:

> This general principle is inherent in the very definition of government, and essential to every step of the progress to be made by that of the United States, namely: That every power vested in a government is in its nature sovereign, and includes, by force of the term, a right to employ all the means requisite and fairly applicable to the attainment of the ends of such power, and which are not precluded by restrictions and exceptions specified in the Constitution, or not immoral, or not contrary to the essential ends of political society.[75]

Hamilton conceded that "the moment the literal meaning (of a constitutional clause) is departed from, there is a chance of error and abuse," but he cautioned, "And yet an adherence to the letter of its powers would at once arrest the motions of government."

Hamilton, though the first American statesman to give detailed expression to the doctrine of implied powers, was not the first to use it. Ironically, it had been advanced by two who were now his chief opponents. In Essay 44 of *The Federalist* Madison had written: "No axiom is more clearly established in law, or in reason, than that wherever the end is required, the means are authorized; wherever a general power to do a thing is given, every particular power for doing it is included." And in August 1787 when some insisted that Congress lacked the power to enforce levies on the states, Jefferson himself had argued that no express grant of authority was necessary: "When two parties make a compact, there results to each a power of compelling the other to execute it."[76]

Washington waited anxiously for Hamilton's reply, aware that if ten days elapsed without his taking action the bill would automatically become law. To his concerned inquiries Hamilton replied that Sundays and the day of receipt did not count. The doubts raised by Randolph's, Madison's, and Jefferson's arguments were offset by Hamilton's, which were given additional force by Washington's habit of assigning extra weight to views issuing from the department head most involved. Perhaps also he shared Jefferson's "just respect for the wisdom of the legislature." In any event the veto message prepared by Madison was never used. Just under the wire, Washington signed the bill into law.

Neither Jefferson's nor Hamilton's letter was published at the time. But in the two writings before him Washington had the record of the beginnings of what he most dreaded in American political life—the growth of factionalism. Implicit in Jefferson's letter was his faith in a democratic and agrarian society whose exemplar was the individual freeholder. Explicit in other letters that he wrote relative to the bank was his distrust of metropolitan growth and financial power structures. In *Notes on Virginia* he had described great cities as festering sores on the body politic and had predicted that growth in disease, crime, and class strife would accompany urban development. He feared the concentration of wealth, especially in hands that neither produced nor directed production but merely shuffled papers—stocks, bonds, certificates, currency. Implicit in Hamilton's letter was his often stated faith in an oligarchic society exemplified by the captain of finance and the industrial entrepreneur. Explicit was his desire for urban growth and concentrations of financial power as essential to the development of a strong nation. Jefferson's concern for debtor interests was countered by Hamilton's regard for creditors as a source of both energy and stability. Jefferson's advocacy of a diffusion of both wealth and governmental power was countered by Hamilton's call for the centralization of each and the combination of the two.

The diametrical opposition of the two statesmen on strict and loose construction of the Constitution was less real than apparent. Hamilton was indeed as earnest an advocate of broad construction as he appeared to be in his carefully reasoned letter. But Jefferson's fears of liberal construction in the hands of a Hamilton-dominated Congress caused him to assume in his communication to Washington a stance just once removed from rigor mortis. As we have seen, Jefferson had recognized the practical necessity of implicit powers even under the old Articles of Confederation. His own frustrating experience as a strict constructionist Governor of Virginia had taught him a good deal. Nevertheless, there was a significant difference of degree in Hamilton's and Jefferson's ideas about the occasion and frequency of resort to implied powers. To Hamilton they were the great facilitators of political and economic growth. For Jefferson they were, as he had said in the Declaration of Independence of changes in government, not to be resorted to "for light and transient reasons." Jefferson was even more disturbed by the direction in which Hamilton was moving the nation than by the means which the Treasury Secretary employed.

The differences between Hamilton and Jefferson were publicized and dramatized by something that happened in May. In that month appeared the American edition of Thomas Paine's *The Rights of Man*, a spirited reply to Edmund Burke's eloquent *Reflec-*

tions on the Revolution in France. As might be expected, Paine, who had declared, "Where liberty is not, there is my country," was as vociferous in support of the French Revolution as the great conservative was in opposition to it. During Jefferson's stay in France, Paine had discussed the American Constitution in company with the Virginian and Lafayette and afterwards had corresponded with the American minister regarding events in England. Jefferson admired the quotable style of the irascible English corset-maker turned pamphleteer for liberty: he once closed a letter to Paine with the expressed conviction that the author of *Common Sense* was the best writer then living in America with the possible exception of "your obedient servant, Th. Jefferson." The American did not share some of Paine's bristling attitudes, but it was his habit to emphasize the points of agreement between himself and others. And he did in truth share Paine's hopes that much good would come from the French Revolution, which had not yet proved very bloody.

Though their association was by no means close, the diplomatic Jefferson and the contentious Paine were soon to be linked in the American imagination. This fateful circumstance arose from Jefferson's predilection for saying and writing pleasant things to friends, acquaintances, and strangers. In this case his letter was addressed to a stranger, Jonathan B. Smith, to whom he was returning a copy of the English edition of Paine's *The Rights of Man* which Madison had borrowed. Learning that Smith's brother, a Philadelphia printer, was bringing out an American edition of the work, the Secretary of State wrote:

> I am extremely pleased to find it will be reprinted here, and that something is at length to be publicly said against the political heresies which have sprung up among us.
> I have no doubt our citizens will rally a second time 'round the standard of Common Sense.[77]

Without asking Jefferson's permission, the printer quoted this note in the American edition, coupling it with praise of the Secretary for "that Republican firmness and Democratic simplicity which endear their possessor to every friend of the Rights of Man."[78] The quotation from Jefferson was read by many who never read Paine's book. It was reprinted on May 14 in the *Philadelphia Gazette of the United States* and, reproduced in paper after paper, quickly made its way up and down the Atlantic seaboard.

Almost as soon as the American edition appeared Hamilton began loudly to deplore Jefferson's indiscretion. He believed that the Secretary of State's praise of Paine and the French Revolution would irritate a British government to which both were anathema. Hamiltonians were quick to cite the reference to "political heresies which have sprung up among us" as a thinly veiled allusion to a series of articles by John Adams that had been published in a Philadelphia newspaper. Much less disturbed by the prospect of giving offense to the British than by the fear that he had hurt the feelings of his old colleague of 1776, Jefferson wrote to Washington:

> I am afraid the indiscretion of a printer has committed me with my friend Mr. Adams, for whom, as one of the most honest and disinterested men alive, I

have a cordial esteem, increased by long concurrence in opinion in the days of
his republicanism; and even since his apostasy to hereditary monarchy and nobility,
though we differ as friends should do. . . . I am sincerely mortified to be thus
brought forward on the public stage, where to remain, to advance, or to retire
will be equally against my love of silence and quiet, and my abhorrence of
dispute.[79]

As Hamiltonians worked overtime to exploit the breach between Jefferson and
Adams, Jefferson turned to Madison for advice. The congressman averred that the Vice
President, if injured, had simply gotten what he deserved: "Surely if it be innocent and
decent in one servant of the public thus to write attacks against its government, it cannot be very criminal or indecent in another to patronize a written defense of the principles on which that government is founded."[80] Madison advised his friend not to
communicate with Adams regarding the matter, and Jefferson managed to keep silent
until July when he dispatched a letter of explanation to the sensitive sage of Braintree,
concluding, "That you and I differ in our ideas of government is well known to us both;
but we have differed as friends should do, respecting the purity of each other's motives,
and confining our difference of opinion to private conversation."[81] The lettter brought
from Adams a conciliatory reply.

But by that time Jefferson's and Adams's private differences had become a public
issue. Hamilton and Adams were seen as members of one faction dedicated to strengthening the central government and remodeling it along British principles. Now in various
states scattered local groups that viewed with dismay what they regarded as a march
toward monarchy thought that they had found a leader. They had been appreciative
of Madison's fight in the House of Representatives and had been aware of that cocklebur
spokesman for democracy, Senator William Maclay of Pennsylvania. But they had not
found a national captain. Now, to Jefferson's dismay, they looked to him. What a position for a man who hated controversy! He was not only thrust into disputes with old
friends and current colleagues, but was hailed as a brother in arms by some whose rabid
radicalism was abhorrent even to his tolerant mind—those motivated more by hatred
of the classes than by love of the masses.

No wonder Jefferson was much troubled again with headaches. His yearning for
escape had been evident for weeks when he wrote his daughter Polly about the spring
chorus of the frogs, the sky-winged flash of a bluebird, and the greening of the
willows.[82] He had been dreaming of a vacation trip up the Hudson with Madison. On
May 17, with Congress in recess and the business of his department slackened, he rode
out of town to meet his friend, who was already in New York. He welcomed the country
sound of a whippoorwill, familiar to him since his Virginia childhood, as he rode past
the outskirts of Philadelphia.[83]

He began to relax but his restless mind was as active as ever. Every revolution of
the carriage wheels carried him farther from the capital's preoccupation with revolutions of another sort, but every turn was registered on an odometer[84] so that he could
record the mileage between landmarks. He used his account book not only for its
designated purpose, but also, once he and Madison left New York behind, to record
trees and shrubs and flowers with the thoroughness of a botanist, make detailed observations of the fauna, describe the topography with a cartographer's eye, and note the

nuances of soil coloration with the same practiced skill he had exhibited in his European travels.

The most delightful part of their trip began on May 29 with their arrival at Fort George. The clear waters mirrored virgin forests of blue-green giants. An Indian on the shore looked out upon a scene no less familiar to the first of his race to greet a white man there, no less familiar indeed to that aboriginal welcomer's grandsire's grandsire. His headache long gone, Jefferson drank in the beauty of what he described to his Patsy as "without comparison the most beautiful water I ever saw." But the loyal Virginian who had found even the Alps inferior in beauty to his native Blue Ridge was compelled to qualify his praise of New York scenery with a criticism of the humidity and a reminder that there was "nothing anywhere else, in point of climate, which Virginia need envy to any part of the world."[85]

Jefferson even found the patience to fish. But upon his return to Philadelphia through New England after extending the journey to Lake Champlain he discovered that many people were convinced that the speckled trout, salmon trout, and bass of which he wrote meticulously were really so many red herring to cover his angling for votes. One news dispatch from Albany noted that the Secretary of State was traveling with "the Charles Fox of America, the celebrated James Madison."[86] One of Hamilton's supporters wrote to him: "There was every appearance of a passionate courtship between the Chancellor [Robert Livingston], Burr, Jefferson, and Madison when the two latter were in town. . . . Upon this subject, however, I cannot say that I have the smallest uneasiness. You are too well seated in the hearts of the citizens of the northern and middle states to be hunted down by them."[87]

From Connecticut another supporter informed Hamilton that the Virginia travelers had "scouted silently through the country, shunning the gentry, communing with and pitying the Shayites. . . . They are supremely contemned by the Gentlemen of Connecticut, which state I found on a review right as to national matters."[88]

The linking of Jefferson with Paine at the same time as his "botanizing expedition" through the Northern states, the fact that the trip was made in the company of the chief congressional opponent of Hamilton's policies foreign and domestic, and the close association between the Secretary of the Treasury and British diplomats all conspired to direct international as well as national attention to the Secretary of State's little vacation. Sir John Temple, His Majesty's consul in New York, informed his London superior, the Duke of Leeds: "I am sorry to inform Your Grace that the Secretary of State's party and politics gains ground here, and I fear will have influence enough to cause acts and resolves which may be unfriendly to Great Britain, to be passed early in the next session of Congress. The Secretary of State, together with Mr. Madison. . . (is) now . . . gone to the Eastern States, there to proselyte as far as they are able to a commercial war with Great Britain."[89] As significant as Sir John's assumption regarding the true purpose of the trip was his conviction as early as May 1791 that there was an opposition political party headed by Jefferson.

George Beckwith, the informal British representative to the United States, reported to London that he believed Jefferson and Madison had undertaken the tour to gain support for an anti-British policy. Beckwith assured his superiors, however, that since then he had personally toured the same area, undoing all the mischief done by the Virginians.[90]

Were there even a few mischievous sparks to account for so much smoke? Apparently not. Jefferson, true to habit, kept detailed and voluminous notes on his journey. He had a passion for recording everything he saw, every person he met, as if experience itself, and not merely the record of it, could be preserved in this way. Yet Jefferson's notes for his private use show little time spent with politicians in the course of his journey. Most of the time his mind seems to have been far removed from the political battles whose tactics he supposedly was plotting. The only battlefields he appears to have contemplated on his journey were those of Saratoga, Crown Point, Ticonderoga, and Bennington, scenes that symbolized the once united struggle of patriots now divided. Even there, he confessed, his attention often strayed from accounts of historic advances and dramatic charges to the plants that were nature's quiet vanguard in the retaking of fields originally hers. His notes suggested that he spent far more time researching methods for combating the Hessian fly, an insect pest on which he would report to the American Philosophical Society, than in devising tactics to discomfit the Hamiltonians.

But what Jefferson knew about his own activities and what he thought he knew about his motives were as chaff in the winds of public opinion. Washington might cling stubbornly to the belief that the United States as yet had no political parties, and Jefferson might repeatedly tell his friends and himself that, even if there were political parties, he was not the leader of one. The public, including both his opponents and his adherents, had decided otherwise. If it was not yet true that the reluctant Virginian was the head of a political party it soon would be. As so often in a democracy, popular belief foreshadowed reality.

Of course, however innocent Jefferson's vacation amid rural delights, he had not concentrated all his attention on the woodland voices of whippoorwill and thrush. He was not at all oblivious to the strident voice of the *Philadelphia Gazette of the United States*. Its publisher, John Fenno, had made the newspaper practically a house organ for the Hamiltonians, shrilly trumpeting charges of political connivance against Jefferson and his friends. Hamilton partly subsidized the publication by giving Fenno the printing contracts for the Treasury Department. There were in Philadelphia two newspapers, one edited by Benjamin Franklin's grandson, which were generally favorable to the views expressed by Jefferson and Madison. But their editors did not seem to be a match for Fenno. Madison cherished the hope of gaining for the capital the services of the man he regarded as the foremost journalist in America, his old college mate Philip Freneau. Madison's hope accorded well with Jefferson's wish to see a "whig vehicle of intelligence" to compete for national influence with Fenno's "paper of pure toryism."[91]

Jefferson was impressed with Freneau's credentials and, before leaving on his Northern tour, had offered him the post of translator for the State Department. The salary was small but it would be a valuable supplement to his earnings if he should establish a newspaper in Philadelphia and he would have access to foreign journals and a pipeline to one of the two most important departments of the executive branch. Freneau had declined, saying he was busily engaged in building the circulation of his weekly in East Jersey.

Jefferson was disappointed. More than that, he was chagrined—as he always was when one of his charmingly made proffers was rejected or when one of his designs was frustrated. He evidently solicited Madison's aid in changing Freneau's mind and rejoiced when he received a letter from the congressman saying that the journalist was en route to Philadelphia. Some days later Jefferson exasperatedly wrote Madison that his letter about Freneau had not been followed by Freneau himself. Several months later Jefferson importuned Madison directly: "I am sincerely sorry that Freneau has declined coming here. Though the printing business is suffiently full here, yet I think he would have set out on such advantageous ground as to have been sure of success. His own genius in the first place is so superior to that of his competitors. I should have given him the perusal of all my letters of foreign intelligence and all foreign newspapers, the publication of all proclamations and other public notices within my department, and the printing of the laws, which added to his salary would have been a considerable aid. Besides this, Fenno's being the only weekly or half weekly paper, and under general condemnation for its toryism and its incessant efforts to overturn the government, Freneau would have found that ground as good as unoccupied."[92]

The generation of Americans who had pledged "to each other our lives, our fortunes, and our sacred honor" were truly more honorable than many of their counterparts in most of the nineteenth and twentieth centuries, but they were not nearly so concerned about conflict of interest. Besides, the Jeffersonians, recalling the Hamiltonians' subsidizing of Fenno through Treasury Department printing orders, would probably have resorted to the time-honored defense of children, party leaders, and chiefs of state: *They* did it first. Another interesting aspect of Jefferson's letter is its revelation that he, popularly regarded as leader of the opposition, in turn saw the Hamiltonians as dedicated to overturning the government.

In any event, Jefferson's indirect approach through Madison was properly baited. The journalist accepted the position of translator for the State Department and began publishing the *National Gazette*. Madison had written to Jefferson: "In the conduct and title of the paper it will be altogether his (Freneau's)[93] own," but both Virginians knew that the strength of the journalist's anti-Hamilton convictions would insure an editorial policy acceptable to them.

Jefferson soon rejoiced in a letter[94] to Patsy that Freneau's two papers a week "contained more good matter" than the six published by Franklin's grandson. Freneau attacked Hamilton and his schemes with a cleverness and erudition rare in American journalism, and sometimes with a personal invective all too common. Freneau himself proved a welcome addition to Philadelphia society, at least to that portion sympathetic to Jefferson and Madison. Jefferson took at once to the short, wiry man with the dark gray eyes. Of French Huguenot parentage, he exemplified the energy, efficiency, and animated charm for which the breed was famous. He had published in 1786 his first volume of poems, among them "The Wild Honey Suckle" and "The Indian Burying Ground," works that would help to make him famous as "the father of American poetry." His interest in the Indians, and his blend of classicism and what would come to be known as romanticism, were congenial to the Virginian. Besides, the journalist's own life as a Revolutionary blockade–runner, prisoner of war, and master of a merchant ship had provided him with a rich fund of anecdotes.

Freneau assumed his duties as the State Department's "clerk of foreign languages" in mid-August of 1791. Nine weeks later another man's assumption of new duties in Philadelphia provided grist for Freneau's editorial mill and, quite literally, headaches for the Secretary of State. The newcomer was George Hammond, freshly accredited British minister to the United States.

Only twenty-eight years old, he had the self-confidence of a young man who has risen rapidly in the employ of a great empire and has ample reason to anticipate still greater success. Instructed by his government to cultivate Americans with political clout, he had entered upon the task with such enthusiasm that he had talked with many senators before his official reception by the Secretary of State and President. Hammond had waited until a week after his arrival to call on Jefferson, only to find the Secretary out. When Jefferson returned the call, he found the minister out. Not until November 11 did the Secretary of State present the British minister to the President. Hammond's closest conferences with a member of the executive branch would not be with the Secretary of State but with the Secretary of the Treasury.[95]

Having become accustomed to Hamilton's secret conversations with Beckwith, the informal representative of the British government, Jefferson was prepared for the probability of such conferences between the New Yorker and Hammond, the official representative. But nothing had suggested to him that Hamilton, who so decried possible French influence in American affairs, might be conferring privately with Jean Baptiste Ternant, the newly accredited French minister to the United States. He was disconcerted when such proved the case.

At first, while England had seemed indisposed to cooperate with the United States, France had given no signs of such an attitude. Jefferson thought that, even if revolution-forged sentiment did not dictate French cooperation, enlightened self–interest would. But France surprised him by fixing the handicap of a discriminatory tariff on American tobacco imported in American, as opposed to French, ships. Writing to Short to request Lafayette's intervention, Jefferson described the French policy as "such an act of hostility against our navigation as was not to have been expected from the friendship of that nation." He branded it as worse even than the British Navigation Act, which, though "so much and so justly complained of," left "to all nations the carriage of their own commodities free."[96] Still he used diplomatic restraint when he complained directly to the French, saying, "We presume the National Assembly must have been hurried into the measure, without being allowed time to reflect on its consequences."[97]

Jefferson had anticipated no difficulties with Ternant, a former officer in the American Revolution of whom Lafayette had said in a letter of commendation, "He in a great measure belongs to both countries." But Jefferson had been undercut by Hamilton's conferences with the Frenchman, the first one a four-hour discussion when the Secretary of State was out of town. Ternant had brought to Hamilton and Knox the appeals of French colonials for aid against black insurrectionists in St. Domingo; money and arms had been provided at once. Hamilton undoubtedly had impressed the minister as one who could get things done. The Treasury Secretary also had impressed him as a reasonable man sympathetic to French interests. This impression was strengthened by Hamilton's private assurance that all the questions troubling Franco-American relations could be disposed of in a new treaty of commerce, a method which the American said he favored. Hamilton even confided to Ternant some of the conditions of an American approach to a new treaty of commerce with the British, assuring him of his own attachment to the French. Ironically enough, Ternant found Jefferson, who was so often accused of being a Francophile, cool and reserved by comparison with

Hamilton.[98]

When Hamilton revealed something of his conversations with the French minister, Jefferson resented not only the fact that he had been bypassed but also the fact that the American bargaining position had been weakened by Hamilton's frustration of United States plans to let Paris make the first move toward a commercial treaty. Jefferson believed that in this instance American initiative was especially unfortunate in view of Ternant's admission that he had not been authorized by his government to discuss a treaty with the United States and did not expect such authorization.[99] Discussion of a treaty, he indicated, would have to take place in Paris.

Hamilton, it turned out, had so far intervened in the matter as privately to suggest to the Frenchman that he discuss terms informally with Jefferson and send any resulting agreement to Paris for acceptance or rejection. The very active Secretary of the Treasury urged the same idea upon Washington, who transmitted it to Jefferson. The Secretary of State pointed out that a tentative agreement approved by him with the President's knowledge would be a thoroughgoing commitment while Paris would not be at all bound by the decisions of a minister not even authorized to discuss a treaty.[100]

Washington, however, was convinced by Hamilton. So Jefferson drafted a treaty proposal which provided that the citizens, ships, produce, and manufactures of each country should be accorded the same treatment within the borders of the other as if they had indeed been native to the receiving country. The only exception would be in regard to tariffs: import duties in each nation would remain at the maximum then existing; if either nation reduced its duties, the other must follow suit in like proportion.[101]

Hamilton opposed this plan with one of his own which would raise American duties, apparently by 25 to 50 percent with respect to French duty levels. Jefferson disgustedly summarized: "So they were to give us the privileges of native subjects, and we, as a compensation, were to make them pay higher duties."[102] Not surprisingly, negotiations fell through.

Jefferson suspected that Hamilton had never been sincerely interested in promoting a treaty between the United States and France. Why had he bothered to put on an act? Jefferson thought he knew the answer when Hamilton came forward with another proposal. The Treasury Secretary urged that, since France had turned down the chance for a reciprocal treaty, the same opportunity should be offered to Britain. The Virginian believed that Hamilton had initiated and then aborted negotiations with the French simply to pave the way for the kind of treaty he wanted with London. Far from sharing his fellow Virginian's suspicions, Washington embraced Hamilton's proposal as sensible.

Jefferson's arguments that the United States should refrain from commercial treaty negotiations with either France or Britain made no dent in Washington's position. The Secretary of State reluctantly began addressing to Hammond questions which by mid-December elicited the Englishman's admission that he was empowered only to discuss, not to conclude, a commercial treaty. By then Jefferson had ample evidence that Britain preferred the status quo in commercial relations so long as her privileges were protected by an American pledge against discrimination. Fruitless correspondence between Jefferson and Hammond continued into the spring of 1792.[103]

Meanwhile the Secretary of State had found himself in other contests for which he had little enthusiasm. He had successfully defended a spate of Washington's diplomatic appointments before a Senate committee headed by Caleb Strong of Massachusetts. Even so, the full Senate's approval of one of them, the appointment of Jefferson's protégé Short as minister to The Hague, had snagged on a tie vote until Vice President Adams cast the decisive aye.

But Jefferson's satisfaction in his former secretary's success, and in the approval of Thomas Pinckney of South Carolina as minister to London, were mitigated by his having to labor to win endorsement of Washington's choice for minister to Paris, a personally and politically distasteful Hamiltonian—Gouverneur Morris. The strength and vehemence of Senate opposition to Morris had caused Washington to share some of Jefferson's doubts about the tactless New Yorker. Jefferson wrote the new appointee a letter stressing the importance of his staying out of political strife among Frenchmen and especially refraining from complaints about "government founded on the will of the people." But Washington wrote an even more emphatic letter, so sternly admonitory that Jefferson suggested moderating its tone.[104]

Not long after helping to nudge these appointments through the Senate, the Secretary of State confided to Short his "unalterably fixed" determination to resign from the cabinet at the conclusion of the President's first term on March 1, 1793.[105] He had already informed Washington, who had sought to discourage him.

Despite his longing to resign and a sense of futility, Jefferson permitted himself no relaxation in his labors as Secretary of State, showing imagination and initiative as well as dogged determination. Corresponding with Spanish officials in an effort to secure United States control of the mouth of the Mississippi, he sometimes wrote in the manner of a bold caballero. Very different in tone was the closely reasoned, meticulously researched, ninety-five page reply which he addressed to Hammond's voluminous "abstract of such particular Acts of the United States as appear to me infractions on their part of the definitive treaty of peace."[106] Jefferson submitted the work to the criticism of Madison, Edmund Randolph, and Hamilton. The two Virginians wholeheartedly approved. Hamilton raised only one cavil but Washington dismissed that. With minor revisions the document was dispatched to the British minister May 29, 1792. Attorneys and scholars have admired it ever since, but it had no practical influence on negotiations between the United States and Great Britain. Jefferson had been as industrious in its preparation as if he had entertained real hopes of its success.

Hammond went personally to Hamilton to complain of "the general acrimonious style" of "this extraordinary performance." "This gentleman," the minister informed his superior, Lord Grenville, "treated me (as he has done upon every occasion) with the strictest confidence and candour. After lamenting the intemperate violence of his colleague, Mr. Hamilton assured me that this letter was very far from meeting his approbation, or from containing a faithful exposition of the sentiments of this government." The President, he said, had not read Jefferson's statement but had merely trusted his Secretary of State's assertion that it voiced the consensus of the cabinet.[107] If even the greater part of Hammond's report may be believed (and it is difficult to see what he could have gained by misrepresenting the matter to his own government), Hamilton had in effect told the diplomat that Great Britain might safely disregard an official communication from the United States. Alert observation, not paranoia, inspired Jefferson's conviction that Hamilton would subvert the policies of his own government in behalf of what he, the Secretary of the Treasury, deemed its own best interests. There is no need to wonder, as some writers have, at Jefferson's privately recorded belief that Hamilton "communicated to Hammond all our views and knew from him in return the views of the British Court."[108]

Adding to Jefferson's frustrations at a time when the Spanish were intriguing with the Creek Indians was the fact that the American Chargé d'Affaires in Madrid, William Carmichael, seldom bothered to correspond with his own government. Jefferson was not the only one frustrated by Carmichael. In writing to his Secretary of State concerning the errant diplomat, Washington completely abandoned his usual measured prose: "I believe we are never to hear *from* Mr. Carmichael, nor *of* him but through the medium of a third person. His ____ (I really do not know with what epithet to fill the blank) is to me amongst the most unaccountable of all the unaccountable things!"[109]

When Short, in accordance with Jefferson's plan, joined Carmichael on a special commission in Madrid to deal with Spanish claims to part of Georgia and disputed navigation rights on the lower Mississippi, dependable lines of communication were established. There was also hope that the competent Short would be able to conduct helpful discussions with the Spanish. But instead there was more frustration, justifying Washington's suspicion that "there is a very clear understanding in all this business between the Courts of London and Madrid; and that it is calculated to check, as far as they can, the rapid increase, extension and consequence of this country."[110]

Jefferson might have hoped that one of his domestic responsibilities as Secretary of State would provide some relief from the frustrations of foreign affairs. Service as the President's righthand man in the planning and construction of "the Federal City" on the banks of the Potomac was a task for which he was well qualified by his architectural studies. At first he had seized with alacrity the opportunity to produce a planned city. Interestingly enough, in view of his spirited defense of strict constructionism, he gave the most liberal interpretation to grants of executive authority for carrying out such a design. Jefferson favored enough allowance for individual tastes to prevent "a disgusting monotony" but he did advocate parallel streets and a limit on building heights.[111] He was pleased when Major Pierre Charles L'Enfant, a former officer of the Continental Army and a brilliant French engineer, was engaged to lay out the future capital. But L'Enfant's impressive gifts did not include a talent for diplomacy. After considering Jefferson's tentative plans for parallel streets, he wrote: "Such regular plans indeed, however answerable they may appear upon paper or seducing as they may be on the first aspect to the eyes of some people must. . . become at last tiresome and insipid, and it never could be in its origin but a mean continuance of some cool imagination wanting a sense of the real grand and truly beautiful. . . ."[112]

Jefferson continued to favor a gridiron design but now pressed his ideas mainly in regard to the architecture of public buildings. For the capitol, he wrote, he would "prefer the adoption of some one of the models of antiquity, which have had the approbation of thousands of years, and for the President's House I should prefer the celebrated fronts of modern buildings which have already received the approbation of all good judges. Such as the Galerie du Louvre, the Gardes meubles, and two fronts of the Hotel de Salm."[113] It is interesting that Jefferson, though adhering to the idea of classical design for the national capitol, as he had earlier for Virginia's state house, thought a modern design appropriate for the executive mansion. Though he was strong in his own preferences, he recognized L'Enfant's superior experience in engineering and deferred to him in most professional matters.

For a time, it seemed that Jefferson had enough tact to supply the Frenchman's lack. But then the engineer, singleminded in dedication to what he considered the best plans and procedures, began bypassing the commissioners supervising the project and demonstrated complete willingness to push around homeowners to get what he wanted. The whole business cost Jefferson many vexatious hours of conference and labor before, after warnings from both the Secretary of State and the President, L'Enfant resigned.[114]

Central Washington would be shaped to the Frenchman's distinctive plan, but he had not remained long enough to design the Capitol and President's House. Jefferson proposed that the commissioners stage a competition for these architectural sketches and they adopted the idea. The Secretary of State's suggestion that the spherical designs of the Pantheons in Rome and Paris be taken into account in planning the chief government building was influential in the domed final design and ultimately in that of many state capitols. When the winning sketches, by Dr. William Thornton, promised to be too costly in execution, Jefferson guided a committee of architects and builders to an esthetically acceptable compromise that would save half the cost of construction. Jefferson anonymously entered a Palladian rotunda design for the President's House, but the President and the commissioners favored the more conservative and austere sketches of James Hoban. On balance, while Jefferson certainly did not dominate plans for the future capital, it seems safe to say that no one was more influential than he in determining the neoclassical inspiration of the most prominent federal buildings.[115]

Trying as it was, Jefferson's work in creating the federal city carried with it the special satisfaction of being associated with the President in an enterprise in which they often thought alike. Jefferson had not only tremendous respect, but also an almost filial affection, for the great man who combined marmoreal majesty with the easy graces of a Virginia country squire. Jefferson found special satisfaction in April when Washington followed his advice to veto a congressional apportionment bill. The Secretary's counsel was based partly on belief that the measure was unconstitutional and partly on his conviction that Presidential forcefulness would have a salutary effect on Congress and the burgeoning American political tradition.[116] Hamilton had urged Washington to sign. Most of the time, though, it was Hamilton rather than Jefferson who convinced Washington on matters of public policy. The position of the Secretary of State was a lonely one.

Nevertheless Hamilton felt threatened. Despite his triumphs within the Administration and in Congress, there were signs that he was losing some of the battles of public opinion. As editor of *The National Gazette* Freneau subjected the Treasury Secretary to an unremitting bombardment that was echoed elsewhere in the American press. Hamilton was convinced that Jefferson and Madison were directing the fire and his anger against them mounted weekly.

The President was no happier than his two chief secretaries. On May 5, preparing to leave the capital for a brief trip to Mount Vernon, Washington conferred with Madison.[117] Underscoring earlier expressions of his wish to retire from office upon completion of his term, he said that he did not deem his services essential to the federal government. Moreover, he thought that others could do a better job than he. There were those who did not suffer from his "inexperience in the forms of public business," his "unfitness to judge of legal questions, and questions arising out of the Constitution." There was another matter, one that must have been difficult for him to talk about. He was becoming an old man (sixty in his day was about the equivalent of eighty today). The seemingly tireless general who had been able to outlast his young officers in the saddle, and then listen to hours of conflicting counsel which he could digest and summarize with uncanny accuracy, now felt the hand of mortality upon him. His health problems were multiplying and he even feared the failing of his faculties. The "fatigues and disagreeableness" of office were "scarcely tolerable." Nor was only the role of gentleman farmer preferable to that of President. To escape from the office he would willingly "go to his farm, take his spade in his hand, and work for his bread."

Madison was reassuring in his usual quiet way. Admittedly the President lacked legal training, but expertise in the law could be supplied by his counselors. With their knowledge at his command, his decisions had always been at least as good as those of anyone else who might have been Chief Executive and often had been better.

To the President's statement that he was weary with the problems of rising factionalism Madison replied that Washington could do more than anyone else to unite the contending groups. Who might conceivably be worthy to succeed him? Madison could think of only three: Adams, Jay, and Jefferson. Adams' "monarchical principles" and stands on legislation, he argued, had made the Vice President's name anathema to Southerners and to all republicans. Jay, he thought, was scarcely more popular than Adams. Besides the onus of sharing Adams' philosophy, the New Yorker had offended on the questions of British debts and navigation of the Mississippi. What of Jefferson? Madison knew him better than anyone else in Philadelphia did, perhaps anyone else anywhere, and Madison was convinced of his friend's "extreme repugnance to public life and anxiety to exchange it for his farm and his philosophy." And viewing the matter dispassionately, Madison noted that Jefferson had strong enemies in the North, especially among Pennsylvanians who resented his role in removing the capital to the South. Madison concluded by urging the President to serve a second term.

Some days later Madison by chance met Washington on the road when the President was on his way to Mount Vernon. The Chief Executive then handed Madison a letter which he had addressed to the congressman. It reiterated Washington's determination to retire and asked his fellow Virginian to draft a farewell address along certain clearly indicated lines. Only one thing could make him reconsider his decision to leave office—substantial evidence that a contest over succession would further imperil national unity.[118]

Jefferson on May 23 wrote Washington urging him to accept a second term.[119] He sincerely wanted the President to continue in office but he seized the occasion to press another point equally important to him. In arguing that Washington should remain as a force for unity in a time of widespread public dissatisfaction, he could explain that Hamilton was responsible for the unrest.

The Secretary of State assumed a pose of objectivity quite at variance with his real feelings about Hamilton. Even so, Jefferson was not simply carrying on a personal vendetta. Though his rivalry with Hamilton may have added piquancy to the attack, it was not a principal motive. Having made up his mind to withdraw from public life, he was not jockeying for personal political advantage. He was genuinely disturbed over what he regarded as a "monarchical" trend encouraged by Hamilton. He was so agitated that even as perceptive and sympathetic a Jefferson biographer as Nathan Schachner, lacking access to certain Hamilton correspondence advocating monarchy, pronounced the Secretary of State's concern on this score "almost pathological."[120]

In his assumed objectivity Jefferson listed the "real or imaginary" causes of discontent. He was supposedly simply relaying a catalog of things troubling the people without presuming to attest the validity of most of the items. He listed twenty-one complaints, all related directly or indirectly to the financial policies of the federal government. He made it clear that he held Washington blameless in all instances. Indeed, his praise of the President has been deemed excessive by some unaware of the effusiveness with which Jefferson customarily lauded anyone, high or low, who seemed deserving.

Having cleared the way by separating the President from the policies of the Treasury Secretary and his congressional followers, and even disarmingly admitting that his own fears might be excessive, Jefferson charged that the national debt had been grossly mishandled. It had become too large to be taken care of by the ordinary sources of revenue, so that the impost had been raised to such a height that the collectors might have to bear arms. Even so, the sums obtained were still insufficient to service the debt, and the federal government had to resort to excise taxes. This expedient was so unpopular as to invite mass resistance. To the Revolutionary generation, revolt against taxation was not inconceivable.

In obedience to the principle so often attributed to Sir Thomas Gresham, paper money issued by the National Bank was driving out dependable coinage. This ghost currency served only the lenders, whose annual profit of 10 to 12 percent was "taken out of the pockets of the people." The bank, which was supposed to stimulate commerce and insure national prosperity, was imperiling both commerce and agriculture by substituting "paper speculation" for true production.

The political and social effects of the bank, he argued, were even worse than the economic. The institution's policies had created in Congress a "corrupt squadron." The term now conjures up visions of outright bribery but Jefferson meant simply conflict of interest in that Congressmen who were stockholders in the bank were also framing the legislation that governed it. As we have seen, conflict of interest was not so damning in the eighteenth century as in some later periods. It might not have troubled Jefferson so much in this instance if he had not seen the "corrupt squadron" as deliberately eroding constitutional limitations, not solely for convenience but as part of a predetermined plan to convert the "present republican form of government to that of a monarchy, of which the English constitution is to be the model." Probably more of the "corrupt squadron" than Jefferson supposed were moved by exigency rather than by deep-seated philosophical convictions, but the great brain of the coalition—Hamilton—had confessed to intimates that he desired just such transformation.[121]

There was some hope, Jefferson conceded, that the upcoming congressional elections would return a majority dedicated to liberty. But the elections themselves posed a danger. The division of the electorate promised to be geographical as well as ideological. He could envision the eventual dissolution of the Union on North-South lines. If present policies reached far into the future, the South might have some excuse for seceding. The federal government, he said, had consistently "sacrificed" Southern interests, satisfying the North's commercial creditors at the expense of the South's agricultural debtors. The charge was not a very diplomatic one in view of the fact that Washington had been President during the entire life of the government. But there was a good deal of truth in it. Hamilton saw the future of the nation as resting principally with Northern commercial interests and favored them constantly. Washington was so determined to be free of sectional prejudice that he often acquiesced in the sacrifice of his own region.

Injustices to the South and to debtor interests, Jefferson maintained, now lent strength to the arguments of those who had gone down to defeat fighting against ratification of the Constitution. Suppose some of the true-blue Republicans who had supported ratification of that instrument now joined with opponents to destroy it? Jefferson said, "This is an event at which I tremble, and to prevent which I consider your continuance at the head of affairs as of the last importance." He said, too: "The confidence of the whole Union is centered in you. Your being at the helm will be more than an answer to every argument which can be used to alarm and lead the people, in any quarter, into violence or secession. North and South will hang together if they have you to hang on."

On July 10, after Washington's return to the capital, he discussed Jefferson's letter with him.[122] The President repeated his determination to retire. He feared that if he did not persist in that intention the public might conclude that "his former professions had been mere affectation, and that he was like other men: when once in office he could not quit it."

Washington was solemn, even sad. He did not feel fit to continue four more years. His hearing was increasingly impaired, he said. Suppose other faculties became similarly impaired without his being aware of the fact.

Then he sought to assuage Jefferson's fears. He assured him that monarchists constituted an insignificant proportion of the population. His own observations had not led him to conclude that dissatisfaction with the government was widespread, but if such was the case there might be no general desire that he continue in office.

Now the old eagle revealed something that had been sticking in his craw. He believed that much of the opposition to the excise law was being stirred up by Freneau's paper. Furthermore, he regarded many of the incendiary pieces as personal attacks on him. As for this fiction of his Administration being guilty of offenses in the financial sector while he himself remained innocent, "if they thought there were measures pursued contrary to his sentiment, they must conceive him too careless to attend to them or too stupid to understand them." Jefferson knew that Washington, in saying what he would like to say to Freneau, was really criticizing the Secretary himself. The President was angry when he said that he personally "must be a fool indeed to swallow the little sugar plums here and there thrown out to him." Honey laced with the gall of criticism obviously was a sickening dose. When Washington asserted that talk of his innocence in actions of his own Administration was an allegation of carelessness or stupidity, he impatiently swept aside the sophistry in Jefferson's letter.

The President had not ceased to hold the younger man in high regard (his lengthy confidential conversation proved that), but he was displeased with him. Jefferson had a filial affection for Washington and, besides being disappointed at the failure of his own arguments, he was hurt by the old chief's displeasure. Jefferson's optimism salvaged one compensation. He might have convinced the chief executive that a contest to succeed him would indeed breed great discord in the nation. Maybe Washington would consent to serve again.

Washington was a father figure to Hamilton too. That fact made more emotional the Treasury Secretary's reaction to a letter of July 19 in which the President listed Jefferson's 21 objections to federal financial policy.[123] Washington did not attribute these objections to Jefferson, but Hamilton seems to have had no doubt of their origin. In a lengthy reply composed of roughly equal parts of fiscal erudition and hauteur, he declared, "I have not fortitude enough always to hear with calmness calumnies which necessarily include me. . . I acknowledge that I cannot be entirely patient under charges which impeach the integrity of my public motives or conduct." He defended every item of his policy and apparently convinced Washington.

Though Hamilton insisted that he "in no degree" deserved any questioning of his motives, he had recently been impugning Jefferson's motives and attempting to destroy his Cabinet colleague's influence in Virginia. To Edward Carrington, United States Marshal for Virginia, he addressed a bulky letter saying: "Mr. Madison, cooperating with Mr. Jefferson, is at the head of a faction decidedly hostile to me and my administration; and actuated by views, in my judgement, subversive to the principles of good government and dangerous to the union, peace, and happiness of the country." Madison, he asserted, far from being "the simple, fair, candid one" he seemed, was an embittered schemer egged on by Jefferson. The Secretary of State's opposition, according to the Treasury Secretary, was personal, based partly on jealousy because the Virginian had wanted the Treasury post for himself. He was also trying to destroy Hamilton as an obstacle in his path to the Presidency. The Secretary of State, Hamilton warned, was "a man of profound ambition and violent passion." The amateur psychologist may be pardoned for seeing here a clear case of projection.

Hamilton did not succeed through this, or other efforts, in his attempt to build within Virginia a political machine hostile to Jefferson and Madison. Edward Carrington would seem, on the face of it, an unlikely foundation stone for such a structure. His office as marshal had been secured for him by Madison.

But Hamilton was attacking Jefferson in other quarters. Even before receiving Washington's letter based on the Secretary of State's 21 objections, the New Yorker had been writing letters against the Jeffersonians which he circulated widely under various pseudonyms. In the context of the times there was nothing especially cowardly about pseudonymous attacks; they were an accepted part of eighteenth-century political life. But the vehemence and violence of the assault was unusual when directed against a Cabinet colleague. And it was inconsistent in Hamilton to find Jefferson's opposition more irritating than Madison's because it was less frank, while he himself continued to sign various fictitious names to diatribes against Jefferson.

Jefferson had left Philadelphia for Monticello in mid-July and apparently was remaining aloof from political battles, even in his own state. The only significant contest between Federalists and Republicans was in New York, where Hamilton was backing Jay against George Clinton, incumbent candidate for Governor. Jefferson thought it unfortunate that Republican politicians had seen fit to support Clinton, and hence took no active interest in that fight. On August 12 he wrote to one of his favorite Philadelphians, David Rittenhouse: "I am here indulging in reverie and rural occupations, scarcely permitting anything to occupy my mind seriously. When I count the days I still have to remain here, I wish I could see at their end only the pleasure of meeting you again, and keep behind the curtain the table piled with papers, and the eternal sound of the door bell.''[124]

While the master of Monticello indulged in rural reverie Hamilton was busy in Philadelphia vilifying him. Sometimes using the initials "T.L.," sometimes signing himself "An American," he published six letters in July and August in the *Gazette of the United States*. First "T.L." made the charge that Freneau, editor of the Republican *National Gazette,* was in the employ of the State Department as a translator. This accusation, of course, was the simple truth. But he went too far when he charged that Freneau, long an enthusiastic Republican, had sold out his principles.

Freneau probably suspected that Hamilton was the author of the attack in the *Gazette of the United States* when he replied that not one line appearing in his own paper had been written by Jefferson. Freneau also countercharged that John Fenno, editor of the rival newspaper, was a well-rewarded "vile sycophant" of the Hamiltonians. In the ensuing verbal fencing with Freneau, the pompous Fenno was punctured by a score of well-aimed thrusts. Wearing one mask or another, Hamilton continued to insert himself into the fray, his chief target a straw man of his own construction labeled "Jefferson." This Jefferson was an enemy of the Constitution and an apostle of disunion. But Hamilton, encouraged by the applause of his followers, became reckless. He said that Jefferson was the head of a political party. The news surprised many of his readers, but some were as delighted as they were astonished and professed themselves ready to enlist under the new banner. Ironically, Hamilton had suggested that his rival, though pretending to "profound knowledge," was "ignorant of the most useful of all sciences— the science of human nature.''[125]

No matter how strongly Washington wished to exclude factionalism from the government of the United States, he could no longer ignore the existence of warring factions personified in his two principal Cabinet members. That they would ever again move properly in tandem seemed daily more unlikely, but he would not willingly part with either. He must play the peacemaker. Writing to Jefferson about the threat of an Indian war, he appended an appeal for cooperation in the Cabinet: "How unfortunate ...that whilst we are encompassed on all sides with avowed enemies and insidious friends...internal dissensions should be harrowing and tearing our vitals." If there is not greater tolerance, he said, "I believe it will be difficult, if not impracticable, to manage the reins of government or to keep the parts of it together." The experiment in union must be given every chance. If not, "in my opinion, the fairest prospect of happiness and prosperity that ever was presented to man will be lost, perhaps forever." He was not pointing an accusing finger at anyone. "My earnest wish and my fondest hope...is that instead of wounding suspicions and irritable charges, there may be liberal allowances, mutual forbearances and temporizing yieldings on *all sides*. Under the exercise of these, matters will go on smoothly and, if possible, more prosperously.''[126] Three days later, but Jefferson had no way of knowing it, Washington sent to Hamilton a letter in similar vein and partly identical wording.[127]

Hamilton and Jefferson rarely did anything in unison, but both answered Washington on September 9.

Hamilton wrote that if the President could not reconcile his two chief ministers "the period is not remote when the public good will require substitutes." It was also clear who Hamilton thought should make most of the concessions. He described himself as "the deeply injured party" and said that Jefferson had made him "the frequent subject of the most unkind whispers and insinuations." Hamilton complained: "I have long seen a formed party in the Legislature under his auspices, bent upon my subversion. I cannot doubt from the evidence I possess that the *National Gazette* was instituted by him for political purposes and that one leading object of it has been to render me and all the measures connected with my department as odious as possible." Despite this conspiracy, Hamilton said, he had long refrained from counterattacking Jefferson and had even protected him from attack.

But recently his patience had been exhausted. "I cannot conceal from you that I have had some instrumentality . . . in the retaliations which have fallen upon certain public characters and that I find myself placed in a situation not to be able to recede for the present." Duty had actuated his efforts "to draw aside the veil from the principal actors." This assertion that it would be necessary for him to continue his attacks for the present (until the elections were past?) made virtually worthless his assurance: "If you shall hereafter form a plan to reunite the members of your administration upon some steady principle of cooperation, I will faithfully concur in executing it during my continuance in office. And I will not directly or indirectly say or do a thing that shall endanger a feud."[128]

Jefferson wrote to the President from the peace and comfort of Monticello, which he must soon forsake. In a lengthy, logical letter he said that he had opposed Hamilton's economic and political system because it "flowed from principles adverse to liberty, and was calculated to undermine and demolish the Republic by creating an influence of his department over the members of the Legislature." He said that he had scrupulously refrained from interfering in Hamilton's department whereas Hamilton had repeatedly interfered in the conduct of foreign policy.

For the first time, Jefferson complained to Washington that the Secretary of the Treasury had entered into "cabals" with legislators and confidential conferences with foreign diplomats to frustrate the policies of the State Department and substitute Hamilton's own. When the New Yorker's policies predominated, "their execution fell, of course, to me; and I can safely appeal to you, who have seen all my letters and proceedings, whether I have not carried them into execution as sincerely as if they had been my own, though I ever considered them as inconsistent with the honor and interest of our country . . . . So that if the question be by whose fault is it that Colonel Hamilton and myself have not drawn together, the answer will depend on that to two other questions: Whose principles of administration best justify, by their purity, conscientious adherence? And which of us has, notwithstanding, stepped farthest into the control of the department of the other?" Contrasting his conduct with Hamilton's in another instance, he said that while he had secured subscriptions for Freneau's paper he had never written for it nor gotten anyone else to write for it. On the other hand Hamilton was responsible for the "late charges against me in Fenno's *Gazette;* for neither the style, matter, nor venom of the pieces alluded to can leave a doubt of their author." He asked, "Is not the dignity, and even decency, of government committed when one of its principal ministers enlists himself as an anonymous writer . . . ?"

Jefferson did not promise to gratify the President's wish for "temporizing yieldings." He reminded Washington that he was resigning as Secretary of State at the end of the President's first term. He did not feel free until then to deal with Hamilton's charges as he would like. He did not say precisely what he would do after March 4, 1793 but he did declare: "I will not suffer my retirement to be clouded by the slanders of a man whose history, from the moment at which history can stoop to notice him, is a tissue of machinations against the liberty of the country which has not only received (him) and given him bread, but heaped honors on his head."[129]

The frequency and animosity of Hamilton's published attacks increased in September. Under the classical pseudonyms Amicus and Catullus, he filled the columns of Fenno's paper with praise of himself and abuse of Jefferson. In one article he pictured the Virginian as "the intriguing incendiary, the aspiring, turbulent competitor," like Caesar "coyly refusing the proffered diadem" while "grasping the substance of imperial domination."[130] The derogatory reference to Caesar is interesting in view of Hamilton's earlier statement to Jefferson that Caesar was the greatest man in the history of the world.

When Edmund Randolph volunteered his services as a penman to answer the protean Hamilton, Jefferson replied that he had long held to a policy of never writing anonymously for publication and that he would not engage in controversy with anyone who did. "Every fact alleged under the signature of 'an American' as to myself is false, and can be proved so; and perhaps will be one day. But for the present, lying and scribbling must be free to those mean enough to deal in them, and in the dark."[131]

Randolph appears to have entered the fray anyway under a pseudonym, as did such loyal friends of Jefferson as Madison and Monroe. Over his various pen names Hamilton replied to them all, sometimes descending to the lowest level of personal gossip, as when he looked forward to the day "when the plain garb of Quaker simplicity is stripped from the concealed voluptuary."[132]

On his way back to Philadelphia from Monticello Jefferson stopped over at Mount Vernon. There on the morning of October 1 he and Washington talked at length about their common desire to retire from office.[133] Washington said that he was sorry to see his guest so fixed in that intention. He would be "extremely sorry" for the resignation to come during his Presidency. He "could not see where he should find another character to fill (the) office." The Secretary's interest quickened when his chief added that he personally was "quite undecided whether to retire in March or not. His inclinations led him strongly to do it. Nobody disliked more the ceremonies of his office, and he had not the least taste of gratification in the execution of its functions." The sunken look of the eyes and the sag at the corners of the mouth of that still majestic face reinforced the sincerity of the disavowal. He said that he was happy only at home and that his presence there was now "peculiarly called for" by the probably terminal illness of his nephew, who had been running the Mount Vernon farms for him. He did not believe his presence necessary in Philadelphia, but if it proved so for the principal cause to which he had devoted his life he would "make the sacrifice of a longer continuance." He would reserve his decision awhile. It "would be in time if made a month before the day of election."

The President said he had asked his personal secretary, Tobias Lear, to "find out from conversation, without appearing to make the inquiry, whether any other person would be desired by anybody." Lear had reported that Washington's continuance in office "was the universal desire." "But this," said Washington, "was only from the North; it may be very different in the South." Jefferson thought the President was providing a convenient opening for him to talk of opinion in the South. He replied, "As far as

I know, there is but one voice there, which is for your continuance."

Jefferson then talked of his own situation: "I have ever preferred the pursuits of private life to those of public, which have nothing in them agreeable to me." He talked of having been drawn reluctantly into public affairs by the circumstances of the late war and again, in the postwar period, being called "from a retirement on which I had determined. I have constantly kept my eye on my own home and can no longer refrain from returning to it." He insisted that Washington's situation was quite different: "His presence was important; . . . he was the only man in the United States who possessed the confidence of the whole; . . . government was founded in opinion and confidence; and . . . the longer he remained, the stronger would become the habits of the people in submitting to the government, and in thinking it a thing to be maintained; . . . no other person would be thought anything more than the head of a party."

Mention of parties opened the way for Washington to discuss his concern over the disagreements between Hamilton and Jefferson. Until very recently he had never suspected that their differences were personal as well as political. "He wished he could be the mediator to put an end to it." He said that Jefferson was needed in the Administration "in order to keep things in their proper channel, and keep them from going too far."

Once again he deprecated Jefferson's fear of a movement toward monarchy. "He did not believe there were ten men in the United States whose opinions were worth attention who entertained such a thought." Jefferson retorted that there were many more than the President imagined and recalled monarchist sentiments expressed by company at the President's own table "a little before we left Philadelphia." "Though the people are sound, there is," Jefferson insisted, "a numerous sect who have monarchy in contemplation. The Secretary of the Treasury is one of these. I have heard him say that this Constitution was a shilly-shally thing of mere milk and water which could not last and was only good as a step to something better." Jefferson found these words disturbing particularly when he "reflected that (Hamilton) had endeavored in the convention to make an English constitution of it, and when, failing in that, we saw all his measures tending to bring it to the same thing."

Fears were especially justified, Jefferson argued, "when we saw that these measures had established corruption in the legislature, where there was a squadron devoted to the nod of the Treasury, doing whatever he had directed, and ready to do what he should direct. . . . If the equilibrium of the three great bodies, legislative, executive, and judiciary, could be preserved, if the legislature could be kept independent, I should never fear the result of such a government; but . . . I cannot but be uneasy when I see that the executive has swallowed up the legislative branch."

Washington countered, "As to that interested spirit in the legislature, it is what cannot be avoided in any government unless we are to exclude particular descriptions of men, such as the holders of the funds, from all office."

Jefferson came back: "There is a great difference between the little accidental scheme of self-interest, which would take place in every body of men, and influence their votes, and a regular system for forming a corps of interested persons who should be steadily at the orders of the Treasury."

Washington began speaking in a placating way about the possible advantages of some of the federal fiscal measures, admitting that there was room for differences of opinion. He then began exhorting Jefferson to remain in office. At that moment a call to breakfast ended the conversation and it was not resumed at table.

In ensuing months attacks by Hamilton and his followers made retirement seem all the more attractive to Jefferson. The Secretary of State had designed for himself a swivel chair, which Hamilton now adopted as the symbol of what he regarded as the Virginian's weathervane policies. Sometimes he wrote cleverly on the subject, sometimes vulgarly with slang references to the portion of "his Honor's" anatomy occupying the seat. A South Carolina Hamiltonian who borrowed the same image also wrote that those seeking evidence of Jefferson's prowess as a warrior should consider "his exploits at Montecelli [sic]."[134] Here was a revival of the old canard that the Governor had fled in cowardly fashion before the approach of Tarleton's cavalry; in reality, the chief fault of Jefferson's conduct on that occasion was his near foolhardiness in delaying his departure.

But Jefferson's friends, particularly Madison and Monroe, dealt effectively with Hamilton's charges, citing from the records to prove his inaccuracy in statements of fact. The Secretary of State did not believe it necessary to remain in office to defend either his honor or his political philosophy, especially after learning in mid-November that Republicans had gained in the congressional elections. Anti-Federalist victories in nine of Pennsylvania's eleven districts should end Hamiltonian domination of the House. Informed opinion in the capital already assumed that Washington would accept another term. Jefferson instructed various United States diplomats in Europe to address future communications merely to the Secretary of State, not to him by name, as he might soon have a successor. Early in December he informed his Philadelphia landlord that he would be ending his lease in March, and he sold some of his furniture. Shortly after New Year's Day he began the joyous labor of packing for home.

Meanwhile, Jefferson had troubles that the public knew nothing about. These, too, were connected with Hamilton. In December 1792 the Secretary of the Treasury revealed to James Monroe and two other Republican congressmen that he had had an illicit affair with a Mrs. James Reynolds. The confidential revelation, in which Hamilton threw himself upon the honor of the trio as gentlemen, was made only to explain away as blackmail the charges which the woman's husband was preparing to make regarding the Secretary's operations within the Treasury. Probably as a way of silencing Jefferson and his colleagues regarding the Reynolds affair, Hamilton let them know that he knew of the Virginian's conduct with Mrs. Jack Walker in 1768 and might divulge it to others. Of course, the single embarrassing incident with Betsey Walker, whatever its exact nature, had not led to physical consummation whereas Hamilton's relationship with Mrs. Reynolds had been physically intimate, protracted, and sordid. There was no proper balance for a tradeoff unless one concluded that in personal conduct Jefferson had more reputation to lose than his cabinet colleague. Monroe did signal that the Secretary of State and his friends were not crouched in fear and trembling at the Treasury Secretary's threats when he invited the pseudonymous Catullus to "exhibit himself to the public view that we might behold in him a living monument of that immaculate purity to which he pretends, and which ought to distinguish so bold and arrogant a censor of others."[135]

So the thread of controversy with Hamilton stitched together the old year and the new. And if the new brought for Jefferson the bracing prospect of escape from onerous employment it brought also a whole train of events that almost weekly made such retirement less consistent with duty. New Year's Day itself brought in Philadelphia a popular celebration of the creation of the French Republic. Many of the celebrants called themselves Jacobins as well as Republicans and, embarrassingly if flatteringly, looked to Jefferson for leadership. Americans were becoming divided over the new French government, some eager to embrace their Gallic brothers in revolution, others recoiling in horror from those who had overthrown the monarchy. Almost every sort of public occasion provided an opportunity for display of sentiment on one side or the other. On January 9 Jefferson, apparently accompanied by fourteen-year-old Polly, saw the first balloon ascension in the United States. Jean-Pierre Blanchard, the French aeronaut, waved both the United States flag and the French tricolor as he took off in his yellow silk balloon before a Philadelphia audience of thousands. But the political aspects intrigued Jefferson less than the utilitarian. To Martha, back in Virginia, he wrote: "The security of the thing appeared so great that everyone is wishing for a balloon to travel in. I wish for one sincerely, as instead of ten days I should be within five hours of home."[136]

Though determinedly antimonarchical and bitterly opposed to Hamilton, Jefferson was far from being an ideologue. He did not favor every candidate who wore the Republican label, nor wish ill to every Federalist rival. Certainly John Adams was a Federalist and, Jefferson suspected, more than half a monarchist; but the Virginian was not sorry to see his old friend reelected Vice President over Republican George Clinton when Washington was returned to the Presidency by unanimous vote of the electors. In a letter to Thomas Pinckney, American minister to England, the Secretary of State had correctly predicted: "There will be a strong vote against Mr. Adams, but the strength of his personal worth and his services will, I think, prevail over the demerit of his political creed."[137] Adams had received 77 electoral votes, Clinton 50. Jefferson, though not a candidate, had received four votes from Kentucky.

With all Jefferson's worries, things were still going better for him than for his archrival. Not only was Hamilton at least half sick for most of January 1793, but his operations of the Treasury were being subjected to intense and hostile scrutiny both in the Congress and outside. On January 23 William Branch Giles, a young Virginia congressman who had rapidly won distinction at the bar after studying under George Wythe, introduced resolutions in the House of Representatives. There had been in the Senate unpublicized requests for an accounting by the Treasury Secretary and Giles himself had previously moved for a general accounting. But the new Giles Resolutions, besides being publicized, went farther than anything from the Senate in demanding a full and detailed report. They charged Hamilton with defying the House's formal request for information, with borrowing from the bank at five percent interest when public funds were available, and with ignoring orders in the transfer of funds. They also accused him of misapplication of appropriated funds and of dereliction in office.

Working with the remarkable speed and efficiency which he could bring to fiscal reports, Hamilton soon submitted, in rapid fire installments, a complete accounting with vouchers and other documentation. These revealed that the Secretary had violated certain legal technicalities and had acted highhandedly but they did not support any suspicions of dishonorable conduct. Of course, they also did nothing to eradicate the impression that he had been contemptuous of the Congress's right to be informed.

While the investigation of the Treasury was in progress, Jefferson visited the President on February 7 on State Department business and took occasion to tell him of a change in personal plans. He said that doubts about whether the Senate would vote for continuance of United States diplomatic establishments in Europe had caused him to suspend speaking with him "on the subject of my going out of office." If the Senate had ended the operation of ministries "the remaining business of the department would be too inconsiderable to make it worth while to keep. But. . . the bill being now passed, I was freed from the considerations of propriety which had embarrassed me." Jefferson offered, if the President had made "no arrangement to the contrary, to continue somewhat longer." How long he could not say, "perhaps till summer, perhaps autumn."[138]

Washington replied that, "so far from [making] arrangements on the subject, he had never mentioned to any mortal [Jefferson's] desire of retiring, till yesterday." Then, hearing that the Secretary had given up his house and that it was "rented by another," he had mentioned the fact to Edmund Randolph, had asked him if he knew that Jefferson's retirement had been talked of, and whether he had heard any successors suggested. Washington expressed his pleasure that such considerations were now unnecessary and confessed his earlier "apprehensions that [Jefferson's] retirement would be a new source of uneasiness to the public." That very day Governor Lee of Virginia (Lighthorse Harry of the Revolution) had told the president of "the general discontent prevailing in Virginia." Until then the Chief Executive had never had "any conception" of it, "much less sound information." He found it "very alarming." Once again he expressed his "earnest wish" that the Secretaries of State and Treasury "could coalesce in the measures of the government" and repeated his arguments of former conversations. Now he added that he had reasoned in the same way with Hamilton, who had "expressed his readiness." Washington thought that such a "coalition would secure the general acquiescence of the public."

At first Jefferson was a little evasive: "My concurrence is of much less importance than you seem to imagine. I keep myself aloof from all cabal and correspondence on the subject of the government, and see and speak with as few as I can."

Then he spoke more directly: "As to a coalition with Mr. Hamilton, if by that is meant that either is to sacrifice his general system to the other, it is impossible. We have both, no doubt, formed our conclusions after the most mature consideration. And principles conscientiously adopted cannot be given up on either side." He declared his "wish to see both Houses of Congress cleansed of all persons interested in the bank or public stocks; a pure legislature being given us, I should always be ready to acquiesce under their determinations, even if contrary to my own opinions, for. . . I subscribe to the principle that the will of the majority, honestly expressed, should give law."

He confirmed what Governor Lee had said about discontents in the South and said they were "grounded on seeing that their judgements and interests were sacrificed to those of the Eastern states on every occasion, and their belief that it was the effect of a corrupt squadron of voters in Congress, at the command of the Treasury." How Jefferson loved that phrase "corrupt squadron"! This time he gave it new force by pointing out that if "those members who had any interest distinct from and contrary to the general interest of their constituents" had disqualified themselves from voting on the concerned issues, "the laws would have been the reverse of what they are on all the great questions." He cited the new Assumption bill, which had passed in the House only by the Speaker's tie-breaking vote.

At this point the President must have looked inexpressibly weary. He ceased to argue. He had agreed to remain in office, he said, because of "strong solicitations" after he returned to Philadelphia from his visit to Mount Vernon. He spoke of the "extreme wretchedness of his existence." Now people were even attacking him for the royal formality of the levees at which he recently had granted audiences in New York. He had been "led into them by the persons he consulted" there. "If he could but know what the sense of the public was, he would most cheerfully conform to it."

A few days later, Edmund Randolph told Jefferson something learned from Tobias Lear. For three weeks after arriving in New York, the President had resisted pressure to introduce levees. When he did yield he "left it to (his aid David) Humphreys and some others to settle the forms. Accordingly, an antechamber and presence room were provided, and when those who were to pay their court were assembled, the President set out, preceded by Humphreys." When he had passed through the antechamber, "the door of the inner room was thrown open, and Humphreys entered first, calling out with a loud voice, 'The President of the United States.' The President was so much disconcerted with it that he did not recover from it the whole time of the levee, and when the company was gone, he said to Humphreys, 'Well, you have taken me in once, but by God you shall never take me in a second time.' "[139]

After witnessing Washington's misery a few days before and now hearing this anecdote, Jefferson had a new appreciation of what his chief was enduring. Jefferson himself was committed only to serving till summer or, at most, autumn. When he saw Washington, clad in a velvet suit and silk stockings (both as black as mourning garb), stand to take the oath of office on March 4 for a second term, he knew that the President was accepting a sentence of four more years of hard labor and abuse.

Jefferson, too, was beginning a new term, even though he was not committed to completing it. As statesman and politician, he was actively concerned with events in his own Virginia, in the nation, and in the world. In the Old Dominion, things were much to his liking. Monroe was now the senior senator from the Commonwealth, Richard Henry Lee having resigned and been replaced by John Taylor of Caroline. Tall, lean, redheaded, the forty-year-old Taylor might have been taken for Jefferson's brother. Their philosophical profiles were even more alike: Taylor believed that the security of the Republic rested with the tillers of the earth and he had written a pamphlet decrying moneyed influence in Congress and the specific evils of Hamiltonianism. The most influential member of Virginia's delegation in the House continued to be Madison. Alexander White, the only member who sided with Hamilton, had been defeated. From Virginia Monroe sent encouraging news about the General Assembly and the mass of voters: "In every respect, so far as we have heard, we find the public mind perfectly sound in regard to those objects of national policy at present most interesting. Every member (of the legislature) is either as he should be, or has gained his place by fraud and imposition."[140]

On the national scene Jefferson did not find the situation so satisfactory. Speculation about his association with the Giles Resolutions ranged from theories that he was their author to assumptions that he was merely an interested spectator of this latest effort to embarrass Hamilton. Of his emotional involvement in the whole matter there can be no doubt. Jefferson was a shrewd political analyst and he had a long list of congressmen whom he believed members of the "corrupt squadron." He can have held little hope that the Giles Resolutions would actually pass, and may have believed that their chief value lay in alerting a sizeable minority, in and out of the Congress, to the necessity for watching Hamilton. Nevertheless, when the resolutions failed by wide margins, Jefferson's chagrin at defeat probably almost equaled Hamilton's joy of vindication. In private correspondence the Virginian blamed the result on complacency, ignorance, and malice.

He found no comfort in the international scene. Two weeks before the inauguration, Colonel William S. Smith, John Adams's son-in-law, recently returned from Paris, had called on the Secretary of State. Seven years before, Smith had observed, "I know of no gentleman better qualified to pass over the disagreeables of life than Mr. Jefferson."[141] The news he brought now severely tested Jefferson's reputation for equanimity. The French ministers had "entirely broken with Gouverneur Morris, shut their doors to him, and will never receive another communication from him."[142] Smith had declined the request that he be the bearer to the United States government of a message to this effect from the President of France. The messenger, therefore, would be a newly appointed French Minister to the United States, Edmond Charles Genêt.

There was encouragement in Smith's information that Genêt would have full powers to give the United States "all the [commercial] privileges we can desire in their countries, and particularly the West Indies." There were even grandiose plans to "emancipate South America" from Spain, for which purpose forty-five ships of the line would be sent in the spring. These glittering possibilities did not counterbalance the hard fact of Gouverneur Morris's failure in his mission, a failure foreseen by Jefferson when he reluctantly backed the appointment out of loyalty to Washington.

Only five or six days before the conversation with Smith, the Secretary of State had received from Ternant a collection of extracts from the letters of officials in Paris. These were highly critical not only of Morris, but also of Short. Jefferson was especially sorry to see his former secretary in line for a reprimand, but the older man had earlier been disturbed by his protégé's growing antipathy for the government in Paris, as had Washington. In a letter perfervid in reproof of what Jefferson regarded as the apostasy of a disciple of liberty (perhaps a disciple of his own), he wrote: "The liberty of the whole earth was depending on the issue of the contest, and was ever such a prize won with so little innocent blood? My own affections have been deeply wounded by some of the martyrs to this cause, but rather than it should have failed, I would have seen half the earth desolated. Were there but an Adam and an Eve left in every country, and left free, it would be better than as it now is."[143]

Fortunately, Jefferson was always far more levelheaded and discreet in public actions and statements than in some of his personal letters. He apparently translated personally the papers furnished by Ternant rather than entrusting them even to Freneau. He may have been moved by a general awareness of the need for discretion or by a specific desire to protect Short. On the day of the conversation with Smith he sent these translations to the President together with an extract from a private letter in which Short sought to justify himself. That evening Jefferson called on the President.[144] Washington was fully impressed with the seriousness of the situation and said that Morris must be recalled. Yet he saw opportunities for the United States if the situation was dealt with properly. Unfortunately, he was "extremely at a loss what arrangement to make." Jefferson asked if Morris in Paris and Pinckney in London might not change places. Washington said that "would be a sort of remedy, but not a radical one." Then he revealed what he really had in mind. He said that, though Jefferson had "unfixed the day" on which he intended to resign as Secretary of State, he appeared "fixed in doing it at no great distance of time." He thus would be free to replace Morris as Minister to France. Jefferson had the confidence of both factions in France and "might do great good." Washington wished that Jefferson would accept "were it only to stay there a year or two."

Jefferson was emphatic: "My mind is so bent on retirement that I could not think of launching forth again in a new business. I could never again cross the Atlantic. As to the opportunity of doing good, this [Philadelphia] is likely to be the scene of action, as Genêt is bringing power to do the business here. I cannot think of going abroad."

"You pressed me to continue in the public service," Washington said, "and refuse to do the same yourself."

"The case is very different," Jefferson retorted. "You unite the confidence of all America and are the only person who does . . . . for myself, my going out would not be noted or known. A thousand others could supply my place to equal advantage. Therefore I feel myself free. As to the mission in France, I think Pinckney perfectly proper."

Washington pressed the point no more.

Later Jefferson began to think more about the opportunities than the troubles presented by the French crisis. Smith had said that the French planned to begin their attack on Spanish America at the mouth of the Mississippi and sweep southward along the Gulf of Mexico. "They would have no objection to our incorporating into our government the two Floridas."[145] Jefferson, previously prepared to guarantee Spain's possessions west of the Mississippi in exchange for a cession of those to the east, now instructed Short and his fellow commissioner in Madrid to make no such offer.

In marked contrast to his emotional "Adam and Eve" letter to Short, Jefferson soon began writing letters to American representatives in Europe prudently advising them that the United States could be expected to observe strict neutrality if there should be a general war. Early in April, Jefferson learned that France on February 1 had declared war on Great Britain and Holland. A little later he would learn that France was also at war with Spain. Though his sympathies were engaged by the infant republic's struggle against the imperial dynasties seeking to crush it, the Secretary of State was not at all disposed to see half the earth devastated in the interest of French liberty.

He was certainly not disposed to see an acre of United States soil bloodied. No one was more aware than he that the American alliance with a France allied against the mightiest powers in the world placed his country in grave danger. The United States was not strong enough and stable enough to wage another war. Jefferson heard in the blast of the trumpet no call to glory. He listened to no "ancestral voices prophesying war." His counsel was consistently for peace. In his letter of April 7 informing the President of the outbreak of general war in Europe, the Secretary of State said that the United States must "take every justifiable measure for preserving our neutrality."[146]

Jefferson's letter had called Washington back from a vacation at Mount Vernon. On April 18, one day after his return, Washington submitted a set of thirteen questions for the consideration of each cabinet member and called a meeting for their discussion.[147] Jefferson confided to his personal journal: "Though those sent me were in his own handwriting, yet it was palpable from the style, their ingenious tissue and suite, that they were not the President's, that they were raised upon a prepared chain of argument, in short, that the language was Hamilton's, and the doubts his alone. They led to a declaration of the executive that our treaty with France is void." Edmund Randolph, having heard Hamilton run through "the whole chain of reasoning" the day before, had no doubts whatsoever of the authorship.

When the Cabinet were assembled with the President, they unanimously answered in the affirmative the first question, whether Genêt should be received as minister from France. Hamilton did express strong regret that the United States was obliged to recognize the new French government. The next question was whether Genêt "should be received absolutely or with qualifications. Here Hamilton took up the whole subject and went through it in the order in which the questions sketch it." Jefferson was not charitable in his private notes. He wrote, "Knox subscribed at once to Hamilton's opinion that we ought to declare the treaty void, acknowledging, at the same time, like a fool as he is, that he knew nothing about it." Jefferson summarizes his own opinion with a terse, "I was clear it remained valid." Randolph at first agreed with Jefferson but, after Hamilton quoted the jurist Emmerich von Vattel in opposition, the Attorney General said he would take further time to consider. The Cabinet determined unanimously that Congress should not be called into special session to supply an answer. Jefferson noted: "There having been an intimation by Randolph that in so great a question he should choose to give a written opinion, and this being approved by the President, I gave in mine April 28th. Hamilton gave in his. I believe Knox's was never thought worth offering or asking for."

While all the conferees were prepared to endorse a policy of neutrality, at least in theory, there was disagreement as to whether neutrality should be publicly proclaimed or merely observed without proclamation. Hamilton was strong for a proclamation. Jefferson argued that it should at least be deferred. A declaration of neutrality, he said, would amount to an official statement that the United States would not go to war. Since a declaration of war was constitutionally the responsibility of Congress, a declaration that the nation would not go to war was not within the province of the Executive. He also cited a practical reason for postponing such a statement. Would it not be wise "to hold back the declaration of neutrality as a thing worth something to the powers at war [so] that they would bid for it, and we might reasonably ask a price, the broadest privilege of neutral nations?" When all others present agreed with the Secretary of the Treasury, however, Jefferson assented. He had gained a minor compromise: the actual word "neutrality" would not be used in the official document.

There remained for final decision by the President the question of whether the treaty with France was void. Jefferson's written opinion, supported later by Randolph's, prevailed. It is a milestone document in American diplomatic history.[148] He wrote: "I consider the people who constitute a society or nation as the source of all authority in that nation, as free to transact their common concerns by any agents they think proper, to change these agents individually, or the organization of them in form or function whenever they please: that all the acts done by those agents under the authority of the nation are the acts of the nation, are obligatory on them, and inure to their use, and can in no wise be annulled or affected by any change in the form of the government or by the persons administering it." The United States did not have a treaty with the late Louis Capet but with the sovereign nation that he had once represented.

Jefferson here foreshadowed one aspect of the doctrine of self-determination of peoples which would be enunciated by a later Virginia-born President, Woodrow Wilson. Jefferson countered Hamilton's citation of Vattel with a quotation from the same authority: "He who does not observe a treaty is assuredly perfidious since he violates his faith." He also buttressed his position with quotations in parallel columns from three authorities in international law: Grotius, Pufendorf, and Wolff. Jefferson maintained that Hamilton's argument was based on a quotation contrary to the context from which it was lifted. He was contemptuous that "this scrap should have been culled, and made the hook whereon to hang such a chain of immoral consequences." He believed that morality was important among nations as well as among individuals.

When the two chief Secretaries wrote opinions on fiscal matters, Hamilton sometimes made Jefferson seem naive. But in this matter of international law Hamilton's diffuse opinion, lacking in substance, compared most unfavorably with Jefferson's well-researched and compact writing.

Washington issued a foreign policy proclamation on April 22. Drafted by the Attorney General, it carefully avoided the word "neutrality." It proclaimed that the United States was at peace with both France and Great Britain and warned American citizens against hostile acts toward either belligerent.

Jefferson obtained less of a compromise in another matter. Hamilton proposed that the customs inspectors, who were under his department's jurisdiction, be the chief agents to enforce neutrality. Jefferson was disturbed that men owing their jobs to the Secretary of the Treasury should be official informers and spies on fellow citizens. He thought that, if Americans were to be prosecuted for violations of neutrality, it should be through the operation of grand juries and judges, not through "the secret information of a collector." Jefferson believed that, because of his quarrel with Hamilton, he could not make the case as appropriately as Randolph. But when he urged Randolph to take the initiative, he found the Attorney General's views equivocal. Jefferson did not like Randolph's proposal, accepted by Hamilton, that the customs collectors serve as agents but report to the district attorneys. Jefferson reminded Randolph that the customs collectors had "been suspected to be a corps, trained to the arts of spies, in the service of the Treasury." Jefferson was offended by Randolph's airy assurance that Hamilton had said he was not "prying into the conduct of individuals."

The final decision was that the customs men should report violations of neutrality to district attorneys and governors. No longer keeping to himself his disgust with his Virginia cousin, Jefferson wrote Madison that the decision had rested on the opinion of a single person, "the most indecisive one I ever had to do business with. He always contrives to agree in principle with one but in conclusion with the other."[149] Jefferson told Monroe that on most matters now the cabinet divided two and one-half to one and one-half. This odd reckoning was made possible by the fact that one member, Randolph, was a divided man.[150]

At best, the official policy of "strict and impartial neutrality" would have involved the Secretary of State, as Jefferson said, in matters "equally delicate, difficult and disagreeable."[151] But it soon became clear that the task would be enormously complicated by the character and activities of the new French ambassador. Citizen Genêt, as he preferred to be titled, arrived in Charleston, South Carolina, aboard a 36-gun French frigate. The thirty-year-old diplomat had the great curved beak of a bird of prey,[152] but everything about him looked good to the enthusiastic crowd that greeted him. Governor William Moultrie, a veteran major general of the American Revolution, gave substance to his effusiveness by permitting the Frenchman immediately to arm some privateers. Genêt reported to Paris that this outfitting was facilitated "while taking certain precautions in order still for a while to safeguard the neutrality of the United States."[153]

By ironic coincidence, word of Genêt's arrival reached Philadelphia on the very day that Washington's proclamation of neutrality was issued. The Frenchman's triumphal progress northward to the capital took thirty-nine days. Amid all the toast-filled evenings that delayed his progress along a path bestrewn with blossoming branches and flowery compliments, he found time to equip and arm four privateers, recruit Americans to sail them, turn them loose upon British merchant ships, and arrange to have their captured prizes brought back to American ports. He also commissioned American citizens for military service against Spanish Florida and Spanish-held Louisiana.

Jefferson knew only about the convivial aspects of Genêt's tour. Unaware of the flagrant breaches of United States neutrality and sovereignty, he rejoiced that the visit had stirred anew the "spirit of 1776." His joy was moderated only a little by consideration that partisan hearts might imperil national neutrality. Accordingly, when Genêt, fresh from cheering crowds in the streets of Philadelphia, presented his credentials to the Secretary of State, Jefferson gave him a warm welcome. The Secretary then escorted him to the President, who received him with cool politeness.[154]

Washington's coolness was partly habitual reserve but also partly his reaction to a recent event. The *Embuscade,* the same French frigate that had brought Genêt to Charleston, had come ahead of him up the coast to Philadelphia, bringing the captured British merchant ship *Grange.* In letters to his son-in-law[155] and his nephew,[156] Jefferson had enthusiastically described the "prodigious joy" of thousands of Pennsylvanians who, "when they saw the British colors reversed and the French flag flying above," "rent the air with peals of exultation." Very different was the mood of Hammond when he called on the Secretary of State to protest that the *Grange* had not been captured on the high seas but in Delaware Bay. These circumstances were new to Jefferson. Instantly he promised that, if the capture had indeed taken place in American territorial waters, the United States would not tolerate it. When investigation confirmed the validity of Hammond's complaint, Jefferson immediately insisted that the French return ship and cargo to the British and free the prisoners. The formal request from the Secretary of State had been addressed to Ternant, but Genêt acquiesced after presenting his credentials.

Hammond protested again. Another captured British vessel had been carried into Charleston, where the French consul had condemned it and offered it for sale. If the report was correct, the Secretary of State assured him, the proceeding was a legal nullity and the consul had committed "an act of disrespect towards the United States." The report was confirmed. Jefferson diplomatically but firmly told the French minister that "an error in judgement" had been committed by a "particular officer" and asked him to prevent similar "errors."[157]

There were many more such cases, not all so clear-cut as the first two. Hammond claimed that American neutrality was violated when privateers, equipped in Charleston by Genêt and manned by American sailors, captured British ships at sea and brought them into American ports. On May 20 Washington's Cabinet faced the question: "Shall the privateer fitted out at Charleston and her prizes be ordered out of the ports of the United States?"[158] The word "privateer," as soon became evident, might as well have been pluralized.

In the meeting Jefferson defended Genêt. He said that the Frenchman might very well have been operating under Article XXII of the old treaty between the United States and France, which stated that it "shall not be lawful for enemies of France to fit out privateers." The "implication," he argued, was that it "shall be lawful for the French." Perhaps such actions now were forbidden but, until the French were apprised of this fact, they must be only a "slight offense." What right did the federal government have to order the privateer away? Article XVII of the old treaty made it "lawful to enter with prizes and stay." He would concede that the treaty provided no justification for condemning and selling the prizes of war. As to the accusation that French privateers were manned by Americans, Jefferson accepted the French claim that they were manned by Frenchmen resident in the United States. French citizens, he said, even in a foreign country, "retain fidelity to their own." They had a "right to return to defense of (their) country by sea or land," might buy a vessel with their own money, and "man her themselves on condition (that they commenced) no hostilities within limits of the United States." As soon as they were out of limits, they and their vessel would be "free as any other."

Jefferson urged that it would be a mistake to enter upon a "policy of this touchiness" when the first minister from the Republic of France was "newly arrived." He cited the popularity in the United States of the "French nation and cause" and the welcome proposals, brought by the French minister, to grant free trade with France and its colonies. "Should such a mission (be received) with reprimand?" And for whom would we be spurning France? "For England? For (the) Confederate princes?" He concluded, "The party wishing that is very small."

This impassioned plea had little influence on Jefferson's colleagues. Hamilton and Knox said that France should be forced to give up the prize. "If that could not be," then both privateer and prize should be ordered away. "If that could not be, then order away the privateer." Randolph argued for "ordering away the privateer and nothing more." Washington agreed so readily that Jefferson assumed the President had been of that opinion before hearing all the discussion.

Jefferson called on the President on May 23, the day after sending him the drafts of letters he had prepared for the Chief Executive's signature.[159] They were largely routine correspondence with officers of the French government incident to Genêt's replacement of Ternant. The President did not routinely approve. He said there was an expression in one of them which he had "never before seen in any of our public communications"—"our republic." In the phrase "your minister plenipotentiary to *our republic*" the President, or somebody, had underscored the offending words. "He said that certainly ours was a republican government, but yet we had not used that style in this way; that if anybody wanted to change its form into a monarchy, he was sure it was only a few individuals, and that no man in the United States would set his face against it more than himself; but that this was not what he was afraid of; his fears were from another quarter; that there was more danger of anarchy being introduced."

Washington then referred to an article that had appeared the day before in Freneau's newspaper. The President said that he "despised" all the personal attacks on himself, but that there never had been "an act of the government, not meaning in the executive line only, but in any line, which that paper had not abused."

At home a little later, Jefferson recorded the conversation in his journal, and wrote:

> He was evidently sore and warm, and I took his intention to be that I should interpose in some way with Freneau, perhaps withdraw his appointment of translating clerk to my office. But I will not do it. His paper has saved our constitution, which was galloping fast into monarchy, and has been checked by no one means so powerfully as by that paper. It is well and universally known that it has been that paper which has checked the career of the monocrats.

He added: "The President, not sensible of the designs of the party, has not with his usual good sense and *sang froid*, looked on the efforts and effects of this free press, and seen that, though some bad things have passed through it to the public, yet the good have preponderated immensely." Jefferson's criticism was confided to the private pages of his *Anas* and even then was moderated by a compliment. At that, it marked, so far as we know, the first interruption of that filial reverence which he had always shown to the older man whose sturdy resourcefulness in both wilderness and forum was reminiscent of Jefferson's own father. Unremitting responsibility and uninterrupted criticism had frayed the nerves of both President and Secretary of State. They were tired of each other.

Jefferson was disenchanted with the world in which he labored. Even home was no longer a settled place of refuge but temporary quarters on the Schuylkill River where he existed amid packing cases ready for removal to Monticello. The connotations that the word "republican" had for Washington evidenced conclusively that the President and the Secretary of State quite literally did not speak the same language. The most influential member of the Cabinet, Jefferson wrote Monroe, was Hamilton, who was "panic-struck if we refuse our breech to every kick which Great Britain may choose to give it. He is for proclaiming at once the most abject principles, such as would invite and merit habitual insults. And indeed every inch of ground must be fought in our councils to desperation in order to hold up the face of even a sneaking neutrality."[160] Knox he saw as an empty-headed echo of the Treasury Secretary. Even Randolph's suave and swarthy charm now seemed an alien oleaginousness to grease his way between contending factions. None of Jefferson's colleagues seemed very attractive now. His private writings suggest that at times he did not particularly like himself.

He did not even have the comfort of Madison's understanding presence. But he could still unburden himself in correspondence with his friend, now back at Montpelier, his Virginia home. Madison replied: "I feel for your situation but you must bear it. Every consideration, private as well as public, requires a further sacrifice of your longings for the repose of Monticello." Madison explained the "private consideration": "You must not make your final exit from public life till it will be marked with justifying circumstances which all good citizens will respect, and to which your friends can appeal. At the present crisis, what would the former think, what would the latter say?"[161]

Jefferson replied with uncommon eloquence that still touches the heart:

To my fellow citizens the debt of service has been fully and faithfully paid.
I acknowledge that such a debt exists, that a tour of duty, in whatever line he
can be most useful to his country, is due from every individual. . . . I have now
been in the public service four and twenty years, one half of which has been spent
in total occupation with their affairs and absence from my own. I have served
my tour then. No positive engagement, by word or deed, binds me to their further service. . . .

The motion of my blood no longer keeps time with the tumult of the world.
It leads me to seek for happiness in the lap and love of my family, in the society
of my neighbors and my books, in the wholesome occupations of my farm and
my affairs, in an interest or affection in every bud that opens, in every breath that
blows around me, in an entire freedom of rest or motion, of thought or incog-
itancy, owing account to myself alone of my hours and actions.[162]

He concluded with a threnody for dead hopes, picturing himself

Worn down with labors from morning to night and day to day; knowing them
as fruitless to others as they are vexatious to myself, committed singly in desperate
and eternal contest against a host who are systematically undermining the public
liberty and prosperity, even the rare hours of relaxation sacrificed to the society
of persons in the same intentions, of whose hatred I am conscious even in those
moments of conviviality when the heart wishes most to open itself to the effusions of friendship and confidence, cut off from my family and friends, my affairs
abandoned to chaos and derangement, in short, giving everything I love, in
exchange for everything I hate, and all this without a single gratification, in possession or prospect, in present enjoyment or future wish.

One measure of Jefferson's loneliness and unhappiness is the degree of indiscretion with which he warned Genêt that Hamilton was really pro-British and anti-French
and to be avoided. He was determined that the Secretary of the Treasury should not
intervene as he had in discussions between the Secretary of State and Ternant. If Genêt's
own account may be trusted, Jefferson even went so far, in transmitting unpleasant communications to the French minister, as to assure him that the Secretary of State was
only "the passive instrument of the President."[163]

Genêt continued to flatter. With a grandiloquence that greatly exceeded his mastery
of the English language and produced a ludicrous result, he wrote Jefferson that Paris
proposed to the United States the establishment "in a true family pact, that is, in a national compact, the liberal and fraternal basis on which she wishes to see raised the
commercial and political system of two People, all whose interests are confounded."
In ensuing weeks the interests of the United States and France became increasingly
"confounded."[164]

Genêt was not pursuing the possibility of a commercial alliance with the United
States nearly so energetically as he was prosecuting a war from American shores. The
taking of the British ship *Catharine* two and a half miles off the Atlantic Coast of the

United States led to a proclamation that American sovereignty extended three miles out to sea, the maximum distance of cannon fire at the time. Precedent after precedent in the implementation of American neutrality was established by Jefferson as he dealt with Genêt in connection with repeated violations. Upon mature reflection, the Secretary of State had revised his interpretation of Article XXII of the old treaty between the United States and France. If the enemies of France were not allowed to outfit privateers in American ports, he now said, "we ought not therefore to permit France to do it, the treaty leaving us free to refuse, and the refusal being necessary to preserve a fair and secure neutrality."[165]

Jefferson's sympathies with French republicanism did not seduce him from tough-minded enforcement of American neutrality. Neither did the blandishments and appeals of American voters who claimed him as their leader. Genêt protested to the Secretary the removal from the French privateer *Citizen Genêt*, in Philadelphia, of two "French" officers, Gideon Henfield and John Singletary, and demanded their immediate release. Actually, they were Americans commissioned in Charleston by the French. The Secretary of State explained that the men were in custody of the civil authorities, over whom the executive branch of the federal government exercised no control.

Indicted by a grand jury in Pennsylvania, Henfield was prosecuted by the federal district attorney in Philadelphia with the aid of Attorney General Randolph. The three lawyers for defense were members of the Republican Party, which increasingly looked to Jefferson for leadership. One of them was the son-in-law of his old friend Rittenhouse. The jury, apparently caught up in Republican sympathy, reported "not guilty," a verdict enthusiastically saluted by Freneau's paper. In effect, the editor saw the erection of a milestone in American jurisprudence, one proclaiming in deeply etched letters: "Henceforth there can be no doubt that a citizen of the United States has a perfect legal right to board a French privateer."

Lest silence be mistaken for acquiescence Jefferson wrote to Gouverneur Morris, "No citizen has a right to go to war of his own authority; and, for what he does without right, he ought to be punished."[166] The Secretary of State viewed the verdict as a pardon for one "ignorant of the unlawfulness of his undertaking." The United States government could not tolerate individual actions that violated neutrality out of sympathy for either Britain or France.

When Genêt protested the President's decision that privateers be ordered out of American ports, Jefferson told him there would be no concessions on this point. Several weeks later, Genêt told Jefferson that he would not arm any more privateers in American ports but point blank refused to give up those already commissioned. By this time the Secretary of State had had more than enough of this agitator who waved his diplomatic credentials with one hand and with the other paid out gold to suborn American citizens.

When Jefferson instructed the federal district attorney in New York to prosecute both citizens and noncitizens involved in the outfitting and arming of a sloop in that city to prey on British commerce, Genêt vehemently protested that the vessel had been armed for defensive, not offensive, action. The Secretary of State replied that even France's own consul in New York had admitted otherwise; then he cited both the laws of man and the laws of nature to support the United States government's policy of neutrality.[167]

Genêt replied: "Let us not lower ourselves to the level of ancient politics by diplomatic subtleties." As for Jefferson's arguments, "I do not hesitate to tell you that they rest on a basis which I cannot admit."[168]

Henfield had become a hero to some of the more radical Republicans in the United States. In reference to that officer's case Genêt had appealed to Jefferson: "Do not punish the brave individuals of your nation who arrange [range?] themselves under our banner, knowing perfectly well that no law of the United States gives to the government the sad power of arresting their zeal by acts of rigor. The Americans are free; . . . they may change their situation when they please."[169] So the French minister admonished on United States law the American Secretary of State; so he lectured on Americanism the author of the Declaration of Independence. Now he addressed his inflammatory invocations to "all Republican Americans." Jefferson wrote to Madison, "He will sink the republican interest if they do not abandon him."[170] He also wrote to his friend during the vexatious summer of 1793: "Never in my opinion was so calamitous an appointment made as that of the present Minister of France here. Hotheaded, all imagination, no judgement, passionate, disrespectful and even indecent toward the President in his written as well as verbal communications. . . . He renders my position immensely difficult."[171]

When Hamilton returned to the pseudonymous writing of public letters, this time under the name Pacificus and with French violations of neutrality as an excuse for attacking the Republicans, Jefferson appealed to Madison to reply to the Treasury Secretary and "cut him to pieces in the face of the public."[172] Using the name Helvidius, Madison debated with Hamilton on the division of executive and legislative responsibility in foreign affairs. The series of letters by the two still further defined areas of Federalist and Republican disagreement, Hamilton emphasizing executive power and Madison stressing legislative authority.

Meanwhile Genêt, embracing Republicans with the same meddlesome hands with which he constantly stirred trouble in the federal government, was doing more to discredit Jefferson's party than Hamilton possibly could. On July 5, when both the President and the Attorney General were out of town, Jefferson, Hamilton, and Knox met to deal with possible defiance of the United States government by the French minister. There were rumors that the *Little Sarah*, a captured British brigantine renamed the *Little Democrat*, was being armed under Genêt's direction. Jefferson and Hamilton both approved a letter of inquiry from Knox to Governor Thomas Mifflin to determine the truth of the report.

Later that day Genêt paid a call on Jefferson to communicate with him "not as Secretary of State, but as Mr. Jefferson."[173] The Frenchman said that he had prepared addresses to the inhabitants of Louisiana and Canada, urging insurrection against their imperial masters. He personally proposed to commission officers in Kentucky who would rendezvous outside the United States and attack the Spanish stronghold of New Orleans. Jefferson "told him that his enticing officers and soldiers from Kentucky to go against Spain was really putting a halter about their necks; for . . . they would assuredly be hung [sic] if they commenced hostilities against a nation at peace with the United States." He added, "Leaving out that article, I do not care what insurrections should be excited in Louisiana."

Two days later, a Sunday, with the President still absent, Jefferson conferred with Mifflin and Pennsylvania Secretary of State Alexander James Dallas at the governor's urgent request.[174] The *Little Democrat*, Mifflin said, now was outfitted with fourteen cannon, ten more than when she first had docked in Philadelphia. The ship was lying in the Delaware River between Philadelphia and Mud Island. On hearing the night before that the brigantine was about to sail, the Governor had sent Dallas to Genêt at midnight. According to the Pennsylvania Secretary, Genêt, as soon as he was asked to detain the *Little Democrat*, "flew into a great passion, talked extravagantly, and concluded by refusing to order the vessel to stay."

When Knox, who was supposed to meet with them, was late in arriving at the Sunday conference, Jefferson went directly to Genêt. The Secretary of State told the minister of his information that the *Little Sarah*—significantly, Jefferson refused to use the name *Little Democrat*—was "armed contrary to the decision of the President" and would sail that day. He asked Genêt to detain the ship until Washington came back to the capital on Wednesday. As Jefferson himself told the story, Genêt "took up the subject instantly in a very high tone, and went into an immense field of declamation and complaint. I found it necessary to let him go on, and in fact could do no otherwise, for the few efforts which I made to take part in the conversation were quite ineffectual."

The Frenchman charged the United States with having violated treaties with France. He complained that the Americans "suffered (their) flag to be insulted and disregarded by the English," who removed French provisions from American vessels. He demanded that, if the United States was incapable of protecting French vessels in American ports or French property on the high seas, it should permit the French "to protect it themselves." He had been so "thwarted and opposed" in all dealings with the United States government that he "sometimes thought of packing up and going away." Genêt must indeed have been divorced from reality if he expected Jefferson to tremble at this threat.

The voluble diplomat recalled the "friendly propositions" he had brought from his own government and said that the President ought not to have replied to them "without consulting Congress." Upon the President's return, Genêt said, he would certainly "press him to convene Congress." By this time he had gotten into a sufficiently moderate tone for Jefferson to stop him to explain that the Constitution divided "the functions of government among three different authorities, the executive, legislative and judiciary, each of which was supreme in all questions belonging to its departments, and independent of the others; that all the questions which had arisen between him and us belonged to the executive department and, if Congress were sitting, could not be carried to them, nor would they take notice of them."

Were they not the sovereign? Genêt demanded. They were sovereign only in making laws, Jefferson explained. "The executive is sovereign in executing them, and the judiciary in construing them where they relate to their department."

"But, at least," said Genêt, "Congress are bound to see that the treaties are observed."

"No,...the President is to see that treaties are observed."

"If he decides against a treaty, to whom is the nation to appeal?"

"The Constitution has made the President the last appeal."

Genêt bowed, dipping his beaked head as if he were a mechanical bird. "Indeed I will not make you my compliments on such a constitution."

After he "expressed the utmost astonishment" over this document, he "was now come into perfect good humor and coolness, in which state," Jefferson said, "he may with the greatest freedom be spoken with." So Jefferson talked to him about the "impropriety" of his "persevering contrary to the will of the government" of the United States in matters "wherein unquestionably they had a right to be obeyed."

"But," Genêt insisted, "I have a right to expound the treaty on our side."

"Certainly," Jefferson agreed, "each party has an equal right to expound treaties. You, as agent of your nation, have a right to bring forward your exposition, to support it by reasons, to insist on it, to be answered with the reasons for our exposition where it is contrary. And when, after hearing and considering your reasons, the highest authority in the nation has decided, it is your duty to say you think the decision wrong, that you cannot take upon yourself to [accept] it, and will represent it to your government to do as they think proper. But in the meantime, you ought to acquiesce in it, and to do nothing within our limits contrary to it."

Genêt was silent for a moment, and Jefferson interpreted this unusual circumstance as a sign of his unspoken recognition that the Secretary of State was right on this point. Jefferson now pressed the minister to detain the *Little Sarah*.

"Why detain her?" Genêt demanded.

"Because she is reported to be armed with guns acquired here."

Genêt said the guns were "all French property." Surely the Americans did not "pretend" to control the French "in the disposal of their own property"? He could name to Jefferson the French vessel from which he had taken each gun.

Jefferson replied, "I will be obliged to you for any evidence of that fact which you will furnish me." And he repeated his request for detention of the ship.

Genêt was "embarrassed and unwilling." He said he "should not be justified in detaining her."

"It would be considered a very serious offense indeed if she should go away," Jefferson said. "The government is determined on that point and, thinking it is right, will go through with it."

In the ensuing conversation Genêt said that the vessel was not in readiness to sail, but when Jefferson asked if he might depend on her not being ready before the return of the President, the Frenchman would say only that she would not be ready "for some time." Jefferson later noted: "Whenever I tried to fix it to the President's return, he gave the same answer, that she would not be ready for some time, but with the look and gesture which showed he meant I should understand she would not be gone before that time." Then he added, "But she is to change her position and fall down the river today, but she will not depart yet."

"Will she fall down to the lower end of the town?" Jefferson asked.

"I do not exactly know where," said Genêt, ". . . but let me beseech you not to permit any attempt to put men on board of her. She is filled with high-spirited patriots, and they will unquestionably resist. And there is no occasion, for I tell you she will not be ready to depart for some time."

Saying that he would take for granted the vessel would not be ready before the President's return, that in the meantime he would "have inquiries made into the facts," and that the case would be "laid before the President the day after his return," Jefferson took his leave and returned to the Governor. The Secretary told Mifflin of his conversation with Genêt, and said that he personally was satisfied the ship would not sail.

The Governor then ordered the militia, which had been summoned, to be dismissed.

Now for the first time Dallas told Jefferson that, in his conversation with Genêt the night before, the Frenchman had said that he would appeal from the President to the people. This was a serious threat indeed.[175]

The next day Jefferson met with Hamilton and Knox in the Governor's office.[176] Both Hamilton and Knox proposed the immediate erection of a battery on Mud Island. If the *Little Democrat* attempted to pass, they said, she should be fired upon and sunk.

Jefferson dissented vigorously. The President was expected within forty-eight hours. The Secretary was sure that the vessel would not sail before then. "Erecting a battery and mounting guns to prevent her passage might cause a departure not now intended, and produce the fact it is meant to prevent." If she were fired on "in the present ardent state of her crew just in the moment of leaving port, it is morally certain that bloody consequences would follow. No one could say how many lives would be lost on both sides. And all experience has shown, that blood once seriously spilled between nation and nation, the contest is continued by subordinate agents, and the door of peace is shut. At this moment, too, we expect in the river twenty of their ships of war, with a fleet of from one hundred to one hundred and fifty of their private vessels, which will arrive at the scene of blood in time to continue it, if not to partake in it.

"The actual commencement of hostilities against a nation, for such this act may be, is an act of too serious consequence to our countrymen to be brought on their heads by subordinate officers, not chosen by them nor clothed with their confidence." It would be "too presumptuous on the part of those officers, when the chief magistrate, into whose hands the citizens have committed their safety, is within eight and forty hours of his arrival here, and may have an opportunity of judging for himself and them, whether the buying and carrying away two cannon (for according to information, the rest are the nation's own property) is sufficient cause of war between Americans and Frenchmen."

American citizens aboard the ship, Jefferson thought, should be prosecuted. Such action would be an indication of the government's determination to enforce neutrality. He thought Hamilton's fears of British retaliation if the ship should escape were unjustified. American actions had proved American intent.

With the President absent and the Cabinet so sharply divided, Governor Mifflin hesitated to act. Meanwhile, the *Little Democrat* slipped downstream to a new anchorage, out of reach of any battery that might be placed on Mud Island.

When Washington returned on Thursday morning, July 11, to find a sheaf of papers bearing the label "instant attention" in Jefferson's neat handwriting, he was irritated to discover that Jefferson himself was not in town. The Secretary of State was actually nearby in his Schuylkill home, sick and running a fever. The President was placated when he learned these facts in response to his abrupt solicitation of a written opinion on the crisis "before tomorrow."

Jefferson had supplied the President with all necessary documents on the *Little Democrat* crisis, including statements of the positions of all three conferring Secretaries, before the Cabinet meeting next day. Though still loyal and admiring in his attitude toward Washington, Jefferson no longer saw him as immune to human foibles. He surmised that the President wished that armed force had been used in the ship crisis, but believed that if Washington had been in the capital he himself would not have used guns.

Jefferson agreed with Hamilton, Knox, and the President that the federal government had the right and duty to prevent the arming of vessels in United States ports by either belligerent and to prosecute those of its citizens who participated in hostile actions against either. But the Secretary of State clashed with his Cabinet colleagues in defending the right of a belligerent to increase its armament while in an American port by mounting guns it already owned or to augment its forces by recruiting its own citizens resident in the United States.

Since these problems involved knotty legal issues, Jefferson urged that they be referred to the Supreme Court. Pending an official opinion, both the *Little Democrat* and the British *Jane*, said to be increasing its armament, would be instructed not to depart. In the President's name, Jefferson formally requested a consultation with the Court. Chief Justice John Jay and the Associate Justices turned down the invitation on the grounds that such consultation in the preparation of executive decrees would violate "the lines of separation drawn by the Constitution between the departments of the government." The precedent thus established still prevails.[177]

Of greater immediate interest than the establishment of a constitutional precedent was the fact that the *Little Democrat*, in defiance of the President's orders, slipped out to sea. From Dallas and Mifflin, and then through the energetic efforts of the Hamiltonians, word spread that the French minister had threatened to appeal to the people of the United States over the head of their President. From many quarters there were demands that Paris be asked to recall Genêt. Hamilton voiced the demand in the Cabinet. Knox proposed that, while the government awaited a reply from France, it should suspend recognition of Genêt. Jefferson's counterproposal was that the French government be sent copies of its minister's correspondence so that it might perceive his unfitness and take appropriate action. No decision was reached immediately although Jefferson, no less than Hamilton and Knox, realized that, one way or another, Genêt must go.[178]

The problems surrounding Genêt were dealt with in a series of Cabinet meetings tense with suspicion and resentment.[179] At the meeting on July 23 Jefferson submitted two letters to be addressed to Genêt in answer to his protests. The first was approved *in toto* but the second was deferred after Knox proposed adding some comment on the Frenchman's disrespectful references to the President. Washington then said that they must shortly determine what was "to be done with Mr. Genêt." In his own opinion, he said, the minister's "whole correspondence" should be sent to Gouverneur Morris for transmission to the authorities in Paris. With it should go "a temperate but strong representation of his conduct, drawing a clear line between him and his nation, expressing our friendship to the latter." So far the President was advocating exactly what his Secretary of State had suggested. Now he went farther than Jefferson had gone in previous statements, but possibly not a great deal farther than he had already gone in private thinking. Washington said he thought that the United States should insist on the recall of Genêt, "and in the meantime that we should desire him either to withdraw or cease his functions."

Hamilton launched upon a long speech exhorting the President to firmness, saying that the handling of the crisis at hand could determine whether the government would continue or be overthrown by a faction. He wanted the people to be told of all the infuriating things that the French minister had done. Otherwise the incendiaries in the

United States might soon take sides with the French.

Knox could not marshal facts and bend logic to his will as Hamilton could, but he made his own contribution to the argument. As Jefferson recorded in his journal, "Knox told some little stories to aggravate the President, to wit, that Mr. [Rufus] King had told him, that a lady had told him, that she heard a gentleman say that the President was as great a tyrant as any of them, and that it would soon be time to chase him out of the city." And then, too, "Mr. Stagg, lately from New York," had told him that the St. Tammany Society, a New York City organization of those who called themselves Democrats or Republicans, "now had meetings to the number of five hundred persons" and that the French consul "appeared to be very intimate with them."

Washington retained his outward composure and, before adjourning the session, calmly asked the Cabinet members to reflect on the question of whether Congress should be convened.

At a Cabinet meeting on August 1 there was unanimous agreement that Genêt's correspondence and a full statement of his conduct be forwarded through Morris to the Executive Council of France, and that his recall should be "required." Jefferson suggested that the request be made "with great delicacy." The others saw no need for delicacy. Knox proposed that Genêt should be "sent off" in the meantime. No one concurred. Next it was proposed that the Secretary of State write a letter to Genêt telling him that the government had applied for his recall. Jefferson opposed the idea for fear that "it would render [Genêt] extremely active in his plans, and endanger confusion." Here he stood alone and had to give in. The final proposal, that the Genêt correspondence be published "by way of appeal to the people," was supported by Hamilton in a speech of three-quarters of an hour that Jefferson said was "as inflammatory and declamatory as if he had been speaking to a jury." The Secretary of State's journal noted: "E. Randolph opposed it. I chose to leave the contest between them. Adjourned to next day."

Equally laconic was the opening of the next day's entry: "Met again. Hamilton spoke again three-quarters of an hour." His subject again was the desirability of carrying the case against Genêt to the people. This time Jefferson opposed him. Addressing the New Yorker's fears of the "democratic society" formed in his own state, Jefferson assured him that it had been organized in connection with the gubernatorial campaign and that, far from extending its connections over the continent, would "die away" after the election if left alone. Opposition or proscription "would give it importance and vigor; would give it a new object, and multitudes would join it merely to assert the right of voluntary associations." Any move against the Democratic or Democratic-Republican political associations would "make the President assume the station of the head of a party instead of the head of the nation."

As for the proposal that the proceedings leading up to Genêt's recall be spread before the public in an appeal to the people, Jefferson thought the idea dangerous. "There have been great differences of opinion among us," he reminded, "sometimes as many opinions as persons. This proves there will be ground to attack the decisions and Genêt will appeal also; it will become a contest between the President and Genêt." The alert and sensitive Hamilton could not fail to appreciate the extra meaning when Jefferson said there would also be "anonymous writers." The differences of opinion in the Cabinet, he saw, would be reproduced among the public and in Congress. Such a course as an appeal to the people, therefore, would foment the same troubles at home that the Treasury Secretary sought to prevent. And how would such an appeal work abroad? "Why appeal to the world? Friendly nations always negotiate little differences in private, never appeal to the world but when they appeal to the sword." The princes of the Confederacy of Pilnitz had formed a conspiracy to spread the fear that the French Republican government was trying to excite insurrections in other nations. "Colonel Hamilton supposes Mr. Genêt's proceedings here are in pursuance of that system; and we are so to declare it to the world and to add our testimony to this base calumny of the Princes. What a triumph to them to be backed by our testimony! What a fatal stroke at the cause of liberty! *Et tu Brute*."

In a more practical strain, he warned: "We indispose the French Government and they will retract their offer of the treaty of commerce."

Washington did not take an unequivocal stand but his talk of promised support if there should be an appeal to the public convinced Jefferson that the President was inclined to that procedure. The Secretary of State suddenly saw a yawning ideological chasm between himself and his chief. He told himself, "The President has not confidence enough in the virtue and good sense of mankind to confide in a government bottomed on them, and thinks other props necessary."

The meeting, according to Jefferson, took a startling turn: "Knox, in a foolish, incoherent sort of a speech, introduced the pasquinade, lately printed, called 'The Funeral of George W_____n,' " where the President was placed on a guillotine. At this Washington "was much inflamed, got into one of those passions when he cannot command himself, ran on much on the personal abuse which had been bestowed on him, defied any man on earth to produce one single act of his since he had been in the government which was not done on the purest motives. . . . He had never repented but once the having slipped the moment of resigning his office, and that was every moment since. . . . By God! He had rather be in his grave than in his present situation. . . . He had rather be on his farm than to be made *Emperor of the World*, and yet. . . they are charging him with wanting to be a King. . . . That *rascal Freneau* sent him three of his papers every day, as if he thought he would become the distributor of his papers. . . . . He could see in this nothing but an impudent design to insult him."

There was a pause. Evidently even Knox, who had deliberately excited the President's anger, was stunned by the force of the reaction. Everyone found it difficult to resume the discussion. The question "was, however, after a little while, presented again." The President said there seemed to be "no necessity for deciding it now." The propositions already agreed on "might be put into a train of execution, and perhaps events would show whether the appeal would be necessary or not." He proposed that they meet next day in Mr. Jefferson's office "to consider what should be done with the vessels armed in our ports by Mr. Genêt and their prizes."

At the next meeting Hamilton proposed to suppress the privateers by military force and return the prizes to their owners. Jefferson proposed, on the other hand, that Mr. Genêt be required to deliver the prizes to the owners. If he should fail to do so, the United States should pay the British for them, and then subtract the sum from the debt it owed to France. Also the French minister should be informed that "we would allow no further asylum in our ports to the said privateers." Jefferson's arguments carried the day.

The President asked whether Congress should be called. Knox and Randolph were against it. "Hamilton said his judgement was against it, but that if any two were for it, or against it, he would join them to make a majority." Jefferson was for it. They agreed to submit separate opinions in writing. Knox said sarcastically, "We should have had fine work if Congress had been sitting these last two months."

Jefferson thought then and wrote later in his journal, "The fool thus let out the secret." The implication was that Hamiltonian policies were more easily executed without the watchdogs of the people looking on. Jefferson recorded, "Hamilton endeavored to patch up the indiscretion of this blabber by saying he did not know; he rather thought they would have strengthened the executive arm."

Four days later, when Jefferson was at his house in the country, Washington called on him.[180] The visit was prompted by a letter from the Secretary of State announcing that he would resign on the last day of August. Once again the President expressed his own regret at not having resigned and said that it was "increased by seeing that he was to be deserted by those on whose aid he had counted." He did not know "where he should look to find characters to fill up the offices; . . . mere talents did not suffice for the Department of State, but it required a person conversant in foreign affairs, perhaps acquainted with foreign courts; . . . without this, the best talents would be awkward and at a loss."

Now the President revealed something new. "Colonel Hamilton had three or four weeks ago written to him, informing him that private as well as public reasons had brought him to the determination to retire, and that he should do it toward the close of the next session" of Congress. Having two Secretaries leave at different times deprived him of the flexibility he would have in gratifying various geographical constituencies if he could fill both places at once. "He expressed great apprehension at the fermentation which seemed to be working in the mind of the public; . . . what it would end in he knew not. A new Congress was to assemble, more numerous, perhaps of a different spirit." It would "relieve him considerably" if Jefferson would stay until the end of the next session.

Jefferson spoke of his "excessive repugnance to public life" and again recited the litany of his reasons. He referred also to "the particular uneasiness of my situation in this place, where the laws of society oblige me always to move exactly in the circle which I know to bear me peculiar hatred; that is to say the wealthy aristocrats, the merchants connected closely with England, the new[ly] created paper fortunes." Such talk of not being at home with "wealthy aristocrats" might seem strange from the master of Monticello, scion of the lordly Randolphs. But in this instance, as well as in Jefferson's references to John Adams' having "become aristocratical," it is clear from the context that the Virginian was referring to attitude rather than breeding. As for wealth, Jefferson, despite his vast acres, apparently did not think of himself as "rich." His indebtedness was heavy and, like many Virginia planters of his day, he was land poor. Jefferson added that, as the President saw, "there is such an opposition of views between myself and another part of the Administration as to make it peculiarly unpleasing and to destroy the necessary harmony."

He sought to reassure his chief about the next Congress. He thought they "would attempt nothing material but to render their own body independent." The Republican Party, he said, were "firm in their disposition to support the government. . . . The maneuvers of Mr. Genêt might produce some little embarrassment, but . . . he would be abandoned by the Republicans the moment they knew the nature of his conduct; and on the whole, no crisis existed which threatened anything."

Washington said he "believed the views of the Republican Party were perfectly pure, but when men put a machine into motion, it is impossible for them to stop it exactly where they would choose, or to say where it will stop." He insisted, "The constitution we have is an excellent one, if we can keep it where it is. It is, indeed, supposed there is a party disposed to change it into a monarchical form, but I can conscientiously declare there is not a man in the United States who would set his face more decidedly against it than myself."

Jefferson interrupted: "No rational man in the United States suspects you of any other disposition. But there does not pass a week in which we cannot prove declarations dropping from the monarchical party that our government is good for nothing, is a milk and water thing which cannot support itself. [They say that] we must knock it down and set up something of more energy."

"If that is the case," said the President, "I think it a proof of their insanity, for the republican spirit of the Union is so manifest and so solid that it is astonishing how anyone could expect to move it."

Returning to the problem of finding Jefferson's successor, the President dismissed several possibilities: Madison (probably not available), Jay (loath to leave his present office), Thomas Johnson (inexperienced in foreign affairs), Robert Livingston (his appointment would mean New Yorkers would occupy both of the two highest Cabinet posts).

Jefferson asked why not make an interim appointment: "Mr. Randolph, for instance."

"Yes," said Washington, "but there you would raise the expectation of keeping it, and I do not know that he is fit for it, nor what is thought of Mr. Randolph."

Jefferson "avoided noticing the last observation" until Washington asked for a direct answer.

Then the Secretary admitted that "the embarrassments in Randolph's private affairs had obliged him to use expedients which had injured him with the merchants and shopkeepers, and affected his character of independence; that these embarrassments were serious, and not likely to cease soon."

As if all other possibilities were exhausted, Washington pressed: "If you would only stay in till the end of another quarter [the last of December], it would get us through the difficulties of this year. And I am satisfied that the affairs of Europe will be settled with this campaign; either France will be overwhelmed by it, or the confederacy [of princes] will give up the contest. By that time, too, Congress will have manifested its character and view."

Jefferson was firm: "I had set my private affairs in motion in a line which powerfully called for my presence last spring, and they suffered immensely for my not going home. I have now calculated them to my return in the fall, and to fail in going then would be the loss of another year and prejudicial beyond measure."

The President asked whether Jefferson could not arrange his affairs by going home for awhile.

"I do not think the public business would admit of it," the Secretary said. "There never is a day now in which the absence of the Secretary of State would not be inconvenient to the public.''

Washington then asked him to take "two or three days to consider" whether he could not postpone his leavetaking "till the end of another quarter." Washington, with the peculiar charm of an indomitable old hero confessing his dependency, said, "Like a man going to the gallows, I am willing to put it off as long as I can. But if you persist, I must then look about me and make up my mind to do the best I can." Then he walked away.

Five days later Jefferson, disrupting all his plans, agreed to stay in office until the end of the year. This time both he and Washington recognized the decision as definitive. Though disappointed and frustrated, Jefferson was relieved to have the matter settled.

He was hard at work on the long letter[181] that Gouverneur Morris would transmit to the French government. He presented a draft of it at a Cabinet meeting August 15. Even Hamilton and Knox could find nothing significantly wrong with his work. He separated Genêt's actions from the policies of France and, without waffling on a single point of contention, gave Paris every opportunity to save face. By skillful use of quotations, he made Genêt the principal witness against himself so that it was unnecessary for the United States government to say many harsh things about the French minister. From a jumble of materials, Jefferson brilliantly produced a mosaic of Genêt's words and his own that presented an unmistakably clear picture.

When the Cabinet met on August 20 they considered Jefferson's final draft paragraph by paragraph.[182] On only one phrase was there disagreement, but here the difference was sharp. Jefferson had said that if Genêt's activities were permitted to "embroil" the United States and France, such a conflict between two republics would "draw on both a reproach which it is hoped will never stain the history of either, that of liberty warring on herself." Hamilton moved to strike out the words "that of liberty warring on herself." He said that the expression would give offense to the powers at war with France, that it "amounted to a declaration that they were warring on liberty." Furthermore, "we were not called on to declare that the course of France was that of liberty." He had at first been with the French "with all his heart," but had "long since left them." He did not believe in "encouraging the idea here that the cause of France was the cause of liberty in general, or could have either connection or influence in our affairs."

Knox promptly endorsed Hamilton's views. Then, to Jefferson's delight, "the President, with a good deal of positiveness, declared in favor of the expression. He said that "he considered the pursuit of France to be that of liberty, however they might sometimes fail of the best means of obtaining it . . . . He had never at any time entertained a doubt of their ultimate success if they hung well together."

Jefferson argued the need for including words of friendliness in a stern demand for the recall of a friendly nation's accredited representative, and also said he thought it was a good idea to disabuse those at home of any idea that the Executive was "tainted with a hankering after monarchy."

Randolph joined with Hamilton, saying he "thought it had been agreed that this correspondence should contain no expressions which could give offense to either party." Jefferson retorted that the letters that had already been exchanged by France and the United States were so barren of friendly expressions that they were "as dry and husky as if written between the generals of two enemy nations . . . . There is not from beginning to end of the letter one other expression, or word, in favor of liberty, and I should think it singular, at least, if the single passage of that character should be struck out." Washington intervened to say that France was the only nation the United States could count on and once again declared his "strong attachment to the expression." But he left the final decision to the Cabinet. As Jefferson wrote in his journal, "It was struck out, of course."

With this single alteration, Jefferson's letter was sent to Morris by special messenger three days later. Subsequently, perhaps as much as three weeks later, the Secretary of State sent a copy to Genêt, explaining in a note to him that the French minister to the United States must be a person "disposed to respect the laws and authority of the country." Pending the arrival of his successor, he might continue to exercise his diplomatic functions so long as they were "restrained within the limits of the law." The exercise of restraint upon the French consuls in the United States would no longer be Mr. Genêt's responsibility, Jefferson told him. Control would be exercised by the President.[183]

Jefferson had delayed sending the notice to Genêt so as to shorten the period of the minister's service after learning of his dismissal. He had supposed correctly that Genêt would be angry and vengeful. The letter found the Frenchman in New York. He dashed off to the Secretary of State a threat to appeal to Congress.

The Virginian did not receive the letter until December. A yellow fever epidemic had disrupted communications. From the waterfront the sickness spread all over Philadelphia. The custom of shaking hands was abandoned and people began to walk down the middle of the streets as if contagion might leap out at them from doorways and alleys. The roll of the dead grew daily. Washington, in accordance with plans made before the epidemic, left Philadelphia on September 10. Knox left. Hamilton was absent from public haunts. Jefferson, who had reached the point where he gave little credence to anything emanating from the Treasury Secretary, wrote Madison, "Hamilton is ill of the fever, as is said. He had two physicians out at his house the night before last. His family think him in danger, and he puts himself so by his excessive alarm. He had been miserable several days before from a firm persuasion he should catch it. A man as timid as he is on the water, as timid on horseback, as timid in sickness, would be a phenomenon if his courage of which he has the reputation in military circles were genuine."[184] Evidently Jefferson still smarted at the charges of cowardice made against him by the Hamiltonians.

Jefferson had said that he would leave on October 1 for a visit to Monticello. He now admitted to Madison, "I would really go away, because I think there is rational danger, but that I had before announced that I should not go till the beginning of October, and I do not like to exhibit the appearance of panic." Besides, some ranking member of the executive branch should remain. But soon he was left with only one clerk, and so many people had departed the capital that there was no point in staying for government business. On September 17 he left for home, pausing to visit Washington and Madison en route. At Monticello the hills blazed with the red and gold of autumn beneath a smoke-like haze of blue. He found it hard to leave his home, all too soon, on the twenty-fifth day of a Blue Ridge October but he expected to return within a little more than two months.

He did not go back to Philadelphia. The offices of government had abandoned that plague-ridden city for Germantown. From Baltimore on, the journey was made with

Washington, but even the pleasure of restored companionship with his old chief did not keep him from complaining about the heat, the cold, the dust, and the rain. Finding no stage for this segment of the trip, he was "fleeced of seventy odd dollars" by the owner of a private vehicle. He found Germantown filled with those who had fled Philadelphia, and this most private and fastidious of men was reduced to sleeping in a bed placed in a corner of a tavern's public room.[185] Cabinet rank was no great help in obtaining accommodations in the overcrowded little town when a prominent man considered himself lucky to obtain a shared bed. But resourcefulness and charm could accomplish something. Before long Jefferson had secured adequate accommodations, not only for himself but also for Madison and Monroe.[186]

At a Cabinet meeting on November 8 Washington said that "Mr. Genêt's conduct continued to be of so extraordinary a nature" that he thought they should give "serious consideration whether he should not have his functions discontinued and be ordered away."[187] Hamilton and Knox argued vehemently for dismissal. Randolph opposed, and even Jefferson gave him credit for doing so "with firmness and pretty lengthily." The President also argued at length but, saying that he did not "wish to have the thing hastily decided," postponed the matter until his return from a trip to Reading and Lancaster.

When they met again on November 18 there were more letters from Genêt to be entered in evidence, for some had been received in the President's absence.[188] Jefferson vigorously opposed the abrupt dismissal of the minister before his own government could recall him. He called France "the only nation on earth sincerely our friend" and said that the proposed measure was "so harsh a one that no precedent is produced where it has not been followed by war. Our messenger has now been gone eighty-four days. Consequently, we may hourly expect [a reply from Paris] and to be relieved by their revocation of him." Any such action on the part of the United States would take eight to ten days. "This would bring us within four or five days of the meeting of Congress. Would it not be better to see how the pulse of that body, new as it is, would beat?"

Hamilton urged that the federal government's "conduct now would tempt or deter other foreign ministers from treating us in the same manner." He did not believe France "would make it a cause of war; if she did we ought to do what was right and meet the consequences."

Knox chimed in to say he thought it "very possible Mr. Genêt would either declare us a department of France or levy troops here and reduce us to obedience."

Randolph joined with Jefferson, saying that a precipitate ouster of Genêt might resurrect his popularity. Now he was "dead in the public opinion if we would but leave him so." Lamenting the equal division of his cabinet, Washington dropped the matter.

A thorny question in the last days before the convening of Congress was the President's message to the national legislators, particularly with reference to a Presidential declaration of neutrality. Genêt was continually protesting publicly that the Chief Executive had no right to issue such a proclamation without congressional consent, and the Frenchman might be winning converts among the members themselves.

Both Jefferson and Randolph were against a formal proclamation, at this point, of future neutrality. Jefferson still believed that the belligerent nations should be induced to "bid for our neutrality." Randolph, as Attorney General, prepared a paper on the subject for Washington. Hamilton attacked it vigorously. Washington gave the Treasury

Secretary the assignment of preparing a covering paragraph to be inserted into the Presidential message. Jefferson might legitimately have considered this a snub, but nothing in the President's manner indicated that it was meant to be.

Jefferson was, however, asked to prepare the section on foreign affairs as a whole.[189] It would follow an opening message prepared by Randolph. Hamilton declared his "in toto" opposition to Jefferson's draft: "the contrast drawn between the conduct of France and England amounted to a declaration of war." Not surprisingly, he found it too favorable toward the French, too prejudiced against the British. The Secretary of State toned down his references to both nations, but Hamilton still declared the message unacceptable. Though Randolph approved Jefferson's message, he opposed appending to it certain documents relating to the conduct of affairs, as Jefferson had proposed. Like Hamilton and Knox, he thought they should be kept secret. Jefferson argued for openness. He was delighted by the next turn of events. He recorded in his journal, "the President took up the subject with more vehemence than I have seen him show" and argued for even greater openness than the Secretary of State had advocated. "This was the first instance I had seen of his deciding on the opinion of one against that of three others, which proved his own to have been very strong."

Jefferson recorded another cause for satisfaction, this one connected with the address which Randolph had written for Washington. "I was happy to see that Randolph had, by accident, used the expression 'our republic,' in the speech. The President, however, made no objection to it, and so, as much as it had disconcerted him on a former occasion with me, it was now put into his own mouth to be pronounced to the two houses of legislature."

A bit of gossip which Jefferson heard on December 2 strengthened his hope that the President was being educated concerning the real objectives of the Hamiltonians. The Secretary of State gave it the dignity of a separate entry in his journal:

> Langdon, Cabot, and some others of the Senate, standing in a knot before the fire after the Senate had adjourned, and growling together about some measure which they had just lost; "Ah!" said Cabot, "things will never go right till you have a President for life, and an hereditary Senate." Langdon told this to Lear, who mentioned it to the President. The President seemed struck with it, and declared he had not supposed there was a man in the United States who could have entertained such an idea.[190]

By this time, cold weather having ended the plague, the government had returned to Philadelphia. On December 3 the President, in company with the Cabinet, appeared at the capitol to deliver his message to Congress. On December 5 he submitted in writing the message on foreign policy which Jefferson had prepared. Attached were documents comprising the correspondence between the Secretary of State and Genêt and the message transmitted to the French government through Gouverneur Morris. For the first time Jefferson's role as the conductor of foreign relations was clearly revealed. Hamilton had wanted "the veil" removed. Now it was. Not only were intelligent Republicans inspired with gratitude for the salvation of their party's reputation, not only were Adams and other old friends among the Federalists relieved to discover that Jefferson was "as little satisfied with the conduct of the French minister as anyone," but also one of the most loyal Hamiltonians, New York politician Robert Troup, declared: "Jefferson's letter to Gouverneur Morris has blotted all the sins of the former out of the book of our remembrance; and with the sentiments and temper Jefferson appears at present to possess we would much regret that he should quit his post until the clouds which threaten a storm be dispersed."[191]

In this last month in office he presented to the House of Representatives his long-awaited report on commerce, written in obedience to the resolution adopted in the first Congress of the United States. It was a survey of the trade of the Western world with particular reference to the needs of the United States.[192] Madison and Tench Coxe had helped with the statistical research, but Jefferson himself had conceived the grand scope of the report and executed it with unusual insight and objectivity. He even had the ministers from the Netherlands, Spain, France, and Great Britain check the accuracy of the separate sections devoted to their nations. Hammond took exception to some things but did not convince Jefferson.

The Secretary of State charted a course by which the United States might eventually escape from economic colonialism. He used simplified statistical tables of a sort not then common in state papers. The facts spoke for themselves to demonstrate how other nations, most especially Great Britain, conducted trade with the United States, a newcomer to international marts, on terms disadvantageous to the young Republic. Jefferson advocated a protective tariff for American manufactures, a tit for tat system in which the United States would respond in kind when another country placed high duties on American goods or prohibited them. High tariffs would be imposed first on foreign products most competitive with American and secondly on important manufactures most easily produced at home or obtained from nations other than the offending one. It is ironic that Jefferson, the agriculturist and foe of centralized power, advocated such use of federal trade regulations as a stimulus to manufacture whereas Hamilton, the spokesman for commerce and centralization, opposed it. What appears to be a paradox dissolves, at least insofar as Jefferson is concerned, when one reflects that, though an idealist, he was pragmatic in pursuit of his ideals. In his *Notes on Virginia* and in various private letters Jefferson had revealed his detestation of large-scale manufacturing and the great marts. But five years' experience representing American interests in Europe, plus service as Secretary of State at a time when the struggle between England and France sometimes seemed most significant in terms of economic consequences, had educated the Virginia planter to a far broader concept of the world and its work. Jefferson held fast to his ideal of an American republic strong enough to command respect throughout the world. He was prepared to subordinate his personal prejudices to the attainment of that goal.

In the last days of the year Washington appealed once more to Jefferson to stay on. But the President accepted the fact that this time the Secretary of State could not be deflected from his determination to retire.[193]

In those closing days, Genêt forwarded to Jefferson documents which he demanded be presented to Congress. When Jefferson transmitted the letter and papers to the President, Washington replied, "Every day, more and more, discovers the intention of this agent to perplex this government, and to scatter thick and wide the seeds of dissension."[194]

On his very last day in office, Jefferson returned the papers to the French Minister with a note saying: "Your functions as the missionary of a foreign nation here are con-fined to the transactions of the affairs of your nation with the Executive of the United States. . . . The communications which are to pass between the Executive and Legislative branches cannot be a subject for your interference. . . . The President must be left to judge for himself what matters his duty or the public good may require him to propose to the deliberations of Congress."[195]

Even one who hated unpleasantness in personal relations as much as Jefferson did must have found some satisfaction in discharging this last duty. At least the classicist in him must have found appropriate, simultaneously with the ending of his tour as Secretary of State, the completion of his dealings with the man who had created his greatest problem in that office.

There were other satisfactions. Jefferson must have wondered at times whether his service in the Cabinet, with its many attendant frictions, had not lowered him in Washington's originally high estimation. There was comfort, therefore, in a note from the President saying, "The opinion, which I had formed, of your integrity and talents, and which dictated your original nomination, has been confirmed by the fullest experience."[196]

The verdict of history Jefferson could not know. Though he probably anticipated vindication in large degree, he almost surely never suspected it would be so generous. One of the greatest of his successors as Secretary of State, John Quincy Adams, many years later wrote of the Virginian's handling of the Genêt crisis that he had "triumphantly sustained and vindicated the administration of Washington without forfeiting the friendly professions of France." Adams even went so far as to say, "Mr. Jefferson's papers on that controversy present the most perfect model of diplomatic discussion and expostula-tion of modern times."[197] George Canning, who served brilliantly as Britain's Foreign Secretary while Adams headed the United States Department of State, perhaps paid Jef-ferson the highest tribute of all. In 1823 when the Englishman took his country out of the Holy Alliance and began steering an exacting course between contending powers, he told the House of Commons, "If I wished for a guide in a system of neutrality, I should take that laid down by America in the days of the Presidency of Washington and the Secretaryship of Jefferson, in 1793."[198] Historians have echoed the praise of these great diplomats.

On the fifth day of the new year, 1794, Jefferson undoubtedly was more occupied with the immediate future than with his place in history. He was sick of unfriendly words and faces. He looked forward to enjoying the company of Madison and Monroe in Virginia rather than among the snipers of Philadelphia. His political and social experiences as Secretary of State had been made more disagreeable by contrast with the happy days he had known in Paris. But where were the friends of those days? Lafayette, the happy warrior for freedom, had been imprisoned by the revolutionists.[199] Madame de Cor-ny, who had entertained the greatest minds and talents of Paris, was now a widow in humble circumstances in Rouen. Once, when Madame de Corny had left Paris to visit Maria Cosway in London, Jefferson had written to Maria from France to say that he wished the visitor could return to him with her hostess in her pocket. Recently he had written to Angelica Church, in London, asking, "Where is Mrs. Cosway? I have heard she was become a mother; but is the new object to absorb all her affections?"[200] Mrs. Church's reply brought from Jefferson the exclamation: "Madam Cosway in a convent! I know that to much goodness of heart she joined enthusiasm and religion. But I thought that very enthusiasm would have prevented her from shutting up her adoration of the god of the Universe within the walls of a cloister, that she would rather have sought the *mountain-top*. How happy should I be that it were *mine* that you, she and Mde. de Corny would seek."[201]

But at least Jefferson himself was headed back to that mountaintop in Virginia, from which detached height he was determined to look down upon the struggles of public life as he had so often looked upon nature's storms rumbling and flashing in the valley below. He could not conceive of anything that might lure him away from his friends, his books, his music, any ambition that might take him from his vast, uncluttered vistas of eye and mind.

XVI

'THE ONLY VICE'

I F "LIVING well is the best revenge," Jefferson in early 1794 was thoroughly revenged on the Hamiltonians and all who had made his life miserable in Philadelphia. From the day of his return on January 16 he became immersed in the affairs of Monticello. Replying eighteen days later to an invitation to visit General Horatio Gates in New York, he said: "The length of my tether is now fixed from Monticello to Richmond. My private business can never call me elsewhere and certainly politics will not, which I have ever hated both in theory and practice. I thought myself conscientiously called from those studies which were my delight by the political crisis of my country. . . . In storms like those all hands must be aloft. But calm is now restored, and I leave the bark with joy to those who love the sea. I am but a landsman, forced from my element by accident, rejoining it with transport, and wishing to recollect nothing of what I have seen but my friendships."[1]

So determined was he to separate himself from the rude world that he even refused to read newspapers. In April, with green life pushing up through the red earth, he wrote to John Adams: "I return to farming with an ardor which I scarcely knew in my youth, and which has got the better entirely of my love of study. Instead of writing 10 or 12 letters a day, which I have been in the habit of doing as a thing of course, I put off answering my letters now, farmer-like, till a rainy day and then find it sometimes postponed by other necessary occupations."[2] This most diversely intellectual of Americans even began to sound anti-intellectual—up to a point. He professed to believe that ignorance was "the softest pillow" on which a man could rest his head, but characteristically he cited Montaigne in support of the proposition.[3]

Once again he thrilled to the marvel of white dogwood cascading down his mountain and foaming in great billows at its base. The deep pink glow of redbud illumined the dark green recesses of the forest. And as spring glided into summer, on warm nights the plaintive note of the whippoorwill, that in Philadelphia had struck at his heart like the song of the nightingale at Ruth's amid the alien corn, spoke comfortingly of home to the returned native.

His own voice added to the music of the day as he rode over the red fields and under the pink boughs of his orchards, singing songs of France and Italy as exotic to the Virginia countryside as the vines and trees he had transplanted from Europe.[4] He rejoiced in the opportunity to restore to productivity the lands which had languished in his absence. And there was equal joy in the remodeling of the great house itself in accord with sophisticated architectural concepts he had brought back from Europe. Jefferson's right hand never recovered the dexterity it had known before he injured it while leaping over a Parisian fence on a memorable day with Maria Cosway; nevertheless, he apparently joined in the family musicales[5] that sent strange sounds as well as beams of yellow candlelight through the long windows, astonishing wild creatures that ventured under cover of darkness onto the level lawns.

Polly Jefferson, who had just turned sixteen and in newfound dignity was increasingly called Maria, was a constant part of the family circle. Shortly before Jefferson's return home Martha and her husband, Thomas Mann Randolph, had moved from Henrico County to Edgehill near Monticello. They and their two children seem to have spent as much time in Jefferson's home as in their own.

Part of Jefferson's time was spent in soothing worries and healing breaches among the Randolphs, who were blood kin as well as in-laws. There were misunderstandings between Thomas Mann Randolph and his father, Colonel Randolph of Tuckahoe, who had married a woman younger than some of his children and was raising another family. As a childhood playmate of the father, Jefferson was in a privileged position for the practice of diplomacy. A still more serious problem in the Randolph family proved agonizing for both Thomas Mann and Martha. Nancy Randolph, Thomas Mann's unmarried sister, had made her home with another sister, Judith, living in Cumberland County. Judith was a Randolph by both blood and marriage, her husband being Richard Randolph, brother to the brilliant and eccentric John Randolph of Roanoke. The story was soon widely circulated that Nancy had conceived a child of which Richard was the father. According to one version she had suffered a miscarriage. A more sensational version gained credence when Richard was formally charged with infanticide. Before Jefferson's return to Monticello, Richard had been tried and, after able defense by Patrick Henry and John Marshall, acquitted.

But the public had not pronounced "not guilty." Though many may have been ready to acquit him of murder, they still believed him guilty of seducing his sister-in-law and her guilty of succumbing to his seductions. Society had not decided what its attitude toward her should be. Jefferson did not know whether adultery had been committed but he had never had any doubts about how Nancy should be treated. Before the trial he had written to Martha who, like her husband, was not only sorry for Nancy but also worried about the contagion of scandal. Jefferson referred to the unfortunate young woman as a "pitiable victim, whether it be of error or of slander," and admonished his daughter, "Never throw off the best affections of nature in the moment when they become most precious to their object, nor fear to extend your hand to save another lest you sink yourself."[6]

Jefferson did not have to take on others' problems because he had none of his own. In 1792 he had written that he was "haunted nightly by the form of our friend Hanson."[7] He referred to Richard Hanson, a representative of the English firm of Farell & Jones, to whom Jefferson was heavily indebted as a result of his wife's inheritance in 1774 of her father's obligations along with his property. Another large debt, stemming originally from his mother's estate, was owed by Jefferson to the Glasgow house of Henderson, McCaul & Company.

Though Jefferson's major debts were innocently acquired and he worked conscientiously to pay them off, his life-style was not conducive to financial recovery. He had made some concessions to economy, notably dispensing with the services of Adrien Petit, the efficient *maître d' hôtel* who had served him in Paris and Philadelphia. Transferring to the servant a note received from one of Jefferson's debtors and adding some money to it, Jefferson was able to discharge a debt which he had owed the Frenchman for some time. But generous hospitality in the Virginia tradition, with no wayfarer of any class turned away, was costly, especially when the eminence and popularity of the host attracted so many mere acquaintances and even strangers. And the perpetual stocking of his cellar with the finest imported wines was expensive. His intellectual tastes also played havoc with his household economy. On October 23 he wrote to George Wythe that the next time his old teacher visited Monticello there would be at his disposal a library "now certainly the best in America."[8]

The same letter told of another expensive occupation, the transformation of Monticello into perhaps the most elegant, though not the largest, home in America. Jefferson did not think that it was very elegant at the time of transition. "We are now living in a brick kiln," he wrote, "for my house, in its present state, is nothing better." A much more favorable estimate came from a distinguished foreign visitor, the duc de la Rochefoucald-Liancourt, who pronounced it "infinitely superior to all other houses in America" and predicted that the completed structure would equal "the most pleasant mansions in France and England."[9]

Jefferson had scrapped his original plans for a two-story portico at the entrance façade of Monticello and was converting to the now familiar one-story portico topped by an octagonal dome. Some architectural historians believe that it was the first dome on any building in the United States. Though traditional in its Palladianism, the house was innovative. When completed it would contain four stories, but three would be hidden, one underground and two in the roof line. As Nigel Nicolson has said, "A house was given the shape of a pavilion." The same writer says of Jefferson, "With extraordinary skill, he contrived to make the house seem smaller while actually doubling its size." Nicolson has also paid felicitous tribute to Jefferson's use of octagon rooms. He had made a modest start along these lines in his design for the foyer of the Governor's Palace in Williamsburg. Now he was building a series of ingeniously integrated octagons. Nicolson notes: "They not only gave great variety to the rooms by providing wall-spaces for standing furniture at different angles and windows opening on different views, but from outside they imparted 'movement' to the whole building. Interesting effects of light and shade were thereby achieved, softening and humanising the classicism of the porches, and giving the house distinction from every angle, like a piece of sculpture."[10]

The visiting duke was as enthusiastic about the life led on the plantation as about the house itself. In his *Travels through the United States,* he wrote: "Mr. Jefferson displays a mild, easy and obliging temper . . . in every situation of life."[11] Completing the idyllic picture, the duke reported that Jefferson's daughters were "handsome, modest, and amiable women" and that his son-in-law was like a son.

Actually, all was not quite that idyllic. Thomas Mann Randolph, an intelligent, attractive man who had begun a promising public career by filling the usual local offices, was suffering from some unidentified malady which caused him to travel northward in the summer of 1794 and to resort to the springs of Augusta County in 1795 and 1796. He regained his health during the last of these three vacations, but he was often beset by melancholy. He appears to have suspected at times that, no matter what his accomplishments, he would always be known principally as Jefferson's son-in-law. He may have realized that, even in his wife's affections, he would come second to the great man. In 1798 she wrote to her father, "The first sensations of my life were affection and respect for you and none others in the course of it have weakened or surpassed that."[12] No later bonds, she wrote, could "weaken the first and best of nature." The whole relationship was complicated by the fact that Randolph, who revered Jefferson, became heavily dependent on his approval and advice.

Physical suffering also intruded upon Jefferson's peace. In September 1794 he was confined to his bed by rheumatism, apparently aggravated by his constantly riding over his farms in all kinds of weather. At this time Washington asked him to return to public service. Spain was now ready to negotiate in earnest with the United States but wished to deal with someone of greater stature than William Carmichael and William Short, two commissioners who had lost face while cooling their heels in Madrid. As an internationally famous American, an accomplished diplomat, and the initiator of policies that had brought Spain to the bargaining table, Jefferson seemed an ideal choice. But to Secretary of State Edmund Randolph, who had transmitted the President's request, Jefferson replied that he was in a "paroxysm of rheumatism," and explained that even if he were to recover completely, "No circumstances, my dear Sir, will ever more tempt me to engage in anything public. I thought myself perfectly fixed in this determination when I left Philadelphia, but every day and hour since has added to its inflexibility."[13]

One of Jefferson's closest friends had already accepted a diplomatic post abroad. Monroe had replaced Gouverneur Morris as United States minister to France. Jefferson was torn between rejoicing at the timely replacement of a bad diplomat with a good one and bemoaning the personal loss of a close companion.

His worries were of an opposite kind in the case of his closest friend, Madison. The congressman was threatening to leave public office and Jefferson felt that his own selfish joy in having his Orange County friend near him again would be insufficient compensation for the nation's loss of so brilliant and conscientious a statesman. Madison had reason to be distracted from public affairs. On September 15, shortly after a visit to Monticello, the shy little forty-three-year-old bachelor married a statuesque twenty-five-year-old widow, the fascinating Dolley Payne Todd. To her the "father of the Constitution" was "the great little Madison."[14]

Madison's letters would have kept Jefferson informed on public affairs even if he had been able to hold to his resolution not to touch a newspaper. When Britain, desperate in its war with France, forbade United States trade with the French West Indies and began seizing defiant American vessels, Madison proposed House resolutions to exclude England from American commerce. When an obscure Congressman astonished the House with an uncommonly eloquent speech in opposition, Jefferson wrote Madison: "Every tittle of it is Hamilton's except the introduction."[15]

Only publicly, however, could Jefferson remain aloof when Hamilton's internal excise tax on distilled liquors brought bitter ferment in October 1794. Western Pennsylvania farmers resisted collection of the duty, and Washington was persuaded to crush them with military force. Appropriately, Hamilton, handsome on horseback, commanded the 14,000 militia from four states who marched through rural Pennsylvania under the banners of war. The New Yorker celebrated the move as a well-timed assertion of federal authority, cited the collapse of resistance as evidence of complete success, and seemed to think it a good thing that the occasion had arisen. Jefferson believed that the federal government had overreacted. To Madison he deplored "such an armament against people at their plows" and wondered how "an appeal to arms" could be "justified before that to the law had been tried and *proved* ineffectual."[16] To Monroe, Jefferson wrote that "an insurrection was announced and proclaimed and armed against, but could never be found."[17]

From his mountain retreat, and with Madison as his agent, Jefferson proposed a more constructive use of federal power. He submitted to the President and Edmund Randolph, now Secretary of State, a plan for a national academy of sciences. He proposed recruiting a faculty from some of Europe's best minds.[18] Washington received the idea cordially; he himself had thought a federal university desirable, partly as a means of promoting national unity. But economic developments and the pressure of other problems frustrated the proposal. Nevertheless Jefferson's advocacy of a national undertaking of the kind that he had urged upon his state at the start of the Revolution was another evidence of the pertinacity with which he pushed his favorite concepts. It was reasonable to assume that he would nurture the seedling in silence until he found the climate suitable for bringing it forth.

He was lured back to the paperwork he had forsworn by a letter of inquiry from Christopher Daniel Ebeling, a German who was writing a *Biography and History of North America.* The request for information did not draw from Jefferson a volume comparable to the *Notes on Virginia* which he had written in response to the questions of a Frenchman, but it did elicit far more advice than Ebeling could have anticipated. Among other things, Jefferson warned the German not to trust two of his Northern contributors, Jedidiah Morse and Noah Webster, when they wrote about the South. "To pass once along a public road through a country . . ., to put up at its taverns, and get into conversations with the idle, drunken individuals who pass their time lounging in these taverns is not the way to know a country, its inhabitants or manners. To generalize a whole nation from these specimens is not the sort of information which Professor Ebeling would wish to compose his work from."[19]

One of Jefferson's own answers showed him no less prejudiced than Morse and Webster. He described America's two political parties in highly colored terms reminiscent of Samuel Johnson's most notorious definitions. Republicans he identified as "1. The entire body of landholders throughout the United States" and "2. The body of laborers, not being landholders, whether in husbandry or the arts." He wrote that the wealth of these people was "the foundation of that of their antagonists." "The Anti-Republicans," he said, "consist of 1. The old refugees and Tories. 2. British merchants residing among us and composing the main body of merchants. 3. American merchants trading on British capital. Another great portion. 4. Speculators and holders in the banks and public funds. 5. Officers of the federal government with some exceptions. 6. Office-hunters willing to give up principles for places. A numerous and noisy tribe. 7. Nervous persons, whose languid fibers have more analogy with a passive than active state of things."

Jefferson anticipated the likely question: why didn't the Republicans—the industrious, virtuous, and perceptive majority—take control from their badly flawed enemies? He explained that the Republicans were scattered on their separate farms whereas their opponents held the cities as citadels and disseminated their propaganda from the many presses which they controlled.

Obviously the partisan in Jefferson was triumphing over the scholar. It was also prodding the recluse. Admittedly he wrote to a friend on November 30, 1795, that he was "in a retirement I dote on, living like an Antediluvian patriarch among my children and grandchildren, and tilling my soil."[20] But on December 31 he wrote to William B. Giles, "Where the principle of difference is as substantial and as strongly pronounced as between the Republicans and the Monocrats of our country, I hold it as honorable to take a firm and decided part, and as immoral to pursue a middle line, as between the parties of honest men and rogues into which every country is divided."[21]

Jefferson fretted as the Republicans fumbled in their attempts to exploit the unpopularity of the treaty recently negotiated with England by John Jay, one of the principal Federalists. Public ire was stirred because the document granted the United States only neglible trading privileges with the West Indies while giving the British unrestricted rights of trade between that colony and the American Republic.

But Hamilton, writing a series of newspaper articles over the pseudonym "Camillus," answered criticism of the treaty so skillfully that he blunted its effect. In grudging admiration of the New Yorker, Jefferson wrote to Madison: "Hamilton is really a colossus to the Anti-Republican Party. Without numbers he is a host within himself. They have got themselves into a defile where they might be finished; but too much security on the Republican part will give time to his talents and indefatigableness to extricate them. We have had only middling performances to oppose to him. In truth, when he comes forward, there is nobody but yourself who can meet him. . . . For God's sake, take up your pen. . . ."[22] How long could Jefferson sit on his mountaintop without lifting the proven lance that was his own pen?

Jefferson had hoped for the success of efforts in the House to block the treaty by denying appropriations for its implementation, thus circumventing the constitutional provision that only the Senate could act on ratification. The attempt was frustrated, but Jefferson was revealing to his friends, perhaps even to himself, that when the stakes were high he was not always a strict constructionist.

Once again he was pouring his energies into a variety of tasks, but he still held back from political activity. He no longer helped to enact laws or administer them, but instead labored to preserve them—quite literally. He was collecting and codifying the statutes and public papers of Virginia, many of which were in private hands, sometimes careless hands. He no longer sought to make changes in either house of Congress, but undertook revolutionary changes in the house that was his dwelling. In the spring of 1796 he demolished the attic to substitute the octagonal dome, transforming his home into something startlingly new on the American landscape though solidly rooted in Palladian and classical tradition. During the reconstruction, Jefferson reported to a friend, he and his family were camping "under the tent of heaven." In view of Jefferson's love of comfort and penchant for drama, it is possible that his reference implied little more than picnicking in good weather. He was no longer drawn to Philadelphia by the operations of government but he did accept the presidency of the American Philosophical Society which was headquartered there. His pleasure in elevation to the office was mitigated by the fact that the vacancy had been created by the death of his friend David Rittenhouse.

The construction of a dome and the speculations of philosophy were not enough to rivet Jefferson's attention on celestial clouds when the dust clouds of political conflict boiled up from below. He kept sending advice to the Republican warriors in Congress to exacerbate dissatisfaction with the Jay treaty. To Madison he admitted vexation with Washington, bemoaning "the incomprehensible acquiescence of the only honest man who has assented to it," and saying, "I wish that his honesty and his political errors may not furnish a second occasion to exclaim, 'Curse on his virtues; they've undone his country.' "[23] Indicative of the strength of Jefferson's indignation was the indiscreet note that he wrote to Mazzei, who had returned to Italy. He did not call Washington by name but the reference was plain: "It would give you a fever were I to name to you the apostates who have gone over to these heresies, men who were Samsons in the field and Solomons in the Council, but who have had their heads shorn by the harlot England. In short we are likely to preserve the liberty we have retained only by unremitting labors and perils."[24]

Shifting from Old Testament to Swiftian imagery, he added a more positive note: "But we shall preserve them, and our mass of weight and wealth on the good side is so great as to leave no danger that force will ever be attempted against us. We have only to wake and snap the Lilliputian cords with which they have been entangling us during the first sleep which succeeded our labors."

With Jefferson's feelings so intense, the "we" could not much longer remain purely editorial. The pressures to become involved in the great political struggle were suddenly magnified by the fact that 1796 was an election year and Washington had declined to accept a third term. As Vice President, John Adams was first in line for consideration as his successor. But Hamilton essayed the role of kingmaker and he pushed for Thomas Pinckney of South Carolina, who had recently completed a tour of duty as minister to England. So strong, however, was New England prejudice against Pinckney that Hamilton was forced to compromise, agreeing to a ticket of Adams for President and Pinckney for Vice President.

Of course, there could be no straightforward offering of such a ticket. At that time the Constitution's provisions for election of a President made no allowance for the existence of political parties. Each state, either by legislative action or popular vote, chose electors equal in number to the total of its representatives and senators in Congress. Each elector then voted for two persons for President. The one receiving a majority would be elected to the top position and his nearest competitor would be Vice President. There was the very real possibility that the newly chosen President and Vice President would embody antagonistic philosophies, that they might indeed be arch rivals.

Who would be the Republican standard bearer? The *Aurora,* a much quoted Philadelphia newspaper edited by Benjamin Franklin Bache, namesake of his famous uncle, declared on September 13: "It requires no talent at divination to decide who will be the candidates for the chair. Thomas Jefferson and John Adams will be the men, and whether we shall have at the head of our executive a steadfast friend to the rights of the people, or an advocate for hereditary power and distinctions, the people of the United States are soon to decide."[25]

Jefferson had suggested that Madison be a candidate, much as he had earlier been urging him to take the lead in rebuttal of Hamilton's arguments. But it was generally acknowledged that Madison could not carry Pennsylvania or New York, states crucial to success in an election in which Southern support of the Republicans would be counterbalanced by New England support of the Federalists. Madison had urged Jefferson to accept the nomination and the request had became a chorused demand.

Active candidacy was distasteful to Jefferson. On August 30 he had confided to Mann Page: "I do not believe with the Rochefoucaulds and Montaignes that fourteen out of fifteen men are rogues. I believe that a great abatement from the proportion may be made in favor of general honesty. But I have always found that rogues would be uppermost, and I do not know that the proportion is too strong for the higher orders, and for those who, rising above the swinish multitude, always contrive to nestle themselves into the places of power and profit."[26]

What cynicism! Those who raised themselves above the multitude were mostly rogues. Those who didn't were swine. No wonder he had little appetite for political contests.

If Jefferson still subscribed to the Enlightenment faith in the perfectibility of man, he must have seen that achievement as aeons distant. But he had repeatedly testified that he did not believe the cause of liberty hopeless. The persistence with which he had so often urged Madison and others into the fray was testimony to his faith that the actions of one good man would make a difference. How much of his reluctance to return to the arena was to be explained by a revulsion against politics? Certainly there was a great deal in politics to find revolting, especially if you were both a high-minded patrician and a perfectionist artist-scholar given to indiscreet utterance of unpopular views. But was such an aversion the sole cause of Jefferson's silence as others pressed his candidacy? Long after the conclusion of his service as Governor he remembered his administration with embarrassment. In his own mind, though not in that of any objective observer, such achievements in the State Department as his successful maintenance of American neutrality were outweighed by the fact that even in his own sphere of diplomacy he had sometimes been thwarted by Hamilton. Perhaps he feared rejection by his fellow citizens, a rejection particularly painful if he assumed the role of ardent suitor and if his defeat were engineered by Hamilton. So Jefferson chose to do nothing to launch his candidacy . . . but also he did nothing to escape any current of public opinion that might carry him to the Presidency.

Many Federalists refused to believe that he was not "rowing toward his objective with muffled oars." Aaron Burr, the brilliant leader of Tammany, the Republican machine in New York City, was often mentioned as a candidate. When it was learned that New York Republicans had reached agreement with their Southern brethen to back a ticket headed by Jefferson with Burr as the Vice Presidential candidate, rumors were rife about deals. Burr had stopped by Monticello to see Jefferson briefly in the course of a Southern journey the year before. Two of the Virginian's neighbors swore to an affidavit that the two politicians had never been alone and that political strategy had not been discussed.[27]

The event was not to be determined in a single national election day. Popular balloting for Presidential electors took place on different days in different states, and even those states whose legislatures directly chose electors acted on different days. Suspense mounted as observers variously predicted that the Presidency would go to Adams, Pinckney, or Jefferson. When the Virginian received from his son-in-law, Thomas Mann Randolph, a letter brimming with confidence that Jefferson would be the victor, the older man replied promptly despite chill-stiffened fingers. "It is so cold," he wrote, "that the freezing of the ink on my pen renders it difficult to write." He was equally cold to the enthusiastic assumptions that he would be the next President: "Few will believe the true dispositions of my mind on that subject. It is not the less true, however, that I do sincerely wish to be second on that vote rather than the first. The considerations which induce this preference are solid, whether viewed with relation to interest, happiness, or reputation. Ambition is long since dead in my mind. Yet even a well-weighed ambition would take the same side."[28]

As the balloting proceeded with agonizing slowness in state after state, Jefferson conceived another worry—that he and Adams might be tied. The Constitution provided that, in such an instance, the winner should be determined by vote of the House of Representatives. He authorized Madison, in that event, "to solicit on my behalf that Mr. Adams may be preferred. He has always been my senior from the commencement of my public life, and the expression of the public will being equal, this circumstance ought to give him the preference."[29]

An emotional note crept in ten days later when Jefferson wrote Edward Rutledge that his candidacy had been "without concert or expectation on my part; on my salvation I declare it. . . . On principles of public respect I should not have refused; but I protest before my God that I shall, from the bottom of my heart, rejoice at escaping." Then, in words reminiscent of Washington's after accepting command of the Continental Army, he said: "I know well that no man will ever bring out of that office the reputation which carries him into it." Then he went beyond: "The honeymoon would be as short in that case as any other, and its moments of ecstacy would be ransomed by years of torment and hatred. . . . I have no ambition to govern men, no passion which would lead me to delight to ride in a storm."[30]

The electors in Pennslyvania, the last state to ballot, had already voted, but Jefferson did not yet know the results. Adams had received one vote, Pinckney two, Burr 13, Jefferson 14. Nationally the total was Burr 30, Pinckney 59, Jefferson 68, and Adams 71. Some New England Federalists, fearful that Pinckney might eclipse Adams, had cast their second votes for Jefferson. He would be the next Vice President of the United States.

Would he, now philosophically at odds with Adams, agree to serve with him? Madison, who knew Jefferson so well, was not sure. He urged his friend to accept so that he would be in a position to influence Adams' administration. Madison told Jefferson that the President-Elect "is said to speak of you now in friendly terms and will no doubt be soothed by your acceptance of a place subordinate to him."[31]

Doubtless impelled by generous impulse and his habit of "taking things by the smooth handle," as well as by more subtle reasons, Jefferson wrote to Adams: "The public and the papers have been much occupied lately in placing us in a point of opposition to each other. I trust with confidence that less of it has been felt by ourselves personally. . . . I have never one single moment expected a different issue (of the election); and though I know I shall not be believed, yet it is not the less true that I have never wished it. My neighbors as my compurgators could aver that fact, because they see my occupations and my attachment to them. . . . I leave to others the sublime delights of riding in the storm, better pleased with sound sleep and a warm berth below, with the society of neighbors, friends, and fellow laborers of the earth than of spies and sycophants. . . . I have no ambition to govern men. It is a painful and thankless office. . . . That your administration may be filled with glory, and happiness to yourself and advantage to us, is the sincere wish of one who, though in the course of your own voyage through life various little incidents have happened or been contrived to separate us, retains still for you the solid esteem of the moments when we were working for our independence, and sentiments of respect and affectionate attachment."[32]

Jefferson did not mail the letter to Adams but to Madison. Did Madison think it should be sent to Adams? "If Mr. Adams can be induced to administer the government on its true principles," Jefferson said, "and to relinquish his bias to an English constitution, it is to be considered whether it would not be on the whole for the public good to come to a good understanding with him as to his future elections. He is perhaps the only sure barrier against Hamilton getting in."[33]

Madison thought the letter unnecessary, believed that it came on a little too strong, and deplored its critical reference to Hamilton. The letter was never sent to Adams.

While Jefferson was confiding to Madison his hopes of steadying Adams, the President-Elect was revealing similar hopes regarding his influence over the Virginian. Encouraged by reports of friendly comments from Jefferson, Adams wrote a friend: "Mr. Jefferson's letters and declarations are no surprise to me. We labored together in high friendship in Congress in 1776 and have lived and dined together very frequently since that time. His talent and information I know very well, and have ever believed in his honor, integrity, his love of his country and his friends."[34]

He added something that he said was "entre nous": "I may say to you that his patronage of Paine and Freneau, and his entanglements with characters and politics which have been pernicious, are and have long been a source of inquietude and anxiety to me, as they must have been to you. But I hope and believe that his advancement and his situation in the Senate, an excellent school, will correct him. He will have too many French friends about him to flatter him, but I hope we can keep him steady."

If Jefferson was susceptible to flattery, he certainly did not seem flattered by the prospect of the vice presidency. At first he suggested that there was no need for him to take the oath of office in Philadelphia and certainly no need for a formal ceremony of notification there. He could be notified by mail. Surely some officeholder could administer the oath to him at Monticello. A trip northward in winter would be a "tremendous undertaking." Traveling had long been an ordeal for him. Despite his fondness for nautical figures of speech, he dreaded travel on large bodies of water. Rough roads—and virtually all roads were rough in winter—could be just as bad. Jefferson had never traveled more than twenty miles west of Charlottesville. Now he was even more out of the habit of journeying. In the three years since leaving Philadelphia after resigning the office of Secretary of State, his longest trip from home, with the exception of a single journey to Richmond, had measured less than seven miles.

Eventually Jefferson's fear that he might seem to be sulking if he remained at home caused him to travel to the federal capital. He wrote Madison: "I shall escape into the city as covertly as possible. If Governor Mifflin should show any symptoms of ceremony, pray contrive to parry them." Nevertheless, when the Virginian arrived in Philadelphia by public coach after ten days on the road, he was saluted by the discharge of sixteen rounds from two twelve-pounders manned by an artillery company. A banner proclaimed "Jefferson the Friend of the People."

Even before going to the Madisons', where he would spend the night, he called on John Adams. Returning the visit the next day, Adams entered into a review of Franco-American relations, which were at their worst point since the Genêt crisis. Repeatedly victorious over England and her allies in continental contests, France was energetically exporting revolution and in the process was ignoring American neutrality. Merchants, financiers, and shipowners were talking of war with France as a possible solution to the crisis and Hamilton was inflaming the public. Paris had increased the tension by refusing to accept the new American envoy, Charles Cotesworth Pinckney. The President-Elect said that he would like to send Jefferson to France but supposed that he was needed in his own country. Jefferson averred that he was.

The next morning he took the oath of office in the Senate chamber. His lightly powdered hair tied in a queue, his tall frame clad in a long blue frockcoat buttoned to the waist, he held back his sometimes stooping shoulders and stood superbly erect. As could have been predicted, Jefferson spoke modestly of his own qualifications and feelingly of his "cordial and uninterrupted friendship" with Adams. He not only declared that he had no further political ambitions—a statement regretted by his friends and disbelieved by his enemies—but also revealed his view of the Vice Presidency as an office of very limited responsibilities. On this point he was certainly a strict constructionist, regarding his own duties as solely the constitutionally prescribed ones of presiding over the Senate and of succeeding to the duties of the Presidency in the event of the death, resignation, or incapacity of the President. Undoubtedly Jefferson derived less satisfaction from his inauguration as Vice President of the United States than from his installation the evening before as president of the American Philosophical Society.

A few days later Jefferson sat as presiding officer of the society while his paper on the Megalonyx, or Great Claw, was read by the secretary. Jefferson had chosen the name because of what appeared to be the most distinguishing feature of a prehistoric creature that he sought to reconstruct from fossil remains found in Greenbrier County, Virginia. Noting the leonine characteristics of this prehistoric animal, three times larger than an African lion, he speculated that nature had "formed the larger animals of America, like its lakes, its rivers, and mountains, on a greater and prouder scale than in the other hemisphere."[35] He used qualifying phrases but his speculations, prodded by his patriotism, ventured a little far afield. Nevertheless, his treatise was an important pioneering effort, and he followed it with productions of more restraint and precision so that today he is honored as the father of American paleontology. The distinguished twentieth-century scientist Harlow Shapley, famed for his researches in photometry, spectroscopy, and cosmogony, has written to the Virginian: "He had, as they say, pretty nearly everything. In the field of natural philosophy he had caution and daring, inquisitiveness and willingness to change his mind in the light of new facts or as a result of further thought. What we would now call proper scientific methods appeared to be instinctive with him."[36]

Those same qualities of mind Jefferson brought to the practice of statecraft. But they were not to be available to the Adams administration. Two days after the inauguration, the new President and Vice President had been entertained at dinner by General Washington, affable in his efforts to bridge any gap between administrations and cheerful at release from the burdens of office. When Jefferson had confirmed Adams' supposition that he would not be interested in serving as an envoy to France, he had promised to find out whether a fellow Virginian, James Madison, would accept the appointment.

Now, as the new President and Vice President left Washington's quarters, Jefferson revealed that Madison had no interest in the assignment. Adams seemed embarrassed and said more than was necessary in the circumstances—that unanticipated opposition to Madison had developed. The two men walked on together for awhile, physically an ill-matched team—Adams short, round-headed, rotund; Jefferson tall, long-headed, lean. If they had been horses instead of men, nobody would have expected them to pull together in harness. After a few minutes they went their separate ways.

The two men later recalled the conversation and the parting. Their accounts are essentially the same. Adams said, "We parted as good friends as we had always lived; but we consulted very little together afterwards."[37] Jefferson said that he was never consulted. The President's explanation was that "party violence soon rendered it impracticable, or at least useless."[38] At the time he may have been disposed to blame this state of affairs mostly on some of Jefferson's followers who, he said, undermined him with "misrepresentation and insinuation." But upon maturer reflection he concluded that "this party violence was excited by Hamilton more than any other man."[39]

Though it is true that Hamilton and other Federalists on the one side and some Republicans on the other made easy conference between President and Vice President almost impossible, Jefferson contributed nothing toward bridging the gap but a personal friendliness. It was unlikely that his advice would be sought very often when in his address upon taking the oath of office he had interpreted his duties as minimal and had emphasized that he did not consider himself part of the administration. Adams himself as Vice President had not played a prominent role in either of Washington's administrations. Jefferson's concept of the Vice Presidency—so different from that of Adams who saw its holder as inevitably elevated above what he called "the common major generals, simple bishops, earls and barons" and "common trash of ambassadors, envoys, and ministers plenipotentiary"[40] —must have contributed to the downgrading of that office in the formative years of the Republic.

Just nine days after his inauguration as Vice President, Jefferson left Philadelphia, arriving at Monticello March 20. All too soon, this miserable traveler was on the return road, on May 5 leaving a flowering Virginia spring for a special session of Congress where only ambitions would bloom and political reputations would blossom. On the fifth day of his journey, when he paused for breakfast at Bladensburg, Maryland, he read a newspaper article that took his appetite. It contained a garbled version of the letter to Mazzei in which he had implied that Washington was one of those "who were Samsons in the field and Solomons in the council but who have had their heads shorn by the harlot England." He would have found it painful enough to read an accurate reproduction of his letter. This version was still worse. Mazzei had translated the original into Italian and given it to a Florentine newspaper. A Parisian paper had in turn translated it into French. The *Minerva*, a New York paper edited by Noah Webster, an ardent Federalist, had translated it back into English, and publications in Philadelphia and elsewhere had eagerly copied it. In Paris the letter had acquired an extra sentence which the *Minerva* innocently translated along with the rest of the French text. It made Jefferson declare the necessity "that we arrest the progress of that system of ingratitude and injustice towards France, from which they [the Federalist government] would alienate us to bring us under British influence." Jefferson had protested the "forms," or ceremonies, of the United States government. An error in translation had transformed the word from plural to singular so that he appeared to object to the "form," or system, of government in his country.[41] Webster called the letter treasonable.

Jefferson's first impulse was to "take the field of the public papers." But he soon decided against this course. There were demands that he either confess to authorship of the letter or disown it. He could not easily do either. If he denied its authenticity, he would have to point out the respects in which published versions differed from the original. To do so would be to increase circulation of his disparaging comments on Washington. Also it would be difficult to explain his position without alluding to Washington's confidential correspondence with his Cabinet. When Jefferson arrived in Philadelphia two days later he discovered that his letter was the principal subject of scandal in the capital.

Despite the admiration of his Philadelphia friends in the American Philosophical Society, Jefferson had often felt an alien in the Federalist-dominated society of the city. There may well have been nothing paranoid in his assumption that now he was being ostracized. Monroe begged Jefferson to explain the circumstances of the letter, saying that his silence brought upon him "all the odium of having written it" whereas a bold defense of it would raise "the spirits of the honest part of the community." Nevertheless, Jefferson chose silence, not even indulging in his letters to Monroe and Madison what must have been an inclination to blame Mazzei. Perhaps the Vice President was all too aware that the principal cause of his embarrassment had been his own indiscretion.

Surely no less painful than widespread public disapproval was the deadly threat to his friendship with Washington. As disputatious members of his Cabinet, Jefferson and Hamilton had not only been representatives of opposing philosophies but also something very like sibling rivals for parental approval. In the preceding year Jefferson had fallen under suspicion when leaks of Washington's memos from those cabinet days had fueled Republican charges. Then Washington had accepted the younger man's denial and his explanation that someone was attempting to "sow tares between you and me, by representing me as still engaged in the bustle of politics, and in turbulence and intrigue against the government." The incident of the letter might well confirm earlier suspicions and add too great a strain to the former President's severely taxed generosity.

Ostracized by the Federalists and loudly praised by Republican editors and congressmen, Jefferson soon consented to play the hero for those who saw him as one. Not as the result of a dramatic decision, but by a rapid succession of small acquiescences, cooperative responses, and gently proffered counsels, he shouldered the leadership of the Republican Party.

The dominant issue between the parties was one of foreign policy. With France and England at war and both displaying their contempt for American neutrality, not to say American sovereignty, many Federalists were saying that it might be necessary to fight the French. Some Republicans were asserting that Great Britain was the earlier and greater offender and therefore more in need of a lesson. Before the convening of Congress, Jefferson stated his views in a letter to Elbridge Gerry. The Virginian, ever since his first Northern trip, had been friendly with the Massachusetts politician, but he probably wrote to him now because he knew that Adams was likely to name him to the commission to negotiate with the French. The Vice President doubtless hoped to reach through his letter to Gerry a larger audience than one. The note was one of those that Jefferson prepared with the same care that he might lavish on a state paper.

"I do sincerely wish with you," he said, "that we could take our stand on a ground perfectly neutral and independent towards all nations." To this ideal, he said, he had always remained true as a public official. But the English had always been dissatisfied with attempts to deal evenhandedly with the belligerents. "They have wished a monopoly of commerce and influence with us and they have in fact obtained it." He argued that, through their influence over American industrialists, financiers, and politicians, the British continued to direct the policies of their former colonies. The impersonal wording did not disguise the personal frustration underlying his assertion that British domination of most of the American press brought upon those who wished "merely to recover self-government the charge of subserving one foreign influence because they resist submission to another."[42] American independence was only an illusion.

A few weeks later, after Gerry had been appointed a commissioner, Jefferson wrote him another letter, even more passionate for peace than the first but more objective in its discussion of the belligerents. "The insults and injuries committed on us by the belligerent parties, from the beginning of 1793 to this day, and still continuing, cannot now be wiped off by engaging in war with one of them. As there is great reason to expect this is the last campaign in Europe, it would certainly be better for us to rub through this year, as we have done through the four preceding ones, and hope that on the restoration of peace we may be able to establish some plan for our foreign connections more likely to secure our peace, interest and honor, in future. Our countrymen have divided themselves by such strong affections, to the French and the English, that nothing will secure us internally but a divorce from both nations; and this must be the object of every real American, and its attainment is practicable without much self-denial. But for this, peace is necessary. Be assured of this, my dear Sir, that if we engage in a war during our present passions, and our present weakness in some quarters, our Union runs the greatest risk of not coming out of that war in the shape in which it enters it."[43]

Jefferson's attitude was realistic and his moral stance was that of a statesman above petty factionalism. But the tone in which he addressed Gerry, even allowng for this Virginian's habitual effusiveness in personal communication, smacked of the wooing politician. "It was with infinite joy to me," he wrote, "that you were yesterday announced to the Senate as Envoy Extraordinary, jointly with General [C.C.] Pinckney and Mr. [John] Marshall, to the French Republic. . . . My reliance for our preservation is in your acceptance of this mission." He even added that, while he must return home from Philadelphia before receiving assurance of Gerry's acceptance, "it will reach me in my retirement and enrich the tranquility of that scene." Was Jefferson impelled to such flattery solely by desperate concern for his country? Or was there also a strong admixture of a desire to impress the powerful Massachusetts politician with the idea that the Vice President was a moderate with the vision and temperament to unite warring factions?

Whatever Jefferson's motives, Hamilton for once thought there was little to fear from him. When Adams, just two days after taking office, had requested the opinions of his Cabinet on policies toward France, they had forwarded the questions to the New Yorker before replying. Hamilton saw everything under control—his control. He wrote to his friend Rufus King, now in England as United States Minister: "Mr. Adams is President, Mr. Jefferson Vice President. Our Jacobins say they are well pleased, and that the Lion and the Lamb are to lie down together. Mr. Adams' personal friends talk a little in the same way: Mr. Jefferson is not half so ill a man as we have been accustomed to think him; there is to be a united and vigorous administration. Skeptics like me quietly look forward to the event, willing to hope but not prepared to believe.''[44]

Another Federalist leader, Fisher Ames, had a different view of Jefferson's role: "In a Senate that will bring him into no scrapes, as he will have no casting votes to give, responsible for no measures, acting in none that are public, he may go on affecting zeal for the people; combining the antis, and standing at their head, he will balance the power of the chief magistrate by his own. Two Presidents, like two suns in the meridian, would meet and jostle for four years, and then Vice would be first.''[45]

Jefferson was not finding it that simple. Now that he was in the capital and Madison, declining reelection to Congress, had returned to Virginia, their roles were reversed. Madison was dependent upon Jefferson for reliable information on national politics. Only ten senators, Jefferson said, were dependable in their devotion to Republican principles whereas eighteen would stand firm for the Federalists. Republican strength in the House approximated that of the Federalists but was weakened on some days by excessive absences and renegade tendencies.[46]

Jefferson certainly saw himself as leader of the opposition rather than as an ally of the President. In answer to a letter from a Maryland man with the fascinating name Peregrine Fitzhugh, the Vice President wrote: "It is possible from the complexion of the President's speech that he was disposed or perhaps advised to proceed on a line which would endanger the peace of our country.... The nomination of the envoys for France does not prove a thorough conversion to the pacific system.''[47]

Jefferson cautioned his correspondent that these words were not for publication but, advised by his father that the Vice President surely would not mind their being shared with the faithful, Peregrine held his friends fascinated with his revelations. Eventually Jefferson's comments, exaggerated in transmission, reached Adams himself.

Thanking his informant, the President wrote that the news would give him an additional motive "to be upon my guard." He added: "It is evidence of a mind soured yet seeking for popularity, and eaten to a honeycomb with ambition, yet weak, confused, uninformed and ignorant. I have been long convinced that this ambition is so inconsiderate as to be capable of going great lengths.''[48] Obviously, the breach between President and Vice President was complete.

In distorted form, Jefferson's comments reached the general public. Apparently not remorseful for his own epistolary indiscretion even while the echoes of his Mazzei letter still reverberated, Jefferson lamented to Peregrine Fitzhugh: "I have been for some time used as the property of the newspapers, a fair mark for every man's dirt. Some, too, have indulged themselves in this exercise who would not have done it had they known me otherwise than through these impure and injurious channels. It is hard treatment, and for a singular kind of offense, that of having obtained by the labors of a life the indulgent opinions of a part of one's fellow citizens. However, these moral evils must be submitted to, like the physical scourges of tempest, fire &c.''[49]

He was feeling sorry for himself without blaming himself. Vice President Jefferson was sounding very much like President Adams.

By now Jefferson had become the party leader that the Federalist press had accused him of being. He no longer restricted his partisan activities to advising friends in Virginia and Republican colleagues in the Congress. He sought to strengthen his ties with Aaron

Burr, with whom his candidacy had been linked in the elections for President and Vice President, but for whom he had evinced little admiration. A Federalist victory in New York had ousted Burr from his seat in the United States Senate, giving it to Philip Schuyler, Hamilton's father-in-law. Burr, however, was an active leader in the State Assembly and remained the most prominent Republican in his state. If Jefferson was to weld a strong alliance of Republicans, North and South, he needed Burr's support. So he wrote him, giving him a "general view of [the Republican] situation and prospects," saying that he was sure the colonel already knew these things, but adding: "At any rate, it will give me an opportunity of recalling myself to your memory, and of evidencing my esteem for you."[50]

He reported that the majority in the House of Representatives was "very equivocal indeed. A few individuals of no fixed system at all, governed by the panic or the prowess of the moment, flap as the breeze blows against the republican or the aristocratic bodies, and give to the one or the other a preponderance entirely accidental." He said that, largely because of events in Europe, the "threatening propositions" contained in the President's bellicose address had been "abandoned one by one, and the cry begins now to be that we have been called together to do nothing. The truth is, there is nothing to do, the idea of war being scouted by the events of Europe; but this only proves that war was the object for which we were called. It proves that the executive temper was for war; and that the convocation of the Representatives was an experiment of the temper of the nation, to see if it was in unison."

Jefferson expressed his disappointment that the Adams administration had proved as secretive as its predecessor in dealing with Congress. "I had always hoped," he said, "that the popularity of the late President being once withdrawn from active effect, the natural feelings of the people towards liberty would restore the equilibrium between the executive and legislative departments."

"I consider the future character of our republic as in the air," he said. "Indeed its future fortune will be in the air, if war is made on us by France, and if Louisiana becomes a Gallo-American Colony." Already he was thinking of the risks to the United States of having Louisiana remain in foreign hands. He feared England, too, particularly when the Administration seemed to be succumbing to her wiles. He confessed himself "almost oppressed with apprehensions that fraud will at length effect what force could not, and that what with currents and counter-currents, we shall, in the end, be driven back to the land from which we launched twenty years ago. Indeed, my dear sir, we have been but a sturdy fish on the hook of a dexterous angler who, letting us flounce till we have spent our force, brings us up at last."

All was not hopeless, however. "I have been much pleased," he told Burr, "to see a dawn of change in the spirit of your State. . . . If a prospect could be once opened upon us of the penetration of truth into the Eastern States, if the people there (who are unquestionably republicans) could discover that they have been duped into the support of measures calculated to sap the very foundations of republicanism, we might still hope for salvation, and that it would come, as of old, from the East."

Jefferson asked whether Burr believed that the East would "awake to the true state of things. Can the middle, Southern and Western States hold on till they awake? These are painful and doubtful questions; and if, in assuring me of your health, you can give me a comfortable solution of them, it will relieve a mind devoted to the preservation of our republican government in the true form and spirit in which it was established. . . .''

In a single letter, the Vice President in effect had outlined a platform for the Republican Party and provided it with several rallying cries. He had made a well-timed overture toward Northern Republicans by addressing Burr in friendly terms, stressing the areas of agreement between them, and seeking his counsel. Jefferson still wrote ''republican'' with a lower case ''r'' but his activities insured that the letter would soon be capitalized.

Burr's response was all that the Virginian could have wished. The colonel said, ''The moment requires free communication among those who adhere to the principles of our revolution.'' Suiting his actions to his words, he said that for this purpose face to face conversation was better than writing and therefore he hoped to see Jefferson soon in Philadelphia.[51]

That June, when Monroe returned from France to the jeers of the Federalists and the cheers of his fellow Republicans, Burr was in Philadelphia to see him and Jefferson. For two hours Monroe, the Vice President, Albert Gallatin, and Burr discussed the fate of the Republic and the duties and opportunities of Republicans. Fresh from Europe with news that only he could impart, Monroe was listened to eagerly. Gallatin's shrewd observations, uttered in the impeccable English he had acquired in America but with the French accent of his native Swiss canton, drew the respect merited by their author's cosmopolitan wisdom. Burr, less than five-feet four-inches tall, slender as a yellow jacket, his great, grave eyes contradicting the flippancy of his leprechaun smile and elfin ears, would have been compelling as a curiosity even if he had not been commanding as an intellect. But the focus of attention in this remarkable group of Republican chiefs was Jefferson. His questions prompted the most significant answers and his nod confirmed their pertinence. Another important leader, Madison, was far away in Virginia but he too awaited the word from Jefferson.

The Vice President was astonished by the motley ranks of those who offered him allegiance. Burr told him of the mechanics who were flocking to the Republican banner in New York City. Could these urban ironsmiths and coopers walk the paths of freedom as truly as the plowman in his fields? Jefferson wasn't sure, but he thought it would be folly not to find out.

The Republicans gave Monroe a testimonial dinner in Philadelphia on July 1. The writers of *Porcupine's Gazette,* wielding appropriately sharp quills, called each participant ''Monsieur'' rather than ''Mister'' and disgustedly reported a toast to ''The Man of the People, Thomas Jefferson.''[52] Jefferson had retired from the banquet before his name was proposed but, even if he should have inhibiting second thoughts, he obviously would not be permitted to retire from the battle for the Presidency which was shaping up three years ahead. *Porcupine's Gazette,* in an advertisement for a pamphlet warning of the Virginian's ''pretensions'' to the Presidency, said: ''Mr. Jefferson's acknowledged *Letter to Mazzei* having rent the veil that concealed from the partial and prejudiced many of his political deformities, the PRESENT CRISIS demands that they should now be exposed without reserve.''[53] As Jefferson headed home from Philadelphia on July 6 he could scarcely have avoided a wistful thought back to that July twenty-one years earlier when he and John Adams had worked together for American independence.

While Jefferson, in retreat at Monticello, contemplated events from his cool mountaintop, Monroe and Hamilton were caught up in hot and dusty combat. A newly published history of the United States, anonymously written by James Thomson Callender, revealed sordid details of Hamilton's adulterous affair with Mrs. James Reynolds and of Mr. Reynolds' attempts to blackmail the New Yorker. Earlier, to refute the suspicions of some congressmen that he had indulged in improper activities as Secretary of the Treasury, Hamilton had revealed to three of them the story of his indiscretions with the married woman. To clear away certain mysteries about his public procedures, he found it necessary to make damaging revelations about his private conduct. He did so, however, with the understanding that the facts he imparted would not go beyond the ears of his three visitors.

Publication of the secret facts, in complete violation of a gentlemen's agreement, enraged Hamilton. Since Monroe was now the object of attacks by the Federalists, Hamilton and his friends leaped to the conclusion that Monroe, one of the original conferees, was the betrayer of confidence. Actually, someone else had told Callender, but Monroe was unable to convince Hamilton.

With rumor outrunning fact, Hamilton published the original records with all their embarrassing details. That proud and fastidious man may have suffered as much from revealing to the world the bad grammar of his mistress as from sharing with the public the more physical aspects of their couplings. He grandiosely declared that attacks on his morals, public and private, were attacks on the nation itself. He saw himself soaring in public nobility above all the little peccadilloes of private life. He was, he asserted, the victim of a Jacobin "conspiracy of vice against virtue." He cited as chief members of the "Jacobin Scandal-Club" Monroe and Jefferson.[54]

Monroe entered into a series of public arguments with Hamilton that threatened to bring the two of them to the dueling ground. Jefferson, however, was not tempted into debate. Perhaps he agreed with his friend Madison who wrote privately that Hamilton's attack on Jefferson was "a masterpiece of folly, because its impotence is in exact proportion to its venom."

Callender, however, eventually wheedled out of Jefferson small financial contributions in support of future publications. The partisan pamphleteer boasted that if he could find another person to do one-half of what Mr. Jefferson has "already done, I would make myself heard very distinctly for a considerable distance."

Before the summer was over, Jefferson could no longer regard the gathering storm as a dull rumbling from the North. Early in August danger struck in Virginia with the suddenness of summer lightning. Even before Jefferson had left Philadelphia he had learned of the trouble that had befallen the Congressman from his district, Samuel J. Cabell. A Republican, Cabell had criticized the Adams administration in circular letters to his constituents. A grand jury of the federal circuit court in Richmond had drawn a presentment against him for disseminating, in time of public danger, "unfounded calumnies against the happy government of the United States," all in the interest of France. In ensuing weeks excitement and resentment mounted in Virginia over reports that jurymen of British birth had been instrumental in charging the congressman with being a tool of French interests.

Jefferson drew up a petition to the Virginia House of Delegates and circulated it among the voters of his district. It denounced both the indictment and its judicial instigation as violations of the Constitution and requested the Delegates to impeach and punish the grand jurors so as to protect the constitutional rights of the citizens of

Virginia.[55] The action was a bold one, but Jefferson kept his own name out of the business, having Peter Carr present the petition to the voters.

Before taking this step, the Vice President submitted the paper to the judgment of Madison and Monroe. Madison suggested small amendments. Monroe questioned the right of a state legislature to intervene in the relationship between a citizen and his representative to the federal government. He suggested that the petition be addressed to the United States House of Representatives.

In answering Monroe's objections Jefferson once again revealed that he was selective in the practice of strict construction and again placed his reliance in that natural law which he had cited in the Declaration of Independence. He told his friend that he had anticipated the objection, "but I knew that to send the petition to the House of Representatives in Congress would make bad worse; that a majority of that house would pass a vote of approbation. On examination of the question, too, it appeared to me that we could maintain the authority of our own government over it."[56]

He argued: "A right of free correspondence between citizen and citizen, on their joint interests, whether public or private, and under whatsoever laws these interests arise . . . is a natural right; it is not the gift of any municipal law, either of England, or Virginia, or of Congress; but in common with all our other natural rights, it is one of the objects for the protection of which society is formed, and municipal laws established."

"The courts of this Commonwealth . . . ," he argued, "still retain all their judiciary cognizances not expressly alienated by the federal Constitution."

But the triumph of his pragmatism in pursuit of his ideals was revealed in his additional comment: "Were the question even doubtful, that is no reason for abandoning it. The system of the General (federal) government is to seize all doubtful ground. We must join in the scramble or get nothing. Where first occupancy is to give right, he who lies still loses all." Ironically, Jefferson regarded as an enemy the government which an increasing number of Americans believed he was destined to head. He envisioned the states' interposing to protect individual liberties from a tyrannical central power.

After much argument, in and out of legislative halls, the House of Delegates adopted a resolution condemning the action of the grand jury as "a violation of the fundamental principles of representation" and "a subjection of a natural right of speaking and writing freely."[57] But the Delegates made no move toward impeachment.

In the long run, the most significant aspect of Jefferson's efforts was the revelation of his philosophy and modus operandi. Though his distrust of the Federal government was greatly heightened by the fact that his own party was out of power, he believed quite apart from partisan considerations that big government was likely to be the master rather than the servant of the people. Moved by this fear, he laid more stress than ever before on states' rights. Though he was successful in securing the passage of resolutions embodying his views, he was frustrated in his attempt to give operative force to the resolutions. In fighting for what he believed to be the most vital freedoms he was prepared to sacrifice what he regarded as lesser ones: when told that grand jurors born in England had been active in the usurpation of power, he suggested that only native citizens be permitted to serve on juries.

At this point, even more than at earlier times in his career, Jefferson's proceeding was to incite others to action while keeping his own involvement secret. He had long believed in "taking things by the smooth handle" but as a young revolutionist he had acted boldly in his own name even at the cost of diarrhea and migraine. Had he now begun to think as a Presidential candidate?

Amid public discord from summer to year's end Jefferson had at least one occasion to celebrate domestic concord. At Monticello on October 13 his daughter Maria (now seldom called Polly) was married to her half first cousin John Wayles Eppes. John was the son of that Aunt Eppes who had been a second mother to young Polly during the first part of her father's service in Paris. Like most aristocrats, English and American, Jefferson had no fears of inbreeding in either horses or people so long as the stock was good. He had long held in affection the groom and his family. To Martha, or Patsy, who had remained as close to her father after marriage as before, he wrote: "I now see our fireside formed into a group, no one member of which can ever produce any jarring or jealousies among us. No irregular passions, no dangerous bias, which may render problematical the future fortunes and happiness of our descendants." He was presenting to the newlyweds the plantation called Pantops, which stood right across from Monticello.

But before year's end his idyllic dream was shattered. Maria and John remained at Monticello for days after the wedding, not an unusual procedure in Virginia at the time. But their stay was prolonged beyond their original intention, first by a fall in which the bride suffered a sprain. Jefferson's concern over his daughter, a bad cold which he caught, and rain-swollen rivers that made travel difficult, all conspired to keep him at Monticello until December 4, several weeks after the convening of the Senate in Philadelphia. By that time, Maria and John had gone to his parents' home. It gradually became evident that they would never occupy the house at Pantops.

Jefferson was unhappy as he set out for Philadelphia. His alterations to Monticello had literally involved raising the roof, and the chestnut shingles and other roofing material had not arrived in time, so that except for the study and the parlor the house was open to the rains and snows of winter. He described himself as "houseless."[58] Certainly no quarters in Philadelphia could be a home. Shortly before leaving the capital in the past summer he had written Edward Rutledge about the intolerable atmosphere of the city: "You and I have formerly seen warm debates and high political passions. But gentlemen of different politics would then speak to each other, and separate the business of the Senate from that of society. It is not so now. Men who have been intimate all their lives cross the streets to avoid meeting, and turn their heads another way lest they should be obliged to touch their hats. This may do for young men with whom passion is enjoyment. But it is afflicting to peaceable minds. Tranquility is the old man's milk."[59]

Jefferson's primacy among Republican leaders would alone have been enough to make him the man most hated by ardent Federalists. Now there was an added factor to earn the enmity of many who, though lukewarm party men, loved and revered Washington. The clerk of Albemarle County, a Federalist and enemy of Jefferson's, had written to Washington to warn him that a seemingly innocuous letter addressed to the former President had been signed with a false name and was somehow part of a plot against him inspired by Jefferson. The informant assured Washington that he knew whereof he spoke. After all, he lived "in cannon shot of the very headquarters of Jacobinism."[60]

Remembering Jefferson's letter to Mazzei, disapproving highly of many of his former Cabinet member's utterances and associates, and now goaded by this latest report, Washington told a relative that if the new charge could be proved against Jefferson "it would be a pity not to expose him to public execration."[61] The clerk may have been sincere in his accusation, but Jefferson was innocent. Nevertheless, Washington from this time forward regarded Jefferson as a personal enemy and a menace to the Republic. Word got around. Some who had merely resented Jefferson as too French, too philosophical, or too clever, now had a comfortably respectable reason for hating him.

For Jefferson, the scorn of Washington was harder to bear than the enmity of his followers. The hostility between Jefferson and Hamilton had been exacerbated by their having competed like sibling rivals for the older man's approval.

On January 11, 1798, almost a month after checking into his rooms at Francis's Hotel, Jefferson wrote Angelica Church, "Party animosities here have raised a wall of separation between those who differ in political sentiments."[62] He remembered her fondly from the days when she and his beloved Maria Cosway had been rival beauties, though friends, and he had gotten into minor trouble by writing to each that he wished he might be hand in hand with her as he traveled down the Rhine. Mrs. Church probably had heard many hard things said about her old Virginia friend. After all, she was Hamilton's sister-in-law.

Now a piece of work which had won Jefferson much praise during those happy days in Europe was being picked apart in an effort to shred his reputation and his following. The famous *Notes on Virginia* had contained a supposedly accurate rendering of the Mingo Chief Logan's address to Lord Dunmore at the conclusion of Dunmore's War. Jefferson had commented, "I may challenge the whole orations of Demosthenes and Cicero, and of any more eminent orator, if Europe has furnished any more eminent, to produce a single passage superior to the speech of Logan."[63] In one of the Indian's most famous sentences he had blamed the murder of his family on one Colonel Cresap. Jefferson had identified the criminal as Michael Cresap, "a man infamous for the many murders he had committed on those much injured people." The speech had been thrust into new prominence when it was declaimed in Philadelphia in successive performances by a professional elocutionist. Cresap was dead, but his son-in-law Luther Martin, known as "the Federal Bulldog," saw an opportunity to help his party and defend the family honor at the same time. He charged that the speech was a fiction and Jefferson's identification of Cresap a defamation of an honorable man.

Jefferson immediately sought further information on Cresap's complicity or innocence and promised to make any warranted correction in the next edition of the *Notes*. Martin seemed far more interested in injuring Jefferson than in obtaining a correction or apology. He made the incident an excuse for circulating in the press letters abusing Jefferson and suggesting blots on the Vice President's character.

Despite all provocation, Jefferson refused to be drawn into a debate in the press, much to the chagrin of his old friend John Page who warned him not to "indulge" so much his "philosophical disposition."[64] To one friend, Jefferson quoted, "Oh! that mine enemy would write a book!"[65] He was inclined to retreat from all public expression, literary or political.

Private expression was another matter. Each day he dined with members of Congress. Frequently among them was Gallatin, who now, in the absence of Madison, became despite his foreign accent the principal Republican spokesman in the House. As presiding officer of the Senate, Jefferson could, on principle, stand above the fights in that chamber. He could be the adviser, and sometimes the mentor, of leading combatants in the House. Though constant public criticism weighed heavily upon Jefferson, his role under other circumstances could have been satisfying. He was more happily cast as seer than as gladiator.

Astute leadership was especially important for Republicans in the House, where their precarious majority was sometimes wiped out by absenteeism and where, according to Gallatin, they had fewer effective speakers than the Federalists.[66]

Even the most adroit leadership could make little difference in the Senate. There the Republicans were outnumbered more than two to one. This fact seemed to influence Jefferson's approach to a constitutional question posed by Federalist efforts to impeach Tennessee's Senator William Blount for conspiracy to invade Spanish territory with British support. One of the most extraordinary aspects of the affair was that a Republican senator should be accused of conspiring with the British rather than the French. Behind the scenes Jefferson furnished Virginia Senator Henry Tazewell with legal references indicating that impeachment was a criminal prosecution. Impeachment, he argued, violated the Bill of Rights provision for jury trials in all cases of criminal prosecution. Tazewell shared Jefferson's view but most senators didn't. Not even the loyal Madison was convinced by the series of arguments that Jefferson dispatched to Montpelier. The Vice President's zealous defense of his opinion was fueled by fear. He wrote Madison: "I see nothing in the mode of proceeding by impeachment but the most formidable weapon for the purposes of a dominant faction that ever was contrived. It would be the most effectual one for getting rid of any man whom they consider as dangerous to their views."[67]

As Congress tensely awaited return of the American envoys from France with news that could mean new problems, or even war, irritation flared in many ways. When some Federalists stayed away from a Washington's Birthday Ball on the grounds that it was an insult to the incumbent President, Jefferson rejoiced that the occasion had "sown tares among the exclusive federals."[68] Jefferson was disgusted when argument between two New England members of the House led one to spit in the face of the other and culminated a few days later in a duel in the House with one wielding a cane and the other a pair of fire tongs. Mingled with Jefferson's distaste for the behavior of both combatants was his concern that one of them—a Republican—had very nearly been expelled from the House. He was confirmed in his fear that expulsion would be a majority weapon for further reducing a minority.

The best indication of Jefferson's views on party factionalism at the time comes not from his letters to friends already familiar with his attitudes from personal conversation but from his reply to a fellow Virginian he did not know well but whose right to disagree he respected. John Wise, a prominent Virginian, hearing that the Vice President had described him as being "of Tory politics," requested an explanation. As the term "Tory" had commonly been applied to defenders of the Crown during the Revolution, calling a patriot a tory could cause a fight in some bars.

In his reply to Wise, Jefferson expressed wonder that his comment, lightly made in the company of daily dining companions in Philadelphia, should have found its way back to Virginia. He admitted that he had spoken without personal knowledge and might have been mistaken. In any event, he believed that Mr. Wise was entitled to an explanation of Jefferson's own understanding of the appellation. He wrote:

> It is now well understood that two political sects have arisen within the U.S., the one believing that the executive is the branch of our government which the most needs support, the other that (like the analogous branch in the English government) it is already too strong for the republican parts of the constitution, and therefore in equivocal cases they incline to the legislative powers. The former of these are called federalists, sometimes aristocrats or monocrats, and sometimes tories, after the Corresponding sect in the English government of exactly the same definition. The latter are styled republicans, whigs, jacobins, disorganizers, etc.[69]

To this point, the tone of the letter was pedantic. But now Jefferson made a more provocative observation:

> Both parties claim to be federalists and republicans, and I believe with truth as to the great mass of them. These appelations therefore designate neither exclusively, and all the others are slanders, except those of whig and tory which alone characterize the distinguishing principles of the two sects as I have before explained them.

Jefferson was already at work on the concept that the basic unity of most Americans could be expressed in terms of their adherence to both federalism and republicanism. He would whittle away the excess verbiage, leaving the clean-cut statement: "We are all Republicans; we are all Federalists." Even while one part of his mind wore the blinders of partisanship, another retained the vision of a statesman.

Nevertheless, many in the House of Representatives did not see him in that role. There, according to Theodore Sedgwick of Massachusetts, "Philippics" were "pronounced against the author of the letter to Mazzei."[70] He saw Jefferson as "the very life and soul of the opposition" and, in amusing contrast to the Vice President's concept of his own congressional following as often negligent and inattentive, described them as "a well organized and disciplined corps, never going astray, or doing right even by mistake."

Federalist congressmen gleefully read aloud in the House from twisted versions of the Mazzei letter, and Federalist editors found in the proceedings enough fuel to warm the hearts of their readers in a Philadelphia February. Some of Jefferson's friends proved more embarrassing than his enemies. Rushing to his defense, the *Aurora*, edited by Franklin's radical grandson, accepted the most notorious version of the Mazzei letter and praised the Vice President for exposing Washington.[71]

Debate ostensibly was centered on foreign policy and specifically on United States relations with France, but in the popular mind Jefferson was so closely identified with French interests that the fires of argument made of him a conveniently illuminated target.

The Virginian's anxiety extended far beyond matters of personal reputation or political success. Though war between France and the United States seemed to him improbable, it was at least a distinct possibility. The French Directory was still angry over Jay's treaty, which had placed British trade with America on a most-favored nation basis. Wily Foreign Minister Talleyrand had contrived to delay negotiations for a treaty of commerce and amity with the United States, wielding etiquette as a fencing sword and holding the American Commissioners at bay with aggressive politeness. The French might at any moment resume interference with ships flying the American flag in the Atlantic.

On March 5 President Adams told Congress of a report from the American Commissioners that the Directory seemed sure to adopt a proposal now before it to declare neutral ships subject to seizure if they carried British merchandise or products. Two weeks later, Adams, without revealing the texts of communiques from the American negotiators, announced that these reports made it clear that his government's best efforts in Paris had proved futile. The United States should no longer indulge in dreams of friendship with France. He urged Congress to act without delay to protect American shipping and territory and to provide supplies and revenue for an augmented army and navy. Seeing the President's message as a summons to war, Jefferson described it to Madison as "almost insane."[72]

The Vice President believed that Congress should prohibit the arming of merchant vessels and then adjourn. Adjournment would not only make hasty legislative action impossible but would also return congressmen to their constituents, whom he believed less bellicose than the representatives. Though Congress did not follow Jefferson's prescription, it did declare its opposition to war with France.

It took another action which raised his hopes. It called on the President to share with the legislators the actual texts of reports from the American commissioners in Paris. Surely free examination of the actual documents would reveal the irresponsibility of the Chief Executive's analysis. Hatred of France would cool and unhealthy excitement would subside. The Congress made its demand on April 2. Jefferson's supporters should have become uneasy when Federalists joined their ranks to sweep the resolution through by a large majority. The next day the President complied.

The documents revealed the Americans' repeated exposure to snubs and insults, climaxed by the suggestion of three French agents (identified in the dispatches as X, Y, and Z) that the United States, as the price of negotiation, make a loan to France and stimulate their own efforts with a $240,000 bribe. Though United States Minister Charles Cotesworth Pinckney's reply was not the oratorical "Millions for defense but not one cent for tribute" soon ascribed to him, his "Not a sixpence!" was equally bold and clear. The situation revealed was made to order for those who wished to whip up war sentiment. There were insults that rankled, and there was a patriotic response that would appeal to a nation hungry for heroic action.

The House voted more than three to one against publication of the XYZ papers but unreliable reports of the documents were already circulating and the Senate released the original texts. Jefferson favored publication as putting an end to "artful misrepresentation." To Monroe he wrote, "At this moment my name is running through all the city as detected in a criminal correspondence with the French directory."[73] Many Republicans who had regarded the French as brothers in arms were dismayed. Had Jefferson, despite his superior opportunities to know France, been as gullible as they? Or was there a more sinister explanation of his being in league with these enemies of his country? Garbled reports, Jefferson wrote Madison, had "produced such a shock on the republican mind"[74] as had not been felt since the dawn of American independence.

Even now, though, Jefferson's concern for his country overrode his fears for himself. He was afraid that many Republicans, revolted by the French assumption that they would put France above their own homeland, might support the war measures of the Federalists to refute the "imputation of being French partisans." Such a movement among Jefferson's own followers might provide the margin necessary to form a majority for war.

Jefferson was as shocked as his supporters. At first he could not accept the idea that the Directory had been responsible for the conduct of Talleyrand and of X, Y, and Z, or had even known about it. But the shock did not deflect him from the path of peace. He used his considerable powers of persuasion and drew on his surviving reservoir of goodwill to keep his fellow Republicans from becoming warmongers. Meanwhile he refrained from public debate on the XYZ affair. Though repeatedly indiscreet in private correspondence despite the proven costliness of the habit, he was generally cautious about getting involved in public arguments.

The Federalists "will carry what they please,"[75] he wrote Madison on April 26, explaining that many Republicans were leaving the House without waiting for adjournment. Four representatives from Virginia had already left and another was preparing to leave. He doubtless wished that one of the remaining Virginia Republicans had headed for home, for that one had now joined the "war party." Gallatin fought against the Federalist horde as skillfully and valiantly as Horatius at the bridge—and as futilely.

Though opposed to the program of the "war party," Jefferson was not diametrically opposed. He said that rightminded Republicans were "willing to indulge the war-gentry with every reasonable measure of internal defense and preparation" but would "oppose everything external."[76] We do not know how he defined the difference, but the actions of Republicans in Congress suggest that he may have regarded a navy as more likely to be used "externally" than an army and therefore potentially a more aggressive force. For all his idealism, he admitted the necessity of military as well as moral defense and, as in his days as Secretary of State, believed in meeting any genuine threat to American sovereignty regardless of the quarter from which it came. "If our house be on fire," he wrote one correspondent, "without inquiring whether it was fired from within or without, we must try to extinguish it. In that, I have no doubt we shall act as one man."[77]

Encouraged by Federalist applause, Adams breathed out threatenings and slaughter in his public addresses, excoriating the French hardly more than the Republicans, whom he accused of "all lengths of profligacy, falsehood, and malignity."[78] Jefferson's protégé Monroe he described as a "disgraced minister, recalled in displeasure for misconduct."[79]

In contrast, John Marshall, returning in June from his mission to Paris, was escorted by three corps of cavalry and treated to a demonstration second in the memory of Philadelphians only to that accorded George Washington. Was he not one of those stouthearted Americans who had withstood the blandishments and bullying of the French? In salute, bells rang far into the night. Their clamor could not have been very agreeable to Marshall's cousin Thomas Jefferson.

Nevertheless, the Vice President punctiliously called on Marshall twice in one morning, the second time leaving a visiting card with the notation that he was "so lucky as to find" him out on both occasions. He had to insert an "un" before the "lucky" to correct a serious error of execution if not of fact.[80]

Before the end of June, Jefferson, who earlier had lamented the exodus of Republicans from Philadelphia, himself returned home. A president pro tempore could preside as well as he in a chamber where action on all major legislation was foreordained by a Federalist majority now three to one.

Two days before he left, Congress had passed the Alien Act, authorizing the President to deport from the United States any aliens believed dangerous to public peace and safety or even suspected of "treasonable or secret" predilections. Jefferson had predicted in April that oppressive acts dealing with aliens and sedition would be passed by the Congress. The Alien Act was followed by an Alien Enemies Act authorizing the Chief Executive, in time of declared war, to imprison or deport aliens subject to an enemy power.

On July 4, the day Jefferson arrived at Monticello, the Senate passed the Sedition Bill, which would make it a high misdemeanor, punishable by fine and imprisonment, for citizens or aliens to enter into unlawful combinations opposing execution of federal laws, to aid or attempt "unlawful assembly," or to do what Adams had already accused the Republicans of—publishing "false, scandalous, and malicious writing" bringing into disrepute Congress or the President. The irony of the July 4 date of passage did not escape at least one of Jefferson's supporters, Congressman Henry Tazewell. We may be sure it was painfully obvious to the author of the Declaration of Independence. The bill actually became law on July 14, Bastille Day, which must have seemed quite appropriate to its advocates.

Jefferson's anxiety for the preservation of American freedom was shared by his friends Madison and Monroe. Madison's observation in anticipation of passage of the oppressive measures had been characteristically penetrating and philosophical: "Perhaps it is a universal truth that the loss of liberty [at] home is to be charged to provisions against danger real or pretended from abroad."[81] Monroe, whose political maturity had been furthered by his experiences in Paris, was equally philosophical. Of the Federalists, he said: "The more... that party is left to itself, the sooner will its ruin follow."[82] Always skillful in personal relations, he now revealed sophisticated psychological insight. He said: "I am very much inclined to think that the patient must find out his own disorder, if not by himself yet that he must think so: that the physician must not appear, or if at all by no means as a prominent character."

If Jefferson was tempted to more vigorous intervention by such demonstrations of public support in Virginia as the sixteen-gun salute and banquet accorded him in Fredericksburg, his two friends would add their restraining counsels to his natural inclination to avoid fruitless conflict. Even amid his tribulations in the Federalist citadel of Philadelphia he had retained enough perspective to write to John Taylor of Caroline, "A little patience and we shall see the reign of witches pass over, their spells dissolve, and the people, recovering their true sight, restore their government to its true principles."[83] But he was not in a mood to cherish ties with France or any other part of the Old World. In the same letter he said that Americans should "haul off from Europe as soon as we can, and from all attachments to any portions of it."

Though still sure that France planned no invasion of the United States, he had expected that hysteria would cause the United States to declare war on France. At Monticello he learned that his gloomy anticipation had nearly been realized. The more bellicose Federalists had decided to press for a declaration on July 4. People of every faction were sensitive to the vibrations of that anniversary! Some Federalists in the Senate hesitated at the last moment, and the date passed. The next day the House, by voice vote, indicated its opposition to war. Conflict between French vessels and armed American merchantmen occurred from time to time on the high seas. But there was no declared war and Jefferson began to suspect that, while the war fever still burned in some parts of the body politic, the crisis was past.

Not so, however, the crisis of liberty. Jefferson saw the Alien Act as "a most detestable thing" that would subject aliens in the United States to the terrors of "absolute government."[84] The painfulness of the realization was exacerbated for him by the vulnerability of personal friends. Comte Constantin de Volney, whose philosophical conversation had brightened the dinner table at Monticello and who dreamed that humankind were becoming "a single family governed by the same spirit," deemed it prudent to flee the United States. Jefferson's cherished confidant Joseph Priestley, the eminent scientist and philosopher who had taken refuge in Pennsylvania from the violence visited upon him in his native England, was almost certain to be a victim of the new law. A man of Jefferson's intellectual associations had many endangered friends.

A still greater number of his active supporters were threatened by the Sedition Act. Jefferson had foreseen the arrest of Republican editors, especially his radical friend Benjamin Franklin Bache, and even the persecution of Republican congressmen who sent circular letters to their constituents. As month succeeded month, twenty-five editors and printers were prosecuted.

Maybe intervention by Jefferson in the conflict between the Adams Administration and France would smack too much of the adventures of one of his favorite fiction heroes, Don Quixote. He had written in 1795, "I have laid up my Rosinante in his stall."[85] But the war at home was another matter. The federal government was supreme in foreign policy, but the states could intervene against domestic oppression. Even if Jefferson had not yet memorably expressed the idea, he had already sworn eternal hostility to every form of tyranny over the mind of man. He could not ignore the opportunity to bring the state legislators up to the firing line for liberty.

He had no doubts about the constitutionality or patriotism of such a course. Even the great seer of Federalism, Alexander Hamilton, had argued in *The Federalist*: "It may safely be received as an axiom of our political system that the State governments will, in all possible contingencies, afford complete security against the invasions of the public liberty by the national authority."[86]

Of course, Jefferson did not delude himself that every state could be converted into a bastion of freedom. The Federalists were strong enough in many to at least neutralize any clamor for boldly unprecedented action. And in New England they were in control. This galling fact he admitted in replying to a letter from John Taylor of Caroline who said that some Southern Republicans were advocating secession. The Vice President conceded, "It is true that we are completely under the saddle of Massachusetts and Connecticut, and that they ride us very hard, cruelly insulting our feelings, as well as exhausting our strength and substance."[87] But, pointing out the folly of secession and the extreme unlikelihood that seceding states would live in ideal harmony with each other, he defused the proposal with that subtle humor so characteristic of him, a sense of the comic so gentle that to this day he is often mistakenly thought of as humorless. "Seeing that we must have somebody to quarrel with," he wrote, "I had rather keep our New England associates for that purpose than to see our bickerings transferred to others."

While intervention by state governments to protect the liberties of their citizens would be perfectly legitimate, there might well be some question of the propriety of his leading a movement opposed to the measures of the government which he was sworn to serve as Vice President. Accordingly, beginning sometime in September, he laid his plans and began their execution in utmost secrecy—a secrecy so deep that many years later when he sought to recall the steps by which he had proceeded he found he had covered them so carefully that he himself was baffled.

It must be assumed that Jefferson had given some hints of his plans to Madison and Monroe, but he did not make them his confidants and aids. Undoubtedly this omission was an important part of his strategy. Jefferson had worked so closely with these two friends that, if he were suspected of leading opposition to the government, they would surely be accused of abetting him. For their protection as well as his own, he was making it possible for them in all honesty to declare ignorance of his activities.

Jefferson needed the help of an honest, intelligent, and loyal Republican versed in politics, and conveniently located in Virginia, who had nonpolitical reasons to travel in other states. Fortunately, just such a man was available. Wilson Cary Nicholas was bound as loyally to Jefferson in friendship as to the Republican Party in principle. A discreet and evidently persuasive man, he had been Jefferson's choice to talk with Edmund Randolph and give him "a strong and perfect understanding of the public mind" in 1793 when the Attorney General seemed to vacillate between the views of the Secretary of State and those of Hamilton. Nicholas' business activities occasionally carried him into neighboring states. His dealings there were usually with politically influential people. As Nicholas was on the fringe of great events rather than in their center, few would think of him as the Vice President's agent.

Whether or not Jefferson had communicated his plans to Nicholas before September 21, that gentleman had already concluded that the various town and country protest movements against the Alien and Sedition Acts were insufficient. "The disease has gained too much strength to be destroyed by anything they can do," he wrote to his brother in Kentucky. "All that can be expected from them is to prepare the people to give their support to the state governments."[88]

Perhaps by then Jefferson had already formulated resolutions of protest appropriate for action by a state legislature. The protest that he drew up asserted that the Alien and Sedition Acts violated the compact of the states in forming the federal government and therefore were unconstitutional. "The several states composing the United States of America are not united on the principles of unlimited submission to their General Government. . . . By compact under the style and title of a Constitution for the United States . . . , they constituted a General Government for special purposes, reserving, each state to itself, the residuary mass of right to their own self government. . . . Whensoever the General Government assumes undelegated powers, its acts are unauthoritative, void, and of no force."[89]

Essentially the same thing had been said by many Republicans and even, in earlier times, by so ardent a Federalist as Alexander Hamilton. But Jefferson now went a step farther than most. He said: "The government created by this compact was not made the exclusive or final *judge* of the extent of the powers delegated to itself, since that would have made its discretion, and not the Constitution, the measure of its powers; but . . . as in all other cases of compact among parties having no common judge, each party has an equal right to judge for itself, as well of infractions as of the mode and measure of redress.''

He cited the constitutional amendment declaring "that the powers not delegated to the United States by the Constitution, nor prohibited by it to the states, are reserved to the states respectively, or to the people.'' He asserted that therefore the Sedition Act "and all other . . . acts which assume to create, define, or punish crimes other than those enumerated in the Constitution are altogether void and of no force, and . . . the power to create, define, and punish such other crimes is reserved, and of right appertains solely and exclusively to the respective states, each within its own territory.''

Jefferson also argued that the Sedition Act violated the Bill of Rights declaration that "Congress shall make no law respecting an establishment of religion, or prohibiting the free exercise thereof, or abridging the freedom of speech or the press.''

In opposition to the Alien Act, he wrote: "Resolved, that alien friends are under the jurisdiction and protection of the laws of the state wherein they are; that no power over them has been delegated to the United States, nor prohibited to the individual states . . . .''

With an eloquence that might have given away the secret of his authorship he insisted that violation of the rights of the alien was a threat to the rights of every citizen. "The friendless alien has indeed been selected as the safest subject of a first experiment, but the citizen will soon follow, or rather has already followed, for already has a Sedition Act marked him as its prey. . . . These and successive acts of the same character, unless arrested on the threshold, may tend to drive these states into revolution and blood, and will furnish new calumnies against Republican governments, and new pretexts for those who wish it to be believed that man cannot be governed but by a rod of iron. . . . It would be a dangerous delusion were a confidence in the men of our choice to silence our fears for the safety of our rights. . . . Confidence is everywhere the parent of despotism; free government is founded in jealousy and not in confidence. It is jealousy and not confidence which prescribes limited constitutions to bind down those whom we are obliged to trust with power. . . . Our Constitution has accordingly fixed the limits to which, and no further, our confidence may go; and let the honest advocate of confidence read the Alien and Sedition Acts, and say if the Constitution has not been wise in fixing limits to the government it created and whether we should be wise in destroying those limits?

"Let him say what the government is if it be not a tyranny, which the men of our choice have conferred on the President, and the President of our choice has assented to and accepted. . . . The men of our choice have more respected the bare suspicions of the President than the solid rights of innocence, the claims of justification, the sacred force of truth, and the forms and substance of laws and justice. In questions of power, then, let no more be heard of confidence in man, but bind him down from mischief by the chains of the Constitution.''

Jefferson had come a long way from his Enlightenment faith in the perfectibility of man, an assumption nurtured in his days at William and Mary and not directly challenged by the genial Episcopal environment in which he had grown to manhood. It had been shaken in the tribulations of his governorship to the extent that he warned during the Revolution that reforms must be pushed through in the unity born of a struggle for life and liberty before the winning of security invited full resumption of selfishness. Later, in the salons of Paris, his faith in the perfectibility of man seemed to be restored. But now he talked of the necessity of promoting man's happiness, not by releasing him from restraints but by "binding him down from mischief by the chains of the Constitution."

His disappointment in Adams and his own alienation from the administration of which he was theoretically a part were certainly in some measure responsible for his disillusionment. But his concept of man as a creature born to err who must be protected from his own excesses must have owed something to his association with Madison. Reared in the traditions of Scottish Calvinism and an enthusiastic student of Calvinist theology at Princeton, Madison in later life supplied his more optimistic friend with nudging reminders of the human animal's selfishness. Not that the dour-looking little statesman despaired of reform; he simply believed that individual selfishness must be controlled in ways that would make it serve the public good. The Constitution of which he was the father sought to serve the people by balancing categories of self-interest.

Jefferson's resolution on the Alien and Sedition Acts, like his Declaration of Independence, was at once a catalogue of injuries, an invocation of philosophical principles, and a demand for specific reforms. The most controversial thing about his resolution was its proposed instrument of reform. "Where powers are assumed which have not been delegated," he wrote, "a nullification of the act is the rightful remedy." All states, he argued, had "a natural right in cases not within the compact . . . to nullify all assumptions of power by others [including the federal government] within their limits. . . . Without this right they would be under the dominion, absolute and unlimited, of whosoever might exercise this right of judgement over them."[90] Thus he was prepared to introduce the doctrine of nullification, citing in support both constitutional grounds and, as in the Declaration of Independence, natural right. Also, again harking back to the revolutionary experience, he called for committees of correspondence among the several states.

Jefferson probably expected the resolutions to be adopted first by the Virginia and North Carolina state legislatures, though not necessarily in that order, with Kentucky following their example. Whether because of a rumor spread northward or one deliberately planted by a Jefferson follower, the Philadelphia *Aurora* reported in August that the Virginia General Assembly was likely to take steps against the Sedition Act. By the end of September Jefferson apparently had concluded that his resolutions should be introduced first in North Carolina.

The anticipated order of procedure was changed when fate presented Nicholas with an irresistible opportunity. While he had Jefferson's resolutions in hand, he was visited by John Breckinridge, Speaker of the Kentucky House. A former resident of Albemarle County and member of the Virginia House of Delegates, he had been elected to Congress in 1793 but instead of taking his seat had left to try his fortunes in Kentucky, the new state carved from the Old Dominion. There he had quickly moved to the forefront in law and politics. Nicholas' brother George was in Kentucky engaged in land speculation with Breckinridge. Moreover, George was now being hounded by federal authorities because of a pamphlet which he had written against the Alien and Sedition Acts.

Breckinridge would be in a position to push or guide Jefferson's resolutions through the Kentucky legislature. His association with the Nicholases would be enough to account for any Virginia influence in the matter, if one was suspected. For that matter, opposition to the hated acts was at least as strong in Kentucky as in its mother state.

Nicholas was already troubled by fears that the North Carolinian with whom Jefferson wished him to communicate was likely to be suspected of working as the Vice President's agent. How much safer to deal with Breckinridge, a trusted friend of Jefferson's who nevertheless was little associated with him in the public mind. Then, too, sentiment against the acts was not nearly so strong in North Carolina as in Kentucky. A little uneasy because he could not be sure of Jefferson's reaction, Nicholas nevertheless showed the resolutions to Breckinridge, revealing their authorship but pledging his visitor to secrecy.

Breckinridge at once conceived the idea of going to Monticello to pay his respects to the author. Realizing that such a visit might jeopardize all of the efforts to conceal Jefferson's role in the affair, Nicholas persuaded the Kentuckian to defer that pleasure. As he set out for home with the manuscript in hand, Breckinridge told his host that he could count on Kentucky's acting on the resolutions before the General Assembly of Virginia convened.

Nicholas dashed off a letter to Jefferson explaining the change of plans and anxiously awaited a reply. To his relief, Jefferson assured him that he had acted correctly. He himself now thought passage by the North Carolina legislature was unlikely. He did wish that Nicholas would tell Madison about the whole project. "You know of course I have no secrets from him. I wish him therefore to be consulted as to these resolutions."[91]

Nicholas was prevented by illness from seeing Madison, and apparently it was Jefferson himself who first acquainted Madison with the particulars, probably in late October at Monticello.

Orchestration of the protest had proceeded apace in Kentucky. On November 7, addressing that state's newly convened legislature, Governor James Garrard called upon them to register their "protest against all unconstitutional laws and impolitic proceedings." Breckinridge was named to a committee of three to reply to the gubernatorial address, and announced that he would introduce resolutions in response to the call for protest. The very next day the House went into committee of the whole and Breckinridge introduced the resolutions.

They had been much edited. Perhaps Breckinridge, in desiring to call on Jefferson before returning to Kentucky, had been motivated as much by a desire to propose changes as to pay his respects. He presented the first seven resolutions exactly as written by Jefferson. But the eighth resolution, the climactic one calling for specific action to combat the evils described in the first seven, was considerably toned down. For Jefferson's call for a committee of correspondence to address other states was substituted a provision that Kentucky congressmen be asked to work for repeal of the "unconstitutional and obnoxious acts." Some of the defiant eloquence of the original eighth resolve was placed in a ninth. Amputated from it, however, was Jefferson's assertion that "every state has a natural right in cases not within the compact . . . to nullify of their own authority all assumptions of power by others within their limits." An invitation to other states to join with Kentucky in requesting the Congress to repeal the Alien and Sedition Acts was substituted for the bold doctrine of nullification.

There is no indication that Jefferson lamented the tempering in tone and substance of his original resolutions. In fact, by November 17, when he mailed a copy of the amended Kentucky resolves to Madison, he wrote, "I think we should distinctly affirm all the important principles they contain, so as to hold that ground in future, and leave the matter in such a train as that we may not be committed absolutely to push the matter to extremities, and yet may be free to push as far as events will render prudent."[92] Though an ardent idealist, Jefferson anticipated the maxim that politics is the science of the possible.

Madison, undoubtedly influenced by his earlier conversation with Jefferson, was already at work on a set of kindred resolutions to be introduced in the General Assembly of Virginia. The final product was more concise than Jefferson's, for Madison held to his customary terseness whereas Jefferson had been unaccustomedly prolix in his resolves. Madison's paper held, like Jefferson's, that the powers of the federal government were "no further valid than they are authorized by the grants enumerated" in the Constitution. He also wrote that "in case of a deliberate, palpable, and dangerous exercise of other powers, not granted by the said compact, the states who are parties thereto have the right, and are in duty bound, to interpose for arresting the progress of the evil, and for maintaining within their respective limits, the authorities, rights, and liberties appertaining to them."[93] The point was essentially the same as that urged by Jefferson, but Madison's use of the word "interpose" gave, to this argument for action by the states to protect their people from federal tyranny, its historic name: the doctrine of interposition. Madison's resolves lacked the inspiring eloquence of Jefferson's, but their more conciliatory tone doubtless made them more acceptable to those who feared the threat of national disunion even more than they feared the Alien and Sedition Acts.

Though Jefferson had acquiesced in the final form of the Kentucky resolutions, he may have been motivated partly by acceptance of a fait accompli as well as by prudent second thoughts. But when Madison acquainted him with his proposed Virginia resolutions, Jefferson seized upon the possibility of changing something still in the making. The Vice President was not content that his friend had only gone so far as to state the theoretical right to interposition. Jefferson was impatient that Madison had raised no threat of nullification and had not even called for committees of correspondence.

Still covering his tracks from the public, Jefferson addressed Madison indirectly through Nicholas. To his Albemarle neighbor he wrote, "The more I have reflected on the phrase in the paper you showed me, the more strongly I think it should be altered. Suppose you were, instead of the invitation to cooperate in the annulment of the acts, to make it an invitation 'to concur with this commonwealth in declaring, as it does hereby declare, that the said acts are, and were ab initio, null, void, and of no force or effect.' I should like it better."[94]

But Madison did not like it better. As introduced in the Virginia Assembly by John Taylor, the resolutions contained the phrase which Jefferson had substituted for Madison's own. But, as finally passed, they did not contain the Vice President's addition. Instead of Jefferson's declaration, ringing like a steel gauntlet thrown down at the door of the federal temple, there was an appeal to other states to concur with the commonwealth "in declaring, as it does hereby declare, that the acts aforesaid are unconstitutional.''[95] As these words were the same originally used by Madison, it is virtually certain that he was responsible for their restoration. The resolutions also expressed confidence ''that the necessary and proper measures will be taken by each [state] for cooperating with this state in maintaining the authorities, rights, and liberties reserved to the states respectively or to the people.''

Thus, thanks to Jefferson, Virginia on Christmas Eve of 1798 lent its great weight to the movement opposing the Alien and Sedition Acts. And, thanks to Madison's prudence, that influence was exerted in such a way that no one could claim subversion of the judiciary or even incitement to subversion. The doctrine of interposition could, and would, be cited in support of measures that many deemed subversive of the federal executive as well as the federal judiciary. But Madison had not spelled out how a state should initiate the process of interposition, and his reference to it as a right of the ''states'' could have been interpreted as an indication that it was a function to be exercised by the states in concert rather than by a single state.

As the instigator of both the Kentucky and Virginia Resolutions, Jefferson played an important role in organizing significant opposition to the Alien and Sedition Acts. In each case, the prudence of another statesman—in the first instance, Breckinridge; in the second, Madison—subordinated zeal to realism. The two sets of resolves, by no means identical, soon became so confused with each other in the public mind that they became inseparable. Eventually they became recognized as planks in the Republican Party platform and as such had as little individuality in the eyes of the casual observer as any one of the random width boards in a courthouse floor.

There is no record of Jefferson's ever having fumed over modification of his ideas in either set of resolutions. Indeed, his good-humored acceptance of amendment makes one wonder whether he might not have moderated his own expressions if nobody else had.

Jefferson appears to have enjoyed thoroughly his clandestine role as fomenter of opposition to the threat of tyranny. There were sound reasons for his policy of concealment, but it also seems to have accorded well with the disposition of the man who, at least since the days of his youthful correspondence with John Page, had delighted to communicate in code. It is hard to imagine that no smile crossed Jefferson's face when, deep in engineering actions by the Virginia and Kentucky Assemblies, he wrote Stephens Thompson Mason: ''The Alien and Sedition Laws are working hard. I fancy that some of the state legislatures will take strong ground on this occasion. For my own part, I consider those laws as merely an experiment on the American mind to see how far it will bear an avowed violation of the Constitution.''[96]

In the first month of the new year of 1799, he wrote to Elbridge Gerry, a federalist now leaning toward republicanism, one whose support would be useful in the building of a united Republican front:

I do then, with sincere zeal, wish an inviolable preservation of our present federal constitution, according to the true sense in which it was adopted by the states, that in which it was advocated by its friends, and not that which its enemies apprehended, who therefore became its enemies. And I am opposed to the monarchising of its features by the forms of its administration, with a view to conciliate a first transition to a President and Senate for life, and from that to a hereditary tenure of these offices, and thus to worm out the elective principle. I am for preserving to the states the powers not yielded by them to the Union, and to the legislature of the Union its constitutional share in the division of powers; and I am not for transferring all the powers of the states to the general government, and all those of that government to the executive branch.[97]

In letters such as this, almost as much as in the Kentucky Resolutions that he wrote and the Virginia Resolutions he instigated, Jefferson provided the platform for the newly emergent Republican Party in what would be its first national campaign. The documents, formal and informal, for which he was responsible set forth the issues on which the coming battle would be waged. His messages did not detail the methods by which he would preserve the Constitution. By eschewing precise prescriptions they avoided boring the superficially interested and fragmentizing the ranks of the deeply concerned. Like any shrewd national leader, Jefferson produced the sort of messages inevitably hailed by supporters as bold statements of major principles and disparaged by opponents as glittering generalities.

Jefferson's letter to Gerry was written from Philadelphia. He had left Monticello for the capital on December 18 and had arrived on Christmas Day, one day after adoption of the Virginia Resolutions.

Jefferson's acute discomfort at being once again surrounded by Federalists might cause us to suspect paranoia if a reading of the newspapers and correspondence of the time did not reveal the close watch kept on all Republican leaders, and especially on him. Considerable ingenuity was employed in both detection and imagination. Jefferson explained to his friends that he would write them seldom because of what he described to John Taylor as "the infidelities of the post office." He cautioned both Madison and Monroe to examine the seals on letters from him to see if they had been opened.

While Jefferson now had to be extremely guarded in his utterances, words which had earlier been inspired by him soon were widely circulated. The General Assembly of Virginia ordered five thousand copies of its resolutions printed and distributed in all the counties of the commonwealth. Other copies, of course, would be sent to all the other states.

Jefferson repeatedly urged Madison to lance the swollen pretensions of the Federalists with his pen. The Vice President tried to get his friend to publish his notes on debates in the Federal Convention that had produced the Constitution.[98] Jefferson hoped that the record would remind Americans how far their government had strayed from the intentions of the founders. Madison, perhaps partly because he had moved from some of his own stands in the convention, demurred. Jefferson then pressed his friend to write a series of topical commentaries on events, promising that he himself would attend to the details of publication so that the author could remain anonymous. "The engine is the press," he insisted. "Every man must lay his purse and his pen under contribution."[99] But Madison, having written both the Virginia Resolutions and an extended address to the people to be circulated with them, thought that for the time he had done enough.

Jefferson had more success with Edmund Pendleton. Impressed by the quality and spirit of the judge's plea for Republicanism addressed to the citizens of Caroline County, the Vice President asked him to prepare a summary of the Adams Administration's threats and failures. Jefferson said that he would have 10,000, perhaps even 20,000, copies printed for distribution by sympathetic congresssmen. He refused to accept Pendleton's demurrer, and the jurist produced an address to the American people. Though it was not ready for publication before the congressmen left for home, it was widely reprinted in newspapers as well as in a pamphlet. The vehemence with which the Federalists attacked the author testified to their estimate of its effectiveness. Jefferson also sent back to Virginia copies of a pamphlet by George Nicholas presenting the views of Kentucky Republicans and declaring, "If no other state in the union thinks as we do, Virginia, the ancient, the great, the powerful, the rich and the republican state of Virginia, still remains free and independent." Jefferson cautioned the Virginia distributor, "Do not let my name appear in the matter."[100]

The Vice President had no fear that the Virginians and Kentuckians would remain alone in opposition. A Philadelphia newspaper attacked the pronouncements of the Virginia Assembly as "little short of high treason," but opposition to the Alien and Sedition Acts was boldly voiced in various communities of Pennsylvania. With Jefferson's confidence rising, his own voice of protest lost its shrillness. Even in writing to Madison, before whom he sometimes indulged in self-conscious and transparent hyperbole, he said, "Anything rash or threatening might check the favorable dispositions of these middle states, and rally them again around the measures which are ruining us."[101] To Pendleton he was even more emphatic: "Anything like force would check the progress of the public opinion and rally them round the government. This is not the kind of opposition the American people will permit. But keep away all show of force, and they will bear down the evil propensities of the government, by the constitutional means of election and petition."[102]

To those now coming to be called the High Federalists, the Hamiltonians, whose dogmatic zeal far exceeded the President's, the resolutions inspired by Jefferson seemed anything but moderate. Hamilton longed for a professional army and knew how he would use it. With such a force, he told a Federalist senator, he would "subdue a *refractory and powerful state*." The federal government, he said, should "act upon the laws and put Virginia to the test of resistance."[103]

Quite obviously Hamilton was not disposed to let Virginia either defy the federal government from within the Union or depart from that Union in peace. For his own part, Jefferson seems to have had no doubts about the constitutionality of secession. After all, Virginia had made its ratification of the Constitution contingent upon the right to secede. But he was also convinced of the folly of secession unless the states were subjected to insufferable tyranny with no hope of legal respite. The threat of war between the United States and France had not been completely dissipated. It was unthinkable that the United States, a fledgling republic in a world hostile to republicanism, should suffer schism at such a time. In a letter to Kosciuszko, the Polish patriot who had aided the Americans in the Revolution, Jefferson said: "If we are forced into a war, we [Americans] must give up political differences of opinion and unite as one man to defend our country, but whether at the close of such a war, we should be as free as we are now, God knows." If granted peace, however, Americans could make their government "a model for the protection of man in a state of freedom and order."[104]

In that very February of 1799 when Jefferson wrote of his fears and hopes for the republic, foreign and domestic crises were interacting to bring both to accelerated conclusions. At this time John Adams asserted himself against the High Federalists led by Hamilton and assumed the mastery of his own administration. When he perceived that the Hamiltonians hungered for war with France, would indeed be frustrated by an honorable settlement of the French crisis, he resolutely turned his face from them and dismissed some within the executive branch.[105] Adams' resentment against the French ran deep, but deeper still was his fear that war, whether justified or not, would necessitate bold government actions to forestall mobocracy and that such actions would destroy the system of checks and balances among the executive, legislative, and judicial branches. Upon this fragile balance, he believed, rested much of the hope for preservation of free government in the United States. He took charge of negotiations for peace, nominating William Vans Murray, a man of his own choice, as minister to France. Adams knew that Murray believed the French sincerely desired peace. With Adams' backing, but with his Cabinet kept in ignorance, negotiations moved steadily toward peaceful settlement. Though Jefferson rejoiced in the resolution of the crisis, he was not prepared to view the President in a generous light. In a letter to Monroe the Vice President said of Adams' accomplishment, "You will perceive that this measure has been taken as grudgingly as tardily."[106]

Even this measure of delight was mitigated for Jefferson by his having to preside impartially over Senate debates in which he and his followers were maligned or ridiculed. The scene in the House, which he had by report, he described as "scandalous." There Republicans trying to speak in opposition to the Alien and Sedition Acts were shouted down.[107]

In lieu of a war with France, Hamilton and his followers had to extract what satisfaction they could from the domestic employment of force to crush Fries' Rebellion, an uprising of several hundred Pennsylvanians in opposition to a direct federal property tax levied in anticipation of such a war. Hamilton's appetite was not appeased. He wrote to Secretary of War James McHenry, who was more his agent than the President's, "Besides eventual security against invasion, we ought certainly to look to the possession of the Floridas and Louisiana, and we ought to squint at South America."[108]

Daily jibes in the Senate and the Federalist press heated Jefferson's temper. His resentments boiled to the surface in correspondence with political allies. But one letter from a college student tapped in him a deep well of idealism undefiled. William Green Munford received from Jefferson a more eloquent and noble letter than had any of his elders:

> I am one of those who think well of the human character generally. I consider man as formed for society, and endowed by nature with those dispositions which fit him for society. I believe also, with Condorcet, as mentioned in your letter, that his mind is perfectible to a degree of which we cannot as yet form any conception. . . .
>
> I join you therefore in branding as cowardly the idea that the human mind is incapable of further advances. This is precisely the doctrine that the present despots of the earth are inculcating, and their friends here re-echoing; and applying especially to religion and politics; . . . But thank heaven; the American mind is already too much opened to listen to these impostures; and while the art of printing is left to us science can never be retrograde. What is once acquired of

real knowledge can never be lost. To preserve the freedom of the human mind then and freedom of the press, every spirit should be ready to devote itself to martyrdom, for as long as we may think as we will, and speak as we think, the condition of man will proceed in improvement.[109]

Perhaps Jefferson's attainment of the long view was facilitated by the fact that when he answered the student's letter he was back for the summer, on his mountaintop. Even so, he was far from isolated. Monticello had become a command post in his country's political wars. He still directed fire on his old targets, the Alien and Sedition Acts, but he now had found a new target as well. To Edmund Randolph, who had expressed concern over the federal government's claims to common law jurisdiction, he wrote: "Of all the doctrines which have ever been broached by the federal government, the novel one of the common law being in force and cognizable as an existing law in their courts, is to me the most formidable. All their other assumptions of ungiven powers have been in the detail. The bank law, the treaty, the Sedition Act, Alien Act, the undertaking to change the State laws of evidence in the State courts. . . have been solitary, unconsequential, timid things, in comparison with the audacious, barefaced, and sweeping pretension to a system of law for the United States, without the adoption of their Legislature, and so infinitely beyond their power to adopt. If this assumption be yielded to, the State courts may be shut up, as there will then be nothing to hinder citizens of the same State sueing each other in the federal courts in every case. . . ."[110]

But he did not abandon the old targets. He was busy molding shot for the Virginia and Kentucky legislatures to fire at the Alien and Sedition Acts. Wilson Cary Nicholas, preparing for a trip to Kentucky, offered to carry Jefferson's words of guidance to the lawmakers soon to convene in Frankfort. The Vice President believed that both Kentucky and Virginia should reiterate their protests as a reply to Federalist criticisms provoked by their original resolutions. He outlined his ideas and mailed them to Madison to get his comments before replying to Nicholas. Once again Madison urged greater moderation than Jefferson had shown. Madison readily accepted the suggestion that an attack on the federal government's "new pretensions" to common law jurisdiction be added to the list of complaints. And he had no objection to Jefferson's description of the Alien and Sedition Acts as a "palpable violation of the federal compact." But he was disturbed by the suggestion that this violation could be made "the ground of doing in future whatever we might now rightfully do, should repetition. . . render it expedient."[111]

That Jefferson was thinking of secession as an eventual resort after a succession of abuses is confirmed by the letter to Nicholas in which he accepted excision of the offending reference. There was no need, the Vice President said, to cite in advance the grounds for secession "as we should never think of separation but for repeated and enormous violations," and "these, when they occur, will be cause enough of themselves." Jefferson wrote Nicholas that he believed the legislators should declare their devotion to the Union, stressing at the same time that "we are willing to sacrifice to this everything but the rights of self-government in those important points which we have never yielded and in which alone we see liberty, safety, and happiness."[112]

His proposal that the legislators declare themselves "not at all disposed to make every measure of error or of wrong a cause of scission" was reminiscent of his statement in the Declaration of Independence that "Prudence, indeed, will dictate that government long established should not be changed for light and transient causes; and accordingly all experience hath shewn that mankind are more disposed to suffer, while evils are sufferable, than to right themselves by abolishing the forms to which they are accustomed."

Jefferson had gone further in his letter to Madison. In it, after urging the importance of laboring to preserve the Union and the Constitution, he advocated a statement of determination, "were we to be disappointed in this, to sever ourselves from that union we so much value, rather than give up the rights of self government which we have reserved, and in which alone we see liberty, safety, and happiness." This statement recalls still another from the Declaration of Independence: "But when a long train of abuses and usurpations, pursuing invariably the same object, evinces a design to reduce them (the people) under absolute despotism, it is their right, it is their duty, to throw off such government, and to provide new guards for their future security."

There is every reason to believe that Jefferson, like other American statesmen of his day, accepted the right of secession. But the ease and grace with which he accepted Madison's recommendation that all references to secession be excised from the proposed new legislative resolutions suggests that Jefferson contemplated with horror the prospect of a broken union. At the same time, dearly as he loved the Union, he loved freedom more.

Even in immediately practical terms, Jefferson did well to submit to Madison's moderating influence. The New York legislature had officially declared its opposition to the resolutions already adopted by Virginia and Kentucky. And Rhode Island, Massachusetts, Connecticut, New Hampshire, New Jersey, Pennsylvania—even the Old Dominion's neighbor Maryland—had indirectly expressed disapproval. Perhaps Jefferson, seldom radical in his public pronouncements even when there was no one to whisper words of restraint, enjoyed indulging in heartfelt but unwise rhetoric in private communication with a sage friend sure to preach caution.

Jefferson finally was so prudent as to decline Nicholas's suggestion that he actually draft the second series of Kentucky Resolutions. The Vice President wished "to avoid suspicions (which were pretty strong in some quarters on the last occasion)" and insisted "there remains still . . . a mass of talents in Kentucky sufficient for every purpose." Jefferson's messages, however, doubtless played a part in overcoming the initial reluctance of Kentucky legislators to adopt a second set of resolutions in reply to hostile responses to the first. With John Breckinridge presiding as Speaker, the House passed the new resolves in November without a dissenting vote. Moreover, though Jefferson, in compliance with Madison's suggestion, had eliminated from his proposal any reference to "nullification," the House declared "a nullification of those acts (Alien and Sedition) by the States to be the rightful remedy." The words which had gone down so easily in the House stuck in the Senate's craw and were swallowed only after a wrenching debate.

Jefferson had hoped to meet with Madison for the actual drafting of the new Virginia resolutions but Monroe persuaded him not to because of the danger of arousing public suspicions. Madison's composition took the form of a "Report" in which he denied that the earlier Virginia Resolutions had supported nullification and said that they had been composed for the purpose of "exciting reflection" on threats to liberty. It assailed the doctrine of federal assumption of the common law, answered many objections to the earlier Resolutions, and declared it to be the legislators' "duty to renew, as they do hereby renew, their protest against 'the Alien and Sedition Acts,' as palpable and alarming infractions of the Constitution."[113]

Before the Virginia Assembly could act on Madison's Report, another event focused national attention. On December 14 Washington died. People who had never seen the first President mourned as for a lost father. For Jefferson, of course, the pain was personal and intense. Now there could never be a reconciliation with the man whom, more than any other since the death of his own parent, he had revered as a father figure. There would be no opportunity to regain the trust of Washington that he had once earned and then, largely through the chicanery of others but partly through his own indiscretion, lost forever. Jefferson had become impatient with Washington, even resentful toward him, as he saw him lending the weight of his reputation to the plans of the Hamiltonians. Yet, in the *Notes on Virginia*, he had described Washington as one "whose memory will be adored while liberty shall have votaries, whose name shall triumph over time, and will in future ages assume its just station among the most celebrated worthies of the world." Now he thought that some of the eulogies of Washington were so excessive as to excite disgust in their subject if he could read them. But later he would write of his old chief:

On the whole, his character was, in its mass, perfect, in nothing bad, in few points indifferent; and it may truly be said that never did nature and fortune combine more perfectly to make a man great, and to place him in the same constellation with whatever worthies have merited from man an everlasting remembrance. For his was the singular destiny and merit of leading the armies of his country successfully through an arduous war for the establishment of its independence, of conducting its councils through the birth of a government, new in its forms and principles, until it had settled down into a quiet and orderly train; and of scrupulously obeying the laws through the whole of his career, civil and military, of which the history of the world furnishes no other example.[114]

He added, "These are my opinions of General Washington, which I would vouch at the judgment seat of God, having been formed on an acquaintance of thirty years."

Having set out for Philadelphia on December 21, Jefferson arrived on the 28th, two days after the day of formal mourning proclaimed by act of Congress. A Federalist–dominated city swept up in grief for the loss of Washington was not disposed toward tolerance for the leader of the Republicans.

The hostile environment probably doubled Jefferson's pleasure in welcoming to the city on January 17 Du Pont de Nemours, a French devotee of liberty prepared to begin life anew in America. After his life under the French Directory, even life in a United States with Alien and Sedition laws seemed enviable freedom. To Jefferson he had written before leaving France: "I wish to die in a country in which liberty does not exist only in the laws—always more or less well, more or less badly, carried out—but chiefly in the fixed habits of the nation."[115] John Adams had refused to receive Du Pont's son as consul general of France. The President had feared that the Du Ponts would be a radicalizing force in the United States. Jefferson welcomed the elder Du Pont as an old friend, a fellow intellectual, and one who, like himself, had thought long and constructively about education.

Education was still his concern the day after welcoming the Frenchman. Then, as on a former occasion, he sought advice from Joseph Priestley, specifically asking what subjects the Englishman believed should be taught in a university. Despairing of remolding his alma mater, William and Mary, to his heart's desire, Jefferson cherished the idea of establishing a new university in central Virginia. He proposed, for a faculty, "to draw from Europe the first characters of science." Of course, in Jefferson's day, the term science embraced not only what later generations denominated by the term but also every discipline of scholarship. If in welcoming Du Pont the Vice President was showing friendliness to a family suspect in the eyes of the Federalists, in communicating with Priestley he was consorting with a foreigner whom rumor said the Alien Laws had been designed to entrap.

Meanwhile even the second sets of Kentucky and Virginia Resolutions were overshadowed by the death of the man whom Virginia's Lighthorse Harry Lee had described in congressional ceremonies as "first in war, first in peace, and first in the hearts of his countrymen." There was criticism of Jefferson's absence from this program and others honoring Washington. The Vice President could not escape daily reminders of the national mourning. For a month the chair from which he presided over the Senate was draped in black.

Other deaths afflicted him. Jupiter, his devoted manservant of many years, had insisted, despite Jefferson's fears for the slave's health, on accompanying his master on the return to Philadelphia. At Fredericksburg the old servant had become too sick to continue and Jefferson had "engaged the tavernkeeper to take care of him till he should be quite well enough to proceed."[116] But Jupiter had recovered only enough to return to Monticello and later, after one more short journey, had died. Jefferson wrote to his son-in-law Thomas Mann Randolph, "I am sorry for him as well as sensible he leaves a void in my domestic administration which I cannot fill up."[117]

This loss was engulfed by another that was announced to Jefferson on the same day in a letter from his other son-in-law, John Wayles Eppes. His little granddaughter, the first born of Maria, or Polly, was dead just a few weeks after Jefferson had rejoiced at her birth. Moreover, the mother herself was ill with an abscessed breast and had lost the use of both arms. Jefferson was not reassured by news of the medical care she was receiving. "The system of physicking as subsidiary to the aid of surgery," he wrote, "is very questionable. For every good effect it can produce, I am sure two bad ones will result."[118]

Earlier Jefferson had declared that debts caused him to lose sleep. Now his nights were haunted by new financial worries. A nonsmoker, he did not like to grow tobacco but, finding himself short of funds for both clothes and tax payments about the time he became Vice President, he had returned to cultivation of the crop. When the price seemed likely to keep rising, he withheld his tobacco from the market a little longer, only to become the victim of a market ruined by the suspension of commerce with France and the unsettled state of affairs in Europe. In 1800 he had the frustration of having to accept seven dollars per hundred for the tobacco he sold in Philadelphia and six dollars per hundred in New York. "And thus," he wrote Thomas Mann Randolph, "ends this tragedy by which we have both lost so much."[119] But it didn't end there.

Randolph, unable to meet the mortgage payments on his plantation, had taken a short-term loan from a merchant and now asked Jefferson's help in repaying. At great peril to his own finances, Jefferson let his son-in-law have more than $1,800. Only Jefferson's reputation for integrity and his known skill as a farmer restrained the impatience of his own creditors.

For Jefferson 1800 was a strange year. Winds of change were sweeping the land, and every wind seemed to bring libelous rumors or promises of glory. Whether he walked the streets of Philadelphia or sat on his mountaintop in Virginia, they whispered of mortality and financial ruin but they also carried the call of history. The very Federalist policies that contributed to his financial misfortunes stirred the ire of fellow planters in Virginia and other Southern states and made ardent anti-Federalists of lukewarm politicians. Even President Adams' wisdom and fortitude in dismissing powerful members of his Administration and acting decisively to end the troubles with France, while benefiting the nation, divided his party at a time when growing numbers of Republicans were ready to take advantage of the breach.

Jefferson embodied all that many Americans feared and all for which many others hoped. He was at once one of the most hated and one of the most idolized men in America. When a badly informed Baltimore newspaper printed on June 30 an account of the Vice President's death, there was mourning in some quarters, rejoicing in others.

By this time, the national election, in its strangely disorganized fashion, had already begun. Republican triumph in state legislative contests in New York made virtually certain, despite Hamilton's efforts to change the method of choosing electors, that the electors from that state would be of Jefferson's party. Republican congressional leaders, in caucus, had selected Burr as their candidate for Vice President. It had long been taken for granted that Jefferson would be their candidate for President. Federalist leaders had pledged support to a ticket of Adams and Charles Cotesworth Pinckney.

While the contest for control of the executive branch waxed hot through the summer, Jefferson, in his cool mountain retreat, worked on the parliamentary manual that would be his greatest legacy to the legislative branch. Drawing on both British and American precedents, he prepared a rule book for the Senate that ever since has furnished succinct guidance not only to both houses of Congress but also to the state legislatures. This accomplishment alone would have been enough to earn him a place in history.

His health thrived and so did his crops. He even seemed to achieve a large measure of philosophical detachment in assessing the calumnies heaped upon him by the opposition.

As would be expected, many Hamiltonians attacked Jefferson as a betrayer of Washington and a traitor to his country. But the most persistent and heated attacks were directed against his private, rather than his public, life. He was charged with obtaining his handsome estate by defrauding widows and orphans, with feeding his lust on slave girls, and with living his life in complete freedom from the restraints of religious belief. A letter signed Burleigh, printed in the *Connecticut Courant* and reprinted at least fifteen times in New York, summarized the questions hurled from many New England pulpits: "Do you believe in the strangest of all paradoxes—that a spendthrift, a libertine, or an atheist is qualified to make your laws and govern you and your posterity?"

Jefferson did not deign to answer publicly the charges of libertinism and atheism, but he did refer to them in a remarkable letter[120] to a friend who was, like him, both scholar and statesman. His words to Dr. Benjamin Rush, besides including one of the most memorable sentences Jefferson ever composed, afforded revealing glimpses into both his religious and his political faith. Alluding to the ravages of yellow fever in Baltimore, Norfolk, and Providence, he wrote: "When great evils happen, I am in the habit of looking out for what good may arise from them as consolations to us, and Providence has in fact so established the order of things, as that most evils are the means of producing some good. The yellow fever will discourage the growth of great cities in our nation, and I view great cities as pestilential to the morals, the health, and the liberties of man. True they nourish some of the elegant arts, but the useful ones can thrive elsewhere, and less perfection in the others, with more health, virtue, and freedom, would be my choice." This from no Shaker who saw beauty only in utility, but from a man who had composed paeans to the sculptures of Houdon and confessed that he sorely missed the great orchestras of Europe!

There followed a paragraph that would have surprised many who recalled his fears that the Society of the Cincinnati might evolve into an aristocracy deriving undue influence from the Revolutionary leadership of its forebears. Joining with Rush "in condemning the mania of giving names to objects of any kind after persons still living," Jefferson wrote: "Death alone can seal the title of any man to this honor, by putting it out of his power to forfeit it. There is one other mode of recording merit, which I have often thought might be introduced, so as to gratify the living by praising the dead. In giving, for instance, a commission of Chief Justice to Bushrod Washington, it should be in consideration of his integrity, and science in the laws, and of the services rendered to our country by his illustrious relation. . . . A commission to a descendant of Dr. Franklin, besides being in consideration of the proper qualifications of the person, should add that of the great services rendered by his illustrious ancestor, Ben Franklin, by the advancement of science, by inventions useful to man. . . ."

The letter gained in eloquence as it turned directly to questions of religious and political faith and revealed the ironic fact of their inseparability in the mind of this man devoted to the separation of church and state. "I promised you a letter on Christianity, which I have not forgotten. On the contrary, it is because I have reflected on it that I find much more time necessary for it than I can at present dispose of. I have a view of the subject which ought to displease neither the rational Christian nor Deists, and would reconcile many to a character (his own) they have too hastily rejected." He did not believe, however, that it would reconcile some of the clergy. They cherished, he said, "a very favorite hope of obtaining an establishment of a particular form of Christianity through the United States; and as every sect believes its own form the true one, everyone perhaps hoped for his own, but especially the Episcopalians and Congregationalists. The returning good sense of our country threatens abortion to their hopes and they believe that any portion of power confided to me will be exerted in opposition to their schemes. And they believe rightly; for I have sworn upon the altar of God eternal hostility against every form of tyranny over the mind of man."

Jefferson did not set that last clause apart as if he had envisioned that it would sometime be chiseled into the stone of a great memorial. Only a semicolon separated it from the preceding thought. And he barely paused after uttering the famous words, continuing in the same paragraph: "But that is all they have to fear from me: and enough too in their opinion, and this is the cause of their printing lying pamphlets against me, forging conversations for me . . . which are absolute falsehoods without a circumstance of truth to rest on. . . ." But, as in *A Summary View of the Rights of British America* and more than once in the Declaration of Independence, Jefferson had embedded in the dull clutter of contemporary minutiae a shining sentence for the ages. "I have sworn upon the altar of God eternal vigilance against every form of tyranny over the mind of man."

Of course, Jefferson had the balm of praise as well as the sting of criticism. John Beckley, his personal loyalty to the Vice President intensified by heightened hatred of the Federalists, who had fired him as Clerk of the House of Representatives in 1797, had produced a laudatory pamphlet[121] on the great Virginian. Jefferson fully appreciated the character and competence of this English knight's son educated at Eton and William and Mary. But as Secretary of State, Jefferson had said, "Beckley is a man of perfect truth as to what he affirms of his own knowledge but too credulous as to what he hears from others." The Vice President could hardly fail to be grateful for the pamphlet's rhetorical salute: "Jefferson, mild, amiable, and philanthropic, refined in manners as enlightened in mind, the philosopher of the world, whose name adds luster to our national character, and as a legislator and statesman stands second to no man's— *Jefferson still lives.* On him then concentrate your present views and your future hopes." But Jefferson believed that in some instances Beckley's credulity and enthusiasm had caused him to give the Vice President more credit than was due.

This consideration led him to draw up, for his own assessment as well as for posterity, "A Memorandum (Services to My Country)."[122] Confronted by the extremes of opprobrium and adulation, and apparently more fearful of the second, he wrote: "I have sometimes asked myself whether my country is the better for my having lived at all? I do not know that it is. I have been the instrument of doing the following things; but they would have been done by others; some of them, perhaps, a little better."

Proceeding in chronological order, he listed first an accomplishment of his early twenties: "The Rivanna had never been used for navigation; scarcely an empty canoe had ever passed down it. Soon after I came of age, I examined its obstructions, set on foot a subscription for removing them, got an Act of Assembly passed, and the thing effected, so as to be used completely and fully for carrying down all our produce."

"The Declaration of Independence" he listed next without embellishment. Then he recorded his efforts in support of religious freedom, citing the Act of 1776 exempting dissenters from contributions to the Anglican church, and his preparation of the Act for Religious Freedom in 1777, with final passage in 1786 "and then by the efforts of Mr. Madison."

He next listed four other acts: one "putting an end to entails," one "prohibiting the importation of slaves" (he could have pointed out that Virginia was the first state in modern history to pass such a law), one "concerning citizens, and establishing the natural right of man to expatriate himself at will," and one "changing the course of descents and giving the inheritance to all the children, & c., equally."

He cited the "act for apportioning crimes and punishments" which he had drawn up as part of the general revision of Virginia laws but which had been defeated by a single vote when proposed to the legislature by Madison in 1785. He noted that "the public mind was ripe for this in 1796, when Mr. [G.K.] Taylor proposed it," and accordingly it had passed. The measure substituted labor for the death penalty in various crimes.

Some people might have been surprised that Jefferson listed, among the greatest contributions of his life, having olive plants "of the best kind" sent from France to South Carolina and Georgia in 1789 and 1790, and in 1790 also having "a cask of heavy upland rice" sent from Africa for planting in the same two states. But he explained, "The greatest service which can be rendered any country is to add a useful plant to its culture, especially a bread grain; next in value to bread is oil."

Not at all surprisingly, he listed his authorship of "the act for the more general diffusion of knowledge," though admitting, "Whether . . . [it] will ever be carried into complete effect, I know not." He noted: "It was received by the legislature with great enthusiasm at first; and a small effort was made in 1796, by the act to establish public schools, to carry a part of it into effect, viz., that for the establishment of free English schools; but the option given to the courts has defeated the intention of the act."

Foreshadowing his self-written epitaph, he said nothing about having been a state legislator or congressman, except by implication when he mentioned his authorship of various acts and of the Declaration of Independence, and nothing whatever about having been Governor, United States Minister, Secretary of State, and Vice President. These deliberate omissions seem to reflect his frequently expressed resentment of politics as a distraction from the serious enterprises of cultivating the mind and the earth.

And what of the next office that might be his? However ambivalent Jefferson's attitude toward public position, there was nothing ambivalent about his desire to win any contest in which he was engaged. The electoral process was still unreformed—not only cumbersome and inefficient but definitely of the sort not favored by scriptwriters with a strong dramatic instinct. The news of the election came in isolated reports of choices of electors in separate states or even of choices of those who would choose the electors—all of this with agonizing slowness over a period stretching from spring into fall. And then the final result would remain in doubt at least until the casting of ballots by the electors in their various state capitols on December 3.

Republican triumph in New York's legislative elections in the spring presaged that state's choice of Republican electors. Of course, Burr's activities had a great deal to do with Republican prospects in New York, and he was also busy campaigning in New England. He assured Jefferson and Madison that, although Adams would carry Rhode Island, it would give one or more electoral votes to Jefferson. Burr said that he personally would receive no votes from that state. He saw that Jefferson and Madison both got the impression that certain votes would be withheld from Burr in the North, thus insuring that there could be no tie between the two chief Republican candidates.[123] Of course, with the system of the Presidency going to the candidate receiving the most votes and the Vice Presidency to the second highest contender, there was the possibility that two men of the same party would arrive neck and neck at the finish line. Then the final determination would be left to the United States House of Representatives.

Burr conveyed to both Jefferson and Madison his fears that the Republican electors in the South would desert the New Yorker, thus depriving him of the Vice Presidency. Madison, on his own initiative and with Jefferson's encouragement, worked to see that Burr was not betrayed by Southern electors.[124]

Republican hopes rose when Hamilton divided Federalist ranks by publishing a pamphlet castigating Adams. Hamilton hoped to end Adams' tenure in the Presidency and at the same time keep Jefferson and Burr out. To obtain these ends he promoted the candidacy of a South Carolina Federalist, Charles Cotesworth Pinckney. But Pinckney's own cousin, Senator Charles Pinckney, was the leader of South Carolina Republicans and he assured Jefferson that the next legislature, which would name the electors, was sure to be Republican.[125]

The largest state of all, Jefferson's own Virginia, was strong in support of its native son. From other states came encouraging reports. When Jefferson left Monticello for Washington on November 24, 1800, he had come to believe what his followers all over the country had been telling him—that he was likely to be the next President of the United States. Stopping at Montpelier overnight, he offered Madison the position of Secretary of State.[126]

Jefferson arrived in Washington on the evening of November 27 and checked into Conrad's boardinghouse, sometimes more formally known as "Messrs. Conrad and McMunn's apartments." The address, New Jersey Avenue and C Street, although it was near the capitol, was not nearly so urban as it sounded. Even Pennsylvania Avenue was little more than a good country road through a near-swamp. But there were advantages as well as disadvantages in the bucolic setting. From Jefferson's rear windows, the land sloped down toward a forest. This was not Monticello, but the Vice President was fortunate to have both bedroom and parlor in a town so crowded by the opening of Congress that some dignitaries did not even have private bedrooms. He had purposely arrived late to avoid a formal meeting with Adams on the occasion of the President's address to a joint session of Congress, but his quarters had been reserved for him by a friendly congressman.[127]

Of course, Jefferson might not stay long at Conrad's. He might soon be moving into the Executive Mansion. In at least one respect, life there would be reminiscent of Monticello. The house was still under construction. In fact, Abigail Adams was said to use the East Room as a laundry room.

As Jefferson supped with the congressmen at the boardinghouse and presided over the sessions of the Senate, there was inevitably a subtly altered relationship because of the knowledge that he might soon be President of the United States. There could be no certainty, however, for some weeks at least. The results of the balloting would not be known immediately after the electors cast their votes in the separate states on December 3. And even when results had been obtained in the state capitals, suspense would build as politicians awaited their arrival in Washington. Of course, the reports from Virginia were quickly received but they had been a foregone conclusion. The *National Intelligencer* of December 12 carried under the head "Splendid Intelligence" a report that immediately became the principal topic of conversation at Conrad's and every other establishment in Washington that housed members of the Senate and House of Representatives. Noting that the South Carolina Assembly had chosen the Republican electoral slate by a comfortable majority, the newspaper said, "Mr. Jefferson may, therefore, be considered as our future President."[128]

The paper's editor, Samuel Harrison Smith, was a Jefferson supporter and this fact may have prompted a bold assessment. Jefferson seems never to have doubted a

Federalist sweep of New England and none of the returns from there contradicted his judgement. In fact, Federalist strength in that region was so great as to pose an impediment to effective administration if he were elected. Republican hopes for victory in the Middle States were shattered when New Jersey chose seven Federalist electors and Pennsylvania, in a tortured compromise between the two houses of its legislature, selected eight Republicans and seven Federalists. Some people had forecast that the South would be almost solid for the Republicans, but Maryland's slate of electors was almost evenly divided between the two parties, and the Republican victory in North Carolina was two to one rather than nearly unanimous.

Before the votes of all the electors were known it became evident that the Federalist vote had topped out at 65, with Adams receiving that number and Pinckney receiving 64, as one Rhode Island elector had voted for Adams and Jay rather than for both standard-bearers of his party. The Republicans were virtually certain of 73 electoral votes, giving them victory by a respectable margin. Of course, there was the possibility that Jefferson and Burr had tied, but the Virginian had received private word at the behest of South Carolina's Republican chairman that one of the state's electors would vote for George Clinton rather than Burr, apparently for the express purpose of preventing a tie. On December 14 Jefferson was sufficiently assured of victory to offer the post of Secretary of the Navy to Robert Livingston. The next day he wrote to Burr, "I understand several of the high-flying Federalists have expressed their hope that the two Republican tickets (Jefferson and Burr) may be equal, and their determination in that case to prevent a choice by the H[ouse] of R[epresentatives] (which they are strong enough to do) and let the government devolve on a President. . . ."[129] selected from the Federalist majority in the Senate.

But Jefferson took pains to point out to Burr what had been said about a South Carolina elector voting for Clinton and said he also had been told, though he could not vouch for the accuracy of the reports, that a Tennessee elector and one from Georgia would do the same thing. In any event, he said, the matter of preventing a tie should not have been left to chance. Things had been "badly managed." That Jefferson should write to Burr in this vein suggests that he experienced some lingering or revived doubt as to whether a tie had been prevented, and also that he may have been reminding the New Yorker of an obligation to bow out if by some chance a tie had occurred, throwing into jeopardy not only Jefferson's victory but also the success of the Republican Party.

In his official capacity as president of the Senate, Jefferson received the final returns on December 28. The belated Christmas present was an unwelcome one. He and Burr were tied. Jefferson duly reported these returns to the Secretary of State, his cousin John Marshall, a staunch Federalist who might be expected to delight in the opportunity presented to his party. Jefferson feared that Marshall's interest might be even more personal. There were reports of a Federalist plan to place the Secretary of State in the Presidency if the House were unable to decide between rival candidates. Soon the *Aurora* reported a Federalist "conspiracy" to make the Chief Justice the chief executive.

Anxiety intensified as the new year dawned with rumors rife of various schemes to thwart the popular majority of the Republicans. Virginia's Governor, the levelheaded James Monroe, reported great distress and anger in his state over rumored machinations by the Federalists and wrote Jefferson, "If the union could be broken, that would do it."[130] Jefferson had earlier expressed his frustration to Monroe: "After the most energetic efforts, crowned with success, we remain in the hands of our enemies by want of foresight in the original arrangement."[131] As when writing to Burr about the possibility of a tie, Jefferson seemed to think that the negligence was something for which he shared no responsibility. Perhaps, consistent with his actions in some other matters, he deemed that the candidate should remain aloof from the machinery essential to his election.

Some people thought that the electoral crisis had not been precipitated by a "want of foresight" so much as by keen foresight on the part of Burr and his henchmen (one always has supporters, but one's opponent always has henchmen). Madison believed that the tie had resulted from "false assurances dispatched at the critical moment to the electors of one state that the votes of another would be different from what they proved to be."[132] In other words, individual electors in various states felt no need to withhold their votes from Burr to prevent a tie with Jefferson, because they had been informed that electors in other states were doing so.

If Jefferson himself had previously harbored suspicions of Burr, he now dismissed them. On New Year's Eve, General Samuel Smith of Maryland, with Burr's authorization, released to a Washington newspaper quotations from a letter in which the colonel had said that if a tie should occur he would "utterly disclaim all competition."[133] The colonel found it painful to countenance any suggestion that he might be a party to "counteracting the wishes and expectations" of his countrymen. As Smith was, like Jefferson, a boarder at Conrad's, it is reasonable to assume that he had shared these comments of Burr's with the Vice President even before transmitting them to the press. On New Year's Day, Jefferson received direct assurances from Burr. The colonel said that the Virginian had no reason to fear the outcome of a contest in the House. Jefferson could rely on the support of members from at least nine states. Voting in the House would be by states, not individuals, and a majority of nine states was required. "As far forth as my knowledge extends, it is the unanimous determination of the Republicans of every grade to support your administration with unremitted zeal."[134] As for Burr himself, "My personal friends are perfectly informed of my wishes on the subject and can never think of diverting a single vote from you." The colonel professed that he was motivated "as well by the highest sense of duty as by the most devoted personal attachment."

To his daughter Maria, Jefferson wrote that the Federalists had tried to "debauch Colonel Burr from his good faith by offering him their vote to be President" but that "His conduct has been honorable and decisive and greatly embarrasses them."[135]

Meanwhile Burr, learning that a tie with Jefferson was not merely a theoretical possibility but actual fact, had written another letter to Samuel Smith. The colonel considered "unreasonable, unnecessary, and impertinent" a suggestion that, in the interest of justice and party harmony, he announce that if elected President by the House, he would resign.[136] Burr was a hard man to pin down, but after General Smith talked with him in Philadelphia he concluded that the colonel thought that the House should elect him if it was not going to elect Jefferson. Whether or not Burr had acted to advance his own candidacy for the Presidency, he certainly did not make an unequivocal renunciation that could have ended Federalist maneuvering and the resultant crisis in transferring power in the young Republic.

The Federalists had until the second Wednesday in February to plot and plan.

Though the votes of the electors were already known, the law prescribed that they be officially tabulated on that day. In the meantime, Jefferson presided as usual over the deliberations of the Senate, which this time included confirmation of the Chief Justice. But the daily sessions were usually short and Jefferson found time early in January to pay his respects to Martha Washington at Mount Vernon, and too much time in both January and February to ponder his political fate. Most of the important business in Congress was being conducted in the House and even more in boardinghouses and private dwellings where Federalist politicians foregathered. Before the end of January it was well known that the Federalists in the lower chamber had indeed committed themselves to Burr's support.

Adams revealed his contempt for these proceedings in a letter to Elbridge Gerry, an old friend of the President's who was also a friend to Jefferson: "Mr. Burr's good fortune surpasses all ordinary rules, and exceeds that of Bonaparte. All the old patriots, all the splendid talents, the long experience, both of federalists and antifederalists, must be subjected to the humiliation of seeing this dexterous gentleman rise, like a balloon filled with inflammable air, over their heads. . . . What a discouragement to all virtuous exertion, and what an encouragement to party intrigue, and corruption!"[137]

More important than Adams' disgust with the proceedings, in terms of potential to affect the outcome, was Hamilton's vigorous opposition. He wrote to leader after leader of his party, insisting that Jefferson was preferable to Burr. One to whom he wrote was James A. Bayard, the sole representative of Delaware in the House. As voting would be by states, his vote alone would be as influential as that of the entire delegation from Virginia, most populous of the states. Jefferson was sure that eight states would be in his column. He needed a ninth. If Bayard broke with the Federalist majority, Jefferson's election as President would be virtually assured. Jefferson may not have known that Hamilton wrote to Bayard to dissuade him from voting for Burr, but the Virginian knew that Hamilton was campaigning against the colonel and he did hope for Bayard's support.

Hamilton, in his letter to Bayard, called Jefferson a "contemptible hypocrite" and made no secret of his enmity toward him but said that there was "no fair reason to suppose him capable of being corrupted."[138] To the charge that the Virginian was a perpetual revolutionary, Hamilton retorted that his observations of the Vice President suggested for a Jeffersonian administration "the expectation of a temporizing rather than a violent system." In colorful letters to Bayard and others, Hamilton admitted that he would not be loath to have a part in Jefferson's "disappointment and mortification." But he called Burr "as unprincipled and dangerous a man as any country can boast—as true a Catiline as ever met in midnight conclave." The substance of each highly rhetorical missive boiled down to the commonplace argument that the Virginian was the lesser of two evils. Hamilton's known hatred for Jefferson lent force to this argument.

By February 11, when balloting was scheduled to begin in the House, the nation was rapidly running out of time for a peaceful settlement before the inaugural date of March 4. The Philadelphia *Gazette of the United States* reported that Jefferson's supporters were prepared to march on Washington and seize control of the government. Editorially, it demanded, "Are they then ripe for civil war and ready to imbrue their hands in kindred blood?"[139] The paper warned that the Virginians would be no match for seventy thousand armed men from Massachusetts. In Virginia, Governor Monroe said that he would convene the General Assembly to deal with "any plan of usurpation" by the Federalists. He was not comforted when Jefferson's son-in-law reported that some of the arms and military stores had been removed from the federal arsenal in Bedford County and that he feared the Federalist Administration in Washington was "disarming the state in order to secure an usurpation."[140] Old horror stories of Royal Governor Dunmore's removal of munitions from the powder magazine in Williamsburg were, because of the active role of Thomas Mann Randolph's ancestors in the resulting crisis, a prominent part of Randolph family lore.

As if fate had refined the torture of suspense which Jefferson had to endure, his position as Vice President required him to preside over the joint session of the two houses of Congress on February 11 and, with all eyes focused on him, physically open the sealed certificates from the electors of the sixteen states. There were, of course, no surprises when the tellers completed the official tally and Jefferson announced the vote: Jefferson—73, Burr—73, Adams—65, Pinckney—64, Jay—1. He must have been relieved that this act ended his part in the proceedings, but must have speculated anxiously as members of the House retired to their own chamber for the decisive vote. Their deliberations were closed to the public, though seats were reserved for the President and senators. Though Vice President of the United States and presiding officer of the Senate, Jefferson did not fit into either of the two categories provided for. Surely he had no desire to have to steel himself to sit unblinking in that overcrowded chamber while its members considered his merits and demerits. Waiting in absentia would be hard enough. But maybe it would not be long; rules prohibited adjournment of the House before election of a President and Vice President.

On the first ballot, Jefferson, as he had expected, won the votes of eight states: New York, New Jersey, Pennsylvania, Virginia, North Carolina, Kentucky, Georgia, and Tennessee. Burr won the votes of six states: New Hampshire, Massachusetts, Rhode Island, Connecticut, South Carolina—and Delaware. Hamilton's arguments had not convinced Bayard. Two states, Vermont and Maryland, unable to reconcile differences within their own delegations, cast blanks. Jefferson needed the support of one more state. Actually, in individual votes he trailed Burr 51 to 55, but the determination would be by states, not by individuals.

The members had only their tempers to keep them warm while, in their unheated chamber pierced by winds that piled up snowdrifts outside, they answered 27 roll calls, beginning at one o'clock in the afternoon, extending through the night and until eight o'clock the next morning, without changing a single vote.

Though bound by the requirement that they not adjourn before electing a President, the Representatives did what many legislators had done before and have done since. They relied on a legal technicality and declared the session suspended but not adjourned. Returning at noon, they took another roll call. The vote was unchanged. At this point, Bayard later told Hamilton, the members "looked banged badly."[141]

The balloting continued. There was a chance that the vote would change very soon. Maryland's Joseph Nicholson, ill before the voting began, was worse after exposure to the storm. If he withdrew, the deadlock within the Maryland delegation would be broken and the state's vote would go to Burr. But as Nicholson's fever mounted to a dangerous height, he lay on a cot and kept voting. Harrison Gray Otis, a Boston Federalist active for Burr, looked at the Marylander in wonder. "It is a chance that this kills him," he wrote to his wife. "I would not thus expose myself for any President on Earth."[142]

When the session was suspended until the following morning, not a vote had changed. On February 14, after 33 ballots, there was no change. The next day being Sunday, the Representatives suspended proceedings until Monday.

Jefferson anticipated an end to the stalemate on that day. If the Federalist leadership in the House had been able to muster enough votes to name a president pro tempore as chief executive, he reasoned in a letter[143] to Monroe, it assuredly would have done so. Obviously Republican threats from the Middle States to resort to arms in such an eventuality had given pause to the Federalist plotters. He had other reasons for thinking that the Federalists did not have the strength to carry the day for Burr. "Many attempts," he told Monroe, "have been made to obtain terms and promises from me [in exchange for support in the balloting]. I have declared to them unequivocally that I would not receive the government on capitulation, that I would not go into it with my hands tied." As Burr had not withdrawn from the contest, Jefferson assumed that he was actively campaigning. He knew that Bayard was in communication with Burr, and he believed that the Delaware congressman had offered federal appointments to several of the Republican congressmen if they would switch their votes to the New Yorker.

Jefferson would have been surprised therefore to know what Bayard would report to Hamilton about conversations with Burr: "The means existed of electing Burr but this required his cooperation. By deceiving one man (a great blockhead), and tempting two (not incorruptible), he might have secured a majority of the States. He will never have another chance of being President of the United States; and the little use he has made of the one which has occurred, gives me but a humble opinion of the talents of an unprincipled man."[144]

When the House reconvened on Monday, February 17, and balloted for the thirty-sixth time, Bayard refrained from casting Delaware's vote for anyone. The South Carolina delegation also refrained. Federalist delegates from Vermont and Maryland cast blank ballots, thus permitting the Republican delegates to carry those states for Jefferson. The four New England states that voted continued to support Burr. The remaining ten states balloted for Jefferson. He was the next President of the United States.

The approach of his inauguration on March 4 was awaited with apprehension by Federalist leaders and with sickening fear by many citizens whom a scurrilous campaign had taught to regard him as a human concatenation of every vice. But many plain citizens were singing songs of hope dedicated to Jefferson. And one who epitomized the often excoriated, philosophically sophisticated, alien-born friends of the Vice President wrote to him, rejoicing that henceforth he could omit the "Vice" from the title of the "greatest man" in the United States. "You never had but one *Vice*," said Du Pont de Nemours. "I compliment your country and both hemispheres that you have at last lost it."[145]

XVII

'THE CHILD IS FATHER OF THE MAN'

AS THOMAS Jefferson, accompanied by friends, walked in his usual shambling, loose-gaited fashion from his boardinghouse to the Capitol, he was fully aware of the contrast between his informal approach and the august business which awaited him—his inauguration as President of the United States. No appropriate symbols of the day, and no ironies of the occasion, escaped his observation. Whether a spectator or an actor, he was one who always noticed.[1]

Of course, when in Washington, Jefferson usually depended on his own long legs to get from his living quarters to his work. There was no reason to do differently now. But, however casual his manner, no one was more conscious than he of the democratic symbolism of his colloquial progress to the capitol in contrast to the regal processions of his two predecessors. Jefferson had long believed that the trappings of monarchy encouraged the philosophy of tyranny. He had dreamed of a growing American society that would burst the old husk of privilege. Now the seeds were being warmed by a rising sun. On this very day of March 4, 1801, Republicans were singing a new song that proclaimed:

Now entering on th' auspicious morn,
In which a people's hopes are born,
What joy o'erspreads the land. . . .

In Jefferson's childhood, March, rather than January, had been officially the first month of a new year. Nature, oblivious to man's calendars, still began the new year in March. And Jefferson's term as chief magistrate would begin with a new century.

The nineteenth century had not begun in 1800 as so many unthinking persons had assumed. Jefferson, with his interest in astronomy and his penchant for computation, would never have made such a mistake. He knew that 1801 was the first year of a new century, knew it literally and figuratively. After the inauguration he would write to his friend Joseph Priestley: "We can no longer say there is nothing new under the sun. For this whole chapter in the history of man is new. The great experiment of our Republic is new. Its sparse habitation is new."[2] Jefferson was one of the most ardent converts to the idea that the human race could begin anew in America. As historian and philosopher, and in the long view almost always consistently an optimist, he was convinced that his actions as chief magistrate of the western republic, and therefore guardian of "the great experiment," would establish precedents not only for his own country but also for democratic societies yet unborn.

If the Republic was still under construction, so was its Capitol. Only the north wing was finished, and into it were crowded the Senate, the federal courts, and the library. An inchoate central structure linked this wing with a temporary one on the south occupied by the House of Representatives. Its oval shape and brick construction earned it the nickname "the Oven," a designation that invited jokes about half-baked products.

Jefferson did not hasten to his appointment with destiny. An uninformed bystander, seeing him shamble along with his group of friends just ahead of the company of Maryland artillery sent to do him honor, might have surmised the progress of marching soldiers had been slowed by a group of strolling civilians who had gotten in the way. But Jefferson's advance was not as casual as it seemed. Habitually punctual and long practiced in pacing himself, he mounted the steps of the north wing right on time for the noon ceremony, apparently oblivious to the salutes fired by the cannon which the Marylanders had dragged to the scene. He entered the chamber where he had presided over the Senate and suffered so many irritations and humiliations at the hands of once dominant Federalists. Now in this room members of both houses awaited him.

In the presiding officer's seat, the central of three chairs, was Aaron Burr, sitting as tall as his small frame permitted. He quickly stood and with a gesture offered his chair to the President-Elect. Jefferson took it and Burr sat on his right. John Marshall, who had been named Chief Justice by Adams in a "midnight appointment"[3] just before the President's term expired, sat on Jefferson's left. In the company of friends, the President-Elect often sat on the end of his spine, with one shoulder dropped, but on this public occasion he sat erect. Burr was dwarfed by the two tall, rangy Virginians.

No one knows for sure what each of the three men was thinking in the ensuing minutes of silence. We do know that Marshall was thankful Burr had not been elected President, but had deep forebodings about Jefferson. To get to the inauguration on time, he had left off writing a letter to his friend Charles Cotesworth Pinckney. In it he had said: "The new order of things begins. . . . There are some appearances which surprise me. I wish, however, more than I hope, that the public prosperity and happiness may sustain no diminution under democratic guidance. The democrats are divided into speculative theorists and absolute terrorists. With the latter I am not disposed to class Mr. Jefferson. If he arranges himself with them it is not difficult to foresee that much calamity is in store for our country—if he does not they will soon become his enemies and calumniators."[4]

Conspicuously absent from the ceremonies was the man who had appointed Marshall. John Adams, traveling alone, for Abigail had preceded him, had left Washington before dawn. Weighed down by the recent death of Charles, the son whom he had renounced as "a mere rake, blood, and beast,"[5] the President was equally disillusioned with the office he was leaving. "If I were to go over my life again," he had told another son, "I would be a shoemaker rather than an American statesman."[6]

As Jefferson rose, manuscript in hand, even those who had known and worked with him for years looked at him with the minute attention of renewed curiosity. Before he left this room he would be President of the United States. Standing tall and still in his plain dark suit, he had a monumental dignity not evident when he was walking. He was little more than a month short of his fifty-eighth birthday in a generation when age came on more quickly than in our own time, but his face was almost completely unlined except for parentheses around the firm but sensitive mouth and the suggestion of crowsfeet by the large, luminous, hazel eyes. The heavy eyebrows remained reddish brown, but his hair, which formerly he had worn lightly powdered, was now almost uniformly gray. The bold nose and chin seemed fresh from the sculptor's chisel. His cheeks were as ruddy as the apples from his Monticello orchards.[7]

Jefferson's voice projected so badly that those seated in the middle of the chamber heard him only poorly and those toward the back not at all. But even this defect had at least one advantage: a Washington resident in the audience found it impossible to believe that "this man so meek and mild, yet dignified in his manners, with a voice so soft and low, with a countenance so benignant and intelligent," could be "the violent democrat, the vulgar demagogue, the bold atheist and profligate man I have so often heard denounced by the Federalists."[8]

After modest professions of inadequacy and of reliance on the wisdom and virtue of the Congress, all wrapped up in one of the nautical metaphors so dear to this landlubber statesman, Jefferson addressed the mood of the nation. "During the contest of opinion through which we have passed," he said, "the animation of discussions and of exertions has sometimes worn an aspect which might impose on strangers unused to think freely and to speak and to write what they think; but this being now decided by the voice of the nation, announced according to the rules of the Constitution, all will, of course, arrange themselves under the will of the law, and unite in common efforts for the common good."[9]

The comment was appropriate but not unexpected. Victors usually want everybody to fall in line. But Jefferson now went an important step further: "All, too, will bear in mind this sacred principle, that though the will of the majority is in all cases to prevail, that will to be rightful must be reasonable; that the minority possess their equal rights, which equal law must protect, and to violate would be oppression." He was serving notice to both his enemies and his followers that vengeance would not be visited upon the Federalists. He was determined that his own party would be a shining exception to that gloomy social law that those just freed from persecution rush to persecute others.

Friends familiar with Jefferson's frequent laments over the role of politics as a destroyer of friendships recognized as more than diplomatic rhetoric his plea: "Let us restore to social intercourse that harmony and affection without which liberty and even life itself are but dreary things. And let us reflect that, having banished from our land that religious intolerance under which mankind so long bled and suffered, we have yet gained little if we countenance a political intolerance as despotic, as wicked, and capable of as bitter and bloody persecutions."

He said:

During the throes and convulsions of the ancient world, during the agonizing spasms of infuriated man, seeking through blood and slaughter his long-lost liberty, it was not wonderful that the agitation of the billows should reach even this distant and peaceful shore; that this should be more felt and feared by some and less by others, and should divide opinions as to measures of safety. But every difference of opinion is not a difference of principle. We have called by different names brethren of the same principle. We are all republicans, we are all federalists.

Here was an important thought clothed in some of the finest Jeffersonian eloquence. The first sentence was long and in a cadence that suggested the billows which it described. But a continuation in the same style would quickly have degenerated into oppressive grandiloquence. Instead Jefferson followed it abruptly with sentences of contrasting brevity, phrases whose careful balance suggested tranquility following tumult. The eloquent simplicity of the last three sentences anticipated the style that would be called Lincolnian. To some people such literary artistry in public discourse suggests, quite unfairly, the insincerity of Chaucer's Pardoner. But Jefferson had expressed the same thought in words of no calculated eloquence more than three years before when he had written to John Wise: "Both parties claim to be federalists and republicans, and I believe with truth as to the great mass of them: these appellations therefore designate neither exclusively."

If Jefferson had left unqualified his statement about all being both republicans and federalists, he would have been a fair target for reproach from those who had heard his complaints about the monarchial sentiments of Hamilton and others. He addressed the problem in words as eloquent as any in the Declaration of Independence and far less derivative:

If there be any among us who would wish to dissolve this Union or to change its republican form, let them stand undisturbed as monuments of the safety with which error of opinion may be tolerated where reason is left free to combat it. I know, indeed, that some honest men fear that a republican government cannot be strong, that this government is not strong enough; but would the honest patriot, in the full tide of successful experiment, abandon a government which has so far kept us free and firm, on the theoretic and visionary fear that this government, the world's best hope, may by possibility want energy to preserve itself? I trust not. I believe this, on the contrary, the strongest government on earth. I believe it the only one where every man, at the call of the law, would fly to the standard of the law, and would meet invasions of the public order as his own personal concern.

Jefferson closed the argument with a device suggestive of the concluding couplet of a Shakespearean sonnet, summarizing the preceding lines in words that seemed to address the auditor more directly than their predecessors:

Sometimes it is said that man cannot be trusted with the government of himself. Can he, then, be trusted with the government of others? Or have we found angels in the form of kings to govern him? Let history answer this question.

Using phrases that linked him to both his friends and his opponents, he appealed: "Let us, then, with courage and confidence pursue our own federal and republican principles, our attachment to union and representative government." He cited the special advantages of Americans, including possession of "a chosen country" that was "kindly separated by nature and a wide ocean from the exterminating havoc of one quarter of the globe" and "a due sense of our equal right to the use of our own faculties, to the acquisitions of our own industry, to honor and confidence from our fellow citizens, resulting not from birth, but from our actions and their sense of them."

Too proud in the campaign to answer charges that he was an atheist, Jefferson now professed his faith by citing as one of the advantages of the United States the fact that its people were "*enlightened* by a benign religion, professed, indeed, and practiced in various forms, yet all of them inculcating honesty, truth, temperance, gratitude, and the love of man; acknowledging and adoring an overruling Providence, which by all its dispensations proves that it delights in the happiness of man here and his greater happiness hereafter." By using the phrase "enlightened by a benign religion" Jefferson refuted the contention that his philosophy held enlightenment and religion to be irreconcilable enemies. Generalizations about Enlightenment philosophy were as common and as inaccurate in the eighteenth century as generalizations about Existentialism in the twentieth.

"With all these blessings," Jefferson asked, "what more is necessary to make us a happy and a prosperous people? Still one thing more, fellow citizens—a wise and frugal government, which shall restrain men from injuring one another, shall leave them otherwise free to regulate their own pursuits of industry and improvement, and shall not take from the mouth of labor the bread it has earned. This is the sum of good government, and this is necessary to close the circle of our felicities."

The unelaborated statement would seem to anticipate by a quarter of a century the classic *laissez-faire* philosophy of government. It could be neatly summarized in the quotation often attributed to Jefferson but not discovered among his writings: "That government is best which governs least." But he made a significant addition in the list of "essential principles" which he said "should be the creed of our political faith, the text of civic instruction, the touchstone by which to try the services of those we trust." After listing "equal and exact justice to all men, of whatever state or persuasion, religious or political; peace, commerce, and honest friendship with all nations, entangling alliances with none," he called for "the support of the State governments in all their rights, as the most competent administrations for our domestic concerns and the surest bulwarks against anti-republican tendencies." His view of the federal government as almost solely a provider of protection from foreign aggression and domestic crime did not necessarily imply a similarly limited role for the state governments, which, being nearer to the people, would be less capable of tyranny. Jefferson himself had advocated a state system of schools and even a state library and state museum.

His plea for strong state governments was followed by a call for "the preservation of the General Government in its whole constitutional vigor, as the sheet anchor of our peace at home and safety abroad." He was fully conscious of the duality of the federal system and apparently saw the tensions of the opposing national and state forces as not only an inevitable, but also a desirable, concomitant of that system. Though he did not use the precise analogy, he apparently saw them as comparable to the tensions produced by opposing forces in architecture. Out of balance, they might cause the collapse of the federal republic; in balance, they would sustain the structure.

Still dealing with what he regarded as essential, Jefferson admonished his hearers to have "a jealous care of the right of election by the people—a mild and safe corrective of abuses which are lopped by the sword of revolution where peaceable remedies are unprovided; absolute acquiescence in the decisions of the majority, the principle of republics, from which is no appeal but to force, the vital principle and immediate parent of despotism."

He called for "a well-disciplined militia, our best reliance in peace and for the first moments of war till regulars may relieve them" and stressed the need for "supremacy of the civil over the military authority."

"Economy in the public expense, that labor may be lightly burthened," and "the honest payment of our debts and sacred preservation of the public faith" were next on Jefferson's list. His growth from the days when he had wanted to preserve a nation of farmers, "God's chosen people," from the contamination of trade was marked by his call for "encouragement of agriculture, and of commerce as its handmaid." The reference was important for another reason. Obviously a government charged with encouraging agriculture and commerce could not be restricted to the primary functions of repelling foreign attack and keeping peace at home.

Jefferson completed his list of essentials with "the diffusion of information and arraignment of all abuses at the bar of the public reason; freedom of religion, freedom of the press, and freedom of person under the protection of the habeas corpus, and trial by juries impartially selected. These principles form the bright constellation which has gone before us and guided our steps through an age of revolution and reformation. The wisdom of our sages and blood of our heroes have been devoted to their attainment."

Jefferson's habitually diffident manner in public speaking reinforced the sincerity of his statement: "With experience enough in subordinate offices to have seen the difficulties in this the greatest of all, I have learnt that it will rarely fall to the lot of imperfect man to retire from this station with the reputation and the favor which bring him into it." He may have been mindful not only of the frustrations and disappointments of Adams' administration as President but also of his own as Governor of Virginia. But, as if Adams were as much removed from his thoughts as he was physically absent from the proceedings, Jefferson omitted any reference to his immediate predecessor and paid a tribute to Washington that must have appeased his own sense of justice as well as reassured a large part of his audience: "Without pretensions to that high confidence you reposed in our first and greatest revolutionary character, whose preeminent services had entitled him to the first place in his country's love and destined for him the fairest page in the volume of faithful history, I ask so much confidence only as may give firmness and effect to the legal administration of your affairs."

Though he had stressed his reliance on the wisdom of the Congress and the importance of majority rule in the Republic, Jefferson was not prepared to concede that others would always be right whenever they differed with him, simply because they outnumbered him and his cabinet. While admitting "I shall often go wrong through defect of judgement," he added, "When right, I shall often be thought wrong by those whose positions will not command a view of the whole ground."

He concluded: "May that Infinite Power which rules the destinies of the universe lead our councils to what is best, and give them a favorable issue for your peace and prosperity." How would these words be received by New Englanders who had been warned to hide their Bibles to avoid confiscation by the Arch Atheist moving into the Executive Mansion? Maybe some thought the whole performance akin to the Devil's reputed practice of quoting scripture when it served his purposes.

Chief Justice Marshall stepped forward to administer the oath of office. The two Virginia cousins, both towering figures physically and mentally, stood face to face in an ironic confrontation of political enemies. Marshall as a Federalist and Jefferson as a Republican had in mind different interpretations as the new President repeated after the new Chief Justice a pledge that he would, "to the best of my ability, preserve, protect, and defend the Constitution of the United States."

A short while later Marshall added a postscript to the letter he had been writing to General Pinckney. "I have administered the oath to the President. You will before this reaches you see his inauguration speech. It is in the general well-judged and conciliatory. It is in direct terms giving the lie to the violent party declamation which has elected him, but it is strongly characteristic of the general cast of his political theory."[10]

Though Marshall was still apprehensive about a Jefferson administration, the change of tone between the reference to it in the main body of the letter and the comment in the postscript indicated that the inaugural address had significantly reduced the urgency of his fears. One of Jefferson's chief purposes in his address had been to allay the apprehension of his enemies. His partial success with so longtime an opponent, chief of the Virginia Federalists and recipient of the highest appointment bestowed by the retiring Federalist President, augured well for his success with less dedicated and intransigent members of the opposition.

There was also an augury for the success of one of Jefferson's other purposes—to present an image of republican simplicity. When he entered Conrad's boardinghouse for dinner, all places at the head of the table, comfortably near the fireplace, were already taken. When no man offered the President his seat, Mrs. John Brown, wife of a United States Senator from Kentucky, offered him hers. Jefferson, of course, politely refused, and took his usual chair at the foot.[11]

Evidence of the success of the inaugural address was soon available from many quarters. Jefferson had released a copy to the press in advance, and it had been set in type before delivery. The Rev. Manasseh Cutler, who had feared a reign of atheism and Jacobinism if Jefferson were elected, now wrote: "There is a fair opening, and I think a hope, that he may prove a prudent man, and, though the next Congress will have a majority of Jacobins, the administration may not be greatly changed."[12] George Cabot, a Massachusetts Federalist leader, wrote to Rufus King that Jefferson's speech was "so conciliatory that much hope is derived from it by the Federalists; it certainly contains some foolish and some pernicious as well as many good ideas. In the whole, however, its temper entitles it to respect and, whatever may be the sincerity of its professions, good policy requires that they be trusted till contradicted by actions."[13]

Of course, many were not won over. Jefferson had expected this would be the case. He wrote to a supporter: "The Eastern states will be the last to come over, on account of the dominion of the clergy, who had got a smell of union between Church and State, and began to indulge reveries which can never be realized in the present state of science."[14]

What of Jefferson's third great purpose—to·set forth the philosophy that would animate his administration? It is not particularly surprising that many who heard or read his inaugural address were later surprised by some of his actions as President. He presented his purposes briefly, saying that he would "compress them within the narrowest compass they will bear, stating the general principle but not all its limitations." But it is a little surprising that those who had followed his career were unprepared for his major moves as chief executive. And it is much stranger that historians with access to his public record and private letters as well as the inaugural address of March 4, 1801 should see any contradiction between his professions before that date and his practices afterward.

The address was the result of much thought. Though one of the most distinguished American historians has said, "Since the House of Representatives did not elect him until February 17, Jefferson had only a little more than two weeks in which to prepare his inaugural address,"[15] it is difficult to believe that the methodical statesman, realizing the strong possibility of his election, did not use the interval for preparation. But whether he did or not, his whole career and the productions of his tireless pen were preparation. Daniel Webster, when praised for the excellence of his impromptu speeches in the Senate, insisted that he had never delivered an impromptu speech in that chamber. Whatever public business was introduced, he said, was always something that he had studied and pondered. Jefferson would have found himself in such a position in making an inaugural address.

A review of his expressions and actions through the decades before his assumption of the Presidency will show that they, the inaugural address, and his performance as chief magistrate are all united in a general consistency. Indeed, his juvenile correspondence and his recollections of childhood show clearly that the child was father of the man. Both the private and public character of Jefferson had been not only foreshadowed but formed when he became the third President of the United States. The Republic itself was not even near such a stage of maturity. He would exert considerable influence on both its physical form and its psyche.

Admittedly there was paradox, at least on a superficial level, in the man who was accused of having little stomach for war in the Revolution and who had declared his lifelong "passion for peace," waging against the Barbary States a war which the great and ancient states of Europe had painstakingly avoided. There was wonder in the spectacle of the national debt being reduced drastically by the prudent management of one who lay awake nights tortured by visions of his own creditors. No less paradoxical was the action of this strict constructionist who, though operating under a Constitution with no provision for the purchase and assimilation of foreign territory, boldly initiated and carried through the Louisiana Purchase, at one stroke of his pen doubling the size of the United States. The irony was underlined when prominent citizens of New York, New Jersey, and the five New England states protested the supposed unconstitutionality of the President's action by threatening to lead their states out of the Union to form a Northern Confederacy. And of course, it is amusing as well as strange that the man who never traveled more than 25 miles west of his birthplace should evince a strong and sympathetic interest in the West and sponsor the great Western expeditions of Lewis and Clark and Zebulon Pike.

There was some cause for surprise when the President, who had long advocated "taking things by the smooth handle," directly challenged the authority of the Supreme Court in a controversy culminating in the celebrated case of Marbury v. Madison. It also seemed paradoxical to some, although not at all inconsistent with Jefferson's inaugural pledge to encourage commerce, that the man famous for advocating a self-sufficient society of free farmers should pursue a foreign policy that sent both American exports and imports soaring to new heights. And it was doubly ironic that another step in that policy, imposition of the Embargo, should so far reverse those gains that New Englanders, once horrified by Jefferson's doctrine of interposition, should now threaten to invoke it against his administration.

Examination of each of these paradoxes shows it to be more apparent than real. A case in point is the instance of Jefferson the peacemaker reversing the policy of Washington and Adams, who had paid tribute to the Barbary States to protect American commerce from their depredations, and instead waging war against Tripoli until attainment of victory more than four years later. His action seemed the more remarkable because even Great Britain and France stooped to pay protection money to these North African pirates and all of Europe accepted this practice as a way of life. But Jefferson, while truly passionate for peace, had never called for "peace at any price." This fact should have been obvious to anyone who recalled that in 1774, at the age of 31, he had published *A Summary View of the Rights of British America* which implied that liberty was more precious than peace. And though a reluctant rebel, he had been one of the most active revolutionists in the great war for independence, becoming indeed the voice of his nation's aspiration to independence and the author of its apologia for taking up arms.

In the specific matter of dealing with the Barbary States, Jefferson showed complete consistency, his advocacy of war in preference to tribute dating from his service as a United States Commissioner in 1785 and continuing through his tenure as Washington's Secretary of State. In 1785 he clearly explained his reason for this stand and his belief that peace could not be pursued through weakness: "Weakness provokes injury and insult, while a condition to punish it often prevents it. This reasoning leads to the necessity of some naval force, that being the only weapon with which we can reach an enemy. I think it to our interest to punish the first insult, because an insult unpunished is the parent of many others."

The connection between Jefferson the private debtor and Jefferson the President whose retrenchment policies reduced the national debt 30 percent within eight years despite a war and the Louisiana Purchase is more logical than might appear at first blush. The sleepless hours that he dedicated to his own finances may well have strengthened his determination that the federal government avoid such pitfalls. It should be remembered, too, that while Jefferson's financial woes often were exacerbated by the extravagance of his tastes in architecture and interior decoration, they stemmed to a greater extent from the debts which he inherited from his father-in-law. Jefferson was always a careful steward of other people's property; it is not surprising that he should have been especially frugal when acting as steward for all citizens of the United States.

The action by President Jefferson most often cited as paradoxical was his use of a broad construction of the Constitution to justify the Louisiana Purchase. Historians of subsequent generations have been as busy as politicians of his own in quoting strict constructionist statements from Jefferson in order to prove that he betrayed his philosophy because he could not resist the temptation to double the area of the United States. Their task is an easy one because he spoke and wrote often in favor of strict construction. But his adherence to the principle, so unswerving that it straitjacketed his administration as Governor of Virginia, became far more flexible long before he was President. Contemplation of the frustrations of his gubernatorial service, always a painful memory for Jefferson, probably played a part in his growing flexibility. Another factor was Jefferson's pragmatic idealism, his habit in his maturity of weighing the probable benefits to society of a given proposal instead of making a purely doctrinaire decision. He did not abandon his ideals; he served them the hard way, determining in each instance what he believed most likely to advance them and acting accordingly regardless of labels.

Jefferson had supported, and even advanced, moves based on a broad construction of the Constitution and of the earlier Articles of Confederation. In 1785, when the emissary from the Continental Congress to the Barbary States was long delayed, Jefferson suggested to Adams that the two of them, being already in Europe and aware of the Congress's intentions, should exercise their own powers as ministers plenipotentiary and appoint someone who would bargain hard with the pirate kings. Though many of his fellow Virginians in 1790 protested Alexander Hamilton's assumption scheme on the grounds that they could "find no clause in the Constitution authorizing Congress to assume the debts of states," Jefferson accepted the New Yorker's broad construction and shepherded a compromise by which Southern congressmen approved it in exchange for an agreement to move the national capital to the Potomac. When the federal city was being built and Jefferson as Secretary of State supervised layout and construction, he greatly enhanced his influence over the esthetics of the process by giving the most liberal interpretation to grants of executive authority.

In 1793 Jefferson—ironically enough opposed by Hamilton—had proposed a protective tariff for American manufactures, a tit-for-tat system in which the United States would respond in kind when another country placed high duties on American goods or prohibited them. Jefferson was no lover of tariff barriers and he preferred strict construction when practical, but he saw a protective tariff as the only means of rescuing the fledgling republic, a newcomer to international marts, from economic colonialism. Jefferson had resorted to the "implied powers" of the Constitution, a doctrine always associated with Hamilton. Remarkably enough, Jefferson had advanced this doctrine in August 1787, well before Hamilton, when some had insisted that Congress lacked the power to enforce levies on the states. The Virginian had said that no express grant of authority was necessary: "When two parties make a compact, there results to each a power of compelling the other to execute it."

Repeatedly Jefferson, though preferring strict construction, had been unwilling to let it stand in the way of important opportunities for his country. Anyone familiar with his advocacies and actions in these instances should have realized that Jefferson, given the chance to add the Louisiana Territory to the United States, would not be held back by his strict constructionist sympathies if convinced that the opportunity was important to the welfare of the United States. As Secretary of State, he had recognized the importance of control of the Mississippi, saying that the moment France took possession of Louisiana we must "marry ourselves to the British fleet and nation."

In a letter to John Breckinridge, he said: "I would not give one inch of the Mississippi to any nation, because I see in a light very important to our peace the exclusive right to its navigation. . . . The Constitution has made no provision for our holding foreign territory, still less for incorporating foreign nations into our Union. The Executive, in seizing the fugitive occurrence which so much advances the good of their country, have done an act beyond the Constitution. The Legislature, in casting behind them metaphysical subtleties, and risking themselves like faithful servants, must ratify and pay for it, and throw themselves on their country for doing for them unauthorized what we know they would have done for themselves had they been in a situation to do it."[16]

No impenetrable mystery shrouds Jefferson's sponsorship of the most famous Western expeditions in American history despite his own failure to explore the West except in study and imagination. His interest in that great region was sincere and virtually lifelong. It was sparked in early childhood by his father's tales of cartographic expeditions that carried him into the wilderness where he was confronted by angry bears, made friends with Indians, and on at least one occasion slept in a hollow tree. The interest was fanned when Indians were guests in young Jefferson's boyhood home and when, as a student at the College of William and Mary, he heard a chief standing in the cold light of the moon and the ruddy glow of a council fire bid his tribe an eloquent farewell before sailing across the great sea. As American Minister in Paris, eager to refute Buffon's claims that all creatures degenerated in size in the environment of the New World, Jefferson eagerly sought impressively large zoological specimens from the West. Of course, his tremendous intellectual curiosity thirsted for any knowledge of the New World's own new world. And, as we have seen, he was fully aware of the importance of the Louisiana Territory to the security and prosperity of the United States.

Why then did Jefferson not see the West for himself? The answer seems to be that, unlike such associates as Washington and Monroe, who traveled up and down the roads and rivers of the republic, Jefferson was a bad traveler. Despite his frequent use of nautical imagery, he dreaded ocean voyages, either declining or only reluctantly accepting appointments that would carry him overseas. And though he was a good horseman, extended land travel was fatiguing to him. It is not surprising that, in an era when only the hardiest frontiersman ventured far to the West, he eschewed the pathless wilderness. And Jefferson, while an unsparing taskmaster for himself, was far more inured to mental labor than to physical discomfort. He could not have emulated his father and found sleep after trading his four-poster for a hollow tree.

Close friends of Jefferson's—such comrades as Madison and Monroe—were not surprised when this man who loved to be loved and advocated "taking things by the smooth handle," challenged the authority of the Supreme Court. As Vice President, Jefferson had passionately and repeatedly declared his belief that the security of American democracy depended upon preservation of the balance of powers among the three branches of government—legislative, executive, and judicial. Jefferson, whenever he was in a position of responsibility, acted on his deeply held convictions. Unpopularity, personal attacks, and the possibility of defeat, though bitterly painful, could not deter him. Under pressure of these misfortunes, he suffered psychosomatic illnesses ranging from diarrhea to migraine; but from the controversial *A Summary View of the Rights of British America* in 1774, to the Declaration of Independence in 1776 that he understood would place a price on his head, through a series of stands since that had caused old friends to snub him, he had persisted in his duty as he saw it. As President, when migraine would hold his head in a tightening vise for weeks on end, he would make no compromise with duty in either choosing a course or pursuing it. And he made some hard choices—from trying to convict his former Vice President of treason to proclaiming a hated embargo. He would plan and calculate when pain dictated seclusion and perform his executive functions in the few pain-free hours allotted him.

That Jefferson should keep his inaugural promise to "encourage commerce" should not have surprised anyone who had followed his public career. Admittedly, he had been narrowly agrarian as late as February 1791 when, alarmed by Hamilton's proposal for a national bank, he wrote, "The only corrective of what is corrupt in our present form of government will be the augmentation of the numbers in the lower house, so as to get a more agricultural representation, which may put that interest above that of the stock-jobbers." His was a Romantic, Wordsworthian idealization of those who worked with the soil and he brought a zealot's intensity to the task of driving the money changers from the temple of democracy. By 1793, however, his duties as Secretary of State had caused him to study international trade and his appreciation of commerce had increased tremendously. It was then that, in obedience to a resolution of the Congress, he submitted a survey of the trade of the western world with particular reference to the needs of the United States—a masterpiece as remarkable then for its use of simplified statistical tables as for its grand scope. In it he advocated federal trade regulations as a stimulus to manufacturing. A true product of the Virginia plantocracy, he never lost his agricultural bias but had so far advanced in breadth of view before his election as President as to believe that urban mechanics might make an important contribution to the Republican Party.

On examination, most of the so-called inconsistencies between Jefferson's actions as President and his previously expressed convictions melt away. His changes of opinion are not revealed as whimsical or erratic but as aspects of the evolution of a powerful intellect.

But some may say there is a major inconsistency, one so diametrically in conflict with his expressed "eternal hostility to every form of tyranny over the mind of man" as to invite the charge of hypocrisy and to expose as sacrilege his claim to have sworn this opposition "upon the altar of God." For Jefferson lived and died a slaveholder, participating in a system that exercised tyranny over both the minds and bodies of fellow humans. Yet no one has argued more eloquently and realistically than he that "The whole commerce between master and slave is a perpetual exercise of the most boisterous passions, the most unremitting despotism on the one part, and degrading submissions on the other." In the same chapter of his *Notes on Virginia*, he wrote: "Indeed I tremble for my country when I reflect that God is just; that his justice cannot sleep forever; that considering numbers, nature and natural means only, a revolution of the wheel of fortune, an exchange of situation, is among possible events; that it may become probable by supernatural interference." Jefferson had attempted to write into the Declaration of Independence a condemnation of slavery. He argued that it was inconsistent to deny to others the freedom for which the colonists declared that they were fighting as a God-given right, but slaveholders from the Deep South and slavetraders from New England defeated him.

Jefferson repeatedly proposed the gradual abolition of slavery but he believed firmly that blacks and whites could not live together peaceably in a free society. He therefore supported various schemes for the colonization of freedmen and even for the creation of a black territory west of the Mississippi that would be encouraged to achieve statehood. He would not free his own slaves so long as he lived because the laws of Virginia then exiled freed slaves. Jefferson believed they were better off in his care. His attitude was paternalistic but it was still far too liberal for most of his contemporaries. If we abide by the sensible cliché that one should be judged in the context of his times, Jefferson is relieved of the charge of hypocrisy.

Still there remains, some insist, one overriding inconsistency that transcends categorization. It is the occasional conservative statement or action that seems to run counter to his lifelong career as a liberal. Before we can assent to the justice of the accusation, we must ask one question: Was Jefferson truly a liberal?

The temptation is to say that he was. Certainly many politicians and most writers and historians of the twentieth century have said so. If liberalism is the advocacy of progressive change, one can, without too much semantic subtlety about the nature of progress, cite a long list of Jefferson's achievements that would deserve the liberal label.

Starting in 1774 as the author of *A Summary View* with its denial of Parliamentary authority over the North American colonies and its sharp criticism of the King's policies, and moving on to the authorship of the Declaration of Independence with its assertion that "all men are created equal" and that revolution under some circumstances is a natural right, Jefferson was launched upon a career that most would call liberal if not radical. In October 1776 he began to work on a revision of the statutes of Virginia, a process involving repeal of the laws of entail and primogeniture, establishment of a state-supported system of education, and disestablishment of the Church of England. He also played a prominent part in the abolition of capital punishment except for murder and treason and secured passage of an act prohibiting importation of slaves. His proposed ordinance for the government of the Northwest Territory, which became the basis for the Ordinance of 1787, provided that slavery be banned from the territory after 1800. When enacted into the Ordinance of 1787, this provision established the precedent for federal authority over slavery in the territories. As American Minister to France in the 1780s he was a favorite in Enlightenment salons and took a sympathetic and helpful interest in the intelligentsia's efforts to promote political reform. His patient dealings with France's revolutionary regime when he was Secretary of State, his opposition as Vice President to the Alien and Sedition Acts, and his leadership of the opposition party that saw monarchism in the Federalist Administration and demanded simple republicanism instead—all helped to form the popular image of liberalism which Jefferson brought to the Presidency.

His performance as President, some would argue, further enhanced the liberal image. They see his use of a broad construction of the Constitution to justify the Louisiana Purchase as evidence of vigorous liberalism. They see enlightened liberalism in the course of neutrality that he pursued as President during the Napoleonic Wars, a course for which he himself had set a masterly precedent as Secretary of State, a precedent cited in later years by both the United States and Great Britain. Some say that the humane spirit of liberalism is epitomized by the generosity with which at the start of his Administration he not only removed restrictions on civil rights of his opponents but extended the hand of partnership.

His activities after eight years as President are generally construed as further affir-
mation of his liberalism. He spoke out for freedom, encouraged learning, and founded
the University of Virginia. This last contribution, and his authorship of the Declaration
of Independence and the Statute of Virginia for Religious Freedom, were the only
achievements that he chose to list on his tombstone.

And so we have, neatly summarized, the career of a liberal. A little too neatly. We
would do well to remember how protean the term liberal is. In its political sense, as
applied to persons or measures favoring change, the word was just coming into use
in the Anglo-American world about the time Jefferson became President. In the generations since, nobody has been able to compose an unchanging list of specific measures
that are "liberal." Well into the twentieth century, "economic freedom" as opposed
to state regulation was commonly cited in both the United States and Great Britain as
one of the principal elements of political liberalism. Then, in the third decade of this
century, increased governmental regulation of the economy came to be labeled liberal
and resistance to this movement came to be called conservative. A still more abrupt
shift of terminology took place in the United States during the Korean War. At the start
of the action those who favored military intervention were called liberal because they
"recognized the need for the United States to assume its international responsibilities,"
and those who opposed intervention were called conservative because they were "isola-
tionists." Yet, before the war ended, those who favored military action were called
conservative because they were seen as "defenders of the old imperialism," and those
who demanded withdrawal were seen as liberals because they favored "the self-
determination of peoples." Yesterday's liberalism is today's conservatism. Liberalism
and conservatism are parts of a system of relativity in which each is defined in terms
of the other.

Categorization becomes more stable if we compare statesmen performing in the
same arena at the same time. But even that procedure presents difficulties. If Jefferson's
authorship of the Declaration of Independence is to be cited as evidence of his radicalism,
then John Adams' spirited advocacy of such a declaration should make him a radical
too. So should his insistence that Jefferson be the author, partly because of Jefferson's
literary prowess and partly because he wanted a Virginian deeply involved so that the
most populous of the American colonies would not compromise with Parliament. Yet
Adams is frequently presented as a conservative foil for Jefferson the liberal. If Jefferson's
A Summary View is to be cited as evidence of his radicalism, it must be remembered
that Patrick Henry's fiery orations had outdistanced Jefferson's pamphlet nine years
before its publication. Yet Henry is customarily presented as the conservative nemesis
of Jefferson's liberal programs in the Virginia legislature. Henry was one of the first to
call for separation from England but he had no revolutionary desires beyond national
independence. There is another point to be considered: some believe that the Founding
Fathers—middle or upper class to a man—sponsored a conservative revolution because
the status quo of colonial society was threatened by imperial policies originating in
London. Jefferson's colleagues agreed with him—some in praise and some in criticism—
that he had not presented in the Declaration of Independence any ideas peculiarly his
own but simply had expressed "the sense of the Congress." How could Jefferson's stand
for independence make him radical without making radical all the other delegates who
shared it?

Perhaps an examination of differences would be more enlightening than a consideration of unanimity. One of the most liberal actions of Jefferson's life, it is often said, was his work on Virginia's Committee to Revise the Laws of the Commonwealth. When the group assembled on January 13, 1777, Edmund Pendleton, though known as "Old Moderation," called for a completely new code of laws and the proposal was seconded by Thomas Ludwell Lee. Jefferson's position probably was taken for granted; he had said that the real revolution would be in the forums where laws were made. But one member argued that if a completely new code were produced "every word and phrase in that text would become a new subject of criticism and litigation until its sense should have been settled by numerous decisions; . . . in the meantime the rights of property would be in the air." This more conservative view prevailed. Some have said that Jefferson's most liberal act was his formulation of the most seminal proposal in the history of American public education—a plan calling for free instruction from grammar school to university "without regard to wealth, birth or other accidental condition or circumstance." A prominent statesman insisted that the program be highly selective in view of the unequal distribution of abilities among the human race, arguing, "By this means twenty of the best geniuses will be raked from the rubbish annually."

When Jefferson was being urged to be a candidate for President, when he was being told that he offered the one best opportunity for liberal reform, a prominent Republican statesman complained of "those who, rising above the swinish multitude, always contrive to nestle themselves into the places of power and profit." Far more surprising than the implied criticism of leaders was a Republican's characterization of the majority as "the swinish multitude." Though in his inaugural address in 1801 Jefferson called for "a jealous care of the right of election by the people," and though on other occasions he had declared that the republicanism of a government could be measured by the degree to which individual citizens participated in its decisions, a Republican statesman, in opposing direct election of United States Senators, had written: "I have ever observed that a choice by the people themselves is not generally distinguished for its wisdom. This first secretion from them is usually crude and heterogeneous. . . . I could submit, though not so willingly, to an appointment for life, or to anything rather than a mere creation by and dependence on the people."[17] Jefferson opposed formation of the Society of the Cincinnati because he feared that a membership based on descent from American Revolutionary officers could lead to an hereditary privileged class, yet one Republican statesman called for special consideration for the descendants of revered Revolutionary leaders in appointing people to high federal office.

Who was the statesman who, in this instance proving more conservative than "Old Moderation" himself, opposed Pendleton's proposal for a completely new code of laws, saying that so much change could, for a while, leave property rights "in the air"? None other than Jefferson himself.

Who said that a program of public education should be so planned that "the best geniuses will be raked from the rubbish annually"? Not some gimlet-eyed Federalist doing violence to Jefferson's dream but again Jefferson himself.

And what of the Republican leader who referred to the mass of voters as "the swinish multitude"? Could Jefferson remain in the same party with him? He did more than that; he inhabited the same skin.

And of course it was Jefferson who opposed direct election of United States Senators on the grounds that "a choice by the people themselves is not generally distinguished for its wisdom."

Again, it was Jefferson who urged that the inheritors of great old Revolutionary names be given preference for federal appointments when the qualifications of rival candidates were substantially equal.

So Jefferson sounds like a conservative in the matter of statutory reform, public education, evaluation of the electorate, direct election of Senators, and visiting the honors of the fathers upon the sons. Only the knowledge that he was a liberal keeps us from seeing him as a conservative. One is reminded of Governor Fauquier, one of Jefferson's earliest patrons, who was surprised by the throng of protesters that confronted the Stamp Act Distributor on his arrival in Williamsburg in 1765. They jostled like a mob, shouted like a mob, threatened like a mob. "This concourse of people," the Governor reported to his superiors in London, "I should call a mob did I not know that it was chiefly, if not altogether, composed of gentlemen."

Yet for virtually every conservative quotation from Jefferson a matching liberal one can be found—sometimes in the same document.

Was Jefferson schizophrenic? Was the famous "Dialogue of Head and Heart" he addressed to Maria Cosway only a sample of the debates he perpetually waged with himself? Not at all. Like most contemplative people of high intelligence, he was capable of seeing more than one side of each issue. By lifting some of the most extreme statements from the context of his voluminous writings on every matter of major concern in his day, and by ignoring the particulars of time and place that he had to consider, he can be made to seem either liberal or conservative. The game is played all the time with Jefferson's words. Both liberal and conservative politicians have played it. Jefferson's name turned up more than any other in a 1985 poll of United States Senators to determine their favorite heroes. Both liberals and conservatives felt an affinity with him.[18]

Among writers and historians of recent decades, however, the tendency has been overwhelming to begin with the assumption that Jefferson was a liberal and then either to exclude from consideration or treat as an anomaly any of his words and actions inconsistent with the liberal image. In few if any cases is the distortion willful. Most biographies of Jefferson in recent years have come from either academe or journalism at a time when the bias of both professions has been distinctly liberal.

In death as in life, except among the few antagonistic to him, Jefferson attracts intense loyalty. He is not only the patron saint of a political party. He is also the patron saint of a host of ideologists, most of them of the liberal persuasion. Many of them approach the task of telling Jefferson's life story as if it were that of a revered father. Each conservative thought attributable to this Founding Father is an isolated slip from grace. To reveal it to the public, they seem to feel, would be as disloyal and as pointless as exposing to general gossip the few instances in which a beloved parent, deservedly respected for sobriety, indulged too heavily in drink.

A respectable case can be made that Jefferson philosophically is close to prominent self-avowed conservatives in our own time. Editing a 1967 symposium on *The New Conservatives*,[19] Professor Leonard Lief of Hunter College found that the seven participants, all professed conservatives, agreed on seven issues. The participants were three philosophers, Russell Kirk, Richard M. Weaver, and Frank Meyer; two historians, Clinton

Rossiter and Peter Viereck; a journalist, William F. Buckley; and a United States senator, Barry Goldwater.

The first issue on which they found common ground was: "For the most part, a deep belief in God and a concern with religion in the daily affairs of men." Many of Jefferson's contemporaries believed that his concern with religion was either small or hostile. We now know that he was a closet theologian who anticipated some of the theories of Albert Schweitzer, that he read daily from his own multilingual edition of the New Testament, and that, though hostile to what he regarded as priestly tyranny, he believed religion to be vital to society.

"A suspicion of big government and a reliance upon local administration of public affairs" was the second point of agreement. Jefferson is more closely identified with this view than any other famous American.

"A belief in the imperfect nature of man and a hostility to any scheme—political or social—that suggests a Utopian world" was the third point on which symposium participants agreed. At first blush this view may not seem compatible with Jefferson's. Was he not a representative leader of the Enlightenment and as such a believer in the perfectibility of man? The fabled optimism of this philosophy's adherents was not so boundless as we are sometimes inclined to think.[20] Hume pessimistically observed, "When the arts and sciences come to perfection in any state, from that moment they naturally, or rather necessarily decline, and seldom or never revive in that nation, where they formerly flourished." Montesquieu said that "Almost all the nations. . .travel this circle" of advance and decay. Voltaire saw perfection as unattainable because "No advantages. . .are pure and unmixed." Wieland despairingly wrote that "the epoch of brightest enlightenment is always the very epoch in which all sorts of speculations, madness, and enthusiasm, flourish most."

Jefferson's own optimism about the perfectibility of man was tempered by association with Madison who, deeply steeped in Calvinist theology, was well aware of the human tendency to backslide. By the time of the American Revolution, Jefferson was convinced that he must work quickly to secure enactment of reforms because as soon as the immediate common danger was past the opportunity for unselfish cooperation would be lost. He grew to believe that the most important purpose of a constitution was to protect man from himself. Jefferson may not have been as hostile to Utopianism as most twentieth-century conservatives, but long before he became President he was distrustful of it.

"A conviction that social equality is not, in and of itself, a desirable end" was the fourth point on which the symposiasts agreed. Whether Jefferson believed social equality desirable probably must remain unknown. He indicated many times that he regarded it as impossible, given the many natural disparities among human beings, and therefore in his utilitarian way spent little time pondering its desirability.

"An admiration for tradition and the past" was the fifth item on which the symposium reached common ground. Though not a slave to the past, Jefferson drew inspiration from it. Advising President Washington about construction in the new Federal City, he wrote, "Whenever it is proposed to prepare for the Capitol, I should prefer the adoption of some one of the models of antiquity, which have had the approbation of thousands of years." From the citations in reams of his correspondence it was apparent that he also believed that those planning and deliberating within the Capitol should be mindful of the "models of antiquity."

When we come to the sixth point agreed on by the symposium, "a respect for the importance of property and free enterprise in stabilizing society and spurring individual incentive," we are dealing with the very warp and woof of Jefferson's political philosophy. We have seen that he was unwilling in 1774 to undertake the creation of a completely new code of laws for Virginia because he was unwilling to have the commonwealth enter upon a period of litigation in which property rights would be "in the air." He fully accepted the argument that voting should be restricted to property owners because only they would have a sufficient economic stake in society to be attentive to its needs. Repeatedly through the years Jefferson portrayed the small, independent landholder as the chief stabilizing element in a nation.

"An abhorrence of communism" was the last of the seven points on which the conservative symposiasts agreed. Though communism of a sort had existed in the early days of Christianity in the Roman Empire and subsequently in other places, even including a brief period in seventeenth-century Virginia, Marxist Communism was more than four decades in the offing when Jefferson became President. It is easy to see, however, that he would have considered it a "form of tyranny over the mind of man."

So in at least five of the seven areas of agreement reached by the twentieth-century conservatives, we find Jefferson sharing their views. In the other two, he is at least partially sympathetic. Certainly a respectable case can be made that Jefferson was more conservative than liberal.

Can an equally good case be made, in twentieth-century American terms, that Jefferson was as much liberal as conservative? Determining whether someone is a liberal is in some ways a more complicated process than deciding whether he is a conservative. Though conservatism is not monolithic, the differences among its adherents are largely matters of degree, whereas avowed liberals now declare allegiance to either of two schools often in conflict. In the 1920s Vernon Parrington, in *Main Currents in American Thought*, argued that "liberals" in the United States could be divided between those who believed in the "English philosophy of laissez-faire," depending on the adjustments of the acquisitive instinct and commonsense self-interest, and those who believed in human perfectibility and anticipated an egalitarian society "in which the political state should function as the servant to the common well-being." In subsequent decades the second school seems to have borrowed from German liberalism an idea succinctly expressed by Guido de Ruggiero in his *History of European Liberalism*: if "obedience to the moral law is freedom," then obedience to a state imbued with moral values can be "the highest expression of liberty." In 1909 Herbert Croly, in *The Promise of American Life*, captured the imagination of Progressives with his vision of a strong central government transferring power from the few to the many. By 1967, at the time that Leonard Lief was publishing his summary of the conservative creed as agreed upon by a distinguished American symposium, Maurice Cranston was publishing in *The Encyclopedia of Philosophy* his conviction that in the United States "one might divide liberals into those who see freedom as something which belongs to the individual, to be defended against the encroachments of the state, and those who see freedom as something which belongs to society and which the state, as the central instrument of social betterment, can be made to enlarge and improve."[21] Of course, the dichotomy is not absolute. Some who claim the liberal label borrow first from one school, then from the other.

Though Jefferson, as we have seen, invoked the doctrine of implied powers even before Hamilton, we cannot without procrustean distortion fit Jefferson into the second school of American liberalism. He definitely did not see the national government as "the central instrument of social betterment."

Much stronger are Jefferson's affinities with the first school of American liberalism as defined by Cranston. He did "see freedom as something which belongs to the individual, to be defended against the encroachments of the state." This kind of liberal is increasingly described as *libertarian*, a more precise and therefore more useful term than the contradiction-embracing *liberal*.

Jefferson, however, is not an entirely representative libertarian. For example, his belief that the right to vote should be restricted to those with a property interest in society, and with a modicum of education, does not square well with the convictions of those whose libertarianism is incontestable.

When we say that Jefferson defies philosophical categorization it is not because his particular pigeonhole is hard to find but because it does not exist. Genius when united with imagination—and perhaps it always is—cannot be so confined. To be constructive it must have its consistencies; but it cannot, for the sake of consistency, abdicate all its options. Such abdication would make creative statesmanship impossible. Croly argued that the United States would fulfill its promise to its people when the means of Hamilton were used to attain the ends of Jefferson. The truth is that Hamilton's means were sometimes used for Jeffersonian ends by Jefferson himself. Witness the acquisition of the Louisiana Territory.

The fact that Jefferson was not willing to be consistently wrong in order to be consistent does not, however, mean that he was inconsistent with abnormal frequency. Most of the extreme statements that are cited to make him seem either radical or reactionary are culled from his private correspondence. In private communications with relatives and friends he indulged the artist within and escaped the restrictions of lawyer's prose to revel in the delights of colorful metaphor and outrageous hyperbole. Thus, intoxicated with his own rhetoric in a 1787 letter to William Stevens Smith, Jefferson wrote: "What country before ever existed a century and a half without a rebellion? . . . . The tree of liberty must be refreshed from time to time with the blood of patriots and tyrants. It is its natural manure." Yet in 1784, solemnly warning against glorification of revolution, he admonished that America's armed rebellion against the mother country had been an atypical revolt because of the quality of Washington's leadership: "The moderation and virtue of a single character has probably prevented this revolution from being closed, as most others have been, by a subversion of that liberty it was intended to establish." So great is the volume of Jefferson's correspondence that even a tiny proportion of it written with unguarded hyperbole affords numerous quotations for the use of those who portray him as an extremist.

A review of Jefferson's life reveals far more consistencies than inconsistencies. Of course, the fact that one looking back over the great man's career can see each major decision as part of a recognizable pattern does not mean that the pattern would have been apparent to any acute observer in Jefferson's early manhood. It does not even mean that, in the full course of his career, the next major step at every turn would have had about it the kind of inevitability that makes prediction more than guesswork.

Jefferson's life was like that of the most fascinating characters in fiction, marked now and then by actions which provide jolting surprises for the observer but which upon examination are seen to have been foreshadowed.

The first thread of consistency to become apparent in Jefferson's story is his large capacity for affection. This is evident in his loving reverence for his father and his great devotion to his sister. His companionship with his sister, marked by sensitivity to feminine sensibilities and epitomized by shared delight in music, foreshadowed his friendships with women throughout his life. He courted his wife by singing with her as she played the piano, and tradition says that two suitors waiting in Martha Skelton's hallway left in despair when they heard her voice joined in harmony with Jefferson's. Maria Cosway's musicianship was a strong factor in her attraction for Jefferson, and the shared pleasures of music nurtured their romance. When Jefferson and his daughters made music together at Monticello, he was happy in an ambience of love.

And of course, he was capable of strong masculine comradeship, as evidenced by his early friendship with John Page; his brotherhood of the spirit with Peter Carr; his lifelong gratitude to one of his teachers, William Small, and his continued devotion to another, George Wythe; his intellectual intimacy and affectionate bond of trust with James Madison; his paternal interest in such young disciples as William Short; and in the end his fraternal relationship with John Adams, born in sacrifice and risk for a common cause, outlasting the animosities of politics, so that at last the two aged survivors of a generation of giants found comfort in the thought of each other's existence.

Jefferson would never have echoed Jonathan Swift's statement: "All my love is towards individuals. . . . But principally I hate and detest that animal called man; although I heartily love John, Peter, Thomas, and so forth." The Virginian's compassion embraced not only relatives and friends, but strangers of every race and class. His sympathies were as universal as humanity itself.

Almost as old as the tug of affection with Jefferson was the habit of hyperbole for dramatic effect. It is evident in many of his earliest letters, particularly in his adolescent effusions to John Page compounded of exclamations, rolling periods, classical quotations, and eschatological despair over the loss of his fair Belinda. Hyperbole is not unusual in adolescent correspondence, and grandiloquence is not rare among the very young if they are intellectually inclined. But Jefferson's mature style is inchoate in his youthful letters. The rhythms are the same or similar.

With the passage of years, there are more short sentences among the long, more pithy phrases and striking figures of speech; and true eloquence replaces rococo. As the years pass, hyperbole appears only now and then, but when it does it burns its mark like a lightning strike. Frequently the mature letters are pregnant with wisdom, but even when they are it sometimes is expressed with an exaggeration more appropriate to poetic license than to scholarly discipline or magisterial reserve. And even when he sent shrewd observations from Europe as a diplomat, dispatched word of Federalist schemes to friends in Virginia as Vice President, and anonymously rallied opposition to the Alien and Sedition Acts, his use of code seemed to be more than a simple necessity. Sometimes there were signs of the same relish in the glamor of mystery with which adolescent Tom addressed coded letters to his friend John Page.

In opposition to his habit of hyperbole was his passion for precision. Everything must be measured. As a young man on his honeymoon he was aware that the distance between two landmarks was 4.9 miles, not five. When one he loved was buried, he noted how long it took two men shoveling to make a grave and figured how long it would take them to dig a given plot. He outfitted one of his carriage wheels with a device to measure the number of its revolutions. He provided his home with an anemometer that could be read indoors and surrounded himself with thermometers, barometers, and rain gauges. He invented devices for the more precise measurement of time. His *Notes on Virginia* and his voluminous report on international trade bristled with statistics. It would not have been strange if he had died, as Washington did, after measuring his own pulse.

Balancing Jefferson's scientific and technical approach was his strong esthetic sense. Probably he himself could not have told when he first came under beauty's sway, but his thralldom was for life. The white clouds of dogwood, the pink glory of redbud, and the cool blue of distant mountains became part of him before he knew what beauty was. All his life his heart beat faster to the blaze of autumn leaves, the blond glory of a woman's hair in sunlight, the chaste facade of a neoclassical temple, the rich reds and blues of Renaissance painting, the polished perfection of an Houdon sculpture, the cadence of sonorous verse, and the long-drawn note of a well-tuned cello. Beauty heightened his joys, assuaged his sorrows, and provided escape from the minutiae of an overburdened life.

Sobriety—ironically enough in view of partisan legends of Jefferson's carousing with a seraglio—seems to have been a lifelong characteristic. Some of his fellow students at the College of Wiliam and Mary complained of the dullness of his sober habits, and at least one, when he returned from his own nightly adventures, used to overturn the book-laden table at which young Tom labored. At different stages of his life various people testified to the fact that he did not smoke, preferred wine in moderation to any other alcoholic beverage, eschewed sexual innuendo in the presence of ladies, and refrained from cursing in company of either sex.

Some historians have gone so far in emphasizing Jefferson's sobriety as to assert that he had no sense of humor. What a strange conclusion about a man who included Latin puns in his correspondence, laughed at himself in his love letters, recalled with rueful amusement the rescue of a fiddle from the burning of his house, said that certain footmen were the most incorruptible of men because no payment of money could induce them to hurry, and claimed among his favorite books *Don Quixote* and *Tristram Shandy*! In fact, he carried Sterne's masterpiece on journey after journey and read it over and over. Was this because, lacking a sense of humor, he perused it repeatedly in futile efforts to determine why other people thought it was funny?

It is good that he was sober and industrious because his love of comfort was such that he might easily have become a sybarite. Though born near the frontier, he was reared with abundant servants and in childhood moved to the home of his Randolph cousins, where he enjoyed such luxuries as were known to the great planter families of Tidewater and Piedmont. In early years he was a great walker and all his life he was a good horseman, but he did not participate in the sports that hardened many of his peers to a more rugged way of life. He spoke contemptuously of Patrick Henry's wasting time in hunting. He would have agreed with Oscar Wilde's description of fox-hunting as "the unspeakable in pursuit of the uneatable." As a young man, delighting in the marital happiness of a friend, he reflected that domestic bliss required little except a loving mate. It could be found in a tiny cottage with a single table, two chairs—and a few servants. Though most of Jefferson's indebtedness was not his fault, he often exacerbated the problem by surrounding himself with costly elegance. He even spent a great deal of money in refurbishing very temporary quarters in Paris.

A tempered optimism was characteristic of Jefferson at every stage of his life except for the period immediately succeeding his wife's death. Ordinarily he tackled each problem with hope but without the easy assumption that success could be won without effort. Early academic achievement did not keep him from working as hard at his studies as if he had been a slow student. He always prepared for each law case as thoroughly as if the advantage of the law were on the other side and Blackstone were his opponent. At the age of seventy-three he realistically admitted, in a letter to John Adams, "My hopes, indeed, sometimes fail; but not oftener than the forebodings of the gloomy."[22] In the same letter, he said, "there are, indeed, . . . gloomy and hypochondriac minds, inhabitants of diseased bodies, disgusted with the present and despairing of the future, always counting that the worst will happen because it may happen. To these I say, how much pain have cost us the evils which have never happened! My temperament is sanguine. I steer my bark with Hope in the head, leaving Fear astern."

Jefferson had more than hope to sustain him when he became President. He had behind him a solid record of accomplishment that would have entitled him to an honored place in history if he had never become Chief Executive. His authorship of the Declaration of Independence alone would have guaranteed that his fame would last as long as the Republic itself. Of course, if Jefferson had not written that document, somebody else would have. But it is highly improbable that any other member of the Congress would have produced so eloquent a statement and one so successfully transcending the transient and the parochial. His Statute for Religious Freedom has been international in its influence. The friendships that he formed in Europe while Minister to France accelerated the exchange of Enlightenment ideas between the old world and the new. As Secretary of State he not only did a great deal to keep the fledgling republic out of the war between England and France but established a model of neutrality followed in later years by his own country and Great Britain as well. His leadership of the new Republican Party, which later became the Democratic Party, wrote an important chapter in American political history and helped to arrest the national drift toward autocracy. As the nation's most influential architect, he gave to its federal city the neoclassical forms that he favored, and they inspired copies throughout the United States. He also, of course, framed a plan for the addition of states to the Union and insured that some would be admitted as free states. And he planted in the minds of his fellow Americans a plan of public education that bore fruit at a later date.

The character and abilities that enabled Jefferson to achieve so many things before becoming President were fully developed by the time of his inauguration. The Presidency brought new applications of his talents, but no significant changes in him. If his character and abilities were already formed, so was his philosophy. Of course that philosophy was nowhere presented, in academic fashion, as a formal system. Its perimeters altered shape from time to time in response to the stimuli of events or the inner impulse toward growth. It had the structure of a multicellular organism composed of shifting subordinate elements in which four nuclei may be discerned.

One nucleus is the passionate belief that knowledge, while not a panacea, provides the means to solve most of the world's ills. This view was an article of faith with many Enlightenment philosophers, and Jefferson was encouraged in this belief by the instruction he received from Professor William Small, who had come to William and Mary as an apostle of the Scottish Enlightenment, as well as by his readings from British thinkers, and his participation in the salons of Paris. But these experiences did not so much inspire an attitude as confirm a predilection. Jefferson shared the faith of Bacon—one of his three chief heroes—that "knowledge is power." But even if Jefferson had not believed in the usefulness of knowledge he would have pursued it because of his insatiable need to know. Long before the cliché "A mind is a terrible thing to waste" Jefferson felt the truth of it in every fiber of his being. There was an organic union between Jefferson's personal aspiration for knowledge and his philosophical belief in it. As an article of political philosophy it found concise expression in his dictum, "If a nation expects to be ignorant and free, in a state of civilization, it expects what never has been and never will be."[23]

That he linked knowledge and freedom is not surprising because another nucleus of Jefferson's philosophy is expressed in words that we already have had occasion to quote several times: "I have sworn upon the altar of God eternal hostility against every form of tyranny over the mind of man." He chose as the motto on his seal ring, "Rebellion to tyrants is obedience to God." He became, as we have seen, sophisticated enough to realize that rebellions are always in grave danger of subverting the very freedoms which they are intended to secure. He learned that the defeat of tyranny is sometimes best achieved by evolution but he was sure that the struggle must be unremitting.

Indeed, like most geniuses celebrated for achievement, he believed in almost unremitting toil in pursuit of excellence in everything he deemed important. The thoroughness with which he prepared legal briefs and government reports was evidence of this attitude as was the care he lavished on personal letters, those to the unknown and the very young as well as those to the influential. In full cry, he pursued excellence with an enthusiasm to match his peers' in chasing the fox. He urged excellence upon his children, his neighbors, his beloved Commonwealth of Virginia and the Republic whose independence he had asserted. In the interest of excellence he improved the plant stock of the nation, invented a superior plow, and transformed public and domestic architecture. He advocated a public educational system offering greater rewards for excellence than any the western world then knew. And he was aware that the potential for excellence was not the property of a single class; he was passionately concerned that it not be wasted wherever it appeared. To say that less than one's best was good enough was a sure way to provoke the wrath of this normally equable man. He believed that civilization was a constant struggle against the primordial pull of barbarism. And though we have not found the specific figure of speech in his writings, Jefferson seems to have believed that any member of civilized society who did not strive for excellence in the pursuit of his duties was as criminally negligent as a shirking dike-builder standing on land precariously reclaimed from an angry sea.

The fourth nucleus of Jefferson's philosophy is one he shared with Edmund Burke, the concept of society as a compact among past, present, and future generations. He believed that each generation owed to its predecessors the preservation and utilization of their creations for human good. He also believed that each generation owed to its successors the improvement of its own heritage and the creation of new benefits for transmission to them. No man was more zealous in preservation of cultural treasures from the past and none was a more zealous promoter of invention. Nor did he, as some have, compartmentalize chronologically the arts and the sciences, looking only to the past for artistic inspiration while ready scientifically to invade new frontiers. His favorite sculptor was his contemporary Houdon who, although grounded in classicism, was the most innovative wielder of a chisel in his day. In architecture, government, and literature, Jefferson looked to classical models, but he was ready to adapt these models to the needs of his own time and of an envisioned future. "The earth belongs to the living," he insisted. In their stewardship of earth's resources, natural and cultural, the living must be responsible but they must not be bound by the dictates of their predecessors nor must they attempt to fetter their successors.

No antiquarian delighted more than Jefferson in old books (he haunted the stalls by the Seine in search of them), old ruins (like a lover he stared transfixed at the temple at Nimes), old tongues (he insisted on adding to the university curriculum one more "dead" language, Anglo-Saxon). Yet no man participated more fully in the life of his time, leaving his mark in law, politics, literature, linguistics, historical scholarship, the sciences, and sampling with eager appetite all that music and the graphic arts could offer. Nor did he neglect the social life of his time, fully participating in society in both the superficial and the deeper contexts of that term. His conversation charmed in the parlors of Williamsburg, the assembly room of the American Philosophical Society in Philadelphia, and the salons of Paris, and the two most celebrated beauties of Europe were his devoted admirers. Probably nobody in the western world in his time gave dependable friendship to a greater number or variety of people, ranging from unsophisticated youths to Hessian prisoners of war, English clergymen, Italian rebels, and French philosophers. His confidants ranged from slaves to nobles, from illiterates to savants.

Yet his passion for the past and his intense involvement in the present were not all absorbing. Near the end of his life he regretfully suspended for a time his readings in ancient classics in order to acquire a familiarity with the most recent scientific literature. A man must keep up. In the last letter that he wrote, ten days before his death, his enthusiasm was for the future: "All eyes are opened, or opening, to the rights of man. The general spread of the light of science has already laid open to every view the palpable truth that the mass of mankind [have] not been born with saddles on their backs, nor a favored few booted and spurred, ready to ride them, by the grace of God."[24]

Once again we are faced with a Jefferson paradox. He clung to the old and familiar. He chose to end his life where it had begun, in a little corner of Albemarle County, and on his beloved mountaintop where the happiest hours of his youth had been spent and where he said his thoughts always lingered. Though he sometimes spoke deprecatingly of his long pedigree, he cherished ancestral links with the past and was pleased when one of his daughters married a relative. He could be content to remain for years within a few miles of his familiar fields. Yet this same man's mind roamed the world and he sought out the alien, not just for novelty, but because of the opportunity to learn. He not only walked unafraid toward the future; he leaned forward to meet it. More than any other American statesman, Jefferson exemplifies that tension between the pull of the familiar and the lure of adventure which is the principal source of vitality in a society.

This exemplum is perhaps his greatest legacy to successive generations. When Jefferson wanted the General Assembly of Virginia to approve his design for a capitol, he stressed his plan's indebtedness to a classical model rather than its significant variations. He knew that people are much more willing to accept the new and strange when familiar aspects are emphasized. He used the same technique in presenting political ideas, citing both Athenian and Anglo-Saxon experience in arguing for an enlarged electorate, and drawing upon his capacious memory to present at least a partial precedent for each legal reform. Back of this artifice was a basic sincerity. Despite his fascination with new possibilities, he also sought the comfort of the familiar. But the practice of holding on to the old while reaching for the new is more than an instrument of individual conversion or a source of individual comfort. It is the secret of keeping a society or a culture alive.

Jakob Burckhardt maintained that "man, divorced from tradition, is too weak and too poor a creature to create greatness out of himself. . . . Without his past man is a barbarian."[25] Alfred North Whitehead argued that the idea of adventure belonged "to the essence of civilization."[26] History supports both views. Heraclitus said, "As with the bow and the lyre, so with the world: it is the tension of opposing forces that makes the structure one." The society that attempts to cut itself off from its heritage and the society that resists adventure both destroy the balance of tension essential to survival.

The stimulus of cross-fertilization so necessary to the healthy growth of a society comes not just from contacts with other contemporaneous societies but also with the past. A society that has overcome geographical parochialism may still suffer from temporal parochialism. The challenges provoking life-renewing responses can come from other times as well as other places.

A tension produced by a precariously maintained balance between the pull of tradition (even if it be only habit glorified) and the urge to adventure characterized such diverse civilizations as those of Egypt under the fourth dynasty and the greater part of the eighteenth, Babylonia under Hammurabi, Athens in the fifth century B.C., the Italian cities in the Renaissance, England in the Elizabethan and Jacobean periods, and the United States in the Revolutionary and Early Federal eras of which Jefferson was so prominent a part.

The questing spirit is a mark of life in a society as in an individual. But concentration upon the unfamiliar necessitates a counterbalancing awareness of the familiar. Societies, no less than the individuals comprising them, can have crippling identity crises.

The life-preserving balance between tradition and adventure is not simply an acquired characteristic of humanity in a state of civilization. James Harvey Robinson observed in 1929 that virtually all animals, including *homo sapiens*, evidence a "dogged obstinacy in clinging to (their) habits" and a "general suspicion of the unfamiliar."[27] He commented, "This trait has served to slow down the process of change but at the same time has greatly increased the security and permanence of each achievement." He also notes: "Among animal proclivities there is, however, from the one-celled organisms upward, a lifesaving tendency to make random movements, extensions and contractions, to hasten hither and thither, in the pursuit of food and mates. The restlessness and groping are among man's legacies also. They affect his routine and static habits, and lie behind and back of the inventions and discoveries he has made."

How can one tell when a society is threatened by too much alteration of tension between tradition and adventure? More than forty centuries of experience suggest that there are at least four danger signals of too strong an impulse for change, and at least three warning signs of too strong a pull toward tradition. The impulse to change is dangerously strong when people are uncertain of their identity and manifest a general rootlessness; when there is little curiosity about the past, even in relation to the present, and a tendency to consider "irrelevant" everything not here and now; a compartmentalized view of past, present, and future that prevents a perception of continuity; and the absence of a common cultural language for the educated. Danger signs of too strong a pull to tradition include unreasonable suspicion of "outsiders"; the existence of large underprivileged elements who feel excluded from the society's heritage; and a tendency to consider "irrelevant," and hence not a proper element of formal education, everything not fitted to existing forms of the culture. With varying degrees of understanding and success, Jefferson addressed each of these seven dangers.

His fight against these threats revealed him to be a man of vision. The eloquence with which he stated his views, and his ability to inspire concern in others, prove his skill in communication. American historians are generally agreed that vision and skill in communication are the two characteristics that most often distinguish a great President from a merely good one. Jefferson, along with Lincoln, Wilson, Theodore Roosevelt, and Franklin Roosevelt, is often cited in support of this premise.

That Jefferson was a great President is as far beyond dispute as almost any subjective judgment of human abilities can be. Would he be a great President today if his knowledge could be updated? Shoving aside the inevitable consideration that to alter any factor in the chain of events is potentially to alter all subsequent ones, it seems safe to say that Jefferson's great vision, glowing eloquence, tremendous industry, honorable character, and wide-embracing humanity would make him a great national leader today.

Could he get elected? Certainly not if he adhered to the wish that he expressed to James Madison, that American candidates would always "stand" for office, not "run" for it. Success in politics today demands a much more aggressive approach. It has become a cliché that, to win, the aspirant must have "fire in his belly." When one recalls that Jefferson despised the custom of candidates' providing free drinks on election day but complied with it as a device necessary to success, it seems likely that he would have altered his insistence on "standing" rather than "running" if he really wanted office. What of his ability to communicate? His word mastery would be impressive in any age and he was extraordinarily persuasive in committee and in private conversation, but even his best friends, and certainly Jefferson himself, admitted that he was ineffective as a public speaker. His chief problem in addressing large audiences was a voice which, even when strained to the point of harshness, was inaudible beyond the first few rows. Public address systems would solve this problem with large audiences. Radio and television would provide the one to one encounters in which he was so successful.

Another pertinent question is whether Jefferson would be willing to enter politics today. Although he was the product of a social class and a society that stressed *noblesse oblige* and translated the sentiment directly into political terms, he was often reluctant to be a candidate and was jealous of the time that politics took from scholarship. In American society today, when it is no longer presumed that the best minds will find their way into politics, when more enter business, scholarship, or the arts, it is by no means certain that Jefferson would seek office. Such contemporaries of his as Madison, George Mason, Richard Henry Lee, George Washington, John Adams, and Franklin might feel a comparable reluctance. The weakness is perhaps not so much in the Founding Fathers as in our society. A situation in which virtually all the best minds went into politics certainly would not be desirable today. But if politics were attractive to a larger proportion of outstanding intellects, our society would be better off.

Those concerned about the survival of our civilization can find few more instructive models than Thomas Jefferson. Not all the apparent inconsistencies in his character and career yield to investigation. Any introspective person discovers puzzling inconsistencies in himself. As Jefferson was a man of extraordinary subtlety, it is not surprising that some of his inconsistencies defy analysis. But the major contradictions, as between tradition and innovation, can be seen as strengths rather than weaknesses when viewed as part of the tension essential to vitality.

James David Barber, whose seminal work *The Presidential Character* has provided the most commonly used scholarly apparatus for classifying Presidents of the United States, has described Jefferson as clearly "active-positive." He explains that "active-positive Presidents want most to achieve results" as distinguished from passive-positives, "who are after love." Interestingly enough, while Jefferson projected an active-positive image and was, as Professor Barber indicates, active-positive in terms of accomplishments, he was strongly tempted toward the passive-positive role. What great leader's correspondence shows more than Jefferson's an almost insatiable hunger for love? Or evidences more convincingly the internal struggle between the urge to determine the course of public events and the longing to lose himself in art and scholarship, not only for renewal but also for refuge? United in Jefferson were the adventurer of Tennyson's "Ulysses" and the esthetic recluse of his "Palace of Art."

Yet this same dichotomy may well have helped to shape him philosophically to the delicate balance of venturing and conservation. No amount of speculation on the origins of his attitudes can destroy the validity of his philosophy. That philosophy gains relevancy from catholicity. His sympathy, like his curiosity, was universal. His principles were consistent but his applications were varied; so, like most great minds, his is not easily pigeonholed. In this fact lies its greatest strength.

In this circumstance, too, lies the opportunity for distortion. Not all of it has been the work of politicians either deliberately or overzealously twisting words from their context to exaggerate a single aspect of Jefferson's thought. Equally at fault are twentieth-century scholars who in overardent discipleship have ignored any utterances of the Monticello master that are inconsistent with true-blue liberalism. They have not heeded the advice which he gave to the scholars he selected to teach at the University of Virginia: "This institution will be based on the illimitable freedom of the human mind. For here we are not afraid to follow truth wherever it may lead." Hence, we have in Thomas Jefferson one of American history's strangest cases of mistaken identity.

Nevertheless there is some truth in virtually all the claims put forth by Jefferson's admirers for, whatever their philosophical persuasion, there is something in him that answers the demands of their minds and hearts. We may, paraphrasing Jefferson's "we are all Republicans, we are all Federalists," say, "we are all Jeffersonians." Some will cite one aspect (perhaps opposition to central power), others another (perhaps faith in public education), but each—liberal, moderate, or conservative—will find enough affinity for Jefferson to claim allegiance. Of no other American statesman can this be said. No one could say: we are all Washingtonians, all Lincolnians, all Wilsonians, or Rooseveltians. No other American statesman's name provides a common roof under which the diverse peoples of the Republic can foregather.

Notes for
Thomas Jefferson

CHAPTER II

1. *The Adams-Jefferson Letters,* Vol. II, ed. Lester J. Cappon, (Chapel Hill: University of North Carolina Press), 464.

2. Ibid., 467.

3. Ibid., 469 (Adams to Jefferson, May 3, 1816).

4. Ibid., 483-484 (Jefferson to Adams, Aug. 1, 1816).

5. Ibid., 612 (Jefferson to Adams, Dec. 18, 1825).

6. Henry S. Randall, *The Life of Thomas Jefferson,* Vol. I (Philadelphia: J.P. Lippincott & Co., 1865), 612. The date was recorded in Col. Peter Jefferson's *Book of Common Prayer.* Before 1752, dates in Great Britain and her colonies differed from those on the Continent because of the English lag in adopting the Reformed Calendar of Gregory XIII. The difference was one of ten days in the seventeenth century and eleven in the eighteenth. The Gregorian dating is known as New Style (N.S.) whereas the older calculation is called Old Style (O.S.).

7. Dumas Malone, *Jefferson and His Time,* Vol. I; *Jefferson the Virginian* (Boston: Little, Brown and Co., 1948), 27.

8. Of course, estimable scholars close to early sources have accepted the more spectacular version. Note especially Randall, I, 15. Randall heard the popular account from Thomas Jefferson's own grandchildren.

9. Randall, *The Life of Thomas Jefferson,* I, 15.

10. Ibid.

11. *Autobiography of Thomas Jefferson* (Boston, 1948), 19.

12. E.M. Sanchez-Saavedra, *A Description of the Country: Virginia's Cartographers and Their Maps, 1607-1881* (Richmond: Virginia State Library, 1975), 25-39.

13. Nathan Schachner, *Thomas Jefferson, A Biography,* Vol. I (New York: Thomas Yoseloff, 1957), 3-5. Information on Thomas Jefferson II is derived from this volume as well as from Malone, I, 8-9, and *Burke's Presidential Families of the United States* (London: Burke's Peerage Limited, 1975), 97.

14. Information on Thomas Jefferson I and his antecedents is derived from Schachner, I, 2-3, and especially from *Burke's Presidential Families,* p. 97.

15. *The Writings of Thomas Jefferson,* ed. Paul Leicester Ford, Vol. I (New York: G.P. Putnam's Sons, 1892), 388-389.

16. Virginius Dabney, *Virginia the New Dominion* (Garden City, New York: Doubleday, 1971), 46-47; Jonathan Daniels, *The Randolphs of Virginia* (Garden City, New York: Doubleday & Co. Inc., 1972), 16-33, 333-335; H.J. Eckenrode, *The Randolphs: The Story of a Virginia Family* (New York: The Bobbs-Merrill Co., 1946), 31-43.

17. Marquis de Chastellux, *Travels in North America in the Years 1780, 1781 and 1782,* trans. Howard C. Rice, Jr., Vol. II (Chapel Hill: University of North Carolina Press, 1963), 151.

18. David S. Jordan and Sarah L. Kimball, *Your Family Tree* (Baltimore: Genealogical Publishing Co., 1968), 97, 135, 159, 161-162; Arthur Adams and Frederick L. Weis, *The Magna*

Charta Sureties, 1215: The Barons Named in the Magna Charta 1215, and Some of Their Descendants Who Settled in America, 1607-1650, 2nd authorized ed. with revisions and corrections by Walter Lee Shepard, Jr., (Baltimore: Genealogical Publishing Co., 1968), 60, 114, 123-124. *Burke's Presidential Families,* 128, 611.

19. Account of Jane Randolph based on Randall, I, 15-17.

20. Malone, *Jefferson and His Time,* I, 435-437.

21. Randall, *The Life of Thomas Jefferson,* I, 17. See table of births copied from Peter Jefferson's *Book of Common Prayer.*

22. Ibid., 41.

23. Ibid., 11.

24. Ibid., 17.

25. Sarah N. Randolph, *The Domestic Life of Thomas Jefferson* (New York: Frederick Ungar Publishing Co., 1958), 39.

26. Sanchez-Saavedra, *A Description of the Country,* 26-27.

27. Sarah Randolph, *The Domestic Life,* 19-20.

28. Sanchez-Saavedra, *A Description of the Country,* 30-39.

29. Malone, *Jefferson and His Time,* I, 26-27.

30. Randall, *The Life of Thomas Jefferson,* II, 192; Malone, I, pp. 39-40.

31. Randall, *The Life of Thomas Jefferson,* I, 13.

32. Ibid., 46.

33. Ibid., Randall, I, 14.

34. Malone, *Jefferson and His Time,* I, 45.

35. Ibid., I, 42.

36. Randall, *The Life of Thomas Jefferson,* I, 41.

37. Thomas Jefferson, *The Papers of Thomas Jefferson,* ed, Julian P. Boyd, Vol. I, 1760-1776 (Princeton, N.J.: Princeton University Press, 1950), 3. This is the earliest known letter written by Thomas Jefferson.

38. The account of Thomas Jefferson's visit with Colonel Dandridge is based on Ford, IX, 339-345n, 475-476n; X, 59-60, information that Jefferson himself furnished William Wirt; and on Randall, I, 20-21.

The physical description of Jefferson is based largely on Randall, I, p. 34. That historian had the benefit of conversations with Jefferson's family and had before him as he wrote several locks of the statesman's hair which had been cut at different ages. In addition, the failure of people who saw Jefferson to agree on the color of his hair is sufficient evidence of the subtlety of its coloring.

39. Philip Vickers Fithian, *Journal and Letters, 1767-1774,* ed. Hunter Dickinson Farish (Colonial Williamsburg, Inc. 1957), 177.

CHAPTER III

1. Edward Dumbauld, *Thomas Jefferson: American Tourist,* (Norman: University of Oklahoma Press, 1946), 4-5.

2. Alf J. Mapp, Jr., *The Virginia Experiment,* 2nd ed. (La Salle, Ill. 1974), Plate XII.

3. Description of Duke of Gloucester Street as it would have been in 1760 is based on personal examination of both restored and reconstructed buildings and examination of the architectural drawings and archeological findings of Colonial Williamsburg, Inc.

4. Dumbauld, 31.

5. Ibid.

6. Ibid., 79.

7. Thomas J. Randolph, ed., *Memoir, Correspondence, and Miscellanies from the Papers of Thomas Jefferson* (Charlottesville, VA: F. Carr and Co., 1829), Vol. I, 2.

8. Profile sketch reproduced in Lally Weymouth, ed., *Thomas Jefferson: The Man, His World, His Influence* (New York: G.P. Putnam's Sons, 1973), 15, where the caption incorrectly gives Small the title "Rev."

9. J.E. Morpurgo, *Their Majesties' Royall Colledge,* (Williamsburg: Endowment Association of the College of William and Mary, 1976); 133. The account of Small's activities is based on 135-40 of the same work.

10. Psalm XIX, 1.

11. Ralph Ketcham, "Thomas Jefferson," in *The Encyclopedia of Philosophy,* ed. Paul Edwards, 1967, Vol. 4, 259.

12. Ibid.

13. Crane Brinton, "The Enlightenment," in *The Encyclopedia of Philosophy,* ed. Paul Edwards, 1967, Vol. 2, 520.

14. Morpurgo, *Their Majesties' Royall Colledge,* 133.

15. Description based on portrait of Fauquier by Benjamin Wilson in collection of the Thomas Coram Foundation for Children, London. Reproduced in William Howard Adams, *The Eye of Thomas Jefferson,* National Gallery of Art, Washington, 1976, 12.

16. Mapp, *The Virginia Experiment,* 190-220, 328-29.

17. Description based on Catherine Carter Critcher reproduction of earlier portrait of Wythe. Reproduced in David John Mays, *Edmund Pendleton* (Cambridge: Harvard University Press, 1952), Vol. 2, opp. 294.

18. Ibid., Vol. I, 226.

19. Letter of January 15, 1815, to L. H. Girardin in A.E. Burgh, ed., *The Writings of Thomas Jefferson,* The Jefferson Memorial Edition, Washington, D.C., 1907, Vol. XIV, 231.

20. *Virginia Historical Register* (July 1850), 151.

21. Henry S. Randall, *The Life of Thomas Jefferson* (Philadelphia: J. B. Lippincott & Co., 1865), Vol. I, 22-23.

22. Ibid., 16-17.

23. Ibid., 34-35.

24. William Wirt Henry, *Patrick Henry, Life, Correspondence and Speeches* (New York, 1891), 29-30; William Wirt, *The Life of Patrick Henry* (Philadelphia, 1836), 28-30. Details of W.W. Henry and Wirt versions have been questioned. See Robert Douthat Meade, *Patrick Henry: Patriot in the Making* (Philadelphia: J. B. Lippincott, 1957), 96-98.

25. Governor of Virginia, 1808-1811; father of John Tyler, tenth president of the United States.

26. Lyon Gardiner Tyler, *Letters and Times of the Tylers* (Richmond, Va., 1884), Vol. I, 55.

27. Morpurgo, *Their Majesties' Royall Colledge,* p. 134.

28. *The Papers of Thomas Jefferson,* ed. Julian P. Boyd (Princeton: Princeton University Press, 1950), Vol. I, 76-81; Randall, *Life of Thomas Jefferson,* I, 24-30.

29. *The Papers of Thomas Jefferson,* I, 77.

30. *Adams-Jefferson Letters,* ed. Lester J. Cappon (Chapel Hill: University of North Carolina Press, 1959), Vol. II, 307.

31. *The Papers of Thomas Jefferson,* I, 3-4.

32. Ibid., 5-6.

33. Ibid., 7-9.

34. Ibid., 9-11.

35. Ibid., 11.

36. Ibid., 12.

37. Ibid., 13-14.

38. Ibid., 15.

39. Ibid., 15-16.

40. Randall, *Life of Thomas Jefferson,* I, 53-55

41. Ibid., 40.

42. *The Papers of Thomas Jefferson,* I, 2.

43. A more detailed description of the ensuing legislative scene is in Mapp, *The Virginia Experiment,* 299-303. Evidence supporting the exact wording here given for Henry's resolutions is discussed in Freeman, *Washington,* III, 131, n. 29, and Appendix III-3, 592-595.

44. It is popularly believed that Henry, instead of finishing his sentence as here quoted, shouted, "If this be treason, make the most of it." This more dramatic version, followed by Robert Douthat Meade (*Patrick Henry,* I, 175-81), is derived from William Wirt Henry, whose *Patrick Henry, Life, Correspondence and Speeches,* though a valuable work, puts strong trust in uncertain family traditions and is marred by notable errors. Our version is drawn from the manuscript "History of Virginia" by Edmund Randolph, who lived in the house of his uncle, Peyton Randolph, one of the chief participants in the legislative scene, and is corroborated by the earwitness account of an unidentified Frenchman whose journal was discovered by M. Abel Doysie in the *Archives* of the Hydrographic Service of the Ministry of the Marine in Paris. See Mapp, *The Virginia Experiment,* 529-30, n. 87.

45. Thomas J. Randolph, *Memoir,* 3.

CHAPTER IV

1. *Journals of the House of Burgesses, 1761-65,* 359-60. Hereafter cited as J.H.B., 1761-65.

2. Ibid., lxvi.

3. Ibid., lxvi-lxvii.

4. Douglas Southall Freeman, *George Washington,* III, 140.

5. David Mays, *Edmund Pendleton,* I, 164, 330, n. 41.

6. Letter of September 20, 1765, to Francis Dandridge, quoted in Freeman, *Washington,* III, 143-44.

7. *J.H.B., 1761-65,* lxix.

8. Randall, *Life of Thomas Jefferson.* I, 41.

9. Ibid.

10. Randolph, *Domestic Life,* 39.

11. *Papers of Thomas Jefferson,* Julian P. Boyd, ed. I, 21.

12. Ibid., 18-19.

13. Ibid., 19.

14. Ibid., 20.

15. Ibid., 18.

16. Thomas J. Wertenbaker, *Norfolk, Historic Southern Port,* 188-89.

17. The description of Dr. Morgan's appearance is based on the 1764 portrait by Angela Kauffmann reproduced in *The Eye of Thomas Jefferson,* ed. William Howard Adams (National Gallery of Art, Washington, 1976), 97. Information on Morgan and his meeting with Jefferson is from 80-81, 97, and 211 of the same work.

18. Ibid., 80-81.

19. Randall, *Life of Thomas Jefferson,* I, 46.

20. *Papers of T.J.,* I, 21.

21. Frank L. Dewey, "Thomas Jefferson's Law Practice," *Virginia Magazine of History and Biography,* LXXXV (July 1977), 289. Mr. Dewey's article has proved wrong the assumptions of generations of Jefferson biographers. His research with the Casebook and Fee Book and the Account Books for 1771, 1772, and 1774 has opened the way to a startling reevaluation of the significance of Jefferson's legal experience to his political career. All of my own research on this subject was stimulated originally by Mr. Dewey's work.

22. Mays, *Pendleton,* I, 224.

23. Dewey, "Thomas Jefferson's Law Practice," 289.

24. James Parton, *Life of Thomas Jefferson* (Boston, 1874), as quoted in Dewey, 290.

25. John W. Davis, "Thomas Jefferson, Attorney at Law," address to Virginia State Bar Association, 1926, as quoted in Dewey, 290.

26. Marie G. Kimball, *Jefferson: The Road to Glory, 1743 to 1776* (New York, 1943), 90.

27. Malone, I, 119.

28. *Papers of T.J.,* II, 235.

29. Malone, I, 439-40.

30. Ibid., 115-16.

31. *Thomas Jefferson's Garden Book, 1766-1824,* annotated by Edwin M. Betts (Philadelphia: American Philosophical Society, 1944).

32. Ibid., Aug. 3, 1767.

33. John Hammond Moore, *Albemarle: Jefferson's County* (Charlottesville, Va., 1976), 35-40, 68-86. The Walkers and their relationship with the Jeffersons and their county are discussed in the foregoing pages.

34. Jefferson did not admit to greater offenses in the following episode than are here recorded. Charges of greater offenses with Mrs. Walker were made by political enemies during his Presidency. These charges do not come within the scope of this volume. They are printed in Malone, I, Appendix III, 447-51.

35. Ibid., 129.

36. Charles S. Sydnor, *Gentlemen Freeholders* (Chapel Hill, 1952), 53-54.

37. "Chairing" of the victors was a custom in Virginia as in England.

38. Alf. J. Mapp, Jr. *The Virginia Experiment* 2nd ed. (La Salle, Ill., 1974), 332.

39. Ibid.

40. *J.H.B., 1766-69,* 188-89.

41. Mays, *Pendleton,* I, 250.

42. Albert Ellery Bergh, ed., *The Writings of Thomas Jefferson* (Washington, D.C., 1905), Vol. XIV, 339.

43. This description of Pendleton is based on the excellent Mays, *Pendleton,* I and II.

44. *Papers of T.J.,* I, 26-27.

45. Lipscomb and Bergh, *Writings of Thomas Jefferson,* XIV, 339.

46. *J.H.B., 1766-69,* 168, 170-71.

47. Ibid., 171.

48. Ibid., 173-74.

49. The description of Nicholas is based on Hugh Blair Grigsby, *The Virginia Convention of 1776* (Richmond, Va., 1855), 63-68.

50. Lipscomb and Bergh, *Writings of Thomas Jefferson,* XIV, 339-40.

51. *J.H.B., 1766-69,* 214.

52. The description of Blair is based on Grigsby, *Virginia Convention,* 68-74.

53. The description of Lee is based on the portrait reproduced as Plate XIII in Mapp, *The Virginia Experiment;* Grigsby, *Virginia Convention,* 130-43; Burton J. Hendrick, *The Lees of Virginia* (Boston, 1935), 80, 86-87, 100-102; John Adams' description in *Letters of the Continental Congress,* ed., Edmund Cody Burnett (Washington, D.C., 1921), I, 2.

54. *J.H.B., 1766-69,* 216.

55. Ibid., 218.

56. The description of George Washington is based largely on Douglas Southall Freeman, *George Washington,* Vols. I-VI (New York, 1948-1954), especially Vol. III; James Thomas Flexner, *George Washington,* Vols. I-IV (Boston, 1972); various oil portraits, and especially the Houdon statue in the State Capitol in Richmond and Houdon busts.

57. The description of Mason is based largely on Kate Mason Rowland, *The Life of George Mason,* Vols. I-II (New York, 1892); *The Papers of George Mason,* ed. Robert A. Rutland (Chapel Hill, 1970); Robert A. Rutland, *George Mason—Reluctant Statesman* (Charlottesville, 1963).

58. *J.H.B., 1766-69,* xl.

59. Letter of July 12, 1736, to Lord Egmont, in Beverly B. Munford, *Virginia's Attitude Toward Slavery and Secession* (Richmond, 1909), 16-17.

60. *The Commonplace Book of Thomas Jefferson,* int. and notes by Gilbert Chinard (Baltimore, 1926).

61. *J.H.B., 1766-69,* xl.

62. Freeman, *Washington,* III, 223-24.

63. Mapp, *The Virginia Experiment,* 337.

64. Malone, I, 137.

65. *J.H.B., 1766-69,* 226-27.

66. Ibid., 227.

67. Freeman, *Washington,* III, 250.

68. Ibid., 241-42.

69. Obituary address by William Wirt, printed in Bergh, *Writings of Thomas Jefferson,* XIII, xiii.

70. *J.H.B., 1766-69,* 228.

71. Agnes Rothery, *Houses Virginians Have Loved* (New York, 1954), 165. Malone, I, 144.

CHAPTER V

1. Malone, I, 126.

2. T.J. to John Page, February 21, 1770; *Papers of T.J.,* I, 34-35.

3. Ibid., 36.

4. John Page to T.J., March 6, 1770; *Papers of T.J.,* I, 38.

5. Thomas Nelson, Sr., to T.J., March 6, 1770; *Papers of T.J.,* I, 37.

6. Thomas Nelson, Jr,. to T.J., March 6, 1770; *Papers of T.J.,* I, 37.

7. George Wythe to T.J., March 9, 1770; *Papers of T.J.,* I, 38.

8. *The Commonplace Book of Thomas Jefferson, A Repertory of His Ideas on Government, With an Introduction and Notes by Gilbert Chinard* (Baltimore, 1926).

9. Ibid., 5.

10. T.J. to Robert Skipwith, July 17, 1771; *Papers of T.J.,* I, 74-75. Although we have examined Jefferson's writings for literary sources both before and since reading Garry Wills' *Inventing America: Thomas Jefferson's Declaration of Independence* (New York: Doubleday, 1978), his scholarship has been so thorough and so valuable that it deserves a special acknowledgement apart from the customary end notes.

11. T.J. to Robert Skipwith, August 3, 1771; *Papers of T.J.,* I, 76-77.

12. Thomas Jefferson, *An Essay Towards Facilitating Instruction in the Anglo-Saxon and Modern Dialects of the English Language For the Use of the University of Virginia* (New York: John F. Trow for the Board of Trustees for the University of Virginia, 1851), introductory letter to Sir Herbert Croft, October 30, 1798 (letter to Croft reproduced in Lipscomb and Bergh, *Writings of T.J.,* XVIII, 361-364.)

13. Ibid.

14. Alf J. Mapp, Jr., *The Golden Dragon: Alfred the Great and His Times* (La Salle, Ill.: Open Court, 1974), 85-91.

15. Ibid., 166-169; F.M. Stenton, *Anglo-Saxon England,* 2nd ed. (Oxford, 1971), 635-636; Dorothy Whitelock, *Changing Currents in Anglo-Saxon Studies* (Cambridge, 1958), 24.

16. Thomas Jefferson, *Notes on the State of Virginia* (Chapel Hill, N.C., 1955), 164-169.

17. T.J. to John Adams, April 11, 1823 (*Thomas Jefferson: Writings,* 1466: The Library of America, N.Y., 1984). Chinard notes the similarity between Voltaire's statement and Jefferson's.

18. Anthony Ashley Cooper, 3rd Earl of Shaftesbury (1671-1713).

19. E. Millicent Sowerby, comp., *Catalogue of the Library of Thomas Jefferson,* 5 vols. (Washington, D.C.: The Library of Congress, 1952-1959), Vol. II, 11.

20. Wills, *Inventing America,* 169-171.

21. Alf J. Mapp, Jr., *The Virginia Experiment,* 2nd ed. (La Salle, Ill. 1974), 15-16.

22. Wills, *Inventing America,* 238.

23. *Commonplace Book,* entry 721, 182-183.

24. *Commonplace Book,* entry 718, 182-183.

25. Ibid.

26. T.J. to Robert Skipwith, August 3, 1771; *Papers of T.J.,* I, 78, 81.

27. Randall, *Life of Thomas Jefferson,* I, 63. Sarah N. Randolph, *Domestic Life,* 4. "Memoir of a Monticello Slave," as dictated to Charles Campbell by Isaac; in James A. Bear, Jr., ed., *Jefferson at Monticello* (Charlottesville: University Press of Virginia, 1967), 5.

28. Randall, *Life of Thomas Jefferson,* I, 63.

29. Ibid., I, 64.

30. Thomas Jefferson Randolph, ed., *Memoir, Correspondence, and Miscellaneous,* I, 3. Ford, I, 6.

31. T.J. to Thomas Adams, February 20, 1771; *Papers of T.J.,* I, 62.

32. T.J. to Thomas Adams, June 1, 1771; *Papers of T.J.,* I, 71.

33. T.J. to Thomas Adams, February 20, 1771; *Papers of T.J.,* I, 62.

34. T.J. to Thomas Adams, June 1, 1771; *Papers of T.J.,* I, 71.

35. John may have died before the wedding. See Schachner, 86, 526-527, n. 1. But one must

consider that the placing of orders for imported goods and the receipt of those goods were often far apart on the calendar. Even after John's death, Jefferson may have been billed for goods ordered for the child when he was alive. T.J.'s own memorandum gave the death date as June 10, 1771.

36. Malone, I, 157-160.

37. Randall, *Life of Thomas Jefferson*, I, 64. Jefferson, in his January 26, 1772, entry in the *Garden Book* (55), takes special notice of the snow, calling it "the deepest snow we have ever seen in Albermarle."

38. Description by T.J.'s elder daughter, Martha Jefferson Randolph, who heard the story from both parents. Randall, *Life of Thomas Jefferson*, I, 64, n. 1; Also Sarah N. Randolph, *Domestic Life*, 44-45.

39. T.J. to Thomas Mann Randolph, October 19, 1792; Jefferson Papers, Library of Congress, Document No. 13465, microfilm series 1, reel 17.

40. In the letter to Randolph, Jefferson said, "Having little confidence myself in medicine and especially in the case of infants, and a great deal in the efforts of nature, I direct my hopes towards them."

41. Nigel Nicolson, *Great Houses of the Western World* (London, 1968), 257-260; Thomas Tileston Waterman, *The Mansions of Virginia* (Chapel Hill, 1945), 341-346, 386-396; Fiske Kimball, *Thomas Jefferson, Architect* (Boston, 1916).

42. Margaret Bayard Smith, *The First Forty Years of Washington Society* (New York: Charles Scribner's Sons, 1906), 65.

43. "How sublime to look down into the workhouse of nature, to see her clouds, hail, snow, rain, thunder, all fabricated at our feet!" T.J. to Maria Cosway, 1786, Ford, IV, 315.

44. Mapp, *The Virginia Experiment*, 340-341.

45. *Virginia Cavalcade*, I, 20-22; *Journal of the House of Burgesses, 1770-72*, 119, 122-123, 127-129, 131, 134-136, 137-138; Mapp, *The Virginia Experiment*, 341.

46. Ibid., 342; Robert L. Scribner, "Nemesis at Gwynn's Island," *The Virginia Cavalcade*, II (Spring, 1953), 42. The physical description of Dunmore is based on the portrait by Sir Joshua Reynolds, a copy of which, by Charles X. Harris, is owned by the Virginia Historical Society.

47. Freeman, *Washington*, III, 289-290.

48. J.H.B., 1773-1776, 22.

49. Ibid.

50. Thomas Jefferson Randolph, I, 4.

51. Sarah N. Randolph, 46, Ford, I, 7-9.

52. Malone, I, 160-161.

53. Thomas Jefferson Randolph, I, 4-5.

54. *J.H.B., 1773-1776*, 39.

55. Freeman, *Washington*, III, 316.

56. Ibid.

57. Ibid.

58. Sarah N. Randolph, 45.

59. Ibid.

60. Ibid., 47.

61. Malone, I, 161.

62. Ibid., 431, n. 3.

63. Virginius Dabney, *The Jefferson Scandals* (NY, 1981), 26-27. This is the definitive work on T.J.'s relationship with Sally Hemings.

64. A genealogical chart of the Hemings family appears in Bear, *Jefferson at Monticello*, following 24. Regarding the paternity of Betty's children, see John Chester Miller, *The Wolf by the Ears: Thomas Jefferson and Slavery* (New York: The Free Press, 1977), 162-163.

65. Ford, I, 6; Malone, I, 441-445.

66. Malone, I, 164.

67. Schachner, 108.

68. Ellen Randolph Coolidge memoir, ms. 66, U. Va., quoted in Fawn McKay Brodie, *Thomas Jefferson, an Intimate History* (New York: Norton, 1974), 81.

69. Both the details of the flood and of the transaction with the minister were meticulously recorded by T.J. in his Account Book.

CHAPTER VI

1. David John Mays, *Edmund Pendleton, 1721-1803; a Biography* (Cambridge: Harvard University Press, 1952), 262, 272.

2. George Mason to Martin Cockburn, May 26, 1774; in *The Virginia Historical Register,* III (January 1850), 28.

3. Thomas J. Randolph *Memoir,* I, 5.

4. John Rushworth (c. 1612-1690), author of *Historical Collections of Private Passages of State.*

5. Thomas J. Randolph, I, 6.

6. *J.H.B., 1773-1776,* 124.

7. Ibid., 132.

8. Ibid.

9. Ibid., xiv.

10. Mapp, *The Virginia Experiment,* 349.

11. Freeman, *Washington,* III, 354.

12. *Calendar of Virginia State Papers and Other Manuscripts, 1652-1781,* ed. W.P. Palmer (11 vols. Richmond, Va., 1875-1893), VIII, 53.

13. *Papers of T.J.,* I, 116.

14. *Papers of T.J.,* I, 117. This sentence does not appear in all versions. See *Papers of T.J.,* I, 137, n. 34.

15. *Papers of T.J.,* I, 137, n. 34.

16. A complaint against this assertion would be made in the Declaration of Independence.

17. Thomas J. Randolph, I, 7.

18. Ibid.

19. Ibid.

20. *Papers of T.J.,* I, 671-672.

21. Thomas J. Randolph, I, 101.

22. All quotations from "A Summary View" are based on the text in *Papers of T.J.,* I, 121-137.

23. Matthew P. Andrews, *Virginia, the Old Dominion,* 233.

24. Beverly B. Munford, *Virginia's Attitude Toward Slavery and Secession (Richmond, 1909),* 17.

25. *Papers of T.J.,* I, 670-671.

26. Thomas J. Randolph, I, 101.

27. Ford, I. 13-14. *Papers of T.J.,* I, 676.

28. Thomas J. Randolph, I, 7.

29. Argument in the Case of Howell vs. Netherland, April, 1770; Ford, *Writings of T.J.,* I, 380, 381.

30. Peter Force, *American Archives* (9 vols.; Washington, D.C., 1837-1853), Series 4, II, 167.

31. Moses Coit Tyler, *Patrick Henry* (Ithaca, NY: Great Seal Books, 1962), 147-149.

32. Edward Carrington. His wish was carried out more than three decades later.

33. Edmund Randolph, "Edmund Randolph's Essay on the Revolutionary History of Virginia (1774-1782)," *Virginia Magazine of History and Biography,* XLIII (1935), 223.

34. *Papers of T.J.,* I, 159-160.

CHAPTER VII

1. The account of the gunpowder episode is based largely on Force, *Archives,* Series 4, II, 168-170, 371-372; Freeman, *Washington,* III, 414-415; and *The Virginia Gazette* (Dixon & Hunter), April 29, 1775, supplement.

2. Robert Donald to Patrick Henry, April 18, 1775; in Mays, *Pendleton,* II, 354, n. 34.

3. See Fairfax Harrison, "The Equine F.F.V.'s," *Virginia Magazine of History and Biography, XXXV* (October 1927), 351-361. Also Jefferson, *Account Books,* May 7, 1775.

4. The phrase is Dumas Malone's, Malone, I, 197.

5. T.J. to William Small, May 7, 1775; *Papers of T.J.,* I, 165-166.

6. *Papers of T.J.,* I, 174.

7. *Papers of T.J.,* I, 171.

8. Richard B. Morris, ed., *Encyclopedia of American History* (New York: Harper & Row, 1970), 99.

9. John Adams to Timothy Pickering, August 6, 1822; in Adams, *The Works of John Adams,* ed. with notes by Charles Francis Adams (10 vols.; Boston: Charles C. Little and James Brown, 1850-65), II, 512-514, n. 1.

10. Ibid.

11. Mapp, *The Virginia Experiment,* 402-403, 540, n. 92.

12. Freeman, *Washington,* III, 438-440.

13. Henry Steele Commager, ed., *The Heritage of America* (Boston: Little, Brown & Co., 1949), 150; Freeman, *Washington,* III, 436.

14. Ford, *Writings of T.J.,* I, 464, n.

15. *Papers of T.J.,* I, 187.

16. Comparison of T.J.'s original ms. with both Dickinson's draft and the document eventually approved by the Committee is greatly facilitated by the annotated texts in *Papers of T.J.,* I, 187-219.

17. *Autobiography,* 28.

18. *Papers of T.J.,* I, 231.

19. T.J. to Francis Eppes, June 26, 1775; *Papers of T.J.,* I, 174-175.

20. T.J. to John Randolph, August 25, 1775; *Papers of T.J.,* I, 240.

21. Ibid.

22. John Randolph to T.J.; *Papers of T.J.,* I, 244.

23. *Papers of T.J.,* I, 144-145.

24. T.J. to Ebenezer Hazard, April 30, 1775; *Papers of T.J.,* I, 164.

25. T.J. to John Randolph, November 29, 1775; *Papers of T.J.,* I, 268.

26. Ibid.

27. *Papers of T.J.,* I, 276.

28. T.J. to Francis Eppes, November 7, 1775; *Papers of T.J.,* I, 252.

29. Mays, *Pendleton,* II, 70.

30. John Page to T.J.; *Papers of T.J.,* I, 259.

31. Malone, I, 216.

32. Re survey: to Thomas Nelson, May 16, 1776; *Papers of T.J.,* I, 292. Letter to Jefferson from Dr. James McClurg; *Papers of T.J.,* I, 286-287.

33. John Page, to T.J.; *Papers of T.J.,* I, 109.

34. Mays, *Pendleton,* II, 109.

35. Ford, *Writings of T.J.,* I, 18.

36. T.J.'s "Notes of Proceedings in the Continental Congress"; *Papers of T.J.,* I, 309.

37. T.J. to Thomas Nelson, Jr., May 16, 1776; Ford, *Writings of T.J.,* II, 1-2.

38. Mapp, *The Virginia Experiment,* 431.

39. T.J. to Samuel Kercheval, July 12, 1816; Ford, *Writings of T.J.,* X, 37.

40. Mapp, *The Virginia Experiment,* 431.

41. William M.E. Rachal, "Virginia Declaration of Rights," *Virginia Cavalcade*, I (Summer, 1951), 14.

42. Mapp, *The Virginia Experiment*, 429.

43. Ibid., 433.

44. Ford, *Writings of T.J.*, I, 24.

45. In 1818, Jefferson would gratefully recall Franklin's words, "I have made it a rule, whenever in my power, to avoid becoming the draftsman of papers to be reviewed by a public body"; Carl Becker, *The Declaration of Independence; the History of Political Ideas* (New York: Knopf, 1942), 208.

46. John Adams to Timothy Pickering, August 6, 1822; Adams, *Works*, II, 514, n.

47. T.J. to Thomas Nelson, May 16, 1776; *Papers of T.J.*, I, 292.

48. John H. Hazelton, *The Declaration of Independence: Its History* (New York: Dodd, Mead & Co., 1906), 149-154.

49. T.J. to Ellen W. Coolidge, November 14, 1825; Lipscomb and Bergh, *Writings of T.J.*, XVIII, 349.

50. T.J. to Henry Lee, May 8, 1825; Ford, *Writings of T.J.*, X, 343.

51. Garry Wills, *Inventing America*, 248.

52. Ibid., 181-192.

53. Ibid., 207-217.

54. John Adams to Abigail Adams, July 3, 1776; Adams, *Works*, IX, 420.

55. Carl Becker, *The Declaration of Independence* (NY, 1940), 208.

56. *Papers of T.J.*, I, 427.

57. This circumstance is ironic in view of the fact that, after Adams and Jefferson were political opponents, the New Englander criticized the wording as unoriginal. After the two were reconciled, however, Adams defended the wording against a similar charge by others.

58. Adams to Timothy Pickering, August 6, 1822; Adams, *Works*, II, 514, n.

59. Garry Wills, *Inventing America*, 88-90.

60. Julian P. Boyd, ed., *The Declaration of Independence; the Evolution of the Text as Shown in Facsimiles of Various Drafts by Its Author* (Washington: The Library of Congress, 1943), 13.

61. Ibid.

62. Carefully collected evidence that Shakespeare based his description of the hurricane in *The Tempest* on Secretary William Strachey's account of the West Indian hurricane that wrecked the *Sea Venture* was published in 1917 by Charles Mills Gayley in a volume entitled *Shakespeare and the Founders of Liberty in America*. Some passages of the play so closely parallel Strachey's report that the narrative details are almost identical, though transferred from particular to universal significance by the transcendent creative genuis of the poet." Mapp, *The Virginia Experiment*, 497, n. 45.

CHAPTER VIII

1. Edmund Pendleton to T.J., August 10, 1776 *Papers of T.J.*, I, 489.
2. Malone, I, 240.
3. T.J. to William Fleming, July 1, 1776; *Papers of T.J.*, I, 412-413.
4. T.J. to Edmund Pendleton, July, 1776; *Papers of T.J.*, I, 408.
5. John H. Hazelton, *The Declaration of Independence: Its History* (New York: Dodd, Mead & Co., 1906), 454-456.
6. John Hancock to T.J.; *Papers of T.J.*, I, 523.
7. Ibid.
8. Ibid., 524.
9. *Autobiography*, 55-56.
10. Edmund Pendleton to T.J., July 22, 1776; *Papers of T.J.*, I, 471-472.
11. T.J. to John Adams, October 28, 1813; Merrill D. Peterson ed. *Thomas Jefferson: Writings*, 1307-1308.
12. Thomas Jefferson, *Notes on the State of Virginia*, ed. with an Introduction and Notes by William Peden (Chapel Hill: University of North Carolina Press, 1955), 161.
13. T.J. to Skelton Jones, July 28, 1809; Lipscomb and Bergh, *Writings of T.J.*, XII, 298.
14. Ibid., 299.
15. Malone, I, 239.
16. Beverly B. Munford, *Virginia's Attitude Toward Slavery and Secession* (Richmond: L.H. Jenkins, 1909), 25.
17. *Papers of T.J.*, II, 306.
18. Ibid.
19. Ibid., 307.
20. Ibid., 315.
21. T.J. to Skelton Jones, July 28, 1809; Lipscomb and Bergh, *Writings of T.J.*, XII, 299-300.
22. Plan Agreed Upon By the Committee of Revisors at Fredericksburg, January 13, 1777; *Papers of T.J.*, II, 325.
23. *Asser's Life of King Alfred*, ed. with Introduction and Commentary by William Henry Stevenson (Oxford: The Clarendon Press, 1959), 93-94.
24. Jefferson, *Notes*, 46.
25. Ibid., 146-147.
26. *A Short Account of the School in Kingswood Near Bristol* (Bristol: Printed by William Pine, 1768).
27. Jefferson, *Notes*, 147.
28. Ibid., 147-148.
29. Ibid., 148.
30. Ibid.
31. Ibid., 149.
32. Eudora Ramsay Richardson, ed., *Virginia: a Guide to the Old Dominion* (New York: Oxford University Press, 1941), 154.
33. Landon Carter to George Washington, October 31, 1776; in Peter Force, *American Archives* (9 vols., Washington: 1837-1853), 5 ser., II, 1304-1307.
34. Richard Henry Lee to T.J., June 16, 1778; *Papers of T.J.*, II, 200-201.
35. Edmund Pendleton to T.J., May 11, 1779; *Papers of T.J.*, II, 266.
36. Malone, I, 248-249.
37. *J.H.B.*, October 7, November 23, December 12, December 14, 1778.
38. John Adams to T.J., May 26, 1777; *Papers of T.J.*, II, 22.
39. Richard Henry Lee to T.J., August 25, 1777; *Papers of T.J.*, II, 29.
40. Virginius Dabney, *Virginia, the New Dominion* (Garden City, NY: Doubleday, 1971), 144.
41. Henry Timrod, "Ethnogenesis."

42. John Hammond Moore, *Albemarle, Jefferson's County, 1727-1976* (Charlottesville: University Press of Virginia, 1976), 57 et seq.

43. Friederike Charlotte Luise (von Massow) Friefrau von Riedesel, *Letters and Journals* (New York: New York Times, 1968), 154-160.

44. T.J. to Benjamin Franklin, August 13, 1777; *Papers of T.J.,* II, 27.

45. T.J. to Patrick Henry, March 27, 1779; *Papers of T.J.,* II, 238-243.

46. *Papers of T.J.,* II, 278, n.

47. Ibid.

48. John Page to T.J., June 2, 1779; *Papers of T.J.,* II, 278.

49. T.J. to John Page, June 3, 1779; *Papers of T.J.,* II, 279.

CHAPTER IX

1. J.R.V. Daniel, ed., *A Hornbook of Virginia History* (Richmond: Virginia Department of Conservation and Development, 1949), 101; Louis Knott Koontz, *Robert Dinwiddie: His Career in American Colonial Government and Westward Expansion* (Glendale, Calif.: The Arthur H. Clark Company, 1941), 39, 169-170.

2. Thomas Tileston Waterman, *The Mansions of Virginia, 1706-1776* (New York: Bonanza Books, 1945), 32-33, 51, 394, 396-398.

3. T.J. to Richard Henry Lee, June 17, 1779; *Papers of T.J.*, II, 298.

4. T.J. to Major General William Phillips, June 25, 1779; *Papers of T.J.*, III, 14-15.

5. T.J. to William Fleming, June 8, 1779; *Papers of T.J.*, II, 288.

6. Ibid.

7. Ibid.

8. Ibid.

9. Milo M. Quaife, ed., *The Capture of Old Vincennes* (Indianapolis: Bobbs-Merrill, 1927), xix.

10. T.J. to Theodorick Bland, June 8, 1779; *Papers of T.J.*, II, 286.

11. T.J. to Theodorick Bland, June 14, 1779; *Papers of T.J.*, II, 291.

12. Order of Virginia Council Placing Henry Hamilton and Others in Irons, June 16, 1779; *Papers of T.J.*, II, 292-293.

13. T.J. to Richard Bland, June 18, 1779; *Papers of T.J.*, II, 299.

14. Richard Henry Lee to T.J., July 8, 1779; in Richard Henry Lee, *Letters*, ed. J.C. Ballagh (2 vols.; New York: Macmillan, 1911-1914), II, 86.

15. T.J. to George Washington, July 10, 1779; *Papers of T.J.*, III, 30.

16. T.J. to George Washington, July 17, 1779; *Papers of T.J.*, III, 40-41.

17. T.J. to George Washington, October 8, 1779; *Papers of T.J.*, III, 104.

18. Malone, I, 312.

19. Schachner, I, 184.

20. Hugh Blair Grigsby describes Madison in *The Virginia Convention of 1776*, 83-89. See also reference to Madison on 81.

21. Schachner, 185-188.

22. T.J. to Samuel Huntington, December 16, 1779; *Papers of T.J.*, III, 226.

23. T.J. to Benjamin Harrison, December 23, 1779; *Papers of T.J.*, III, 241.

24. Ibid.

25. T.J. to James Wood, May 17, 1780; *Papers of T.J.*, III, 377.

26. Freeman, *Washington*, V, 163.

27. T.J. to Richard Henry Lee, September 13, 1780; *Papers of T.J.*, III, 643.

28. T.J. to General von Steuben, February 15, 1780; Schachner, 191.

29. T.J. to William Campbell, July 3, 1780; *Papers of T.J.*, III, 479; T.J. to Charles Lynch, August 1, 1780; ibid., 523.

30. Schachner, 193.

31. Horatio Gates to T.J., July 21, 1780; *Papers of T.J.*, III, 499.

32. T.J. to James Madison, July 26, 1780; *Papers of T.J.*, III, 507.

33. T.J. to George Rogers Clark, January 29, 1780; *Papers of T.J.*, III, 276.

34. T.J. to Horatio Gates, September 3, 1780; *Papers of T.J.*, III, 588.

35. T.J. to La Luzerne, August 31, 1780; *Papers of T.J.*, III, 577.

36. Marshall Butt, *Portsmouth Under Four Flags* (Portsmouth, Va.: Messenger Printing Co., 1971), 16-17.

37. Malone, I, 324.

38. *Official Letters of the Governor of the State of Virginia, Vol. II: The Letters of Thomas Jefferson*, ed. H.R. McIlwaine (Richmond: Virginia State Library, 1928), 254; *Journals of the Council of the State of Virginia, 1776-1781*, ed. H.R. McIlwaine (2 vols.; Richmond: Virginia State Library, 1931-1932), II, 269.

39. William Tatham to William Armistead Burwell, June 13, 1805; *Papers of T.J.*, 273-274.

40. Schachner, I, 200-201.

41. These and subsequent details of Jefferson's activities in the emergency drawn from Jefferson's Diary; Ford, III; *Journals of the Council*, II, 269; *Official Letters of the Governors*, II, 254.

42. T.J. to J.P.G. Muhlenberg, January (29) 31, 1781; *Papers of T.J.*, IV, 487.

43. Ibid., 487-488.

44. T.J. to Samuel Huntington, January 17, 1781; *Papers of T.J.*, IV, 386.

45. Horatio Gates to T.J., February 2, 1781; *Papers of T.J.*, IV, 501.

46. T.J. to Horatio Gates, February 17, 1781; *Papers of T.J.*, IV, 637.

47. Ibid.

48. Butt, *Portsmouth Under Four Flags*, 16-17.

49. Steuben to T.J., February 11, 1781; *Papers of T.J.*, IV, 584.

50. T.J. to Steuben, February 12, 1781; *Papers of T.J.*, IV, 593. Full letter appears on 592-594.

51. Ibid., 592.

52. T.J. to Benjamin Harrison, November 30, 1780; *Papers of T.J.*, IV 169.

53. Ibid., n.

54. T.J. to Steuben, February 12, 1781; *Papers of T.J.*, IV, 593.

55. This practice is illustrated by his correspondence, especially *Papers of T.J.*, IV, 536-696.

56. Physical description based on C.W. Peele portrait, Independence Hall; reproduced in Freeman, *Washington*, IV, between 617 and 618.

57. T.J. to Steuben, February 16, 1781; *Papers of T.J.*, IV, 633.

58. Benjamin Franklin Stevens, ed., *The Clinton-Cornwallis Controversy* (London: 1888), I, 10-13.

59. Henry P. Johnston, *Yorktown Campaign and the Surrender of Cornwallis*, 1781 (New York: Harper & Bros., 1881; reprint published by the Eastern National Park and Monument Associations, 1958), 37.

60. Ibid., 38.

61. T.J. to Lafayette, March 12, 1781; *Papers of T.J.*, V, 129.

62. Virginius Dabney, "Jack Jouett's Ride," *American Heritage*, XIII (December 1961), 56-57.

63. Christopher Ward, *The War of the Revolution*, II (2 vols.; New York: Macmillan, 1952), 701.

64. In the National Gallery, London, England; reproduced in full color in Richard M. Ketchum, ed., *The American Heritage Book of the Revolution* (N.Y., 1958), 342.

65. The account of Tarleton's raid and Jouett's ride is based on Moore, *Albemarle*, 63-65; Virginius Dabney, "Jack Jouett's Ride," *American Heritage*, XIII (December 1961), 56-59; Virginius Dabney, "From Cuckoo Tavern to Monticello," *The Iron Worker*, XXX (Summer, 1966), 1-13; John Cook Wyllie, "Writings About Jack Jouett and Tarleton's Raid on Charlottesville, in 1781," *The Magazine of Albemarle County History*, XVII (1958-1959), 49-56.

66. Moore, *Albemarle*, 65.

67. Handed down by word of mouth, the story is still told in the Charlottesville area.

68. *Journal of the House of Delegates of the Commonwealth of Virginia, 1781-1786* (Richmond: Thomas W. White, 1828), June 12, 1781.

69. Ibid.

70. Betsy Ambler to Mildred Smith, 1781; in "An Old Virginia Correspondence," *Atlantic Monthly*, LXXXIV (October 1899), 538.

71. Schachner, I, 218.

72. Jefferson, *Notes*, xiv.

73. Schachner, I, 218-219.

74. T.J. to George Nicholas, July 28, 1781; *Papers of T.J.*, VI, 105.

75. George Nicholas to T.J., July 31, 1781; *Papers of T.J.*, VI, 105.

76. *J.H.D.*, December 12, 1781, 37.

77. T.J. to Isaac Zane, December 24, 1781; *Papers of T.J.*, VI, 143.

78. Matthew Page Andrews, *Virginia, the Old Dominion* (New York: Doubleday, Doran & Co., 1937), 300.

79. T.J. to Edmund Randolph, September 16, 1781; *Papers of T.J.*, VI, 118.

CHAPTER X

1. Gilbert Chinard, *Thomas Jefferson, the Apostle of Americanism* (Boston: Little, Brown, 1929), 118.

2. T.J. to Marbois, March 4, 1781; *Papers of T.J.*, V, 58.

3. Jefferson, *Notes*, xiv, xv.

4. Ibid., 7.

5. Ibid., 19.

6. Ibid., 24-25.

7. Ibid., 25.

8. Ibid., 152-153.

9. Ibid., 153.

10. Ibid.

11. Ibid.

12. Nigel Nicolson, *Great Houses of the Western World* (New York: Putnam, 1968), 257-258.

13. *AIA Journal* (July 1976), 91.

14. Chastellux, *Travels*, II, 42.

15. Jefferson, *Notes*, 73-78; Jefferson, *Garden Book*.

16. Jefferson, *Notes*, 279-280, n. 4.

17. Jefferson, *Notes*, 284, n. 16.

18. Ibid., 151.

19. Ibid., 289-290, n. 3.

20. Embodied in Albert Marckwardt and James L. Rosier, *Old English Language and Literature* (New York: Norton, 1972).

21. Jefferson, *Notes*, 63.

22. Ibid., 230.

23. Ibid., 47.

24. Ibid., 47-48.

25. Ibid., 47.

26. Ibid., 199-202.

27. Ibid., 101.

28. Ibid., 92-93.

29. Ibid., 98.

30. Ibid.

31. Ibid., 99-100.

32. Ibid., 281, n. 8; Karl Lehmann-Hartleben, "Thomas Jefferson, Archaeologist," *American Journal of Archaeology*, XLVII (April 1943), 161-163.

33. Though Byrd had inherited slaves, he disapproved of slavery. Louis B. Wright, *The First Gentlemen of Virginia: Intellectual Qualities of the Early Colonial Ruling Class* (San Marino, Calif., 1940), 343-344.

34. Jefferson, *Notes*, 87.

35. Ibid.

36. Ibid., 162-163.

37. Ibid., 137-138.

38. Ibid., 138-139.

39. Ibid., 139-140.

40. Ibid., 140.

41. Ibid.

42. Ibid.

43. Ibid., 140-141.

44. Ibid., 142.

45. Ibid.

46. Ibid., 142-143.
47. Ibid., 143.
48. Ibid.
49. Ibid., 60.
50. *Papers of T.J.,* I, Appendix II, 677-679.
51. T.J. to Benjamin Rush, September 23, 1800; Ford, VII, 460.
52. Jefferson, *Notes*, 158.
53. Ibid., 159.
54. Ibid., 161.
55. Ibid., 159.
56. Ibid., 159-160.
57. Ibid., 223.
58. Ibid., 223-224.
59. Ibid., 224.
60. Ibid., 224-225.
61. Ibid., xvii.
62. The culture of this generation of Virginia leaders is discussed in Mapp, *The Virginia Experiment*, Chapter VII, 175-220.

CHAPTER XI

1. Chastellux, *Travels*, II, 41.
2. Ibid., II, 42.
3. Ibid., II, 46.
4. T.J. to Overton Carr, March 16, 1782; *Papers of T.J.,* VI, 166-167.
5. T.J. to Charles McPherson, August 12, 1773; *Papers of T.J.,* I, 96.
6. Chastellux, *Travels*, II, 45-46.
7. T.J. to the Speaker of the House of Delegates, May 6, 1782; *Papers of T.J.,* VI, 179.
8. Ibid., n.
9. Schachner, 237.
10. John Tyler to T.J., May 16, 1782; *Papers of T.J.,* VI, 183-184.
11. James Monroe to T.J., May 6, 1782; *Papers of T.J.,* VI, 179.
12. James Monroe to T.J., May 11, 1782; *Papers of T.J.,* VI, 183.
13. T.J. to James Monroe, May 20, 1782; *Papers of T.J.,* VI, 184-185.
14. Ibid., VI, 185.
15. Ibid., VI, 185-186.
16. Malone, I, 394-395.
17. See *Papers of T.J.,* VI, 184-195. In this definitive edition of Jefferson's writings, the next letter penned by Jefferson after that to Monroe (May 20, 1782) was to Benjamin Harrison, August 7, 1782.
18. Randall, I, 382.
19. Ibid.
20. Ibid., I, 383.
21. Ibid.
22. Malone, I, 397.
23. Randall, I, 384.
24. Ibid.
25. Robert R. Livingston to T.J., enclosing Jefferson's Appointment as a Peace Commissioner, November 13, 1782; *Papers of T.J.,* VI, 202.
26. Ibid., n; also James Madison, *The Papers of James Madison*, V, ed. William T. Hutchinson and William M.E. Rachal (a projected work of "some twenty volumes," of which 12 have been published; Chicago: The University of Chicago Press, 1962-   ), 268-269.
27. T.J. to Robert R. Livingston, November 26, 1782; *Papers of T.J.,* VI, 206.
28. T.J. to Chastellux, November 26, 1782; *Papers of T.J.,* VI, 203.

CHAPTER XII

1. T.J. to James Madison, January 31, 1783; *Papers of T.J.*, VI, 225-227. T.J. to James Madison, February 7, 1783; Ibid., 230-232. T.J. to Chevalier de la Luzerne, February 7, 1783; Ibid., 227-228. T.J. to Robert R. Livingston, February 7, 1783; Ibid., 228-229.

2. Schachner, 240.

3. T.J. to James Madison, January 31, 1783; *Papers of T.J.*, VI, 225.

4. T.J. to James Madison, February 7, 1783; *Papers of T.J.*, VI, 230.

5. Ibid.

6. Ibid., 230-232.

7. James Madison to T.J., February 11, 1783; *Papers of T.J.*, VI, 235.

8. Concerning his boredom in Baltimore, Jefferson concluded an unusually long letter to Randolph, February 15, 1783, "You feel by this time the effects of my idleness here." *Papers of T.J.*, VI, 249.

9. Ibid., 247.

10. Ibid., 247-248.

11. Ibid., 248-249.

12. Ibid., 249.

13. Resolution of Congress, February 14, 1783; *Papers of T.J.*, VI, 240.

14. T.J. to James Madison, February 14, 1783; *Papers of T.J.*, VI, 240.

15. T.J. to Abner Nash, March 11, 1783; *Papers of T.J.*, VI, 255.

16. T.J. to Robert R. Livingston, March 13, 1783; *Papers of T.J.*, VI, 257.

17. Ibid.

18. Robert R. Livingston to T.J., April 4, 1783; *Papers of T.J.*, VI, 259.

19. "Honorary Degree Conferred on Jefferson by the College of William and Mary"; *Papers of T.J.*, VI, 221.

20. Jefferson, *Notes*, 210.

21. Ibid., 214.

22. Ibid., 219.

23. Ibid., 220.

24. Ibid., 213-214.

25. Ibid., 220.

26. *Catalogue of The Library of Thomas Jefferson*, 5 vols., ed. E. Millicent Sowerby (Washington, D.C.: Library of Congress, 1952-1959).

27. G.E. Hastings, *Life and Works of Francis Hopkinson* (Chicago: 1926), 331-335.

28. T.J. to Martha Jefferson, November 28, 1783; *Papers of T.J.*, VI, 360.

29. An equally spartan schedule is set forth in *A Short Account of the School in Kingswood, Near Bristol* (Bristol: 1768), with the assurance (p. 6): "Neither do we allow any time for play on any day. He that plays when he is a child will play when he is a man."

30. T.J. to Marbois, December 5, 1783; *Papers of T.J.*, VI, 374.

31. T.J. to Martha Jefferson, December 11, 1783; *Papers of T.J.*, VI, 380-381.

32. T.J. to Martha Jefferson, December 22, 1783; *Papers of T.J.*, VI, 417.

33. T.J. to Peter Carr, December 11, 1783; *Papers of T.J.*, VI, 379-380.

34. T.J. to James Madison, December 11, 1783; *Papers of T.J.*, VI, 381.

35. Ibid.

36. James Tilton to Gunning Bedford, December 25, 1783; George Washington, *The Writings of George Washington, 1745-1799*, ed. John C. Fitzpatrick (39 vols.; Washington, D.C.: United States Government Printing Office, 1931-1944), XXVII, 285-286, n.

37. Washington returned his commission to Congress on December 23, 1783. The ceremony is reported in Freeman, *Washington*, V, 474-477

38. T.J. to Benjamin Harrison, December 24, 1783; *Papers of T.J.*, VI, 419.

39. Ibid.

40. T.J. to James Madison, January 1, 1784; *Papers of T.J.*, VI, 438.

41. Thomas Jefferson, *Autobiography*, printed in Thomas Randolph, I, 47.

42. Ibid., I, 47-48.

43. T.J. to James Madison, February 20, 1784; *Papers of T.J.*, VI, 545.

44. Ibid.

45. Report of the Committee on Jefferson's Compromise Motion Concerning Ratification, January 3, 1784; *Papers of T.J.*, I, 442. Jefferson's original motion appears on pp. 439-440; as reported by the committee, pp. 441-442.

46. Jefferson, *Notes*, 161.

47. T.J. to Martha Jefferson, February 18, 1784; *Papers of T.J.*, VI, 543.

48. T.J. to James Madison, February 20, 1784; *Papers of T.J.*, VI, 544-550.

49. Malone, I, 410.

50. An annotated text of "The Virginia Cession of Territory Northwest of the Ohio and Plan for Government of the Western Territory" may be found in *Papers of T.J.*, VI, 571-617.

51. Jefferson's Notes on Coinage, *Papers of T.J.*, VII, 150-203, also includes Robert Morris' report to the president of Congress (January 15, 1782), Gouverneur Morris' letter to William Hensley (April 30, 1783), and Robert Morris' letter to Jefferson (May 1, 1784).

52. *Papers of T.J.*, VI, 516, 522.

53. T.J. to George Washington, April 16, 1784; *Papers of T.J.*, VII, 105-106.

54. Ibid., VII, 106-107.

55. Ibid., 108.

56. Freeman, *Washington*, VI, 9-12.

57. G.K. van Hogendorp to T.J., c. April 6, 1784; *Papers of T.J.*, VII, 80.

58. Ibid., 82.

59. T.J. to G.K. van Hogendorp, May 4, 1784; Ibid., 208-209.

60. John Tyler to T.J., May 20, 1784; Ibid., 278.

61. James Madison to T.J., April 25, 1784; Ibid., 121-122.

62. Ibid., 122.

63. Ibid.

64. T.J. to James Madison, March 16, 1784; Ibid., 30.

65. T.J. to James Madison, May 8, 1784; Ibid., 233-234.

66. Ibid., 232-233.

67. T.J. to William Short, April 30, 1784; Ibid., 148.

68. William Short to T.J., May 14, 1784 (first of two letters of this date); Ibid., 253.

69. Schachner, 261-262.

70. Ibid., 261.

71. T.J. to George Rogers Clark, December 4, 1783; *Papers of T.J.*, VI, 371.

72. *Papers of T.J.*, VII, 302-312.

73. Roger Sherman to Ezra Stiles, May 11, 1784; Ibid., 303 n.

74. Extract from the Diary of Ezra Stiles, June 8, 1784; *Papers of T.J.*, VII, 303.

75. *Maryland Journal and Baltimore Advertiser*, July 9, 1784; quoted in Dumbauld, 58.

76. Dumbauld, 59.

77. T.J. to Elbridge Gerry, July 2, 1784; *Papers of T.J.*, VII, 357-358.

78. Ibid., VII, 358.

CHAPTER XIII

1. Sarah N. Randolph, *The Domestic Life*, 73.
2. Schachner, 264.
3. Ibid.
4. Edward Dumbauld, *Thomas Jefferson, American Tourist*, 60-61.
5. Howard C. Rice, Jr., *Thomas Jefferson's Paris* (Princeton, N.J.: Princeton University Press, 1976), 13.
6. Ibid., 15.
7. Dumbauld, 61.
8. Rice, *Thomas Jefferson's Paris,* 77.
9. Ibid., T.J. to Samuel H. Smith, September 21, 1814.
10. John Quincy Adams, *Memoirs* (Freeport, N.Y.: 1969 reprint), I, 317.
11. Rice, 78.
12. Ibid.
13. T.J. to L.H. Girardin, January 15, 1815; Lipscomb and Bergh, *Writings*, XIV, 231-232.
14. Rice, 78.
15. T.J. to Rev. James Madison, July 19, 1785; *Papers of T.J.*, XIII, 379-383.
16. Rice, 86.
17. T.J. to William Short, March 29, 1787; *Papers of T.J.*, XI, 253-255.
18. Malone, II, 5.
19. Rice, 91.
20. Jack Shepherd, *The Adams Chronicles, Four Generations of Greatness* (Boston: Little, Brown and Company, 1975), 96.
21. Rice, 39.
22. Rice, quoting Abigail Adams, 40.
23. Elizabeth Wayles Eppes to T.J., October 13, 1784; *Papers of T.J.*, VII, 441.
24. Francis Eppes to T.J., October 14, 1787; *Papers of T.J.*, VII, 441-442.
25. T.J. to Elizabeth Thompson, January 19, 1787; *Papers of T.J.*, XI, 57.
26. John Adams to T.J., January 22, 1825; Lester J. Cappon, ed., *The Adams-Jefferson Letters* II, (2 vols.; Chapel Hill: University of North Carolina Press, 1959), 606-607.
27. Benjamin Franklin to John Adams, July 4, 1784; Adams, *Works*, VIII, 206-207.
28. Paul C. Nagel, *Descent From Glory* (N.Y.: 1983), 17.
29. Malone, II, 9.
30. Jefferson's "General Form of a Treaty, September 4 to November 10, 1784," Editorial Note; *Papers of T.J.*, VII, 463.
31. Ibid., 464.
32. Jefferson's treaty drafts and notes found in *Papers of T.J.*, VII, 463-490.
33. Draft of a Model Treaty; *Papers of T.J.*, VII, 486.
34. Ibid., 487.
35. Ibid.
36. Jefferson's "General Form of a Treaty, September 4 to November 10, 1784," Editorial Note; *Papers of T.J.*, VII, 465.
37. American Commissioners to De Thulemeir, with Observations on Treaty, November 10, 1784; *Papers of T.J.*, VII, 491.
38. Ibid.
39. John Adams to De Thulemeir, February 13, 1785; *Papers of T.J.*, VII, 465, n.
40. T.J. to John Adams, July 28, 1785; *Papers of T.J.*, VIII, 317.
41. Jefferson's "General Form of a Treaty," VII, 470.
42. *Papers of T.J.*, VI, 226, n. 1; 233.
43. T.J. to James Madison, December 8, 1784; *Papers of T.J.*, VII, 558.
44. T.J. to Benjamin Harrison, January 12, 1785; *Papers of T.J.*, VII, 600.

45. Jefferson recorded his meeting with Houdon in a letter to Washington dated December 10, 1784; *Papers of T.J.*, VII, 567. Our description of the artist is based on "Houdon in His Studio," a painting by Brilly, reproduced in Rice, 59. In a letter to Benjamin Harrison, dated January 12, 1785, Jefferson reports his conversation with Franklin; *Papers of T.J.*, VII, 600.

46. T.J. to Benjamin Harrison, January 12, 1785; *Papers of T.J.,* VII, 600.

47. Ibid.

48. T.J. to Washington, December 10, 1784; *Papers of T.J.*, VII, 567.

49. William Howard Adams, ed., *The Eye of Thomas Jefferson* (Washington, D.C., 1976), 182.

50. Rice, 57.

51. T.J. to Washington, August 14, 1787; *Papers of T.J.*, XII, 36. The tricorn hat was referred to as a "chapeau bras" because it could be carried under the arm.

52. T.J. to Charles Bellini, September 30, 1786; *Papers of T.J.*, VIII, 568.

53. Ibid., 568-569.

54. T.J. to John Bannister, Jr., October 15, 1785; *Papers of T.J.*, VIII, 636-637.

55. T.J. to David S. Franks, June 17, 1785; *Papers of T.J.*, VIII, 225.

56. John Jay to T.J., March 15, 1785; *Papers of T.J.*, VIII, 33. Also see Jefferson to John Jay, May 11, 1785; *Papers of T.J.*, VIII, 145-146.

57. T.J. to James Madison, January 30, 1787; *Papers of T.J.*, XI, 95-96.

58. T.J. to John Jay, June 17, 1785; *Papers of T.J.*, VIII, 226.

59. The foregoing estimate is amply supported by the correspondence in *Papers of T.J.*, X and XI.

60. Lafayette to T.J., October 11, 1784; *Papers of T.J.*, VII, 439.

61. Rice, 63.

62. Ibid., 110.

63. T.J. to James Madison, January 30, 1787; *Papers of T.J.*, XI, 95.

64. Ibid.

65. T.J. to Vergennes, August 15, 1785; *Papers of T.J.*, VIII, 385-389.

66. T.J. to Vergennes, November 20, 1785; *Papers of T.J.*, IX, 51.

67. Schachner, 279-280. Jefferson's reply to Vergennes is switched here from the past to the present tense.

68. Lafayette to T.J., March 18, 1786; *Papers of T.J.*, IX, 337.

69. Vergennes to T.J., May 30, 1786; *Papers of T.J.*, IX, 597-598. The background of the tobacco problem is discussed informatively in *Papers of T.J.*, IX, 457-460, n.

70. John Adams to T.J., February 21, 1786; *Papers of T.J.*, IX, 295.

71. Ibid.

72. T.J. to Nathanael Greene, January 12, 1786; *Papers of T.J.*, IX, 168. This letter is misdated 1785 by Jefferson.

73. T.J. to John Jay, August 23, 1785; *Papers of T.J.*, VIII, 427.

74. T.J. to James Monroe, November 11, 1784; *Papers of T.J.*, VII, 511-512.

75. Draft of a Treaty of Amity and Commerce; *Papers of T.J.*, VIII, 347-353.

76. T.J. to John Adams, August 6, 1785; *Papers of T.J.*, VIII, 347.

77. Ibid.

78. T.J. and John Adams to John Jay, March 28, 1786; *Papers of T.J.*, IX, 358.

79. Ibid.

80. For a description of the pipe and smoking habits of the ambassador, see Jack Shepherd, *The Adams Chronicles*, 133-136.

81. In a letter to James Madison, dated January 30, 1787, Jefferson describes his changed insight into Adams' character: "A seven months' intimacy with him here, and as many weeks in London, have given me opportunities of studying him closely. He is vain, irritable, and a bad calculator of the force and probable effect of the motives which govern men. This is all the ill which can possibly be said of him. He is disinterested as the being who made him: he is profound in his views; and accurate in his judgement, except where knowledge of the world is necessary to form a judgment. He is so amiable that I pronounce you will love him, if you ever become acquainted with him"; *Papers of T.J.*, XI, 94.

82. T.J. to Abigail Adams, September 25, 1785; *Papers of T.J.*, VIII, 548.

83. Mather Brown's portrait of Abigail Adams is reproduced in Shepherd, *Adams Chronicles*, 134.

84. Writing to T.J. of her reluctance to leave Paris, Abigail Adams said, "I was still more loath on account of the increasing pleasure and intimacy which a longer acquaintance with a respected friend promised, to leave behind me the only person with whom my companion could associate with perfect freedom and unreserve . . . ." Abigail Adams to T.J., June 6, 1785; *Papers of T.J.*, VIII, 198.

85. Shepherd, *Adams Chronicles*, 120.

86. T.J. to John Adams, May 25, 1785; *Papers of T.J.*, VIII, 164.

87. Shepherd, *Adams Chronicles*, 121-122.

88. John Adams, *Works*, I, 420.

89. T.J. to William S. Smith, September 28, 1787; *Papers of T.J.*, XII, 192-193

90. Richard Price to T.J., March 21, 1785; *Papers of T.J.*, VIII, 53.

91. T.J. to John Jay, April 23, 1786; *Papers of T.J.*, IX, 402. Schachner (p. 2810) mistakenly assumed that Jefferson referred to France in this letter.

92. Benjamin Rush to T.J., January 24, 1783; *Papers of T.J.*, VI, 223.

93. T.J. to Charles Thompson, April 22, 1786, and September 20, 1787; *Papers of T.J.*, IX, 400, and XII, 159-161.

94. Archibald Bolling Shepperson, *John Paradise and Lucy Ludwell of London and Williamsburg* (Richmond: The Dietz Press, 1942).

95. Edwin M. Betts, ed., *Thomas Jefferson's Garden Book*: Philadelphia, 1944, 110-111.

96. Ibid., 111.

97. Ibid.; Randall, I, 447; T.J. to John Page, May 4, 1786; *Papers of T.J.*, IX, 445.

98. "Notes of a Tour of English Gardens"; *Papers of T.J.*, IX, 369.

99. Ibid., 372.

100. Ibid., 373.

101. Ibid., 369.

102. The entire description of the burial ground and related garden plans is taken from Betts, *Garden Book*, 25-27, reprinted from *Account Book*, 1171.

103. Betts, *Garden Book*, 114.

104. Ibid., 112-113.

105. Ibid., 111.

106. Shepherd, *Adams Chronicles*, 136.

107. Ibid., 137.

108. For a general comment on his increased sophistication in art, see Kimball, *Jefferson, the Scene of Europe*, 115.

109. Reproduced in color in Shepherd, *Adams Chronicles*, 138. For information concerning the portrait, see Malone, II, 62-63. Also see letter to Jefferson from Abigail Adams, July 23, 1786; *Papers of T.J.*, X, 161.

110. Kimball, *Jefferson, the Scene of Europe*, 9.

111. Like John and Abigail Adams, Smith corresponded with T.J. afterwards, sometimes, as in his letter of February 20, 1793, on affairs in France, providing him with valuable information.

112. See *Papers of T.J.*, VIII, 485-492, for an annotated reprint of leases of the Hotel de Langeac.

113. Rice, 51.

114. Ibid., 52.

115. Ibid.

116. *Papers of T.J.*, XI, 373, 383; XII, 135; XIII, 343.

117. T.J. to James Currie, September 27, 1785; *Papers of T.J.*, VIII, 558.

118. Malone, II, 12, 133-134.

119. T.J. to Francis Eppes, August 30, 1785; *Papers of T.J.*, VIII, 451.

120. Malone II, 133-135; Mary Jefferson to T.J., c. September 13, 1785; *Papers of T.J.*, VIII, 517.

121. T.J. to Mary Jefferson, September 20, 1785; *Papers of T.J.*, VIII, 532-533.

122. William Short to William Nelson, October 25, 1786; *Papers of T.J.*, X, 3, n. Related papers (including Demeunier's queries and Jefferson's answers) may be found in *Papers of T.J.*, X, 3-65.

123. Relevant notes and correspondence may be found in *Papers of T.J.*, X, 363-383.

124. Jefferson's comments on François Soule's *Histoire; Papers of T.J.*, X, 368, n.

125. Ibid.

126. Though Richmonders, loving classical allusions, said that their city was built on seven hills, subsequent generations have not been able to agree on which of the hills now within its borders were so designated.

127. A plaster model for the capitol, constructed in Paris under Jefferson's direction, is displayed now in the capitol itself.

128. T.J. to William Buchanan and James Hay, January 26, 1787; *Papers of T.J.*, IX, 220.

129. T.J. to James Currie, January 28, 1786; *Papers of T.J.*, IX, 220.

130. T.J. to Madame de Tesse, March 20, 1787; *Papers of T.J.*, XI, 226.

CHAPTER XIV

1. This painting, titled "The Declaration of Independence," is in the rotunda of the capitol, Washington, D.C.

2. Rice, 18. For further information on the Halle aux Bleds, see W.J. Adams, *The Eye of Thomas Jefferson*, 260; also, *Papers of T.J.*, X, xxix and pictures opposite 434.

3. Rice, 19.

4. Ibid., 19-20.

5. *Thomas Jefferson: Writings* (Library of America), 867.

6. Ibid.

7. So the Heart describes the Halle aux Bleds in Jefferson's famous "Dialogue Between Head and Heart," written to Maria Cosway, October 12, 1786; *Papers of T.J.*, X, 445.

8. Fawn Brodie, *Thomas Jefferson: An Intimate History*, 254-258.

9. T.J. to Maria Cosway, October 12, 1786; *Papers of T.J.*, X, 445.

10. Rice, 14. The couple did not dine at St. Cloud as Malone (II, 71) says. See *Papers of T.J.*, X, 445 ("after dinner, to St. Cloud").

11. For an idea of Richard Cosway's appearance, it is unwise to rely on his flattering self-portrait. See George C. Williamson, *Richard Cosway, R.A.* (London, 1905), 37-39, where it is revealed that both J.T. Smith and Peter Pindar thought he looked like a monkey. In fairness, though, it should be noted that to Ozias Humphrey he was "the kindliest of friends" and to Andrew Plimer "my beloved master." See Helen Duprey Bullock, *My Head and My Heart: A Little Chronicle of Thomas Jefferson and Maria Cosway* (New York: G.P. Putnam's Sons, 1945), 171.

12. Rice, 96.

13. Rice, 43-44.

14. She was the wife of Johann Baptiste Krumpholtz, even more celebrated as composer and harpist.

15. T.J. to Maria Cosway, October 12, 1786; *Papers of T.J.*, X, 445.

16. Kimball, *Jefferson, the Scene of Europe*, 164.

17. Ibid., 163.

18. Bullock, *My Head and My Heart*, 15.

19. Lady Victoria Manners and George C. Williamson, *Angelica Kauffmann, R.A.: Her Life and Her Works* (New York: Hacker Art Books, 1976), 26.

20. Implicit in Helen D. Bullock, *My Head and My Heart: A Little Chronicle of Thomas Jefferson and Maria Cosway* (N.Y., 1945).

21. It should be noted, however, that Cosway had at least one mistress—Mary Moser. See Bullock, *My Head and My Heart*, 144-145.

22. T.J. to Maria Cosway, October 12, 1786; *Papers of T.J.*, X, 445.

23. Ibid., 446.

24. George C. Williamson, *Richard Cosway, R.A.* (London, 1905), 28-49.

25. See Shippen's description of Jefferson at Court; Rice, 99.

26. A picture of the Bagatelle is reproduced in Rice, 102; see also Kimball, *Jefferson, the Scene of Europe*, p. 164. The name "casino" does not necessarily refer to gambling.

27. Desmond Seward, *Prince of the Renaissance: The Golden Life of François I* (New York: Macmillan, 1973), especially 70, 91-98.

28. Kimball, *Jefferson, the Scene of Europe*, 166.

29. Ibid., 165.

30. Evident at Monticello and elsewhere.

31. Kimball, *Jefferson, the Scene of Europe*, 166.

32. Ibid.

33. T.J. to Maria Cosway, October 12, 1786; *Papers of T.J.*, X, 445-446.

34. Ibid. Jefferson may have combined in his memory two visits to St. Germain and vicinity. The description of the column is based partly on Kimball, *Jefferson, the Scene of Europe*, 167,

but especially on sketches reproduced in Rice, 110-111.

35. T.J to Maria Cosway, October 12, 1786; *Papers of T.J.*, X, 446.

36. Ibid.

37. Kimball (p. 168) mistakenly says Jefferson was "trying to leap over a large kettle." Jefferson's granddaughter says that he was with a "companion" (Randall, I, 456). Bullock (p. 24) misdates the accident as September 14 and says without equivocation that Jefferson sustained the injury "while in Maria's company." See also L.H. Butterfield and Howard C. Rice, Jr., "Jefferson's Earliest Note to Maria Cosway With Some New Facts and Conjectures on His Broken Wrist," *The William and Mary Quarterly* (series 3, volume V, January 1948, 26-33), and their later letter to the editor printed on 620-621 of the same volume.

38. T.J. to William Stephens Smith, October 22, 1786; *Papers of T.J.*, X, 478.

39. Maria Cosway to T.J., September 20, 1786; *Papers of T.J.*, X, 393-394.

40. T.J. to Maria Cosway, October 5, 1786; *Papers of T.J.*, X, 431-432.

41. Maria Cosway to T.J., October 5, 1786; *Papers of T.J.*, X, 433.

42. Rice, p. 4.

43. T.J. to Maria Cosway, October 12, 1786; *Papers of T.J.*, X, 443-444.

44. Ibid., 453, n.

45. Ibid., 444.

46. Ibid., 453, n.

47. T.J. to Maria Cosway, October 13, 1786; *Papers of T.J.*, X, 458.

48. Maria Cosway to T.J., October 30, 1786; *Papers of T.J.*, X, 496, n. This translation is from the original Italian which appears on 494-495.

49. Maria Cosway to T.J., November 17, 1786; *Papers of T.J.*, X, 538-540. The letter appears both in the original and in English translation.

50. William Short to William Nelson, October 25, 1786; *Papers of T.J.*, X, 416, n.

51. *Papers of T.J.*, X, 416, n.

52. Calonne to T.J., October 22, 1786; *Papers of T.J.*, X, 474-478.

53. T.J. to the ambassadors of Portugal and Russia, "Jefferson's Proposed Concert of Powers Against the Barbary States (July-December, 1786)"; *Papers of T.J.*, X, 559-570.

54. Elizabeth Eppes to T.J., May 7, 1787; *Papers of T.J.*, XI, 356.

55. Andrew Ramsay to T.J., July 6, 1787; *Papers of T.J.*, XI, 556.

56. T.J. to Francis Eppes, July 2, 1787; *Papers of T.J.*, XI, 524-525.

57. Abigail Adams to T.J., July 6, 1787; *Papers of T.J.*, XI, 550-552.

58. T.J. to Abigail Adams, July 1, 1787; *Papers of T.J.*, XI, 514-515.

59. T.J. to Abigail Adams, July 10, 1787; *Papers of T.J.*, XI, 572.

60. Abigail Adams to T.J., July 10, 1787; *Papers of T.J.*, XI, 572-573.

61. T.J. to Abigail Adams, July 16, 1787; *Papers of T.J.*, XI, 592.

62. T.J. to Abigail Adams, October 4, 1787; *Papers of T.J.*, XII, 201-202.

63. T.J. to Wilson Miles Cary, August 12, 1787; *Papers of T.J.*, XII, 23-24.

64. T.J. to George Gilmer, August 11, 1787; *Papers of T.J.*, XII, 24-26.

65. Ibid.

66. T.J. to John Jay, May 4, 1787; *Papers of T.J.*, XI, 338-343.

67. Jefferson's description is quoted in Kimball, *Jefferson, the Scene of Europe*, 185; T.J. to William Short, March 15, 1787; *Papers of T.J.*, XI, 214.

68. T.J. to Lafayette, April 11, 1787; *Papers of T.J.*, XI, 283-285.

69. T.J. to Madam de Tott, April 15, 1787; *Papers of T.J.*, XI, 271-272.

70. "Notes of a Tour into the Southern Parts of France, &c," March 9, 1787; *Papers of T.J.*, XI, 415-428.

71. T.J. to John Jay, May 4, 1787; *Papers of T.J.*, XI, 339-342.

72. "Notes of a Tour into the Southern Parts of France, &c"; *Papers of T.J.*, XI, esp. 427-429 (March 29).

73. T.J. to Gaudensio Clerici, August 15, 1787; *Papers of T.J.*, XII, 39.

74. "Notes of a Tour into the Southern Parts of France, &c," April 29, 1787; *Papers of T.J.*, XI, 441-442.

75. T.J. to William Short, May 21, 1787; *Papers of T.J.*, XI, 372.

76. Lipscomb and Bergh, XVII, 229; "Notes of a Tour into Southern Parts of France, &c,"; *Papers of T.J.*, XI, 457-458.

77. Lipscomb and Bergh, XVII, 232-35.

78. T.J. to Maria Cosway, July 1, 1787; *Papers of T.J.*, XI, 519.

79. Ibid., 519-520.

80. Jefferson's affinity for mountaintops is evident not only in his choice of a homesite but throughout his writings.

81. T.J. to Maria Cosway, December 24, 1786; Bullock, 60.

82. Maria Cosway to T.J., July 9, 1787; *Papers of T.J.*, XI, 567-569, including Italian original and English translation.

83. John Trumbull to T.J., September 17, 1787; *Papers of T.J.*, XII, 139.

84. Ibid.

85. T.J. to John Trumbull, October 4, 1787, Ibid., 206-207.

86. T.J. to John Trumbull, November 13, 1787; *Papers of T.J.*, XII, 358.

87. Maria Cosway to T.J., December 1(?), 1787; Ibid., 387.

88. Maria Cosway to T.J., December 7, 1787; Ibid., 403.

89. Maria Cosway to T.J., December 10, 1787; Ibid. 415.

90. T.J. to Maria Cosway, January 31, 1788; Ibid., 539-540.

91. Maria Cosway to T.J., December 25, 1787; Ibid., 459-460.

92. T.J. to Maria Cosway, January 31, 1788; Ibid., 539-540.

93. John Trumbull to T.J., March 6, 1788; Ibid., 647.

94. T.J. to John Trumbull, Bullock, 87.

95. Maria Cosway to T.J., March 6, 1788; *Papers of T.J.*, XII, 645.

96. *Autobiography*, 93.

97. T.J. to John Adams, March 2, 1788; *Papers of T.J.*, XII, 637-638.

98. T.J. to William Short, March 10, 1788; Ibid., 659.

99. John Adams to T.J., February 12, 1788; Ibid., 581.

100. Schachner, 356-357.

101. Ibid.

102. See "Memorandums on a Tour from Paris to Amsterdam, Strasburg, and back to Paris, March 3, 1788, to March 30, 1788"; *Papers of T.J.*, XIII, 8-33.

103. T.J. to John Trumbull, March 27, 1788; Bullock, 89.

104. Memorandums on a Tour from Paris to Amsterdam, Strasburg, and back to Paris, March 3, 1788, to March 30, 1788; *Papers of T.J.*, XIII, 14.

105. Ibid., 16-24. T.J. to William Short, April 9, 1788; *Papers of T.J.*, XIII, 48.

106. "Memorandums on a Tour from Paris to Amsterdam, Strasburg, and back to Paris, March 3, 1788 to March 30, 1788"; *Papers of T.J.*, XIII, 27.

107. T.J. to Maria Cosway, April 24, 1788; *Papers of T.J.*, XIII, 103.

108. Ibid., 103-104.

109. Brodie, 231-232.

110. Ibid., 229.

111. Ibid., p. 230. Mrs. Brodie (p. 523, n. 6) cites Freud's observations of the "phallic symbolism, in dreams, of ploughs, hammers, rifles, revolvers, daggers, etc." (*Complete Psychological Works*, V, part 2, 356).

112. Garry Wills, *Inventing America*, 119.

113. Brodie, 349-350.

114. Dumas Malone, *Jefferson the President, First Term 1801-1805* (Boston: Little, Brown and Company), 497-498. Hereafter referred to as Malone IV. The definitive summation of evidence concerning Jefferson's relationship with Sally Hemings is Virginius Dabney, *The Jefferson Scandals* (N.Y.: Dodd, Mead, 1981).

115. Kimball, *Jefferson, the Scene of Europe*, 279.

116. Ibid.

117. T.J. to William Carmichael, May 8, 1789; *Papers of T.J.*, XV, 105.

118. Quoted from H. Taine, *Nouveaux Essais de Critique et d'Histoire,* in Malone, II, 233.

119. T.J. to John de Crevecoeur, May 20, 1789; *Papers of T.J.*, XV, 140-141.

120. T.J. to Lafayette, June 3, 1789; *Papers of T.J.*, XV, 165; "Draft of a Charter of Rights"; Ibid., 167-168.

121. T.J. to John Jay, June 17, 1789; *Papers of T.J.*, XV, 189.

122. T.J. to John Jay, June 29, 1789; *Papers of T.J.*, XV, 223.

123. Kimball, 286; T.J. to Lafayette, July 7, 1789; *Papers of T.J.*, XV, 254.

124. T.J. to Lafayette, July 7, 1789; *Papers of T.J.*, XV, 254.

125. *Papers of T.J.*, XV, 253.

126. Lafayette to T.J., July 8, 1789; *Papers of T.J.*, XV, 254.

127. Lafayette to T.J., July 9, 1789; *Papers of T.J.*, XV, 255.

128. Malone, II, 233.

129. Malone, II, 224.

130. T.J. to James Madison, September 6, 1789; *Papers of T.J.*, XV, 292-297.

131. *Papers of T.J.*, XV, 384-386, n.

132. Proposition submitted by Richard Gem; *Papers of T.J.*, XV, 391-392.

133. *Papers of T.J.*, XV, 390, n.

134. T.J. to James Madison, August 28, 1789; *Papers of T.J.*, XV, 366.

135. Lafayette to T.J., August 25, 1789; *Papers of T.J.*, XV, 354.

136. Malone, II, 230.

137. *Autobiography of Thomas Jefferson* (Capricorn Ed.), 113.

138. Ibid., 114.

139. Ibid.

140. Ibid. Montmorin's reply, relayed in the third person by T.J., is here given in the first.

141. Ibid. T.J.'s reply, related by him in the past tense, is presented here in the present.

142. Ibid., 107-108.

143. T.J. to Montmorin, July 8, 1789; *Papers of T.J.*, XV, 260-261.

144. *Autobiography*, 106.

145. Ibid., 106-107.

146. Ibid., 111.

147. In Burke, *Reflections on the Revolution in France, and on the Proceedings in Certain Societies in London Relative to That Event, in a Letter Intended to Have Been Sent to a Gentleman in Paris* (1790).

148. *Autobiography*, 110.

149. Ibid., 115.

150. T.J. to John Trumbull, September 9, 1789, *Papers of T.J.*, XV, 407; John Trumbull to T.J., September 11, 1789, Ibid., 417-418; T.J. to John Trumbull, September 16, 1789, Ibid., 435-436; John Trumbull to T.J., September 22, 1789, Ibid., 467-469.

151. Randall, I, 558-559.

152. Malone II, 234.

153. H.H. Arnason, *The Sculptures of Houdon* (N.Y.: Oxford, 1975), 87.

154. *Autobiography*, 115-116.

CHAPTER XV

1. T.J. to John Trumbull, November 25, 1797; *Papers of T.J.*, XV, 560.

2. Martha Jefferson Randolph's phrase, from her manuscript "Reminiscences of TH.J by MR," Ibid., 560, n.

3. Ibid., 560, n.

4. Ibid., 560-561, n.

5. Freeman, *Washington*, XI, 236.

6. Address of Welcome of the Officials of Norfolk, November 25, 1789; *Papers of T.J.*, XV, 556.

7. Thomas J. Wertenbaker, *Norfolk: Historic Southern Port* (Durham, N.C.: Duke University Press, 1931), 77-81.

8. Jefferson's Reply to the Foregoing Address of Welcome, November 25, 1789; *Papers of T.J.*, XV, 556.

9. Martha Jefferson Randolph, "Reminiscences of TH.J by MR"; *Papers of T.J.*, XV, 561.

10. T.J. to William Short, December 14, 1789; *Papers of T.J.*, XVI, 25-26.

11. Ibid., 26. Richmond is built on many hills and there is little agreement on which were the original seven, but residents have long cherished the reference that links them to classical Rome.

12. S.F.T. Kimball, "Thomas Jefferson and the First Monument of the Classical Revival in America," *Journal of the American Institute of Architecture* (1915), 23.

13. Ibid., 23.

14. *AIA Journal* (July 1976), 91.

15. T.J. to George Washington, December 15, 1789; *Papers of T.J.*, XVI, 34-35.

16. Randall, I, 552-553; Randolph, *Domestic Life*, 552-553.

17. Randall, I, 552-553.

18. Randolph, *Domestic Life*, 552-553.

19. Malone, II, 246.

20. Malone, II, 247.

21. James Madison to George Washington, January 4, 1790; *Papers of T.J.*, XVI, 118, n.

22. George Washington to T.J., January 21, 1790; *Papers of T.J.*, XVI, 117.

23. James Madison to T.J., January 24, 1790; *Papers of T.J.*, XVI, 126.

24. William H. Gaines, Jr., *Thomas Mann Randolph: Jefferson's Son-in-Law* (Louisiana State University Press, 1966), 26.

25. Ibid., 24, 50.

26. Ibid., 25-26.

27. T.J. to Thomas Mann Randolph, Sr., February 4, 1790; *Papers of T.J.*, XVI, 154.

28. *Papers of T.J.*, XVI, 189-191. The number of families of slaves is mistakenly given as 12 in Malone, *Jefferson and the Rights of Man*, 252; Marriage Settlement for Martha Jefferson; *Papers of T.J.*, XVI, 189-191.

29. Ibid., 253-254.

30. T.J. to "Mr. Fitzhugh," March 11, 1790 (Schachner, 390).

31. "Autobiography of T.J."; Lipscomb and Bergh, I, 161-162.

32. Ibid., 162-163.

33. *The Diaries of George Washington*, IV, (Boston: 1925), 106.

34. Freeman, *Washington*, VI, 255-256.

35. Hugh Blair Grigsby, *The Virginia Convention of 1776* (Richmond: 1855), 54, 65; Alf J. Mapp, Jr., *The Virginia Experiment*, 424.

36. Merrill D. Peterson, *The Jefferson Image in the American Mind* (New York: Oxford University Press, 1962), p. 222.

37. Ibid., 222.

38. Ibid., 223.

39. Ibid., 226.

40. James Thomas Flexner, *The Young Hamilton* (Boston: Little, Brown and Company, 1978), 13 and 16.

41. Claude Gernade Bowers, *Jefferson and Hamilton: The Struggle for Democracy* (New York: Houghton, Mifflin Co., 1925), 22-23.

42. Ibid., 22.

43. Flexner, *The Young Hamilton*, 446.

44. Bowers, 24.

45. Flexner, 318.

46. Ibid., 449.

47. T.J. to Benjamin Rush, January 16, 1811; Lipscomb and Bergh, XIII, 4.

48. Flexner, *The Young Hamilton*, 331-336.

49. T.J. to Thomas Mann Randolph, Jr., April 18, 1790; *Papers of T.J.*, XVI, 351.

50. T.J. to Thomas Mann Randolph, Jr., June 20, 1790; *Papers of T.J.*, XVI, 541.

51. Account of the conversation is from Thomas Jefferson, *The Anas of Thomas Jefferson, 1791-1809*, Franklin B. Sawvel, ed. (New York: The Round Table Press, 1903), 33-34.

52. Ibid., 34.

53. *Journal of William Maclay, United States Senator from Pennsylvania, 1789-1791*, Edgar S. Maclay, ed. (N.Y.: 1890), May 24, 1790 entry, 272.

54. All sources cited agree on this point.

55. Jefferson, *Anas*, 34.

56. Ibid.

57. Richard B. Morris, ed., *Encyclopedia of American History*, 123.

58. T.J. to William Short, January 8, 1825; Lipscomb and Bergh, XVI, 92.

59. T.J. to Lafayette, April 2, 1790; *Papers of T.J.*, XVI, 293.

60. Harold Syrett et al. eds., *Papers of Alexander Hamilton* (New York: 1961-73), XVI, XVII.

61. T.J. to Thomas Cooper, October 27, 1808; Lipscomb and Bergh, XII, 180.

62. Final State of the Report on Weights and Measures; *Papers of T.J.*, XVI, 653-654.

63. Postscript to the Report on Weights and Measures; *Papers of T.J.*, XVI, 675.

64. Malone, II, 280.

65. T.J. to Isaac McPherson, August 13, 1813; Lipscomb and Bergh, VIII, 151-152.

66. *Papers of T.J.*, XVIII, 38, n.

67. Schachner, 403-404; Malone II, 321-323.

68. *Papers of T.J.*, XVII, 378-379.

69. T.J. to Francis Kinloch, November 26, 1790; *Papers of T.J.*, XVIII, 80.

70. T.J. to Gouverneur Morris, August 12, 1790; *Papers of T.J.*, XVII, 127. The italics are Jefferson's.

71. T.J. to James Madison, March 13, 1791.

72. Malone, II, 324.

73. T.J. to George Mason, February 4, 1791 (Ford, V), 274-276.

74. Cabinet opinion, February 15, 1791 (Ford, V), 284-289.

75. Alexander Hamilton to Washington, February 23, 1791; *Papers of Alexander Hamilton*, VIII, 62-135.

76. T.J. to Edward Carrington, August 4, 1787, *Papers of T.J.*, 678-679.

77. T.J. to Jonathan B. Smith, April 26, 1791, Ibid., XX, 290.

78. Extended "Editorial Note," Ibid., 268-290.

79. T.J. to Washington, May 8, 1791, Ibid., 291-292.

80. James Madison to T.J., May 12, 1791, Ibid., 294-295.

81. T.J. to John Adams, July 17, 1791, Ibid., 302-303.

82. T.J. to Mary (Polly) Jefferson, March 31, 1791, Ibid. XIX, 644-645.

83. Schachner, 436.

84. Displayed by the Smithsonian Institution, Washington, D.C., as part of its American Revolutionary Bicentennial exhibit on "Thomas Jefferson, Scientist."

85. T.J. to Martha Jefferson Randolph, May 31, 1791; *Papers of T.J.*, 463-464.

86. Malone II, 361.

87. Robert Troup to Alexander Hamilton, June 15, 1791; *Papers of Alexander Hamilton*,

Harold C. Syrett, ed. (N.Y. 1965), VIII, 478-479.

88. Nathaniel Hazard to Alexander Hamilton, November 25, 1791; Ibid., IX, 529-537.

89. Sir John Temple to the Duke of Leeds, May 23, 1791; Samuel Flagg Bemis, *Jay's Treaty: A Study in Commerce and Diplomacy* (New York: 1924), 84n.

90. George Beckwith to Grenville, June 14, 1791, summarized, Ibid., 83.

91. T.J. to Washington, September 9, 1792, (Ford, VI), 101-109.

92. T.J. to Madison, July 21, 1791; *Papers of T.J.*, XX, 657-658.

93. James Madison to T.J., July 24, 1791; Ibid., 667.

94. T.J. to Martha Jefferson Randolph, November 13, 1791 (Schachner, 443).

95. Bemis, *Jay's Treaty*, 104-105.

96. T.J. to William Short, July 28, 1791; *Papers of T.J.*, XX, 686-687.

97. Schachner, 451.

98. Ternant to Montmorin, October 27, 1791; Malone, II, 396.

99. *Anas*, November 1791, (Ford, V, 397-400).

100. Ibid., 397-400, 436-437, 451-452.

101. "Clauses for Treaty of Commerce with France" and "Questions to be Considered of," November 1791, (Ford, V, 397-400).

102. Ford, I, 185.

103. Ford, V, 400-405.

104. Washington to Gouverneur Morris, January 28, 1792, with letter to T.J. (Fitzpatrick, XXXI), 467-470.

105. T.J. to William Short, January 28, 1792 (T.J. *Papers*, L. of C., Series I, Reel 15).

106. T.J. "to the British Minister", May 29, 1792 (Ford, VI), 7-69.

107. Hammond to Grenville, June 8, 1792; Bemis, *Jay's Treaty*, 106-107.

108. *Anas*, March 11, 1792.

109. Washington to T.J., August 23, 1792 (Fitzpatrick, XXXII), 128-130.

110. Ibid.

111. T.J. to Washington, November 29, 1790 (Ford, V), 252-253.

112. Malone, III, 375.

113. T.J. to L'Enfant, April 10, 1791; *Papers of T.J.*, XX, 86.

114. T.J. to L'Enfant, February 27, 1792 (T.J. *Papers*, L. of C., Series I, Reel 15).

115. *Papers of T.J.*, XX, 3-87.

116. Opinion on the Bill Apportioning Representation (Ford, V), 493-501.

117. *Papers of James Madison*, XIV, in Robert A. Rutland and Thomas Mason, eds. (Charlottesville, Va.: 1983), 229-303. This account may be accepted as especially reliable because Madison composed it as a memorandum following his conversation with Washington.

118. Ibid., 304.

119. T.J. to Washington, May 23, 1792 (Ford, VI), 1-6.

120. Schachner, 464.

121. Gouverneur Morris, who delivered the eulogy at Hamilton's funeral, July 14, 1804, had confided to his diary the day before: "He was on principle opposed to republican and attached to monarchical government." *Papers of Alexander Hamilton*, XXVI, 324.

122. *Anas*, July 10, 1792.

123. Freeman, *Washington*, VI, 364.

124. T.J. to David Rittenhouse, August 12, 1792; (Malone, II), 459.

125. Henry Cabot Lodge, ed., *The Works of Alexander Hamilton*, II, (New York: 1904), 288-289.

126. Washington to T.J., August 23, 1792, Freeman, *Washington*, VI, 368.

127. Washington to Alexander Hamilton, August 26, 1792, Ibid.

128. Alexander Hamilton to Washington, September 9, 1742; *The Works of Alexander Hamilton*, IV, 303-305.

129. T.J. to Washington, September 9, 1792, Freeman, *Washington*, VI, 369-370.

130. Amicus, September 11, 1792; *Papers of Alexander Hamilton*, XII, 354-356; Catullus, September 15, 19, 29, Ibid., 379-385, 343-401, 498-506, 578-587. In Catullus, September 29, Hamilton saw T.J. as "Caesar, who overturned the republic." Ibid., 505-506. There was contem-

porary dispute as to whether Hamilton intended to refer to T.J. as an "intriguing incendiary"; Ibid., 379, n. 2; 502, n. 7. Previous biographers of T.J. have incorrectly attributed to Hamilton writings against T.J. under the pseudonym "Scourge."

131. The actual author was William Loughton Smith (Ibid., 411-412); T.J. to Edmund Randolph, September 17, 1792 (Ford, VIII) 151-152.

132. *Papers of Alexander Hamilton*, XII, 505-506.

133. *Anas*, October 1, 1792.

134. Malone, II, 473.

135. Ibid., 476.

136. T.J. to Martha Jefferson Randolph, January 14, 1793 (Randall, II), 191.

137. T.J. to Thomas Pinckney, December 3, 1792 (Ford, VI), 143-144.

138. *Anas*, 103-105.

139. Ibid., 105-106.

140. James Monroe to T.J., March 27, 1793.

141. William S. Smith to T.J., May 21, 1786. For record of conversation see *Anas* (Feb. 20, 1793), 106-108.

142. *Anas* (Feb. 20, 1793), 106-108.

143. T.J. to William Short, January 3, 1793; T.J. *Papers*, L. of C., Series I, Reel 17.

145. T.J. to William Carmichael and William Short, March 23, 1793; T.J. *Papers*, L. of C., Series I, Reel 17.

146. T.J. to Washington, April 8, 1793 (Ford, VI), 212.

147. *Anas* (April 18, 1793), 118.

148. T.J. to Washington, April 28, 1793 (Ford, VI), 218-231.

149. T.J. to James Madison, May 12, 1793 (Ford, VI), 251.

150. T.J. to James Monroe, May 5, 1793 (Ford, VI), 239.

151. T.J. to Gouverneur Morris, June 13, 1793 (Ford, VI), 299-300.

152. Portrait by Ezra Ames in collection of the Albany Institute and Historical and Art Society.

153. Schachner, 488.

154. Genet to T.J., September 18, 1793; *American State Papers, Class I, Foreign Relations*, I, 172-174.

155. T.J. to J.W. Eppes, May 12, 1793; T.J. *Papers*, L. of C., Document no. 14772, Series I, Reel 18.

156. T.J. to Thomas Mann Randolph, May 6, 1793 (Ford, VI), 241.

157. T.J. to M. Ternant, May 15, 1793; *American State Papers, Class I, Foreign Relations*, I, 147.

158. *Anas* (May 20, 1793), 122-125.

159. Ibid.

160. T.J. to James Monroe, May 5, 1793 (Ford, VI), 238-239.

161. James Madison to T.J., May 27, 1793 (Ford, VI), 268-269.

162. T.J. to James Madison, June 9, 1793, (Ford, VI), 290-294.

163. Genet to Minister of Foreign Affairs, Oct. 7, 1793 (Schachner), 492.

164. Genet to T.J., May 23, 1793; *American State Papers, Class I, Foreign Relations*, I, 147.

165. Schachner, 493.

166. T.J. to Gouverneur Morris, August 16, 1793 (Ford, VI), 381.

167. T.J. to Genet, June 17, 1793; *American State Papers, Class I, Foreign Relations*, I, 154-155.

168. Genet to T.J., June 22, 1793; Ibid., 155-156.

169. Ibid., 156.

170. T.J. to James Madison, August 3, 1793 (Ford, VI), 361.

171. T.J. to James Madison, July 7, 1793 (Ford, VI), 338.

172. Ibid.

173. *Anas* (July 5, 1793), 129-131.

174. Ibid. Some quotations from T.J. in this passage and subsequently from *Anas* (July 10, 1793), 136-144, are transposed from past to present tense to reproduce as nearly as possible the actual words he spoke.

175. *Anas.*

176. Ford, VI, 339-344.

177. T.J. to Chief Justice Jay, July 18, 1793; *Correspondence and Public Papers of John Jay*, Henry P. Johnston, ed. (N.Y.: 1891) III, 486-487. Jay to Washington, July 20, 1793, Ibid., 487-488; Jay to Washington, August 8, 1793, Ibid., 488-489.

178. Information on cabinet meetings from July 23, 1793, through August 2, 1793, is taken from *Anas*, 148-161.

179. *Anas* (July 23, 1793), 148-153.

180. Ibid., et seq.

181. T.J. to the U.S. Minister to France (Ford, VI) 371-393.

182. Memorandum, August 20, 1793 (Ford, I), 259-260.

183. T.J. to Genet, September 15, 1793 (Ford, VI), 429-430.

184. T.J. to James Madison, September 8, 1793 (Ford, VI), 419.

185. T.J. to James Madison, November 2, 1793 (Ford, VI), 439.

186. T.J. to James Madison, November 17, 1793 (Ford, VI), 449-450.

187. *Anas* (Nov. 8, 1793), 174-175.

188. Ibid. (Nov. 18, 1793), 175-178.

189. Ibid. (Nov. 28, 1793), 181-183.

190. Ibid. (Dec. 1, 1793), 193.

191. Malone, III, 153.

192. *Report on the Privileges and Restrictions on the Commerce of the United States in Foreign Countries*, (Ford, VI), 470-484.

193. Washington to T.J., January 1, 1794; *The Writings of George Washington*, ed. John C. Fitzpatrick (Washington, D.C.: 1940) XXXIII, 231.

194. Washington to T.J. (received Dec. 28, 1793); Schachner, 515.

195. T.J. to Genet, December 31, 1793; Ford, VI, 496.

196. Washington to T.J., January 1, 1794; Fitzpatrick, XXXIII, 231.

197. John Quincy Adams, *Parties in the United States* (New York: 1941), 17.

198. Malone, III, 80.

199. Angelica Church to T.J., August 19, 1793; Schachner, 510.

200. T.J. to Angelica Church, June 7, 1793; Ford, VI, 289.

201. T.J. to Angelica Church, November 27, 1793; *Thomas Jefferson: Writings* (Library of America), 1013.

CHAPTER XVI

1. T.J. to Horatio Gates, February 3, 1794 (Jefferson Papers, L. of C., microfilm, Series I, Doc. 16571, Reel 20).

2. T.J. to John Adams, April 25, 1794 (Ford, VI), 504-505.

3. T.J. to E. Randolph, February 3, 1794 (Ford, VI), 498-499.

4. *Thomas Jefferson's Farm Book*, Morris Betts, ed. (Charlottesville: 1976), xiv.

5. For an expert opinion on this point, I am indebted to conversation on January 13, 1985, with Dr. Helen Cripe, author of *Thomas Jefferson and Music* (Charlottesville: 1976).

6. T.J. to Martha Jefferson Randolph (Randall, II), 221.

7. During the Revolution, Farrell and Jones had refused Jefferson's tender of payment in Virginia currency.

8. T.J. to George Wythe, October 23, 1794 (Jefferson Papers, L. of C., microfilm, Series I, Doc. 16749, Rec 120).

9. Schachner, 568.

10. Nigel Nicolson, *Great Houses of the Western World* (London: 1972), 260.

11. Schachner, 569.

12. Martha Jefferson Randolph to T.J., received July 1, 1798; E.M. Betts and James A. Bear, Jr., eds., *The Family Letters of Thomas Jefferson* (Columbia, Mo.: 1965). On April 4, 1790, she had written her father concerning her husband, "I have made it my study to please him in everything and do consider all other objects as secondary to that except my love for you." (Ibid., 52-53)

13. T.J. to E. Randolph, September 7, 1794 (Ford, VI), 512-513.

14. Caroline Holmes Bivins, *Dolley and the Great Little Madison* (Washington, D.C.: 1977), 1.

15. T.J. to James Madison, April 3, 1794 (Jefferson Papers, L. of C., microfilm, series I, Doc. 16604, Reel 20). The congressman was William Smith of South Carolina, not to be confused with the William Smith who was son-in-law to John and Abigail Adams.

16. T.J. to James Madison, October 30, 1794 (Schachner), 566.

17. T.J. to James Monroe, May 26, 1795 (Ford, VIII), 15-22.

18. T.J. to James Madison, February 23, 1795; James Madison to T.J., March 23, 1795 (Jefferson Papers, L. of C. microfilm series I, Doc. 16804, Reel 20).

19. "Notes on Professor Ebeling's Letter of July 30, '95, " (Ford, VII), 44-49.

20. T.J. to Edward Rutledge, November 30, 1795 (Ford, VII), 39-40.

21. T.J. to William B. Giles, December 31, 1795 (Ford, VII), 41-44.

22. T.J. to James Madison, September 8, 1795 (L. of C. microfilm, Series I, Doc. 16916, Reel 20).

23. T.J. to James Madison, March 27, 1796 (Ford, VII), 68-69.

24. T.J. to Phillip Mazzei, April 24, 1796 (Ford, VII), 72-78.

25. Philadelphia, Pa. *Aurora*, September 13, 1796 (Malone, III, 276).

26. T.J. to Mann Page, August 30, 1795 (Ford VII), 23-25.

27. Malone, II, 277.

28. T.J. to Thomas Mann Randolph, November 28, 1796 (Jefferson Papers, L. of C., microfilm, Series I, Doc. 16280, Reel 20).

29. T.J. to James Madison, December 17, 1796 (Ford, VII), 91-92.

30. T.J. to Edward Rutledge, December 27, 1796, Ibid., 93-95.

31. James Madison to T.J., December 19, 1796 (Schachner), 585.

32. T.J. to John Adams, December 28, 1796 (Ford VII), 95-97.

33. T.J. to James Madison, January 1, 1797 (Ford VII), 98-100.

34. John Adams to "Mr. Dalton," January 19, 1797, first quoted in Schachner, 587.

35. T.J. to James Madison, The description of the oath-taking in the Senate Chamber is based on the Edward Thornton account (Henry Adams, *History*, I, 196-199), and the report in *National Intelligencer*, March 6, 1801.

36. Malone, III, 345.

37. C.F. Adams, ed., *The Works of John Adams*, IX (Boston: 1854), 284-285.

38. Ibid.

39. Ibid., 285.

40. John Adams to Elbridge Gerry, April 6, 1797; *The Works of John Adams*, VIII (1853), 538-539.

41. Malone, III, 303.

42. T.J. to Elbridge Gerry, May 13, 1797 (Ford VII), 119-124.

43. T.J. to Elbridge Gerry, June 21, 1797 (Ford VII), 149-151.

44. Alexander Hamilton to Rufus King, February 15, 1797 (Charles R. King, *The Life and Correspondence of Rufus King* II, N.Y., 1895), 147-148.

45. Fisher Ames to Chistopher Gore, December 17, 1796 (*Works of Fisher Ames*, Seth Ames, ed., Boston, 1854) I, 211.

46. T.J. to James Madison, May 18, June 1, June 8, June 15, 1797 (Ford, VII), 124-127, 131-134, 140-141, 142-144.

47. T.J. to Peregrine Fitzhugh, June 4, 1797 (Ford, VII), 134-138.

48. John Adams to Uriah Forrest, incorrectly dated June 20, 1797; Adams, *Works*, VIII, 546-547.

49. T.J. to Peregrine Fitzhugh, February 23, 1798 (Ford, VII), 208-211.

50. T.J. to Aaron Burr, June 17, 1797 (Jefferson *Papers*, L. of C., microfilm Series I, Doc 17429-17431, Reel 20).

51. Aaron Burr to T.J., June 21, 1797, Ibid., Doc. 17438.

52. *Porcupine's Gazette*, July 5, 1797, quoted in Malone, III, 324.

53. Ibid.

54. *The Works of Alexander Hamilton*, Henry Cabot Lodge, ed., (N.Y., 1904), VII, 369-479.

55. Ford VII, 158-164; VIII, 322-331.

56. T.J. to James Monroe, September 7, 1797 (Jefferson *Papers*, L. of C., microfilm Series I, Doc. 17483-17484, Reel 21).

57. Adrienne Koch and Harry A. Koch, *William & Mary Quarterly*, 3rd Series, V (April 1948), 153.

58. T.J. to Martha Jefferson Randolph, February 8, 1798 (Randall, II), 405; T.J. to Maria Jefferson Eppes, March 7, 1798, Ibid., 406.

59. Thomas Jefferson to Edward Rutledge, June 24, 1797 (Jefferson *Papers*, L. of C., microfilm Series I, Doc 17444-17446, Reel 21).

60. John Nicolas to G. Washington, November 18, 1797 (Flexner, IV), 384. For discussion of the letter's implications, see Ibid., 384-388.

61. G. Washington to Bushrod Washington, August 12, 1798, *The Writings of George Washington*, John C. Fitzpatrick, ed., XXXVI (Washington: 1941), 408-409.

62. T.J. to Angelica Church, January 11, 1798 (Jefferson papers, L. of C., microfilm Series I, Doc. 17553-17554, Reel 21).

63. T.J., *Notes on Virginia*, 62.

64. John Page to T.J. June 21, 1798 (Jefferson *Papers*, L. of C. microfilm Series I, Doc. 17806-17808, Reel 21).

65. Quoted by T.J. to Dr. Samuel Brown, March 25, 1798 (Ford VII), 222-223.

66. Albert Gallatin to Mrs. Gallatin, February 18, 1798 (Henry Adams, *The Life of Albert Gallatin*, Philadelphia: 1879), 193-194.

67. T.J. to James Madison, February 15, 1798 (Ford VII), 201-203.

68. T.J. to James Madison, March 2, 1798, Ibid., 211-213.

69. T.J. to John Wise, February 12, 1798 (Malone, III), 364-465.

70. Theodore Sedgwick to Rufus King, April 9, 1798, *The Life and Correspondence of Rufus King*, Charles R. King, ed., II (N.Y.: 1971), 310-312.

71. Malone, III, 367.

72. T.J. to James Madison, March 21, 1798 (Jefferson *Papers*, L. of C., microfilm Series I, Doc. 17648-17649, Reel 21).

73. T.J. to James Monroe, April 5, 1798, Ibid., Doc. 17700.

74. T.J. to James Madison, April 6, 1798, Ibid., Doc. 17704-17705.

75. T.J. to James Madison, April 26, 1798, Ibid., Doc. 17740-17741.

76. T.J. to Thomas Mann Randolph, April 12, 1798 (Malone, III), 375.

77. T.J. to James Lewis, Jr., May 9, 1798 (Ford, VIII), 250-251.

78. John Adams to the Mayor, Aldermen and Citizens of Philadelphia, April 1798, *The Works of John Adams*, Charles Francis Adams, ed., IX (Boston: 1854), 182.

79. John Adams to "the inhabitants of the County of Lancaster, Pennsylvania," May 8, 1798, Ibid., 190.

80. Albert J. Beveridge, *The Life of John Marshall*, II (Boston: 1916), 346-347.

81. James Madison to T.J., May 13, 1798 (Malone III), 379.

82. James Monroe to T.J., June 1798 and June 16, 1798; S.M. Hamilton, ed., *Writings of James Monroe,* III (N.Y., 1898), 128-136, 127.

83. T.J. to John Taylor, June 1, 1798 (Ford VII), 263-266.

84. T.J. to Madison, June 7,, 1798, Ibid., 266-269.

85. T.J. to Mann Page, August 30, 1795, Ibid., 23-35.

86. *The Federalist*, Benjamin F. Wright, ed. (Cambridge, Mass., 1966), No. 28, 255.

87. T.J. to John Taylor, June 1, 1798 (Ford, VII), 263-265.

88. W.C. Nicholas to George Nicholas, Sept. 21, 1798 (Nicholas Papers, University of Virginia). Quoted in Malone, IV, 400-401.

89. James J. Kilpatrick, ed., *We the States: An Anthology of Historical Documents, etc.* (Virginia Commission on Constitutional Government, Richmond 1964), 143-151. For comparison of rough draft, fair copy, and facsimile of resolution as adopted, see Ford, VII, 288-309.

90. Ford, VII, 301.

91. Malone, III, 401.

92. T.J. to Madison, November 17, 1798 (Lipscomb and Bergh), 62-63.

93. Kilpatrick, *We the States*, 152-153.

94. T.J. to W.C. Nicholas, November 29, 1798 (Ford VII), 312-313.

95. Kilpatrick, *We the States*, 154.

96. T.J. to Stephen T. Mason, October 11, 1798 (Ford, VII), 282-283.

97. T.J. to Elbridge Gerry, January 26, 1799 (Ford, VII), 327.

98. T.J. to James Madison, January 5, 1799 (Ford, VII), 318.

99. T.J. to James Madison, January 5, 1799 (Ford, VII), 344.

100. T.J. to Archibald Stuart, February 13, 1799 (Ford, VII), 354.

101. T.J. to James Madison, January 30, 1799 (Ford, VII), 341.

102. T.J. to Edmund Pendleton, February 14, 1799 (Ford, VII), 356.

103. Alexander Hamilton to Theodore Sedgwick, February 22, 1799.

104. T.J. to Kosciuszko, February 21, 1799 (Lipscomb and Bergh, X), 116.

105. Paul C. Nagel, *Descent from Glory* (N.Y.: 1983), 76-77.

106. T.J. to James Monroe, February 19, 1799 (Ford, VII), 366.

107. T.J. to James Madison, February 26, 1799, Ibid., 371.

108. Alexander Hamilton to James McHenry, June 27, 1799, *The Works of Alexander Hamilton*, John C. Hamilton, ed. (N.Y.: 1851), 283-284.

109. T.J. to William Green Mumford, June 18, 1799 (Jefferson *Papers*, L. of C. microfilm Series I, Doc, 18037-18039, Reel 21). Document in L. of C. is a copy; original in library of Teachers College, Columbia University, N.Y.

110. T.J. to Edmund Randolph, August 18, 1799 (Lipscomb and Bergh, *Writings*, 1903), 125-129.

111. T.J. to James Madison, August 23, 1799 (Adrienne Koch, *Jefferson and Madison: The Great Collaboration*, N.Y.: 1950), 196-198.

112. T.J. to W.C. Nicholas, September 5, 1799 (Ford IX), 79-81.

113. Kilpatrick, *We the States*, 157-226.

114. T.J. to Dr. Walter Jones, January 2, 1814 (*Thomas Jefferson: Writings*, The Library of America, 1984), 1319-1320.

115. Du Pont de Nemours to T.J., August 27, 1799 (Jefferson Papers, L. of C., microfilm Series I, Doc 17848, Reel 21).

116. T.J. to Thomas Mann Randolph, February 4, 1800 (Jefferson Papers, L. of C., microfilm Series I, Doc. 18172, Reel 22).

117. Ibid.

118. Ibid.

119. T.J. to Thomas Mann Randolph, March 14, 1800, *Thomas Jefferson's Farm Book*, E.M. Bates, ed., (Charlottesville: 1976), 274.

120. T.J. to Benjamin Rush, September 23, 1800 (*Thomas Jefferson: Writings*, Library of America, 1984), 1080-1082.

121. *Address to the People of the U.S.: With an Epitome and Vindication of the Public Life and Character of Thomas Jefferson.*

122. Ford VII, 475-477; *Thomas Jefferson: Writings* (Library of America), 702-704.

123. James Nicholson to Albert Gallatin, May 6 and May 7, 1806, and Mrs. Gallatin to Gallatin (Adams, *Gallatin*), 241-243.

124. James Madison to T.J., October 21, 1800, *Letters and Other Writings of James Madison* (Published by Order of Congress, Philadelphia, 1867) II, 162.

125. Sen. Charles Pinckney to T.J., October 12, 16, and 26, 1800 (Jefferson Papers, L. of C. microfilm Series I, Doc. 18411-18421, Reel 22).

126. Malone III, 490.

127. Ibid., 491.

128. Ibid., 142.

129. T.J. to Aaron Burr, December 15, 1800 (Ford, VII), 466-468.

130. James Monroe to T.J., January 6, 1801 (*The Writings of James Monroe*, Stanislaus M. Hamilton, ed., N.Y.: 1900) III, 253-255.

131. T.J. to James Monroe, December 20, 1800 (Jefferson Papers, L. of C., microfilm Series I, Doc. 18511, Reel 22).

132. James Madison to T.J., January 14, 1824; Irving Brant, *James Madison*, IV (Indianapolis, 1957), 26.

133. J.S. Pancake, "Aaron Burr, Would-Be Usurper," *William and Mary Quarterly*, 3rd Series, VIII (April 1951), 205.

134. Aaron Burr to T.J., December 15, 1800 (Jefferson *Papers*, L. of C. microfilm, series I, Doc. 18494, Reel 22).

135. T.J. to Maria (Mary Jefferson) Eppes, January 4, 1801 (Ford, VII), 477-479.

136. *William and Mary Quarterly*, 3rd Series, VIII, 204-213.

137. John Adams to Elbridge Gerry, December 30, 1800 (Adams, *Works*, IX), 577-578.

138. Alexander Hamilton to James A. Bayard, January 16, 1801; Harold C. Syrett, *Papers of Alexander Hamilton,* XXV (N.Y.: 1977), 319-320.

139. *Gazette of the United States*, February 16, 1801 (Malone, III), 503-504

140. Thomas Mann Randolph to James Monroe, February 14, 1801 (Malone, III), 503.

141. James A. Bayard to Alexander Hamilton, March 8, 1801 (Syrett, *Papers* XXV), 345.

142. Schachner, 657.

143. T.J. to James Monroe, February 15, 1801, (Ford, IX), 178-180.

144. James A. Bayard to Alexander Hamilton, March 4, 1801 (Syrett, *Papers*), XXV, 345.

145. DuPont de Nemours to T.J., February 20, 1801 (Malone, III), 505.

CHAPTER XVII

1. Details of Jefferson's inauguration, where not otherwise annotated, are based on Henry Adams, *History of the United States of America from the First Administration of Thomas Jefferson*, I (N.Y.: 1917), 196-199. The most valuable part of this record is the letter of Edward Thornton, in charge of the British Legation at Washington, to Lord Grenville, Foreign Secretary, March 4, 1801.

2. T.J. to Joseph Priestley, March 21, 1801 (Ford VIII), 22.

3. The phrase, Jefferson's own, should not be taken quite literally, although Adams was signing commissions the evening before the inauguration.

4. John Marshall to Charles Cotesworth Pinckney, March 4, 1801 (*American Historical Review*, Vol. 53, no. 3, 518-520). Note that the letter is misquoted in Albert J. Beveridge's famous *Life of John Marshall* (1919). Omission of the word "not" reversed the meaning of the last sentence in the quotation. Discovery of this and other errors in the letter as reproduced by Beveridge was the work of Richard J. Hooker, who examined the original document in archives of the Charleston Library Society, Charleston, S.C.

5. Paul C. Nagel, *Descent from Glory: Four Generations of the John Adams Family* (New York: Oxford, 1983), 78-79.

6. Ibid., 81.

7. The description of Jefferson on this occasion is based principally on the portrait painted by Rembrandt Peale a few months earlier.

8. Bernard Mayo, *Jefferson Himself* (Charlottesville: 1970), 219.

9. Ibid., 221-224. A more generally accessible source for the First Inaugural Address is *Thomas Jefferson: Writings* (Library of America, 1984), 492-496.

10. John Marshall to Charles Cotesworth Pinckney, March 4, 1801, *American Historical Review*, Vol. 53, no. 3, 518-520.

11. Margaret Bayard Smith, *The First Forty Years of Washington Society* (N.Y.: 1906), 12.

12. Schachner, 665, quoted from W.P. Cutler and J.P. Cutler, *Life, Journals and Correspondence of Rev. Manasseh Cutler*, II (1888), 43-45.

13. George Cabot to Rufus King, March 20, 1801; Charles R. King, *The Life and Correspondence of Rufus King*, Vol. III, N.Y., 1971, 407.

14. T.J. to Moses Robinson, March 23, 1801; Schachner, 666.

15. Malone, V, 17.

16. T.J. to John Breckinridge, August 12, 1803; *Thomas Jefferson: Writings (Library of America, N.Y., 1984)*, 1136-1139.

17. T.J. to Edmund Pendleton, August 26, 1776, Ibid., 755-756.

18. *Washington Dossier* (May 1985).

19. Leonard Lief, *The New Conservatives* (Indianapolis and N.Y.: 1967). The list of common ground issues is from 7-8.

20. The following statements by Hume and Montesquieu are quoted in support of this proposition in Peter Gay, *The Bridge of Criticism* (N.Y.: 1970), 74-75. The Voltaire quotation is from the "Miscellany" section of *The Portable Voltaire*, ed. Ben Ray Redman (N.Y.: 1977), 225.

21. *The Encyclopedia of Philosophy*, (N.Y. and London: 1967), IV, 460-461.

22. T.J. to John Adams, April 8, 1816, *Thomas Jefferson: Writings* (Library of America), 1381-1384.

23. T.J. to Col. Charles Yancey, January 6, 1816 (Ford X), 4.

24. T.J. to Roger C. Weightman, June 24, 1826, *Thomas Jefferson: Writings* (Library of America), 1517.

25. As summarized in Karl J. Weintraub, *Visions of Culture* (Chicago: 1966), 135.

26. Alfred North Whitehead, *Adventures of Ideas* (N.Y.: 1933), 380.

27. James Harvey Robinson, "Civilization and Culture," *Encyclopedia Britannica*, 1929.

Select Critical Bibliography

BY FAR the most important sources of information on Thomas Jefferson are his formal writings, his journals and record books, and his massive correspondence with men, women, and children on three continents over a period of sixty-seven years. The originals of these writings are to be found chiefly in the Library of Congress, the Alderman Library of the University of Virginia, the Virginia State Library, the Massachusetts Historical Society, the Henry E. Huntington Library in San Marino, and the Earl Gregg Swem Library of the College of William and Mary. Jefferson papers from all these repositories are available on microfilm or in photostat from the Library of Congress. Many of these writings, from 1760 to August 1791, are in print in *The Papers of Thomas Jefferson*, published by Princeton University Press, beginning in 1950 under the brilliant editorship of the late Julian P. Boyd, who saw the work through its first twenty volumes. Since 1983 the work has gone forward under the editorship of Charles T. Cullen. Volume XXII of the project's sixty-volume collection is now (1986) in preparation.

Amplifying and explaining much in the Jefferson Papers are those of his associates, especially James Madison, George Washington, James Monroe, John Adams, and Alexander Hamilton.

Second in importance only to such original sources is Henry S. Randall's *The Life of Thomas Jefferson*, published in three volumes in 1858. Though technically a secondary source, it is in effect, because of the author's acquaintance with Jefferson's relatives and friends and access to personal artifacts, a primary one.

Next in significance for the scholar of Jefferson's life is Dumas Malone's six-volume *Jefferson and His Time*. Though discovery of additional facts since completion of Professor Malone's work; and my own insights, have compelled me to differ with his interpretation of some points, they have not dimmed my respect for his biography as a monument of American scholarship. All of us who write about Jefferson today are in Professor Malone's debt.

We are indebted also to the late Nathan Schachner, whose *Thomas Jefferson* was published in two volumes in 1951. Mr. Schachner derived fresh insights from the varied activities of a life of both practical affairs and scholarship and from the fact that before writing a biography of the Virginian he had written one of Jefferson's arch rival, Alexander Hamilton.

Even though buildings are not listed in this bibliography, much of my research has involved detailed examination of homes and public structures. This kind of preparation, whenever possible, is often valuable in reconstructing scenes in a biographee's life. It assumes unusual importance in the case of Jefferson, because he was especially sensitive to his surroundings and also because, as architect and landscape gardener, he left his impress on some of these settings. I have studied with special care buildings and grounds in Charlottesville, Albemarle County, Williamsburg, and Richmond, in Virginia, as well as others in the District of Columbia and Philadelphia.

I. *Jefferson's Writings*

Betts, Edwin M., ed. *Thomas Jefferson's Farm Book.* Princeton, 1953.
_____. *Thomas Jefferson's Garden Book.* Philadelphia, 1944.
_____ and Bear, James A., Jr. *The Family Letters of Thomas Jefferson.* Columbia, MO, 1965.

Boyd, Julian P., ed. *The Papers of Thomas Jefferson.* Vols. I-XXX. Princeton, 1950–1982. Vol. XXI, Index, published 1983, Charles T. Cullen, ed. This is by far the most ably and thoroughly edited collection of Jefferson's letters but at this time (1986) extends only to August 1791.

Cappon, Lester J., ed. *The Adams-Jefferson Letters: The Complete Correspondence Between Thomas Jefferson and John and Abigail Adams.* Chapel Hill, NC, 1959.

Ford, Paul Leicester, ed. *The Writings of Thomas Jefferson.* 10 vols. New York, 1892–1899. Competently though not always objèctively annotated, this collection suffers from large gaps in the correspondence. It is valuable chiefly as a printed source of Jefferson letters after August 1791, the latest date so far covered by the Princeton edition edited by Boyd and Cullen.

Jefferson, Thomas. *An Essay Towards Facilitating Instruction in the Anglo-Saxon and Modern Dialects of the English Language for the Use of the University of Virginia.* New York, 1851.

Lipscomb, A.A. and Bergh, A.E., eds. *The Writings of Thomas Jefferson.* 20 vols. Washington, DC, 1903. These volumes include letters not to be found in Paul Leicester Ford and not yet within the compass of the Princeton edition, but annotation is sparse and portions of printed letters are omitted without textual indication of that fact.

Malone, Dumas, ed. *Autobiography of Thomas Jefferson.* Boston, 1948.

Mayo, Bernard, ed. *Jefferson Himself.* Charlottesville, VA, 1971.

Peden, William, ed. *Notes on the State of Virginia.* By Thomas Jefferson. Chapel Hill, NC, 1955.

Peterson, Merrill D., ed. *Thomas Jefferson: Writings.* (The Library of America), New York, 1984.

Presidential Papers, Library of Congress, Washington, DC. Thomas Jefferson Papers, Series I, Reels 14–22. For those years not yet included in the Princeton Edition, this collection is the essential source. Even for those letters available in the Princeton Edition, the L. of C. collection offers the added testimony of variations in handwriting and of Jefferson's suggestive emendations of his first drafts.

Sawvel, F.B., ed. *The Complete Anas of Thomas Jefferson.* New York, 1903.

II. *Contemporary Writings*

Adams, John. *Works.* Ed. C.F. Adams. 10 vols. Boston, 1856.

Ames, Seth, ed. *Works of Fisher Ames.* Boston, 1854.

Bland, Richard. *An Inquiry into the Rights of the British Colonies.* Williamsburg, Alexander Purdie & Co., 1776. (Reprint, Richmond, VA, 1922).

Burnaby, Rev. Andrew. *Travels Through the Middle Settlements in North America in the Years 1759 and 1760.* 2nd ed. London, 1775.

Burnett, Edmund Cody, ed. *Letters of Members of the Continental Congress.* Washington, D.C., 1921.

Burr, Aaron. *Memoirs of Aaron Burr with Miscellaneous Selections from His Correspondence.* Ed. Matthew L. Davis. 2 vols. New York, 1836–1837.

Carter, Landon. *The Diary of Colonel Landon Carter of Sabine Hall, 1752–1778.* Ed. Jack P. Greene. 2 vols. Charlottesville, VA, 1965.

Chastellux, Marquis de. *Travels in North America, 1780, 1781, and 1782.* Ed. Howard C. Rice, Jr. Chapel Hill, NC, 1963.

Fithian, Philip Vickers. *Journal and Letters of Philip Vickers Fithian.* Ed. Hunter Dickinson Farish. Williamsburg, VA, 1943.

Hamilton, Alexander. *Papers.* Harold Syrett, et al. 17 vols. New York, 1961–1973.

_____. *Works.* Ed. John C. Hamilton. 7 vols. New York, 1850–1851.

_____. *Works.* Ed. Henry Cabot Lodge. 12 vols. New York, 1904.

King, Charles R. *The Life and Correspondence of Rufus King.* Vol. II. New York, 1895.

Maclay, Edgar S., ed. *Journal of William Maclay, United States Senator from Pennsylvania, 1789–1791.* New York, 1890.

Madison, James. *Letters and Other Writings of James Madison.* 4 vols. Published by Order of Congress. Philadelphia, 1867.

_____. *Papers.* Vols. I-XIV. Eds. Robert A. Rutland and Thomas A. Mason. Chicago, IL, and Charlottesville, VA, 1983.

_____. Papers of the Presidents. The James Madison Papers. Library of Congress Microfilms.

Marshall, John. "John Marshall to Charles Cotesworth Pinckney, March 4, 1801."*American Historical Review.* Vol. 53, no. 3.

Mason, Frances Norton. *John Norton & Sons, Merchants of London and Virginia, Being the Papers from Their Counting House for the Years 1750–1795.* Richmond, VA, 1937.

Monroe, James. *Writings.* Ed. Stanislaus M. Hamilton. 7 vols. New York, 1898–1903.

Moreau de St. Mery. *Moreau de St. Mery's American Journey.* (1793–1798). Ed. and trans. by Kenneth and Alma M. Roberts. New York, 1947.

Oswald, Richard. *Memorandum on the Folly of Invading Virginia, the Strategic Importance of Portsmouth, and the Need for Civilian Control of the Military.* Ed. W. Stitt Robinson, Jr. Charlottesville, VA, 1953.

Stevens, Benjamin Franklin, ed. *An Exact Reprint of Six Rare Pamphlets on the Clinton-Cornwallis Controversy with Very Numerous Important Unpublished Manuscript Notes by Sir Henry Clinton, K.B..* Vols. I & II. London, 1888.

Virginia Gazette (Williamsburg, J. Royle, microfilm), 1765–1766. Colonial Williamsburg, Inc.

Virginia Gazette (Williamsburg, Purdie and Dixon, photostats), 1766, 1774. Colonial Williamsburg, Inc.,and Library of the College of William and Mary.

Virginia Gazette (Individual issues, 1775–1776), Virginia Historical Society and

Colonial Williamsburg, Inc.

Washington, George. *Writings*. Ed. J.C. Fitzpatrick. 39 vols. Washington, D.C., 1931–1941.

III.   *Official and Semi-official Collections*

American Archives. Ed. Peter Force. 9 vols. Washington, D.C., 1837–1853.

Calendar of Virginia State Papers. Richmond, VA, 1875.

Journals of the Continental Congress. 34 vols. Washington, D.C., 1904–1936.

Journals of the Council of State of Virginia. 2 vols. Richmond, VA, 1931–1932.

Journals of the House of Burgesses of Virginia, 1619–1776. Richmond, VA, 1905–1915.

Journals of the House of Delegates of Virginia, 1776. Richmond, VA, 1828.

Official Letters of the Governors of the State of Virginia. Vols. I–III. Gen. ed. H.R. McIlwaine. Richmond, VA, 1926–1929.

The Statutes at Large, Being a Collection of All the Laws of Virginia. 13 vols. Ed. W.W. Hening. Richmond, VA, 1809–1823.

IV.   **Secondary Sources**

Abernathy, P. *Western Lands and the American Revolution*. New York, 1937.

Adair, Douglass. *Fame and the Founding Fathers*. New York, 1974.

Adams, Arthur and Weis, Frederick L. *The Magna Carta Sureties, 1215: The Barons Named in the Magna Carta and Some of Their Descendants Who Settled in America, 1607–1650*. 2nd authorized edition with revisions and corrections by Walter Lee Shepard, Jr. Baltimore, 1968.

Adams, Henry. *History of the United States During the Administrations of Jefferson and Madison*. 9 vols. New York, 1891–1893.

_____. *History of the United States of America From the First Administration of Thomas Jefferson*. Vol. I. New York, 1917.

_____. *The Life of Albert Gallatin*. Philadelphia, 1879.

Adams, William Howard. *The Eye of Thomas Jefferson*. Washington, D.C., 1976.

Ambler, Charles Henry. *Sectionalism in Virginia From 1776–1861*. Chicago, 1910.

Andrews, Matthew Page. *Virginia, the Old Dominion*. New York, 1937.

Arnason, H.H. *The Sculptures of Houdon*. New York, 1975.

Bear, James A., Jr., ed. *Jefferson at Monticello*. Charlottesville, VA, 1976.

Becker, Carl. *The Declaration of Independence*. New York, 1940.

Bemis, Samuel Flagg. *Jay's Treaty: A Study in Commerce and Diplomacy*. New York, 1924.

Beveridge, Albert J. *The Life of John Marshall*. 4 vols. Boston, 1916.

Bivins, Caroline Holmes. *Dolley and the Great Little Madison*. Washington, D.C., 1977.

Bowers, Claude Gernade. *Jefferson and Hamilton: The Struggle for Democracy*. New York, 1925.

Boyd, Julian P., ed. *The Declaration of Independence; the Evolution of the Text as Shown in Facsimiles of Various Drafts by Its Author.* Washington, D.C., 1943.

Bridenbaugh, Carl, *Seat of Empire.* Williamsburg, VA, 1958.

Brinton, Crane. "The Enlightenment," *The Encyclopedia of Philosophy.* Vol. V. Ed. Paul Edwards. New York, London, 1967.

Brodie, Fawn. *Thomas Jefferson: An Intimate History.* New York, 1974.

Brown, Robert Eldon, and B. Katherine. *Virginia, 1705–1786. Democracy or Aristocracy?* East Lansing, MI, 1964.

Bullock, Helen Duprey. *My Head and Heart: A Little Chronicle of Thomas Jefferson and Maria Cosway.* New York, 1945.

Burke's Presidential Families of the United States of America. London, 1975.

Burnett, Edmund Cody. *The Continental Congress.* New York, 1941.

Butt, Marshall W. *Portsmouth Under Four Flags.* Portsmouth, VA, 1971.

Butterfield, L.H., and Rice, Howard C., Jr. "Jefferson's Earliest Note to Maria Cosway with Some New Facts and Conjectures on His Broken Wrist," *William and Mary Quarterly.* Series 3, Vol. V. January 1948.

Chinard, Gilbert. *Thomas Jefferson, the Apostle of Americanism.* Boston, 1929.

Chitwood, Oliver Perry. *Justice in Colonial Virginia.* Baltimore, 1905.

_____. *Richard Henry Lee, Statesman of the Revolution.* Morgantown, WV, 1967.

Coke, Edward. *The First Part of the Institute of the Laws of England; Or, a Commentary Upon Littleton.* Philadelphia, 1853.

Commager, Henry Steele, ed. *The Heritage of America.* Boston, 1949.

Cranston, Maurice. "Liberalism," *The Encyclopedia of Philosophy.* New York and London, 1967.

Cresson, William Penn. *James Monroe.* Chapel Hill, NC, 1946.

Cripe, Helen. *Thomas Jefferson and Music.* Charlottesville, VA, 1976.

Dabney, Virginius. "From Cuckoo Tavern to Monticello," *The Ironworker.* Vol. XXX (Summer 1966).

_____. "Jack Jouett's Ride," *American Heritage.* Vol. XIII (Dec. 1961).

_____. *The Jefferson Scandals.* New York, 1981.

_____. *Virginia the New Dominion.* New York, 1971.

Daniel, J.R.V., ed. *A Hornbook of Virginia History.* Richmond, VA, 1949.

Daniels, Jonathan. *The Randolphs of Virginia.* New York, 1972.

Dewey, Frank L. "Thomas Jefferson's Law Practice," *Virginia Magazine of History and Biography.* Vol. LXXXV (July 1977).

_____. *Thomas Jefferson, Lawyer.* Charlottesville, VA, 1986.

Dowdey, Clifford. *The Golden Age: A Climate for Greatness, Virginia 1732–1775.* Boston, 1970.

_____. *The Great Plantation.* New York, 1957.

_____. *The Virginia Dynasties.* Boston, 1969.

Dumbauld, Edward. *Thomas Jefferson, American Tourist.* Norman, OK, 1946.

Eckenrode, H.J. *The Randolphs: The Story of a Virginia Family.* New York, 1946.

_____. *The Revolution in Virginia.* Boston and New York, 1916.

Flexner, James Thomas. *The Young Hamilton.* Boston, 1978.

Flippin, Percy S. *Royal Government in Virginia, 1624–1775*. New York, 1919.

Freeman, Douglas Southall. *George Washington*. Vols. I–VI. New York, 1948–1954.

Gaines, William H., Jr. *Thomas Mann Randolph: Jefferson's Son-in-Law*. Baton Rouge, LA, 1966.

Gipson, Lawrence Henry. *The British Empire Before the American Revolution*. 13 vols. New York, 1936–1967.

_____. *The Coming of the Revolution, 1763–1775*. New York, 1954.

Greene, Jack P. *The American Colonies in the Eighteenth Century, 1689–1763*. New York, 1969.

_____. *The Quest for Power: The Lower Houses of Assembly in the Southern Royal Colonies, 1689–1776*. Chapel Hill, NC, 1963.

Griffith, Lucille. *The Virginia House of Burgesses, 1750–1774*. Rev. ed. University, AL, 1970.

Grigsby, Hugh Blair. *The History of the Virginia Federal Convention of 1788*. 2 vols. Richmond, VA, 1890–1891.

_____. *The Virginia Convention of 1776*. Richmond, VA, 1855.

Harrison, Fairfax. "The Equine F.F.V.'s" *Virginia Magazine of History and Biography*. XXXV (October 1927).

Hastings, G.E. *Life and Works of Francis Hopkinson*. Chicago, 1926.

Hazelton, John H. *The Declaration of Independence: Its History*. New York, 1906.

Hendrick, Burton J. *The Lees of Virginia: Biography of a Family*. Boston, 1935.

Henry, William Wirt. *Patrick Henry, Life, Correspondence, and Speeches*. New York, 1891.

Isaac, Rhys. *The Transformation of Virginia, 1740–1790*. Chapel Hill, NC, 1982.

Johnston, Henry P. *Yorktown Campaign and the Surrender of Cornwallis, 1781*. New York, 1881.

Jordan, David S., and Kimball, Sarah L. *Your Family Tree*. Baltimore, 1968.

Jordan, Winthrop D. *White Over Black*. Chapel Hill, NC, 1968.

Ketcham, Ralph. "Thomas Jefferson." *The Encyclopedia of Philosophy*. Vol. V. Ed. Paul Edwards. New York, London, 1967.

Kimball, Fiske. *Thomas Jefferson, Architect*. Boston, 1916.

_____. "Thomas Jefferson and the First Monument of the Classical Revival in America," *Journal of the American Institute of Architecture*. 1915.

Kimball, Marie G. *Jefferson: The Road to Glory, 1743 to 1776*. New York, 1943.

Koch, Adrienne. *Jefferson and Madison: The Great Collaboration*. New York, 1950.

Koontz, Louis Knott. *Robert Dinwiddie: His Career in American Colonial Government and Westward Expansion*. Glendale, CA, 1941.

Lehmann-Hartleben, Karl. "Thomas Jefferson, Archaeologist," *American Journal of Archaeology*. XLVII (April 1943).

Levy, Leonard W. *Jefferson and Civil Liberties: The Darker Side*. Cambridge, MA, 1963.

Lief, Leonard. *The New Conservatives*. Indianapolis and New York, 1967.

Lundeberg, Philip K., and Siddall, Abigail T., eds. *Soldier-Statesmen of the Age of the Enlightenment: Records of the 7th International Colloquy on Military*

History. Manhattan, KS, 1984.

McIlwaine, H.R., ed. *Journals of the Council of the State of Virginia, 1776–1781.* 2 vols. Richmond, VA, 1931–32.

Malone, Dumas. *Jefferson and His Time.* 6 vols. Boston, 1948–1981.

Manners, Lady Victoria and Williamson, George C. *Angelica Kauffmann, R.A., Her Life and Her Works.* New York, 1976.

Mapp, Alf J., Jr. *The Golden Dragon: Alfred the Great and His Times.* LaSalle, IL, 1974.

——————. *The Virginia Experiment.* 2nd edition. La Salle, IL, 1974.

Marckwardt, Albert and Rosier, James L. *Old English Language and Literature.* New York, 1972.

Marshall, John. *The Life of George Washington.* 5 vols. Philadelphia, 1804–1807.

Mason, George. *Papers.* Ed. Robert A. Rutland. 2 vols. Chapel Hill, NC, 1970.

Mays, David. *Edmund Pendleton.* 2 vols. Cambridge, MA, 1952.

Meade, Robert D. *Patrick Henry: Patriot in the Making.* Philadelphia, 1957.

——————. *Patrick Henry: Practical Revolutionary.* Philadelphia, 1969.

Miller, John C. *Origins of the American Revolution.* Boston, 1943.

——————. *The Wolf by the Ears.* New York, 1977.

Moore, John Hammond. *Albemarle: Jefferson's County.* Charlottesville, VA, 1976.

Morgan, Edmund S. *Prologue to Revolution.* Chapel Hill, NC, 1959.

——————. *The Stamp Act Crisis.* Chapel Hill, NC, 1963.

Morris, Richard B., ed. *Encyclopedia of American History.* New York, 1970.

Morpurgo, J.E. *Their Majesties' Royall Colledge.* Williamsburg, VA, 1976.

Munford, Beverley B. *Virginia's Attitude Toward Slavery and Secession.* Richmond, VA, 1909.

Nagel, Paul C. *Descent from Glory: Four Generations of the John Adams Family.* New York, 1983.

Nicolson, Nigel. *Great Houses of the Western World.* New York, 1968.

Peterson, Merrill D. *The Jefferson Image in the American Mind.* New York, 1960.

"Poll of American Institute of Architects," *AIA Journal.* July 1976.

Quaife, Milo M., ed. *The Capture of Old Vincennes.* Indianapolis, 1927.

Randall, Henry S. *The Life of Thomas Jefferson.* 3 vols. Philadelphia, 1865.

Randolph, Edmund. "Edmund Randolph's Essay on the Revolutionary History of Virginia (1774–1782)," *Virginia Magazine of History and Biography.* XLIII (1953).

Randolph, Sarah N. *The Domestic Life of Thomas Jefferson.* Cambridge, MA, 1939.

Randolph, Thomas Jefferson, ed. *Memoir, Correspondence, and Miscellaneous from the Papers of Thomas Jefferson.* Charlottesville, VA, 1829.

Richardson, Eudora Ramsay, ed. *Virginia: a Guide to the Old Dominion.* New York, 1941.

Robinson, James Harvey. "Civilization and Culture," *Encyclopaedia Britannica.* 1929.

Rothery, Agnes. *Houses Virginians Have Loved.* New York, 1954.

Rowland, Kate Mason. *The Life of George Mason.* 2 vols. New York, 1892.

Rutland, Robert A. *George Mason—Reluctant Statesman.* Charlottesville, VA, 1963.

Sanches-Saavedra, E.M. *A Description of the Country: Virginia's Cartographers and Their Maps, 1607–1881.* Richmond, VA, 1975.

Schachner, Nathan. *Thomas Jefferson, A Biography.* 2 vols. New York, 1951.

Schlesinger, Arthur M. *The Colonial Merchants and the American Revolution, 1736–1776.* New York, 1957.

Seward, Desmond. *Prince of the Renaissance: The Golden Life of Francois I.* New York, 1973.

Shepherd, Jack. *The Adams Chronicles, Four Generations of Greatness.* Boston, 1975.

Shepperson, Archibald Bolling. *John Paradise and Lucy Ludwell of London and Wiliamsburg.* Richmond, VA, 1942.

A Short Account of the School in Kingswood Near Bristol. Bristol, England. (Printed by William Pine), 1768.

Smith, Margaret Bayard. *The First Forty Years of Washington Society.* New York, 1906.

Smith, Page. *A New Age Now Begins. A People's History of the American Revolution.* 2 vols. New York, 1976.

Sowerby, E. Millicent. *Catalogue of the Library of Thomas Jefferson.* Charlottesville, VA, 1983.

Stenton, F.M. *Anglo-Saxon England.* 2nd ed. Oxford, England, 1971.

Stevens, Benjamin Franklin, ed. *The Clinton-Cornwallis Controversy.* London, 1888.

Stevenson, William Henry. *Asser's Life of King Alfred.* Oxford, England, 1959.

"Survey of Senators," *Washington Dossier.* May 1985.

Sydnor, Charles S. *Gentlemen Freeholders.* Chapel Hill, NC, 1952.

Tyler, Lyon Gardiner. *Letters and Times of the Tylers.* Richmond, VA, 1884.

Tyler, Moses Coit. *Patrick Henry.* Ithaca, NY, 1962.

Ward, Christopher. *The War of the Revolution.* 2 vols. New York, 1952.

Waterman, Thomas Tileston. *The Mansions of Virginia, 1706–1776.* New York, 1945.

Weintraub, Karl J. *Visions of Culture.* Chicago, 1966.

Wertenbaker, Thomas J. *Norfolk, Historic Southern Port.* Durham, NC, 1931

Weymouth, Lally, ed. *Thomas Jefferson: The Man, His World, His Influence.* New York, 1973.

Whitehead, Alfred North. *Adventures of Ideas.* New York, 1933.

Whitelock, Dorothy. *Changing Currents in Anglo-Saxon Studies.* Cambridge, England, 1958.

Wills, Garry. *Inventing America.* Garden City, NY, 1978.

Wirt, William. *The Life of Patrick Henry.* Philadelphia, 1836.

Wright, Louis B. *The First Gentlemen of Virginia: Intellectual Qualities of the Early Colonial Ruling Class.* San Marino, CA, 1940.

Wyllie, John Cook. "Writings About Jack Jouett and Tarleton's Raid on Charlottesville in 1781," *The Magazine of Albemarle County History, SVII.* 1958–1959.

INDEX

About the Author

An 11th generation Virginian in both paternal and maternal descent, Alf J. Mapp, Jr. grew up steeped in the lore of the Old Dominion. As a 16-year-old student at the College of William and Mary, Mapp was thrilled to be attending classes in the same building in which Thomas Jefferson had studied. For 30 years he has researched and written about Jefferson and his associates and the colonial and national environments that produced them. For six years he has pored over thousands of letters written by and to Jefferson to produce this, the most important of his books to date.

Alf Mapp's writings have circled the globe in nine languages, earning the praise of scholarly critics for their literary quality and fresh insights, and winning the plaudits of the public for their high entertainment value. Since 1961, Mapp has been on the faculty of Old Dominion University, where he holds the endowed rank of Eminent Professor. He lives at Willow Oaks in Portsmouth, Virginia.